47.50

Gubernatorial Transitions

Gubernatorial Transitions
The 1982 Election

Edited by Thad L. Beyle

DUKE PRESS POLICY STUDIES
Duke University Press, Durham
1985

Library of Congress Cataloging in Publication Data
Main entry under title:
Gubernatorial transitions.
(Duke Press policy studies)
Bibliography: p.
Includes index.
1. Governors—United States—Election—Case studies.
I. Beyle, Thad L., 1934–   II. Series.
JK2447.G8   1985   324.973′0927   85-6748
ISBN 0-8223-0642-5

Contents

Acknowledgments

Many people were part of this project and contributed in many ways. Obviously the analysts in the gubernatorial transition states were the most important contributors, and we thank them for their time, insight, and analyses. Dan Garry, director of the Office of State Services, National Governors' Association, and Jim Tait, director of the Governors' Center at Duke University, provided support and advice throughout the project. Bob Huefner of the University of Utah and Don Sprengel of Saint Louis University provided advice and crosscutting analyses of the state chapters that were most helpful to me as editor. Tina Carter and Belinda Hedgepeth of the Governor's Center provided assistance at the word processor, as did Dawn Lewis of the Department of Political Science at Chapel Hill.

Finally, I appreciate the good humor and editorial skills of Reynolds Smith at Duke University Press, who has been down this road with me before.

I thank all of them for staying the course on this project—and hope this book is worth their support and perseverance. If it is not, that is my problem and I accept that.

Thad L. Beyle
Chapel Hill, N.C.
October 1984

Preface

There is no force, other than the President's, that can move this country forward as much as the force of the fifty governors. There is no power within the individual state as persuasive as the power of the governor. Those involved in assuming the governorship should know first that there is much good that can come from the exercise of this power and should plan their administrations with this in mind.

I have never understood the debate about whether a governor should be a leader, a manager, or a caretaker because the governorship is, of course, a position of leadership, and governors should attempt to assert that leadership. There is a great opportunity in the office to act as spokesman for the best interests of the state. Don't let that leadership slip away.

Time is the most precious thing a governor has. He does not need to spend time on truck inspections or on wresting power from mayors; much in government takes care of itself. The most important message I can give a new governor is to do those things that will not get done if you do not give them the direction that only the governor can. Look for the things that can be done only because of you.

I am a strong advocate of planning, but as governor you should not sit around waiting for the planning process to tell you what to do. Your term will run out more quickly than you think. You are capable of refining your own thinking and giving direction. Take an inventory of what is wrong with your state. Cast it in the light of opening up opportunities for the people. Use the "Twenty-Year Rule," which is to look ahead to what the state will look like twenty years out. What, at that time, can be said of your stewardship?

In the early 1960s we in North Carolina tried the twenty-year view.

Of course if action taken is valid after twenty years, it is likely to be proper action for all time. We needed a stronger economic and industrial base. We shied away from tax breaks, yet undertook an aggressive industrial recruitment effort. We did not deal with the legislative process but used the power of prestige and leadership of the governor's office to mobilize resources. We pushed in the direction in which the state should go, and the continuing momentum is obvious.

The Research Triangle Park had been created under the administration of Governor Luther Hodges (1954–61). We added the Board of Science and Technology, and Governor Jim Hunt (1977–85) was able to use that base to bring microelectronics to North Carolina, with emphasis on changing the industrial base. We created technical institutes and community colleges to provide technical skills and training beyond the high school. Governor Hunt was able to create the competency test to place emphasis on the level of training in kindergarten through high school. We created the North Carolina School of the Arts; Governor Hunt created the North Carolina School of Science and Mathematics. We created the North Carolina Fund to address the problems of people caught in the cycle of poverty. Improved education, neighborhood leadership, community awareness, and official concern can be observed in all parts of the state today.

The test for every governor in his daily decisions should be, "Have I used my power as governor to make a real difference in the lives of the people of my state?" You have a tremendous power. Do not squander it.

—Comments made by Terry Sanford, President of Duke University and former Governor of North Carolina, 1961–65, at the Seminar for New Governors at Park City, Utah, on November 14, 1982

Gubernatorial Transitions:
Lessons from the 1982–1983 Experience

THAD L. BEYLE

American governments operate in such a manner that changes in the leadership of the executive branches are very systematic. Except for death, incapacity, impeachment, or removal of the president, governor, or mayor, we as a people know exactly when our elected chief executive will be up for reelection or his or her tenure will end. This orderly transfer of power in governmental succession means that the transition is a period of stability yet uncertainty, of transferring legitimacy from one leader to another in a rather open environment.

Such scheduled change means that plans—personal, political, and governmental—can be made years in advance for a specific election and for the way an incumbent leader exits and the newly elected leader assumes office. The governors of most states run on a four-year cycle, with only those in Arkansas, New Hampshire, Rhode Island, and Vermont running every two years. Four other states, Kentucky, Mississippi, New Mexico, and Virginia, do not allow their governors to succeed themselves. Recent attempts to move from two-year to four-year terms have been rejected by voters in Vermont in 1974, and in New Hampshire and Rhode Island in 1982. In 1984 Arkansas voters adopted and New Hampshire voters rejected four-year terms for their governors.

Thirty-two states schedule their gubernatorial elections in the even-numbered years not coinciding with the four-year presidential cycle (voters in North Dakota rejected an amendment to move their election to the off-presidential cycle in 1982); five others hold their elections in odd-numbered years; and nine states' gubernatorial contests follow the presidential calendar; the four states with two-year cycles hold their elections in each even-numbered year. Thus, in 1981, there were two gubernatorial elections; in 1982, thirty-six; in 1983, three; in 1984, thirteen; and in 1985 there will be two.

The focus of this volume is on how the states handle the transition of gubernatorial power, authority, and responsibility. How well do these transitions occur after years, decades, even centuries of experience with regularly scheduled transfers of office between incumbent governors and newly elected governors? Have the states been able to establish institutional processes and procedures to make them as smooth and professional as possible? Or is each one different, with politics the common denominator? Or is there a subtle mix of the political and the professional that can vary by the state, actors, and situation involved?

The Role of the National Governors' Association

Following the 1982 elections, eleven newly elected state governors, sixteen incumbent governors, and three former governors met in Park City, Utah, November 12–14. Representatives of two other newly elected governors also participated. The meeting was neither a partisan celebration nor a media event, but a school for the newly elected governors, sponsored by the National Governors' Association (NGA). Attending this meeting is one of the first of many small steps in the transition from winning the governorship to being governor.

Since 1968 the NGA has conducted a Seminar for New Governors within two weeks of the general elections in even-numbered years. (The first seminars were conducted cooperatively with the Council of State Governments.) The faculty for these seminars are incumbent governors, and every effort is made to inform newly elected governors of the seminar, its importance for their new role, and the value of attending as students. The subjects discussed at the 1982 seminar in Park City included organizing the governor's office, press and public relations, management of the executive branch, executive-legislative relations, intergovernmental relations, a retrospective view of the governorship, the governorship as a partnership involving one's spouse, and the transition period.[1]

NGA began developing printed materials for newly elected governors with the 1974 seminar.[2] In addition, the NGA Office of State Services has established an on-site consulting service for the new governors and their staffs at no cost during the transition period. The consultants are NGA staff members and others who have served in governors' offices in the states and who can provide advice and counsel on a wide range of concerns.

The materials prepared by the NGA are intentionally prescriptive. Options are presented, but the main goal is to prepare governors to hold the reins of power. In his introduction to the 1982 seminar publication, Democratic Governor Scott M. Matheson of Utah indicated that "the perspective . . . is that of focusing the processes of state government and the activities of the people around the governor as a means of accomplishing the governor's goals."[3]

The chapter summaries of NGA's 1982 seminar publication indicate the emphases of NGA's prescriptions. They include the expected—making appointments, developing messages, building relationships, managing programs, and addressing and managing the budget.

Setting Up a Successful Transition
Appoint a transition coordinator
Take a few days' vacation
Attend the Seminar for New Governors
Review personal management style

Transition in the Office of Governor
Choose management style
Develop internal office procedures
Designate staff positions
Establish external office relations

Developing the Team
Review executive branch appointments
Develop the recruitment and screening system
Focus on making executive appointments
Build the team

Taking Over the Policy Process
Review the existing policy tools and personnel available
Test all parts of the system
Manage agencies

Taking Control of the Budget
Arrange for governor-elect's involvement in the incumbent governor's budget process
Determine the extent of personal attention to the budget decision-making
Order review of all budget proposals
Make decisions on budget or budget revision

Withstanding the Assault or Enjoying the Honeymoon
Develop state of the state message
Build relationships with legislators, interest groups, party leaderships,
media, agency officials
Manage legislative program

Taking Another Breath
Evaluate first six months
Set the course

Of interest, though, is the way in which these tasks are directed toward
the political goal, variously worded, of assuming the responsibilities of
government. Also, great attention is paid to the importance of the governor's personal management style in accomplishing that goal. The transition period is regarded as lasting from the election and the inauguration
to at least six months into an administration and after the first legislative
session is held. As one midwestern governor notes, "The most important
goal of the transition is the long-term effect. In other words, the new
governor should not allow short-term pressures and demands for immediate results to overshadow the absolute necessity of establishing a solid
administrative base for the entire term of office."[4]

The Study of Gubernatorial Transitions

The Park City new governors' seminar is a unique but not an isolated example of increasing concern for the process of gubernatorial transition.
Gubernatorial transitions have come to be regarded, by incoming and
outgoing governors alike, not simply as an interregnum or a preinaugural
period but as the critical first stage in the development of a new administration. For the outgoing governors it is a chance to close out an administration in style and document their legacy.

The NGA seminars represent one effort to institutionalize the transition
process by formulating prescriptive lessons of success that draw on learning from past mistakes. Efforts in this direction are growing, but much
of the process still varies considerably from state to state, because of state
politics and personal style.

One important area of variation among states is the nature and scope
of state laws and informal practices concerning gubernatorial transitions.
(See appendix A, which indicates the extent of variation.) Of the seventeen states in which the 1982 elections resulted in a gubernatorial transi-

tion, only Alabama had no provision (legal or informal) concerning the transition process of the governor-elect. Nine of the seventeen transition states had legislation pertaining to the transition itself; seven others provided support for the governor-elect in various ways. Support for the governor-elect might include one or more of the following: appropriating state funds, using state personnel, making available office space in state buildings, acquainting his or her staff with office procedures, transferring information (such as records and files), and—most important—enabling the governor-elect to participate in preparing the budget that he or she will have to submit to the legislature. In a few states (notably, California, Minnesota, and Wisconsin), the extensive adoption of these provisions has served to institutionalize the transition process in many respects. However, in most of the other states, the transition proceeds on an ad hoc basis.

Because practices vary so much from state to state, much of the research on gubernatorial transitions is based on case studies.[5] There is at least one comparative study of gubernatorial transitions[6] and one on transition planning.[7] Two participants have discussed their experiences during a transition,[8] and several state agencies have conducted studies for use within their states.[9] Although much of the literature on gubernatorial transitions remains anecdotal or prescriptive, most findings point toward the persistence of several basic political factors:

1. *The magnitude of the transition task is considerable, with few guidelines to help the new governor.* In 1961 Charles Gibbons concluded, "One of the first surprises of a newly elected Governor-elect is the size of the task which confronts him in preparing to take office." Ten years later Wayne F. McGown observed, "Some states and many municipalities continue to practice the traditional approach to the transition between administrations which boils down to essentially letting the new executive find his own way." And in 1982 one former governor wrote, "No corporation, even in a hostile take-over situation, would ever handle transition the way we do in the states. It is as though you fired the president of a company, plus all the heads of operating divisions and the staff of the corporation central office all at once."[10]

2. *The transition process is a political process that requires knowing or learning how to share power and when to exert influence.* As Ahlberg and Moynihan found, "the new governor takes office only to find he must share power. . . . Having won the mandate of the people for his program, the governor now finds he must ask permission of the legisla-

ture to enact it." Though gubernatorial success cannot necessarily be judged by how well governors work with their legislatures, "the common denominator of transition is politics, pervading all attendant activities. . . . The duration of the transition is politically, rather than structurally defined."[11]

3. *Although a transition by definition denotes change, in reality there may be less change than meets the eye.* As Long noted, "The newcomer to office frequently forgets that he is dealing with a system . . . [that, to maintain stability,] . . . must be highly resistant to change." The changes that may occur will be incremental because "the functioning system is by nature a conservative entity." As a consequence, political goals to "change what is going on in state government" prove to be more rhetorical than real. Further, Blair and Savage argue that the critical importance of transitions must be balanced by a projection of "continuity, stability, knowledgeability, and purpose if the fragile underpinnings of the democratic political system are not to be exposed or threatened."[12]

4. *Commentators seem to agree on the importance of controlling the budget process and the difficulty of inducing major budgetary change.* "The theme," suggest Ahlberg and Moynihan, "is the difficulty of change; the difficulty of devising new programs, of financing them, of winning support for them, of implementing them." Yet, as Long explains, "The built-in requirement that [the governor] propose a budget and that some kind of a State of the Union message be delivered provides compelling points in time when he must perform his basic function of uncertainty absorption and provide at least his tentative *definition of the situation.*"[13]

5. *Though prescriptions abound, many seem to center on the extent to which the new governor can use the transition period to "define the situation."* As John Wickman and I have suggested, "The basic problem of transition is one of communicating interests and directions, both between the old and the new administrations, and within the new." Long explains the importance of the governor's first budget and budget message in these terms. He also views the staffing of the cabinet as "likely to be the first major symbolic step toward defining the situation." However, the opportunities for defining the situation in programmatic terms are limited. One governor urges, "Keep your agenda short. You'll only have time to build the necessary coalitions around three or four major priorities."[14]

With these findings in mind, this book surveys the process of gubernatorial transition in sixteen of the seventeen transition states of 1982–83 during the period between the elections of November 1982 and the post-inaugural adjustments of 1983. The survey is based on individual state studies conducted by a network of state analysts directed by this writer. The state analysts followed a broad outline of research topics and questions (see appendix B) and relied primarily on interviews and press coverage of the transition in their respective states. Ohio's gubernatorial transition is omitted in this study, and the reason speaks to the importance of politics in a transition. There was apparently a political incompatibility between the new governor's administration and the potential state analysts, which closed the doors to access and information.

The 1982 Gubernatorial Elections

The 1982 general elections included thirty-six states in which the governorship was at stake. Seventeen of these states elected a new governor, either because the incumbent governor failed in his renomination or re-election bid or because the incumbent chose not to seek, or was constitutionally unable to seek, another term. Over one third of the transitions took place in the Midwest, with the remainder spread throughout the country. The midwestern states were particularly hard hit during the recession of the early 1980s by their declining economies, which in turn led to decreased state tax revenues and increased demand for state services.

Thirteen states of the thirty-six had high unemployment rates (10 percent or more as of August 1982), and the Democratic candidates fared considerably better than their Republican counterparts by winning eight of these thirteen races (62 percent). Six of these high unemployment state races were won by incumbent governors, two Democrats and four Republicans; one Republican incumbent lost.[15]

These gubernatorial elections and transitions were conducted when there was no presidential race to overshadow state-level candidates or supplant state-level issues. Even so, voter reaction to the presidency of Ronald Reagan (R) may have been a factor in inducing voters across the nation to shift to the Democrats for leadership partly in response to the record of the national Republican administration. Democrats won twenty-seven of the thirty-six seats up for election, a three-to-one ratio that gave the Democrats a net gain of seven gubernatorial chairs. This compares with the five seats they gained in 1974 during the Nixon-Ford presidency and the ten in 1970 during Nixon's first term. The general trend during the 1950–82 period has been for Democrats to lose only 4.8 seats in a midterm election when their party controls the presidency; the Republicans lose 7.4 during Republican presidential midterm elections.[16]

In this section we examine those characteristics of the 1982 elections that influenced the transition process experienced by sixteen of the seventeen new governors during the closing months of 1982 and the opening months of 1983.

THE POLITICS OF THE TRANSITIONS

Table 1 brings together some of the more important electoral characteristics affecting the transition period. These characteristics include the margin of victory, the occurrence of a party or a factional shift, the role of the incumbent governor, and the nature of the campaign issues. Taken together, they address the character and intensity of the political battle.

In the 1982 elections, twenty-five incumbent governors ran for re-election, the highest number since 1962, and six were defeated in either their party's primary (Massachusetts) or the general election (Arkansas, Nebraska, Nevada, New Hampshire, and Texas). Five other incumbent governors, who did not seek or were constitutionally unable to seek re-election, backed the losing candidate in their party's primary (Alaska, Michigan, and New York) or in the general election (California and Ohio). In these eleven states the personal politics of the campaigns, either in primary or general elections, had the potential of setting significant roadblocks for these transitions. However, defeated incumbent Governor Hugh Gallen (D) of New Hampshire died unexpectedly before Governor-elect John H. Sununu (R) was inaugurated. This led to a confusing transition within a transition but did remove Gallen's and Sununu's personal politics as a roadblock to the transition.

Party shifts occurred in eleven of seventeen states, with Democrats gaining control of nine formerly Republican-held seats and Republicans overturning Democrats in two states. Moreover, in three other states where the same party maintained control there were factional shifts, which in many states can mean as many or more potential changes and turmoil than if there were a party shift. Therefore, in fourteen of the seventeen transition states there was either a party or a factional shift, which created the expectation of substantial changes in the politics, co-alitions, and agendas of the governorships as the new administrations took office.

The margin of victory achieved by the governors-elect in the fourteen shift states might be interpreted as an indicator of whether or not the voters gave the new governor a mandate. The victory margins varied widely. In four states (Alabama, Georgia, Massachusetts, and Ohio) the governor-elect won by what must be considered a landslide (i.e., over 20 percent). However, George Wallace's win in the second Democratic primary (the crucial race in Alabama) was the closest in years. In ten states the results indicated a very competitive election with margins of less than 10 percent. In the most competitive states, such as California (1 percent), Nebraska (2 percent), New York (3 percent), and New Hampshire (4 percent), the mandate would have to be fashioned by the governor's performance on the job.

The issues involved in a gubernatorial campaign can embitter the climate in which a transition is to take place. In eight of the 1982 races the outgoing governor's style and record were at issue (Alaska, California, Massachusetts, Michigan, Nebraska, Nevada, New Mexico, and Texas). The incumbent's performance was also tied to other issues—notably, tax-ation, the budget deficit, and reducing government—in three of the aforementioned states (California, Michigan, and Nevada) and three other states (Arkansas, New York, and Wisconsin). Thus, in eleven of the seventeen transition states, campaign issues involved implicit or ex-plicit questioning and criticizing, if not outright condemnation, of the incumbent's policies and record—hardly an easy opening to a dialogue between the outgoing and incoming governors.

THE COSTS OF BECOMING GOVERNOR

Seeking a gubernatorial office was an expensive enterprise in the 1980s. As table 2 indicates, none of these 1982 gubernatorial campaigns cost less than $1 million and three cost over $22 million. These are only the officially reported cash outlays by the candidates' organizations; what the campaigns cost in donated time and services can never be known.

Although it might seem that a candidate can buy the office if he or she spends enough, only ten of the seventeen winners actually spent more money than their opponents. Of the five defeated incumbents in

Table 1. Politics of the 1982–1983 Gubernatorial Transitions

State	Candidates Democratic	Republican	Victory margin	Party shift
Ala.	*George C. Wallace Former governor	Emory Folmar Mayor, Montgomery	20%	No
Alaska	*Bill Sheffield Businessman	Thomas Fink Businessman, former speaker of the house	6	Yes
Ark.	*Bill Clinton Former governor	Frank D. White Governor	10	Yes
Cal.	Tom Bradley Mayor, Los Angeles	*George Deukmejian Attorney general	1	Yes
Ga.	*Joe Frank Harris Businessman, state rep.	Robert Bell State senator	26	No
Iowa	Roxanne Conlin Former Ass't Att. gen. and federal D.A.	*Terry Branstad Lt. governor	6	No
Mass.	*Michael S. Dukakis Former governor	John W. Sears Former Boston city councilor	23	No
Mich.	*James J. Blanchard Congressman	Richard H. Headlee Insurance executive	7	Yes
Minn.	*Rudy Perpich (DFL) Former governor	Wheelock Whitney Businessman (IR)	18	Yes
Neb.	*Robert Kerrey Businessman	Charles Thone Governor	2	Yes
Nev.	*Richard Bryan Attorney general	Robert F. List Governor	11	Yes
N.H.	Hugh Gallen Governor	*John H. Sununu Academic and business consultant	4	Yes
N.M.	*Toney Anaya Former attorney general	John B. Irick Former state senator	6	No
N.Y.	*Mario M. Cuomo Lt. governor (D, L)	Lewis Lehrman (R, C, I) Businessman	3	No
Ohio	*Richard F. Celeste Former state rep., Lt. Governor	Clarence J. Brown Congressman	21	Yes
Tex.	*Mark White Attorney general	William Clements Governor	8	Yes
Wis.	*Anthony S. Earl Former state rep. and administrator	Terry J. Kohler Businessman	15	Yes

* Winner.

Key to party abbreviations: C—Conservative, D—Democratic, DFL—Democratic Farmer-Labor, I—Independent, IR—Independent-Republican, L—Liberal R—Republican.

Key to major issues of the campaign: a. the economy, b. jobs, c. unemployment, d. the candidate, e. taxes, revenue raising, f. pardons and commutations, g. utility

Faction shift within party	Who incumbent governor supported	Party of incumbent	Campaign issues General election	Primary (if relevant)
Yes	No one	D	a, c, d (Wallace) b, n	
—	Loser in party primary	R	capitol relocation; subsistence hunting & fishing	
—	He lost	R	e, f, g, h, b	
—	Winner in party primary Loser in election	D	h, i, d (Bradley)	
No	Winner	D	j, k, l	
No	Winner	R	a, b, i, m, e, d (Conlin)	
Yes	He lost in primary to winner	D	j, n	r, n
—	Loser in primary No one in election	R	a, b, o, m, n, j	n, r
—	No one	R	a	
—	He lost	R	a, n	
—	He lost	R	e, a, b, n	
—	He lost	D	e, j, t	e
Yes	No one in primary Winner in election	D	p, k	
No	Loser in primary Winner in election	D	g, e, r	d (Koch), Mayor of NYC
—	Loser in general election	R	not available	
—	He lost	R	r	d (both), n, g, p, u, a, b
—	No one	R	b, r, e, s	

rates/regulation, h. gun control, i. budget deficit, j. party control, k. continuity vs. change, l. crime and corruption charges, m. abortion and ERA/women's rights, n. previous experience/incumbency/incumbent's record, o. downsizing government, p. previous administration's style (contrast), q. death penalty, r. contrasting ideologies (liberal vs. conservative), s. environment, t. succession, u. education (salaries).

Table 2. 1982 Campaign Expenditures, Gubernatorial Transition States

State	Major Candidates	Primary Election		
		Percentage of total vote	Percentage of total primary spending	Cost per vote
Ala.	*Wallace (D)[d]	51.0[e]	N/A	—
	Folmar (R)		Unopposed	
Alaska	*Sheffield (D)	39.7	62.5	$52.17[a]
	Fink (R)	51.3	42.5	13.64
Ark.	*Clinton (D)[d]	41.9	54.5	3.43[a]
	White (R)[b]	82.8	95.6	30.67[a]
Cal.	*Deukmejian (R)	52.3	42.8	3.63
	Bradley (D)	60.8	64.8	1.58[a]
Ga.	*Harris (D)	24.2	32.6	13.94[a]
	Bell (R)	60.2	86.8	32.74[a]
Iowa	*Branstad (R)		Unopposed	
	Conlin (D)	48.0	37.2	2.49
Mass.	*Dukakis (D)[c, d]	53.5	43.1	3.82
	Sears (R)	49.7	21.7	3.69
Mich.	*Blanchard (D)	50.1	31.4	2.92[a]
	Headlee (R)	34.1	33.8	5.21
Minn.	*Perpich (DFL)[d]	50.4	18.1	.48
	Whitney (R)	59.9	81.0	4.95[a]
Neb.	*Kerrey (D)	71.2	83.9	2.05[a]
	Thone (R)[b]	62.6	77.3	2.80[a]
Nev.	*Bryan (D)	53.2	72.1	12.51[a]
	List (R)[b]	70.6	96.0	16.05[a]
N.H.	*Sununu (R)	31.9	27.7	5.73
	Gallen (D)[b]		Unopposed	
N.M.	*Anaya (D)	56.9	46.2	5.12[a]
	Irick (R)	54.6	42.6	6.17
N.Y.	*Cuomo (D)	52.9	31.0	2.42
	Lehrman (R)	80.0	95.0	15.55[a]
Ohio	*Celeste (D)	42.3	32.4	3.65
	Brown (R)	53.6	43.9	3.12[a]
Tex.	*White (D)	45.3	41.7	3.07[a]
	Clements (R)[b]	91.9	100.0	16.33[a]
Wis.	*Earl (D)	45.1	44.3	.88[a]
	Kohler (R)	67.3	79.4	$ 1.13[a]

SOURCES: Malcolm E. Jewell, "Political Money and Gubernatorial Primaries," *State Government* 56, no. 2 (1983): 69–73; Thad L. Beyle, "The Cost of Becoming Governor," ibid., 74–82; and individual chapters.

[a] Spent most money
[b] Incumbent governor
[c] Defeated incumbent in party primary

Percentage of total general election vote	Percentage of total spending, primary & general election	Cost per general election vote	Total campaign expenditures all candidates— 1982
60	28[f]	$ 3.04	$ 6,867,333[g]
40	30[f]	4.76[a]	
46	33	26.24[a]	6,113,881
38	19	17.75	
55	47	3.83[a]	3,584,467
45	35	3.48	
49	33	2.06	23,397,385
48	37	2.34[a]	
63	46	4.06[a]	6,475,316
37	18	2.66	
53	45	1.78[a]	2,183,131
47	35	1.60	
60	40	2.54[a]	7,718,602
37	8	.80	
52	25	1.58[a]	9,985,103
45	24	1.75	
59	23	1.00	4,411,877
41	47	3.02[a]	
51	41	3.19	2,131,916
49	53	4.22[a]	
54	45	9.93[a]	2,825,374
43	45	12.58	
51	53	4.35[a]	1,207,898
47	47	4.31	
53	44	5.68[a]	2,782,481
47	36	5.32	
51	22	2.01	23,558,518
48	59	5.69[a]	
60	64	2.48[a]	7,650,877
39	36	2.11	
54	40	5.36	22,421,471
46	60	9.43[a]	
57	41	1.01	$ 1,880,919
42	44	$ 1.47[a]	

[d] Former governor
[e] Second primary
[f] For general election only
[g] For the two party candidates only
* Winner

the general elections, two were the top spenders while three were outspent by their successful challengers. For some of the winning candidates, the cost of each vote was high: in Alaska it was $26.24; in Nevada, $9.93. But it also cost some losing candidates dearly for their votes: in Alaska, $17.75; Nevada, $12.58; and Texas, $9.43. In sheer dollar amounts the losing candidacies of Lehrman in New York ($13 million) and Clements in Texas ($13.5 million) must be among the highest in the history of gubernatorial races.

Obviously, the most expensive governor's race per vote was in Alaska at $43.99, with its tremendous geographic size, followed by Nevada at $22.51, Texas at $14.79, and New Mexico at $11.00. The least expensive were Wisconsin at $2.48, Michigan at $3.33, Massachusetts at $3.34, and Iowa at $3.38. Clearly, the size of a state and the concentration of voters have much to do with these differences.

In summary, the transitions following the 1982 gubernatorial elections took place under fairly normal conditions: outgoing governors, some defeated, turned the office over to those who beat them or to a member of the opposite party or a leader of an opposition faction within their own party, often after a very expensive and competitive campaign in which the outgoing governor, his performance, and administration were major issues. These are not the best of conditions for an orderly transition, but in the American system these are often the circumstances within which political power is transferred within the states.

One mitigating factor is the past experience of the newly elected governor. Of the seventeen new governors elected in 1982, eleven were current or former holders of state executive office. Their ranks included four former governors (Wallace of Alabama, Bill Clinton of Arkansas, Michael S. Dukakis of Massachusetts, and Rudy Perpich of Minnesota); four current or former state attorneys-general (George Deukmejian of California, Richard Bryan of Nevada, Toney Anaya of New Mexico, and Mark White of Texas); and three current or former lieutenant governors (Terry Branstad of Iowa, Mario M. Cuomo of New York, and Richard F. Celeste of Ohio). Especially in the case of the former governors, the politics of transition was tempered by past experience.

The 1982–1983 Transitions

The newly elected governors had a range of backgrounds, as displayed in table 3. The oldest was Wallace of Alabama, at sixty-three; the youngest, Branstad of Iowa, at thirty-six. Wallace, having served three terms, was the dean. Most were lawyers (eleven of seventeen), four were business-men (one of whom also was an academic), one was a dentist, and one had made public service his calling. Twelve were natives of their states.

The most immediate springboards to the governor's chair in 1983 were positions as former governor (four), attorney general (four), lieutenant governor (three), member of Congress (one), member of the state legis-lature (one) or a state administrator (one). The other three had been involved in state government and politics but did not have a penultimate office from which they sought the governorship. The importance of hold-ing a statewide elective office previously is clear.

In general the class of 1982 came to office fairly well prepared to as-sume the role of governorship. We now turn to the challenges they faced as they moved through the transition into office.

THE FISCAL CHALLENGE

Clearly, the major political fact of life was the economic recession and its impact on state revenues. Both outgoing and incoming governors faced an increasingly bleak fiscal future in which the current fiscal year's budget projected a shortfall of revenues. This created the need for "checkbook fiscal planning" to bring the budget in balance. Cutbacks, layoffs, reductions, fiscal manipulations, and, as the last resort, taxes were the options.

The difference among the transition states was not whether they had a budgetary problem but in the magnitude of the problem. In some states the budgets could be brought into balance by what amounted to tinkering with revenues and expenditures, as in Alaska and Nevada. Other states—California, Michigan, Ohio, and Wisconsin for example—were in such fiscal distress that addressing the budget question was the major issue the governor-elect faced during both the preinaugural period and in the first months in office. The immense size of the projected defi-cits in California and Michigan, for example, meant that significant steps had to be taken, and quickly. In Arkansas the combination of the state's fiscal distress and the spillover from campaign rhetoric led the newly re-elected Governor Clinton's transition team to request less transition funds than were available—thereby hamstringing the transition at the outset.

The Minnesota situation was somewhat unique. Outgoing Governor Albert Quie (Independent Republican) informed newly elected Gover-nor Perpich (Democratic Farmer-Labor) on his first day in his transition

Table 3. The Incoming Governors, 1983

State	Name and party	Date of first service	Present term ends	Number of previous terms
Ala.	George C. Wallace (D)	Jan. 1963	Jan. 1987	3
Alaska	William J. Sheffield (D)	—	Dec. 1986	0
Ark.	William Clinton (D)	Jan. 1979	Jan. 1985	1
Cal.	George Deukmejian (R)	—	Jan. 1987	0
Ga.	Joe Frank Harris (D)	—	Jan. 1987	0
Iowa	Terry Branstad (R)	—	Jan. 1987	0
Mass.	Michael S. Dukakis (D)	Jan. 1975	Jan. 1987	1
Mich.	James J. Blanchard (D)	—	Jan. 1987	0
Minn.	Rudy Perpich (D)	Dec. 1976	Jan. 1987	1*
Neb.	Bob Kerrey (D)	—	Jan. 1987	0
Nev.	Richard H. Bryan (D)	—	Jan. 1987	0
N.H.	John H. Sununu (R)	—	Jan. 1985	0
N.M.	Toney Anaya (D)	—	Jan. 1987	0
N.Y.	Mario M. Cuomo (D)	—	Jan. 1987	0
Ohio	Richard F. Celeste (D)	—	Jan. 1987	0
Tex.	Mark White (D)	—	Jan. 1987	0
Wis.	Anthony Earl (D)	—	Jan. 1987	0

SOURCE: *Governors of the American States, Commonwealths and Territories, 1983* (Washington, D.C.: National Governors' Association, 1983) and *The Book of the States, 1984–85* (Lexington, Ky.: The Council of State Governments, 1984), pp. 49–50.

office that there was a possible revenue shortfall for the current fiscal year. It reached $312 million by mid-November. But Quie accepted responsibility for this shortfall and, working with the legislative leaders (DFL), came to an agreement to cover half of this deficit through budget cuts and shifts, and the rest through increased taxes. The bill passed narrowly and Quie signed it. However, Perpich's distance from the resolution of this issue tended to create budget and leadership problems.

In a sense the fiscal issues in the states framed the transition, forcing all actors to address their attention to coping with the state's financial situation.

THE APPOINTMENTS CHALLENGE

These budgetary problems meant that the other processes and activities of the transition were not as significant or of as high a priority in some states as they might normally have been. However, history seemed to be

Immediate past public position	Occupation	Birthdate	State of birth
Governor	Lawyer	8/25/19	Ala.
	Businessman	6/26/28	Wash.
Governor	Lawyer	8/19/46	Ark.
Atty gen.	Lawyer	8/3/35	Wis.
State rep.	Businessman	2/26/36	Ga.
Lt. gov.	Lawyer	11/17/46	Iowa
Governor	Lawyer	11/8/33	Mass.
U.S. Rep.	Lawyer	8/8/42	Mich.
Governor	Dentist	6/27/28	Minn.
	Businessman	8/27/43	Neb.
Atty gen.	Lawyer	6/16/37	D.C.
	Businessman/ educator	7/2/39	Havana, Cuba
Atty gen.	Lawyer	4/29/41	N.M.
Lt. Gov.	Lawyer	6/15/32	N.Y.
Lt. Gov.	Public service	11/11/37	Ohio
Atty gen.	Lawyer	3/17/40	Tex.
State Admin.	Lawyer	4/12/36	Mich.

Succeeded to governor's office on former Gov. Wendell Anderson's resignation and then appointed Anderson to the U.S. Senate seat vacated by Walter Mondale, who became vice-president.

repeated in some states as incoming governors challenged the late appointments of outgoing governors. In California outgoing Governor Edmund G. (Jerry) Brown, Jr., attempted to fill many judicial appointments, a few of which newly elected Governor Deukmejian was able to block in his role as attorney general and member of the Commission on Judicial Appointments. During the last weekend before the inauguration Brown made 350 appointments.

In Michigan a newly reelected supreme court justice died; outgoing Governor William G. Milliken appointed the Republican candidate, who had run third behind another Democratic candidate. In a complex series of events, incoming Governor James Blanchard challenged the appointment, and a divided court first decided to uphold the appointment. When one justice had second thoughts, the Democratic judges caucused privately and voted to remove the appointee. The new governor then appointed a Democrat.

Similarly, lame-duck appointments made by outgoing Governor Bill

Clements (R) in patronage-rich Texas became an issue in that state. Debate grew among senators and Governor-elect White (D) over whether or not to deny automatic confirmation of Clements's appointments. The decision was to vote on each appointment, thereby leading to confirming fewer than half of them. Further compounding this situation was the resignation of the Democratic chief justice of the Texas Supreme Court just before the general election. Clements sought to appoint a scheduled-to-retire member of the court, who was confirmed only after he agreed to serve the term that would expire in 1984 and not to seek re-election.

But, by and large, staffing the governor's office and state departments was undertaken with considerably less of the media and political spotlight than past experience would have led one to expect. Although the focus on fiscal issues may be part of the reason, another may lie in the fact that many of the initial appointments, described by Long as "the first major symbolic step toward defining the situation," were to management positions.

The governor's key staff—the budget director and the finance director—were often the first named. This was the case in California when Governor-elect Deukmejian's first announcement at his initial press conference on Thursday following the Tuesday election was the designation of his director of finance. This appointment was intended as a signal that the state's budgetary problems were to be the top priority of the new administration. Similarly, Nebraska Governor-elect Robert Kerrey's first major decision was to keep the current budget director and staff, and Kerrey himself surprised observers by his attention to budgetary details, thereby staking out his managerial style. Dukakis of Massachusetts named his first two appointments on the same day—his chief of staff and the secretary of administration and finance. Nevada's to-be-elected Governor Bryan made his first appointment on election day before the polls closed by selecting his budget director and head of the Department of Administration. In symbolic terms the first major cabinet appointment by Governor Clinton of Arkansas in both 1979 and 1983 was a black. Generally, these first symbolic appointments were not to the old patronage positions of heads of highways or economic development.

However, in Alabama this symbolic action was turned on its head. Although the initial appointments by "new" Governor Wallace did define the situation in that he brought back many people from his previous administrations, he himself created the uncertainty by not being available to the press, legislators, interest groups, and others. The cause was his poor health, which has left Alabama state government in a permanent state of transition.

Another aspect of the appointments process is establishing a way to find the right people for the right job, and, at the more mundane level, how to sort through the piles of applications and endorsements from those seeking an appointment or working to retain one. Most transition workers reported frustration at handling the volume of work, some falling considerably behind in categorizing, filing, and reviewing each potential appointee. The process appeared to be one of confusion and chaos.

Some found the promise of new word-processing machines to be a less than fruitful approach. In Massachuetts, Wang Laboratories loaned sophisticated word-processing equipment to the transition staff so that they might handle this problem better. After the staff spent several weeks learning how the machines worked, the equipment did help. In New Mexico such a system broke down and the process had to be done by hand because volunteers proved unable to use the new technology effectively.

A RISE IN PROFESSIONALISM?

Is this tendency to appoint managers early a sign of hard fiscal times, or did it represent a real shift of gubernatorial priorities? The evidence from these studies suggests that, although both interpretations are correct, many of the newly elected governors viewed their management styles as an important way of approaching their role. Some, like new Governor Tony Earl of Wisconsin, were very optimistic: "There are only two things I know of that are unmanageable—New York City and the Chicago Cubs." Moreover, it appears that the governors wanted to have their management support systems in place as they addressed both short-term concerns and long-terms plans. For example, Alaska's Governor Bill Sheffield created a miniature OMB (Office of Management and Budget) in his office, bringing together several units not previously integrated, and appointed a CPA as its first director.

Closely related to this general observation on the importance of the management style is the sense that the 1982–83 gubernatorial transitions were more professional and less political than many that have been reported on in the past. While there were electoral clashes between the outgoing and incoming governors in many of the transitions, the overall record seemed to be more of accommodation on both sides. A few conflicts broke out over outgoing administration appointments, as noted earlier, but these were political and, by and large, the exception.

As a sign of the times, some of the greatest tension points were over the state's financial situation. The questions were of several types: Was the incumbent hiding or not addressing the problem of the state's financial situation and leaving it for the new governor to solve, as the events during the California transition suggested? Could one trust the revenue estimates of the outgoing administration or any revenue estimates in a declining economy? As one incumbent governor suggested at the seminar, "Treat economic estimators like pollsters."[17]

For example, because of technical difficulties in projecting accurate revenues, a 9-percent shortfall in the New Mexico budget ($137 million) was not discovered until two weeks after election day! Were the efforts of the outgoing administration to cope with the fiscal situation (cutbacks, budget shifts) politically motivated, as was alleged in Alabama? In Texas a political twist to the budgetary crisis was the comptroller's simultaneous announcements of three successive revenue estimate reductions, amounting to $3.4 billion, and his candidacy for the Democratic party's gubernatorial nomination in 1986, obviously beginning a campaign that would pit him against the newly elected Governor White four years hence!

The major conclusion is that the transitions were increasingly professional rather than political, even in the cases of those six incumbent governors who had been defeated in their reelection bids. In Arkansas, for example, the Budget Office is turned over to the governor-elect immediately upon election—even if, as in 1978 and 1982, the budget is authorized by the defeated incumbent governor. And in Wisconsin outgoing Governor Lee Dreyfus allowed Governor-elect Earl to appoint an interim budget director the day after the election. Cooperation rather than noncooperation predominated.

In states where a long-time governor was retiring (Georgia, Iowa, Michigan, and New York) this cooperation was tied to the desire, at least on the part of the outgoing governor, to leave a record of long-term accomplishment unblemished by last-minute petty politics or bickering. In Georgia outgoing Governor George Busbee vacated the governor's mansion several weeks early so that the new governor would have time to get settled before the inauguration. And for some governors, such as Jay Hammond of Alaska, Milliken of Michigan, and Hugh Carey of New York, the unhappy memories of their transitions into office guided them in assisting the newly elected governors. Carey set up a two-track transitioning-out process in the early summer of 1982, focusing first on nuts and bolts and second on policy issues. The results in the form of policy option papers, issue papers, and budgetary documents were designed to assist the new governor. Governor Cuomo attested to their help. Even one-term governors such as Dreyfus of Wisconsin took significant steps to prepare for the transition; Dreyfus was fulfilling his vow to plan a smoother transition than he had had.

At the same time, many would probably echo the observation of Governor Kerrey of Nebraska: trying to replace the top management of any organization is difficult; trying to do it in two and a half months during the holiday season is impossible.

THE POLITICAL FACTOR

In many states, professionalism may have been only skin deep in the logistics of the transition process itself and some initial appointments. There is still evidence that politics is a major, if not the major, factor to be considered in the transition. Despite incumbent and former governors' entreaties, and NGA advice, campaign directors and key campaign personnel were often brought into the new administration, either in the governor's office or other administrative positions.

In two states, New Mexico and New York, members of the new governor's family, Steve Anaya and Andrew Cuomo, had prominent roles in the transition and the new administration. Such appointments have sensitive, political symbolism, as affirmed by the younger Cuomo's characterization of them as "the son thing." In Arkansas the governor's office is seen as family, with all the loyalty implied by the word. Long spoke to this point in noting that the family nature of the governor's office is based on personal trust, unbureaucratized relationships and an absolute loyalty to the head of the family. He also suggested that it can be "a psychologically costly affair."[18]

This phenomenon is further demonstrated by Don Sprengel's 1982 survey of gubernatorial staffs, which found "that 56 percent served in the most recent general election campaign, 41 percent had known the governor at least six years *prior* to serving on the office staff, and 36 percent had been politically associated with the governor prior to election." Thus, bringing campaign personnel into the new administration is not a unique phenomenon.

A review of the 1982–83 transitions supports this finding in many of the states. Sprengel argues that "loyalty to the governor-elect, a close working relationship and a willingness to suppress self to the governor," are the key variables. This echoes the advice given by the outgoing chief of staff of the Brown administration in California: "In making selections, never underestimate the importance of loyalty. Get a signed, undated resignation from every appointee. Fire someone as soon as you can to show who is in charge." The advantage, clearly, is that a skilled brokerage team is in place, but the problem is that the loyalty of such a staff can be too narrow, as was the case in Michigan. Or, as in Wisconsin, the initial appointments to major positions, although conveying loyalty, consensus, and low visibility, did not sit well with some of Governor Earl's constituents who wanted innovative and outspoken leaders in key positions.

Among the smoothest transitions were those of the four former governors. Knowledge of the office, the use of previous staff members as key assistants, and the value of reflections on past mistakes—all contributed to these smoother transitions. Dukakis summed it up: "My whole way of dealing with the transition was conditioned by having been through it before." Having undergone a transition out of office, they were also in a better position to understand some of the problems—administrative, political, and personal—that an outgoing governor faces. Therefore, the demands they placed on the outgoing administration were couched in an understanding of the situation.

TIME AS A FACTOR

Time was a significant factor in each of the transitions but in different ways, depending on the situation in the state. Once the election results are known, public attention focuses on the newly elected governor. However, the outgoing governor still has the legal authority, if not the power, to act until the newly elected governor is sworn into office. This legal authority was especially pertinent in Arkansas, where devastating December storms had to be responded to—officially by outgoing Governor White and unofficially by soon-to-be Governor Clinton. And in California outgoing Governor Brown called the legislature into special session to reapportion the state legislature before incoming Governor Deukmejian took over the office.

As is evident from the dates presented in table 4, most newly elected governors did not have much time to prepare for the first major events

Table 4.   Significant Dates in the 1982–1983 Gubernatorial Transitions, Following the November 2, 1983, Election

	Inaugural[a]	Convening of legislature[b]	Submission of budget
Ala.	Jan. 17, 1983	Apr. 19, 1983[c]	Apr. 26, 1983
Alaska	Dec. 6, 1982	Jan. 17, 1983	Jan. 19, 1983
Ark.	Jan. 11, 1983	Jan. 10, 1983	Jan. 10, 1983
Cal.	Jan. 3, 1983	Dec. 6, 1982	Jan. 10, 1983
Ga.	Jan. 11, 1983	Jan. 10, 1983	Jan. 14, 1983[d]
Iowa	Jan. 7, 1983	Jan. 10, 1983	Feb. 1, 1983[d]
Mass.	Jan. 6, 1983	Jan. 5, 1983	Jan. 26, 1983[d]
Mich.	Jan. 1, 1983	Jan. 5, 1983	Jan. 18, 1983
Minn.	Jan. 1, 1983	Jan. 3, 1983	Jan. 24, 1983[d]
Neb.	Jan. 6, 1983	Jan 5, 1983	Jan. 15, 1983
Nev.	Jan. 1, 1983	Jan. 17, 1983	Jan. 28, 1983[d]
N.H.	Jan. 5, 1983	Jan. 5, 1983[c]	Feb. 15, 1983
N.M.	Jan. 1, 1983	Jan. 18, 1983	Feb. 14, 1983[d]
N.Y.	Jan. 20, 1983	Jan. 5, 1983	Feb. 1, 1983[d]
Ohio	Jan. 10, 1983	Jan. 3, 1983	Mar. 15, 1983[d]
Tex.	Jan. 18, 1983	Jan. 11, 1983	Jan. 19, 1983[d]
Wis.	Jan. 3, 1983	Jan. 11, 1983	Jan. 25, 1983[d]

[a] Office of State Services, National Governors' Association, "Gubernatorial Elections in the States and Territories—1982," Oct. 19, 1982.
[b] *The Book of the States, 1982–83* (Lexington, Ky.: The Council of State Governments, 1982), 210–11.
[c] Legislature convened in organizational session: Ala., Jan. 11, 1983; N.H., Dec. 6, 1982.
[d] Or sooner.

they were to face: inauguration, the convening of the legislature, and the submission of the annual or biennial budget. And as one incumbent governor argued: "The budget is the key. . . . you have got to capture it. Budgeting is a process not an event."[19] A major reason is its role in guiding and controlling an administration. For example, the newly appointed budget director for Massachusetts Governor Dukakis sees the budget as a contract-setting mechanism by which the departmental directors buy into the budget.

In Alaska it was barely a month before the administration had to be in place; except for the governor's office staff, it wasn't. In states like California, New York, and Ohio the legislature convenes before the governor's inauguration, and in Arkansas and Texas the budget is submitted to the legislature before the newly elected governor is inaugurated. In several other states the inauguration, the convening of the legislature, and the submission of the budget are virtually simultaneous. In these states the budget submitted to the legislature is clearly that of the outgoing governor and his administration. Suggested changes or shifts usually must be submitted later by the new administration. Georgia and Iowa were clearly different. Outgoing Governor Busbee cooperated by leaving the task of preparing the next fiscal year budget for Georgia to Governor-elect Joe Frank Harris prior to his inauguration; outgoing Governor Bob Ray of Iowa did the same for Governor-elect Branstad.

In states where the governor-elect needed considerable time to assemble his administration, understand the budget and its problems, and get his priorities in order, there was just not enough time, and many had to assume office before they were ready. In some states, the governor-elect and his staff had been so consumed by the politics of winning the election that little time or planning had gone into how to govern. This was especially true in those states in which the election had been highly contested and the outcome was not known until the election results were in.

In California, for example, a team of candidate Deukmejian's campaign leaders began to plan for the transition as early as August. Weekly meetings were held and the plan of action for the transition was developed. But in October, when the campaign was in trouble, planning stopped because full attention had to be given to winning the election. A top Nebraska transition staff member was unwilling to work for a candidate who would dilute his concentration on a winning campaign by starting to plan the transition before the election!

Unusual among the candidates were former Governors Dukakis of Massachusetts and Perpich of Minnesota. Dukakis had spent his four-year interregnum period at the John F. Kennedy School of Government at Harvard, where he was able to teach and to reflect on the problems of public management. He initiated his transition planning process even before the September primary in which he defeated incumbent Governor Bruce King and assigned a Kennedy School colleague to focus on this effort alone and with discretion. The process expanded after his primary win. Perpich established a transition team immediately following his primary victory, as had then Arkansas attorney general Clinton in 1978, who saw his victory as a sure thing. Anaya in New Mexico also took some initial steps to plan the transition because he anticipated victory. In a different yet related vein, Governor-elect Harris of Georgia was able to retain the incumbent department heads because of the similarity of his philosophy and approach to those of outgoing Governor Busbee, thereby removing one of the most difficult steps in a transition.

In states where there was a severe fiscal or other crisis, as in California, Michigan, New York, and Ohio, time was of the essence. The new governor needed to gain control of the levers of government as soon as possible yet was generally unable to do so until officially inaugurated. Here, what seemed to be too much time worked to their disadvantage because they were expected to hit the ground running before the runway had been officially opened to them.

LEADERSHIP STYLE AS A FACTOR

Much of what transpired in gubernatorial transitions appeared to border on chaos because too many people, interests, and issues pressed in on too few people in a very constricted period. There was also an individualized and personal character about each of the transitions. Few people were actually empowered by the governor-elect to take action and make decisions on his behalf; and there was a parochial, or home-state, view of how to work through a transition, staff up, and undertake budget and policy review. Alaska's Governor-elect Sheffield established a transition team and a set of six task forces to assist during the transition. His leadership style was thus seen as very managerial and involved many people representing a variety of concerns. Although an agenda was created, so were problems, which resulted from such wide participation.

In Massachusetts, Governor-elect Dukakis established a twenty-three-member Transition Advisory Committee (TAC), which assisted in making appointments, setting priorities, and maintaining political linkages during the period. In addition, the TAC served the important symbolic function of showing Dukakis as a new person, one who sought counsel and advice; in his first term he was seen as a person who made decisions quickly and listened to no one. Five of the TAC subcommittee chairpersons were then selected as cabinet secretaries.

Although the NGA guidelines provided the new governors with conceptualizations of gubernatorial leadership in terms of command and gaining control, it becomes clear from these studies that the governors conceptualized leadership more in terms of brokerage. The new governors tended to lead, not through the formal powers of the governor's office, but by their ability to lead a variety of independent power sources.

This approach meant that the staffs for the governor's office itself and for the departments and agencies tended to be drawn from the lists of former and current state administrators and other prominent state citizens. There were few, if any, attempts to go outside a state for the best person possible, partly because of the need to appoint people who already knew the workings of the state's political system and who would not need time to learn them. Additionally, these appointees should be able to quickly locate the "old silver foxes" in the agencies (discussed by Massachusetts analyst Martha Weinberg), who know "where all the treasure is buried."

Leadership style can also be conceptualized in terms of how the governor himself performs—the tone he sets for his administration. Some are above the action, moving in as needed or called for. Earl in Wisconsin adopted an FDR decision-making style, getting advice from both the bureaucracy and his personal staff in order to be well informed as a chief executive. His delegation of authority was always partial, tentative, and provisional, allowing him greater control. Others, such as Governors Clinton of Arkansas, Kerrey of Nebraska, and Anaya of New Mexico, immersed themselves in the details of the budget and policy process, thereby sending the signal that they were detail oriented but often at the expense of standing back for a view of the larger picture.

In Anaya's case such attention to details could be interpreted by the media as indicative of a man so petty and consumed by ambition that even the decisions on trivial matters were not delegated. Yet, at another level, Anaya's campaign strategy of abandoning traditional campaign promises led to significant changes in how appointments were made and allowed him to address issues and ideologies rather than the narrow interests of fiefdoms.

Cuomo of New York sought to take a more personal, hands-on style in his administration, partly to indicate how his style contrasted with the more aloof style of former Governor Carey and partly because of his own described background as "a lawyer, a nit-picker, a footnote writer." But he realized that to go too far in the latter direction might lead to his losing policy control. Deukmejian's cabinet system in California was established to give him a thorough and orderly control over policy making and implementation.

THE LEGISLATIVE ROLE

Despite the advice given by one incumbent governor at the seminar, "a governor successful in managing the selection of legislative leadership gains a pyrrhic victory,"[20] several governors-elect did so. In Alabama it is a tradition, especially under oft-elected Governor Wallace. In New

Hampshire intervening in the selection of legislative leadership was an extraordinary act but one that set the activist tone of the Sununu administration. This also obligated one half of the legislative leadership to the governor, which helped him achieve legislative support for his initiatives. In New Mexico it was a rare political act when Governor-elect Anaya supported a more moderate group of legislators in the house to gain control of the speakership and to reduce the power of the Coalition, a bipartisan group of conservative legislators in control since 1978. Having succeeded, he then had considerable success in working with the legislature.

Obviously, these governors felt that intervening in the choice of legislative leadership was part of the calculus they needed to develop a working relationship with the legislature.[21] Although this may have a very positive effect for the governor vis-à-vis the legislature, one incumbent governor further cautioned the newly elected, "Don't necessarily judge your success by your legislative score card."[22]

In a different vein Alaska's Governor Sheffield was caught in a conflict with his legislature that was in reality an interhouse power rivalry over the budget. To have his appointments approved, he and the senate president joined in calling a joint legislative session to vote on his appointments. However, to obtain a quorum, state troopers were called in to force four house members to be present—hardly a way to build a good working relationship.

Former Governor Dukakis of Massachusetts, trying to redress errors of his first administration, began working with the legislature prior to the September primary, was conciliatory in his approach, involved legislators in his policy process, and appointed a former legislator as his director of legislative relations. However, another former governor, Clinton of Arkansas, could not avail himself of a law that allows a governor-elect to recess the legislature for thirty days, providing more time to prepare a legislative program. The political fear of antagonizing the legislature prevailed. The mood of the legislators: We give a new governor a honeymoon period. This is his second term. He has been this way before and should know what he is doing.

Governor Cuomo, as lieutenant governor, had watched former Governor Carey's confrontational style in working with the legislature. Some of Cuomo's earliest steps, which were well received by the legislature, were directed at developing better working relationships and creating an atmosphere of willingness to compromise.

But Governor Deukmejian's legislative relations were difficult at best.

The Democratic-controlled legislature in California did not provide housing for the new governor—a continuing controversy stemming from the Ronald Reagan administration. And their conflict over the budget almost resulted in payment in script for state employees and delayed the adoption of the budget for the longest time in the state's history.

Clearly, legislative relations are important for the new governor and must be addressed carefully so that the goals of the new administration can be achieved, thereby enhancing its image.

THE NGA TRANSITION ROLE

Against this backdrop the transition assistance effort undertaken by NGA had limited yet generally positive results. The new governors' seminar was generally very well received by the governors-elect who attended. Here they could interact personally with their new colleagues and the incumbent governor faculty. However, one incumbent governor with a puckish sense of humor observed at the seminar that "only at the National Governors' Association can you hear so many lectures on management from lawyers."[23] But it should be noted that the governors-elect from the big states (California, Michigan, New York, and Texas) chose not to attend. Perhaps this was because they were snowed under by their new responsibilities at home. Or was it because they did not perceive a seminar in Utah as helpful for the problems they faced in Sacramento, Lansing, Albany, or Austin?

Some new governors used the on-site technical assistance made available to them by NGA (thirteen of the seventeen states were visited by NGA assistance personnel). For example, the NGA on-site assistance in New Mexico is credited with helping to organize the office staffing and tighten the policy and budget schedules to match the legislative calendar requirements. However, most governors-elect preferred to go it alone. There is more than a hint from these studies that state parochialism is still a significant factor in gubernatorial transitions and must be understood and addressed in any outside assistance efforts.

THE INAUGURATION AS POLITICS AND SYMBOL

Each state has elaborate procedures and traditions by which the newly elected governor becomes governor in fact—the inauguration and all the

pomp that goes with it. This event is simultaneously a major governmental, political, and social event. It is costly, needs considerable planning, and involves many people. As an example, in California, Walt
Disney Productions was involved in planning the inaugural and produced the inaugural ball. Yet almost a half-million dollars of the privately raised funds were left over and were eventually used to buy the
governor a residence—resolving by private means one of his legislative
problems.

The inaugural does serve several functions. The first is as a way of
involving those who have worked for and supported the governor-elect
yet who will not have positions in the new administration. In some cases
these individuals do not want such a position; in other cases, placing
them on the inaugural preparation committees is a way of easing them
out of the new governor's state administration.

Inaugurations are also symbolic events where the new in-crowd can be
seen and where, by inference, the old in-crowd may be conspicuous by
their absence. Further, it provides an opportunity for those who supported the wrong candidate to make amends by donating to the costs of
the event.

Third, the style of the inaugural proceedings can be a symbolic statement, as in the Georgia transition. Planned from the outset as a political
event that would stress the no-frills, antiliquor, people's approach of the
new governor, it succeeded in sending such a message to the state. The new
Alaska administration held four inaugural balls—in Juneau, Anchorage,
Nome, and Fairbanks—as a concession to the regional nature of the
state's politics. These balls brought together both supporters and opponents, along with regional notables, to create an air of good feeling. The
New Mexico inaugural was the first to extend beyond Santa Fe, and
events were also held in Albuquerque and Roswell. This was an attempt
by Anaya to reach out to all sectors of the state—geographic, ethnic, and
partisan. And in Arkansas, Diane Blair likened the Clinton inaugurals
of 1979 and 1983 to the differences between the first wedding reception and the second—as different as Camembert and cottage cheese—
and planned that way.

Finally, the inaugural and state of the state addresses can provide the
ringing words by which the new administration will be guided, as
well as a public mandate that may have been unclear in the election
returns. Symbolic messages were just a part of Governor Cuomo's strategy in New York: "I want to convey a certain message in everything I

do." That these symbolic messages attracted the attention of the national press further heightened the effectiveness of his approach.

The Continuing Recession

Finally, we return to the significance of the fiscal issue of framing the 1982 transitions. Clearly, the continuing recession overwhelmed some transitions. But the other side of this coin can be and was turned to the new governor's advantage. Several of the newly elected governors were able to take the issues they and their states faced, frame them in ways that achieved solutions, and in doing so, create the mandate they needed to govern.

The clearest example was Governor Cuomo of New York, who used his handling of the fiscal crisis, a prison uprising, and his major addresses to achieve not only a state mandate but national recognition of his abilities. He obtained legislative agreement on a balanced budget before the beginning of the fiscal year—for the first time in four years— by increasing taxes and cutting programs. He used his image of New York as a family in arguing that the budget was an attempt to "balance our books as a family would, by sharing the burden." His careful handling of the two-and-a-half-day prison uprising at the Ossining Correctional Facility, which he called "the longest week of his life," was successful.

Governor Blanchard of Michigan also used the fiscal crisis and his resolution of it to establish himself as governor in fact. As he said at the time, "If you face the music early, you're better off."[24] Nearby Wisconsin's fiscal situation was of such magnitude (estimated at $330 million by June 30, 1983, and $2.5 billion by mid-1985) that Governor Earl called a special session of the legislature the day after his inauguration. He then successfully guided a major tax package through the legislature, cutting the deficits in half within two days of his inauguration. By striking fast, in his honeymoon period, he appeared to sustain little political damage and provided himself with breathing room. Time will tell whether, as in the presidency, first successes such as these create the context in which later successes can be achieved.[25]

Not all new governors were as successful in turning their efforts at crisis management to their advantage. For example, Governor Deukmejian of California was unable to address his state's fiscal crisis completely in negotiating with the Democratic-controlled legislature, and California remained in fiscal crisis for some time. The hostility between the executive and the legislative branches was probably the greatest since the administration of Culbert Olson (D, 1939–43). Governor White of Texas was unable to generate sufficient legislative support to address the problems created by projected revenue shortfalls and to fulfill his major campaign plank of a significant increase in teachers' salaries. But the evidence from some of these states still indicates that a governor who faces and resolves a crisis directly (i.e., becomes known as a crisis manager) helps define the situation and the nature of his leadership. And clearly the success stories about resolutions of major issues spilled over into the media and—more important—into the legislature.

There were several interesting patterns in the way governors approached their policy agendas; in most states the agendas included the fiscal problems already noted. The NGA advice to new governors is to maintain neutrality, if possible, on national issues[26] and to limit policy agenda so that a clear focus can be developed.[27] Most did shy away from national issues. The exceptions included those who were thrust into the national political arena because of what their victory meant for the Democratic party, because of their liberalism in economically troubled states (e.g., Earl in Wisconsin), or because of the significance of their states in national politics (e.g., Cuomo in New York and Deukmejian in California). Earl became, in fact, the leading spokesman against Reagan policies at the NGA winter meetings in February and was elected chairman of the Conference of Great Lakes Governors—all within two months of having taken office.

Most governors, such as Clinton in Arkansas, Dukakis of Massachusetts, and Sununu in New Hampshire, selected only a few issues on which to focus, usually no more than four or five, and in doing so were generally credited by the analysts with an effective strategy. Governor-elect Perpich's transition staff consciously worked to reduce the policy agenda during the transition. Governor Branstad of Iowa set out and achieved a much longer agenda, but his success was more than balanced by the difficulties of governors who sought a broad agenda but ran into trouble because of a lack of focus. This lack of focus may be a symptom rather than a cause of other problems.

Conclusion

From our analysis, we can distinguish three separate levels of transition at work at the same time, as suggested by Wisconsin analyst Gormley. The first is the logistical transition whereby a viable, functioning office is established for the governor-elect. In most states, this proceeded smoothly except for some critical decisions, such as those made by the governor-elect of Michigan to set up his interim office outside the state capital and by the governor-elect of California to have several interim offices, only one of which was in the state capital.

The second transition is administrative and focuses on personnel selection and institutionalizing the decision-making processes in accord with the governor's personal style. When the new governor has a known track record as an administrator, such as former governors or attorneys general do, this transition can be, and usually was, smoother than when process and style have yet to be determined. In the latter situation, some initial starts and experiments often had to be modified to meet unanticipated problems and to correct processes that were inappropriate to the situation.

For example, Governor Sheffield of Alaska took some early politically inept and unresponsive actions that hurt some of his supporters as he grappled with the revenue shortfalls caused by a decline in worldwide oil prices. He infuriated the agriculture lobby, caused demonstrations among college students, displeased supporters of both the arts and the sciences, and threatened rural and Native Alaskans. He also made an ill-advised fund-raising trip to Houston, which created undermining questions about conflicts of interest in oil company relationships. Governor Anaya's penchant for becoming involved in out-of-state political activities and his excessive attention to the details of his administration led to an image problem with the media that some felt might well interfere with his effectiveness as governor of New Mexico. When Governor Blanchard of Michigan suggested a one-year delay in handling a chemical spill in a small community, the result was a court decision in which a judge ordered the state to act immediately.

The third level of transition relates to policy and refers to the various goals, principles, and programs that the governor wishes to pursue during his administration. This transition embraces the period from the campaign through the process of budget preparation, introduction, and passage, and to the introduction of initial legislative proposals and the assignment of program priorities. This level, or aspect, of the transition was the most important in the 1982–83 transition states because the state budget shortfalls brought fiscal policy to the forefront. These shortfalls supplanted activities in the other transitions at some points and submerged other policy interests and concerns. This third level, or policy transition, also explains why most state observers view the overall transition as incomplete until the legislature has met, considered, and disposed of the governor's budget and policy initiatives. Thus, part of this third transition is political in that it involves relationships with other important actors such as the legislature.

The three transitions appear to form a continuum ranging from the least personal (logistical), through the administrative or managerial, to the most personal (policy). At the least personal end are all procedures, physical amenities, and what might be labeled surface-level communication and cooperation. The administrative transition, in the middle of this continuum, begins to introduce the personal involvement of the governor in bringing his style of management to the state's chief executive office and to the various processes of state government. At the most personal end, the policy transition involves the direct imprint and involvement of the governor himself in setting goals, communicating them, and negotiating with various individuals (agency heads, legislators, interest groups) to achieve them.

Breakdowns and successes in the transition processes become attributed more to the governor himself as one moves from the logistical to the administrative to the policy transition. Although each of these transitions begins well before election day—or they should—they can and do have significant mutual impact. As Alaska analyst McBeath notes, technical and administrative preparations for the gubernatorial transition—the cookbook recipes of the formal transition—are far less important than political preparation by the governor and his staff. Understanding the differences between these levels of transition can be most important for those anticipating, undergoing, assisting, or analyzing a gubernatorial transition. And it must be remembered, as Massachusetts analyst Weinberg notes, it is impossible to enumerate the "dogs that didn't bite" because of the time and attention of the transition staff and the newly elected governor as they work their way into office.

The message from these studies is that there are significant similarities that can be observed and understood, though transitions do vary somewhat from state to state. Although politics still pervades to a considerable extent, there is evidence that transitions are viewed more seriously than in the past by the incoming and the outgoing governors and their staffs, and that in certain areas politics can be set aside. Models of institutionalized transition do not exist in the states. Examples of how to do it and how not to do it are available, and parts of those examples have been adopted and parts avoided. Much, however, is still tied to the politics of a clearly political situation.

Gubernatorial Transition
in Alabama

LAURENCE J. O'TOOLE, JR.

The changing of the guard in the executive mansion in Alabama during 1982 can perhaps be best understood as a transition within a transition. Forrest Hood (Fob) James was replaced by George Wallace at a time of particularly acute uncertainty and confusion in the state. Despite the return to office of Alabama's most durable politician, the gubernatorial transition this time may have been more indicative of flux than at any other period in the state's modern history. Before the shift to the Wallace administration was complete, the signs of political malleability and turmoil were already again abundant.

The Alabama Context:
Political and Economic Underdevelopment

If Alabama is not a "political museum piece," as V. O. Key once characterized the Virginia political system,[1] it is nevertheless a political anachronism. The Heart of Dixie is an underdeveloped society in the midst of a postindustrial nation.

Alabama's one-party political environment has resulted in no-party politics: candidates' support derives from friends and neighbors, plus the loyalty acquired through patronage or other tangible rewards disbursed by electoral victors.[2] In general, the Alabama one-party political system reduces continuity between administrations,[3] creates little incentive for a strong merit system well protected from the vicissitudes of quadrennial electoral contests, and almost necessitates a heavy overlap among key campaign, transition, and gubernatorial office appointees.

Other institutions of the Alabama political order are little further advanced. For instance, slightly more than a decade ago, the legislature was rated by the Citizens Conference on State Legislatures as the least equipped in the nation to perform its function adequately.[4] Some alterations have taken place in the ensuing years, yet today the body is mostly without staff and virtually without offices. By far, most of the information provided to legislators in Montgomery comes from lobbyists.[5]

Major interest groups in Alabama may for simplicity's sake be described as organized into two broad coalitions. The first represents business and prosperous farming interests. The second comprises organized labor, blacks (especially via the Alabama Democratic Coalition), trial lawyers, and personnel in the elementary and secondary school systems of the state. (The latter are represented by the very powerful Alabama Education Association, or AEA.) Neither group would be considered especially liberal by national standards, and both are concerned mostly with issues of fairly narrow self-interest. Yet the former is much the more conservative. During the administration of Governor James (1979–83) legislators connected with or sympathetic to this conservative, business-oriented coalition dominated both houses of the legislature.

Finally, the state government generally, including the operations of the Alabama bureaucracy, has long been reputed to be of poor quality. The merit system is relatively weak; there is no systematic effort to recruit and retain administrative expertise; and, as a study group recently reported, the state has "poor public services in several key areas and inaccessible services in others."[6] The citizenry themselves are not impressed by the performance of their governmental institutions.[7] Any new Alabama governor thus labors under additional handicaps deriving from the character of Alabama government itself.

If the Alabama political system suggests underdevelopment, the state's economic system reinforces that judgment. In 1982–83, a period of great problems for economies all over the nation, a distressed economy in Alabama may seem merely one state's version of the national norm. Yet the picture in the Heart of Dixie is one of the worst in the United States.

The state lacks a diversified industrial structure and a skilled labor force.[8] Dependence on the steel industry has meant disastrous results from the collapse of the domestic automobile market and the increased reliance of American companies on foreign sources. The state's economy also relies heavily on low-wage industry such as textile production and land-based enterprises such as farming and timber. During the 1982 gubernatorial campaign and the subsequent transition period, Alabama's unemployment rate hovered at approximately second worst in the nation. The state's economy was the number one issue in the 1982 gubernatorial campaign.

As scholars studying gubernatorial transition observed some time ago, even in the best of circumstances states possess limited financial flexibility, and this constraint often severely restricts the options available to new governors.[9] Alabama's situation is particularly acute. The property tax, in most states a major source of local government revenue, is the lowest in the nation. As a consequence, the state government finances a much heavier proportion of school costs than is typical elsewhere. Because Alabama's tax capacity and effort are both low, forty-ninth and fortieth in the nation, respectively,[10] the state is hard pressed to cover its obligations. Other major sources of tax revenue are the heavily utilized and regressive sales tax and a nominally progressive income tax. The state has also relied on federal support (more than 45 percent of tax receipts in 1981); thus, because of the cutbacks of federal funds in recent years, Alabama's revenue problems have mounted.

Furthermore, the state's very rigid funding, budget, and political structure make rational allocation decisions nearly impossible. One constraint is the state constitution, now the longest and most cumbersome in the nation. This document requires public approval via referendum before any income tax reform can be enacted. Other problems include the facts that 88 percent of the state budget consists of earmarked revenue, the highest percentage in the nation, and that Alabama's neglect of funding for its prisons and its mental health facilities stimulated the federal district court in Montgomery to assume partial control over these vital state activities—from earlier in the 1970s until this transition period—and to mandate certain state expenditures. In addition state law stipulates that, should revenues not keep pace with projections upon which a budget is based, the governor must order "proration"—the Alabama term for across-the-board budget reductions—in the appropriate proportion, with no ability to distinguish some activities or agencies from others. In September 1982, lame-duck Governor James ordered proration of 10 percent for the Special Education Trust Fund (SETF) and 15 percent for the state's General Fund agencies.

In short Alabama's political and economic systems in 1982 seemed more linked to the state's past then to the pressing problems and opportunities of the current decade. Yet all had not been static. The outgoing governor had arrived in office in 1979 committed to constitutional reform and businesslike government. That he had had little success stemmed partly from his abhorrence of and ineptitude in the political process. Even the election of George Wallace, a man labeled by opponents during the campaign as a throwback to the least attractive times and features of Alabama politics, symbolized a state in transition. For Wallace is, if anything, the quintessentially adaptive politician.

Campaign and Election:
A Fourth Term for Governor George

THE INCUMBENT

James typified the successful entrepreneur. By the 1970s the company he founded had become the nation's leading producer of weight-lifting paraphernalia. James had been active on behalf of Republican causes in Alabama for a number of years. By the late 1970s he became convinced that he could provide the good business sense that was needed to lead the executive branch. He declared himself a Democratic candidate in 1978 (despite protests about his apparent lack of loyalty to that party) and surprised almost everyone by leading a large group of candidates in the primary, winning the runoff, and trouncing the token Republican opposition in November. His inclination was to believe that there were single correct answers to complicated government problems. He had the engineer's view of political life and the businessman's distaste for ambiguity and compromise. James entered the political arena and the governor's office labeling himself nonpartisan and nonpolitical. The transition experience and, later on, early legislative defeats resulted in substantial frustration and an antipolitical stance that he held throughout his tenure. Thus, outgoing Governor George Wallace thrived on the political; James detested it. In taking over the statehouse from Wallace, James aimed to change drastically the way the state's chief executive went about governing.

During the 1978–79 transition, when James and his staff were trying to familiarize themselves with the operations of the governor's office and the circumstances of state government, they felt that the Wallace team had been less than completely cooperative. Almost all James's people had been neophytes in the political process in Montgomery, and they had come away from that experience with the belief that the outgoing administration had not provided much help in such crucial areas as how to handle appointments. Furthermore, they believed that Wallace and his cronies (as they were inevitably called by Alabama critics of the several-term governor) had taken care to commit, or waste, as much state funding as possible shortly before leaving office. As might be expected, the Wallace people of that period remember things differently: they provided plenty of help to the newcomers and left funding for the governor's office and other agencies in fine shape.

The first months of the James administration were somewhat chaotic. The governor announced a number of reform ideas and expected support to develop for them, but he was much less interested in or skillful at dealing with the political realities of Alabama public life. Instead of targeting a few central issues as priorities and working with the legislature on these, the governor pursued issues simultaneously and sporadically.

He also interpreted the principle of separation of powers literally, refusing to exercise the traditional gubernatorial prerogative of helping to organize (and thus acquire some influence within) the legislature. Partly as a result, James had little success with the lawmakers and was viewed with disdain by many of them.

Although many of his initiatives were aimed at "good government," especially redressing what he viewed as the undue politicization of Alabama government under Wallace, James's distaste for the political process and his lack of attention to administration meant that few of his reforms were institutionalized. The governor tried to rationalize much state decision making, but he rarely attempted to solidify these moves through legislation, regulation, or executive order. As a result, succeeding chief executives would be able to return Alabama government to previous practices, should they so desire.

Perceived as uncorruptible but also inflexible, businesslike but disorganized, concerned with progressive government but very conservative on almost all issues, interested in improving services in Alabama but convinced that taxes were too high and that Ronald Reagan's economic program did not go far enough—these ironies described Fob James, the Alabama governor who decided in summer 1982 not to seek another term in office.

THE RACE

The Democratic primary has been the real contest in Alabama for decades, and 1982 was to be no different. Three major candidates vied for support. Another potential, and previous, gubernatorial hopeful, former state attorney general Bill Baxley, decided that because of Wallace's possible candidacy, he would refrain and instead seek election as lieutenant governor.

Joe McCorquodale, longtime member and speaker of the Alabama House of Representatives, declared his interest in the post after receiving assurances, he claimed, that George Wallace planned not to be in the running. McCorquodale represented a rural south Alabama district and in earlier years had tended to draw from some of the same groups as Wallace. During his period as speaker he represented the conservative business coalition and had developed a reputation as an experienced, hardworking legislator without much charismatic appeal.

George McMillan, the state's lieutenant governor, had made no secret of his interest in the state's top post. He developed a well-organized campaign operation and sought to take advantage of his reputation as a "new South" political moderate who would lead the state from its dependence on the politics of the past to an era of racial, educational, and economic progress. McMillan's reference to the politics of the past was a shorthand symbol for George Wallace, who also announced his candidacy—his fifth attempt at the office.

Wallace's announcement surprised McCorquodale and weakened his candidacy. After a desultory campaign—all three candidates promised if elected to stimulate economic recovery for Alabama—McCorquodale was eliminated on September 7, and the field was narrowed to McMillan and Wallace for a runoff. McCorquodale followed his loss with an endorsement of the Republican candidate, Montgomery mayor Emory Folmar.

Shortly after the primary, Governor James placed the state General and SET funds into proration. The race between Wallace and McMillan began to focus more intensively on state economic conditions and the government's finances. Wallace promised no new consumer taxes, suggested that he planned to provide increased state support for education, and claimed that Alabama's economic problems could be solved by attracting industry from out of state. Wallace argued that his earlier experience as a national political figure provided him entré into corporate board rooms and councils of government all over the world.

McMillan argued that he would be more likely to encourage industrial development. If he were governor, Alabama's negative image would no longer be a problem, he said. In short, McMillan tried to make Wallace—his previous policy stands, his health, his past preoccupation with national politics—the real issue; Wallace tried to use his name and experience as assets.

Other issues occasionally altered this pattern slightly. Both candidates openly courted the state's black vote (roughly 30 percent of the expected primary turnout), with McMillan winning endorsement of the major black Democratic political organizations, such as the Alabama Democratic Coalition. Wallace defended himself on the issue, saying that he had made a "mistake" in the past and, in a 1980s version of an old Wallace refrain, promised to be the spokesman for the little guy of either race. "I see the rich getting richer and the poor getting poorer," he asserted on the night of his primary victory.[11] The former governor had used a black female public relations expert as his statewide coordinator with minorities, and his campaign organization contacted black preachers to try to influence the vote.

The race was extremely close overall, with Wallace the winner on September 28 by a 19,000-vote margin, 51 percent to 49 percent. This was the tightest gubernatorial contest in Alabama since the 1930s. Despite the endorsement of McMillan by black organizations, roughly 30 percent of the black vote went to Wallace in the runoff. McMillan, noting that Wallace's campaign tactics had not always been benign, endorsed the winner and suggested that he himself might be heard from again in the future.

The campaign for the general election was less exciting. Wallace played the traditional role of the front-runner in a one-party state: he avoided specifics; he made virtually no promises (the only two recorded and acknowledged by his staff following the election were the guarantee of no increase in consumer taxes and the commitment to work on the economy of the state); he refused to debate his opponent; and, in fact, he appeared publicly only in carefully staged presentations. Wallace spoke at campaign rallies, but he mingled little with the crowds and talked only rarely to reporters. For the most part, Wallace's staff ensured that the aging and nearly deaf candidate would be neither physically exhausted nor carefully scrutinized by outsiders. There were rumors that the former governor was ailing, that his health was deteriorating, that he might be incapable of governance. Yet the press did not amplify these claims much, and the attempts by Wallace's Republican opponent to draw attention to his rival's condition attracted little notice or comment.

Emory Folmar, who ran unopposed in the Republican primary, had originally been considered by Republican faithful and some political pundits the most formidable general election opponent the Democrats would have had to face in quite some time. He seemed to be popular in his home city, he had established a statewide reputation as a tough law-and-order advocate, and his image as a vigorous public official contrasted sharply with that of Wallace in recent years. Yet Folmar had weaknesses too, and these contributed to his defeat. His Republican party affiliation allowed Wallace to paint him as the candidate of the wealthy, a familiar tactic of Alabama Democrats. Then, too, Folmar was an extreme and strident conservative. His reputation among the black community was abysmal, and Wallace was thus able to appeal to a broad coalition of voters, some seeing him as the liberal candidate, others convinced that they knew from experience Wallace's conservative approach to governance.[12]

Neither candidate tied himself to his national party (Wallace pointedly refused an offer of financial assistance by the national Democratic party) or tried to connect his opponent very much with national events, including economic woes. Certainly, however, Folmar was not provided much help by the constant flow of information about the poor state of the national economy and its particularly severe manifestations in Alabama. Unemployment was high and climbing still higher throughout the fall, and each week brought news about plant closings, layoffs, and threatened layoffs.

No other real issues appeared through the campaign, and in the final weeks the candidates sought and staged endorsements, with Wallace receiving support from the state's trial lawyers, the AFL-CIO's political action committee, and the AEA. Both candidates acquired financial support from powerful state business interests, including PAC contributions; Wallace also had significant backing from labor. Overall, Folmar officially outspent Wallace, by roughly a three-to-one ratio for the $2.7 million utilized in the general election (although sufficient additional expenditures were made by Wallace in the primary to render the two candidates' overall totals roughly equal). For both, the major bill was for television advertising.[13] But because of Wallace's extremely high name recognition in the state, Folmar had to wage his campaign almost as if he were running against an incumbent, albeit one to whom none of the state's current ills could be attributed directly.

During the entire period of primary, runoff, and general election Fob

James remained far in the political background. He endorsed no one at any time, he discussed no issues or candidates directly, and his own staff mostly stayed away from the battle. Before his departure he did express some pride at having rid Montgomery of "bagmen" during his tenure. But by this time James had essentially quit the political game and wanted out. All those who had entered office with him had long since fled, he had not been able to get much done, and even many of his supporters had given his performance low marks.

Nor was the outgoing governor himself much of an issue. About the closest that a candidate came to making James or his performance an issue was Wallace's occasional attempt to link James with Folmar via presumed real party loyalty, as in a newspaper ad a few days before the election: "What we've had the last four years is as close to a Republican governor as most of us care to get."[14] James busied himself with certain issues, some of which were clearly affected by his lame-duck status and the forces of transition.

The election of November 2 was a landslide, as most polls in the final days of the campaign had predicted. Wallace won by 58.3 percent to 39.4 percent, with approximately 1.1 million votes cast. The victory was nearly total: the former governor took sixty-two of sixty-seven counties (a few of the state's more urbanized areas went Republican) and the great majority of the black vote. Despite the sweeping victory, Wallace was to enjoy little of the early political influence usually accorded a decisive winner. On election night he announced plans to establish a task force composed of the representatives of various interests in the state; he said he planned to include some of his nonsupporters in this arrangement "because I'm the governor of all the people."[15] But almost prophetically, rumors soon circulated that the governor-elect had been seriously ill for the last few days of the campaign and was in bed with a high temperature on election night. The rumors were promptly denied, but problems were to emerge later. After a fashion, the first portion of the fourth Wallace term peaked on election day; it was to be more than a year before the rocky transition period was really over.

THE WALLACE PHENOMENON

George Corley Wallace is a most remarkable individual. A native of rural Barbour County, Wallace began his political career after World War II as a circuit judge and served in the late 1940s as a state legislator. His first significant policy action, the Wallace-Cater Act, was aimed at the same goal, industrial development, that he trumpeted more than a generation.

In 1958 Wallace ran and lost in a race for governor. His victorious rival portrayed himself as a stricter segregationist during the campaign, and accounts of the period suggest that Wallace decided then not to be out-maneuvered on that issue in the future. Four years later he won the governorship, primarily by using the race issue and attacking federal authorities and outsiders for interfering with life in Alabama. His inaugural address was a demagogic oration still famous in the state, one in which he exhorted his fellow citizens to defend "Segregation now, segregation tomorrow, segregation forever." Shortly after his entrance into office he made further use of the symbol by "standing in the school house door" in a choreographed effort to bar integration at the University of Alabama.

Wallace's first and later terms were marked by more of the same, as he castigated federal judges and bureaucrats for their actions, first on race issues, later on other state policy matters, such as the operation of the prison and mental health facilities, and on symbolic issues such as school prayer. Many in the state blamed him during the first term—and continue to do so—for making political capital of the racial tragedies in Birmingham, Selma, and elsewhere.

During that first administration Wallace was also active in creating a state junior college and technical school system. Then and in succeeding years the network grew so that now Alabama funds twenty junior colleges and twenty-nine technical schools. Defenders of the system point out that whereas twenty years ago Alabama had no structure for junior college education, now it has one of the most elaborate in the nation and one that places postsecondary education well within the geographical reach of all Alabamians. Critics label the arrangement a boondoggle, creating too many underfunded, low-enrollment, low-quality institutions that serve primarily as pork barrels and repositories of Wallace loyalists via patronage slots. Seven colleges bear the Wallace name: five for George, one for his first wife Lurleen, one for his father.

Wallace in the past enjoyed being governor, but he seemed to enjoy seeking office as much, if not more so. In 1964 he conducted a brief campaign for the presidency. In 1966 he sought a constitutional amendment to allow him to run for another term as governor. The legislature did not acquiesce, and Wallace had to resort to running vicariously: his wife Lurleen was the Democratic candidate and ultimate victor. George was, of course, the de facto governor on many matters. In 1968 Wallace mounted his most serious effort for the presidency, running as a third-party candidate. In that same year Lurleen died. Lieutenant Governor Albert Brewer, no Wallace ally, succeeded her and ran a fairly moderate administration. In 1970 Brewer ran for governor and was challenged by Wallace in the Democratic primary. Brewer led but was forced into a runoff with Wallace. The latter appealed to the old racial fears and animosities in the final weeks of the campaign, and Wallace overtook his opponent before the end.

During this next term federal district judge Frank Johnson ruled the state's mental health facilities in violation of the U.S. Constitution and, after providing Alabama some time to alter this state of affairs, imposed detailed standards for administration of the system. Wallace "complained bitterly about federal interference, but did nothing to assume management of the systems from virtually autonomous Corrections and Mental Health Boards."[16] Meanwhile, he embarked on yet another try for the presidency in 1972; this time his effort was cut short by an assassination attempt that occurred in Maryland during May and left him seriously injured and paralyzed from the waist down.

By the time of the election in 1974 the state constitution had been amended to allow gubernatorial succession for one additional term, so Wallace ran and won handily. His third term was marked primarily by unsuccessful policy initiatives and contemplated but aborted political campaigns, and in 1976, Judge Johnson did for the state's prisons what he had done earlier for mental health and imposed a detailed set of requirements on the funding and operation of the system.

Wallace's career has thus been marked by longevity, by a phenomenal ability to appeal to inchoate concerns (especially of the white working class), by dexterity on the issues (most spectacularly, race), by success at building and maintaining a political organization for an extended period in a no-party state, and by a consistent tendency to attribute state problems to the forces of modernization and the influence of alien or complex institutions. In short, George Wallace's political career has been a spectacular achievement, but his success has been inextricably linked to the underdevelopment of the state.

The Transition Period

Clearly, the outgoing and incoming governors in Alabama, despite some common conservative tendencies, were very different in style, in supporters, and in taste for the political life. These differences, when combined with the state's no-party system, the difficult economic circumstances of 1982, the incoming governor's health, and other unanticipated events, combined for a unique transition.

EARLY ACTIVITIES

Wallace's election brought no change in James's steadfast refusal to comment directly on the campaign or the candidates. But within a day of the election James called Wallace to congratulate him on his victory and offer his assistance in the transition. Publicly, the governor announced that he wanted the transition to be "the smoothest in the history of this state,"[17] and he used the image of passing the baton to indicate that he viewed himself and the governor-elect as members of a common team.

Earlier, James's staff, especially his executive secretary, Bobby Davis, who was to coordinate efforts on the outgoing side, had done some preparatory work for the formal transition process. This group drafted some ground rules for how the two administrations might deal with each other between the election and inauguration. James said that he would ensure the assistance of his entire administration, agreed to provide some resources, and suggested a series of briefings in which all cabinet members would eventually participate. James did ask that contacts and requests for information made by the incoming administration to individual departments and agencies be made through the James appointees heading the respective units.

Governor James informed his own staff that he desired a successful transition, and they were asked to provide whatever information and assistance were requested by the Wallace people. Observers on both sides of this transition effort by and large credit James with general sincerity in this directive, although most of the Wallace team believes that on specific topics the governor countermanded his own order by concealing information or excluding the newcomers from certain decisions and that some of the governor's staff were not completely forthcoming. For their part, some of the James staffers remembered the earlier transition (from Wallace) in which they had participated. They viewed their own effort in 1982 as one that would focus primarily on bringing the Wallace group "up to speed" on all the major issues but intended to "stay out of their hair." The avowed position of the outgoing administration was to leave as many issues as possible for the new governor to influence. (Although this was the stated position, the actual results were more varied: some issues were either left for Wallace or were handled with considerable consultation; on other issues James tried to decide himself but could not because his lame-duck status precluded sufficient influence; and on still other matters he successfully took action without consulting the governor-elect or his staff.)

For the most part, the typical transition pattern asserted itself: the governor's office became a much less busy place; phone calls, letters, and traffic shifted to Wallace headquarters; and James's appointees prepared to leave. Some planned to return to the permanent bureaucracy, most sought and obtained positions in the private sector, and a few hoped to garner appointments in the new administration—though the personalized parties of the Alabama system and the gulf separating James and Wallace made such possibilities remote.

The Wallace transition team was headed by two top campaign officials and longtime Wallace allies—Bill Rushton, most recently a financial aid official for one of the state junior colleges and past assistant director of the Alabama Development Office, the state agency charged with luring industry to the Heart of Dixie; and Elvin Stanton, former assistant press secretary to Governor Wallace and a man who remained as chief Wallace aide when he left office in 1980.

Alabama law in 1982 provided no guidance or structure whatsoever for the transition process (though a proposal on the subject was introduced by a Wallace ally in the 1983 legislative session). In fact, aside from the transition four years earlier, there had been little recent precedent. Between 1963 and the arrival of the James administration, the only real transition had been between Brewer and Wallace—an occasion of considerable tension, given the hard feelings generated by the vicious primary fight.

The James administration's preference for informal administrative style, plus the absence of statutory requirements and the weak state of Alabama finances, led the outgoing group to provide some support to the Wallace team but to keep assistance low-key. "It's not that big a job," commented one James insider during the transition period. By mid-November the outgoing governor had placed a few Wallace staffers on state payroll, provided some secretarial staff, and furnished some state cars. A suite of offices for the Wallace transition team was authorized in the State Highway Department Building adjacent to the capitol.

Even before such housekeeping arrangements had been completed, however, the governor-elect and his aides had become the focus of attention among that large portion of the state's politically active citizenry that hoped to attract the attention of the once again powerful. Staffers reported that Wallace was working on his idea to assemble a task force to deal with the state's unemployment problem. Meanwhile, requests for positions with the new administration, or with state government in some capacity, flooded in from the provinces. The entire legislature had been elected at the same time as Wallace under a provisional redistricting plan approved by the federal courts for this election. The old business faction had been considerably weakened by the election, and the AEA-labor-black coalition appeared to be dominant. Wallace met with various senior lawmakers and representatives of certain important interest groups (e.g., AEA, the Farm Bureau, and labor) in the days after the election.

Comments made by the outgoing governor suggested cooperation with Wallace, but there was also a predictable perspective that was likely to create problems before long. "We'll set up a number of formal presentations [by James administration people] where they'll [i.e., the Wallace staff] know precisely where everything is, what the state of the entire government is. He [Wallace] should be able to get his legislative programs ready to go in the April session. That would be invaluable, it could save them a year or two, and we're prepared to pay for it." James spoke in this sanguine fashion out of a belief that "fundamentally the state's in good shape." He reiterated during the early transition period an assertion that he had frequently voiced during his own administration: Alabama had sufficient tax resources; the need was for cuts in spending. This basic viewpoint was to be in marked contrast to that of the incoming administration.[18]

ORGANIZING THE LEGISLATURE

Perhaps the earliest transition issue to be handled was the organization of the legislature. The outgoing governor played absolutely no role here, of course, and the struggle Wallace faced was between his own preferences and those of opponents in the legislative branch.

In the battle for control of the house, Wallace was victorious, just as most new governors in Alabama have been. Former professional wrestler Tom Drake, a longtime Wallace ally, and AEA-proponent Roy Johnson were the incoming chief executive's picks for speaker and president pro tem, respectively. After some attempts by others to test the waters, all opposition withdrew before the house voted on the matter at its organizational session in January. Yet for all practical purposes Wallace's choices were recognized as early as November as the heirs apparent to the positions. Thus, in the crucial slots of leadership in the house (the speaker chooses committee chairs and makes committee assignments, for instance) Wallace's influence would be felt throughout the period. In fact, Drake was known as such a Wallace team player that he sometimes annoyed his colleagues by emphasizing his subservience to the chief executive.

Wallace's influence was seen clearly in the house during the legislative sessions following his inauguration. Perhaps the most obvious evidence of the new governor's control over house affairs, especially in the early days, was the nature of committee assignments. Wallace prevailed upon the all-white house leadership to strengthen substantially the role of blacks in the lower chamber in payment for his electoral triumph. Drake's selections in January included four blacks as committee chairmen, four as vice-chairmen, and substantial black representation on some of the most important house committees.

In the senate, Wallace fared less well. Ever since the state's lieutenant governor became subject to independent popular election in the 1970s, the lieutenant governor has had an incentive to take an active role in selecting the legislative leaders in the senate. (The lieutenant governor presides over the senate and has sole power to name committees.) This pattern continued in 1982. Wallace had selected his choice of Senator Earl Goodwin, yet another old-time Wallace supporter, for president pro tem, but Lieutenant Governor Baxley designated Senator John Teague as his preference. Shortly before the balloting in the upper house, Goodwin withdrew in favor of Teague. The lieutenant governor had exercised some early independence from the governor, and this was to portend actions to come.

THE WALLACE TEAM

If the interim between election and inauguration was an easy period for the James administration, it was less than placid for the Wallace team. By the time this group was established in its offices in the Highway Building, there were more than enough claimants for their attention.

Virtually from the first the Wallace team was organized with a sort of dual staff directorship: Elvin Stanton and Bill Rushton occupied adjoining offices and oversaw the transition activities together. In the early days, Stanton worked on shutting down the Wallace campaign while Rushton organized the process for dealing with the James administration's staff. Others who were to assume prominent roles in the Wallace administration participated before inauguration, though less extensively. There were a number of Wallace people from previous administrations, as well as a few new faces from business and law. Old and new participated in meetings and strategy sessions; however, most disinterested observers concluded that the longtime loyalists were the more prominent in numbers and influence. Even some of the apparent newcomers were apprentices only to government service; they had long been political or personal friends of the state's once and future chief executive. (Legal advisor Ken Wallis, for example, had not worked for Wallace or the state before, yet he had been a close friend for more than twenty years.)

In the latter part of November a series of transition meetings between the two camps was begun. Most sessions were arranged at least a few days in advance and announced publicly. At these, officials from the outgoing administration responsible for one agency or a set of activities briefed the Wallace transition team leaders, plus others who had been invited by the Wallace organizers. The James administration was typically represented by one or more cabinet members (permanent bureaucrats were sometimes present, as well), who provided a briefing paper and an oral presentation. Then the two groups engaged in further discussion.

Some briefings were much more elaborate than others, as might be expected, but most shared certain common features. First, officials of the outgoing administration understandably tended to characterize their own initiatives, operations, and responsibilities favorably. As a result, some of the Wallace team began to discount much of the information obtained via this route. After the inauguration a number of Wallace aides commented that they wished they had talked more with the permanent civil servants rather than the James political appointees so that they could have learned the "truth" about the condition of state government.

Second, most representatives of the various segments of state government under the outgoing administration concentrated on the need for resources for the programs under their responsibility,[19] despite the governor's contention that the state had plenty of resources. This defense and advocacy of programs was not unexpected, but it did highlight the financial crunch that the Wallace administration was going to have to face, and it did create a sense on the part of the incoming staffers that they might have been misled by James's central transition personnel about the seriousness of the situation.

Third, most of the briefings were reactive. Few new policy ideas or options were presented by the departing administration to the incoming one. This fact is partly explained by Alabama's political system itself: the state's administrative apparatus is not strong, and agencies and chief executives have devoted few resources to policy development. Partly, the outgoing group sought to steer clear of seeming to direct the newcomers. And partly, the lack of attention to policy derived from the state's financial condition, which did not seem to allow for many new options, at least in the short run.

Because the core Wallace transition people were intimates of the governor-elect and, in most cases, individuals with extensive experience in earlier administrations, these briefings took on a different character than one might have expected if the outgoing governor had been succeeded by a neophyte staff. There was little discussion of basic information about the political and governmental process in Alabama and much more emphasis on "current facts of life." Some on the Wallace team believed that the experience represented by their staff was greater than that among the James contingent and that their experience was especially helpful during this period. Others in the same group concluded that there may have been costs as well: some of the longtime Wallace people seemed to have had their own views of the issues and may not have learned as much from the "James gang" as they might have had they entered the transition dialogue with open minds and a willingness to be taught.

Other meetings between incoming and outgoing teams were less regular and less formal but certainly no less important. The incoming governor met with the James central staff early in the transition period, for example, to learn the status of certain high-priority issues, including state finances and litigation concerning prisons and mental health. Staffers from both groups met off and on concerning these matters through the period.

The Wallace transition team arranged a third type of meeting, though this did not involve members of the James administration. The incoming group sought to draw ideas and support from, and to buffer the governor-elect from the demands of, various interests in the state. Some major interest groups that were expecting to back proposals in the upcoming session of the legislature tried to attract Wallace's attention through his staff. Some interests also attempted to influence the appointments process or convey quietly to the new administration their own frank assessment of the strengths and weaknesses of the previous administration's efforts in areas of concern to them.

For the most part, the governor-elect remained apart from the day-to-day workings of his team. He spent most of his time at his residence, he visited his transition headquarters only occasionally, he spoke at public functions rarely and was hardly seen during the period between election and inauguration. As the routine briefings were being completed in December, the top Wallace transition group spent less and less time conferring with James people and more and more time on appointments and the Alabama revenue and budget picture. Rushton and Stanton consulted with Wallace daily on these two topics and were widely perceived by those within and without the Wallace camp as particularly influential.

DOMINANT ISSUES DURING THE TRANSITION PERIOD

Between Wallace's election and the end of the transition period, of course, many decisions requiring gubernatorial input had to be made. A few of the dominant issues deserve special attention here.

Appointments. That the monumental task of making political appointments is expected and roughly predictable does not make it much easier. In Alabama an incoming chief executive is confronted with the need to make approximately thirty-five to forty selections for his cabinet (major department heads and professional appointments to gubernatorial staff), to make subcabinet selections, and to make a much larger set of appointments for boards, commissions, and local positions (e.g., license inspectors, boards of registrars). In addition the governor fills vacancies that may appear in elective positions such as public service commissioner or state judgeships. An Alabama governor makes approximately 4,000 appointments during a four-year term.

In most respects the appointments transition from James to Wallace was one of the smoothest aspects of the change in the governorship. Upon James's arrival four years earlier, his administration had had its hands full trying to cope with the appointments process. Some confusion in that new administration, combined with the lack of comprehensive records or assistance from the preceding Wallace group, meant that many of the appointments were delayed for months. Finally, in one of many staff changes to occur during the administration, James hired a hometown friend, Judson Salter, as his appointments secretary (the third person to occupy the slot), and Salter remained until Wallace's inauguration. He established an elaborate system for appointments decision making, and after Wallace's election in 1982 he spent considerable time explaining to the new people the details of his system. Salter provided "great cooperation," in the words of a Wallace insider. As a result, the new administration was able to fill a large number of positions almost immediately.

High-level positions, for example those in the governor's office, were staffed before inauguration. The top transition officials, Rushton and Stanton, spent considerable time on this topic between November and January. They solicited recommendations, checked political and other credentials, and discussed options with the governor-elect. Much public attention centered on the Wallace appointees, for two reasons beyond those that usually stimulate attention to a new governor's selections: Wallace's campaign claim that fresh young faces would play prominent roles in his new administration and Wallace's reliance on black support for his runoff victory. Some young professionals did assume high-level positions, and four blacks were selected to positions in the cabinet or on the governor's staff.

Yet the Wallace "inner cabinet," the small group of staffers that would exercise by far the most influence, was made up mostly of familiar personnel. The smaller circle included Rushton (named just prior to inauguration the director of the Office of State Planning and Federal Programs—a unit to be reorganized, renamed, and strengthened shortly after Wallace took office), Stanton (who was selected as Wallace's executive secretary), Henry Steagall (former executive secretary, now the state's new finance director), plus Billy Joe Camp (former Wallace press secretary, who assumed the position once again). One newcomer but a longtime friend, Ken Wallis, might also be included in this small group; he was named the governor's legal advisor. Most of this group met virtually every day to discuss issues and plan strategy and tactics, though Wallace himself seldom convened staff meetings. His dealings with his staff were mostly one-to-one encounters.[20]

Wallace's governor's office was more heavily staffed than James's outgoing unit (fourteen professionals versus eight) and more clearly organized. The inner circle, especially Stanton and Rushton, were recognized as de facto chiefs of staff, and the jurisdictions of the others were fairly clear. In James's group, the governor's chaotic administrative style had typified the operation: any staffer could pursue whatever he or she wanted. The results under James had been little consistent follow-through on policy matters, few useful staff meetings, high frustration, and rapid turnover.

The remainder of the top selections in the Wallace cabinet were similar to those mentioned above: a sprinkling of new faces mixed with a large number of old Wallace supporters. Some of the latter were reappointed to positions they had occupied under a previous Wallace administration. Although this practice allowed the new administration to capitalize on experience, it created some unique problems. Some selections reminded Alabamians of issues that the new governor had claimed to foresake (e.g., Wallace reappointed his former highway director, a man with a racist reputation). Another cabinet selection, the reappointment of his former director of the Commission on Aging, caused some consternation within the bureaucracy itself. (At the end of the preceding Wallace administration some civil servants alleged confidentially to the State Ethics Commission that this man had violated the Alabama bid law. The ethics panel investigated and forwarded information to the attorney general, who never prosecuted. Now the appointee was returning to his former post and would oversee those who had provided the information!)

A few months into office, Wallace had a chance to fill other state positions, and a number went to relatives (e.g., two judgeships), supporters, and friends. By June, despite the state's fiscal difficulties, the public payroll had expanded by approximately 700 positions. Two high-level appointees had served prison terms, and another had been fined for violating the state's ethics law. Two cabinet members were widely accused of devoting only part of their time to their state responsibilities, and Wallace reorganized several boards and commissions, thus eliminating appointees from the James years and replacing them with his own.[21] The charges of cronyism were insistently made by the media and the governor's political opponents. In short, in at least this aspect of state decision making, the fourth Wallace administration bore the marks of the previous three.

State finances. Gubernatorial transitions stimulate quarrels about money even in the best of times. It is thus no surprise that in Alabama, a state with strained resources and a wide assortment of restrictions on finances, the shift from James to Wallace generated hard feelings. In 1982 it became clear that state revenues would not meet projections, and James ordered proration. He and his staff saw his action as a statesman-like effort to preserve Alabama's fiscal integrity while several months remained in his term.

During the transition period, however, the Wallace staff became convinced that the state's General Fund was in worse shape than they had been led to believe. They concluded that the problem had been created partly by incompetence (bad revenue projections) and partly through malevolence. "They're liars," said one top Wallace staffer in his assessment of the James group, "so we cut ourselves off from them" (in the weeks before inauguration).

Contributing to this difficulty was the fact that during the transition the Wallace group had felt systematically excluded from any decision making that would have monetary consequences. This group believed that it had not gotten information it had asked for and that the outgoing governor and his staff had taken care to commit as much revenue as possible in the last months of the administration—presumably so that the revenue would not be available for Wallace. The complaints from the Wallace people were that the commitment of resources in times of such financial strictures was irresponsible and that the James people, in the words of one Wallace aide, had left the newcomers "out in the cold." From the perspective of the new arrivals, then, the state financial picture was probably the most important and also the roughest aspect of the transition. The conflict and distrust generated here markedly reduced the overall cooperation between the two administrations. By the time the inauguration was near, the high-level Wallace staffers had indeed decided to go it alone rather than to work with the outgoing group.

There seems to be at least some truth to the assertions and accusations of the Wallace side. The James administration did not fully trust Wallace and his group with the wisdom to spend in the best interests of the state. Yet it also seems probable that the Wallace group overstated the restrictions under which they labored. There is certainly an incentive to blame an outgoing administration for the inevitable lack of sufficient resources to satisfy all claimants. And overstating the extent of financial hardship faced by the state may also ease the passage of additional revenue measures.

On the eve of the inauguration the Wallace transition team's report to the governor was leaked to the press. Their analysis blamed the outgoing administration for the state's financial circumstances, labeled James's operations "bizarre," and hinted that new revenues might be needed to salvage the ship of state. This report, combined with the recommendation of one of Wallace's task forces—that the state develop a "more realistic" revenue structure—seemed to be a trial balloon on the tax question. The governor did call a special legislative session immediately after inauguration to handle some short-term financial emergencies (e.g., increasing the state's oil severance tax to help bail out Alabama's perennially strapped Medicaid agency) and asked for an increase in the state's unemployment compensation taxes in a second special session following directly upon the first. (In fact Wallace called four special sessions in 1983, thus tying an Alabama record that he had set in 1975.)

The main item in his legislative package presented to the regular session in April was a bundle of short-term fiscal measures totaling slightly more than $80 million and aimed at solving the most severe revenue problems. (These measures included fee increases, speeded-up collections, and higher charges for alcoholic beverages.) In an attempt to hold to his campaign promise to impose no consumer taxes Wallace labeled these measures revenue enhancements, from the infelicitous phrasing used by the Reagan administration. Before the opening of the regular session there were reports that Wallace may have been considering a push for more significant tax increases; in fact, staffers had been meeting with legislative and interest group leaders on this subject. Yet at that time an unexpected judicial decision ordering new elections for the legislature effectively ended these efforts, at least until 1984. There seemed to be a broadening awareness that tax reform must inevitably come to Alabama, but during the transition the Wallace revenue efforts seemed to propose an interlude rather than to establish a direction.

Litigation. The state's revenue problems illustrate the difficulties that can entangle a transition effort. But on the subject of litigation the outgoing and incoming administrations found it in their mutual interest to reach agreement.

Alabama's prisons and mental health facilities had been the subject of litigation since earlier Wallace administrations. When Fob James took office in 1979, he asked in federal court that he be appointed receiver of the prison and mental health systems. In this capacity the governor would be held responsible for moving them into compliance with federal directives. The court agreed. As his term was ending, James tried to argue in court that the essential goals mandated by Judge Johnson for the prison system had been achieved and that the system should be returned to the jurisdiction of state administration. James further proposed that Wallace or his designee be named receiver for the mental health system.

At the start of the transition James said that he expected "absolutely no conflict" between his own position and that of the governor-elect. The James staff, led by the governor's attorney Jimmy Samford, briefed the Wallace group (Ken Wallis represented Wallace). In this situation, both James and Wallace would be served by settlement. James had made amelioration of the problems a priority of his administration and desired to claim a success before departure. Wallace had earlier used federal intervention to score political points, but inflammation of the issue now would only remind people of an embarrassment.

Less than a week before James's departure, settlements were reached in both cases in federal court. In the ten-year-old prison suit, attorneys for the inmates, Governor James, and the state's outgoing prison commissioner agreed on a plan by which a four-member committee would monitor the state's compliance with federal standards. Full compliance was expected by all parties within less than two years. Wallace's representatives had not been formally included in the last-minute arrangements. This fact provoked some token complaints by Wallace's representatives, but the incoming chief executive seemed relieved not to have to deal with the issue after all. "We're encouraged by the fact that there is a settlement. . . . It's very close to being an acceptable agreement to the incoming governor," Wallis remarked. As one newspaper commented editorially, "when the governor's [i.e., Wallace's] lawyer pronounced his client 'insulted,' it sounded a lot like a sigh of relief."[22] This resolution of the matter solved some but not all of Alabama's problems. Prison overcrowding continued to plague the system and generated both controversy and maneuvering later in Wallace's term, especially by the state's politically ambitious attorney general.

The James administration's proposal in the mental health case was for the system to be returned to full state control, with the new governor or his designee named receiver until regular arrangements could be implemented. Once again, shortly before inauguration, attorneys for the patients and the governor reached agreement on a phasing-out of court controls. The federal judge appointed a receiver for the system, but within a few weeks of inauguration the appeals court had agreed with the Wallace administration's contention that the receiver would have to

have the approval of the new administration. The new governor selected
his legal advisor Ken Wallis as the new receiver of the system, and the
choice was approved by the court.

The Auburn turmoil. The state's important litigation was settled during the transition period because the outgoing governor was not impo-
tent and because both James and Wallace could benefit by a resolution.
Yet in at least one other major item of state business James was hampered by his lame-duck status. A solution required the installation of a
new chief executive.

Auburn University is Alabama's land-grant university and the state's
largest center of higher education. The governor serves as ex officio chairman of the Auburn Board of Trustees, and all other members are appointed by the governor from within the state by congressional district,
thus inevitably involving the university in state politics.

By mid-1982, Auburn's controversial president, originally appointed in
1980 while James was chairman of the board, had antagonized the faculty and administration to such an extent that the campus was in turmoil. James delayed calling the board together to deal with the situation
until after his declaration not to run for reelection. Thereafter, the university president's strongest supporters on the board, who themselves had
been appointed by Wallace in an earlier term, were unmoved by the
governor and insisted on delay.

On election day Auburn's faculty assembled to ask the president to
resign or be fired. The president refused, and there followed a series of
three board meetings between election and inauguration. At each, a minority of the board urged the president's dismissal, to no avail. The controversy escalated, with students, alumni, the Farm Bureau and other
major state interests, plus the legislature and the regional newspapers,
all joining the dispute. National media descended on the rural Alabama
campus, and during the transition period this conflict received more attention in the press than did any other state issue.

Governor James saw his influence reduced to nil but was belatedly
committed to a solution. He held out hope that he might be able to
move the board before he departed office, commenting in his usual ath-
letic metaphor that "a lot can happen in the last two minutes of a ball
game." Yet all he was able to accomplish was a cosmetic change in the
structure of the university, which increased the controversy.

Wallace had maintained that he would have nothing to do with the
matter until he took office, but privately he heard from many interested

parties, including faculty leaders and the president, as inauguration approached. Shortly after he replaced James, Wallace was instrumental in settling the Auburn dispute. His influence stemmed from a number of sources. First, of course, the board would normally be attentive to a new chief executive. Second, a number of board members counted themselves members of the Wallace party. And third, three of twelve trustee slots were available for appointment by the new governor when he assumed office; thus, he could exercise substantial immediate influence over the composition of the board. Wallace first made his trustee selections, including the reappointment of the university president's most ardent supporter and the selection of another, who helped manage the final arrangements. Then, from a hospital bed, he called a board meeting that forced the president's resignation. By late February the Auburn campus was quiet again.

The task forces. During the transition period Wallace undertook one other initiative that deserves discussion. Shortly after election the governor-elect established two task forces. One was to develop ideas for assisting the newly unemployed; the second was to focus on ideas for economic recovery in Alabama. Both were composed of members representing divergent interests and seemed aimed as much at formal cooptation as at generating an agenda for the administration.

The task force on assisting the poor developed relatively tame suggestions in line with the Wallace administration's general approach to social problems; it called upon private charity to aid those in need and made proposals to reduce administrative inefficiencies in the state's system of voluntary agencies. The group studying economic recovery recommended much broader reforms in state policy, including tax reform, more legislative staff, a major overhaul in Alabama's system of higher education, and a reorganization of the state's effort to attract industry. Many of the ideas were not new but had been exceedingly controversial in earlier years.

The groups provided their reports to Wallace near inauguration day, and the governor was said by aides to have been studying the recommendations. Yet he neither adopted nor supported any of the significant suggestions during his first year in office, and none received serious attention in the legislature. (The economic recovery task force was to play a larger role in influencing Wallace's 1984 program.)

The Wallace Reprise:
Administering a State in Transition

George Wallace reassumed the mantle of governor on January 17. His twenty-three-minute address offered few specifics on plans for his term but called for cooperation and harmony, plus individual and institutional charity, to alleviate the effects of the state's economic distress. Wallace attacked eastern banks and some federal agencies for not having the interests of the common people at heart, but these charges lacked the fervor of earlier Wallace orations. The occasion was one of nostalgia for many of the 5,000 people who stood outside the capitol to hear him. Yet on this day, as Fob James quietly slipped out to drive away with his wife and as subdued inaugural festivities were being held in Montgomery for the newcomers, there was little clear sense of how this new administration would make its mark. As it turned out, the fourth Wallace term never did establish an initial direction. The new administration found itself overtaken by unanticipated and uncontrollable events.

The new administration began normally enough. Gubernatorial appointees moved into their offices and experienced the usual hectic confusion of a changeover. Wallace called for a special legislative session (and another right on its heels) to deal with pressing financial matters and with legislative reapportionment, and the governor's top staff met with each other and with legislators to coordinate the operations.

The new governor sought to gain control over the bureaucracy via top aides, especially Bill Rushton. During the second special session in February, Wallace successfully backed legislation merging five agencies, including those that receive most of the state's discretionary federal aid, into a Department of Economic and Community Affairs headed by Rushton. Many observers assumed that this unit would be the Wallace administration's prime mechanism for influencing legislators and local officials on behalf of the governor; as the regular legislative session progressed, these expectations bore fruit. Rushton and the rest of the inner circle used state aid to sway votes and discipline an increasingly restive group of lawmakers.[23]

Wallace himself was hardly seen. He could occasionally be found at his office for a ceremonial occasion, but the top Wallace staff seemed to outsiders to be the major decision makers. There were some flashes of the old Wallace political acumen, yet mostly the governor was invisible.

One reason was revealed on the night of February 21, when Wallace, complaining of discomfort, was hospitalized in Montgomery. His problem was diagnosed as an inflammation of the colon. Wallace was treated and returned home a week later. He was readmitted on March 10 and left on March 16, only to enter another hospital in Birmingham three days later. This time he stayed until April 8, and physicians revealed that the chief executive was in constant and considerable pain stemming from the injuries sustained in the assassination attempt. Further, they indicated, Wallace had been receiving a variety of medications, including an antidepressant and a narcotic for the relief of pain. Of his first eighty-one days in office the governor had been hospitalized for thirty-three.

The status of the governor's health and his fitness for office became the major issue of state politics. Legislators complained of not being able to meet with the governor or discuss matters of policy; gubernatorial staff outside the inner circle were distracted by rumors of the governor's reported death or resignation (some circulated résumés and readied themselves for other employment); and, as Wallace's press secretary commented a month after the governor had returned home, "Probably 40 percent of my work time this week was spent on matters that would be considered rumors."[24]

Once the governor had been released from the hospital, his public visibility did not increase for months. Wallace convened only one press conference all year. He stayed almost always in the executive mansion, canceling virtually all public appearances and sending replacements in his stead; legislators and lobbyists began to perceive the top staff, rather than the governor himself, as the real chief executive. Some asserted that state government was in crisis; others openly questioned whether positions supposedly espoused by the governor were really his own, and he could not appear to answer the query. In earlier Wallace administrations the governor often had seemed less than fully involved in state administration and had left much to the discretion of trusted aides. But he had always been available to settle major disputes and to listen to legislators and lobbyists.[25] A political symbol, especially a living one like Wallace, cannot remain invisible. There were rumors of infighting among the inner circle (denied by all) and reports that some of this group were trying to sneak decisions past the ailing governor. In mid-April the governor did address the opening of the regular legislative session, but his remarks were brief and rambling, and his appearance added fuel to the rumors. George Wallace seemed a new governor in limbo.

As if this were not enough, another unexpected event threw the state political scene into more confusion. The Alabama legislature had been elected in 1982 under a redistricting plan provisionally approved by a three-judge federal panel for that election only. The lawmakers had been ordered to draft a permanent plan by the following March 1 or be subject to a federally imposed one. They did so, and just before the opening of the regular session the panel of federal judges ruled in favor of the plan, but in an unexpected move they ordered new elections for 1983. The most immediate political effect was to virtually eliminate any chance that controversial policy would be considered that year. The new legislature was now running for election, and the governor proposed only three minor matters for consideration: a bundle of crime bills, including many approved in the previous year but nullified by a technicality; the revenue enhancement measures; and a proposal to return to biennial legislative sessions. The Wallace budget was basically level funding with very minor adjustments.

Even this modest package encountered difficulty, especially in the Senate. Lieutenant Governor Baxley, presiding there and anxious to place his mark on Alabama government, was backing a reform of the state's constitution. He allowed virtually no other matters to reach the senate floor for months, and he attempted to hold the governor's program hostage in exchange for favorable consideration of the constitutional revision in the house. Wallace countered with a hurried and relatively tame revision proposal of his own. Insiders reported, further, that the lieutenant governor was preparing to assume the office of chief executive should Wallace take a turn for the worse; some said that he was quietly assembling a staff. To add to the general chaos, Baxley announced at the end of May that he was a candidate for governor in the next election, and McMillan, too, began to prepare his organization for another run at the office.

The lieutenant governor's actions clearly antagonized Wallace, who by the summer had become engaged with Baxley in a struggle for leadership in Alabama government. Many observers speculated that this political battle gave renewed vitality to Wallace, who began to emerge a bit from the isolation of his first several months in office.

As 1983 sputtered to a close Wallace had had limited success in influencing policy. In the general session of the legislature only the revenue portion of his program was approved, despite the governor's ultimate decision to cooperate with the lieutenant governor on a new constitution. (In the end, the state's supreme court struck the document from the

November ballot.) Most substantive matters were delayed until a new legislature was selected. (This activity, too, involved much political maneuvering. Wallace, charged with determining the election time, chose a September date that would have precluded party primaries and, thus, many changes by the group elected in 1982. Under pressure from a federal judge the governor moved the date to November 8, but the Democratic Executive Committee decided not to hold primaries anyway.) The new legislature looked much like the old, albeit with increased numbers of Republicans and independents and the largest black representation per capita of any state legislature.[26]

Wallace had more success in influencing the legislative process during the several special sessions, when a governor has much more formal control over the agenda. Then in 1984, with his health seemingly improved and a new legislature finally in office, he proposed the first real program of his term. Ambitious by Alabama standards, it included property and income tax increases for more affluent citizens (the work of the economic recovery task force had laid the groundwork), a number of reforms in the state's elementary and secondary educational system, and more aid for highways, prisons, and mental hospitals. The burden in new taxes was estimated at $293 million, and the governor was to face a stiff challenge in the legislature. Wallace finally admitted that this program violated his campaign pledge against new taxes and claimed that he had been "absolutely wrong" to make the promise in the first place.[27]

Conclusion

James's tenure had been an interlude between Wallace administrations— and business, or politics, as usual. The transition for Wallace amounted to a reconnecting of the political and administrative linkages of four years earlier. James had made little impact on fundamental structures and processes.

The context in which the governor functions had changed, however, and Wallace's health problems accentuated that difference. Thus, before Wallace's first package had even received consideration by the lawmakers, both he and the legislature seemed in some ways more like transitory than incoming political leaders. The state was rudderless, and the 1983 transition highlighted Alabama's ambiguous situation rather than established a direction. The 1986 gubernatorial campaign had already begun. The state was drifting, apparently in transition, but one worry was that transition might be the permanent state of affairs.

Alaska's Gubernatorial Transition

GERALD A. MCBEATH

On December 6, 1982, Alaska's new Democratic governor, Bill Sheffield, took the reins of a deeply divided state. A businessman turned politician, Sheffield immediately set about designing goals for Alaska and in the process made the governorship the chief issue of the transition period. Ironically, this focus helped defuse the rural-urban tensions of the bitter campaign.

This chapter treats the Alaska transition process in four parts. The Alaska setting—land, people, and politics—is unique and requires an introduction. The transition itself began in the primary and general election campaigns. Its next stage was the executive transition, a brief moment of two months from the general election to the start of the legislative session. The last stage was properly the legislative transition. With respect to the political development of the state, it was the most important, for it provided the new governor a concentrated learning period on which future directions in state policy were based. The chapter concludes with an evaluation of the Sheffield transition.

The Setting of the Transition

Alaska is America's forty-ninth state and the most underdeveloped politically and socially. Sparsity of population explains part of this condition. In 1984 only 465,000 people populated the 375 million acres of the state (one-fifth the size of the total United States), and the population density of less than one person per square mile is perhaps the lowest in the world. Alaska's arctic and subarctic climate explain why so few live in the vast land.

Unlike the other states, Alaska is dependent on a single source of revenue for most of its activities—the super giant Prudhoe Bay oil field, discovered in 1968, which accounts for about 20 percent of domestic U.S. production. Oil and gas severance taxes, royalties, and income taxes supply nearly 90 percent of the state's revenues, and this makes the state highly dependent on changes in the oil market.

Since statehood in 1959, Alaska state government has played a more prominent role in the state's economic and social life than is the case of governments in the other states. Because Prudhoe Bay is situated on lands owned by the state, the state government is the chief means through which oil wealth is distributed. Even before Alaska became oil wealthy, state government was a major agent of change, accounting for nearly 35 percent of jobs in the state.

Another characteristic of Alaska's government and politics is the frontier quality of social and political life. Aboriginal populations of Eskimos, Indians, and Aleuts migrated across the land mass for thousands of years, but no large permanent settlement developed. The more than 200 Native villages that hold a majority of Alaska's rural population are tiny settlements by American rural standards and are separated from one another by hundreds of miles of tundra. Isolated communities with few public services is one definition of the Alaska frontier. A second is the pioneer political culture of the Caucasians who have migrated to Alaska from the contiguous states—from the individualistic and independent miners, fishermen, and trappers of the territorial period to the latest hitchhiker entering Alaska on the road system, with dreams of untold wealth and a free lifestyle. The contradiction between the realities of government protection and the ideals of individualism contributes conflict to state politics and government.

THE MODEL CONSTITUTION

Some of the distinctiveness of Alaska political culture is reflected in the state's constitution.[1] The framers attributed the slow pace of economic development and the lack of social services to federal control over the territory and to the indifference of absentee corporations that exploited Alaska's resources. Statehood promised sufficient authority, but the framers wanted to ensure that government would be unified and could act quickly with force. Thus, they designed a governorship that was stronger than that in most of the American states. The governor and lieutenant governor are the only officials elected statewide, and voters in recent elections have not diluted the governor's power by making the positions of any commissioners, most notably that of attorney general, elective.

A significant part of executive authority is the governor's power to appoint. Nearly 1,000 state officials and board members are appointed by the governor or are subject to the governor's veto. Commissioners (and in some cases, deputy and assistant commissioners and division directors) as well as all civil service exempt members of the governor's office are direct gubernatorial appointees, serving at the governor's pleasure—with commissioners subject to legislative confirmation. The governor appoints more than 500 members of state boards and commissions, some of whom are subject to legislative approval. Finally, he appoints all state judges, basing his appointments on the Missouri system (recommendation through a judicial council, and retention by elections). The governor has substantial reorganization powers, too.

The governor also has major legislative powers. He may call either one or both houses of the legislature into special session. His state of the state and budget messages can be used to set legislative priorities, and the governor's office drafts the executive budget (although in some recent years, the legislature has done the budget over again from scratch).

The strongest executive power is the line-item veto, which enables the governor to redline offensive sections of the operating and capital budgets or to reduce appropriation items. A three-fourths majority of both houses is needed to override the veto, and this is difficult to obtain. Also, the legislature customarily adjourns after passing the state budget, making the governor's actions virtually final.

The state legislature is not without power, however. It retains fiscal authority, enters into major gubernatorial appointments, and may block plans for executive reorganization. Although the tenure of the governor is limited to two consecutive terms of four years, there is no limit on the tenure of legislators but voters in 1984 limited the length of the legislative session to 120 days.

The constitution says little about the transition between administrations. The inauguration of the governor takes place between the November general election and the mid-January onset of the legislative session, timing based on the belief that an executive warm-up is needed before the state's business begins.

ALASKA'S GOVERNORS

Since statehood, Alaska has had only five governors,[2] two of whom (William Egan and Jay Hammond) were reelected, indicating an incumbency effect. But incumbents have also been defeated at the polls, as happened to Keith Miller in 1970 and William Egan in 1974. Miller succeeded Walter Hickel when he became U.S. secretary of the interior, and never established a political base. Egan nearly won the 1974 election and, had he served less long in the executive, might have been victorious.

Notwithstanding the weakness of parties as political organizations in Alaska,[3] the history of the governorship also shows a relatively stable interparty competition, with no party having held power for more than eight years. A majority of voters in Alaska identify themselves as independents, but in recent years the Republican party has tended to outdraw the Democratic at the polls.[4] However, the rise of the Libertarian party in 1976 split the usual Republican vote (affecting the Democratic vote to a much more limited extent), which makes the race for the governorship competitive between candidates of the two major parties.

The immediate setting for the Sheffield transition was the Hammond administration. It oversaw the construction of the trans-Alaska pipeline (1974–77) and was the first administration in the state's (or territory's) history to have huge recurrent revenues. Like most state administrations, the Hammond government could not be easily categorized by ideology. Hammond had been a licensed guide, air-taxi operator, agent for the U.S. Fish and Wildlife Service, and proprietor of a fishing lodge before he was first elected to the state house (as an independent) in 1958. He switched to the state senate in 1967, becoming majority leader in 1970 and senate president in 1971–72. Hammond was mayor of the Bristol Bay Borough at the time he staged his successful campaign for the governorship. In that race he gained the support of rural, Native, and commercial fishing interests, but his most notable support was from the developing environmental constituency in the state.

Hammond saw the state bureaucracy expand from 14,000 to 18,000 workers and state revenues increase from $255 million to over $5.6 billion in 1982. Although his actions and those of the legislature led to growth in state government, Hammond used the executive pulpit to call for diversified economic growth in Alaska, particularly that of renewable resources such as agriculture, fisheries, forests, and tourism. He considered his greatest contribution to the state the creation of the Alaska Permanent Fund, which receives a minimum of 25 percent of oil and gas royalty and bonus earnings (an effective rate of 10 percent of all oil revenues) and which now totals over $5 billion.

Although physically active and energetic, Hammond adopted a style of leadership that was relatively passive. State commissioners were essentially autonomous, as were some special assistants to the governor. The governor intruded little on legislative affairs, but he did use the veto for bargaining leverage and was active in the introduction of bills. Nevertheless, the impression created by some Hammond critics in the 1982 election was that the state government had grown wildly and was out of control. A staff assistant to new governor Sheffield claimed that there were sixty-three governors (the governor, two powerful special assistants, and sixty members of the legislature) instead of the one provided for in the constitution.

Because of his razor-thin margin of victory and the recount in the 1974 campaign, Hammond had had little more than three days' notice before his inauguration, and nothing had been prepared to aid his transition. He vowed to ensure that this would not happen to his successor. Three months before the end of his term, Hammond asked each of the state's fourteen departments to prepare an analytical study for the new administration, focusing on the continuing problems of administration and issues requiring immediate attention. He invited each of the three gubernatorial candidates to send representatives to cabinet sessions, to involve themselves in the preparation of the FY 84 budget (which by law was to be submitted no later than mid-January 1983), and to participate in screening candidates for offices in the administration (such as those for the post of commissioner of education).

This preparation for the state's executive transition should have ensured an orderly change. However, it did not take into consideration the degree to which the Hammond administration was an issue in the campaign and the extent to which the state government was regarded as a highly biased source of information on what Alaska government should be and do.

The Electoral Campaign

The Alaska state election season of mid- and late 1982 was one of the state's most dramatic, but the high points of drama were in the primary and its results. Party and candidate personality played small roles in the campaigns for the governorship. The critical factors were issues but not the usual ones—standard platform positions of candidates; the issues attracting more concern were the Hammond administration and ballot propositions.

THE PRIMARY CAMPAIGN

Governor Hammond actively assisted the primary candidacy of his heir apparent, Lieutenant Governor Terry Miller, who established an independent position as head of a state petrochemical planning project and gained statewide exposure as the governor retired from view. Miller, a Fairbanksan with long experience in the house and senate (and at thirty-eight the youngest candidate for governor in the state's history), was perhaps the most popular candidate in the 1978 election. Then, both the Hammond and Hickel tickets claimed his support.

However, in 1982 Miller could establish little distance from the Hammond administration's record during the campaign. He was associated with the alleged no-growth stance of the Hammond administration, with the permanent fund distribution scheme (which gave $1,000 to each Alaskan resident of six months), with opposition to the capital move initiative, and with support of the state's subsistence laws—all of which were roundly criticized by Anchorage groups and institutions, particularly the *Anchorage Times*.

Alaska's open primaries are a free love system that allows voters to vote in both parties' primaries. Miller lost the primary to Tom Fink, Anchorage insurance man and former house speaker. Fink was supported by Libertarian voters, whose party had not yet been formally recognized by the state and who thus lacked a candidate in the primary, and by Anchorage voters. Fink's positions on the issues were distinctive. He supported capital punishment and pro-life initiatives, and he was the only primary candidate who supported the capital move and subsistence repeal. The magnitude of Miller's loss surprised commentators, who were jolted by the defeat of the person expected to succeed Governor Hammond. ·

The Democratic primary also drew interest, although in contrast to the Republican contest it was a tame affair. Candidates Steve Cowper (Fairbanks lawyer, former representative and chair of the house finance committee) and Bill Sheffield treated one another gingerly, knowing that a party split would deny ultimate victory to a Democrat. Sheffield began his campaign two years before the primary, and he visited communities throughout the state, both large and small, in search of votes. His huge campaign war chest permitted lavish use of print and electronic media to publicize the differences between his position on issues and those of the lame-duck Hammond administration. Yet the Sheffield campaign lacked magic and emotional appeal, and when Cowper entered the race and campaigned in earnest, the Sheffield camp saw its large lead in the polls quickly slip away. Sheffield won the primary by only 260 votes. Cowper graciously conceded defeat to Sheffield and supported him in the general election campaign—unlike Miller, who only begrudgingly acknowledged that Fink had bested him in the primary and then sat out the general election campaign.

THE GENERAL ELECTION CAMPAIGN

The general election was a race between Fink and Sheffield—the two businessmen from Anchorage—with Libertarian Dick Randolph (Fairbanks insurance man and former legislator) playing the spoiler. All candidates opposed Hammond administration policies. What distinguished them to the state's electorate and what led to the electoral coalitions' deciding the race were their positions on the ballot propositions.

The Alaska ballot, like that of other western states, is usually crowded with propositions initiated by interest groups or the legislature itself. The November ballot contained eight propositions, two of which generated widespread debate within the state—the capital-move proposition and the subsistence repeal initiative.[5] The capital-move issue, an old one in Alaska state politics, has appeared on the ballot five times. In 1974 voters opted to move the capital, and in 1976 they selected the site of Willow (some forty miles north of Anchorage on the road system) for a new capital. But an initiative two years later specified that construction could not begin until voters had approved all "bondable costs." A Capital Site Planning Commission produced the cost figure of $2.8 billion to relocate offices, construct new facilities, and indemnify Juneau property owners for their loss from the move. The issue in 1982 was whether the costs should be approved.

Proponents of the move stressed the inconvenience of keeping the capital in Juneau: it is distant from 80 percent of the state's population, who must fly in or ride the ferry and risk being grounded by fog, wind, rain, or snow. Lodged between mountains and the sea, Juneau provides little room for growth. The spacious Willow site is within a 100-mile radius of more than 60 percent of the state's population, who can drive there on the road system. Arguments reduced to the issue of access to government. The Capital Access Committee had strong support from the Anchorage business community and the *Anchorage Times*, and was bankrolled with nearly $1 million.

To opponents of the capital move, the $2.8-billion price tag was prohibitive, even for a rich state. It would give outsiders precisely the wrong image of state policy at a time when government officials were trying to overcome the negative publicity surrounding the state's permanent fund dividend program. Also, moving the capital would deepen the economic depression of southeast Alaska and leave that region—isolated geographically from the Alaska heartland—without a stake in state government. Further, opponents argued that the greater use of telecommunications and the decentralization of state program operations would improve access to government without substantial cost. The anti-move Alaska Committee was supported most heavily by the municipality of Juneau, the southeastern communities, and Fairbanks, as well as by newspapers outside Anchorage and by most of the state's established political leadership. It, too, had a $1 million campaign fund.

Both Fink and Randolph supported the capital-relocation proposition, but Sheffield opposed it. In doing so, he won nearly unanimous support from southeast Alaska—without sacrificing much support in interior Alaska. Sheffield's base in Anchorage was weak, and no issue position was likely to improve it significantly against Fink.

The second major ballot proposition in 1982 was the subsistence issue. Alaska Natives have traditionally engaged in subsistence hunting and fishing. To fulfill one federal condition for the state management of fish and game, the 1978 legislature passed a subsistence law that gave preferential hunting and fishing rights (for personal consumption) to the traditional users of these resources. Some Caucasian sports hunters, fishermen, and many urban residents called this law discriminatory, for they were denied equal rights to hunt and fish. Further, some argued that money flowing into rural Alaska through the Alaska Native Claims Settlement Act (ANCSA) and new state programs reduced the need for subsistence. Sportsmen's associations led the campaign for repeal of the 1978 law. An important development occurred after the primary, when seventy biologists employed by the state's Department of Fish and Game publicly opposed the subsistence law, claiming that it made good biological management of fish and game impossible. Supporters of the subsistence preference charged that government scientists could not be trusted to implement rules fairly. Their trump card was the assertion that if the law was repealed, federal fish and game managers would resume control over Alaska species, protecting aboriginal rights because of the special relationship Natives enjoy with the federal government.[6]

The subsistence repeal initiative pitted Natives against Caucasians and rural interests against urban ones. Native ANCSA corporations, nonprofit organizations, and rural governments launched voter registration drives and effectively exploited the Alaska self-government aspects of the issue. By supporting the 1978 subsistence law, Sheffield gained the very strong support of rural Alaska interests, particularly Natives. Fink and Randolph supported the subsistence repeal, which did not significantly extend their electoral support.

The votes that Alaskans cast for governor on November 6, 1982, were strongly influenced by these two ballot propositions. The capital-move proposition lost by a ratio of 47 percent pro to 53 percent con. In Anchorage and south-central precincts the vote was overwhelmingly for the capital move. Southeast Alaska, rural areas, and over 62 percent of the Fairbanks and the interior electorate opposed the move. The subsistence-repeal initiative lost by a comparable margin—57.6 percent con to 42.3 percent pro. Again, rural areas were almost unanimous in rejecting the proposition, joined by southeast Alaska precincts. Fairbanks and interior Alaska divided on this issue, too; in Anchorage about 50 percent of the voters opted for equal rights, but Fink carried Anchorage handily.

In winning the governorship with 45.1 percent of the three-way vote, Sheffield received critical support from the areas that opposed the capital-move and subsistence-repeal propositions: southeast Alaska, rural areas of the state where Natives are in the majority, and interior Alaska (including a large number of Fairbanks voters). Libertarian candidate Randolph took votes from Fink in Fairbanks (Randolph's hometown) and in the southeast, and cut slightly into Fink's majority in Anchorage.

CAMPAIGN ORGANIZATION, FINANCE, AND STRATEGY

Sheffield is a millionaire hotelier with limited experience in politics. He came to Alaska in 1953, initially working as a television repairman. In the 1960s he bought his first hotel in Anchorage and over a period of ten years added other hotels in Anchorage, Juneau, and in regional centers of rural Alaska. An active member of the Anchorage business community, he headed the state chamber of commerce and was the founding chairman of Common Sense for Alaska, a strongly development-oriented association of Anchorage business and political leaders. Sheffield was active in the Democratic party from the late 1960s but was not a leading party figure until the late 1970s. He began a race for the governorship in 1978 but withdrew before the primary because of the ill health of his wife.

Sheffield was the first to announce his candidacy for the governorship, throwing his hat into the ring in 1980. He left the day-to-day affairs of his hotel corporation in the hands of Al Parrish (his second-in-command, personal friend, and advisor), and began a subdued but quietly effective campaign that resembled, both in timing (early start) and tactics (extensive travel, contacts with small groups of individuals), Jimmy Carter's campaign for the presidency.

Initially, the campaign organization was composed of the Sheffield corporation employees who had become close friends and advisors, and they remain the governor's inner circle to the present. An early addition to the organization was Norman Gorsuch, the state's attorney general under Governor Egan from 1973 to 1974, who became Sheffield's leading political advisor. After the August primary, supporters of Steve Cowper jumped on the bandwagon, and Sheffield was supported by the statewide Democratic committee. He also gained the key staff of the Democratic candidate for lieutenant governor, Steve McAlpine, the young (thirty-four) lawyer and mayor of Valdez who easily outdistanced his opponent in the primary race. (Party candidates for governor and lieutenant governor run separately in the primary but together in the general election.) Thus, a campaign organization founded on business added party support and the services of operatives seasoned in other campaigns. In regional representation, if not political experience, the campaign organization was the best in Alaska.

The 1982 elections in Alaska were the most expensive in the history of the state, with the Sheffield organization spending the most over the course of the campaign—$1.97 million, or $26 per vote (the highest per vote expenditure in the nation). The Fink campaign spent nearly $1 million, and Randolph spent nearly three quarters of a million.[7]

What did the money buy? It bought information, media coverage, staff support, and travel, in that order. Sheffield engaged outside pollsters and campaign consultants—the Rothstein/Buckley campaign firm (an outgrowth of the older Joe Napolitan organization). They developed a sophisticated profile of electoral opinions on major issues. Sheffield's staff then formed issue positions and policies to gain support from the natural constituencies of the Democratic party in Alaska (labor, Natives, other minorities, educators, environmentalists) and to attract other voting blocs (e.g., those interested in resource development or cheap hydropower). The resulting wish book (as it was affectionately called by Sheffield insiders) had something for every significant group in the state.

Money bought direct-mail appeals for campaign donations and the dissemination of the candidate's positions on issues among potential supporters. A large chunk of the treasury—estimated at $400,000—went into television commercials and radio spots. Outside consultants advised the organization on media techniques, and its media campaign was effective. For example, to emphasize the point that Fink would serve Anchorage interests, not those of the state as a whole, one spot juxtaposed the familiar map of Alaska with the city limits of Anchorage, asking whether Fink was running for the governorship of Alaska or Anchorage.

Money paid for a staff of over 100, offices, telephone banks, and other campaign paraphernalia. At state and local levels Sheffield campaign workers coordinated voter registration and campaign work with the offices of the Alaska Committee and with organizations working against the subsistence initiative. Money also paid for extensive travel by Sheffield, McAlpine, and their surrogates.

Who paid the bill? Sheffield and his corporation paid the largest proportion, contributing nearly a half-million dollars to the fund. PACs representing labor, teachers, Natives, and government employees gave large amounts, as did individual businessmen and associates. Many smaller ($5–$200) contributions came from members of supporting organizations.

The strategy of the campaign was to capitalize on the Sheffield positions that were supported by a substantial number of voters—particularly the capital-move and subsistence issues. Attention was given to isolating Fink and his running mate, state senator Mike Colletta, limiting their base of support to Anchorage by contrasting Sheffield as a statewide leader. Finally, the campaign exposed Sheffield (a somewhat reluctant and dry speaker) to small groups instead of large gatherings, building toward larger meetings near the end of the campaign.

Incumbency was an issue in races other than the executive. All but two of the sixty seats in the Alaska legislature were up for election as a result of reapportionment of the two bodies following the 1980 census. The rate of turnover in the twenty-member state senate—30 percent—was lower than that of the forty-member house—62.5 percent, with two legislators changing houses. The new governor thus faced fewer veterans in the house than has usually been the case, and, as we shall see, the structure of power in the two houses was not easy to predict before the election.

The Executive Transition

The movement of the new governor into office took place in two stages. For one month following the election on November 6, there was intensive preparation for government, which brought a crescendo of change at the inauguration of the new governor on December 6. Over the next five weeks new appointments and policies were announced almost daily, with a second spurt of crystallized activity surrounding the formal inauguration balls in January and the beginning of the legislative session.

The Sheffield organization did not begin to think seriously about the transition until mid-September. The research gathered to form position statements for use in the election reflected considerable thought about how Sheffield might govern Alaska, but obviously the concrete process of applying thought to action developed much more slowly.

The guiding forces of the executive transition were the new governor and his transition team. Seven members composed the team, and all were associated with Sheffield personally or were on the statewide campaign committee.[8] Their experiences and connections significantly influenced the way in which the new administration was established. One (Norman Gorsuch) had experience in state government, as head of the Department of Law, and a second (Emil Notti) had been a deputy commissioner. No member of the transition team had been a state legislator, but two had local government experience. Most transition team members had management experience.

Within a week of the election the process of the executive transition was established. The transition team would operate as a managerial team, meeting with Sheffield as a discussion and decision-making body. And the team would organize and manage grass-roots problem identification and personnel selection. Both activities were conducted by task forces, and this was the first time they had been used for transition planning in Alaska.

THE USE OF TASK FORCES

Sheffield adopted task forces because of his experience in campaigning and the recommendations of his transition team. On the campaign trail he had jotted down names of more than sixty individuals whose ideas and suggestions he believed merited serious attention. Directors of the transition team proposed that several transition task forces (instead of one unwieldy committee) make brief forays into state government agencies and make recommendations about crises and problems and also help screen job applicants. By the second week after the election the transition team and governor had selected sixty-four individuals for six task forces: resources, human services, public protection and labor, business management, revenue transfer, and general government.[9]

In general, task force members represented the state elite. Most regions of the state were represented, including a relatively large number of members from outside Anchorage and Fairbanks. Business, labor, education, commerce, banking, and investment communities were present in good numbers. Women, Natives, and other minorities had a voice. The majority of the task force members were Democrats, but Republicans and independents were included.

Two significant interests were absent from the task forces—state agencies and the legislature—and this omission reflected Sheffield's approach to the transition. Transition team members thought career bureaucrats could not investigate state government operations and problems objectively, an observation reinforced by campaign polls that reported highly critical attitudes toward state government. Moreover, Hammond administration agencies had prepared transition documents, and the feeling of the transition team was that these documents incorporated the views of the state bureaucracy. A few former legislators sat on task forces, and transition team members considered them sufficient representatives of the legislature. The overriding thought, however, was that the transition concerned the executive, not the legislature. Also, the legislature was seen as part of the state government problem. What the new administration needed were evaluations from outsiders who were not associated with either branch.

Task force members got copies of Hammond administration reports from the agencies they would investigate and the sections of the Sheffield wish book applying to these agencies. Their instructions were to interview agency heads, identify issues requiring immediate resolution, prepare analyses of problems for each of the state's fourteen departments, and evaluate current and prospective agency personnel.

Most of the six task forces completed their work within two weeks in late November. Task force members were new to the business of objectively evaluating state agency performance, but they had little difficulty identifying major agency problems, which were compiled into a task force report.

THE REPORT OF THE TRANSITION TASK FORCES

The report of more than 300 pages was presented to Sheffield several days before his inauguration, and it was a primary source for the policy decisions that were made before and immediately upon his inauguration. Some of the problems pointed out were the following:

1. *Finance and accounting.* Design of a method of funding public schools, redesign of the state's accounting system, financial and legal questions concerning state grant and loan programs.[10]
2. *Personnel selection.* Membership and policy direction of the state Board of Education, Fisheries Board, Game Board, and regents of the University of Alaska.
3. *State-federal issues.* Need for a maximum security prison, purchase of Alaska Railroad, responsibility for fish and game resource management.
4. *Government organization.* Sorting out departmental functions and responsibilities, organization of the Governor's Office to improve integration with departments, and budget data and planning.

Given the controversial nature of some recommendations and the fact that at least one task force made less than objective recommendations, the transition team considered keeping the materials secret. Rejecting this as impractical, however, they released the transition document to the press, which publicized the recommendations. The publicity raised expectations, but sometimes the direction of influence was not exactly what the new governor or his advisors wanted. This was among the risks attendant upon setting up essentially uncontrolled task forces, which made superficial assessments and evaluations of state government activity.

SELECTING PERSONNEL

While the task forces conducted interviews and prepared recommendations, the transition team and governor engaged in an executive search to select the cabinet. During his campaign, with a few exceptions, Sheffield promised jobs to no one. Upon his election, he indicated that no one would be hired without submitting a résumé and called on qualified Alaskans to apply. The overwhelming response caught the transition team by surprise: within two weeks transition team offices were flooded with more than 1,000 résumés, letters, and calls. By the start of the legislative session, over 1,600 résumés came in, roughly four applicants per post but with the greatest interest, obviously, in positions as commissioner, deputy commissioner, and directors within the governor's office.

The transition team screened cabinet and governor's office positions (the task forces looked at résumés for subcabinet posts), and they did so with the idea that the "best in the state" formed their labor pool. Governor's office positions were filled easily, and by the time of the inauguration this part of the administration bore the Sheffield imprint. The chief of staff, staff assistants for the six functional areas of state government, legislative coordinator, and press officer—those having closest daily contact with the governor—were for the most part selected from operatives in the Sheffield campaign who had directed regional offices (including some former supporters of Cowper, Sheffield's opponent in the primary). Budget and planning officers for the new administration were selected primarily on the basis of expertise in related areas outside state government.

The original conception of the governor's office was that staffers would assist but not direct state affairs, as had allegedly been the case in the Hammond administration. One of Sheffield's criticisms of that administration was that executive decisions were made by special project directors and assistants as often as they were by commissioners or the governor himself. This predilection on the part of the new governor left staff assistants without clear responsibilities and led to confusion in the governor's office until a pattern of influence was sorted out.

The new administration's search for the best ran aground on two realities of government employment in Alaska: many of the state's most talented managers refuse to live in Juneau, and state executive salaries of slightly over $70,000 are a good deal less than resourceful individuals can make outside government. Thus, the first, second, and, in some cases, the third choices refused positions as commissioners, and it was not possible to fill the cabinet by the time of the inauguration.

Governor Sheffield wanted a clean break from the Hammond administration and wanted no holdovers at the rank of commissioner.[11] The new administration called for staged resignations, but it was necessary to continue several officials. Sheffield made the final appointment in March, when he accepted the recommendation of the state Board of Education and named Dr. Harold Reynolds the commissioner of education.

As has been typical in Alaska, the fifteen cabinet-level appointments did not represent a consistent philosophy of government management. Most were Democrats, but fewer than half were strongly identified with the state party organization, and three commissioners were either Republicans or nonpartisans. Two women sat in the cabinet, as did two members of minorities (several Natives held subcabinet positions). Three commissioners were Fairbanks residents, and one had lived most recently in Valdez; rural Alaska and the southeast were not represented on the cabinet. A striking characteristic of the cabinet members was the lack of experience in state government and in the administration of functional areas falling within given departments: one third of the commissioners had no previous significant experience related to the agency they headed. A larger number of businessmen were selected as commissioners than had been the case in the Hammond administration, but there were also three university professors and two local government officials or administrators.

TAKING OVER

At his inauguration on December 6, Governor Sheffield could not present a full cabinet to the state. But by symbolic statements and substantive acts Sheffield established that he was "taking charge" of Alaska government:

> One of my first orders as Governor-elect was to have the picket fence around the Governor's Mansion modified so my two dogs can't get out and terrorize the community of Juneau. So, I asked to see the maintenance man and was told "No, you have to go through the proper channels." I figured that's a good way to get it done slowly, so, much to the amazement of some people, I got together with the maintenance man and discussed with him what I wanted done. And it's done. That's the kind of direct approach you can expect from me as Governor.

Within three days Sheffield froze all ongoing personnel and large financial transactions. He called for the resignations of the Board of Education, the Board of Fisheries, and the Board of Game, declined reappointment of four members of the Board of Regents of the University of Alaska, and quickly appointed replacements who were responsive to him. He froze all out-of-state travel by state employees until a procedure could be developed that was, in his opinion, more accountable. All state contracts for services in excess of $100,000 (and many smaller ones) were frozen until the contracting process could be reviewed. He also appointed a task force to examine immediately the adult corrections division, asking them to propose solutions to the problems of overcrowded prisons and the lack of a maximum security facility in the state.

It is not clear that any of these actions materially affected outcomes— of personnel or programs selected by state boards, of contracted agents hired to do the state's work, or even of the conditions encountered by prisoners in state jails. But the actions immediately told the state's population that there was a new governor in Juneau who would decide state policy.

THE ADMINISTRATIVE TRANSITION—AN ASSESSMENT

The first stage of the executive transition was, in retrospect, successful. In a very short time the new governor amassed a body of information on the operations and problems of state government (omitting the legislature), and he initiated a relatively thorough process for the selection of personnel to run state agencies. The month-long process was also relatively smooth. Some Hammond administration friends complained that they were treated abruptly, and several agency personnel objected strongly to the task force investigations and their superficiality. In general, however, affairs were well conducted.

Two factors explain this smooth administrative transition. Governor Hammond not only required the preparation of transition documents but also insisted that his staff and that of the commissioners cooperate fully with the Sheffield transition staff. The Sheffield staff had space in the capitol and a secretarial service to manage the paper flow. Hammond allocated funds from his contingency reserve to cover Sheffield's transition expenses, and Hammond was receptive to suggestions from Sheffield and his assistants concerning actions he might take that could affect the new administration. The second factor relates to Sheffield's managerial style, as well as to his management experience and that of his chief advisors. The efficiently constructed plan promoted the quick learning of government operations, ready decision making, and prompt action. The one-month administrative transition seemed at the time to be a model for future Alaska governors.

PROBLEMS BEGIN

Then things began to fall apart. From his inauguration until the legislative session began Sheffield was preoccupied with the impact of falling oil prices on state revenue. For this and other reasons, his administration was unprepared for the greatest challenge to a new governor in Alaska— a maverick (and amateur) legislature.

The softening of the oil market was mentioned during the 1982 campaign season, but most debates concerning it were relatively abstract. Given the huge revenue surpluses in 1981 and early 1982, why worry about the future? And a July 1981 special session of the legislature, at the urging of Governor Hammond, proposed a constitutional ceiling on the state budget (which voters approved in the election), which seemed likely to constrain excessive growth in state spending. In fact, the concern up to the inauguration was how, given the expansiveness of Sheffield's campaign promises, new programs could be funded under this limit.

The inability of OPEC (Organization of Petroleum Exporting Countries) nations to hold the price of oil at $34 a barrel and the precipitous drop in oil prices shocked the Sheffield administration revenue officials and planners. Each $1 drop in the price of oil translates into approximately a $150-million decline in Alaska state revenue. Although state fiscal planning is based on estimates with a 70-percent certainty that the amount the state receives will actually be that high, the sizable price drop of late 1982 disturbed the new administration (notwithstanding the fact that most estimates of future revenues were above the ceiling set by the limit). As a result, instead of adding on selected items to the budget document prepared by the Hammond administration, Sheffield decided to revise downward the expenditures of state agencies. This process began during December: some agencies cut budgets on three successive occasions; only Corrections was permitted to increase its request significantly over FY 1983 (1982–83) levels.

Thus, Sheffield faced the legislative season with very pessimistic revenue projections and with no established procedure for gaining concurrence with an austerity budget. This is not to imply that the new administration lacked plans, for it had them in abundance. Perhaps the plan with the greatest long-term significance for the strength of the executive was the development of a miniature OMB (Office of Management and Budget) in the governor's office. Under Hammond there was a division of Budget and Management and a division of Policy Development and Planning, but the functions were not integrated and each unit reported independently to the governor's special assistants. Sheffield brought these functions together into one office and made each division (strategic planning, budget, audit) subordinate to a director whose position was raised to cabinet rank. Of perhaps equal importance, he selected as the state's first OMB director a CPA, Peter McDowell, whose view of policy setting and budget making did not include the legislature.

Discussion in the executive offices before the start of the legislative session focused on capital projects funding. The hope was that the method used to fund capital projects could be rationalized (that is, controlled by the governor's office). Since 1980 this large category of expenditure (totaling $1.38 billion in 1982) had been allocated in equal thirds—the governor, the senate, and the house each compiled a list, which allowed legislators to parcel out projects to communities and other interests in exchange for future support. The governor attacked the pork-barrel system as grossly inefficient and harmful to the state's long-range development, and he proposed that the executive list projects according to priorities of needs (e.g., public safety, health). For example, municipalities were asked to forward their requests for grants (part of the extensive capital budget) *directly* to the governor's office.[12] Plans for future legislative sessions included the implementation of a zero-based budgeting system, again developed in the executive. These plans created apprehension and antagonism among legislators.

The Legislative Transition

While the executive branch underwent some organizational tightening and the formation of an hierarchical management system, legislators in the house bargained over organizational roles in the two-month period between the general election and the start of the new session (the senate organized shortly after the election). In the last session of the Hammond administration both houses were controlled by two-party coalitions, and this pattern continued, with some change of faces in the new legislature. Coalition formation in the Alaska legislature is virtually devoid of political ideology, and party labels have little meaning. Instead, it is a distributional process in which the first group of legislators constituting a majority (generally built around size and split of the budget and developed by trading committee chairmanships and votes on significant fiscal issues) organizes each house. The pattern that can be distinguished in the senate is a temporary alliance of primarily non-Anchorage and some rural Alaska legislators; in the very conservative house the alliance is between Railbelt (communities located along the Alaska Railroad route from Seward through Anchorage to Fairbanks) Republicans and rural Democratic legislators. The administration stayed aloof from legislative organization. It considered this the legislature's business and realized that if the administration interfered and lost, it would pay the price during the session. Thus, at the start of the legislative session a conservative Democratic governor faced two houses in which there were no ruling parties and in which regional and local interests were dominant factors in organization—interests sharply antithetical to those of the new administration.

The formal beginnings of the administration in January 1983 were auspicious. In a concession to the regional nature of Alaska's politics, inaugural balls were held after the New Year in Juneau, Anchorage, Nome, and Fairbanks. These mass events brought Sheffield supporters and some opponents together with regional notables and ushered in the new administration with an air of good feeling. The governor feted legislators at the executive mansion in Juneau, held dinner parties for important leaders such as the "bush caucus" (legislators from rural Alaska), and acknowledged the influence of key lawmakers in some of the subcabinet appointments (for example, in the selection of the head of the Division of Agriculture). The governor's door was open to a wide range of groups and individuals, and he projected an image of accessibility as he moved around Juneau and the state during the inaugural period. Legislators, in turn, offered cooperation to the governor.

Nevertheless, the governor's state of the state and budget addresses took a stance of confrontation that denied him the opportunity for the honeymoon his reforms required. These early reports were calls for submission to executive leadership (and executive budget priorities) that implicitly attacked the special interests on which legislative coalitions were founded. There were also muted calls for financial austerity.

Pursuing his interest in making capital projects funding rational, the executive accumulated requests and then established a list of priorities. This process did not work well; it created conflict and confusion between the executive and legislature, and understandably the proposal was changed substantially. Too, the contradiction between the endorsement of a huge supplemental capital projects budget and falling revenue projections galled the seasoned observers of state government.

Pursuing funds to fatten the operating budget, the governor attacked the sacred cow of the Hammond administration (the state's permanent fund dividend program) by suggesting that revenue sharing, municipal assistance, and part of educational funding be supported through fund earnings—an idea for which there was little support. The administration also proposed a delay in state payments into the fund and cancellation of the "debt" proposed by the legislature,[13] for which there was support. The permanent fund per-capita distribution scheme is no favorite of the executive or many legislators, but a politically acceptable compromise for the disposition of fund earnings has not yet been found.

SOME EARLY STUMBLES

Several early actions of the administration angered major constituent groups. For example, the governor changed the membership of the Agricultural Action Council, and the new members curtailed both the development of a grain terminal at Seward and further agricultural development plans in interior Alaska—actions that infuriated the state's growing and very vocal agricultural lobby. The governor proposed a reduction and tightening of the state's highly popular student loan program (permitting students to borrow up to $7,000 annually at an interest rate of 5 percent, with up to 50 percent forgiveness for students who work in the state for five years after graduation). This proposal evoked demonstrations at university campuses throughout the state and damaged the governor's credibility with the large student population. The governor cut funding of the state Arts Council and the Council on Science and Technology, which displeased supporters of both arts and sciences. And the governor was slow to object to the Interior Department's exploration leasing plans for the Norton Sound (which threatened the subsistence livelihood of Alaska Natives in that region) at a time when cuts were proposed in the state's social welfare programs, particularly those benefiting rural Alaskans and Natives. These and similar proposals, however rational their design given the decline in state revenue projections, were widely perceived as politically inept and unresponsive to those who had supported Sheffield in the campaign.

A QUESTION OF ETHICS

Then one month into the legislative session, when the governor needed broad constituent support, the ethics of the administration were called into question by the governor's fund-raising trip, which became the chief issue of the new administration.

In late January 1983 Governor Sheffield traveled to Washington, D.C., where he met Interior Secretary James Watt and discussed the Norton Sound lease sales. On his return to Alaska the governor stopped in Houston for a fund-raising event. The purpose of the occasion was to raise funds from oil company officials to retire a loan of over $400,000 that the governor had made to his own campaign. The occasion netted $150,000. Accompanying the governor on the trip were the state's attorney general and the commissioner of natural resources.

A powerful Native legislator, alleging that the governor had sold out the state's interests to oil companies, called for a special prosecutor, independent of the executive, to investigate the trip (one section of which was on a privately chartered airplane owned by an oil company with an interest in the Norton Sound leases). This charge was a political bombshell that reverberated throughout the state. (The allegation of executive collusion with oil companies has been a factor in past gubernatorial elections.) The timing of the trip linked executive policy on oil and gas resource development with the interests of oil companies, however innocent the intentions of the administration and however independent its review and recommendations on the lease sales. Moreover, the presence of the state's lawyer and the resource commissioner on the trip spread discredit throughout the administration.

The fund-raising episode further exacerbated legislative-executive relations. Legislative committees refused to report out bills initiated by the administration[14] and held the governor's appointments hostage in committee. After one month the legislature took appropriate advantage of the governor's weakened position. In a series of negotiating sessions the administration conceded to restore equal thirds as the method for allocating capital projects, and the $250 million supplementary measure zipped through the legislature. A supplemental education funding bill that compromised rural and urban interests also passed both houses, and the legislative finance committees began serious work on the state operating budget.

THE CONFIRMATION CONTROVERSY

Although both houses proceeded on the governor's operating budget request, only the senate completed hearings on the governor's appointments. The house Judiciary Committee objected to the governor's nominee for attorney general. The crowning incident was committee chairman Charlie Bussell's call for a public confirmation hearing in Anchorage.

At this point (in early June) the governor's appointments became involved in interhouse rivalry over the budget. Having completed its work the house abruptly adjourned, leaving the senate to accept house spending figures. This action, a house retaliation for the senate's early adjournment in the last session of the Hammond administration, was designed to demonstrate the strength of the house and its ability to schedule legislation. The adjournment also left all gubernatorial appointees hanging, and under the state constitution their names could not be reintroduced by the governor at the start of the next session.

Governor Sheffield then took the "direct approach" promised in his inaugural address. He joined the senate president in calling for a joint legislative session to vote on his appointments. When members of the house coalition declined to attend, the public safety commissioner called in state troopers, who forced four members to be present. The joint session did confirm nominations of all commissioners, including the attorney general, but it balked at appointments to the state Board of Fisheries. The governor gained his objective at the cost of rancor in the house majority and a suit filed against him for alleged unconstitutional practices.

OUTCOMES: WINS, LOSSES—A DRAW

In late June the legislature completed the second-longest session in the state's history. It passed a general fund budget of over $2 billion for operations, $627 million for capital projects, and $180 million for subsidized loans. The governor cut $114 million from the budget, taking the largest chunk from capital construction projects ($90 million). The governor's office maintained that cuts were "even-handed" across the state and that they were necessary to help the permanent fund grow ($150 million was deposited). Critics, however, called the cuts illogical and politically motivated.

The session was acrimonious, and in the words of a veteran legislator it "never quite reached mediocrity." Still, legislators gave the governor some of what he wanted. Appointments were confirmed, albeit requiring the use of extraordinary measures. The operating budget grew at a modest rate of 4 percent over the previous year's figures, indicating that the symbolic messages on fiscal austerity had reached responsive ears. Of equal importance, by the end of the session the administration reached a comfortable working relationship with senate leadership, similar to that used in the latter days of the Hammond administration.

But on proposed large-scale reforms the governor lost. Plans to rationalize capital spending, to void the distribution system of the dividends from the permanent fund, and to alter state loan and benefit programs based on residency requirements—all failed to pass through the legislature. And the governor's plans to reorganize executive government departments, particularly through creating a Department of Corrections, were scuttled. Sheffield's threats to call an immediate special session if this and other priority issues were not resolved had no effect on adjournment. In the end the governor created the new department through an executive order. Enough of the state's business had been enacted during the session, however, that both executive and legislature could claim some credit.

THE LEGISLATIVE TRANSITION—AN ASSESSMENT

Gubernatorial compromise was perhaps a recognition of the political realities of the legislature but was also traceable to the loss of public confidence after the fund-raising trip. The executive's approach to the legislature, regarded by some observers as openly contemptuous before the start of the session, altered somewhat. The executive placed greater reliance on a legislative budget review committee, an interagency continuing committee designed to follow the governor's agenda in the legislature. Too, there was the appearance of greater attention to legislative prerogatives and more skillful legislative lobbying by the governor, his staff assistants, and cabinet officers toward the end of the session. But the governor's remarks after the session—"I'm going to get a lot tougher. I'm not going to roll over to these guys"—suggested that the attitude of confrontation remained. This attitude was understandable, given the raucus and undisciplined behavior of some legislators during the session.

Evaluation of the Gubernatorial Transition

Eighteen months have passed since Governor Sheffield's inauguration—sufficient for an evaluation of the immediate effect of the transition on

the state and to make provisional estimates of the impact of forces—
chiefly economic and political—that influence transitions in other states.
And it is not too early to project the impact that the Sheffield administration may have on the state's political development.

As Governor Sheffield entered the second year of his term, he made
some changes in personnel and approach that addressed problems in his
administration and improved results with the legislature.

Adjusting the bureaucracy. Management problems in four state agencies[15] and the OMB and low morale in the state government work force
renewed attention to executive personnel. The governor fired two heads
of departments upon the anniversary of his election and replaced a
third commissioner five months later. These and related personnel shuf-
fles at the subcabinet level rewarded individuals with experience in state
government administration (although partisan ties remained important
factors in selecting exempt employees). He kept his promise to decen-
tralize decision-making authority in the largest department, an action
popular in interior and rural Alaska.

Changes reached into the office of the governor itself. A new chief
of staff with extensive experience in rural Alaska was recruited, one
whose selection and actions diminished criticism that the governor was
ignoring the needs of rural Alaska and Alaska Natives. An OMB budget
review director regarded as politically naive was replaced by an officer
experienced in working with the budget. Further staff changes were
made in the governor's office in order to coordinate work of departments
and more effectively lobby for the administration's programs in the legis-
ture. The governor held retreats for cabinet-level staff to foster a team
spirit in his administration. Also, he improved his public relations by
expounding his agenda in press conferences and defending it in newspaper guest opinions.

Working with the legislature. In January 1984 Governor Sheffield
gave his second state of the state and budget messages to the legislature.
As in his first addresses, he asked the legislature to contain expenditures
and to rationalize the process for making capital projects appropriations.
In the second-year addresses, unlike those of the previous year, he made
no assault on the popular permanent fund distribution scheme and the
student loan program, and he did not take the legislature (or the state
government) to task for failing to manage the future of declining oil

revenues. Some observers viewed this as an excellent address that exuded leadership and social conscience.

The governor's legislative agenda included four major items: (1) a constitutional amendment to set up a "major projects fund" to finance large-scale capital improvements, such as the Susitna dam, (2) arrangement of long-term debt financing for power projects, (3) purchase of the Alaska railroad from the federal government, and (4) a grant of authority to make a special $450-million deposit to the permanent fund. The governor proposed modest increases in state agency budgets to meet population increases and a major increase in funding for capital projects and state-subsidized loans.

The major initiatives of the 1984 session, however, came from the legislature. The legislature's strategy was to send capital projects funding bills to the governor early so that the legislature would be in session when vetoes came. Also, the legislature hoped to get the governor to sign capital bills before it dealt with substantive legislation: without the threat of vetoing capital bills, the governor has little clout with the legislature.

Capital projects funding thus became the chief issue of the legislative session. At the recommendation of the National Conference of State Legislators (and to keep the governor guessing about how much they wanted to spend), the legislature passed six appropriation bills specialized by function, and a seventh, "sweeper" package for items falling between the cracks and for last-minute add-ons. There was little cooperation between legislature and executive in the design of the six appropriation bills, but for the largest, the catch-all bill, the governor was allocated a large slice of the pie. Nonetheless, the total amount of the bills, $950 million, exceeded the governor's recommendation of $700 million (with an additional $300 million to be reserved for the major projects fund). The governor threatened to veto large amounts unless the legislature acted first on his requests. Some action ensued on the governor's priority list, but the major projects fund was killed.

To ensure that the legislature would not be able to override vetoes, Sheffield struck deals with each of the sixteen minority Democrats in the house and a few senators. (The constitution requires that forty-five of sixty legislators in joint session vote to override appropriation bill vetoes.) Having done his homework, the governor proceeded to veto one quarter of the legislature's projects, saving all those of minority Democrats.[16] Coalition leaders and Republican legislators called foul. They claimed that the vetoes were politically motivated (they were), that Anchorage bore the brunt of the cuts (it did), and that they could override. But, as the governor remarked, he had "learned to count," and the legislature failed to restore any of the vetoed items. The vetoes particularly embittered Anchorage Republicans, who had another complaint: the governor's reapportionment plan changed district lines so that some incumbent Anchorage Republicans would face one another in the 1984 party primaries.

By the end of the session the governor had not achieved most of his presession goals. Sheffield said he was willing to wait and press again on the major projects fund and other proposals, responding to criticism that he had tried too much, too fast in his first year in office.

LESSONS OF THE ALASKA TRANSITION

Most of the states with gubernatorial transitions in 1982–83 had serious economic problems—large deficits, as a result of the national recession, and decline in federal support for state and local programs. Governors, irrespective of their number of years on the job, party affiliation, and political experience, initiated austerity budgets. Alaska had economic problems and funding shortfalls, too, but they were fundamentally different from those of most states, and the executive and legislative responses differed, as well.

Following the drop in oil prices, state revenue projections plummeted (but money kept flowing); using the forecasts, the Sheffield administration began to pare the budget, attempting to roll back some of the state's costlier programs and putting a hold on planning for gigantic capital projects such as the Susitna hydropower project (expected to cost over $15 billion for a start). In the process, however, the administration called for massive supplemental capital projects funding, attempting to justify essentially short-term jobs by the need to create economic development opportunities. Although the standard interpretation is that the new administration lacked consistent direction, it it difficult indeed to imagine a responsive administration resisting the impulse to spend when significant current revenues and a large nest egg were at hand. The sharp drop in state revenue projections seems unlikely to have a direct effect on the state's budget as long as current revenues are adequate. (The 1984 legislature confirmed this assessment by continuing its large-scale funding of capital projects.)

In many states undergoing transitions, the character of the electoral campaign established the ambiance in which executive and legislative change took place. In Alaska the campaign was the most divisive in state history, pitting urban against rural interests, Caucasians against Natives, and Anchorage against the rest of the state. Governor Sheffield made conscious efforts to mend the rifts of the campaign. He ordered state agencies to stay open an additional hour in the afternoon, giving Railbelt residents greater access to government. He asked the legislature for a statement of their resolve to unify time zones and influenced the federal Department of Transportation to act on the issue. He made symbolic gestures, as well, by increasing the number of governor's regional field offices and promising to give regional offices of the state bureaucracy more authority. The governor attempted to replace the entire membership of the fisheries and game boards, and he selected as new commissioner an individual who was trusted by rural Alaskans. Initially, he ducked the subsistence issue by declining to call for a task force (which he had promised to establish if elected) to immediately examine the ramifications of the 1978 law. Then he agreed to form a task force. The delay and confusion over what the governor would do partly defused this issue.

The capital move and the subsistence issues did not disappear after the election, for they express the powerful force of regionalism in state politics. But the governor's confrontation with the legislature in his attempt to establish a strong governorship and the politically embarrassing fund-raising imbroglio made the new administration the focus of attention (as well as the butt of jokes). The fund-raising trip, along with legislative sideshows, diverted energy from regional conflicts and cleavages.

The leadership of Governor Sheffield will be a critical factor as Alaska moves into its second generation as a state. The confusion and political bungling that characterized executive-legislative relations in 1983 were in part a natural result of the new governor's lack of political experience (and that of his top staff and commissioners). The problems camouflaged significant attempted changes in the new administration—the development of an orderly process for a change in government, the design of an integrated budgeting system (controlled by the governor), and the interest in tightening the state bureaucracy and reining in to some extent the maverick legislature, with its independent fiefdoms (a move that may unify that body as it attempts to retain some initiative). The governor's greater success with the 1984 (election year) legislature was an early sign of the impact of these changes.

Alaska's media and political elite criticized the Hammond administration, especially during its later years, for lack of executive leadership and direction. Hammond was not a particularly active governor, but it would be a mistake to view him through the eyes of an ex-governor who said Hammond would have been "a good governor for an established state, like Massachusetts, but [was] a poor governor for a new state like Alaska." Hammond's leadership was important in keeping Alaska intact during the tremendous impact of pipeline construction. He did develop a consensus on some issues, particularly the state's permanent fund, and he was willing to approach problems from the standpoint of their "human" aspects, which was important, given Alaska's divergent cultural groups.

Sheffield has an entirely different style of leadership. It is based on activity, long, hard hours, and involvement in decision making—a willingness to focus on detail, sometimes at the expense of the broader picture, and a vision of the public future. It is the style of a manager turned politician, one in which people are sometimes viewed as impediments or sources of problems. This style promises greater control and perhaps a realistic harnessing of expectations. Development of this leadership depends upon how the political lessons are combined with managerial expertise.

What lessons does Alaska's 1982–83 gubernatorial transition hold for other states? It shows that technical, administrative preparations for office—the cookbook recipes of the formal transition—are far less important than political preparation by the governor and his staff. Indeed, the Alaska case suggests that a "successful" formal transition might handicap a governor if not accompanied by effective political learning,[17] particularly in the arithmetic of legislative power and influence. An easy transition into office may give or reinforce a false sense of control and security. When power is the object, politics must take command.

Two Transitions in Arkansas, 1978 and 1982

DIANE D. BLAIR

Pride and hope. Pride and hope. With these two qualities, we can go a long way. We can bring a new era of achievement and excellence. We can fashion a life here that will be the envy of the nation. The future lies brightly before us.—*Inaugural Address, Governor Bill Clinton, January 9, 1979*

Today we are engaged in a new battle with an old and familiar enemy: hard times. Hard times dominate the long history of Arkansas. We are between a rock and a hard place.—*Inaugural Address, Governor Bill Clinton, January 11, 1983*

In the language of politics certain adjectives have become firmly fixed to the nouns they modify: winning ticket, favorable image, clever ploy, orderly transition. Just as it is the very purpose of a campaign to be persuasive and of a ploy to be clever, so it is the essential function of a transition to bring order and regularity to a temporarily disarrayed political system.

In the earliest days of the Republic the emphasis on smooth and harmonious transitions probably reflected fears as to whether all players understood and accepted the rules of this new elective method for determining the succession to power. Contemporary concerns are more likely to arise from the devastating damage that could be inflicted should our now massive public engines run amok. When even the smallest of states annually allocates hundreds of millions of dollars into vital public services, even the briefest of breakdowns could be severely injurious.

Additionally, today's practitioners and political scientists alike, having grasped the importance of image ("Image, which is filtered through or created by the media, is all-important—not only in reelection but in ability to govern"[1]), have also recognized how critical the transition is in shaping the correct gubernatorial image: "Clearly, the actions taken, appointments made, and images projected by incoming governors between their election and inauguration will reverberate, either positively or negatively, throughout their terms."[2]

For reasons of stability, public service, and political effectiveness, the only good transition is an orderly transition—the more regular and methodical the better. State governments, in recent recognition of the value of orderly transitions, have begun to formalize the process by appropriating public funds and allocating staff, space, and services. The National Governors' Association (NGA), with its new governor seminars, how-to-handbooks, transition assistance teams, and projects such as this one, has been strongly reinforcing and refining the efforts toward more methodical and professional transfers of power.

The assumption behind this particular project is that by having knowledgeable observers closely observing and reporting on the details of transitions in a variety of states, future assistance efforts can be even more usefully fashioned to achieve the well-ordered transition that is everyone's ideal. This chapter, however, follows a somewhat distinctive path (comparative analysis) toward enlightenment. And the major conclusion—that transitions are so inherently individualistic that they place powerful constraints on the regularities that can be either assumed or imposed—may be mildly subversive to the raison d'être of the enterprise.

Ordinarily, single-state studies do not readily lend themselves to comparative analysis. However, in 1982 in Arkansas (as in Alabama, Massachusetts, and Minnesota), the person who was elected governor had been the governor before. These were not the rather routine cases of reelection to a successive term, but restorations to a once-held office. Because Arkansas is one of only four states with a two-year gubernatorial term and because Bill Clinton's restoration was rapid, the interregnum was brief indeed: his first election and transition were in 1978, his second in 1982.

Here, then, are two transitions in which the similarities should far outweigh the differences: many of the usual variables (size of state and government, structural supports available, personality of the principal, media milieu, state timetable and traditions) can be eliminated because they were in fact identical. The same governor-elect prepared to take office in the same state, with only four years separating the two events. Nevertheless, as the following analysis indicates, the two transitions differed rather dramatically in many major respects.

Clinton's Election and Transition, 1978

When Bill Clinton was inaugurated as governor of Arkansas on January 9, 1979, it was to a considerable amount of national as well as state fanfare heralding a political phenomenon. At age thirty-two, Clinton not only was one of the youngest governors in American history, he also seemed contrary to the popular images of Arkansas as one of the most conservative and provincial of the fifty states.

Clinton, an Arkansas native, was educated in the public schools, then moved to Washington, D.C., where he worked on the Senate Foreign Relations Committee (under Senator William Fulbright's tutelage and patronage) and earned a B.S. in international affairs, along with a Phi Beta Kappa key from Georgetown University. After two years at Oxford on a Rhodes scholarship he earned his law degree from Yale University. In 1972 Clinton began returning to Arkansas as a coordinator in the McGovern nomination and presidential campaigns; he returned permanently to the state in 1973 as a professor at the University of Arkansas Law School in Fayetteville.

In 1974 the twenty-eight-year-old Clinton won a primary contest for the Democratic nomination for Congress. He lost the general election to the Republican incumbent but by so close a margin that his political fortunes were advanced rather than diminished by the defeat. In 1976 he easily won his first statewide race, the Democratic nomination for attorney general; with no Republican opposition in the general election, he served as Arkansas campaign manager for the Carter-Mondale campaign in the fall contest, receiving further political glory when Carter carried Arkansas by a bigger majority than any other state but Georgia.

As an activist attorney general, Clinton became even more visible, and as soon as he announced his candidacy for governor, he was conceded to be the front-runner. Predictably, his victory over four opponents in the Democratic primary in July 1978 was by a sufficient majority (59 percent) to avoid a runoff. His victory in the general election over Republican Lynn Lowe was a virtual certainty.

So certain, in fact, was a fall victory that two events that took place between the primary and the general election would have been unthinkable in 1982. First, Clinton injected himself vigorously in a campaign to defeat an initiated constitutional amendment to repeal the sales tax on food and drugs. Although Clinton promised to initiate legislative relief from the sales tax on drugs, the food sales tax should remain, he insisted, until adequate revenue replacements could be enacted. In a year of national taxpayer revolts, the fact that Clinton felt politically secure enough to campaign *for* taxes while simultaneously advancing his own candidacy is a powerful indicator of his confidence during the 1978 campaign.

Even more indicative is the fact that Clinton began his transition during the summer and was in full swing by early autumn. With a large and talented attorney general's staff to assist, Clinton began immediately after the primary to fashion his campaign promises into budgetary priorities and legislative programs. In this effort he had the wholehearted assistance of state agencies, of supportive legislators, and of the NGA. Although most of the $100,000 primary campaign surplus was set aside for the general election, some was diverted to contract for the services of Price Waterhouse, fiscal management specialists who worked with Clinton and his aides on administrative reforms and on the budget, which contained a substantial projected surplus.

As expected, on November 7 Clinton was elected, with 63 percent of the vote; when the Legislative Council began its presession budget hearings one week later, Clinton was well prepared to assert his recommendations and preferences. Because of the ambitiousness of the agenda and the exuberance of Clinton and his team, the pace was hectic, but there was ample time for many public appearances throughout the state, and beyond. The inaugural was a glittering and festive three-day event, including numerous entertainments, and very shortly after the legislature convened, a complete package of administration bills was in the hopper.

Press coverage of the transition was extensive and favorable, celebrating Clinton's youth, his intelligence, and his energy, and noting approvingly that "Clinton would go into office better prepared for the governorship than any of his modern-day predecessors." On inaugural day the *Arkansas Gazette*'s editorial cartoonist George Fisher proudly promoted Clinton from a baby carriage to a shiny new tricycle, and the *Gazette* editorialized that "Mr. Clinton becomes governor today amid brilliant auguries for success. . . . The record that he builds may prove extraordinary . . . before his tenure as governor, presumably four years, is finished."[3]

The Once and Future Governor

The presumption was an especially safe one because only one twentieth-century Arkansas governor had been denied his bid for a second, sometimes called courtesy, two-year term. However, in November 1980, in the most stunning upset in Arkansas political history, Clinton was defeated by Frank White, who got 52 percent of the vote and became Arkansas' second Republican governor since Reconstruction.

Opinions continue to differ on the precise weight of the various factors that led to Clinton's downfall, but each of the following contributed in some measure. A number of legislative and administrative innovations, occasionally devised and implemented by non-Arkansans, had infuriated some of the state's most powerful economic interests, including utilities, timber, trucking, poultry, and medicine. An increase in the vehicle registration and license fees had angered Arkansas' rural, low-to-middle-income Democratic constituency. Important organizational components of Democratic majorities (labor, teachers, Democratic county organizations) had been insufficiently courted and mobilized. Clinton's close ties with the Carter White House did nothing to prevent (and were perceived as having permitted) the decision to locate thousands of highly undesirable Cuban refugees at Fort Chaffee in Arkansas. And unknown thousands of Arkansans, assuming a Clinton victory, decided to vote for White as a way of sending a message to Clinton that they thought he had become too remote, more eager for national acclaim than for Arkansas acceptance, too confident, too arrogant.

For Clinton it was a devastating personal and political defeat; but, although many of his closest friends attempted to dissuade him from an immediate rematch, Clinton, practicing law with a Little Rock firm, almost immediately began making plans to recapture that which he had lost.

Clinton's Election and Transition, 1982

In February 1982, preceding any formal announcement, Clinton began his gubernatorial campaign with two widely broadcast television commercials in which he apologized for what he had done wrong (especially the increases in car-tag fees and some controversial commutations), asked for forgiveness and a second chance, and assured the electorate that he had learned he could not "lead without listening." From then until November, Clinton made hundreds of personal appearances and thousands of personal calls on the long march back to the governorship.

First came a bruising five-man Democratic primary in which Clinton captured 42 percent of the vote, then a heated runoff against longtime Lieutenant Governor Joe Purcell, which Clinton won with 54 percent of the vote; finally Purcell went underground, and his campaign manager emerged as chairman of Democrats for Frank White. Both Clinton and White raised and spent record-breaking amounts, and both waged extensive (and largely negative) media campaigns. The major themes were taxes (who would be least likely to raise them), pardons and commutations (who would be the least lenient), utility rates (who would be the least accommodating to the power companies), gun control (who opposed it most vehemently), and jobs (who would bring the most to Arkansas). Clinton assembled a superb campaign staff, which effectively mobilized teachers, black groups, organized labor, local Democratic organizations, and literally thousands of dedicated volunteers.

Clinton's victory, with 55 percent of the vote on November 2, was a personal and political triumph, and historic first—the first Arkansas governor to have recaptured the office. Considering the vehemence of the campaign, the immediate postelection statements of the principals were not only correct but gracious. Clinton, on his flying round of thank-you's, implored his supporters not to be arrogant in their victory, and at White's campaign headquarters a sign on the marquee read, "Congratulations, Bill." Throughout the transition, relations between the major members of White's staff and Clinton's transition team were cooperative and cordial.

Nevertheless, virtually none of the numerous fortuitous factors that had eased the 1978 transition were present in 1982. The Clinton campaign ended at least $100,000 in debt, and the day after the election, White's director of the Department of Finance and Administration announced a $27-million budget shortfall. Clinton necessarily gave first attention to the budget, on which legislative hearings began soon after the election; but in a drastically collapsed time frame, he had little time for personnel decisions or legislative program preparation. Indeed, not a single bill had been drafted when the legislative session began.

The inaugural was a much more modest, one-day affair, celebrated amid the press theme of a subdued and repentant Clinton's being given his second chance. There were still references to his youth but in phrases such as the "young and grizzled veteran." And following his inauguration, *Gazette* cartoonist Fisher took Clinton off the ten-speed bicycle to which he had been promoted and placed him behind the wheel of a pickup truck, complete with gun rack and coon dog.

The Transitions Compared

TIMETABLE

The most obvious difference between Transitions I and II is the time that was available for transition purposes: seven months in 1978, two and one-half months in 1982. One might assume, therefore, that virtually all transition tasks would have been more thoughtfully and thoroughly concluded in the first transition than in the second. As table 1 demonstrates, however, this was not uniformly the case.

The transition coordinator was named much earlier in 1978, as were the chief of staff and other top aides; and in 1978 work began much earlier on both the budget and the legislative package. Major cabinet appointments, however, were no more quickly made in the first than in the second transition; in fact, decisions to retain incumbent members of the cabinet came forth more quickly in 1982 than in 1978. The major difference in the appointment of agency liaisons was in the number (nine in 1978, three in 1982) rather than the timing.

Table 1. Timetable for Transition Tasks

	NGA recommendation	Clinton transition I	Clinton transition II
Name transition coordinator	Day 1	July	Week 2
Take family vacation	Week 1	Week 7	Weeks 4, 8
Begin consideration of inaugural address	Week 1	Week 9	Week 9
Attend NGA seminar	Week 2	Week 2	No
Decide organization of staff; name chief of staff, press secretary	Week 2	Week 5	Week 8
Name rest of staff	Week 3	Weeks 6, 10	Week 10
Announce budget, administration directors	Week 3	After session	Week 11
Begin budget process	Week 3	Continuous	Continuous
Begin shaping legislative program	Week 3	July	Week 10
Review campaign promises	Week 4	July	Week 1
Make other cabinet appointments	Week 5	Week 10	Week 11 (major)
Designate agency liaisons	Weeks 6–8	Week 9	Week 10
Complete legislative package	Weeks 6–8	Week 10	Week 11, on

In both transitions the dominant focus of the governor's personal time and energy was the budget. Although the 1978 gubernatorial budget review was infinitely more thorough and rigorous (considerable emphasis was placed on writing and distributing an explanatory budget manual to accompany Clinton's recommendations), the process was not completed any more expeditiously than in 1982. In both transitions the inaugural address was written by the governor-elect on the very eve of the inaugural; for Clinton, a gifted wordsmith and orator, speech drafts and writers were neither necessary nor desired; it was the tone rather than the timing that varied.

The single greatest difference between the 1978 and 1982 timetables was in the drafting of legislation for the governor's package, but the 1982 tardiness was caused by many more factors than simply the time available. In neither 1978 nor 1982 did the Clinton transition make personnel decisions (staff or cabinet) as quickly as the NGA timetable suggests. This is due in part to a behavioral characteristic: Clinton is more comfortable with programmatic than with personnel decisions. However, it is even more due to the fact that the Arkansas timetable absolutely demands immediate budgetary decisions, followed quickly by legislative decisions, whereas personnel, especially cabinet, decisions, can be delayed.

STRUCTURAL SUPPORTS (AND POLITICAL CONSTRAINTS)

Over the last decade Arkansas has begun allocating public funds for gubernatorial transitions. The governor-elect may request an appropriate amount from the Governor's Emergency Fund, which the incumbent governor then grants with approval from the Legislative Council, the powerful interim arm of the legislature. The compliance of the governor and the approval of the legislature have heretofore been routine. However, because the actual amount is the governor-elect's responsibility, political considerations are frequently more influential than actual transition needs.

David Pryor, Clinton's immediate predecessor, had requested and received only $30,000 for transition costs in 1974; when he was reelected in 1976, no transition funds were necessary. By the time of Clinton's election in November 1978, the primary campaign surplus had been spent on the general election and transition planning; and expenses, especially for staff and equipment, were mounting. Clinton's transition coordinator, Rudy Moore, decided to request, and promptly received, double the amount that Pryor had been granted (i.e., $60,000).

When Frank White took over from Clinton in 1980, he initially requested, as part of his determination to spend less than Clinton, only $50,000. However, additional supplements had to be requested, first of $4,400, then of $3,500. Logically, then, Clinton could have requested at least $60,000. Because there was a substantial campaign deficit in 1980 (unlike 1978), generous public funding was even more essential. Additionally, Preston Bynum, White's chief of staff (who had been White's transition coordinator) assured Betsey Wright (Clinton's 1982 campaign coordinator and managing member of the 1982 transition team) that a request of anything up to $100,000 would be gladly honored. Indeed, Bynum, because of previous difficulties in dealing with the inadequacies of a $50,000 or even $60,000 budget, urged Wright to request $90,000 or more.

What might have been practically available, however, was politically impossible. The thrust of White's campaign against Clinton in both 1978 and 1980 was that whereas he was a tight-fisted businessman, Clinton had been and would be a loose-reined liberal spender. Additionally, Governor-elect Clinton in 1982 was facing a budget deficit and a straitened economy rather than a budget surplus and projected economic growth as in 1978.

The upshot was that Clinton's transition requested only $60,000 in 1982. As determined by political sensitivities rather than transition needs, then, a much smaller amount was requested than everyone knew would be necessary (which left the 1982 Clinton transition office strictly doling out writing paper and taking turns purchasing toilet tissue for the office).

Political considerations also precluded the use of a potentially invaluable transition device newly available since the Arkansas legislature in 1981 enacted a law permitting nonincumbent governors-elect an additional month of preparation for the legislative session. Under this act, rather than the usual timetable (under which the legislature convenes its regular sixty-day session on the second Monday in January in odd-numbered years and the governor is inaugurated during the first week, customarily on the second day, of the session), a nonincumbent governor-elect may opt to recess the legislature for thirty days immediately after having been sworn in.

Clinton and his key aides were acutely aware of how beneficial this extra month could be in preparing for the biennial session; but when the prospects of employing it were discussed with a diverse sample of legislators, their underlying hostility to such a recess became clear. Farming legislators were concerned about inroads into the planting season. Especially acute were concerns of non–Little Rock legislators who had already made arrangements (and deposits!) for their Little Rock accommodations for the session. Throughout this dialogue there were strong hints that this law was not intended for someone like Clinton, who was no neophyte in need of special considerations.

No governor can wish to begin his term by deliberately provoking a large part of the legislature. Again, therefore, for political reasons rather than transition purposes, a lawful opportunity for useful assistance had to be foregone.

As in 1978, the secretary of state offered transition office space in the Capitol Hill apartments next door to the capitol, an offer that White had gratefully accepted in 1980. (Indeed, Bynum recalled these offices, even with inadequate phones and chairs, as an essential method of separating the White transition from the White campaign. Bynum could summon campaign people to the Capitol Hill operation only if they were truly necessary; otherwise they remained in campaign headquarters winding down the campaign and organizing the inaugural.)

In neither 1978 nor 1982, however, did the Clinton transition utilize this offer. In 1978 Clinton had his commodious and convenient (on Capitol Hill) attorney general's office, which was supplemented by the continued use of campaign headquarters. In 1982, apparently to avoid the time and expense (such as telephone installation and computer transfer) of a move, the transition operated almost exclusively out of campaign headquarters. Clinton used an office in the State Budget Office for some of his budget study and meetings and had an occasional meeting (e.g., with the president of Reynolds Aluminum) in the more impressively furnished offices of his law firm.

Office and funding decisions were not critical; the decision not to delay the legislative session had much stronger reverberations. However, as will be emphasized, even the strongest of structural supports cannot outweigh contrary political realities.

THE BUDGET

Weeks before the general election, that is, before it is certain who the next governor will be, the Legislative Council has begun their budget hearings in which they review and make tentative recommendations on agency requests. This, then, is *the* critical step in the formulation of a biennial state budget. It is critical not only because the Legislative Council recommends budget levels and figures to the Legislative Joint Budget Committee (which in turn recommends a budget to the legislature) but because largely duplicate membership means that the Legislative Council in effect *is* the Joint Budget Committee. If a governor is to have impact on what will become in effect his budget, he must strongly influence the initial recommendations of the Legislative Council. For determined governors who have their own priorities and programs, the budget is—must be—the top priority during any Arkansas transition; and in both 1978 and 1982, so it was for Clinton.

In both years Clinton personally and thoroughly involved himself in virtually every budget decision, and in both years this took by far the largest part of his time and the time of his key aides. By tradition the state Budget Office is turned over to the governor-elect immediately upon his election. This is the closest thing to a permanent, professional transition staff that Arkansas offers, and it proved useful in 1978 (when Budget Office personnel began working with Clinton and his staff well before the general election) and invaluable in 1982. The necessity for immediate and extensive involvement in the budget process and the availability of career staff to assist, then, were the same in both years. However, many other factors with profound budgetary implications were entirely different.

The budget to which Clinton addressed himself in 1978 was one containing a projected surplus of $42 million, expected to reach $80 million by the following July. An additional favorable factor was that Amendment 59, which could have reduced state revenues by as much as $60 million, had been defeated. Anxious to use this largesse in pursuit of his priorities (especially education) and initiatives (a state energy office, a rural health program, a Washington office), Clinton contracted with Price Waterhouse for technical assistance. One permanent and two rotating fiscal management specialists, paid from the primary campaign surplus, were on board by August and worked intensively with Clinton and his staff and with agency personnel not only to shape a Clinton budget but to rationalize and reshape the budget process. The Price Waterhouse personnel also were instrumental in the creation of teams that worked in various state agencies and the governor's office, studying the operation of state government and seeking methods to improve its management.

By the time the Legislative Council began its presession review process, Clinton could appear repeatedly, in person, to argue, knowledgeably and for the most part successfully, for his proposals and priorities. Furthermore, for Clinton personally, it was a superb education in the details of the executive branch that would soon be his.

In 1982 of course, Clinton needed no tutelage in the intricacies of budget making. but this personal expertise was the only factor more favorable in 1982 than in 1978. (Ironically, even this plus had its minus. Because Clinton was by far the most budget-knowledgeable member of his transition team, all of whom were campaign rather than government experts, the budget was absolutely essential work that could not be safely delegated.)

Fortune's smiles had largely turned to sneers by 1982. The Arkansas unemployment figures announced the week of Clinton's election were 9.6 percent, with a prediction that unemployment might reach more than 12 percent by the end of the year. The day after the election the director of the Department of Finance and Administration announced that all state agencies funded through general revenues would have to cut their spending severely as the result of a $27-million shortfall. The originally forecasted 8-percent revenue growth rate had slumped to a 3.5-percent growth rate and was still falling. Furthermore, White had authorized the Corrections Department to overspend its appropriation by as much as $8 million in order to stay in compliance with federal court-ordered standards; White had pledged his support for a supplemental appropriation when the legislature convened, but of course White would now not be around. If the Corrections Department did not get an extra $8.8 million by mid-January, the board chairman announced, two prison units would have to be closed, 200 employees laid off, and 800 inmates turned loose. Because Clinton had been the target of charges throughout the primary and general election that he had been too lenient as governor with his pardons and commutations, he could not afford to begin his new regime by actions resulting in the massive freeing of prisoners.

Bad economic news continued to plague the 1982 Clinton transition. Two weeks after the election, Reynolds Metal Company announced that it was suspending operations at one of its plants, thereby putting over 700 employees out of work. Four weeks after the election, devastating tornadoes and floods raked the state, doing an estimated $500 million worth of damage, some of which (such as road and bridge repairs) would have to be covered by state funds.

Predictably, all those dependent upon state funds began the drumbeats for a tax increase, the source of choice being a 1-percent increase in the state sales tax; and this cry was reiterated almost daily by the state's most widely circulated newspaper, the *Arkansas Gazette*. Again, however, what might have been practically possible (the sales tax is the only major Arkansas tax requiring only a simple majority of the legislature to increase it, and numerous legislators were publicly announcing their willingness to do so) had been made politically impossible by the two preceding gubernatorial elections.

Clinton had made himself politically vulnerable in 1980 by an unpopular revenue-raising measure, the car-tag and license-fee increase. Reminded repeatedly by White that the White administration had not raised taxes and would not do so, Clinton had felt compelled to promise that he would not raise general taxes at least until major economic improvements would permit such action without inflicting undue personal hardship on the average Arkansas taxpayer. Even after his defeat White continued to keep the antitax political pressure on Clinton by repeated statements that he would have managed the shortfall without raising taxes, that it would be interesting to see whether Clinton could keep his promise not to raise taxes, that he suspected Clinton of preparing to ask for a tax increase.

Totally unlike the situation in 1978, then, when a leisurely timetable, a comfortable surplus, a positive campaign, and an optimistic economic atmosphere permitted creative and constructive budgeting, everything in the 1982 atmosphere dictated the necessity of sharp cuts and severe restraints. Whatever Clinton might want to enlarge had to be at the expense of abolishing or cutting back on something else. Because these are acutely political decisions, no outside technical assistance could have done much to ease the process.

There was, perhaps, one fortunate fallout from this nearly exclusive attention to budgets during the 1982 transition, which might be of value to other time-pressed governors-elect who want to move cautiously with their hiring and firing. While the curious press, nervous jobholders, and eager aspirants all clamored for early decisions on staff and cabinet, the transition office and Clinton personally could legitimately refuse any early personnel decisions. As Clinton repeatedly stated his priorities, he would work first on budgets, then staff, then cabinet, then a legislative program. It is with respect to the last item that some of the most obvious differences, again produced primarily by political considerations, distinguished the two transitions.

LEGISLATIVE PROGRAM AND PREPARATION

Progressive in philosophy, activist in temperament, Clinton rode into office in 1978 with large majorities that he, an enthusiastic staff, and an exhilarated press interpreted as a mandate for an imaginative and energetic administration. Clinton had offered a long list of possible improvements in education, energy, economic development, human services, and health care throughout his spring campaign, and in the summer months these proposals began to be shaped into legislative form. An important facilitator to the process was a large and loyal attorney general's staff possessing precisely the expertise necessary for bill drafting. By November, Clinton could begin offering specifics to the Legislative Council on precisely how and why he wanted to reorganize the Industrial Development Commission, upgrade public education, and protect consumers and the environment. Shortly after the legislative session began, each legislator received a packet of thirty-five proposed bills; others were forthcoming, and consideration of these administration measures (eventually over seventy) dominated the legislative session.

In 1982 Clinton's ability to construct a legislative program was constricted by all the circumstances previously noted, especially the much shorter time period, an essentially negative campaign, and an inadequate budget. It was also severely hampered by the total absence of issue people on his transition staff. As in 1978 the staff immediately made a thorough list of all campaign promises. In 1982, however, there was no expert attorney general's staff who could transfer those promises into proposed legislation. To be sure, Clinton's legislative wish list was considerably shorter and simpler than it had been in 1978, but even this shorter list got inadequate presession attention.

The bill-drafting services of the Legislative Council (which had been regarded with suspicion and therefore avoided in 1978) were employed to some extent, as were volunteer members of Clinton's former law firm and that of his wife. None proved a satisfactory substitute for having one's own people drafting one's own legislation. And far more frequently than in 1978, Clinton simply tagged measures introduced by legislators as administration bills, a practice that led to problems when the measures accomplished more or less than Clinton intended.

The 1983 state of the state message got high marks from legislators for virtuoso delivery (a fifty-two-minute unfaltering recitation of technical legislative proposals with no text) and much more "sensible" and "realistic" tone than the 1979 state of the state address. However, the fact that administration bills had still not appeared by the second week in the session led to legislative grumbling over wasted time and a public perception of drift and confusion. Newspaper articles noted that whereas Clinton had sponsored more than seventy bills in all areas of public policy in 1979, by inaugural eve in 1983 "he says he can't even estimate the number of bills he'll offer" and seemed to be concentrating entirely on jobs, the prison system, and utility reform. One *Gazette* story noted that Clinton "has been the epitome of passiveness," and several weeks into the legislative session, *Gazette* cartoonist Fisher pictured the newly acquired Clinton pickup truck on blocks, under the title "Clinton Leadership."

Before, during, and after the session Clinton ardently disputed the caretaker characterization, with a variety of explanations and arguments. First, he said, acknowledging that his previous administration had lacked focus, "I have learned in politics the thing to do is make one important decision at a time. I have determined that it would be best to concentrate on next year's budget." He also explained that although "just getting by" might not sound like the most imaginative program ever offered, it was considerably better than many of the state's citizens were doing. His second administration, he insisted, would not be less aggressive than the first, but it would be more open and accessible, more responsible, careful, and able, and "wiser in its aggressiveness." Above all, directly responding to previous charges of arrogance, of having set his own agenda regardless of popular preferences, of having attempted too much too soon, in 1982 he characterized the major difference in his two administrations: "the populism of his heart now displays itself more in his procedures," that he had learned how to do things "that are achieveable, that are understandable, and, by all means, involve the people in them."[4]

All these sentiments were the product of the disastrous defeat in 1980, the analysis of that defeat during the interregnum, and the strident campaign in 1982, and therefore were politically plausible and strategically defensible. Nevertheless, the entire legislative session, stemming at least partially from lack of preparation, seemed characterized by indecision, sudden shifts, mistaken impressions, and—by previous Clinton administration standards—a low level of accomplishment. What Clinton himself described as the heart of his legislative program, as it had been in many ways the heart of the campaign, was utility reform. Nevertheless, even the utility reform bills were not presented to the legislature until the fourth week of the session; and here, the lack of in-house bill-drafting expertise led to double trouble. Clinton, virtually the only authority on utilities on his transition team, hardly had the time to draft legislation. Finally, in desperation, he contracted out the bill-drafting work to two of the very individuals who had become anathema to and had earned such enmity from utilities in the first Clinton administration.

In this legislative aspect of the 1982 transition Clinton constantly found himself on the horns of a dilemma: his most ardent 1978 backers were disappointed by a contrast in style and substance, which they tried to understand but found difficult to admire; and the legislature, while constantly criticizing the lack of firm leadership, never afforded Clinton the honeymoon with which they had accommodated him in 1978. In fact, the legislators explicitly rejected such a stance. As one leading legislator noted, "The way I see it, he is now starting his second term. He had his honeymoon in his first term. He knows what he's doing. He's smart and he's been this route before. He doesn't need to be treated gently. If its good for the state, I'll be for it. If its good for Bill Clinton, I won't be inclined to go along."[5] An old Arkansas aphorism is that in his first legislative session the governor is a dictator; in the second he is a spectator. Although Clinton was far from being a spectator in 1983, he certainly had fewer legislative successes than in 1979.

If the legislative lapses were largely attributable to inadequate staff support, why didn't Clinton immediately bring such expertise on board? Again, political rather than formal restraints gave Clinton less freedom to choose than in 1978.

PERSONNEL: STAFF, CABINET, AND APPOINTMENTS

There were some rather surprising similarities in the 1978 and 1982 staffing processes. Despite the fact that the first transition was intraparty, between personal and political friends, and the second was interparty, between political opponents, in neither year were more than two of the previous governor's staff retained for the incoming governor's office operation. Whatever the experts may advise, in Arkansas the governor's office is seen as family, and those who have had the total personal and political loyalty expected by the previous governor are not likely to be welcome in the new governor's inner sanctum. However, in both transitions (again belying possible assumptions based on partisanship) the outgoing governors permitted the governor-elect to begin putting new staff on the state payroll as soon as vacancies were created, a kindness that seems to have become a custom.

One minor difference was that those of Pryor's staff who had been unable to locate employment by inaugural time were, at the request of Pryor's office, given "friendly terminations" to ensure their entitlement to unemployment benefits. No such arrangements were requested by White's chief of staff in behalf of his people.

The major differences in staffing, however, were in the size, source, numbers, and functions of those who were officially on board by the time Clinton took office in 1979 and in 1983. Twenty-six people were members of the 1979 staff; the 1983 beginning staff had only fourteen members. The much smaller beginning staff in 1983 was due not only to Clinton's greater cost-consciousness but even more directly to White's repeated assertions in both 1980 and 1982 that Clinton had surrounded himself with much too large and much too liberal a staff. The 1983 beginning staff was not only smaller but much less weighted toward liaison and intergovernmental relations functions (IGR), much more weighted toward constituent relations. The liaison functions were less necessary for two reasons. First, because Clinton had fewer plans for administrative reforms and program redirection, having someone in the governor's office to ride herd on each agency was not essential. Additionally, Clinton's first chief of staff admits that to some extent the 1978 staffing pattern reflected more an effort to find jobs for good people than to find good people for necessary jobs and that the liaison positions provided those jobs.

There is also a sharp contrast in the immediate previous employment of the two staffs: fourteen of Clinton's beginning staff in 1979 came directly from his staff in the attorney general's office, only four from the campaign; in 1983 thirteen of the fourteen beginning staff came directly from the campaign. This contrast is somewhat deceptive because the attorney general's staff was a highly supportive, though necessarily unofficial, component in Clinton's 1978 campaign. The 1979 and 1983 staffs were, however, different types of people. Those from the attorney general's office had been more knowledgeable about issues and eager for change and reform. Those from the 1982 campaign staff were experts on the politics of Arkansas and were primarily oriented toward Clinton's political acceptability.

Only two persons, neither a top aide in the first regime, worked on the first and the second Clinton staffs. Although the expertise of some of the previous staff members might have been useful, especially in legislative preparation, their presence would have inflamed old political controversies and criticisms. Finally, the 1983 beginning staff included slightly fewer females, slightly more blacks, and persons who were slightly older than the 1979 beginning staff; all but one were longtime Arkansans.

Because it is both Clinton's style and Arkansas tradition to make far fewer early cabinet decisions, there is much less to compare, but certain items are noteworthy. First, in both transitions the first major new cabinet appointee announced was black: the director of the Department of Local Services in 1979, the director of the Department of Finance and Administration in 1983.[6] The latter appointment constituted the highest ranking black administrator in Arkansas state government history and was a tribute both to Mahlon Martin's credentials (a very successful city manager of Little Rock) and to the smashing support Clinton got, and needed, from black voters in his 1982 comeback.

Somewhat related was the matter of former Governor Orval Faubus, whom White had appointed (after his campaign assistance in 1980) director of the state Veterans Affairs Department. The appointment had provoked outrage from the state's black leadership (and from liberal whites as well), and especially considering the record-breaking black turnout for Clinton in 1982, it was clear from the outset that Faubus would not be asked to stay. Curiously, the question of when Clinton would terminate Faubus provoked much more press inquiry than did questions of who would be coming on board; and several weeks after his inauguration, Clinton announced Faubus's replacement.

Much earlier in the second than in the first transition, Clinton announced four important cabinet members that he would retain: the directors of Education, Higher Education, Health, and Corrections, and immediately after inauguration Clinton also announced the retention of the director of Human Services, the largest state agency in terms of money and employees. Why was Clinton seemingly so much more agreeable to retaining Republican White's top people than Democratic Pryor's? Clinton gave several explanations for these retentions. First, he noted, all of them had been selected by a board or a commission, with gubernatorial consent, and therefore should be "immune from politics as much as possible." Additionally, he explained, the education director had been his appointee originally, and the higher education director, recently chosen, had been deputy director in Clinton's first regime. Clinton (clearly anxious to avoid another politically costly confrontation with the state's doctors) pointed out that he had promised the state Board of Health greater autonomy in selecting a director. As for the Corrections Department director, Clinton noted that he had been extremely cooperative in attempting to find alternatives to massive funding increases to keep the prisons open and the prisoners confined.

Here, actually, is the crux of the matter. Because of the collapsed timetable, Clinton had to rely much more heavily on incumbent agency heads in 1982 than in 1978; if they proved supportive and useful during the budget-shaping process, they had the opportunity (which few were given in 1978) to prove themselves. Additionally, in contrast to 1978, when Clinton's agenda included significant reshaping (for programmatic purposes) in almost every policy area and making new administrative blood was highly desirable, in 1982 a less revolutionary administrative agenda could tolerate more old hands.

It is somewhat ironic that major appointments seemed to come more quickly in the two-and-a-half-month 1982 transition than in the seven-month 1978 transition, but in 1978 Clinton and his team were searching, in several cases nationwide, for the best possible talent to help shape and implement new programs and goals. Several positions could not be filled until after the legislative session because legislation was necessary to establish the Energy Department, totally reorganize the Industrial Development Commission into an Economic Development Department, and to eliminate the seven-year residence/practice requirement for the Health Department director so that Clinton could hire the West Virginia rural health specialist he especially desired.

The greater number and earlier announcement of retentions was not particularly satisfactory to many 1982 campaign workers eager for top jobs, to previous Clinton people eager to see vengeance done and all White people replaced, or to the press eager for more exciting news. And by late in the legislative session there was some concern among top Clinton aides that the cabinet carry-overs, although promptly and loyally reporting the phone calls and advice they continued to get from White, were not displaying the deference that might have been extended by purely Clinton appointees. Nevertheless, the decisions were entirely congruent with Clinton's new political and programmatic agenda.

Arkansas governors make more than five hundred appointments to boards and commissions of widely varying power and status. Because most of these appointments are highly prized, for an infinite variety of reasons, they are always part of the political bargaining among governors, legislators, interest groups, and interested individuals.[7] Although the competition for and discussion of these appointments is always a major part of any gubernatorial campaign, and was in both 1978 and 1982, in neither year were these appointments a major priority during the transition. In both transitions, procedures were established early to identify vacancies (which are computerized), to acknowledge applicants, and to confirm or deny campaign commitments; rather elaborate procedures for the clearance of potential appointees (with county campaign coordinators, legislators, professional groups) were established and begun. Because these appointments are a bargaining coin and potential anger-inducer with interested legislators, however, governors usually make as few appointments as possible at the front end of legislative sessions.

There were some differences between the two transitions, and they provide an instance in which assuming power from a friend differs considerably from assuming power from a foe. Whereas Pryor had left close to one hundred appointments unmade, very few appointments and certainly no major openings were left unfilled by White. Because most appointments must be confirmed by the senate, which is rarely in session, there are invariably a large number of leftover, unconfirmed gubernatorial appointments when a new governor is elected. Ordinarily, because they have been cleared with the senator from whose district the nominee comes, the leftover appointments are routinely confirmed. In the 1978 transition questions arose over only one of the leftover Pryor appointees, a Workmen's Compensation Commission chairman who had deeply displeased the AFL-CIO. Although the senate (over incoming Clinton's objections) confirmed the appointment, a post-transition adjustment was made in the commission to satisfy organized labor.

In 1982 there was widespread speculation in the press and in political circles that the senate, at Clinton's urging, might deal very harshly with nearly two hundred leftover White appointments—speculation fed by recollections of the first post–Winthrop Rockefeller legislative session when the senate rejected Rockefeller's appointees en masse, and also by White's blocking in 1981 of a Clinton proconsumer appointment to the Public Service Commission, with the cooperation of a state senator who was a utility executive. After weeks of political maneuvering, however, the Clinton forces attempted to block only two of White's nominees— a state insurance commissioner and, as in 1978, a Workmen's Compensation commissioner, again anathema to labor. As in 1979, however, each of these appointees had powerful legislative support and both were confirmed on the second day of the session while Clinton shook hands at his inaugural reception.

More potentially serious problems arose much later in the legislative session when one powerful senator, distributing a list of 115 unfilled positions, proposed a resolution giving the senate power to fill all board and commission vacancies not filled by Clinton in the time set by law. Actually, this was a ploy to attempt to force Clinton into naming a Public Service Commission chairman before the senate adjourned, giving the senate the opportunity to block one rumored choice. However, although the resolution was enacted, by the time it took effect the senate was no longer in session, and especially given its dubious legality, the issue became moot.

Simply sketching the major outlines of personnel decisions in two transitions does not, of course, begin to convey the incessant *sturm und drang* that accompanies this most difficult and delicate of transition tasks. A major part of the calls, correspondence, and requests for the governor-elect's time relates to jobs—persons wanting to keep the positions they have, those desiring (and in many cases feeling entitled to) positions, and those who see a new administration primarily as an opportunity for getting rid of people. In both 1978 and 1982 Clinton spent hours with all these people. In 1982 the pressure for state jobs was especially acute because so many hundreds had worked so long and so devotedly in a closely contested and lengthy campaign; but there was no room in the tight budget for job creation and, in a depressed economy, far less than the ordinary amount of attrition.

Although every governor must feel absolutely confident in and comfortable with his own staff and cabinet, below these levels the emotions and energy are best expended by others. Clinton's 1982 insistence that he was too personally preoccupied with the budget to deal with personnel choices was not a ploy, but its utility as a protective device might be noted by other future governors-elect. Resignations will make some intended but nonetheless awkward terminations unnecessary, and personnel decisions made at leisure may frequently prove superior to those made in haste and under immediate postcampaign pressure.

EXTERNAL RELATIONS

One of the most glaring differences between the 1978 and 1982 Clinton transitions was in the incoming administration's relations with the world outside Arkansas. In 1978 these relations were frequent, open, and welcome; in 1982 they were nonexistent. Partly time but, again, primarily political factors account for the difference.

By mid-summer 1978 the Clinton team had established very close and cooperative relations with the NGA Center for Policy Research and the Council of State Planning Agencies (CSPA) as well as with the NGA itself. Although members of the Clinton transition team read the NGA manuals (particularly the sections on organization of the governor's office) and received some technical assistance in office management, the major subject of these exchanges was policy. The 1978 Clinton transition had an ambitious and complicated policy agenda, especially with respect to economic development and energy, two areas in which the NGA and the CSPA were well versed and eager to assist. The Clinton people and the NGA people quickly discovered a strong mutual interest: here was a governor determined to be much more than a ribbon-cutter; here were innovative policies burning to be implemented. The Clinton administration wanted to establish a Washington office; the NGA could show them how. The Clinton administration intended to aggressively seek federal funds and projects; the NGA could introduce them to the right people at agencies such as EDA (Economic Development Administration) and FHA (Farmers Home Administration). The NGA appreciates articulate and attractive governors who reflect glory on governors in general; Clinton enjoyed the opportunities for national attention and exposure. Not a month passed in the seven-month Clinton transition without either NGA people coming to Arkansas or Clinton people going to Washington.

In 1978 Clinton not only was an enthusiastic participant in the new governors seminar but conferred with Carter at the White House, chaired the session on national health insurance at the Democratic Midterm Convention in Memphis, and on these and other occasions received glowing recognition from the national press. As noted, none of this served Clinton well, in fact became part of the charges against him and possibly contributed to his 1980 defeat.

In 1982 Clinton did not attend the new governors seminar, and virtually no technical or policy assistance (other than the handbooks) was requested or indeed welcome from any out-of-state source. The stated rationale, which certainly has some legitimacy, was that Clinton was not a "new" governor for whom such services were fashioned, and it was doubtful whether anyone (particularly a non-Arkansas anyone) could possibly know as much about the transition period in general and the Arkansas governorship in particular as did Clinton himself.

Obviously influential also, however, is the fact that Clinton's national acclaim, his chairmanship of the Democratic governors, his White House ties, his use of non-Arkansas staff and administrators, had all been hurled against him in both the 1980 and 1982 gubernatorial campaigns. Whether these were decisive factors in his 1980 defeat is problematical, but clearly, at least in the early stages of his 1983 administration, every effort was being made not to provide that kind of ammunition to opponents in the future.

In this connection the staffing arrangements with which Clinton began his governorship in 1978 and in 1982 are noteworthy. Seven of the twenty-six original staff positions in 1978 had included intergovernmental responsibilities; only one of the fourteen original staff positions in 1982 did so.

Clinton did attend and vigorously participate in the NGA winter meeting held in Washington in March. Although he had not, then, entirely gone native, it was obvious that his external relations would be more cautious and constrained than they had been.

THE INAUGURAL

Although intergovernmental relations have great substantive import and are therefore of great concern to political insiders, inaugural activities have great stylistic import and constitute a major symbolic statement to the public. The 1979 and 1983 Clinton inaugurals were as different as Camembert and cottage cheese.

By early December 1978 a large inaugural committee had begun to plan and publicize three days of inaugural events: a Sunday dedicatory service followed by a music-accompanied reception at the Territorial Restoration; a much promoted Monday evening Diamonds and Denim gala featuring Arkansas talent performing rock, opera, gospel, dance, and drama; and a day-long round of activities on inaugural Tuesday, including the formal oath of office, a symphony concert in the capitol rotunda, a reception in the governor's conference room, a public inaugural address on the capitol steps, and a formal inaugural ball. Countless newspaper and television stories described each of these events in advance in colorful detail, and newspaper advertisements invited "all Arkansans" to attend.

Second inaugurals, somewhat in the tradition of second weddings, are likely to be surrounded with much less ceremony, fewer attendant events, and far less public fanfare. In 1982 Clinton's wife worked with a small committee to arrange a much more reserved and traditional, more discreet and modest inauguration. All events took place on inaugural Tuesday, beginning with a dedicatory ceremony, again at Immanuel Baptist Church. Clinton was then sworn in before a joint session of the legislature, which he briefly addressed, and immediately thereafter gave his inaugural address on the steps of the capitol. An afternoon-long reception was held in the governor's conference room while church and school choirs performed throughout the capitol. The day concluded with a reception for campaign county coordinators and the inaugural ball. In outline it was a much less elaborate affair.

However, if the 1979 inauguration had overtones of Camelot, the 1983 inauguration was boisterously Jacksonian. Clinton's inaugural address, as the opening quotation indicates, was a much less elegant, much more homespun affair, and although some from the previous Clinton administration stayed home by their radios and shuddered at a harsh new twang in Clinton's voice, the enormous crowd present cheered mightily when he swung into his familiar campaign attack on selfish utilities. Unprecedented masses attended virtually every event of the day: over two thousand at the dedicatory service (as compared with several hundred at the similar service in 1979); according to the head of gubernatorial security, nearly 4,000 at the outdoor inaugural address, the largest crowd ever gathered at the capitol; and additional thousands in the capitol to shake Clinton's hand at the subsequent reception. Crowds became so enormous at the inaugural ball (where few tuxedos were in evidence) that first one, then a second, ballroom had to be opened, the food and drink quickly disappeared, and the inaugural committee quickly gave up even the pretense of collecting tickets from the more than eight thousand who came to celebrate. Extending the second-wedding analogy, if such events are supposed to be primarily family affairs, Clinton's family had extended enormously in four years' time.

Some attributed the throngs to the massive organizational apparatus that had personally involved thousands of individuals for so many months and given them a real stake in the inaugural events. Others, more cynically, pointed to the low cost of a ball ticket ($10) and the first chance for many Arkansans to examine the elegant new Excelsior Hotel. Others talked about the guilt being expiated by so many who had assumed Clinton's victory in 1980 and had thereby contributed to his defeat. Perhaps most significantly, whereas in 1978 all Arkansans had been invited via newspaper advertisement, in 1982 invitations to the inaugural were mailed to more than 25,000 persons on the Clinton campaign list. Feeling personally invited, they came.

PUBLIC PERCEPTIONS

In both 1978 and 1982, by far the most publicized events of the transition were those numerous occasions when Clinton met with the Legislative Council to argue for his own budget priorities. This was not an artificial scenario created by public relations staff, but a necessity imposed upon all Arkansas governors-elect if they wish to fashion the biennial budget at the beginning. Because Clinton had educated himself extensively in state budgets during the summer of 1978 and was even more experienced in budgetary matters in 1982, the major substantive difference here was that between eagerly shaping a budget with a surplus and forcibly trimming a budget with a shortfall. In both situations the obligations imposed by the inexorable legislative schedule fortuitously produced a public image of a knowledgeable, competent, cost-conscious, take-charge governor.

In amounts and focus of publicity, the major difference between the two transitions stems from the fact that in the 1978 transition there was additional extensive media coverage of many things other than the budgetary process. Articles about Clinton's biographical and behavioral characteristics (especially his youth and intelligence) flowed endlessly from the press. His numerous appearances before various conventions and gatherings were covered exhaustively, as were his trips to Washington, Memphis, and Atlanta. Speculation about staff and cabinet was another favorite topic in 1978, and dozens of articles ballyhooed the elaborate inaugural festivities.

In 1982 Clinton rarely appeared in public except at the budget hearings. After a previous governorship and an extensive campaign Clinton was already known in excruciating detail to the public; biographical and behavioral analyses thus would not have been news of the first order. He made no trips (except for the two brief unpublicized family vacations and an overnight trip to Washington), he and his staff refused to discuss personnel, and the inaugural events were simply announced in the press a short time before their occurrence. In short the transition in general and Clinton in particular kept a very low profile in 1982. When, one month into the transition, Clinton granted his first interviews to the media, he emphasized that he had been totally consumed with trying to trim the budget, that he would keep his campaign commitments (not to raise taxes while the economy was down, not to commute sentences of those convicted of violent crimes, to make the prisons less costly to the state through a prison industry system, to reform the utilities, and bring in more jobs). Only after the budget was in good shape, he said, could he turn his attention to "personalities." Little of this was news, and for much of the following month most of the headlines about Clinton were references to Clinton, Arkansas, which took the brunt of the violent early December storms.

There were, of course, many other events occurring behind the scenes—lengthy sessions with state legislators, peacemaking sessions with those who had been so "shortsighted" as to support White, extensive discussions with agency heads and with the transition team about which of these heads should remain and which should be replaced. Clinton also made ample time available to the groups (especially blacks and teachers) that had been so instrumental in his victory, personally assuring them that their preferences in both personnel and programs would be accommodated. These were private sessions, however, and the public image was that of a governor-elect making slow but steady progress on the fiscal front to the exclusion of everything else.

As Clinton prepared to take office in 1979, his image was that of a dynamic and confident leader who had great dreams and plans for the state and was securing the best and the brightest talent from throughout the nation to ensure their implementation. As Clinton prepared to take office in 1983, his image was that of a highly self-disciplined and focused governor, willing to work hard to make the best of bad times, no longer certain that he could make dramatic changes through the creativity of his intellect and the force of his own personality. In fact, from the moment of his first apology to the hour of his inaugural, he went to great lengths to reshape the image of having been overconfident to the point of arrogance.

On election night he announced that he "felt humbled" by his victory. On a thank-you tour around the state he begged his supporters "not to be arrogant" in their victory and beseeched them to "tell me when I'm wrong as well as when I'm right." Given the pulpit of his church for a postelection sermon, he told the congregation that he "felt unworthy" of the office. Addressing the Democratic State Committee, he announced that his election had been a "humbling and sobering experience," and assured them that above all he would maintain "maximum accessibility." At his first meeting with the Legislative Council he shook hands longer than he spoke, and what he said was how much he would need their advice and assistance. And immediately after his swearing-in he told the assembled legislators that he was "humbled to be given another chance to serve the people."

None of this was pure rhetoric. Clinton had in fact been humbled by his 1980 defeat, but he missed no opportunity to remind the public and the political establishment that he had received their message, learned a painful lesson, and was not likely to forget his fallibility in the future.

CHANGING OF THE GUARD

As Clinton was humble in victory, so White was gracious in defeat, a defeat that he had anticipated, if at all, only in the last weeks of the campaign. White promptly congratulated Clinton and promised a cooperative transition. Especially considering the length and intensity of the campaign and the fierce determination of both principals, the transition coordinators worked harmoniously and were highly complimentary about each other. No useful files were destroyed or necessary information denied. Although the Clinton people were surprised by the size of the shortfall they inherited (and provoked that the press never pounced upon the irony of the businessman governor's having left the state deeply in debt), there was no suggestion that this was a deliberate dirty trick—White had fully anticipated being around to deal with the deficit.

Nevertheless, the politics (both past and future) of the principals permeated the transition. In 1978 a successful Governor Pryor was moving out and up, to a seat in the U.S. Senate. Although there may have been faint thoughts in Pryor's and Clinton's minds that they might meet as adversaries over that senate seat in the distant future, the possibility was remote and certainly not a major factor in the transition.

In stark contrast Governor White had been rejected by the voters, replaced by the man he had defeated previously. Although White moved on to what many would consider an enviable position (with Stephens, Inc., the largest investment banking firm in America outside New York City), he left the office with profound regrets. And although in the immediate aftermath of his defeat he said that he would not seek the office again, that "this is it," as the transition progressed, so did speculation that there would in fact be another Clinton-White rematch in the near future. This speculation was fed by White's remarks throughout the transition—"We'll see if Bill Clinton keeps his word (not to raise taxes)"; "It will be interesting to compare your electric bill today and two years from now"; and "He's a professional politician. I was a businessman."

Despite the correct, indeed cordial, relationships of the transition teams per se, the past (and possibly future) election contests between the principals clearly conditioned what Clinton did, did not, and politically could not do during the transition.

Tensions inevitably arise during any transition, stemming in part from the king's being officially dead but still living on. When the devastating storms hit in early December, it was, of course, Governor White who first toured the state to view the damage, released aid from the Governor's Emergency Fund, and requested all possible assistance from the federal government. However, because in the minds of many, Clinton was really the governor, they turned to him for aid and comfort. It was absolutely necessary that Clinton himself visit the stricken areas and visibly demonstrate his concern. He did so ten days after White's official tour in a National Guard helicopter, which Clinton's transition staff recalls feeling "very awkward" about requesting but which White's office did supply. In substantive response, however, Clinton could do little more than appoint a committee of state legislators to suggest compensatory legislation. This touchy business of a power vacuum was treated thoughtfully by some, less so by others. Asked to respond to reports of criticism by Governor White, the highway director bluntly noted, "I don't have anything to say about what that man says. That's a waste of time. He's not the governor any more."[8]

For the outgoing chief of staff, who remembers relentless confusion and exhaustion when he coordinated White's incoming transition team, the most onerous responsibility in 1982 was keeping White's staff sufficiently "bucked up" to function. There seem to be no handbooks on how to boost the spirits of a defeated and demoralized staff. In fact, Bynum, having watched and thought about transitions from both the incoming and the outgoing perspective, suggested only somewhat facetiously that the single most useful action would be to abolish transitions altogether. For all practical purposes the governor-elect *is* the governor, Bynum observed. If he assumed office immediately, he could immediately have the staff positions, the funds, the agency expertise, the office accommodations and equipment that he so desperately needs. The White transition office, Bynum recalls, was a far busier place in calls, correspondence, and pressures for decision making than the governor's office ever proved to be. Because the transition turns out to be primarily a time for coping with crisis, why not enable the governor-elect to function under the best rather than the worst possible circumstances?

Bynum's suggestion is provocative but probably (for numerous constitutional, traditional, and practical reasons) unrealistic. Within what will undoubtedly continue to be an extremely compressed period of time, what are the factors to which those who would ease the process should be especially sensitive?

Conclusions and Caveats

Because each state has its own unique traditions, each state should have some permanent repository (perhaps the secretary of state's office) as an unofficial Keeper of the Customs to alert the incoming and outgoing governors and/or the transition teams to certain expected rituals. Many are not of great consequence, but an anticipated problem may create less panic than an unanticipated one.

In Arkansas, for example, the governor-elect can expect to be inundated by requests for season passes to the races. These save the holder only $1 in general admission fees, but they are so prized as a status symbol that it is widely considered humiliating to attend the races without one, and the governor's office unfortunately, supplied by the Racing Commission, has the most plentiful supply. At one point in the 1982 transition requests for racing passes were outnumbering four to one all other correspondence at Clinton headquarters. Rumors of prison uprisings are another Arkansas tradition; they do not materialize, which is comforting to know in advance.

It has apparently become customary in recent years for the outgoing governor to leave a personal note for his successor in the governor's office. Pryor left a note to Clinton, attached to two packets of Tylenol: "Good luck, Bill. I am leaving something that may come in handy." Clinton in turn left a note for White: "Frank. Good luck. It's the best job in America." In turn, White left one to Clinton: "People seldom get a second chance. Keep your promises. Good luck." Obviously, the tone may vary (humorous, wistful, admonitory), but the tradition adds a pleasant human touch.

Other state traditions are of considerably greater consequence. Despite the increased professionalism and expertise of those serving in the governor's office, it is still a powerful Arkansas tradition to sweep the office clean in intraparty as well as interparty turnovers. The staff of the outgoing governor should harbor no illusions that keep them from finding new employment, and the governor-elect need suffer no particular qualms of conscience.

The staff of the Budget Office, in contrast, can be seen as a corps of professionals. They will attach their loyalties to the governor-elect immediately after the election, and they will serve faithfully. Given the fact that any Arkansas governor-elect will necessarily give first and foremost attention to the budget, this loyalty is a bureaucratic blessing. The time for budget work will always be insufficient. However, the governor-elect's personal immersion in the budget process is the most thorough education in state government imaginable; it must be done to shape programmatic priorities; it evokes a somewhat unexciting but very favorable press and image; and it is a useful excuse for delaying personnel decisions that may in fact be better made at leisure. Because few Arkansas governors-elect are likely to have the lengthy time and talented staff for bill drafting that Clinton had in 1978 and because legislatures expect the governor's package to be in the hopper in the first week of the session, alternatives must be considered. Private lawyers and law professors are useful only if they can totally set aside their other obligations to meet the governor's timetable and only if their efforts are being strongly coordinated. Otherwise, the Legislative Council staff is willing and able to serve.

It is now routine for a governor-elect to request and receive public transition funds from the Governor's Emergency Fund. Because governors-elect may be reluctant to request more than their predecessors have requested, however, the system would work much more satisfactorily if the legislature authorized the sum in advance and automatically transferred it to a newly elected nonincumbent governor. Similarly, the law permitting a newly elected governor to recess the legislature would be far more functional if it were mandatory.

As these examples and the entire chapter suggest, those assisting with transitions must, above all, be acutely aware of the politics of the particular transition that they are to facilitate. This awareness includes the politics of the past (the preceding campaign, the commitments made therein, the expectations inspired), of the present (the political purposes that must be accomplished by the transition and the political constraints that preclude certain actions and activities), and of the future (the ambitions of the incumbent governor and of the governor-elect, whether there will be a next campaign for either or both, and if so against whom and when).

As the transition comparisons strongly indicate, the political environment permeates the transition and is often the single strongest influence on schedule, substance, and style. What this in turn suggests is that perhaps the greatest need of those who would make themselves useful is superb, up-to-date, in-state political intelligence.

Although the NGA materials are suffused with a stated sensitivity to the inevitable and legitimate individuality of each transition, they also convey a presumption that careful observation and planning can iron out some of the idiosyncrasies and singularities. As these individual state reports are read and reviewed, some effort will be made to extract the commonalities, but perhaps even more attention and weight should be given to the variables.

The 1982–1983 Gubernatorial Transition in California

RICHARD W. GABLE,

MARK SEKTNAN, AND JOEL KING

George Deukmejian became the thirty-fifth governor of California by a margin of 1.19 percent, with 7.88 million votes cast. Only Governor Washington Bartlett's margin of 0.4 percent in the election of 1886 was smaller. In assuming office Deukmejian lacked a clear electoral mandate, replaced a Democratic governor, had no other Republican constitutional officers to support him, and faced a heavily Democratic legislature largely unsympathetic to his programs and his solution to the fiscal crisis that loomed over the state. Greater public support would have to be earned, and its extent will be learned over time. Nonetheless, the electoral victory, regardless of its margin, provided Deukmejian the extensive powers and responsibilities of the governorship in California—what Norton Long referred to as "the symbols of legitimacy to a government."[1]

Gubernatorial transitions are regular occurrences, and transfers of power to another political party have been frequent in California. Yet no standard procedures have evolved, if, indeed, they could be designed, and no legislation to assist transitions was enacted until 1939. Each new governor has been thrown on his own resources and has prepared for assuming the office in his own way.

For much of the time the process was easier than it is today, because the scope of the government was limited and fewer demands were placed on the governor. He had little control over executive functions and slight responsibility for budget preparation until the state's administrative agencies were consolidated under the governor in 1921 and the governor was given much greater control over the budget the following year.

These powers have made California governors more effective once in office, but during the transition greater demands are placed on the governor to select appointees and prepare a budget.

When, in 1938, Culbert Olson became the first Democrat to be elected governor of California in this century, he faced a hostile legislature controlled by Republicans and conservative Democrats. The following year, in recognition of the difficulties encountered, the legislature enacted a measure that gave the governor-elect the power to "require any institution, department, board, bureau, commission, officer, employee or other agency to furnish him with such information, assistance, supplies, transportation and facilities as he may deem necessary in connection with the budget or to assist him in its preparation."

This law remained unchanged until the end of Ronald Reagan's term in 1974. In preparing to assume office in 1966, he had spent $225,000 of privately donated funds for office rental, staff salaries, telephone bills. Consequently, when he was outgoing governor, Reagan proposed a $125,000-item in the 1974–75 budget to assist the new governor. The requested funds were appropriated, and the legislature added $50,000, half of which was to be used by the outgoing governor. The original legislation was also amended. The statement of purpose in the new law was taken directly from the Presidential Transition Act of 1963, and new language expanded on the original legislation to add the following: "The director of finance, after consultation with the governor-elect, shall appoint such persons as necessary to assist the governor-elect in the preparation of the annual state budget and the assumption of the other duties of the governor." Provision was also made for outgoing governors: "The governor may appoint for a period not to exceed 60 calendar days after the conclusion of his term of office persons to assist the governor in concluding matters arising out of his official duties during his last term."

In implementing this legislation, the Department of Finance automatically incorporates in the budget a fund to assist transitions each election year. The amount is based on the 1974 appropriation adjusted by the Consumer Price Index. If the governor-elect is the incumbent governor, no transition funds are appropriated. In 1982 the appropriation totaled $348,000: $296,000 for the incoming governor and $52,000 for the outgoing governor.

Electing the Governor

To gain California's highest office, Deukmejian came from behind in the polls to defeat Lieutenant Governor Mike Curb in the Republican primary and Tom Bradley, the three-term mayor of Los Angeles, in the general election.

THE PRIMARIES

During the primary campaign Attorney General Deukmejian, popularly known as Duke, made an issue of his experience in government in contrast to the outsider image of Curb, a self-made millionaire from the world of entertainment with no experience in government before he was elected lieutenant governor in 1978 at the age of thirty-three. Deukmejian had served in the assembly for four years and in the senate for twelve years when he was elected attorney general in 1978. Yet after twenty years of state service, his Department of Justice letterhead continued to display the phonetic pronunciation of his name—"Duke-may-gin."

As the campaign for the Republican nomination progressed, polls showed Curb ahead at one time by as much as sixteen points; the week before the election the lead was trimmed to eight points, and on the day of the election Deukmejian had surged ahead in the polls. He defeated Curb by 51.1 percent to 44.8 percent in the smallest turnout since the 1946 primary.

Bradley easily won the Democratic primary. Prior to becoming mayor he had been a city councilman and had served for over twenty years on the Los Angeles police force. His strategy was to run a low-key campaign against the senate majority leader, John Garamendi, and Governor Jerry Brown's health and welfare agency secretary, Mario Obledo. He avoided debates and counted on greater recognition to give him the victory. Although his speeches were regarded as lusterless, he proved to be a stolid, methodical campaigner and easily overwhelmed his opponents, receiving 61.1 percent of the votes to Garamendi's 25.2 percent and Obledo's 4.7 percent.

During the primary races the major candidates were briefed about the state's impending fiscal crisis by the top career executive in the Department of Finance, Cliff Allenby, who explained, "We had been going through a process since 1978 of reducing taxes and we had not made any material changes in the level of government services to the extent that taxes had been reduced. So, I felt that it was reasonable to make it clear to all candidates in as consistent and equal manner as possible what the conditions were at that time for the 1981–82 budget and what 1982–83 might look like."

THE GENERAL ELECTION

The campaign for governor started on a low key, in keeping with the character of the two opponents. The *California Journal* headlined the race "Dull Tom and Cautious Duke."² Both candidates stressed their experience. The attorney general focused on his many years in state government; the mayor talked about the similarities between dealing with budgets and other administrative matters for both a large city and the state. Both candidates addressed issues. With different emphases and approaches they agreed on the need to strengthen California's economy, fight crime, improve the educational system, and deal with agricultural and water issues. They disagreed over other issues, especially handgun control and the possible need for new taxes.

Both candidates preferred to avoid a detailed discussion of how they would deal with an apparent budget deficit. Bradley suggested that tax increases might be necessary if the economy did not improve. By contrast Deukmejian took a strong stand, which he has continued to maintain: "I'm going to balance this budget without going to the people for additional taxes." The statements that each candidate expressed in regard to the budget must have been calculated positions because both had the opportunity to gain a full understanding of the projected budget deficit. In mid-August, after the primary and before the general election campaign began, Allenby again briefed both candidates. As before, Allenby and his staff flew to Los Angeles to brief Bradley and his campaign leaders. In Sacramento, Michael Franchetti, later to become Deukmejian's director of finance, and Steve Merksamer, who became the new governor's executive secretary and chief of staff, were also briefed. Allenby identified and explained potential budget changes during the year (welfare court cases, lost federal funds, unitary method of taxation) that could wipe out the reserve and produce a deficit of over $1 billion at the end of FY 1983.

During much of the campaign Bradley held a ten-to-twelve-point edge. In the last two weeks that lead narrowed and held steady at five to seven points for Bradley. Four years earlier Deukmejian was two percentage points behind his opponent at the end of the race for attorney general when he won by ten points. On November 2 Deukmejian received 3,881,014 votes (49.3 percent) to 3,787,669 votes (48.1 percent) for Bradley—a margin of 93,345 votes (1.19 percent). Among the last six governors he is the third attorney general to win the state's highest office.

The Democrats won all the other partisan constitutional offices, including the lieutenant governor's, by substantial majorities, lost one assembly seat (giving them forty-eight to thirty-two seats) and picked up two seats in the senate (giving them twenty-five to fifteen seats). Because money measures require a two-thirds majority in the legislature, six Republicans in the assembly and two Republicans in the senate would have to join unanimous Democratic blocs to raise taxes and approve budget expenditures. (In March 1983 senate Republicans lost one of their members when Ray Johnson switched his registration to independent to protest the Republican approval of a reapportionment plan that gave part of his district, including the city in which he lived, to another Republican senator. He then joined the Democrats in key tax and budget votes.)

THE VICTORY AND ITS MEANING

When a candidate defeats the apparent front-runner, the inevitable question is, How did it happen? Was race an issue? In a state in which blacks constitute about 9 percent of the population, relatively few blacks have been successful in state politics, although their numbers have increased slightly in recent years.

Neither candidate made an issue of Bradley's race. However, the issue did surface a month before the election. On October 7 Bill Roberts, Deukmejian's campaign manager, discussed polls that showed the attorney general trailing 39 to 54 percent. He candidly volunteered, "If we are down only five points or less in the polls by election time, we're going to win." The reason—the hidden antiblack vote. "It's just a fact of life. If people are going to vote that way, they are certainly not going to announce it for a survey taker." Bradley took the comment as an insult. Roberts resigned five days later, but, according to Mervin D. Field, his California Poll found that 5 percent of the voters stated they would not vote for Bradley because he was black. At the same time, 12 percent of the voters polled indicated they would be disinclined to vote for a candidate of Armenian descent. A counterargument could be that Bradley attracted some votes from blacks because he was black rather than because of his stand on issues or his party affiliation. However, the turnout among blacks was somewhat lower than in previous elections in certain Los Angeles areas.

The presence of the handgun registration proposition on the ballot may also have influenced the outcome. The votes for and against this proposition totaled 7.64 million—only a quarter of a million fewer than the 7.88 million votes cast for governor. By contrast, five other ballot propositions drew between 6.6 and 6.8 million votes each; seven more ballot measures received between 7.0 and 7.3 million each. The handgun measure had strong opposition in many of the more rural counties, where the turnout reached as high as 75–80 percent of registered voters, far above the statewide gubernatorial turnout of 68 percent. In these counties the vote for Deukmejian ran as high as 65 percent.

The one certain explanation is that the absentee voters elected Deukmejian. Among the ballots cast in the election booths, Bradley received almost 20,000 more than his opponent. However, the Republicans provided 2 million GOP voters with stamped, addressed cards that they were encouraged to use to request absentee ballots. Of the 525,186 absentee ballots cast, Deukmejian won 61.5 percent to Bradley's 38.5 percent.

A surprising vote was registered for a redistricting initiative on the ballot. The consequences dominated the politics of Deukmejian's first year in office, and beyond. In the June primary three referendum statutes were on the ballot, giving the voters the opportunity to overturn the district lines that the Democratic-controlled legislature had drawn after the 1980 census. These measures, approved by overwhelming majorities, encouraged Republicans, working in cooperation with Common Cause, a public interest group, to place on the November ballot a measure that would take redistricting authority away from the legislature and put it in the hands of a commission. Voters rejected this proposition by 54.5 percent, throwing reapportionment back into the legislature, which was now more heavily Democratic.

Changing Governors

PREPARING FOR THE TRANSITION

Long before the election, steps were taken to prepare for the transition. In Governor Brown's office the first step in May 1982 was to assign the press research officer, a trained librarian, the responsibility of preparing the governor's archives. By contrast, Governor Reagan put staff to work on twenty tons of archival material sixteen months before leaving office.

In early September initial steps were taken to prepare the way for the new administration. During two meetings of the governor's cabinet, B. T. Collins, Brown's executive secretary and chief of staff, and Jim Burton, Collins's deputy, discussed necessary preparations. Each of the units in the governor's office, the five agencies and three cabinet-level departments, and the fifty departments within agencies were instructed to prepare briefing books. This practice was so well established in California state government that over half of the departments had anticipated this action and had begun the preparation. These discussions were followed by a memorandum, dated October 26, from B. T. Collins, expressing the "desire that the transition to the new administration be as smooth and cooperative as possible." After the election, oral briefings were to be scheduled "to insure the smooth continuation of the governmental process." By November 5, three days after the election, briefing books had been completed and reviewed by Burton for appropriateness and completeness.

On the incoming side preparations were also being made. As early as August, during the campaign, Deukmejian, Franchetti, Merksamer, and Ken Khachigian began to discuss the conduct of the transition. Meeting weekly, they attempted to identify some of the problems they would confront if elected and how they might cope with them. Franchetti, who was not active in the campaign full time because he had the responsibility of administering the attorney general's office as deputy attorney general, was asked to develop on his own time a plan of action for the transition. He outlined an approach for appointments, budget preparation, taking over the reins of government in general, and for implementing various policies that Deukmejian was discussing during the campaign. Much more planning had been intended, but the campaign was in trouble in October, and the persons who were supposed to begin work on the transition had to devote full time to the campaign.

In addition all newspaper clippings on the Pat Brown–Reagan transition in 1966, the Reagan–Jerry Brown transition in 1974, and the Reagan presidential transition in 1980 were collected. Merksamer read every clipping dealing with the three months November, December, and January for each of these transitions. Throughout the transition he kept on his desk and used as a guide a recent publication of the National Governors' Association (NGA), *Transition and the New Governor: A Critical Overview.*[3]

CONDUCTING THE TRANSITION

First press conference. Traditionally, the governor-elect holds a press conference the day after the election. Deukmejian did not meet with the press until two days after the election because of a calculated decision made ten days before the election. The campaign team knew that the outcome would be close, so they wanted to give the governor some time to meet with his principal advisors, step back from the campaign, and prepare carefully for the introduction.

The outcome of the contest was uncertain until five o'clock Wednesday morning. That morning Deukmejian met with his key advisors—Franchetti, Merksamer, and Khachigian—to prepare for the press conference. Then he called the Democratic and Republican leaders in both houses to solicit their support. When Deukmejian met the press on Thursday, his first announcement was the appointment of Franchetti as the new director of finance. This appointment was intended to signal that the state's budgetary problems were to be the first priority of the new administration. (By contrast, Reagan, in 1966, did not announce his director of finance until December 15 because his first choices turned him down.) At the same time announcements were made of Merksamer's appointment as chief of staff during the transition and in the new governor's office and of Khachigian's appointment as special consultant during the transition.

Deukmejian went on to express confidence that "this will be a new era of bipartisanship in state government." Having served sixteen years in the legislature, he was certain that he knew "how to work with representatives of the other party." He indicated that he and his wife would be willing to live in the mansion that Governor Reagan had built but never occupied. On another matter of deep concern, he called upon Governor Brown not to fill judicial vacancies before leaving office.

Meeting of incoming and outgoing staff. The following day Merksamer and Franchetti met with Collins and Burton. The 1983–84 budget, then in preparation, was a major subject of discussion. The availability of briefing books was explained. In a display of cooperation Collins said emphatically, "I'll change my schedule to suit yours, because I figure you're going to be busier than me." Thereafter, Merksamer and Collins talked on the phone several times a day and met two or three times a week.

Collins also offered to redecorate the governor's suite of offices before the inauguration. They had not been redecorated for sixteen years and were sorely in need of refurbishing. The generous offer came to plague Brown's staff in the closing weeks because the redecoration kept the offices in turmoil and further disturbed an already distraught staff.

When the subject of appointments was raised, Collins proffered three bits of advice: "In making selections, never underestimate the importance of loyalty. Get a signed, undated resignation from every appointee. Fire someone as soon as you can to show who is in charge." He urged early appointment of the new staff, especially the cabinet officers and key department directors, so that they could benefit from the advice and experience of the outgoing staff. Burton was assigned the scheduling of briefings for various new appointees with their outgoing counterparts. Before adjourning, they made arrangements to bring together the incoming and outgoing governors in a formal meeting, as a symbolic kick-off for the transition.

Meeting of Brown and Deukmejian. The same four staff persons were with the governor and the governor-elect on November 8 when they met in Sacramento, the first of only four times that Deukmejian was in the capital prior to the inauguration. The governor-elect called upon Brown not to fill any judicial vacancies during the remaining weeks of his administration. Deukmejian had considered the quality of Brown's appointments a campaign issue. Having won, he felt that Brown ought not make additional appointments during the remainder of his term. On the other hand, Deukmejian urged Brown, as incumbent, to cope with the serious budget deficit in the waning days of his administration and suggested that Brown call a special session of the legislature for this purpose.

During the meeting Merksamer asked that the governor's office request each agency secretary and department director to prepare a ninety-day calendar (January through March), listing all important due dates (e.g., legislative deadlines, grant applications, policy guidelines, and administrative regulations). The calendars, which had not been prepared before, would give the new leadership specific action agendas. Brown's staff implemented the request at the next cabinet meetings, and a reminder was given at a subsequent meeting.

Transition plans and organization. Immediately after the election Deukmejian's team began to implement its transition plans. Highest priority was given to the preparation of the 1983–84 budget, which was to be balanced without increasing taxes, and to the recruitment and selection of well-qualified appointees who were dedicated to the policies of the new administration. Also high on the agenda were forming a legislative program and establishing effective relations with the legislature, drafting the inaugural address and planning the inauguration, preparing the state of the state/budget message for January 10, and finding a residence for the governor.

Deukmejian and his transition advisors made a conscious decision that he should have only limited media contact prior to taking office. He held only three press conferences, granted no one-to-one interviews, and kept a low profile. All requests by the national media for interviews or appearances were declined. The transition press secretary, Kevin Brett, made most of the announcements to the media while the governor-elect spent his time on transition business. Deukmejian's decision that transition activities should be somewhat removed from the glare of publicity only intensified the curiosity of the press.

Two transition offices were set up, one in Sacramento headed by Merksamer and a second in Los Angeles, near Deukmejian's attorney general office, where he continued to work during the preinauguration period. Merksamer flew to Los Angeles two to three times a week to confer with the governor-elect and talked with him on the phone ten to twelve times a day.

An additional office came into use when a transition appointments coordinator was designated. He worked out of his business office in Torrance as well as the Los Angeles transition office and spent one or two days a week in Sacramento, working with Merksamer. About thirty people worked in the various transition offices.

On November 18 Deukmejian announced the appointment of a statewide, 200-member transition advisory committee that was to give the administration ideas about business, agriculture, law enforcement, education, and finance and to recommend candidates for appointments. The committee met only once during the transition, when about 160 people, at their own expense, convened in Los Angeles.

Four weeks after the election the governor-elect appointed seven transition team advisors to develop firsthand information on operations of the state's major agencies so that incoming cabinet officers would be aware of the issues and problems they would confront when they took office. These persons were instructed to spend two weeks in the agencies, then report their findings to Deukmejian and Merksamer. Most volunteered their time, with the understanding that they were not heirs apparent who would then be appointed to the agencies in which they worked (eventually, three were appointed). This approach contrasted markedly with that of Governor-elect Reagan, who deployed large task forces of businessmen to study the major agencies and departments over a much longer period.

PREPARING THE 1983–1984 BUDGET

The day after the two political leaders met, Franchetti, Deukmejian's designate director of finance, met with Brown's finance director, Mary Ann Graves, to be briefed on the fiscal condition of the state and the status of the budget preparations for the following year. From that moment on, the entire staff of the Department of Finance was turned over to Franchetti to complete work on a budget begun six months earlier.

The budget encompasses a base-line budget and budget change proposals (BCPS). The base-line budget consists of the current year's level of expenditures adjusted for mandatory case-load changes and operating expenses adjusted for inflation. The BCPS are proposals for changes in the base line that involve policy changes. Because of the transition, the process was on a different schedule and additional materials had been prepared. Ordinarily, by November the program budget managers in the Department of Finance would have held hearings on the BCPS and wherever possible would have made decisions; unresolved cases would then be referred to the director of finance. However, the hearings on the BCPS and subsequent appeals were delayed because of the transition, thus giving the new administration the opportunity to examine every change proposed in the base-line budget.

In addition, commencing in late summer, the Department of Finance had prepared "Program Highlights" and "Issue Papers" for use by the new administration. The former is a book of descriptive sheets, each usually no more than one page, summarizing every program in the state that requires a financial outlay. The "Issue Papers" consist of some sixty papers, generally one page each, with flags for expenditure items that may require immediate attention and action.

The budget went to press a few days before Christmas so that it would be ready for submission to the legislature on January 10. During the short period after an election it is virtually impossible to make changes in the base-line budget; at most, the new team can review the BCPS to make the new budget theirs. Franchetti, aided by only a few persons, worked intensively within the Department of Finance for six weeks. They received advice from the seven members of the transition liaison team and other members of their transition team. They were in constant touch with Deukmejian and Merksamer, who spent much of their time on appointments.

STAFFING THE ADMINISTRATION

The new administration had to fill approximately 550 exempt executive positions and positions on state boards and commissions. To help with this task Governor Brown's office provided a massive volume that listed all the positions to be filled, the responsibilities of each, desired qualifications, salaries, and other relevant details.

The governor-elect's choice for transition appointments coordinator was Ted Bruinsma, a prominent businessman, former dean of the Loyola Law School, and candidate for the U.S. Senate in the Republican primary. Although Bruinsma had not been involved in Deukmejian's campaign and did not know him, he agreed to take on the task without pay, until the inauguration.

Merksamer handled the search and screening for persons to staff the governor's office, and Bruinsma had responsibility for cabinet officers and department directors. A timetable called for cabinet selections to be completed by December 15 so that these persons could participate in reviewing candidates for department directors. The goal was to have about sixty top executive positions and ten key policy and administrative posts in the governor's office filled by inauguration. The criteria for selection included competence for the job; experience; ideology consistent with Deukmejian's; ability to articulate the responsibilities of the job and be an effective spokesperson for the governor's program; high moral character; ethnic, sex, and geographic diversity; and ability to manage the bureaucracy.

Nominations were solicited from those known to the governor or working with him on the transition, from the transition advisory committee members, and from major organizations in the state. The openings were not generally publicized (to discourage an excessive number of applications), but all applications were accepted. During the two months after the election some 4,000 résumés reached Bruinsma at the two transition offices, his business office, and even his home. He worked twelve to fifteen hours a day, seven days a week, dividing his time between Los Angeles and Sacramento.

As the résumés accumulated, Bruinsma reviewed them and screened the most likely candidates down to six to ten for a position; in some cases, just four to eight. Frequently, some names reappeared. If it was felt that appropriate persons had not been identified, Bruinsma would solicit more suggestions. Eventually, he interviewed each of the finalists for forty-five minutes to an hour, conducting as many as four interviews a day. He then narrowed the list to only two or three and submitted the names to Deukmejian, through Merksamer. The two interviewed all candidates, occasionally calling for more names. At this time a lengthy form went out to the finalists to get further information about them before a decision was made. The information concerned financial investments and holdings that might relate to the job and other activities and associations that might be seen as affecting performance. Deukmejian and Merksamer then discussed their reactions to the candidates and made a final decision.

The same process was followed in screening department directors, except that nominations were reviewed by the agency secretary before they were submitted to Deukmejian and Merksamer. However, Deukmejian made it clear that the appointment decision was his (the agency secretaries did not have a veto).

The process was much slower than anticipated. The mid-December target for cabinet selections was not met. Eight appointees were chosen by the inaugural date, and the remaining two were selected eight days later. The designation of department directors proceeded even more slowly. Only five of some fifty directors had been designated three months after the election, one month into the new administration. Senior civil servants or former Brown appointees were asked to serve as interim directors. The key positions in the governor's office were filled by January 3, except those of appointments secretary and legal affairs secretary. The appointments secretary was named on January 11, the deputy on February 9; the legal affairs post remained unfilled until April 11.

RELATING TO THE LEGISLATURE

Policy planning. During the two months before the inauguration, in addition to preparing the 1983–84 budget and selecting people for appointment in the new administration, the transition team had to build relations with a heavily Democratic legislature and make plans to initiate policies that would fulfill campaign promises. Even such a routine matter as finding a residence for the governor became a bitter political issue involving relations with the legislature.

Within a month after Deukmejian had been elected, his staff began to prepare for the new legislative session. Rod Blonien, designated the legislative secretary on December 6, was the member of the transition team assigned to compile the legislative goals for the first year.

With the assistance of his deputy, Maureen Higgins, he assembled a report drawn largely from campaign position papers and from a "Goals and Workplan Sheet" prepared by Franchetti during the campaign. The time frame for action was drawn from Franchetti's proposal. Members of the transition advisory committee, which had met in mid-November, were also asked to prepare issue memoranda on topics that required legislative initiative. Over a dozen such proposals were submitted to Art Scotland, Merksamer's assistant during the transition and, later, cabinet secretary. The list of prospective legislation, dated November 30, contained specific and general proposals, with a suggested timetable, in nine policy areas.

This legislative agenda was drafted to prepare the way for the new governor after he took office. Other than keeping the legislature informed about transition plans, Blonien had very little contact with the legislature during these two months. His position was that until Deukmejian became governor, it was inappropriate to initiate contact. He responded to initiatives from the legislature but held back otherwise and refrained from lobbying on any particular issue.

The current year's budget crisis. Prior to the election, officials in the Department of Finance projected a deficit of almost $1 billion by the end of FY 1982–83. In his first press conference after the election Deukmejian charged that Governor Brown was leaving the state in the same desperate condition in which his father, Pat Brown, had left it for Ronald Reagan in 1967. At that time Reagan requested a billion-dollar tax increase, and Deukmejian, then a newly elected senator, carried Reagan's tax bill in the senate. Now Deukmejian reiterated his campaign theme of no tax increase but said that he intended to do nothing about the budget crisis because that responsibility rested with Governor Brown.

A week after the election, controller Ken Cory announced that the state was out of money. It had borrowed all that it could from special funds—about $1.5 billion. To meet November's obligations he would have to borrow $400 million from private banks, the first such borrowing to meet a cash-flow problem in over a decade.

The stage was set for a drama that would unfold over the next three months as the crisis worsened. The projected year-end deficit was now $1.5 billion; some estimates ran as high as $2.5 billion. A loan was negotiated, half of which had to be repaid by February 23, the rest by the following June. Standard and Poor's put the state on a credit-watch, so the treasurer announced that he would not market any of the bonds that had been authorized in the November election until the state's fiscal house was in order. Brown called an extraordinary session to run concurrently with the regular session of the new legislature, which convened on December 8, but the legislators failed to find a solution to the deficit.

In a regular session the legislature can act on any matter it chooses, but it has to abide by rules that would have made it impossible to get bills to Brown's desk before the inauguration. In a concurrent extraordinary session, the legislature can enact bills in that time period but only on issues specified by the governor in his call. Governor Brown requested that the special session deal with both the budget crisis and reapportionment.

December was a month of political posturing. By calling the legislature into special session, the governor made it possible for them to act quickly, but he took no public position on the need for a tax increase. Democratic leaders displayed their concern for a balanced budget but insisted that Deukmejian and/or the Republican legislators should first show their willingness to support a tax increase. The requirement that a two-thirds majority enact a tax increase meant that some Republicans would have to join the Democrats, but assembly Republicans, referred to as the "Proposition 13 babies," were strongly opposed to new taxes. The governor-elect maintained a hands-off position, knowing that his no-tax-increase position had influence on his party members in the legislature. If the budget could not be balanced before he took office, he would have the opportunity to implement his political philosophy in bringing it under control. Ultimately, the legislature took no action. Members of both parties decided to "let George do it."

Reapportionment. Having been called into special session, the legislature did succeed in passing a reapportionment bill for Brown to sign before he left office. It was drafted in haste because voters had invalidated the original Democratic-drawn reapportionment by initiatives on the June primary ballot, then rejected a Republican-supported initiative measure on the November ballot that would have put reapportionment in the hands of an independent commission.

Assembly and senate district lines were redrawn with bipartisan support, but congressional redistricting passed both houses only on straight party votes. The assembly and senate districts were drawn to protect incumbents of both parties and preserve the status quo. The Democrats agreed not to use their majority power to gerrymander Republicans into unfavorable districts. In return, Republicans agreed not to challenge the resultant reapportionment bill with a referendum.

Housing the governor. The strained relations between some prominent members of the Democratic-controlled legislature and the incoming chief executive extended to such a prosaic matter as housing for Deukmejian. In the closing days of the Reagan administration an elegant Spanish-style governor's mansion was built on a $200,000 site of eleven acres donated by Reagan's friends. Throughout his two terms Reagan had lived in a home rented by the state because he regarded the historic governor's mansion as a firetrap. The new mansion, located fifteen miles from the capitol, cost the state $1.3 million to build. This 11,000-square-foot, seventeen-room house was not completed in time for Reagan to occupy it. Governor Brown refused to live in it, dubbing it the Taj Mahal, although some critics suggested that it looked like an old Safeway. Never furnished, it sat vacant, except for caretakers, during the Brown administration. A few days before the election the legislature directed the Department of General Services to sell it.

Even though Deukmejian said he would like to live in the mansion, the legislature failed to enact any of several measures introduced in the special session before the inauguration to halt the sale or provide alternative housing. During the inaugural festivities Governor Deukmejian and his family stayed in a Holiday Inn. Afterward, the family returned to their home in Long Beach. Confronted by this legislative intransigence, which Deukmejian took as a personal affront, he rented a two-bedroom apartment near the capitol and commuted to and from his Long Beach home all year, spending Monday through Thursday in Sacramento.

Thus, when Deukmejian assumed office, an ominous cloud hung over his relations with the legislature, in spite of his long experience in both houses. Unlike the two previous governors, he understood state government, he knew the capital, and he was known and respected in the legislature. He was determined to exert stronger leadership within the legislature, particularly in regard to the budget, than had either Reagan or Jerry

Brown, but he faced what some observers called "four houses" in the legislature. The strained relations between the Democratic leadership of the houses tended to lead the two houses in different directions. Even the members of the governor's own party were at odds with each other. Assembly Republicans, who had supported Curb in the primary, were more opposed to tax increases than were their senate counterparts. Now the governor's office aspired to become a "fifth house" to accomplish political objectives that required legislative approval. Deukmejian could not expect the traditional honeymoon with the legislature as he embarked on his administration.

LEAVING OFFICE: BROWN'S LAME-DUCK ADMINISTRATION

Meanwhile, Governor Brown and his staff continued to fulfill his constitutional responsibilities while they assisted the new team. Jim Burton, the deputy executive secretary and chief of staff, estimates that 25 percent of his time from the election until the inauguration was spent with the incoming administration. Extended discussions were carried on between the staffs of the two teams. The outgoing staff received no complaints about their assistance. Indeed, every member of the incoming team praised the friendly cooperation of the Brown administration. "There were no big issues where tempers flared," one key member of Deukmejian's transition team observed.

However, the conduct of some last-minute business by the Brown administration was a source of friction and drew strong Republican criticism. Brown had failed to keep abreast of his opportunity to fill many vacancies. In the courts alone there were approximately seventy-five openings that he could fill before leaving office. Among them were eighteen new appellate positions the legislature had created. Disturbed by the prospect of more judicial appointments by Brown, Deukmejian asked Brown not to make any more judicial appointments.

In California, judicial appointments must be confirmed by the Commission on Judicial Appointments, composed of the chief justice of the California Supreme Court, the presiding judge of the court to which the appointee has been nominated, and the attorney general. Two votes are required to confirm an appointment. Because three of the eighteen new justice positions were in a newly created district of the court of appeal where there was no presiding justice, a negative vote by Deukmejian, the attorney general, could block their appointments. By the end of November Brown began filling positions, including one on the Supreme Court that had become vacant by a retirement. When the Commission on Judicial Appointments met shortly before Christmas, Deukmejian voted against two of three nominees to the new justice positions and abstained in the third case. The lack of two affirmative votes prevented confirmation of a governor's nominations for the first time in forty-two years. Deukmejian's negative votes against two other nominees did not block their confirmation because the presiding justice voted favorably with the chief justice.

Appointment activity continued over the holiday weekend, until midnight of January 2. In the closing hours a deputy secretary of state moved into the governor's office to process last-minute appointments and bill signings. Over the weekend some 350 appointments to various positions were signed, as well as such bills as those reapportioning the state's legislative and congressional districts. In the crush of these actions, hundreds of pardons that had been processed by the staff were overlooked and not signed by the governor.

Projects high on the governor's agenda were also concluded. As one example, the legislature had passed a law granting unions of state employees the right to have an agency shop. The governor-elect was known to be opposed to such an arrangement, by which employees who are not members of a union that has an exclusive bargaining contract must pay a service fee to the union. Brown could not implement this act until it went into effect on January 1. On December 31 the director of the Department of Personnel Administration began negotiations with nine unions to enter into agency shop contracts. Burton was drawn into these discussions on January 2 and spent eleven hours conducting negotiations. An agreement, not in final typed form, was hammered out between the parties at 11:59 P.M. Every note and scrap of paper used in reaching the agreement was initialed by the governor and the union representatives to ensure legality. In return for permitting the agency shop, the administration succeeded in having some 2,900 state employees classified as supervisors so that they would no longer be covered by union contracts.

The staff of the Brown administration were supposed to be out of the state capitol by the stroke of midnight. At 1:00 A.M. on January 3 a member of the Deukmejian transition team received a call from the state police saying, "They are still here putting their boxes together." He responded, "Give them another hour." At the end of the hour the police ushered out Governor Brown and his staff.

Governing California

If George Deukmejian had scheduled his inauguration at the same time as Ronald Reagan did sixteen years before, he would have been sworn in while Governor Brown and his staff were still working in the governor's office. In 1967 Reagan took the oath of office at one minute after midnight because, according to some reports, he erroneously thought this was required or because he wanted to symbolize that he was taking over the reins of government at the first possible moment. After the ceremony Reagan joked with another former movie actor, Senator George Murphy, "How does it feel to be on the late, late show again, George?" More traditionally, Governor Deukmejian took the oath of office on January 3 at 11:00 A.M. on the steps of the capitol. Supreme Court Justice Frank Richardson, the only remaining member of the high court appointed by Governor Reagan, administered the oath. Walt Disney Productions had assisted inaugural planning and produced the inaugural ball the night before.

In the inaugural address Governor Deukmejian dedicated his administration "in a bipartisan manner . . . to achieving a Common Sense Society that uses its resources wisely to provide improved services to meet the basic needs of the people." He pledged himself to work on four urgent tasks: "the need to create again a strong and growing economy which provides needed jobs; the improvement of education; the restoration of safety to our streets, homes and neighborhoods; and the rescue of our state from its grave financial crisis." In a period of austerity he made a commitment to reduce expenditures and restore fiscal responsibility "without a net tax increase." (Weeks later he explained that phrase: if taxes were to be raised they would later have to be lowered by the same amount below their original level.)

The inaugural festivities were so successful that they raised $490,000 over and above expenses. When a final accounting was made of the $296,000 transition allocation, some $60,000 were unspent and returned to the general fund.

ORGANIZING THE GOVERNOR'S OFFICE

By the time of the inauguration the governor's office was well organized and functioning under the direction of the executive secretary and chief of staff, Steve Merksamer, and his deputy, Sal Russo. Except for the legal affairs and appointments units, all unit heads and their deputies, a total of fourteen, had been selected and had begun working on the transition in November or December. Eight came from the attorney general's office with Deukmejian. Most of them had taken leave to work on the campaign. Four others in this upper echelon had worked on the campaign, including the two, Russo and Doug Watt, who took over the direction of the campaign when Roberts resigned. By the time the legal affairs and appointments secretaries were appointed, twelve lawyers were the ranking members of the governor's office. Over a third of some eighty in the governor's office were from the previous administration. They staffed the correspondence and administrative services units and the clerical secretary and staff assistant position. The new administration thus began its work with a closely knit leadership team: they knew each other well, had worked together, had a common outlook, and they were supported by experienced personnel from the previous administration.

Within a week of inauguration a systematic procedure was ready for all policy communications to the governor. All policy memoranda from a department director were to go through the appropriate agency secretary, to the cabinet secretary, on to the executive secretary/chief of staff, then to the governor. Each was to sign the transmittal letter. The memoranda, in a format reminiscent of Governor Reagan's, briefly describe the subject, summarize the facts of the issue, analyze the significant events, set forth the action recommended (with arguments pro and con), state the effect on existing law, and indicate the necessary deadline. The submission might be for information only, for gubernatorial approval, or for cabinet discussion (in which case it was to be put on the cabinet agenda).

The cabinet meets for two hours every Thursday afternoon; the governor attends every other week. In alternate weeks Merksamer chairs the meeting and the senior staff of the governor's office are present and participate in the discussion. When the governor presides, the senior staff are involved only if they have a presentation to make. That formal procedure will probably continue throughout Deukmejian's administration, subject to modifications required by future experience. By contrast Reagan attended all cabinet meetings, at which decisions were made by consensus. Brown rarely attended the free-form "cabinet events."

Another, more informal procedure evolved as political pressures mounted and conflict with the legislature over the budget and various policy initiatives of the governor intensified. According to Ed Salzman, every weekday evening seven key persons meet to plan strategies for promoting the governor's image through the media and advancing his policies in the legislature.[4] These strategists meet for thirty to ninety minutes under the chairmanship of Merksamer. Also, each morning Merksamer meets with about fifteen members of the governor's office to review the issues of the day. At 10:30 A.M. the governor receives a report on the morning session and the previous evening's strategy meeting. The governor then carefully decides his next steps.

FINANCING THE STATE

Submitting the 1983–1984 budget. As required by the constitution, Governor Deukmejian submitted his budget and delivered his state of the state message on January 10. Reminding the legislature that he felt the citizens deserved "common sense answers arrived at in a spirit of bipartisanship," he announced a plan to return California to solvency in eighteen months. The $1.5-billion deficit would be eliminated by making $750 million in cuts during the current fiscal year and rolling over the remaining $750-million deficit into FY 1983–84. The savings in the current year's budget were to be achieved by freezing state hiring, contracts, and out-of-state travel, by transferring money from special funds into the general fund, and by reducing expenditures in selected programs. His first executive order imposed an immediate 2 percent across-the-board cut.

The proposed budget for 1983–84 would be $458 million less than the total appropriations for 1982–83, a decrease of 1.8 percent. The budget had to cover the $750-million deficit that was to be rolled over and had to provide a total reserve of $800 million. The reduction was to be accomplished by eliminating or scaling down many statutory cost-of-living adjustments, imposing substantial reductions on certain state agencies, raising student fees in higher education, and lowering the amount of fiscal relief promised by statute to local governments.

Resolving the current year's budget crisis. In early 1983 legislators had less time for next year's budget because the current year's budget became their (and the governor's) all-consuming preoccupation. The key deadline was February 23, the date when the first payment of $200 million was due on the $400-million loan that the state had secured after the election.

At the last possible minute the governor signed a measure that was the result of weeks of prolonged negotiations with the legislature. In the final hours assembly Republicans were even more obstructionist than the Democrats. The bill contained $637.5 million in current-year budget cuts and rolled over $900 million into the next year. Two sales-tax triggers were included, which could raise collections from $.06 to $.07 on the dollar: the first if revenues were below projections by $150 million at the end of the first quarter; the second at mid-year if the Department of Finance projected a surplus of less than $100 million by the end of the fiscal year.

The next day several banks agreed to lend the state $428 million to tide it over until a longer-term, $850-million loan could be negotiated to carry the state through the end of the fiscal year. Although the money became available in just one week, it was too late to prevent the controller from making over 100,000 income-tax refund payments and payments to vendors who had registered warrants (IOUs), which were immediately cashed.

Enacting the 1983–1984 budget. The legislature was now able to turn its attention to next year's budget. The governor maintained his strong opposition to a tax increase but supported a number of tax loophole-closing measures and accelerated revenue collections. When eventually approved, they added almost $1 billion to state tax collections. A number of assembly "cavemen," the so-called Proposition 13 babies, uncompromisingly opposed the governor on these measure. Two members of the assembly Republican caucus were removed from their leadership posts for voting in favor of Deukmejian's loophole-closing bill.

Budget deliberations stretched twenty-one days into the new fiscal year beginning July 1, the most protracted deliberations in California history, because the reapportionment controversy reappeared on the scene. Soon after Deukmejian's inauguration, Don Sebastiani, a junior Republican assemblyman and scion of a Sonoma Valley winemaking family, raised $1 million to collect signatures to qualify another reapportionment initiative. Initially, he did not have the backing of the Republican party, the Republican caucus staff did not participate in preparing the plan, nor did the governor take a position on the initiative. If approved by the voters, it might have brought about a shift of three to six congressional seats to Republicans, trimmed the substantial Democratic majority in the California Senate, and turned the California Assembly over to the Republicans. It would have been the third reapportionment initiative in three years, the first having been rejected by the voters in the June 1982 primary and the second having been enacted by the legislature in December 1982, before Brown left office.

When it became apparent that the initiative had qualified for the ballot and the governor might call a special election before the year's end, the Democrats took defensive action and tied the issue into the budget. In California every budget bill is now accompanied by a trailer bill that legally authorizes the expenditures in the budget. The governor may veto individual items in the budget, but he may veto the trailer bill only as a whole. Without the trailer bill, no new budget items can be implemented. The Democrats incorporated into the trailer bill language that prevented the expenditure of public funds (estimated at $14 million) for a special election on the Sebastiani initiative.

The deadlock became so acrimonious that the governor's office posted a sign in the capitol announcing the number of days the state budget had been "held hostage." In retaliation the chairman of the legislative committee supervising capitol facilities denied parking space to the governor's director of finance and his executive secretary. The deadlock was finally broken when the governor scheduled a special election on the Sebastiani initiative for December 13.

The conference committee immediately reported out a $23.1-billion budget, which the governor signed after item-vetoing $1.1 billion. Higher education took 37 percent of the cuts. The final budget was only $370 million above the budget the governor had proposed in January and provided for an end-of-year surplus of $273 million while paying off the $900 million carry-over deficit.

The Sebastiani initiative was immediately challenged in the courts. In mid-September the California Supreme Court ruled, by a 6–1 vote, that the state constitution permits only one reapportionment each decade, thus denying the initiative the ballot. The lone dissenter, the only member appointed to the court by a Republican governor, argued that the public should be given a chance to vote. (This was the first time in thirty-five years that the court had prevented an initiative from going to the voters.)

RELATING TO THE LEGISLATURE

Senate confirmations. Senate confirmation is required for appointments as agency secretary, department director, and certain commissioners. Ordinarily, most gubernatorial appointments are confirmed.

Reflecting the growing tension between the governor and the Democratic legislature, Deukmejian encountered difficulty gaining approval for several key appointments. Appointments of directors of the Industrial Relations Department (a cabinet position) and the Parks and Recreation Department (the nominee was a former assemblywoman and Deukmejian's Republican running mate for lieutenant governor) were flatly rejected by the senate. The former encountered determined opposition from organized labor, which charged that the appointee had an 82 percent antilabor voting record as a Republican state assemblyman and congressman; the latter was turned down on a straight party-line vote because of her "excessive partisanship" as a legislator and charges that she was unqualified to run the state parks system.

The greatest wound was suffered when Deukmejian's key appointment of the director of the Department of Finance failed to be approved within the required year, and the director had to leave office. Within weeks after Franchetti's selection, stories surfaced that he had admitted having leaked a confidential state document containing false information that then Lieutenant Governor Mervyn Dymally was about to be indicted. Dymally claimed that this leak cost him reelection in 1978. Franchetti later apologized to Dymally's campaign aide but not to Dymally. The senate Rules Committee, chaired by the president pro tem, narrowly recommended confirmation, but sufficient votes for confirmation could not be delivered on the floor, possibly because of the pressure of the black caucus. The governor felt that the president pro tem had reneged on a promise and publicly chastised him for not having provided confirmation.

The governor's appointed directors of the Department of Corrections and the Department of Fish and Game resigned when it became apparent that they would not be confirmed. In these cases the problems appear to have arisen from insufficient screening. The former had headed Ohio's Department of Rehabilitation and Correction, but allegations had been made about department racism, discriminatory hiring and promotions, nepotism, and a lock-and-hold prison philosophy. The other appointee was the former owner of a gun shop who had intervened in a poaching case, urging the judge to return confiscated shotguns to friends and customers. There were also charges of derogatory remarks about Vietnamese and the alleged illegal importation of a Nile crocodile hide.

Another cabinet nomination for Secretary of the State and Consumer Services Agency encountered opposition and was confirmed by a narrow margin. The appointment of the head of the Department of Forestry was held up for months by the Republican minority leader, who expressed concern about the nominee's ability to run the department because, as a professor of forestry, he had never had any firefighting experience. A few weeks later the senate Republican caucus removed the minority leader, in part because of this delay. The general counsel of the Agricultural Labor Relations Board was narrowly confirmed as the one-year deadline for his appointment was reached.

A combination of partisan politics and questionable screening accounted for these problems. Deukmejian's predecessors encountered somewhat similar experiences but never in regard to appointments to so many high-level positions. Previously confirmed appointees have now come under investigation for fiscal irregularities. The director of the Office of Economic Opportunities resigned when he came under scrutiny because of allegations that OEO (Office of Economic Opportunity) funds had been directed to Republican supporters of the governor. The Fair Political Practices Commission is investigating charges that the director of Veterans Affairs may have mishandled campaign contributions, and the travel expenses of the director of the Department of General Services are being audited.

Policy initiatives. The tension between the governor and the legislature, which was not confined to appointment confirmations, intensified during Deukmejian's first year of office. The animosity between the branches equaled or exceeded that which had existed when Culbert Olson became the first Democrat to be elected governor of California in this century. The hostility within the legislature extended to the conservative members of the governor's own party. Although his greatest problem has been relations with the Democrats, Deukmejian has also experienced difficulty with members of his own party. A number of the "cavemen" preferred Curb over Deukmejian and took uncompromising ideological positions to budget and tax negotiations. They had not expected a Republican in the governor's office and did not know how to deal with one (only one assembly Republican had served under a Republican governor). A prominent Republican staffer felt that the Proposition 13 babies did not respect Deukmejian because he had no public image except as a crime fighter. The governor joked about the absence of the traditional honeymoon: "It was as short as Zsa Zsa Gabor's marriages."

Under these circumstances the governor's legislative program encountered serious resistance. The "urgent tasks" set forth in his inaugural address guided his policy initiatives: public safety, welfare reform, economic development, and education. The governor announced an anti-crime package of some twenty proposals to close loopholes and accomplish "common sense reform" in the criminal justice system. Much of the package was rejected, not only by the Democrats but also by Republicans, who complained that they had not been consulted. He failed to win early release to ease the crowding in prisons and a number of stricter law enforcement provisions (e.g., proposals to allow life sentences without parole for juveniles, forbid most appeals after guilty pleas, and restrict a judge's authority to reduce murder sentences). However, he did gain a watered-down version of a plan to speed prison construction and increase reimbursement to victims of crime.

The governor proposed a workfare scheme for able-bodied welfare recipients, the improved enforcement of child-support orders, and a statewide plan for the detection of welfare fraud. He failed to get legislative approval for these proposals and, in turn, vetoed the Democratic alternative to his welfare reform package. The legislature did send him bills to put welfare recipients in jobs that are partly subsidized by the government and to give welfare recipients priority in seasonal government jobs.

The governor's plan for economic development and job creation required fewer legislative and more administration actions. He endorsed and made part of his own program several bills that had been introduced by Democrats, and they became law. They increased state funds for small-business loans and established resource centers to provide technical advice and help, permitted small businesses that incur losses in their first two years to apply these losses as a tax credit against profits for the next fifteen years, and established enterprise zones in depressed areas. Bills to speed and consolidate environmental reviews became law, but a bill that would lower environmental standards was stalled.

Although the governor made education improvement a top priority issue in his campaign and his inaugural address, he did not announce any specific proposals for educational reform. While education reform was becoming the hottest policy issue of the year, the governor allowed his fiscal concerns to dominate his position. When the newly elected superintendent of public instruction released his reform package, Deukmejian rejected it as too costly. Even the assembly Republicans, otherwise opposed to increased spending, outdid the governor in supporting increased financing for school reform. Gradually, the governor, who had taken no position on the substantive issues in educational reform, raised (from $350 million to $800 million) the allocation that he would support.

Finally, in mid-June the governor revealed his list of education reforms and implied that he would veto any school-aid bill without them. The legislator whose measure had already passed the senate said, "He's seven months late." A top senate aide complained, "The governor doesn't even have an education guy, and that's the biggest issue of the year." According to Salzman, this person said, "I bet [legislative secretary] Rod Blonien wrote the program on a sheet of yellow paper over a beer one night."[5] Shortly thereafter, the governor did appoint an education secretary.

Now the governor had a program that went beyond the debate over dollars and cents. Although he endorsed many of the reforms the legislature was discussing, he felt that adoption should be voluntary and said that if the legislature appropriated more money than he wanted to spend, he would simply use the line-item veto. The governor was determined to avoid the tax triggers. The governor's strategy was to spread increases over two years, holding down the first year's addition and trusting economic recovery to permit much higher funding the next year.

Deliberations spilled over into the new fiscal year. The governor himself entered into negotiations with Democratic leaders about education reform as well as the budget. The parties moved closer together when the Democrats indicated a willingness to accept the $800-million increase that the governor now supported if he agreed to provide another increase next year. That agreement broke the deadlock. A $2.7-billion school reform and finance bill swept through both houses with nearly unanimous support. The bill ran two volumes, totaling 490 pages, and contained extensive and detailed changes to strengthen public school education. The increased funding for 1983–84 was to be $800 million; $1.9 billion was to be added the next year, the same increase as for the first year plus $1.1 billion for cost-of-living increases and funds needed to implement the many school reforms. However, when the governor signed the legislation, he vetoed all the second-year funding, explaining that the reforms will be monitored "very closely before we agree to further additional financial support."

Nothing in the record of Deukmejian's first legislative year suggests that he achieved strong policy leadership, although he did achieve his budget goal. But as long as the governor is faced with a heavily Democratic legislature, most policy initiatives requiring legislation are likely to move slowly or be rejected. The governor has the authority, and may continue to use it, to veto expenditures when the legislature appropriates money for purposes to which he objects, but he cannot initiate major new policies or materially revise statutory expenditure requirements without legislative cooperation.

Housing the governor (a continued story). After the inauguration the legislature still did not provide housing for the governor, who commuted weekly to Sacramento from his southern California home. Finally, senate hostility melted in mid-May when Democrats decided to let the governor live in the Carmichael mansion "with no strings attached." Legislation was introduced to permit the governor to take occupancy before the start of the school year, but action was deferred by work on the budget and education reform. In the midst of prolonged negotiations over the budget, on July 16 the governor made a surprise announcement that he had decided to pursue other plans and did not intend to move into the mansion. Using the $490,000 left over from the inaugural fund, he intended to find a suitable home to rent or purchase on his own. The governor's executive secretary said, "The governor just got tired of waiting." Early in 1984 the governor's office announced that Deukmejian had purchased a home that he and his family would probably occupy before the new school term began in the fall. The Department of General Services proceeded with the sale of the Carmichael mansion and the legislature explored building a new mansion near the state capitol. The Victorian mansion used by governors before Reagan will continue to be operated as a state park.

The months of petty denial by a few senate leaders can only partly be attributed to the sincere desire to find a better site for a permanent home. If Bradley had been elected and had wanted to live in the Carmichael mansion, there is little doubt that he would have been given speedy occupancy. The governor regarded the frequent senate votes to persist in the sale of the mansion as "a slap in the face." "It appeared to some of us," he said, "that recent actions taken by the Democrats in relation to the mansion and in the rejection of Carol Hallett, seemed directed toward me in a personal sense. I expected tough debate on taxes and welfare but I did not expect that kind of action in those kinds of things. It did not set a cooperative mood." On the other hand Governor Deukmejian himself frequently did not display cooperative behavior on issues involving the legislature. Moreover, Martin Smith reported that President Reagan "has been jerking the strings on Governor Deukmejian" to encourage him to live in the mansion and block efforts to sell it. Although Deukmejian expressed a willingness to live in the mansion, insiders said that initially he was ambivalent; when he visited the president after the election, he became uncomfortable about his willingness to live elsewhere—a willingness his representatives already had communicated to legislators. Reagan's great pleasure at the prospect that the Deukmejians would be living in the mansion apparently caused the governor's shift in position. According to Smith, "the president unquestionably complicated an already complex issue."[6] Politics by any other name would smell no sweeter.

Summing Up: Politics, Policies, and Personality

Gubernatorial transitions begin when the candidate who is eventually successful declares his candidacy and announces his political program. The period from the election until inauguration is often designated *the* transition, but in reality it is the period of preparation for changing governors. The process is formalized when the new governor assumes the authority of office and attempts to introduce changes in state government. A new governor's entire incumbency may be required to accomplish his policy objectives.

When transition studies focus only on how a new governor assumes the responsibility of his office—organizes his immediate staff, selects his first appointees, and forms his initial policy and budget priorities—few accomplishments may be observed. A longer time span must be observed to assess what a new executive has achieved after being ensconced in office. This study has concentrated on the how and the what of Deukmejian's first year in office.

ASSUMING OFFICE: A SMOOTH PROCESS

The formal process by which Deukmejian took over the reins of California government was smooth and orderly. His staff had been thoroughly briefed twice before election so that Deukmejian was well aware of the state's financial plight. Transition legislation assured the cooperation and support of the Department of Finance in preparing the budget and more than enough funds for staff, space, materials, and services to prepare for the assumption of office. Deukmejian returned $60,000 of the transition appropriation to the state treasury. Beyond the legal requirements, Governor Brown's staff eased and assisted the formal process.

The major tension between the outgoing and incoming governors arose over the extent to which Brown should exercise his authority in the waning days of his administration. Deukmejian, in effect, said, fulfill your responsibilities as governor, but only in ways that I would if I were governor. He called on the governor to deal with the budget deficit and convene a special session if necessary. But, he emphasized, the legislature, in special session, should not reapportion the state and should not resolve the budget crisis by raising taxes. Moreover, Deukmejian asked Brown not to make any more judicial appointments.

The assumption of office was smooth in a formal sense also because, in the midst of massive changes—of party, personalities, and policies— an ongoing system of government provides continuity and stability. Most governmental functions and many of the costs are controlled by relevant statutory or case-load provisions, for example, debt service, retirement contractual costs, average-daily-attendance (ADA) costs in public education, full-time-equivalent (FTE) support in higher education. Moreover, a well-trained and responsible career civil service continued the orderly processes of public service, even providing interim directors of operating departments when necessary. In addition, the new governor and his cabinet were the most experienced political leaders to have taken over the state in more than two decades. They were able to cope with the monumental task of carefully and systematically selecting appointees who would be loyal to the governor. The task was more overwhelming and time consuming than anticipated but was achieved to the satisfaction of the governor and his supporters. The structure and decision-making processes developed by the transition team prior to the inauguration were transferred into the governor's office. Many staff members were lawyers. Because most had worked together in the attorney general's office and/or on the campaign, they had evolved procedures and relationships that comfortably fit the governor's style and personality.

The demands of the changeover to a new administration also forced structure onto seemingly fluid events: officials, especially in the cabinet and the governor's office, were appointed before the inauguration; the cabinet and the governor's office were organized and ready to function; the inauguration was planned and the address drafted; the budget was prepared and submitted on schedule; and a legislative program was designed, based initially on campaign promises. The effective conduct of these activities permitted a smooth transfer of authority to the Deukmejian administration, but the governor's ultimate success in achieving his political objectives depends on the total setting within which the transition takes place. From this broader perspective the process has not been smooth or easy, and future success is uncertain. Included in this larger perspective were many influences—legislative and party politics; the budget crisis, which demanded immediate solution; the personality and style of the governor and of his opponents; and the policies the governor is pursuing.

ACCOMPLISHING GOALS: SUCCESSES AND FAILURES

Unlike his two predecessors, Deukmejian was an insider. Curb accused him of being a "career politician." He did not scorn government, as have recent governors—and presidents. Yet in spite of his familiarity with the capital and his experience in the legislature, his greatest problem was in relating to the legislature. Immediately after the election Deukmejian telephoned Democratic leaders in both houses to lay the groundwork for future relations. At his first press conference he talked about "working together" and "talking things over." "The people want bipartisan leadership," he said. "They want the governor and the legislature to resolve problems." In his inaugural address the governor reiterated his pledge of bipartisanship. The plea was futile at a time when the legislature was dominated by the opposite party, members of his own party sometimes rejected his leadership, and both parties had become used to a nonassertive governor.

The governor's executive secretary, Merksamer, complained that the biggest problem was not the budget deficit itself—great as it was—but the lack of civility and the lack of trust that existed in the capitol. Another top aide said, according to Smith, "The problem is everyone hates each other."[7] The administration's relations with the legislature were strained. Even the legislative leaders in the two houses were at odds with each other and with their followers. Senate Republicans dumped their minority leader and the chairman of their caucus in the midst of the budget battle. Assembly Republicans tried, without success, to change minority leaders; a similar unsuccessful move was made against the senate majority leader.

A number of conflicts, many of them unrelated to the transition, have soured relations. The Republicans had defeated a pay raise for legislators in the previous session as punishment for the first reapportionment bill. In turn the assembly Democrats punished the Republicans by stripping the two-thirds vote out of rules (thus denying the one-third-plus minority their power) and took over all committee chairmanships. Also in the previous session, the legislature had created a number of new exempt positions and moved some positions from the lieutenant governor's to the governor's office. Now that a Republican governor was in office, the assembly Democrats attempted to shift a number of appointments (e.g., to the Public Utilities Commission and the Agricultural Labor Relations Board) from the governor to the legislature. Senate Democrats objected to this proposal because they would have to share with the assembly some of the senate authority over appointments. (Similar attempts to weaken the governor's power to appoint had been made in the last two years of Brown's administration.)

These political tensions became especially acute when the governor was denied his appointments, parking spaces for his staff were withdrawn, and the housing question could not be resolved. They also dominated negotiations over the fiscal crisis, which provided the governor the opportunity to challenge the Democrats and make immediate changes in the state's spending plan. Had there been no fiscal crisis when Deukmejian took office, he would have been locked into Governor Brown's budget for six months. If Brown and the legislature had raised taxes during the special session in December, the 1982–83 deficit would not have been as great or might have been eliminated. Because of their inaction, Deukmejian was able to change priorities, first by an executive order that cut spending 2 percent across the board, then by negotiating a resolution that slashed over $600 million from the current budget and rolled over the rest of the deficit into the next year. By opposing tax increases, even with loophole closing, he was able to make further cuts and realign priorities in the 1983–84 budget to absorb the roll-over deficit and hold spending within available revenues.

By the year's end it was apparent that Deukmejian had achieved some significant political successes. Most notably, he put a lid on state spending, something Governor Reagan was never able to accomplish. He overcame an immense—but smaller than first estimated—deficit in eighteen months without increasing tax rates. He did this by means of short-term borrowing, the limited issuance of IOUs, severe spending cuts ($638 million) and item vetoes ($1.1 billion), a standby tax plan, and almost $1 billion in loophole-closing and revenue-enhancing measures that were not called tax increases. Neither tax trigger was pulled as the economic turnaround provided bountiful revenues. The year-end surplus for FY 1983–84 is projected as more than $1 billion and may reach $2 billion next fiscal year.

Through budget cuts the governor has lessened the state's commitment to energy conservation, alternative energy programs, coastal protection, community and family planning clinics, public broadcasting, and the Public Defender's Office—all Democratic favorites. He signed a major school reform act, which included measures he supported but which had been initiated by the superintendent of public instruction and Democratic legislators (the Democrats were able to take as much credit as the governor for this reform). The governor also negotiated, with the Democrats' approval, for a series of measures to spur economic development, modify the welfare program slightly, and begin prison construction with bond money previously approved.

The governor won the budget battle through the use of his blue pencil, and the economic boom erased the deficit, but in the process Deukmejian may not have strengthened his ability to govern. He proved a far tougher negotiator than even some of his most conservative supporters expected. Often his first offer, such as "no tax increase" and the $22-billion ceiling on general fund spending, was his last offer. Only on education reform did he display willingness to compromise; even then, he vetoed the second-year increases that were part of the negotiation. If he wishes to leave his imprint on California, he will probably have to deal. Even Ronald Reagan, ideological as he was a governor, eventually had to compromise with a Democratic legislature.

To accomplish most of his policy objectives Deukmejian needs legislative support and cooperation. Although he has more legislative experience than any recent governor, he has not succeeded in building effective legislative relationships. Martin Smith reported that assembly speaker Willie Brown later admitted that he had made a mistake in cooperating with the governor to solve the state's cash-flow problem early in 1983.[8] Much of Deukmejian's legislative program is yet to be enacted.

At times even the governor's fellow party members did not support him on measures about which he had not consulted them. After the legislature adjourned the 1983 session, senate Republican leader Jim Nielsen accused the governor's aides of having followed their own agenda and having failed to communicate adequately. He told a news conference that "some of us would like to see a little bit better communication between the governor's staff and those of us in the senate." Members of the governor's staff admit that some mistakes have been made in relating to the legislature, especially to the Republicans, and steps are being taken to avoid those gaffes.

Peace may never be made with the Democrats in the legislature if

Deukmejian continues to insist on another reapportionment within the decade. The most serious political setback he encountered was the Supreme Court decision overturning the Sebastiani initiative, a measure about which he had never been enthusiastic. The governor immediately proposed an initiative to amend the constitution and assign reapportionment to a nonpartisan commission. The Democrats announced a counterproposal. However, the major issue that divides the approaches to reforming reapportionment is not who serves on the commission, how its members are selected, its size, or the plurality required for action: the major issue is timing. The governor and the Republicans insist that a commission redraw district lines in time for the 1986 elections. The Democrats are equally insistent that the present districts remain in effect until the 1990 census, when new lines will be drawn for the 1992 elections. The two parties could probably reach a compromise on the nature and functioning of a commission but not on the date when the new lines should be drawn. A head-on collision looms between the governor and the Democratic majority in the legislature. The conflict would "further poison the already bad political atmosphere in Sacramento," according to Martin Smith.[9] (Subsequent to this writing, a gubernatorially supported initiative to this effect was defeated by the voters in November 1984.)

BEING GOVERNOR: PERSONALITY AND STYLE

In addition to legislative and party politics and the dominating budget crisis, Governor Deukmejian's personality and style were important influences on his ability to change the direction of government and accomplish his political goals. Deukmejian is commonly viewed as organized, systematic, deliberate, steady, and predictable. He is "old school" and "goes by the book." Many suggest that he is cautious, not a risk taker. Some see him as aloof, perhaps cool, even dull. But he knows where he wants to go and how to get there. He is a hands-on administrator, one who is knowledgeable about state government and who wants to be involved, as he was in the deliberations of the budget conference committee. Reagan seldom spent more than a day on each year's budget. After his first year Jerry Brown ignored budget preparations. Deukmejian does not fit Treasurer Jesse Unruh's description of the typical governor: "Today you survive by not governing. You run for office, then abandon responsibility." Deukmejian is determined to govern, even if that means conflict and confrontation, by low-key firmness and, when necessary, by statewide radio and television.

As a result of his political and administrative style, he projects a different image than his two predecessors did. Reagan was the great communicator; every action was a media event, but he was removed from many day-to-day details of government. Brown was an idea man, generally uninterested in running government. He was accessible to the press at all hours in many locations, but he manipulated the media for his own ends. In time he was seen as "Governor Moonbeam," "a flake," or "wacko." The press had to adjust to a radically different style when Deukmejian came in. He is not a "performer." According to one member of the capitol press corps, his low-profile, behind-the-scene negotiations and highly organized administration made "normality seem abnormal" after Reagan and Brown.

This is not to say that he ignores press and public relations. Rather, they are different but carefully designed and orchestrated to suit his personality and achieve his ends. His first press conference after the election was delayed a day to permit time for preparation. Prior to the inauguration only two more press conferences were held, and requests for interviews, even from the national media, were declined. As reporters were held off, they became "cranky," according to the governor's press secretary, and there were "a lot of rocky moments."[10] The press conference after Deukmejian's first cabinet meeting turned into a minor disaster when the press secretary gave a "White House briefing" instead of letting reporters interview the governor. That procedure was quickly changed.

Deukmejian now holds a general news conference every three weeks and special conferences from time to time on specific topics. He meets small groups of reporters periodically for on-the-record discussions. In the first six months there was only a handful of one-to-one interviews, a few of which were with the national media. His press staff, however, have explained that they are playing down any suggestion that he has national aspirations, and his two trips to the east coast were not given wide publicity. His presence at the February NGA winter meeting in Washington, D.C., was scarcely noticed. (Opponents insist that his entire budget strategy was calculated to create a presidential image.) Deukmejian's absence from Sacramento on Friday, Saturday, Sunday, and parts of Thursday and Monday further limit his accessibility to the capitol press corps. Even the massive double doors to the governor's outer office, after being open for eight years, are closed—but not locked. In his first year Deukmejian held only thirteen news conferences (compared to thirty-eight for Governor Reagan).

This apparent remoteness has not limited Deukmejian's effectiveness when an issue has required his attention. In the closing weeks of the budget battle the governor and his staff mounted a thorough, far-reaching campaign to sell his solution for holding costs within current revenues. Breakfast interviews, luncheon speeches, a statewide radio address, a call-in radio show, and press conferences in a number of cities carried his message and appeared to put the legislature on the defensive. The blue pencils he sent to each legislator were hardly needed to alert them that he would item-veto expenditures over his $22 billion limit. Never in California history had the blue pencil been so heavily wielded to strike so much from the budget.

Ultimately, Deukmejian's success as a governor may depend on the image he projects and the public's continued support, as well as his ability to relate to the legislature. He has had trouble gaining recognition because, according to pollster Mervin Field, "He's still an unknown guy."[11] In mid-1983 Field's California Poll reported that the proportion who rated Deukmejian as doing either an excellent or a good job had risen from 27 percent in March to 36 percent in June. The proportion who viewed his performance as poor or very poor—just 13 percent— remained almost unchanged. By contrast, when Jerry Brown had been in office the same length of time, 43 percent of the public rated him positively; just 7 percent held unfavorable opinions. Three months later Deukmejian had a 42 percent positive and an 18 percent negative rating; 34 percent judged his performance fair, and only 6 percent offered no opinion.

By contrast, pollster Jack Bentley, of Western Viewpoint Research, reported: "If George doesn't do something in a hurry, he's a lame-duck governor. He's unexciting, a bore."[12] The danger, Bentley said, is that many Californians have no strong opinions about Deukmejian. Undoubtedly, he is becoming more widely known and is gaining greater approval, but, according to Field, his public image is that of a "stubborn steward."

Deukmejian will face a strongly Democratic legislature for all or most of his tenure. The supreme political skill of achieving mutual concessions will be more important than stubbornness. Whereas the Sebastiani initiative was a California wine whose time never came, George Deukmejian may have to sip the bitter wine of compromise with the Democrats to achieve his long-term policy objectives.

The Gubernatorial Transition in Georgia, 1982

DELMER D. DUNN

Georgia's governor in 1982 was George Busbee, who was in the last year of his second four-year term. Busbee's tenure was a record in the state's history. Georgia voters first elected him to office in 1974. They overwhelmingly reelected him four years later, after the state constitution had been changed in 1976 to permit a governor to succeed to a second four-year term. Although Governor Busbee did not take an active public role in its adoption, the 1976 constitutional amendment was widely viewed as a referendum on the first two years of his administration. Busbee thus won three statewide elections. Moreover, he finished his second term in 1982 as a very popular governor. Busbee, in contrast to his immediate predecessors, Jimmy Carter and Lester Maddox, assiduously avoided confrontations. He preferred quiet, behind-the-scenes negotiation, coupled with detailed attention to budgetary matters—a style that enhanced his reputation among Georgia voters as a manager of state government.

Because of Busbee's popularity, his record as governor did not become an issue during the 1982 campaign. All candidates focused upon the future needs of the state, emphasizing some combination of education, economic development, prisons, crime control, and the appropriate level of state taxation. Only two immediate state problems emerged during the general election campaign. As in many states during 1982, Georgia state revenue collections fell below estimated levels. Governor Busbee announced an anticipated shortfall of $66 million and directed agency heads to make appropriate budget cuts. Prison overcrowding was also identified as a problem, but discussion of it was considerably more muted than discussion of the revenue shortfall.

The Candidates

A large field of candidates emerged to compete for the Democratic nomination in the gubernatorial election. Bo Ginn, a ten-year veteran of the U.S. Congress, representing Georgia's coastal district, took the lead in the early phases of the campaign. A second candidate was Jack Watson, an Atlanta attorney who had served as a top aide to President Jimmy Carter in Washington and who as a private citizen had chaired the governing board of Georgia's Department of Human Resources during the Carter governorship. Another Atlanta attorney, Norman Underwood, was a third Democrat in the race. Underwood had been Governor Busbee's top aide during his first administration, served briefly on the Georgia Court of Appeals, and in 1980 in his first statewide election he had run in third place against U.S. Senator Herman Talmadge. A fourth candidate, Buckner Melton, a Macon attorney, had served one term as that city's mayor and was currently a member of the state Board of Industry and Trade. Billy Lovett, who as a member of the state Public Service Commission had consistently opposed all rate hikes requested by Georgia Power Company, was a fifth candidate. Lovett had previously chaired the county governing board in Lowndes County, located in south-central Georgia. Finally, Joe Frank Harris, a businessman from Cartersville in northwest Georgia, was the sixth major Democratic candidate. Harris had served eighteen years in the Georgia House of Representatives, the last eight as chairman of the powerful Appropriations Committee. A number of other candidates contested the Democratic primary, but none campaigned seriously on a statewide basis.

State Senator Bob Bell and former U.S. Representative Ben Blackburn, both from DeKalb County, in the eastern part of metropolitan Atlanta, contested the Republican nomination for governor. Bell had served ten years in the Georgia Senate following four years in the Georgia House. Blackburn had served in the U.S. House for eight years until Democrat Elliott Levitas defeated him in 1974.

The Primary Campaigns

Bo Ginn became the front-runner for the Democratic nomination early in the campaign. He had made friends throughout the state during his tenure in Congress and earlier as administrative assistant to U.S. Senator Herman Talmadge. In the state's sometimes regional politics Ginn had the advantage of campaigning against a field of Democrats that except for Billy Lovett and himself came from the northern half of the state. Moreover, Ginn won the coveted endorsement of the Georgia Association of Educators, probably the most powerful mass-based interest group in the state.

By contrast, Joe Frank Harris began far back in the field, rarely garnering more than 5 percent of the vote in early polls. But Harris had several strengths that proved helpful as the campaign unfolded. Harris enjoyed the friendship and support of most of his fellow house members, as had George Busbee in his campaign eight years earlier. The house support of Harris was even greater than it had been for Busbee in his first campaign for two reasons. First, the house speaker, who was so important in lining up support for Harris, was only in the first months of his tenure as speaker when Busbee first ran. Secondly, one of Busbee's opponents in 1974 was a former speaker, who still enjoyed the support of a number of his former colleagues. In Georgia's loosely organized party structure the alliances among the large number of Democratic members of the house constitute the potentially strongest political organization in the state.

Harris's image was more similar than that of other challengers to the image of Busbee. Both had low-key, nonflamboyant personalities, and Harris, as had Busbee before him, offered himself as a gubernatorial candidate after a long tenure as a powerful house leader. Further, he had expertise in state budgeting at a time when the state was experiencing budgetary problems. He also fit the role of a talented budget manager, a gubernatorial role to which state voters had become accustomed during the Busbee tenure. The Busbee-Harris connection was also enhanced by the close advisor relationship between Harris and Tom Perdue, who was Busbee's chief staff aide.

But the image of Harris as the best copy of Busbee in personality, demeanor, and experience, although important, was augmented by a very effective campaign.

To distance himself from the large field of candidates running for the second berth in the primary runoff (everyone conceded the first position to Ginn), Harris carefully positioned himself as the most conservative of the candidates. In early June, Harris pledged no new taxes if he were elected, as had candidate Busbee eight years earlier. The major candidates in the Democratic primary, including Harris, had earlier avoided such a pledge because of the uncertainties of the economy and the unknown impact of the Reagan administration's "new" federalism program. This pledge distanced Harris from his opponents and marked the turn of his fortunes with Georgia voters. Harris also quietly appealed to the Christian right, a force in Georgia's conservative politics that had not previously been visibly active. Although several of his opponents were also active churchmen, Harris developed this constituency effectively. Finally, Harris attacked Ginn for being a big spender after Ginn received the endorsement of the powerful Georgia Association of Educators, calling him Bo "Can't Say No" Ginn. He carefully reminded Georgia voters of Ginn's Washington connection, arguing, often by inference, that anyone even partly responsible for the "mess" in Washington should not be entrusted with the reins of state government. Harris was helped by his choice of Deloss Walker as his media advisor. Walker's Memphis firm had a record of working with little-known, come-from-behind candidates like Harris. The firm's reputation stretched back to the successful campaign of Dale Bumpers, who became governor of Arkansas in 1970. In 1978 the firm had conducted the successful gubernatorial campaign of Forrest Hood (Fob) James, Jr., in neighboring Alabama.

As expected, Ginn led his foes in the first Democratic primary, with 35 percent of the vote. Harris finished second, with 25 percent of the vote, easily leading Underwood and Watson, who finished with 16 percent and 13 percent of the vote, respectively. Harris, using the same tactics he had used in the first primary campaign, came from behind to defeat Ginn in the primary runoff 55 percent to 45 percent.

The Republican primary was not marked by notable differences between Bob Bell and Ben Blackburn. Both were articulate and conservative candidates. Bell more aggressively attacked the Democratic candidates, stressing that it was time to make some bold moves to take Georgia out of its low ranking among the states in education and other areas. He also more forcefully attacked the speaker of the house, Tom Murphy, a strong and very important supporter of Harris. In the August primary Bell defeated Blackburn with a vote of 59 percent to 41 percent.

The General Election

The general election campaign was hard fought by both sides. Harris enjoyed the advantage of being a Democrat in a state that had elected Democratic governors since Reconstruction. (In 1966 Georgia voters gave a plurality to Republican Bo Callaway in the general election. But at that time Georgia law required the state legislature to select the governor from the top two candidates if no candidate received an absolute majority. The Democratic legislature elected Democrat Lester Maddox.) Harris had already carefully positioned himself as a conservative on most issues, had made himself appear the logical person to assume Busbee's mantle, and had a campaign staff directed by persons who were experienced in statewide races.

Bell nevertheless conducted a campaign that had Harris supporters anxious by the November general election. Bell emphasized the general problems of government in Georgia, indicating that if changes were to come, the Democrats would have to be thrown out of office. He stressed crime and corruption, telling Georgia voters that a public official had been indicted at the rate of one every nineteen days during the past year. He criticized Harris for failing to disclose his personal finances. He also released figures indicating that a concrete company in which Harris had once held a major interest (he later sold it) had shown more profits after Harris became chairman of the house Appropriations Committee than it had before. He attacked Speaker Tom Murphy for the way he ran the Georgia House of Representatives and pointed out his failure to let progressive legislation, especially legislation that related to the criminal justice system, pass the house.

But in the end Bell failed. His criticism of Speaker Murphy failed to attract voters' interest. Bell also failed to make an issue of Harris's integrity. Harris was not vulnerable on this issue and seemed to satisfy doubters by promising to put his assets in a blind trust if elected and explaining that profits in his concrete company stemmed from the timing of interstate highway construction in his area of the state instead of his ascent to a powerful committee post. Bell's support of a 1982 senate bill establishing a mobile electric chair in Georgia, as well as his favorable vote a decade earlier for a bill requiring castration in rape cases, clouded his record. Bell was ultimately unable to capitalize on his extensive knowledge of Georgia government, a knowledge based upon far more experience in state government than that of any recent Republican gubernatorial candidate. Harris defeated him 63 percent to 37 percent.

The Politics of the Principals

With the outcome of the election decided, the transition from the administration of Governor Busbee to that of Governor-elect Joe Frank Harris began. Busbee had not formally endorsed any candidate during the primary campaigns, although it was well known that the major candidate to whom Busbee was closest was Norman Underwood, who had been chief aide during Busbee's first term. Busbee did emerge during the general election campaign as a strong and enthusiastic supporter of Harris. The fact that Busbee's record had not been an issue in the campaign avoided a potential source of animosity. Further, Harris and Busbee enjoyed a cordial personal and political relationship. Philosophically, the two men were close, especially on fiscal matters, and they shared an interest in the process and mechanics of budgeting.

The Busbee-Harris relationship was augmented by close relations between Harris and several Busbee staff members. Busbee's chief aide, Tom Perdue, served as one of a handful of senior advisors to Harris during the campaign. Tom Daniel, Busbee's administrative assistant and coordinator of the second Busbee campaign, left the Busbee staff in August 1981 to begin the task of organizing the Harris campaign. Although not all Busbee staff members supported Harris, most of them did, and they entered the transition period determined to help Harris and his staff.

Most transition planning was done by the Busbee staff. In this they were encouraged by Busbee and spurred by their experience from the transition eight years earlier when there had been meager liaison with the Carter administration, which was already focusing on the national presidential campaign. Busbee was interested in conducting a good transition. He had consciously conducted his administration so that he would be remembered as a good governor when he left office, and he wanted the final chapter to foster that image. He also wanted to be as much help as possible to Harris. One example of Busbee's eagerness to make the transition as easy as possible for Harris was his moving from the governor's mansion several weeks before inauguration day so that Harris could be settled by the time he was sworn in as governor.

Another part of the Busbee effort in transition planning consisted of a briefing book, which was turned over to Harris the day after the election. The book detailed the major functions in the Busbee office and how they were performed. It listed the appointments that could be made directly and those that could be influenced indirectly. Busbee had limited his appointments to boards and commissions in the latter part of his tenure so as to increase the number of appointments that the new administration could make early in its term. Accompanying the list of appointments was a breakdown by time, indicating which ones could be made in, for example, one month, two months, six months. The book also described the important functions within operating departments that might be useful and interesting to the governor and his staff.

The dynamics of the Harris-Busbee relationship and the close interaction of their respective staffs were the most important factors on which the transition process turned.

Transition Procedures

Georgia enacted the Gubernatorial Transition Act in 1971. In it the Georgia General Assembly directs all officers of the state government to be mindful of problems occasioned by transitions in the office of governor, to take steps to avoid or minimize disruptions that might occur as a result of transition, and to otherwise promote orderly transitions (Official Code of Georgia Annotated 45-12-191). The act also authorizes the governor-elect "to use necessary services and facilities," including office space, furnishings, supplies, and equipment; it also authorizes the payment of the staff of the governor-elect, the payment of consultants or experts, the payment of travel expenses, the use of printing and communications services, and the payment of mailing costs. The act further authorizes the governor-elect to pay staff members and to assign any state employee to the governor-elect's staff with the approval of the appropriate agency head (OCGA 45-12-193). Finally, the act authorizes similar service to the former governor for a period not to exceed three months from the expiration of the term of office and authorizes an appropriation not to exceed $50,000 to carry out the activities authorized by the act (Official Code of Georgia Annotated 45-12-194, 45-12-195).

Comings and Goings

The comings and goings between the Busbee and Harris administrations were minimal. Harris announced soon after his election that he would ask all agency heads to stay on through the 1983 legislative session, which convened in mid-January and adjourned in mid-March at the end of its constitutionally limited forty-day session. Although the governor directly appoints only five agency heads, he indirectly exerts great influence over the appointment of other appointed heads. Harris's move stemmed from concern about the timing of the legislative session: the legislature would convene one day before his inauguration, making the time from the election to the beginning of the legislative session very short. He was also concerned about the need for budget cuts: agency heads already familiar with the agency would be in a better position to determine and implement the cuts. Besides, as chairman of the house Appropriations Committee, Harris had worked closely with all of them on budgetary matters in the past, and after being elected governor he received detailed assessments of them from his predecessor. The Harris team also believed that they would not have time to make all the necessary appointments and that continuing the agency heads was better than appointing interim heads. Finally, Harris was concerned that appointing new agency heads would necessitate transition processes within the agencies that would disrupt the smooth transfer of power that he wanted to accomplish. The two or three months between the transition and legislative adjournment would not only give Harris and his staff the opportunity to evaluate each commissioner to determine each one's continued tenure but would also, as Governor-elect Harris explained in a press conference, give the agency heads a chance to determine whether they wanted to work with him. Even after the legislative session Harris was slow to make any personnel changes. In fact no major shifts were made during the first six months of the new administration, and very few were made in the first year.

The smooth flow of the transition process was disrupted by one episode related to the appointment process. After Harris announced that all agency heads had been asked to continue, the governor-elect and some of his top advisors decided to name a new commissioner of the Department of Transportation. The department was headed by Tom Moreland, a professional engineer, who had succeeded Bert Lance in the position after Lance had resigned to run for governor in 1974. In the intervening time Moreland had developed a reputation as an astute manager who had brought a high degree of professionalism to the state's transportation department. But he also was regarded as an independent decision maker—an independence enhanced by his being elected to a four-year term by his board, in contrast to other appointed agency heads who serve at the pleasure of the governor or their governing board or at most for one-year terms. Moreover, the ten transportation board members in Georgia are elected from each of the state's congressional districts by a caucus of the legislators who represent districts within each of the congressional districts, further enhancing Moreland's independence, at least from the governor. Harris and some of his top advisors apparently believed that Moreland should be replaced with someone who would be more loyal to the Harris team.

Three candidates surfaced for the position. One was Joel Cowan, Harris's campaign chairman and close friend. When opposition to Cowan developed, two other candidates emerged, both members of the transportation board. One was a close associate of Bert Lance; the other had close ties to Marcus Collins, chairman of the house Ways and Means Committee. Both Lance and Collins were members of the handful of influential advisors to the governor-elect. This plan was foiled by the eight other members of the transportation board, who stood solidly behind Moreland. Before the fight was over Harris moved to negotiate a settlement. However, during the fray, the new administration moved close to producing an image of disunity among the governor and his key advisors, momentarily casting doubt upon whether Harris was completely in charge of the emerging administration. But this was quickly forgotten and did no lasting damage to the transition effort.

Organizing the Governor's Office

The immediate office of the governor was organized under the new administration as it had been at the end of the Busbee administration. Under the last few governors the office has managed the external relations of the governor—relations with key supporters, legislators, and the general public. The agency management functions of the governor's office have been handled by the staff of the Office of Planning and Budgeting and by Busbee's (and now Harris's) intensive personal involvement in the budgeting process. The key personnel of the Office of Planning and Budgeting, who remained the same under the new administration, work directly with the governor and his chief aide for political direction. With this organization of the governor's office, it should not be surprising that Harris chose many in his campaign staff to become his key office staff. In doing so, Harris was following the practices of his immediate predecessors, Jimmy Carter and George Busbee.

Barbara Morgan, who had served as press secretary for the campaign during the last month and a half, became Harris's press secretary. Morgan had been a member of the statehouse press corps, the representative of a chain of newspapers with outlets in Athens, Augusta, and Savannah. Gracie Phillips, who had served the campaign as treasurer, became the executive assistant responsible for overseeing casework and appointments to boards and commissions. Phillips had not been pursuing a career outside her home immediately prior to the campaign. Earlier, she had held positions in state government, including aide to her father, a veteran member of the Georgia House of Representatives. Rusty Sewell, who had been responsible for coordinating the campaign organization for one area of the state and who was an attorney with nearly a dozen years of experience in state government, became executive counsel. Mike deVetger, a former court administrator who had been responsible for coordinating another area of the state in the campaign, was named the executive assistant responsible for the Governor's Intern Program and for working with important constituent groups for the governor.

Richard Hardon was appointed executive assistant with responsibilities for minority affairs. Hardon had also worked on the Harris campaign staff, joining it after having worked for the Watson campaign before the first primary. Previously, he had worked in the state residential finance program and in Atlanta city government. Early in the Harris term Hardon moved to the Department of Natural Resources as special assistant to the commissioner. At that time he was replaced by Jackey Beavers, a minister from Cartersville, who had run a program for retarded men.

Harris appointed Joel Cowan as his chief of staff. This is an unpaid position first used by former Governor Busbee to honor a close friend and to give him a more formal role in the administration than that of an informal member of the governor's kitchen cabinet. The occupant of the position is an advisor to the governor and performs a variety of tasks at the governor's request. Cowan, a boyhood friend of the governor, is an Atlanta banker and developer. As noted earlier, he served the Harris campaign as campaign chairman. To round out his key staff, Harris appointed Tom Perdue, executive secretary to Governor Busbee, as his principal aide, with the new title chief administrative officer. Perdue, as noted earlier, was a key advisor to Harris during his campaign.

Because the governor's staff in Georgia is not large, Harris knew that not all of his campaign staff could have positions in the governor's office. Harris met with them shortly after the November election and promised that he would find places somewhere in state government for those who wanted them. Eventually, at least three additional campaign aides were employed in his office. The remainder were placed elsewhere, with considerable help from Busbee aides who had been close to the Harris campaign and from some key Harris aides.

The same process was used to place those on the Busbee staff who either wanted to leave the governor's office or would not be carried over to the new governor's staff. Placement was difficult in the fall of 1982 because a hiring freeze had been imposed by Governor Busbee to cope with the state revenue shortfall. However, positions were found in state government or, in some instances, in private industry. The staff of an outgoing governor who has been in office for eight years have ample contacts who can make the placements necessitated by the dismantling of a relatively small campaign staff.

The Harris transition staff was beseiged by supporters' requests for offices. To a considerable extent, this seige was handled by all the staff who remained with Harris. All had a good feel for who the governor's supporters were—who needed to be rewarded and who did not. Gracie Phillips's role as campaign treasurer gave her insight into the governor-elect's support. Those who had served as campaign coordinators knew in detail who had and had not delivered when called upon.

The staff maintained an open-door policy of talking with any office-seeker who visited the transition office. Telephone calls and letters also announced the availability of many talented and not-so-talented Georgians to fill available and unavailable positions. Résumés were taken and office-seekers were told that the staff would be in touch with them if an opening became available. The burden of this task fell upon Gracie Phillips, whose new position was announced soon after the election. But all staff were involved to some extent—they had made their own contacts during the elections and were naturally sought out for whatever favors they could dispense.

The Inaugural

Governor Harris's inaugural as Georgia's seventy-eighth governor was planned from the very first as a political event. About 60,000 invitations, an unusually large number for Georgia, were issued. Much of the planning of the event was conducted by Harris's hometown friends, including as a key planner, for example, Tommy Lewis, the executive director of the Bartow County Chamber of Commerce, the home county of the governor-elect. Lewis, incidentally, was later named executive assistant to run a job-training program for the governor. The inaugural was designed to make three key political statements.

First, it was billed by Harris and his planners as a low-cost, no-frills inaugural. For the first time in twelve years, the event took place on the capitol steps. Costs were reduced by using a trailer bed for a platform rather than building a more elaborate one. In his inaugural address Harris, a fiscal conservative, stressed the necessity of financial restraint. There was a definite effort to portray the event symbolically as a low-cost, low-key affair in a time of state austerity. Second, the inaugural was portrayed as a "people's" inaugural. The outdoor location assured room for as many of the large number of invitees as might choose to attend. The large invitation list was an attempt to reward the faithful and to recruit friends for future fights.

Third, the inaugural reassured the governor-elect's religious-right supporters by banning the serving of alcoholic beverages at official inaugural activities, including the ball. This decision and the announcement by the transition office that the new administration would serve no alcoholic beverages during its tenure contrasted with the practices of the Busbee administration, which had served liquor, and the Carter administration, which had served wine at the governor's mansion. But this policy clearly conformed with the new governor and first lady's private practices and reassured some of his supporters on questions of public morality.

The inaugural was successful. The messages that had been planned were effectively communicated, and the inaugural provided a very good kickoff for the new administration.

Coping with the Processes

Joe Frank Harris came to the governor's chair after a long tenure in the Georgia legislature. Most of his staff came to the office seasoned by the campaign, and most, like Harris, had experience in state government. But even with this knowledge how did they cope with the process? How did they learn to run the office of governor? How did they learn their new responsibilities and duties?

Harris and the members of his staff relied primarily on their counterparts in the Busbee administration for information about their positions and the details of their responsibilities. Busbee and Harris met personally many times, including breakfast meetings. Both attended the National Governors' Association (NGA) new governor's seminar in Park City, Utah—Busbee as a faculty member and Harris as one of the pupils. Thus, there were numerous opportunities for Harris to learn from Busbee, who was an eager teacher.

For his part, Harris emphasized the formulation of the new budget, which was to be presented to the Georgia General Assembly shortly after inauguration. The new budget was actually two budgets. One budget covered the remainder of the current fiscal year. It cut the "in-place" budget by $104 million. Of this amount, $66 million was necessitated by the revenue shortfall stemming from the recession; the remaining $38 million marked a restructuring of priorities in the current budget. The second budget, of course, was the 1984 fiscal year budget, which would take effect July 1, 1983.

In past transitions the incumbent governor has prepared the budgets, leaving the new governor the option of accepting them or preparing new ones emphasizing different priorities. But Governor Busbee considered it unnecessary to prepare the budgets himself, leaving this task to the governor-elect. Thus, after the election Governor-elect Harris presided over the budget sessions in the executive branch, and the budgets introduced in the January legislative session were his.

Harris's ability to quickly write a budget that he could call his own was enhanced by several factors. His legislative experience made him very knowledgeable about state budget processes. He had also retained Clark Stevens, the chief budget officer of the executive branch, as director of the Office of Planning and Budgeting; Stevens's subordinates also retained their positions, as did other agency heads. Thus, the team responsible for formulating the state budget did not change. The only change was that the governor-elect, rather than the governor, conducted the process and made the decisions.

As for the new staff, their primary sources of information about their new positions were the Busbee staff and state agency personnel. Most, but not all, of the Harris staff met repeatedly with their counterparts in the Busbee office. They frequently called the Busbee staff, asked the staff to arrange meetings with key agency personnel, and met with staff members, often several times a day. The new staff also attended the regular Busbee staff meetings, which were led by Tom Perdue. As Busbee staff members left for other positions and as new staff members joined the Harris team, these staff meetings gradually became Harris staff meetings. This process of transition was enhanced considerably by Tom Perdue. As chief aide to both governors he was, in effect, the chief architect of the transition.

The key personnel in the new governor's office, as well as the governor-elect himself, assumed their positions on inauguration day with confidence that they knew and could carry out their responsibilities and duties. Information exchange, moreover, continued after the inauguration. Harris retained from the Busbee office a number of secretaries and other staff assistants who were responsible for the day-to-day functions of the governor's office. Thus, there was no need to train these personnel in new office procedures, and they were readily available to indicate to their new bosses how functions were performed and who could be reached for information. No wonder the new governor was able to conclude several months after the transition that no momentum had been lost as a result of the transition and that the transition itself had actually created new momentum that generated leverage for Harris to use in gaining legislative approval of his budget and legislative program.

The new governor and his staff turned to two other sources for help in the transition. One was the NGA. Governor Harris attended the NGA orientation for new governors and also met with a transition team in Washington. He found these sessions generally helpful, although it is difficult to discover the specific applications to the Georgia transition.

Governor Harris found interacting with other newly elected governors at the orientation sessions to be important. As for the usefulness of the information presented at these sessions, he found the information about policy more important than that about procedures. Procedural information was less important to him because he believed that his state government experience had provided more detailed and useful information about the state's administrative machinery and its budget process than could be gathered from a national program covering these topics in general.

A second organization to which the staff turned for assistance was the Institute of Government at the University of Georgia. At the request of the Harris staff the institute organized a seminar especially directed to staff members who had not previously worked in state government and whose understanding of the legislative process was not so great as that desired by the governor and key staff members. This one-afternoon session was, understandably, general, covering the legislative process and the function of legislative support agencies such as the legislative counsel's office. Most Harris staff members who have been interviewed believe that it was helpful in providing an overview of the Georgia governmental process.

Reaching Out

One hallmark of the early Harris administration was the establishment of closer ties with the state Democratic party. Harris may have developed an appreciation of the state's loosely organized Democratic party in the general election campaign. In what Harris termed his three campaigns (the two primaries and the general election campaigns), he spent a record $3.2 million. The contributors reached through the party were reportedly helpful in the general election, and perhaps this gave Harris an appreciation for the party. At any rate he assigned one of his top campaign aides, Paul Weston, to the post of party executive director, which was the first time in recent history that a Georgia governor had placed a top aide in that position immediately after the campaign. Weston also attended the daily meetings of the governor's staff during the transition period and the first months of the new administration. Another measure of the Harris effort to draw close to the party and to revitalize it as much as possible was his successful support of Bert Lance for the state party chairmanship. Almost alone among state leaders outside the legislature, Lance had endorsed Harris's candidacy early in the campaign, and he became one of the handful of top advisors to the candidate.

The Politics of the New Administration

On January 11, 1983, Governor Joe Frank Harris took the oath of office as Georgia's seventy-eighth governor since statehood in 1776. In his inaugural address he emphasized his dreams for a better Georgia, pledging to strive for excellence in education, human services, and transportation and to improve Georgia's criminal justice system and its economic development. Within the next few days he introduced a legislative package and the two budgets that he had formulated as governor-elect.

Georgia's legislative sessions are limited to forty legislative days annually, which includes weekends unless both houses formally adjourn. Thus, by mid-March the session was over, and Harris was judged by the press and key legislators to have effectively established his image as one who was in charge and who had a sound relationship with the legislature. His budgets had passed with no major changes, and his legislative program was generally well received. He did fail in his efforts to establish a state holiday honoring Martin Luther King, Jr., and also lost a key part of his crime-fighting package, one that would have reduced the number of prospective jurors who could be discarded from a jury panel by defendants in criminal cases to a number equal to that which could be discarded by prosecutors.

General Evaluation

The Georgia transition process in 1982–83 worked well. The retention of all state agency heads, of the previous governor's chief aide, and of several of the Busbee supporting staff minimized the number of positions for which transition was necessary. Where there were changes, the transition proceeded smoothly. By foregoing the opportunity of making personnel changes the new governor also minimized the policy changes that his administration would be likely to make. But this result conformed to the message of the Harris campaign—that he was the closest available copy of George Busbee. In a transition in which the number of changes was minimal, the following factors appear to have been those most critical to the transition process.

The process worked well largely because of informal rather than formal processes. The key provisions of Georgia law providing for transition assistance were the same when power was transferred from Jimmy Carter to George Busbee. Yet, by all accounts, the process was much more thorough and smooth this time than it had been eight years before.

One key factor explaining the smooth transition in Georgia was former Governor George Busbee's personal interest in effecting a smooth transition. The governor consulted with the governor-elect on activities and appointments that were likely to affect the new administration and consciously attempted to make certain that the new governor and his staff would be in a position to govern effectively from inauguration day onward.

The 1982–83 Georgia gubernatorial transition was also enhanced by the support of several key Busbee staff members for the Harris campaign and their willingness and ability to work with incoming staff as they were appointed by Governor-elect Harris. During the campaign the Busbee staff had not supported Harris unanimously, but the number of supporters, especially those in key positions, was large enough that the Busbee staff continued to be highly motivated in providing assistance to the staff of the new governor. Harris's retention of several persons who had day-to-day knowledge of office procedures was also important in continuing the smooth functioning of the governor's office following Harris's assumption of power.

The transition processes were also furthered by Governor Harris's experience, which gave him an excellent working knowledge of state government. Except for thinking in some detail about the appointment of administration floor leaders in the legislature who would introduce and garner support for the new administration's budget and legislative program, he had not thought much about the transition process prior to the general election. Nevertheless, Harris did come to the governor's chair in January with knowledge of how he believed the office should function, and the information exchanged during the transition enhanced his knowledge.

Finally, of course, by making no changes in executive agency leadership, Governor Harris limited the number of persons on his relatively small personal staff for whom a transition process was necessary—and some of these were holdovers from the Busbee staff. The impact of the transition was thus considerably curtailed by the small number of persons to whom it applied.

Recommendations

Although it is difficult to formalize informal processes, especially that of the working relationship between the former governor and his or her staff and the successor, future Georgia transition procedures would be improved by several new provisions. Governor Harris's close involvement in the preparation of the supplementary budget for the current year and the proposed budget for the new fiscal year was critical to his being able to introduce his budgetary proposals within a few days after inauguration. Perhaps this will continue in future transitions, but incorporating it into the law governing transitions would be more likely to ensure its continued practice.

A second factor in the Busbee-Harris transition was the availability of offices for the Harris transition staff that were located close to the governor's office within the capitol. Although the law specifies that the governor-elect and his staff will be supplied offices, there is no guarantee that the offices will be in the capitol itself. Offices located in the capitol facilitate interaction between the new and old staffs. They also provide ready access to the staff by a public that is more familiar with the location of the state capitol than out-of-the-way offices in a far corner of a state office building or in nearby rental space.

Third, the briefing book containing appointment and office organization information was helpful. This was no doubt a product made possible by the enthusiasm of key Busbee staff members in assisting the transition of a candidate whom they liked and supported. That motivation will not always exist, but it may, in fact, be necessary before such information will be prepared. Therefore, the provision of such information would be encouraged if it were required by the state law governing transition.

Finally, the $50,000 appropriation for transition expenses is substantial, greater than that provided in many states. However, the amount has not grown with inflation since the original law was passed more than a decade ago and in future transitions may not be large enough to cover expenses, particularly if the outgoing governor should for any reason require such assistance. There are, of course, many ways to supplement this amount—by borrowing staff from state agencies or placing staff on state agency payrolls or by simply using postage from other accounts. These options are facilitated when a friendly successor is taking over from a friendly predecessor. Because such circumstances will not always occur, the amount should be increased and then tied to an inflation factor such as the cost-of-living index so that it could grow with inflation.

The Gubernatorial Transition
in Iowa, 1982–1983

RUSSELL M. ROSS

The state of Iowa has an image problem. It is almost always thought of as a strictly rural, agricultural state. It is also almost always considered a conservative state, both economically and politically. Actually, Iowa is more urban than rural and, at times, has been more liberal than conservative. More than 55 percent of the population resides within what the U.S. Census Bureau defines as urban areas. In 1978 Iowa had two U.S. senators who were recognized as being among the most liberal in the Senate. Likewise, more Iowans are employed in manufacturing than in agriculture.

Iowa has been traditionally considered a Republican, one-party state. However, in the past twenty years, politics in Iowa has changed. Instead of always being in the Republican column in every election, Iowans have begun to split their tickets and to vote for the individual candidate rather than for the political party at the head of the column.

The election of 1982 was to continue the new Iowa tradition of split-ticket voting and swinging from control by one political party to control by the other. Prior to the off-presidential election, Iowa had a state government dominated by the Republican party. The governor was Republican Robert D. Ray, a five-term governor; a Republican lieutenant governor, Terry Branstad; a Republican secretary of state, Mary Jane Odell; a Republican secretary of agriculture, Robert Lounsberry; a Republican state auditor, Robert Johnson; a Republican state treasurer, Maurice Barringer; and a Democratic attorney general, Tom Miller. The state senate was controlled by the Republicans, as was the state house of representatives.

The Iowa delegation to the U.S. Congress was divided between the two parties: three U.S. House members were Democrats, and three were Republicans. Both of Iowa's U.S. senators were Republicans.

In January 1983 and for the first time in fourteen years, Iowa had a change in the person seated in the governor's chair. Robert D. Ray (R) was the incumbent for three two-year terms and for two four-year terms, 1969–83. No other governor in Iowa history had served more than six years. However, Ray decided in March 1982 not to seek election to a sixth term.

Ray's lieutenant governor, Terry Branstad, immediately announced that he would be a candidate for the Republican gubernatorial nomination. Two other Republicans—Arthur Neu, a lieutenant governor in an early Ray administration, and Tom Stoner, a former chairman of the Republican state central committee—briefly considered running, but both decided not to enter the race. Branstad was therefore unopposed in the 1982 Republican primary election.

Three Democrats contested for the party's gubernatorial nomination. The first to announce was Roxanne Conlin, a former Iowa assistant attorney general and a federal district attorney during the Carter administration. Next to enter the race was Ed Campbell, a former chairman of the Democratic state central committee and an assistant to Harold Hughes while Hughes was Iowa's governor and later a U.S. senator. Hughes had announced that he would seek the Democratic nomination for governor, but he withdrew when Secretary of State Odell ruled that he could not qualify because he had not lived in Iowa for two years prior to the election, as required by the Iowa constitution. (Hughes had voted in Maryland in the 1980 general elections.) The third person in the contest was Jerome Fitzgerald, a former state representative and the Democratic nominee for governor in 1978.

Conlin won the Democratic nomination in the June direct primary election by a wide margin (over Campbell and Fitzgerald) to become the first woman nominated for governor in Iowa by one of the two major political parties.

The Campaign

During the first weeks of the campaign between Conlin and Branstad, Conlin was, according to the Iowa Poll of the *Des Moines Register*, ahead of the lieutenant governor by some twenty points. However, in late June, after the primary election, Conlin disclosed that she and her husband had not been required to pay any state income tax, despite their net worth of over $2 million, because of investments in tax shelters. Her lead in the polls immediately declined, and the race was termed "too close to call" a week before the November 2 election. It is ironic that prior to the revelation of her financial situation, Conlin had condemned the "fat-cat Republicans" who avoid paying taxes by investing in tax shelters and had vowed that she would change the laws that allowed this practice.

Conlin and Branstad agreed that the state faced a financial crisis. However, Branstad said that he believed it could be solved by further governmental "belt-tightening" without raising any major tax, thus following the pattern that Governor Ray had so successfully followed for fourteen years. Branstad reportedly said that a tax increase would be signed only as a "last resort."

Conlin said that she would examine all the taxes and would probably agree to some increase in state taxes to solve the crisis. Late in the campaign she brought forth a plan for selling twenty-year general obligation bonds worth $300 million; the money was to be used to upgrade the Iowa "infrastructure"—its bridges, roads, and sewage systems. This plan, she asserted, would create new jobs for Iowa's unemployed as well as improve the highway transportation system. Branstad opposed the bonding plan but said that he would create 180,000 new jobs in five years by working one day a week with the Iowa Development Commission to attract new industries, particularly high-tech plants. Branstad attempted to identify himself with the Ray programs, pointing to his six years in the Iowa General Assembly and four years as Ray's lieutenant governor.

The two candidates engaged in a series of statewide televised debates in which it became clear that although Branstad was the more conservative of the two, Conlin was certainly not an ultraliberal. The ERA issue did become a part of the campaign: Conlin was the first president of the National Organization for Women (NOW) in Iowa and a staunch supporter of the state and the national ERA. (The equal rights amendment to the Iowa constitution had been defeated by the voters of Iowa in 1980.) The abortion issue likewise separated the two candidates: Conlin supported the U.S. Supreme Court decision; Branstad opposed abortion, except to save the mother's life. Conlin called for limiting the amount of federal income tax payments that could be deducted from the Iowa income tax liability. Branstad again said this plan would be unfair and opposed her limit of $15,000 of federal tax deductibility. Branstad proposed the establishment of an overseas office to promote Iowa products in Southeast Asia, a proposal that Governor Ray had made to the Iowa General Assembly several times. One foreign office has been in existence in West Germany for several years, but its success has been limited, according to most authorities. Branstad pointed to the fact that Iowa, as a leading exporter of agricultural products, needed greater promotion in foreign markets.

Financing the Campaign

In his efforts to become Iowa's thirty-ninth governor, the Republican lieutenant governor raised and spent a record amount, according to reports filed with the Iowa Campaign Finance Disclosure Commission. Branstad's final report disclosed expenditures of $1,004,000, but this did not include a long list of "in kind" contributions for which there is no way of establishing actual value. The Branstad campaign ended with a surplus of $11,000.

More than 10,000 Iowans gave money to the lieutenant governor's campaign for the top position. The figures show that the Branstad campaign had broad support, with no more than 7 percent of his identifiable contributions coming from persons in one occupation. However, owners and employees of state-regulated businesses gave about $1 of every $6 raised. It must be noted that nearly half of Branstad's money came from unidentified contributors who each gave $100 or less, as allowed by law.

Although 10,000 Iowans contributed, fewer than 1,000 contributors provided more than half of the Republican candidate's money. In addition to $48,000 donated by individual bankers and their spouses, Iowans who were directors on bank boards gave another $67,000. Persons identified as manufacturers gave about $60,000. The largest single contribution was $5,000 from Gary Vermeer, chairman of Vermeer Manufacturing of Pella, Iowa—a manufacturer of irrigation and tree-removal equipment. Forty-nine special interest political action committees (PACS) gave Branstad a total of $61,447.

Conlin's final campaign financial report disclosed an expenditure of about $780,000. The last report stated that two people had lent her campaign money—her husband, James Conlin, lent her $14,000, and Charles E. Currey, the treasurer of the Democratic National Committee, lent the candidate $15,000 a few days before the November 2 election. Conlin made a personal loan to the campaign fund of $50,000 before the June primary. Among the PAC contributions were $5,000 from NOW, a PAC of

Des Moines, and $4,650 from the Iowa Committee on Political Education, Des Moines. At the end of the last reporting period, the Conlin campaign had a debt of about $75,000. The three other unsuccessful Democratic candidates—Hughes, Campbell, and Fitzgerald—reported having spent $583,300 during the first six months of the year. Thus, it is certain that more than $2 million was spent in the 1982 Iowa governor's race—by far the most expensive race in the state's history. One of the reasons for the high total was the widespread use of television (the use of the other mass media was relatively limited). The reports indicated that the four major gubernatorial candidates—two Democrats and two Republicans—spent more than $359,000 on television.

Republican Terry Branstad—called Iowa's first million-dollar governor—spent an average of at least $1.83 for each of the 547,700 votes he received in the November 2, 1982, election. The previous record was held by former Governor Robert D. Ray, who spent approximately $500,000 in 1978, or about $1.05 per vote, in winning his final four-year term in office.

The Election Results

In 1982 Iowans turned out in record numbers for a nonpresidential election. Once again, Iowa voters split their ballots between Republicans and Democrats but to an even greater degree than in recent political history. Neither U.S. Senate post was on the 1982 ballot. All six incumbent members of the House (three Republicans and three Democrats) were candidates for reelection, and all six were easy winners. Although 55 percent of the votes for governor went to Republican candidate Branstad, his lieutenant governor, Larry Pope, was defeated by Democrat Robert Anderson. (In Iowa the governor and the lieutenant governor run separately in the election.)

Further evidence of the splitting of tickets by Iowa voters became clear: the Republican incumbent secretary of state, Mary Jane Odell, was overwhelmingly reelected; the longtime incumbent Republican state treasurer, Maurice Barringer, was defeated by Democrat Mike Fitzgerald. The other Democrat to win a statewide contest was incumbent Tom Miller, elected to his second four-year term as attorney general. Two other Republican incumbents that serve on the Iowa Executive Council—Robert Johnson, State auditor, and Robert Lounsberry, secretary of agriculture—won reelection handily.

Thus, a majority of Iowa voters favored Republicans for governor, secretary of state, state auditor, and secretary of agriculture but elected a Democratic lieutenant governor, state attorney general, and state treasurer. To compound the complicated political picture, the Democratic party won control of both houses of the Iowa General Assembly after both had been controlled by the Republicans for four years. The margin in the house was twenty (sixty Democrats and forty Republicans); in the senate the ratio was twenty-eight to twenty-two. The newly elected Democratic lieutenant governor presides over the Iowa State Senate.

The Ray-Branstad Relationship

The 1982 campaign for governor in Iowa made it "perfectly clear" that Republican candidate Branstad would follow the approach that Republican Governor Ray had followed for fourteen years—if at all possible. His entire campaign was based on his support of the Ray administration while he served for four years as the lieutenant governor. "Only as a last resort" would Branstad depart from Ray's course of fiscal responsibility, and he would not increase any major taxes. Likewise, the Branstad campaign included many references to the fact that the lieutenant governor had "total confidence" in the administrators and staff that had served with Ray.

Immediately following the election Ray declared that he would make the transition to the Branstad administration the smoothest possible so that Branstad could "hit the ground running, so to speak." A three-person transition team was named: Wendall Harms, Branstad's campaign manager; Rand Fisher, a campaign staffer; and Branstad's press secretary, Susan Neely. This group of three was assisted by Branstad's staff in the lieutenant governor's office: Jerry Mathiason, his administrative assistant, and Grace Copley, his personal secretary. Campaign funds augmented the $10,000 allowed by Iowa statute for use in the transition from governor to new governor. The transition team worked in the lieutenant governor's offices in the capitol.

Under Iowa law outgoing Governor Ray could have submitted a budget to the 1983 Iowa General Assembly for fiscal years 1983–85, but he announced immediately after the election that he would not do so but would "help Branstad develop his own budget and legislative proposals." Ray further said, "We want to assist him. We are not here to dictate at all. We shouldn't. We couldn't, and we won't." Ray declined to give Branstad any public advice on how to deal with the Democratic-controlled house and senate, saying, "Branstad, as a former legislator and presiding officer in the Senate, has plenty of experience in working with law-makers."

Although Ray did not prepare a budget message, he did present a final "condition of the state" message in January 1983 to the seventieth Iowa General Assembly—his fourteenth such statement. In the thirty-five-minute speech he discussed in relatively general terms some of the highlights of his accomplishments during his five-term administration. Although asserting that he would not suggest a "specific 35-point or a 56-point program," departing Governor Ray did leave several suggestions that the general assembly "might want to consider," such as the recommendations of his high-tech task force, the board of regents' bonding program, the sixty proposals of the Blue Ribbon Transportation Task Force, and the Health Care Cost Containment Task Force recommendations. He also suggested reconsideration of having an office in Washington, D.C., and an Iowa office in Southeast Asia. Likewise, he asserted that the people should be allowed to use a local-option concept to raise revenue for local governmental units. In his last address Ray told the legislature, "Our new governor is experienced and he's prepared for this office. There hasn't been a smoother or better transition in the United States. And Terry, I stand ready to help in any way that you ask."

The Branstad Transition

During the transition, between the November 2 election and his inauguration on January 14, Governor-elect Branstad spent a "most profitable" weekend in Park City, Utah, at the transition seminar sponsored by the National Governors' Association (NGA). (Governor Ray, who had helped start the school and who served on the faculty, addressed the problem of how the governor should deal with reporters.)

During the transition period Bonnie Smalley was in charge of the governor-elect's schedule, and Grace Copley continued as his confidential secretary. They were the gatekeepers who had a "lot to say about what Branstad did with his time; where he went; who he saw and for how long; and who got through to him on the telephone." Mathiason's role in the transition was to coordinate the appointments that Branstad was to make to state boards and commissions and to department head positions. Approximately 1,200 appointments are made by the Iowa governor, but since many positions are for four or more years, only about

400 were to be made during the first six months of the new administration.

Governor-elect Branstad, his assistant for finance, Rand Fisher, and the state comptroller, Ronald Mosher, conducted budget hearings for all state departments, boards, commissions, and agencies during the last part of November and the month of December 1982. These hearings allowed each agency an opportunity to support orally the requests that they had submitted to comptroller Mosher weeks before the November 2 election. Because Iowa's governor must, by law, present a balanced budget to the Iowa General Assembly before February 1 and Governor Ray was not presenting an outgoing budget, it was necessary for the new administration to address the budget questions early and in detail.

Susan Neeley and Rand Fisher, members of the transition team, were the primary assistants in crafting the inaugural speech that was designed to "set the tone, theme and goals for the administration, and the budget message that details how Branstad wants to spend the tax dollars to reach these goals."

Staffing the New Administration

From the very start of the political campaign Terry Branstad had declared that there would be no "wholesale house-cleaning of key personnel." Certainly he followed this pledge to a very high degree. Only two major department heads were discharged. Stanley McCausland, director of General Services, was replaced by Des Moines business executive Jack Walters. William Miller, commissioner of the Public Safety Department, was discharged in favor of Gene Shepard, an attorney from Allison, Iowa, who had had experience as deputy sheriff, city attorney, and county attorney. Personnel who were Ray appointees continued in the roles of state comptroller, social services director, state revenue director, director of the Iowa Development Commission, and director of the Office for Planning and Programming. With these major reappointments Branstad ensured that the administrative policy and style established under the fourteen-year Ray regime would be unchanged, at least during the early months of the new administration.

Even within the governor's personal office staff, an amazing amount of continuity was to be maintained. It is usually recognized that two key members of the governor's personal staff are the person in charge of legislative liaison and the top assistant—the executive assistant to the governor. Governor Branstad asked outgoing Governor Ray's appointees to continue in these pivotal roles: David Oman, as the executive assistant, and Douglas Gross, as the legislative liaison administrative assistant. It must be noted that the remainder of the members of Governor Branstad's personal staff had either served him while he was lieutenant governor or held key roles in the election campaign. Thus, continuity was maintained in every possible way between the Ray and the Branstad eras.

The new governor established his theme by asserting in his inaugural message, "I am committed to continuing Iowa's tradition of open, honest, just and compassionate government. I will be careful and conservative with your tax dollars and caring and compassionate about human needs." Branstad asserted that his top job would be to help the unemployed find jobs and declared that government "can serve as a catalyst to help spur economic growth." He also assured the jobless workers in the state that their unemployment insurance trust fund monies would be forthcoming.

Two former governors, Ray and Hughes, were praised for having moved Iowa government "ahead by light years." The new governor declared that he would build on the "progressive government" that he had inherited. It was made clear in the inaugural message that Governor Branstad was attempting to move from his conservative image as a candidate to the image of a governor in the political center. The new governor also clarified his pledge of full cooperation with the Democratic-controlled legislature, asking them "to meet me halfway."

Among the highlights of the governor's maiden speech were calls for a dramatic change in the way that utility rates are set in Iowa, the establishment of a consumer appellate advocate to protect utility customers before the Commerce Commission, the establishment of an Iowa export office in Asia, the creation of an Iowa fund to encourage citizens to invest in Iowa business, and a narrowing of the tuition gap between the private colleges and the state-supported universities. He also asked that a Citizen's Advisory Commission on Corrections be established and promised to create a Governor's Task Force on Efficiency and Cost Effectiveness.

As former Republican speaker of the house William Harbor said, "It is a continuation of the Ray era, at least initially." Democratic senator Berl Priebe declared that the speech demonstrated that Branstad "is continuing to move toward the political center," adding "when he

[Branstad] first came down to Des Moines, he was a lot further to the right than he is now." Former Governor Ray felt that the speech "was well done. I thought it showed that he can be conciliatory and at the same time have a firm direction. I think he mapped out a modern approach to the problems that is also pragmatic."

The new Democratic lieutenant governor, Robert Anderson, declared that he did not mind Branstad's move to get behind some traditional Democratic issues. "What is important to me as a Democrat are the issues—that the people are taken care of as far as those issues being put into law. As long as it passes and becomes law, I don't really care whose idea it was—and the people on the street don't care either." Republican representative Ray Lageshute possibly summed it up best when he stated, "He sounded like a good moderate Republican."

The Budget Problems

At the completion of the budget hearings held by the new governor and the state comptroller, it became clear that the state treasury would be very nearly in the red by the end of the fiscal year. Iowa law requires that a statewide property tax be instituted if the treasury is depleted. Thus, it became evident that some type of tax increase would be necessary.

Governor Branstad asserted in his budget message of January 21, 1983, that asking for an increase in the sales tax was "the most difficult decision I have ever had to make." He went on to say, "For years I have said raising a tax should be a last resort. I believe that is where we are today. The alternatives are unacceptable." Thus, Branstad departed from the advice of his conservative supporters and took a major turn away from the fiscal conservative game plan favored by former Governor Ray. The recommendation to the Iowa General Assembly called for a 1-cent increase in the sales tax, to be effective on April 1. However, the Democratic-managed legislature in less than one week did even better by making the increase to a 4-percent sales tax effective on March 1. Governor Branstad projected that the increased sales tax would bring in an additional $39 million the 1983–84 budget year and would increase the revenue by $168 million in the new fiscal year.

The governor called for no major cuts in any state programs and predicted a 3.8-percent growth in state revenues for fiscal 1984. Some critics of the governor's plans suggested that this increase was too high and that revenue returns for February 1983 were actually less than for February 1982. However, the proposed budget did call for a freeze on all state employees' salaries. A major series of building projects, primarily at the three state universities, was urged by the governor as a method of creating new construction jobs. He also suggested increasing the Iowa tuition grants to Iowans attending private colleges, increasing vocational-technical grants, and instituting special incentives to teach math, science, and foreign languages.

Some degree of property tax relief would be forthcoming through a sizable increase in state aid to public elementary and secondary schools. Likewise, the budget would have the state assume a greater share of the costs of the state court system, now primarily funded by county property tax levies. The recommended budget also called for increased spending for Aid to Dependent Children; more money for Medicaid, nursing homes, and "homemaker and chore services"; and the continuation of the Unemployed Parent Program, with a new workfare provision. Finally, one new appropriation would allocate approximately $300,000 to start a racing commission to oversee the parimutuel betting law.

Branstad's Legislative Program

Governor Branstad's legislative program fared well in the Iowa legislature. Forty-six of his fifty-four proposals were enacted into law, in spite of the fact that both houses were controlled by the Democrats. The final appropriation figures show that the legislature budgeted about $12.5 million more than the governor had recommended. The final spending recommendations were for $2.048 billion for the first year of the biennium.

Branstad's first veto was a rejection of a bill that would have changed the method that the public school districts used in terminating teachers. The bill was strongly supported by the Iowa State Education Association, whose PAC had endorsed Branstad's opponent, Roxanne Conlin. The governor claimed that he objected to the changes that the bill would make in collective bargaining between school boards and teachers.

The second bill vetoed by Governor Branstad was the state lottery. The governor asserted: "Our state has prided itself on its honest, open and clean government. I fear that involving the government in promoting and profiting from gambling activities that do not have general legal or moral sanction could reduce the strength and effectiveness of our state government." Democratic house speaker Don Avenson responded, "I absolutely can't understand how the governor can say on the one hand [that] parimutuel betting, which has a long history of criminal problems, is good for the state, but a lottery, which is nothing more than a state raffle, is bad for the state." The governor had signed the state parimutuel betting bill into law.

The first item veto exercised by the new governor rejected a clause attached to the appropriations for the state auditor and the state treasurer that their offices be moved from the state capitol to other state office buildings. The legislature planned to take over the vacated space for use by the legislators.

The transition truly came to an end when Governor Branstad used his veto power sixteen times after the adjournment of the Iowa General Assembly. Among the measures sponsored by the Democrats, Branstad vetoed both the state lottery and the establishment of mini-liquor stores. The leaders of the Democrats in the legislature claimed that the governor had broken the cooperative spirit that had prevailed during the legislative session. Majority leader Lowell Junkins (D) and Avenson were particularly critical of the item veto that cut in half the $24.9-million job bill. Avenson said, "Jobs was our number one priority; we said jobs legislation was what this legislature hoped to be judged by."

The Transition: An Assessment

There were many firsts in the 1982–83 gubernatorial election and transition. (1) First gubernatorial election campaign in Iowa in which a candidate spent more than $1 million. (2) First time that a woman was nominated by a major political party to seek the office of governor. (3) First time the governor was the youngest chief executive serving in any state. (4) First time that a member of the Catholic faith was elected to the Iowa governorship. (5) First time that a new Iowa governor retained his predecessor's executive assistant and the administrative assistant for legislative liaison. (6) First time that a retiring governor left his papers in the state archives. (7) First time that an incoming governor faced a treasury deficit within his first six months in office. (8) First time that a new governor's approval rating reached 70 percent in his first term. (9) First time that a Republican held the office of governor while a Democrat held the office of lieutenant governor. (10) First time in thirty years that an Iowa governor was succeeded by a member of his own party.

The transition from Governor Ray to his successor, Terry Branstad, was a textbook operation. All the characters in the scenario followed the script to the letter. Even the suggested timetable was followed almost without deviation. Governor Ray vowed from the night of the election that he and his staff would do everything possible to make the transition the best in the nation. It may have been.

Among the main contributions to the smoothness of the change was the fact that although Branstad appeared to be more conservative than Governor Ray during the campaign, he nevertheless retained nearly all the key members of the Ray administrative team. Branstad, having been a member of the Iowa General Assembly for six years and having served four years as lieutenant governor in the last Ray administration, was totally familiar with all phases of the state governmental operation. Although Ray did not publicly give the new governor advice, it must be assumed that the outgoing governor's influence was extensive during their many private meetings in the weeks following the election. Branstad has asserted that he was impressed by the seminar for new governors and received much valuable information in the sessions. It is quite clear that he followed the recommendations of the NGA publication *Transition and the New Governor*.[1]

The new staff members of the Branstad team appear to have meshed with the members of the Ray staff, who continued to serve in the Iowa governor's office. Even Ray's timetable for press conferences was adopted by the new governor. Another factor that possibly contributed to the successful transition was that former Governor Ray placed all his papers in the state archives, thus making them readily available to the new governor's staff. Many governors in the past had followed the policy that the papers were their personal possessions and had disposed of them. Governor Hughes placed all his papers in the University of Iowa Library.

Further evidence that the gubernatorial transition was of high quality came in the results of the 1983 mid-March Iowa Poll conducted by the *Des Moines Register*. Seventy percent of the 1,005 Iowans included in the sample expressed the opinion that Governor Branstad had performed well in his first ninety days in office. This was a higher approval rate for Iowa's youngest governor than that given either Governor Ray (R) or Governor Hughes (D) after their first six months in office (the two governors recognized as the most popular Iowa chief executives in the twentieth century). It should be noted that when the surveys on Ray and Hughes were taken, the state legislature had completed its session; the Branstad public approval was given more than a month before the legislative session ended.

The satisfaction of Iowans with their new governor surprised some political observers because of his having recommended a 33-percent increase in the state sales tax (from 3 cents to 4 cents). Many conservative supporters had warned Branstad that it would be political suicide to adopt such a position after his political campaign posture of opposing any major tax increase. It is interesting that nearly one-third of the Iowans who expressed approval of the way Governor Branstad was performing could not cite a specific reason for their attitude—a result possibly reflecting their satisfaction with the transition from Ray to Branstad.

Massachusetts:
The Changing of the Guard

MARTHA WAGNER WEINBERG

On November 2, 1983, Michael Dukakis was elected governor of Massachusetts, easily defeating Republican John Sears by a margin of almost 475,000 votes. Dukakis's wide margin of victory in the general election belied the difficulty of a campaign begun almost four years before when Dukakis, the incumbent in the 1978 election, was defeated in the Democratic primary by Edward J. King. Indeed, if there is any single theme that conditioned the style and content of both the 1982 election campaign and the transition, it was Dukakis's continual insistence that he had learned from his defeat and would not make the same mistakes in his second term (mistakes that he felt had led to his defeat in 1978). Unlike most of the nation's governors who had ousted an incumbent, he was not new to the job. Also, unlike the transitions of most of the others, his whole transition effort was characterized by a zealous determination to avoid what he assumed had been his mistakes the first time around. As Dukakis himself put it, "My whole way of dealing with the transition was conditioned by having been through it before. I am a different person: more comfortable in the job, more experienced. And I knew what I had in front of me. You can't know what kinds of problems will confront you until you've actually been elected and have had the experience of trying to take over and manage. It makes all the difference in the world to have been there before."[1]

The Backdrop:
The Candidate, the Context, and the Election

After his surprise defeat in 1978 by Edward J. King (who subsequently defeated Republican Francis Hatch and became governor), Dukakis accepted a senior lectureship at the John F. Kennedy School of Government at Harvard. The Kennedy School served not only as a refuge for Dukakis from the immediate hurley-burley world of politics but also, almost immediately after his arrival, as a base from which to launch his campaign and, ultimately, as an important source for campaign advisors and members of the transition staff and the new administration. Thus, unlike many of his counterparts who took office in January of 1983, Dukakis had spent four years officially out of public life and had had time to reflect on his experience as governor and to teach and think about generic issues of public management. Because of his personal temperament and style and as a result of his belief that crises and complex issues of public policy could and should be managed, a managed process of governance became a hallmark of the Dukakis campaign, transition, and administration.

There were many similarities between the 1978 and 1982 campaigns. Because more than 45 percent of Massachusetts voters are registered Democrats and almost 40 percent are independents who most frequently vote Democratic, the Democratic primary is often the crucial election in Massachusetts. The 1978 and 1982 primary elections were infused with a spirit of cultural and ideological warfare, pitting the more fiscally and socially conservative King Democrats against the more liberal, professional, "Brie-and-white-wine" Dukakis supporters. Both primaries turned on the issue of the incumbent's ability to keep his coalition together and to get out the vote. In 1978 Dukakis had lost crucial support among several groups of Democratic voters who had propelled him to victory over Republican Francis Sargent in 1974. Despite his "lead pipe guarantee" during the 1974 campaign that if he were elected governor there would be no new taxes, in 1975 he signed into law the largest tax increase in the state's history, an act on which King capitalized in the 1978 campaign. In addition, during his first term, he cut back social programs and decreased state spending, actions that cost him support among liberal Democrats and state employees. Finally, Dukakis suffered from a fact of incumbency that can be a disadvantage when it is recognized and used by a skilled challenger: he was the target of a number of disaffected interest groups whose causes he had not championed as governor.

By 1982 the political climate had changed. As governor, King had proposed and carried out a number of conservative social programs, actions that made liberals formerly disaffected from Dukakis take another look and return to the Dukakis camp. Although in 1982 unemployment in Massachusetts was 84 percent of the national average, many citizens were disturbed by the economy and placed some of the blame for its sorry state on King, described publicly by Ronald Reagan as his "favorite Democratic governor." In addition, many cities and towns were reeling under the impact of the loss of property revenue under Proposition 2½, prompting local officials and residents to criticize King for not coming to their aid. Finally, the King administration was plagued by a series of scandals that received extensive media coverage and that focused attention throughout the campaign on the issue of King's honesty and competence. Dukakis, who, according to public opinion polls, was perceived as totally honest, seized the issue of honesty and integrity in government. He also made a major effort to overcome his image of being rigid and aloof, emphasizing again and again what he had "learned" from his previous defeat: being "political" was not necessarily bad, and rewarding friends and supporters who had been loyal and competent was an acceptable, perhaps even intelligent, way of behaving.

The campaign for the Democratic nomination was long and expensive. By the end of the first week in September, King had raised $3 million and Dukakis $2.5. King ran a media campaign, spending $2 million on radio and television advertising. Dukakis, in comparison, spent approximately $800,000 on television and radio and relied on one of the broadest-based field organizations of "donor-activists" that had ever been assembled in a Massachusetts campaign. The average contribution to the King campaign was $250; the average contribution to Dukakis was $70.[2] In addition to building a 50,000-person fund-raising base, which was tapped during the one and one-half years before the primary, Dukakis organizers, to ensure a wide base of support, set up ten issue task forces and divided the state into a 200-area field organization.

Dukakis defeated King in the September primary, winning 53.5 percent of the vote. Turnout was unusually heavy: 1,176,000 voters, 300,000 more than had voted in any previous gubernatorial primary, participated. In comparison, only 178,000 people voted in the Republican primary, which was won by former Boston city councillor John Sears. Though Dukakis continued to push his organization hard and raised $900,000 between the primary and general elections, many observers considered the general election both anticlimactic and dull and accurately predicted the outcome—a landslide victory for Dukakis over Sears.

Transition Policy and Process

The groundwork for a well-thought-out plan for the transition was laid even before the September primary and was initiated by Dukakis himself. According to Dukakis campaign manager (and, later, chief secretary) John Sasso, Dukakis felt that the transition period in his first administration had been chaotic: "He'd come to believe in the importance of the transition period and the first few weeks of a new governor's term. It's the time, more than any other, when you're put under a microscope and you have to know how to perform."[3]

During the summer of 1982 Dukakis asked his Kennedy School colleague Charles Kireker to look at material on transition experiences in the federal government and in other states and, by September, to write a memorandum laying out the tasks necessary to ensure a smooth transition if there should be one. Kireker was a logical choice for several reasons. He had worked with several state governments and had studied transitions while at the Kennedy School. Dukakis had worked with him before and trusted him, an important consideration because of the necessarily low-key nature of an undertaking that assumed victory while a hard-fought campaign was going on. In addition, Kireker had no role in the campaign and had no personal or professional ties to those who were trying to be influential in the campaign. His assignment was designed to be done alone and with discretion.

Not until after the primary did the numbers of those who were thinking about the transition expand, and even their activities were low-key and sharply circumscribed. Paul Brountas, an influential lawyer, longtime Dukakis confidant, and chairman of the campaign, and William Geary, appointments secretary during Dukakis's first term and legislative liaison during the summer of 1982, joined Kireker as members of an informal advisory group that met with Dukakis and campaign director Sasso once a week. The focus of most of the meetings was on clearcut "process" questions: how to manage the logistics of the transition; how to handle the high volume of résumés and mail; how to fund and organize a staff; where to locate transition offices; and how to turn a campaign organization into a working government.

According to both Kireker and Sasso, the pretransition group explicitly decided not to develop policy papers or recommendations for staffing and personnel decisions.[4] The intention was to avoid any diversion of effort from the campaign by those whose long-term objectives might include a position or influence in the new Dukakis administration and to keep attention on the nitty-gritty but important details of the transition. The only consideration that was given to policy development by this group occurred in the few weeks before the general election, when they reviewed positions that the candidate had taken during the campaign and identified four key issues (later picked up in Dukakis's inaugural address) to be the focal point of the last days of the campaign and the early days of the administration. This focus was in keeping with Dukakis's strongly held conviction that he could not come into office with a "laundry list" but, instead, needed to build support within the campaign organization and with external constituencies (particularly the legislature) around a limited number of issues.[5]

This informal transition group continued to advise Dukakis in the days immediately following his election. One week after his election Dukakis officially named campaign manager Sasso the director of the transition, ensuring continuity by linking the transition to the campaign organization. On the day after his election, however, he made it clear that important decisions had already been made about the transition process and about the government. In describing his criteria for selecting personnel, he identified what was to become the "competency and loyalty" theme of the "new" Michael Dukakis, who had learned from his mistakes in his first try at the job: "I think that the principal question has to be competency. The fact that someone worked for me in the campaign is not to disqualify him from serving in the administration. There are thousands of people who were involved in this campaign who are extremely able and extremely competent."[6] In addition, he said that he would soon name a full-time transition advisory committee, a group that was to play a key role in screening personnel and solidifying ties to constituencies.

The twenty-three-member Transition Advisory Committee (or TAC, as it came to be known) was named the following week. The stated purpose of the TAC was "to assist in the selection of key appointees, to serve as a sounding board for setting priorities of the administration and to maintain links with the interest groups that were a vital part of Dukakis' base of support."[7] The membership was drawn from the ranks of business, labor, local government, the legislature, minorities, and women. The TAC was also predominantly made up of individuals who had longtime personal and/or political relationships with Dukakis.

The TAC was to become the principal vehicle to aid Dukakis and his small transition staff in recruitment and screening of top-level personnel in the new government. The group met four times between the announcement of its formation and the first day of December to discuss criteria for the selection of personnel for important government jobs and to produce a list (called the Gang of 100) of persons who should be considered for positions in the cabinet and on the governor's office staff. In addition, the TAC made recommendations and assessed the qualifications of specific candidates for specific jobs and considered how particular clusters of individuals would operate as a group. Finally, five subcommittees of the TAC interviewed almost 100 people during a three-week period and, using these interviews and other material, recommended candidates for eleven cabinet positions. The names and biographical data of those not selected for the cabinet became part of a talent pool from which the cabinet secretaries could draw in staffing their own executive offices.

In addition to accomplishing much of the substantive personnel work of the earliest days of the administration, the TAC also functioned symbolically, providing Dukakis with a forum for articulating what he had learned from his experience as governor and how he had changed. Intent on dispelling his former image as someone who made decisions quickly and listened to no one, he had constructed a slow, deliberate process. One member of the TAC commented: "What you are seeing is a new Dukakis. He is more reflective, less ready to make pronouncements solely out of his own head. He is more interested in counsel and advice. He listens better." Another TAC member agreed: "He is very sensitive to past history: [charges] that he was not sufficiently receptive to constructive ideas, new names, alternative views and criticism. Now he is very amenable, open to hearing it all."[8]

The transition staff and the TAC formed the backbone of the Dukakis transition team during the month after the election. It was not until December 7 that Dukakis named Sasso chief secretary, the title of the chief staff person in the governor's office in Massachusetts. On the same day he announced the appointment of Frank Keefe as secretary of administration and finance, the state's chief fiscal and budgetary officer. This announcement of his first cabinet secretary signaled what the transition team assumed would be the final phase of the transition, the formation of the permanent government, whose members would eventually take over responsibility for running the government. Although this part of the transition did eventually occur, the pace was much slower than the transition group had originally anticipated: the full cabinet was not in place until January 20.

Some critics of the transition process have suggested that in falling behind on his goal of having the cabinet in place by the end of December, Dukakis had lost control of a crucial element of his own strategy. Dukakis felt otherwise:

> I wanted to get good people on board as soon as possible. But my central emphasis was on getting good people. Because of the confusion at Massport [Dukakis had, in a set of stunning moves, taken control of the board of the Massachusetts Port Authority in his first week in office, and, as a result, wanted to coordinate his final cabinet appointments with the appointment of a Massport executive director] I had to slow down a little. But I had believed all along that the world wouldn't come to an end if I hadn't named the full cabinet by January 6. Selecting people for jobs doesn't stop. It's an ongoing process. What's most important is getting excellent people in.[9]

The Mechanics:
Transition Provisions, Procedures, and Support

There are no provisions in Massachusetts law to deal with the transition from one administration to another. In 1974 when Dukakis took over the governor's office from Francis Sargent, Sargent offered him financial support from the Governor's Emergency Reserve Fund, but Dukakis did not accept. In 1978 King requested and received $30,000 (of which he spent $15,000) from Dukakis. In 1982 the Dukakis transition team asked that $60,000 from the Governor's Emergency Fund be allocated for the transition, a request that was approved by the chairmen of the Senate and the House Ways and Means committees and by King.

Despite the ease with which such requests have traditionally received approval, the process of establishing a budget for the transition is not an easy one in Massachusetts. Transition costs are difficult to estimate: as the volume of résumés and job inquiries increased in late November and early December, it became clear that the $60,000 appropriation would not begin to cover expenses. By the end of the transition period the transition organization had had to supplement the budget directly with $30,000 in campaign funds. This supplement led to a second problem of having to keep accounting systems and records that clearly distinguished between the uses of public money and the uses of campaign funds and that documented the legitimacy of both. Finally, according to Kireker, the uncertainty about funding and official procedures for the transition led to delays in getting personnel on board and some scrimping that forced the transition team to rely more on volunteer groups like the TAC to handle all parts of the personnel process than they otherwise might have done.

Although there was no formal provision for housing a transition staff, members of Governor King's staff offered the Dukakis group office space in state buildings. The Dukakis group rejected this offer and chose instead to open a transition office in the building that housed the Dukakis campaign. According to Kristin Demong, finance director of the Dukakis campaign, this choice guaranteed that key people would not be scattered in disparate buildings and helped ensure the smooth shutting down of the campaign and opening up of the government, without the constant scrutiny of state house and press onlookers.[10]

The problems resulting from the lack of an official body of rules and procedures for transitions could have been multiplied many times over had King and his administration decided to be uncooperative in the transition period. Even as early as the end of the primary campaign Dukakis and his chief secretary, Sasso, identified the importance of making certain that relationships with the outgoing governor were as smooth as possible. Dukakis gave a gracious victory speech and followed up with several informal and friendly calls and letters to King. He refrained from publicly criticizing most of King's last-minute appointments to existing and newly created jobs. In addition, as a way of fostering cooperation with agency personnel, he met with each of the outgoing cabinet secretaries. As a result, much of the hostility and undermining that might have been the logical product of a rancorous and bitter campaign were diffused, leaving the Dukakis staff free to concentrate on the job ahead rather than on the campaign they had just successfully concluded.

Despite the fact that the transition group had planned for management of the personnel search process by the staff and the TAC, they had neither anticipated the volume of résumés they would receive nor the time it would take to set up and operate a tracking system. During the week before the general election Dr. An Wang, president of Wang Laboratories, promised to lend the transition team sophisticated word-processing equipment to use to track résumés and to facilitate the personnel searches. The staff took a calculated risk that they could speed up the paper flow by using the equipment, a risk that they felt paid off.[11] Though the equipment eventually proved invaluable, it was not until the third week in November that staff members felt they understood how to use it. As a result, many duplicate names cropped up on lists maintained by the TAC, by the staff, and by key campaign operatives, and there was no single established procedure for submitting applications or suggestions to the new administration. "In retrospect," Kireker said in describing this problem, "I think we should have consulted with more people in the executive search business, or with people who were familiar with the problems of setting up personnel management systems for huge operations."[12]

The search for talented, high-level personnel was always the agreed top priority of the transition staff. Less important in the busy transition period was a systematic attempt to analyze and understand the state's personnel system and the ongoing budget process. The facts that no one from the transition team was assigned to learn the civil service system and that few on the transition team (with the exception of Dukakis) had experience with state personnel systems caused some problems and some delays for the new government. For example, during the hectic and crucial months of November, December, and January, many offices were operating without secretarial support or without any methods of identifying and working with the agency personnel who were carrying out budget and personnel functions in the state's agencies.

Immediately after the election Dukakis did deploy Demong and two members of the campaign staff to analyze and anticipate problems with the state budget that the King administration had already developed and discussed with appropriate committees of the legislature. Demong turned this responsibility over to Frank Keefe when he was appointed secretary of administration and finance. On December 31 Dukakis appointed Barbara Salisbury the state's budget director, leaving Salisbury only the period from January 6 until February 1 (when the budget was due at the printer) to pull together a staff, make contact with the agencies, caucus with the cabinet secretaries who had been appointed, and write the budget. Although Salisbury had had substantial budget experience as the chief manager of the budget of the Department of Public Welfare and although she felt that too much preliminary negotiation with ongoing agency personnel would likely have caused unnecessary unease and extensive politicking within the agencies, she still faced the task—with little staff and little good information—of putting the Dukakis imprint on the budget.[13]

Problems of the Transition:
Choices and Their Implications for Governance

Because the single most important goal of any transition effort is to set up a government that works successfully for those charged with the responsibility of governing for four years, clear-eyed assessments of the strengths and weaknesses of particular transitions can probably be done only after an entire administration has unfolded. In addition, it is difficult to assess systematically the success of much of the activity in a transition because it involves carrying on certain routine functions and anticipating and understanding possible pitfalls that will become noticeable only if they are neglected. It is impossible to enumerate the "dogs that didn't bite," despite the fact that they require enormous time and attention of the transition staff. For example, the policy staff of the transition team made up working groups on the four priority areas, maintained liaison with the King government, kept in touch with the task forces, created briefing books for the secretaries, kept a watchful eye on the legislature, and handled mail on particular issues. They also looked at issues that they deemed of particular significance, such as the status of collective bargaining agreements. In addition, the transition staff had to handle certain routine but critical functions, such as scheduling and managing relations with the press. They chose to perform other functions such as detailed résumé verification and police checks. One might argue that there can be no success stories in handling these routine functions. But the "dogs that don't bite" may be the source of spectacular failures if they go unattended.

However, it is clear that Dukakis and his key aides faced certain generic problems in taking over the government and that the style with which they attacked these problems and the choices they made have implications for the character of the government they run and for the style and substance of the policy for which they will be known. At least four broad categories of problems face all executives in taking over a new administration: those associated with moving from directing a campaign to running a government, those involved with sorting out priorities during the intense period between the election and the inauguration, those associated with getting control of basic systems, and those involved with setting a policy agenda.

MOVING FROM A CAMPAIGN TO A GOVERNMENT

All elected officials face tricky choices in figuring out how to shut down campaign organizations and start up governments. They can pursue one of three strategies: they can fold the campaign organization into the government; they can try to maintain the campaign organization along-side the government; or they can start fresh—walk away from an organi-zation designed to serve one purpose and look ahead to a new task. Du-kakis chose the first option. Having articulated his criteria of competence and loyalty during the campaign, Dukakis opted to rely on his campaign organization for many of his first appointees. Frank Keefe, who had served in his first administration and who had chaired a task force, was named secretary of administration and finance; Frederick Salvucci, sec-retary of transportation in the first administration and the campaign's expert on transportation issues, was appointed to his old job; and Ira Jackson, a key campaign advisor and a Kennedy School colleague of Du-kakis's, was named director of the embattled, scandal-ridden Department of Revenue.

Particularly significant was the designation of John Sasso, the cam-paign manager, first as director of the transition and then as chief of staff in the governor's office. According to Dukakis, the choice of Sasso for a chief of staff position was the product both of his reflections about problems in the first administration and of his own sense of what made him comfortable. "In my first term I had relied too much on the cabi-net and hadn't given enough thought to organizing and managing my own office. This time I decided to have a single chief of staff. I needed some centralization, but I'm not a 'spokes of the wheel,' multiple-deputies man. The idea of bringing on my campaign director fit. John had been excellent. Bringing him in fit with my predispositions about what my office ought to look like this time. And it ensured continuity with the campaign group."[14] Sasso in turn determined the structure of the governor's office, a structure that looked remarkably similar to that of the campaign organization, with eleven staff members reporting di-rectly to Sasso and Dukakis.

The spirit as well as the structure of the campaign organization car-ried over into the government. Dukakis and Sasso had conditioned the campaign organization to operate as a team. As one inside observer of the campaign and the transition put it: "Dukakis and Sasso are both 'detail guys,' retail decision makers if you will. They believe in process.

They want to trust their guys, know them, depend on them, then always be able to rely on the rules of the game to condition the team. There's no room for superstars, for grandstanding, for volatility. They want to go with what they know."[15]

By moving many members of the campaign organization directly into the new administration Dukakis avoided much of the disruption and the loss of energy that often occurs when a new governor's staff is constructed from scratch. He also avoided having to invest time in building a new set of working relationships in a period when his time and attention were at a premium. In addition, he showed his gratitude to those who had orchestrated his all-important electoral victory by giving them the most visible reward—jobs in his new administration.

In choosing to rely on his known and trusted campaign colleagues, he was also limiting his new government in several significant ways. First, he was assuming that those who had effectively run a campaign (where one major issue was the competence of the competition) would also be effective in managing a huge and complicated set of agencies. Second, he was opting to perpetuate an organization characterized by one observer as "made up of experiential learners rather than conceptual thinkers with strong and well conceived ideas about policy and management of governmental processes."[16] Finally, by selecting as his early appointees those with whom he had worked directly, he was foreclosing his options for bringing a whole new coterie into his administration. This decision posed special problems for Dukakis, who had run an exceptionally broad-based campaign, designed to evoke enthusiasm and support from a large number of donor-activists. Although he explicitly recognized the problem of keeping his government in touch with his constituencies by naming key campaign aide Margaret Xifaras to be, as several observers described the position, his "Anne Wexler," he did not use his early appointments to bring new constituencies and persons not well known to him into the government.

Nowhere was the complaint about the bias toward old hands expressed more frequently than on the issue task forces set up during the campaign. The more than 300 loyalists who had worked on the task forces had been summoned to frequent meetings and had also been asked repeatedly for campaign contributions. But because of the campaign managers' sensitivity to the problem of having large groups of enthusiasts who might assume that they were making policy for the new government, the task forces were never allowed to reach a consensus about recommendations or to produce final reports. Although five task force chairpersons became cabinet secretaries, a major blow for many task force activists, who believed that they had demonstrated loyalty and competence, was the feeling that they were excluded from early consideration for jobs in the new administration. As one task force member put it: "I had worked hard. I had given money. I'm a smart professional with experience in government. Despite all this, I couldn't figure out a way to get Dukakis' old buddies to consider my resume. Is this the 'people's government' I worked for? I feel disenfranchised."[17]

SORTING OUT PRIORITIES DURING THE TRANSITION

A second major set of problems faced by any executive taking office is what Kireker called "the reality of the transition": having to make decisions and get systems going in the midst of being deluged by thousands of résumés and phone calls.[18] Because Dukakis had been through one transition, he remembered vividly the confusion of the transition period and with his transition team had made some decisions about what was important. All members of the transition team assumed that the tenor and style of the Dukakis campaign made it imperative that the new government demonstrate its efficiency and its responsiveness, at least to the extent that all letters and phone calls be answered and that a tracking system for résumés be set up. Therefore, one clear priority was to put such systems in place.

All members of the transition team agreed that their single most important focus during the transition period should be on careful and judicious selection of the cabinet. As Sasso described it, "There was no question about it. We all agreed that the picks we'd make for those jobs would ensure our success or doom us."[19] In addition to agreeing that the selection of high-level personnel should receive top priority, Dukakis argued that candidates should be scrutinized not only for their individual talents but also to determine how they would mesh with the other persons under consideration for the cabinet team.

Despite the fact that the transition team had made some choices about their style of operating and their priorities before the election, they still faced the inevitable confusion of the period. Though they obviously knew that they had run a broad-based campaign and expected the applications of many enthusiastic job seekers, they nevertheless had to deal with the difficult problem of processing the applications of "professionals-in-exile," good-government enthusiasts who felt that in the person of Dukakis there was now finally an executive for whom they could work. The transition staff struggled to keep up with the monumental task of tracking résumés, often without success, and, in the process, often angered job applicants by not performing with the efficiency that was supposed to be the hallmark of the Dukakis administration. In addition, they faced the difficult job of cross-referencing résumés from many different sources, including the TAC, campaign staff members, and ongoing government agencies. Kireker, in assessing this period, put it this way:

> We never really got ahead of personnel management—by that I mean the sheer volume of paper. It took us a while to figure out how to use our Wang equipment. In addition, although one of our strengths was having the TAC and "guest interviewers" from the campaign feeding into the process, our system for coordinating these efforts wasn't perfect. If I were to do it all again I would consult earlier with someone who knows how to move this amount of paper in a way that can be directly integrated into the permanent personnel operation of the governor's office.[20]

The fact that staff members were deluged with résumés also affected their ability to devote all their attention to their declared highest priority, selection of high-level personnel. The confusion of the period, coupled with the seriousness with which Dukakis and his staff took the selection process and the value they placed on the contribution of the TAC, slowed the selection process. Although their original goal was to have the entire cabinet in place by Christmas, by the end of December only half of the secretaries had been named. This delay obviously meant that the whole process of staffing the government slowed: for example, as late as mid-March none of the commissioners of such large and often controversial departments as Public Welfare, Mental Health, and Public Health had been named. The potential of having to pay a high price for extending these vacancies through the honeymoon period is great, especially for a governor like Dukakis, who is committed to policy making as a team effort.

GETTING CONTROL OF BASIC FUNCTIONS

With the exception of the extreme importance accorded by Dukakis and his transition team to the recruitment of high-level personnel, the transition team did not spend much time during the transition period on planning how to control the basic managerial and political functions that the governor would have to perform. During the transition they spent little time making efforts to acquaint themselves with the personnel or the ongoing programs of the agencies. According to Sasso, this decision was a conscious one. "At this hectic time establishing our style of conducting ourselves was more important than running around trying to get detailed information. We didn't want to stir things up prematurely or to give anyone a sense that he had cornered the market on a policy area prematurely. First we wanted to get the cabinet in place. We assumed that they would handle their own information gathering."[21]

Although its pursuit of this strategy allowed the transition team to conserve its energy to focus on shaping the new government and smoothing relationships with outgoing Governor King and his chief aides, it had some costs. Because the strategy was based on the assumption that the cabinet secretaries would establish the intelligence-gathering network in the agencies, the delays in appointing top personnel in the secretariats slowed the process of understanding the details of government management. The transition staff did set up a formal liaison with each executive office, asked for debriefing memos, and set up follow-up interviews. The results in the quality and quantity of the information gathered and the identification of key personnel were mixed. As one critic of the new administration's first months in office put it: "They haven't figured out how to locate the 'old silver foxes,' the guys in the agencies who know where all the treasure is buried."[22] In addition, many holdover agency employees believed that the decision to avoid contact with the line agencies, rather than diffusing tension and cutting down on paranoia, actually increased the discomfort of employees. This uncertainty and fear was intensified by the decision of newly appointed secretary of communities and development Amy Anthony to request signed letters of resignation from all division directors, an action that some employees assumed to be a signal of what was to come.

The transition team avoided information gathering about agencies and programs during the transition. They also assumed that the job of building and analyzing the budget should await action by the secretaries. Again, the problem with working from this assumption was that several of the secretaries were not appointed until the budget document was almost complete. Even the early appointees among the secretaries and the personnel of the budget office had a very short time to analyze the budget and make recommendations by February 1, when the budget had to go to the printer. Although the outgoing secretary of administration and finance was cooperative and had directed his employees to prepare backup information for the incoming administration, there was no standard format for presenting this information. In addition, the budget had been prepared without estimates of the costs of maintaining the current level of program operations, with an allowance for inflation, information that the new budget director considered crucial.

Despite the problems associated with lack of information and lack of time, the new budget director Barbara Salisbury felt that the decision not to worry about the budget until the secretaries were appointed was correct. "It was crucial to wait to involve the secretaries. They came up with good ideas about how to manage budgets they were going to have to live with. . . . The meetings were also very successful because they were an important way of establishing our relationship to them. The budget served as a contract-setting mechanism, and allowed the secretaries to 'buy into' the budget."[23]

Dukakis, in his overtures to the legislature during the transition, pursued the same pattern that he had used with the agencies—focusing on issues of style and tone and neither pushing for detailed analyses nor prematurely committing to policy. He believed that the source of many of his problems during his first term had been his rocky relationship with the legislature.[24] During Dukakis's first term the legislative leadership and many members had disliked him, not only because they had disagreed with many of his policy initiatives but also because they had regarded him as aloof, arrogant, and "above politics." As early as the summer before the election Dukakis had assigned a full-time political operative to work with the legislature. During the transition Dukakis and his transition staff refrained from criticizing or even commenting on the creation of new jobs and the pay increases for many continuing employees that were pushed through in the final frenzied days of the legislature's lame-duck session. In addition, the transition team involved legislators (including some who had not worked in the campaign or supported Dukakis) in the working groups set up to put flesh on the bones of the proposals for the four priority areas on which Dukakis wanted to suggest major legislation. Finally, immediately after the election the transition staff assigned one person to monitor legislation closely. In addition, Dukakis gave early, personal, and careful consideration to the requirements of the job of director of legislative relations on his staff; by late December he appointed a well-liked former legislator to the job.

By January, Dukakis had clearly won points for making an effort to change his style. But he had yet to face the first real test of his ability to work with the legislature—his success or failure in passing a tight, no-new-taxes FY 84 budget. The leadership of that legislature would claim in mid-March that the budget was $250 million out of balance, and they seemed to prefer a tax increase in 1983 to the possibility that one might be necessary in 1984—an election year for the legislators.[25]

SETTING A POLICY AGENDA

The policy agendas of incoming administrations are shaped by at least three forces: the personal preferences, style, and choices of the newly elected executive and his close advisors; the issues raised in the campaign; and the broad political environment and the issues that it throws up at any particular time. The policy initiatives of the early days of the Dukakis administration were a product of all of these. Dukakis, Sasso, and Kireker had agreed that when the small transition committee began to operate, it should steer away from articulation of policy. According to Kireker, "From the earliest days of thinking about the transition through the general election, our concern was with process. It was not until mid-October that we looked through the positions we'd taken in the campaign and began to sift them into what became after the election four (later five) priority areas. We knew all along that we didn't want to commit to policy positions prematurely and that even when we made a commitment we didn't want a laundry list. We wanted a focus for our efforts."[26]

The four policy themes that resulted from culling the promises and positions taken during the campaign were the development of a program for jobs and economic growth; the articulation of a focus on law enforcement and crime prevention; a reexamination of state aid to cities and towns hard hit by Proposition 2½; and a commitment to ensure integrity in state government. At the end of November each theme was assigned to a working group consisting of members of the transition, campaign, and governor's office staffs, cabinet secretaries (when they had been appointed), several legislators, and, in the criminal justice working group, the newly elected lieutenant governor. The themes also became the basis for Dukakis's January inaugural address.

Because there was so much overlap among those close to Dukakis during the campaign, during the transition, and in the new government, the process for thinking about policy issues was already smooth and established early in the transition and was in large measure dictated by the way it had been done in the campaign. As one member of the campaign staff put it, "Although Michael is governor now, he doesn't feel like he has to scramble for a policy agenda. He believes that if he put it in a speech in the campaign, he stands for it. His agenda will come from his campaign speeches."[27]

The campaign, particularly the primary fight between King and Dukakis, had also influenced which policy issues were *not* on the early Dukakis policy agenda. King and Dukakis were far apart on social issues, and much to his dismay in his first confrontation with King, Dukakis had found that a majority of Democrats seemed more drawn to King's positions than to his own. In addition, one of the major issues at stake in the King-Dukakis rematch was King's integrity and ability to manage the government. As a result, in his campaign Dukakis steered away from taking positions on controversial social issues or on policies that might be expensive or difficult to implement. As Sasso described this strategy, "We couldn't let King run away with it on his own issues. The issue *was* King and we couldn't allow the focus to be diverted from that."[28] The facts that the policy agenda had been shaped in this way during the campaign and that a healing process had to go on even after the election shifted the focus of Dukakis's early policy agenda away from controversial social programs and initiatives.

In late December a fifth area of emphasis—a commitment to understand and to do something about the plight of the homeless—was added to the four policy priorities. The plight of Americans who had become homeless was made highly visible by the press during the Christmas season, and addressing the issue was something that was one that Dukakis personally felt should be moved to the top of the government's agenda. The identification of the initiative to help the homeless became the fifth focus in Dukakis's inaugural speech, and, in fact, because it involved what was perceived to be such a pressing problem, was the first commitment mentioned in the address. Taking an approach unlike that used with the other priority areas, Dukakis gave high priority to the issue before he had a task force to do the background work. As a result, there was early confusion and some consternation on the part of human services and volunteer groups that were already working on the issue but that had not been consulted on the governor's new policy. Despite the rough beginning for this priority, Dukakis in early January set up a working group of persons inside and outside government to make proposals for alleviating the problem.

Conclusions

Transitions from one government to another can be looked at as rational processes that involve tasks to be accomplished and steps to be taken; in that sense, analyses of them and knowledge about them can be transferred from one executive to another and from one jurisdiction to another. The cautions of those involved in the Dukakis transition that might be passed on to other incoming governors could probably be summed up in three maxims. First, if recruitment of competent, high-level personnel is a high priority, be deliberate but also move quickly: not to do so is to slow down the process of taking control of the government. Second, be extremely careful to estimate realistically the numbers of résumés and personnel issues (and the resulting confusion) that occur and develop a highly sophisticated personnel system as soon as possible to deal with these numbers and to carry the process over to the ongoing work of government staffing. Third, even in the midst of the confusion of the transition period, remember the legacy of the campaign and constantly push to involve new constituencies and new faces in the government: without this involvement, charges of insularity can be leveled early in the administration.

But transitions are more than rationally constructed processes with checklists and caution sheets. They also transmit signals that are taken by a variety of constituencies as symbolic predictors of the direction and tone of the new administration. The style with which the transition is handled provides important cues and images of success or failure to the public as a whole, to the community of political and policy professionals, to the activists in the campaign, and to those involved in governance in the new administration.

The Dukakis administration's success at communicating positive signals to these important constituences cannot be assessed until the administration has unfolded. But it is possible to make preliminary statements about some of the images communicated by Dukakis and his associates at the end of the transition period. The public was pleased: public opinion polls taken by the governor's political staff showed him to have the highest favorability rating during the first two months in office of any Massachusetts governor in the past ten years.[29] Political and policy professionals (persons who work in the government or who, as interested members of the press or lobbying organizations, watch the government carefully) tend to be reluctant to communicate a positive assessment of a process like the transition because they are sensitive to government as a complex process that unfolds over time. Nonetheless, at the end of the transition the consensus among these groups seemed to be that Dukakis had at least not made any major mistakes and that in this respect he was beginning his term in the most favorable possible circumstances.

The signals received by the active campaign workers did not seem to be as positive as those received by the general public or the government insiders. The image of the campaign as a broad-based effort undertaken by citizen-activists whose work was known and valued by Dukakis was not congruent with campaigners' perhaps unrealistic expectations that they would have easy and early access to policies and jobs in the new administration. Despite the transition team's efforts to reinforce the importance of the campaign workers—setting up meetings to thank them and establishing an official liaison position within the governor's office— the harsh reality of fewer than 2,000 jobs and a mobilized army of more than 50,000 people who believed themselves both "loyal and competent" ensured that the signals to the campaign loyalists would be mixed.

To judge the success of the transition in terms of the images conveyed to these important constituencies is problematic; during the course of the administration the images are likely to change for all these groups. Public opinion is ephemeral; policy and political professionals are affected by day-to-day battles and issues as the administration unfolds; and campaign organizations eventually wind down and focus on immediate and particular political issues. As a result, one could argue that the single most important audience receiving signals during the transition period is composed of those actually involved in the new administration. Transitions are psychodramas, involving choices made by the members of the new administration and made in a way that makes them feel secure, comfortable, and competent. In this respect, transitions have to be designed to suit the style and talents of the person who is taking office and are, by definition, successful only if they seem successful to the chief executive and his staff, whose needs the transition is meant to serve.

Michael Dukakis had a particular advantage in ensuring that his transition would fit his style and be a useful and productive experience for him. He had held the office before and had had the luxury of reflecting on what he had done well and what he had done poorly the first time around. He came through the campaign and the transition with a process that reflected a well-thought-out set of views and beliefs: that an orderly process was more important than grandstanding on issues; that the selection of team players was more congruent with this choice than the selection of superstars; that proven loyalty and competence were legitimate and, in fact, exellent criteria for evaluating members of the team; and that a new Dukakis administration could retain the best qualities and people from his first administration while being enriched by his ability to learn from his mistakes. Perhaps the best measure of the success of the Dukakis transition in terms of how well it suited the style and beliefs of the new administration is the consistency of these themes throughout the campaign, the period between the election and the inauguration, and on into the new administration. For Dukakis, the fact that he knew not only what he wanted to accomplish but also that he knew himself and his style meant that he could distinguish among the many pressing problems and opportunities that presented themselves. He could incorporate his assessment into the transition, and so provide a sense of consistency and direction for the new government.

Gubernatorial Transition
in Michigan, 1982–1983

CHARLES PRESS AND KENNETH VERBURG

Perhaps all transitions begin with what the outgoing governor experienced when he or she initially took office—an experience that shapes later attitudes about what a transition should or might be. So we begin with a brief review of how William Milliken, Michigan's longest-serving governor, took office fourteen years ago. The kind of administration he fashioned and the tone it projected provide important clues about his approach to his next transition—leaving office. The transition months, immediately after the election until the inauguration, are the lame-duck months, the months of tension and potential conflict for both governors. Milliken wished to leave office with the style of governing he had followed so long; James Blanchard wished to gain office by setting his own contrasting style and direction. These desires, combined with the unanticipated results of the gubernatorial primaries and the unusual election that followed, were perhaps the most significant aspects of the 1982 transition in Michigan.

Strictly speaking, the transition may be said to end when the new governor is sworn into office. In fact it continues at least until the new governor has established his or her own political tone and style and has begun to achieve major political purposes. For Governor-elect Blanchard, the transition concluded relatively rapidly—very early in the campaign and during the months between election and the January 1 inauguration he had sent out clear signals on how his administration would differ from Milliken's. By the end of March, Blanchard had gotten a massive income tax increase through the Michigan legislature. In April he presented his budget of priorities. By May he had given his "jobs, jobs, jobs" message. At that point we can reasonably say that the transition was over.

The Milliken Years

William Milliken was one of a group of moderate Republican senators who, in the early 1960s, were at odds with conservatives in their party. These conservatives controlled the caucus in Michigan's malapportioned senate. Like other moderates, Milliken was attracted in 1962 by the gubernatorial candidacy of George Romney. Romney chose Milliken as his running mate—an excellent political choice. He was young and intelligent, a member of an old established and wealthy Michigan family, and had grown up in and represented a district in the northern part of the state.

By 1968 Romney had pushed through an income tax and a new constitution and had effectively routed the conservatives of his own party. He then made a try for the presidency and failed spectacularly. But unlike 1964, when Romney shunned Barry Goldwater, Romney campaigned for Nixon in 1968. His reward was the appointment as secretary of the Department of Housing and Urban Development. Thus, Milliken came to the governorship without having earned it on his own. An "accidental governor," he was merely filling out the last two year's of Romney's term.

The immediate transition was not unfriendly, but it was dragged out. Romney was not an executive who could let go easily or before all the strings were tied together to his satisfaction. Milliken waited patiently in the wings—very patiently. His full transition was long—two years, in fact, would pass before some politicians would no longer dismiss him as just a pleasant young man. Some of Romney's former aides presumed to give him unsolicited guidance. Some Republican candidates were openly uncertain about his chances of election. The early public opinion polls indicated that Michigan citizens were unsure about his ability to lead. Milliken won his first election for governor in 1970 by less than 0.2 percent of the vote but six percentage points ahead of the rest of the Republican ticket. At that point his transition was over—everyone recognized that he was indeed governor.

We can only speculate what this experience suggested to Milliken about transitions. It seems safe to say that given his sensitivity, he would consider transition a difficult time for an incoming governor—one that an outgoing governor should try to smooth. He would perhaps remember that in his own case everyone had seemed to pay more attention to the needs and whims of the outgoing governor than to those of the "temporary" new governor. Second, he could also be expected to understand that his successor would want to do things in his or her own way. He could appreciate that the new governor would want the retiring governor and his aides to get and stay out of the way.

He also was aware that a new governor must pick and choose his own staff as well as remove those of doubtful loyalty. Milliken chose carefully, and many of his original choices stayed with him throughout his years as governor. And he reciprocated such loyalty. He insisted, when leaving office, that these principal aides receive decent treatment from the new governor. All signs suggested that the incoming Blanchard administration regarded such demands as reasonable, interpreting decent treatment to mean that a few of Milliken's appointed administrators could move over to civil service jobs to complete minimum employment requirements to vest their retirement benefits.

The Milliken years of governing would reinforce this approach to his successor's problems. What impressed observers most was the Milliken style. His was an administration from which controversy and acrimony were largely absent. Some attributed this solely to the governor's personal qualities. Hugh McDiarmid, *Detroit Free Press* capital correspondent, who wrote biting columns about many Michigan politicians, saluted Milliken as a leader who always projected integrity and a basic decency. To many, Milliken exemplified grace under pressure. Yet what this characterization seems to downplay is the fact that Milliken could make tough decisions and stick to them. He could be very firm and self-assured while being outwardly pleasant and obliging. We suggest that the style and tone of his administration owed as much to the kind of policies he espoused as to the Milliken character and personal charm.

Milliken did not preside over years of inactivity. His term was a period of expansion for an increasingly professional state government, especially in issues affecting the public schools, higher education, and the environment. His administration moved the state steadily from regressive taxation to a more progressive system by such methods as exempting food and drugs from the sales tax and enacting circuit-breaker legislation to reduce property-tax burdens on lower-income persons. His administration also tried to upgrade professionalism in the welfare and mental health programs. Finally, these were years in which a Republican governor, rather than writing off the concerns of the city of Detroit and its black Democratic mayor, began to offer substantial state aid.

As many pointed out, most of these programs were good politics for the 1970s. Educational and ecological concerns appealed to young progressives of both parties. They noted that Milliken was the only Republican governor to carry Wayne County since the days before Roosevelt. In the legislature and within his administration, Milliken's approach was collegial and bipartisan, perhaps even nonpartisan. Democrats headed some state agencies; others served on his staff. His relations with the legislature were those of a compromiser who fashioned bipartisan coalitions, almost issue-by-issue. In his election campaigns he gained the backing of many who usually voted Democratic. Typically, in national politics he supported Gerald Ford and, later, George Bush over Ronald Reagan. Within the Michigan Republican party he held the right wing powerless and put moderates in major positions. He essentially ignored Michigan's growing antitax movement and scorned its conservative leaders.

The core of this record was Milliken's belief that the problems of government should be solved through professionalization rather than partisan politics. His implicit approach to most problems seemed to be, What do the experts think we should do? This approach was good politics because it was difficult to attack—Milliken was not being partisan or personally stubborn. He could disagree with the UAW and the AFL-CIO as easily as he could with those who opposed welfare abortions. Over vigorous union opposition he pushed a revision of workers compensation through the legislature, and ten times he vetoed the bill forbidding state abortions to those on welfare. One could say that in both situations he was merely trying to apply professional expertise to political problems. To him and to many others, that approach just seemed to be common sense.

From such an administration we would expect a smooth transition. This is the kind of governor who would want to do it right, just the way the experts recommend that it be done—a transition that would also reflect his personal inclinations.

Some have argued that Milliken served one term too long. By that they mean that he, for his own good, should have left office in 1978, the year things began to go sour for the auto industry and therefore for many of Michigan's citizens and its professionalized government.

The initial Milliken response to recession, and the traditional one in Michigan, was "Don't panic. Hold on—things will change for the better before too long." The problem was that this time things did not change. This time the answers provided by the professional experts did not seem to help solve the immediate problem of steadily growing deficits. All the experts could propose was the traditional advice that surfaces each time recession hits automobile production—diversify Michigan's economy, this time into robotics and other high-tech industries.

The Milliken administration responded to growing financial troubles by what some called voodoo bookkeeping. For example, the fiscal year-end was pushed from June 30 to September 30, money was borrowed at low interest rates from every state fund available, payments were delayed, and revenue estimates were revised downward two or three times each year. What was at stake was Michigan's professionalized bureaucracy—one of the best in the nation. As long as possible, Milliken resisted cutting the state work force. When cuts could no longer be avoided, he stopped filling vacancies. Meanwhile workers began getting layoff notices, welfare and unemployment insurance costs skyrocketed, and as a final indignity, Reaganomics cut the funds received from the federal government. So here was a governor who had striven to build one of the nation's most professional state work forces having to preside over its gradual disintegration.

It seems fair to characterize Milliken's last two years as governor as years of trying to hold the bureaucracy together until a successor arrived. Every few months or so, with great reluctance, he announced further cuts in the state budget and a reduction in the state work force. In his last year he persuaded the legislature to pass a six-month increase in the personal income tax, but the increase expired just about when Milliken's term did. To keep the ship of state afloat until a new governor could take over, Milliken finally persuaded Japanese banks to underwrite the state's bonds, bonds that Wall Street had rejected.

Thus, along with his own transition experience, his temperament, and his belief in professionalism, Milliken seems to have wanted desperately to get out of the job—as smoothly and honorably as possible. As the primaries and general elections of 1982 approached, Governor Milliken wanted to make the transition an easy one for all concerned—for himself, the new governor, and loyal Milliken aides. He would be most cooperative. The results of the primary and general election helped increase Milliken's cooperative spirit.

The Primary Campaigns

Michigan, like the federal government and several other states, provides campaign funds for primary and general gubernatorial races. For the

1982 campaigns, some $8 million was available. Experience suggests that the availability of public funds leads to a multiplicity of candidates in primary elections—especially because candidates may drop out before the voting without having to return funds that they have already spent.

The 1982 Michigan Republican primary attracted four candidates, but the main battle was seen as that between Lieutenant Governor James H. Brickley and insurance executive Richard C. Headlee. L. Brooks Patterson, Oakland County prosecutor, entered the contest, advocating restoration of the death penalty as his main issue. State senator John Welborn, the acknowledged leader of the ultraconservative wing of the Republican party in the legislature, was the fourth candidate in the Republican primary. All but Brickley, then, were from the anti-Milliken, conservative wing of the party.

James Brickley began his political career as a federal prosecutor in Wayne County and southeastern Michigan. Later, he became a member of the Detroit Common Council. His first statewide race came as Milliken's running mate in 1970. As is true of most lieutenant governors, Brickley kept a low profile. Restless in the job and unhappy with the low pay, Brickley served out the term but did not make himself available for a second one. Shortly after the 1974 election he became president of Eastern Michigan University.

Milliken's choice for a running mate in his second campaign was James J. Damman, a state senator from Oakland County whom Milliken later came to consider a liability. During the campaign, rumors developed about conflicts of interest involving the running mate. The allegations were not enough to bring about Milliken's defeat or even to prevent the lieutenant governor from serving out the term. They were enough, though, to cause Milliken, himself squeaky clean, to turn elsewhere in 1978 for a running mate.

Milliken again chose Brickley. Many assumed that Brickley wanted eventually to become governor himself. We know of no Milliken promise to Brickley that he would step aside by 1983. Yet from Brickley's viewpoint, it seemed a reasonable prospect. After all, Milliken was frequently mentioned as a candidate for national offices, and he would be almost sixty and Michigan's longest-serving governor if he served out the full term. Brickley accepted and served Milliken loyally. Milliken announced in December 1981 that he would not run again. Brickley wasted little time in announcing his own candidacy and immediately received Milliken's blessing. Brickley was a Milliken Republican, a political moderate, handsome and experienced. But there were some major difficulties.

One was that Milliken had lost some favor with the Michigan voters. A high rate of unemployment, the state's teetering on the edge of bankruptcy, unorthodox bookkeeping practices, the temporary rise in the income tax, cutbacks in state programs, and the lame-duck status itself— all diminished Milliken's influence. His control over the Republican party and the independents, on whom he had for so long relied to craft his majority, weakened. Milliken thus was unable to deliver the mantle of party leadership to his chosen successor.

The other problem was that Brickley in mid-1982, as lieutenant governor, cast a key tie-breaking vote in the senate to increase Detroit's payroll tax on suburban commuters who worked in the city. Many of those affected had been Milliken supporters. Perhaps Brickley was reaching out for what he saw as the critical black vote of Detroit in the 1982 general election.

But Brickley did not make it through the primary. Richard C. Headlee, whose only public office was membership on the Oakland University Board of Trustees, won the 1982 Republican primary. (Milliken, who had appointed Headlee earlier, was on record saying that this was the single worst appointment he had made.) Headlee had gained recognition in Michigan in 1976 and 1978 as the leader of two initiative campaigns to limit state and local taxes. His constitutional proposal of 1978 won. It limited state tax revenues to 9.2 percent of personal income and prohibited local tax increases without voter approval. The amendment also assured local units continuation of their share of state tax revenues— 41.6 percent—and forbade the state from making additional demands on local governments unless the state also paid the costs of such programs. Milliken reluctantly supported this Headlee proposal as "something the state can live with." He thus helped defeat another, more drastic constitutional initiative (the Tisch Proposal) similar to California's Proposition 13. Through these tax campaigns Headlee gained a reputation as a responsible combatant against growing government. His fight for reduced taxes stood in stark contrast to Brickley's vote for tax increases.

The Republican campaign was bitter. In widely distributed television ads the three conservatives—Headlee, Patterson, and Welborn—criticized Milliken's tax and program policies. The possible division of the conservative vote would seem to have worked in Brickley's favor. Perhaps it did, but not enough. Brickley, the governor's personal choice, came in second, with about 30 percent of the vote. Headlee won, with 34 percent. Patterson got 28 percent, and Welborn, 7. Thus, less than a third of his own party supported a Milliken moderate.

Brickley's defeat was a bitter pill for Milliken. He passed up attending the state Republican convention, which fills out the remainder of the ticket. The Republican party in Michigan was no longer a Milliken party. The result of the primary further predisposed Milliken to an especially professional transition—if the Democrats won the general election.

THE DEMOCRATIC PRIMARY

The Democratic primary started out with a large crop of gubernatorial candidates. Several of them were state senators who, it was suspected, had announced their gubernatorial candidacies as a way of gaining publicity for another run at their senate seats. In fact, several left the race in time to have their names appear as state senate candidates rather than for the party's gubernatorial nomination.

In the end, only four Democrats appeared on the 1982 primary ballot—former state senator William Fitzgerald, the Democratic nominee for governor in 1978; James Blanchard, member of Congress from south Oakland County; state senator Kerry Kammer from central Oakland County, who had made a reputation on natural resource issues; and Zolton Ferency, former chairman of the state Democrats, a self-proclaimed "democratic socialist" and a professor of criminal law at Michigan State University.

Fitzgerald had been out of the state senate for four years; since 1982 he had established a law firm in Detroit that employed more than 100 attorneys. In 1978, when Fitzgerald was the union-backed candidate, he ran poorly. In 1982 union leaders looked elsewhere for a candidate who could regain the executive office after two decades of Republican rule.

The 1980 census report indicated that Michigan would lose one congressional seat. Early on, it seemed that reapportionment would thus seriously divide Democrats. Not only would it pit two Democratic members of Congress against each other but it would almost certainly result in the loss of a black congressional seat.

The Democratic leadership, working with labor leaders, crafted a plan.

They would recruit one of the southeast Michigan Democratic congressmen for the gubernatorial nomination. William M. Brodhead and James J. Blanchard were the most likely prospects. Ultimately, Blanchard accepted the offer and received almost total labor and party backing in the primary.

Blanchard was not well known in Michigan outside his congressional district. He was young, a New Deal Democrat, generally classed as a pragmatic moderate, who had a likable, down-to-earth personality. He was associated more with the labor wing of his party than with its more trendy liberal faction. And he had recently played an important role in devising a plan to save the Chrysler Corporation from bankruptcy by providing federal guarantees for loans. This plan, he would point out in his campaigns, had already saved 100,000 jobs in Michigan. To a job-starved state, Blanchard promised to save other jobs and, indeed, to create more jobs. It was the kind of proposal that citizens in the nation's leading unemployment state wanted to hear. Blanchard won the primary easily.

Again, from the standpoint of the transition, Blanchard was the type of liberal Democrat whom Milliken could respect. He had in fact recruited some of this type into his own administration. And Milliken was the kind of Republican whom Blanchard could understand and work with. In fact, they had worked together on the Chrysler package.

Michigan's 1982 General Election Campaign: The Issues

What the primary election provided, then, was a race between Richard C. Headlee, Republican, insurance company executive, and citizen-politician, and James J. Blanchard, Democrat, member of Congress, and professional politician. It was also a race between a conservative candidate representing a party in shambles and an FDR liberal who was backed by a party united under union leadership.

A third candidate, running as an independent, presented a potential problem for both Blanchard and Headlee. Robert Tisch, a drain commissioner in a central Michigan county, had gained statewide recognition as the state's leading tax-cut proponent. He had very little chance of winning the governorship but could be a spoiler. His main appeal was to the low-income voters in the rural areas. What was uncertain was just how many votes he might draw and from whom. In the end his under-financed effort did little to affect the outcome.

As we have noted, Michigan's economic condition during 1982 and its outlook for 1983 provided ample basis for attack on the incumbent Republican administration. Had Brickley been the Republican nominee, Blanchard would perhaps have appealed for an end to Milliken-type policies—that it was time for a change. But the Republicans in the August primary had already repudiated the policies of their own governor.

JOBS, JOBS, JOBS

That repudiation left Blanchard with the opportunity to carry on the jobs-creation theme that had served him so well in the primary campaign. And, in many respects, it left him with an appeal not unlike those that Milliken found so successful—Michigan has the natural and human resources necessary to restore its economic well-being if only the people will work together under new leadership. Blanchard thus ran a low-key campaign. The jobs issue afforded him the chance to run an inclusive campaign: he promised an administration that would serve all Michigan interests—labor, business, education, agriculture, government employees, and the poor.

Blanchard offered few specific answers to how he would solve the state's economic woes. He talked of a $1-billion bond issue to create a public jobs program and of the need to establish a state bank. He diffused the tax-increase issue by saying he would consider a tax increase as "a last resort." And while he talked of belt tightening, he avoided harsh references to budget cuts and program reductions.

Blanchard's campaign thus offered hope and avoided creating hostilities. The polls showed him well in the lead at the outset of the campaign. And he correctly saw the task as one of building on the support that would fall to him in this Democratic state. He did not antagonize Governor Milliken or his wing of the Republican party (which would be important in the future transition).

In retrospect it appears that Blanchard left that task to Republican candidate Headlee. If Blanchard was cool and composed, Headlee was boisterous and noisy. Headlee, as we might expect, saw improving the business climate as the main solution to the state's economic mess. He spoke of the need to reform Michigan's liberal unemployment and workers compensation programs—programs he saw as out of step with Michigan's competitor states. Such themes helped drive uncertain union members solidly into the Blanchard camp.

GOVERNMENT CUTBACKS

Headlee also worked hard the theme of cutting back government services. State workers saw that kind of cutback as a threat to their programs and their own jobs. Welfare recipients took such messages as meaning that Headlee would cut their benefit checks drastically. And urban areas, especially Detroit, heard the theme as an end to a state government that cared about distressed cities. This line of campaign rhetoric, especially in the early weeks of the campaign, often cast Headlee in a defensive position, not so much by Blanchard's responses as by media requests for specific details.

WOMEN'S RIGHTS

Headlee's most important campaign problem, however, arose over his handling of the feminist issue. As a Mormon he was from the outset suspect to some on this question. Often repeated lines about "some of my best friends . . ." added to the suspicion of those to whom women's issues were paramount. But perhaps his most significant mistake came in response to a coalition of women's groups who asked each candidate to respond to some eighty-five issues they had identified as important. The media recorded and telecast Headlee's belittling response to the effect that "Well, who is this women's coalition, anyway?" As it turned out, first lady Helen Milliken as well as a former Republican state chairwoman, Elly Peterson, were leaders in the coalition. Helen Milliken responded discreetly; Elly Peterson did not—she led a group of Republican women in support of Blanchard. The episode, we think, also influenced Governor Milliken. He refused to say how he was going to vote. But it became rather evident that at least Helen Milliken was not voting for Headlee.

The Headlee attack on Milliken policies and the later campaign support of Headlee by fellow Mormon and former Governor Romney further drove Milliken and his followers out of their own party. We are not aware of any public statements by Milliken that raised the pitch of the rhetoric. But it seems unlikely that he could have said anything that would have spoken more loudly than his icy silence.

The election turned out to be somewhat closer than one might have expected. Democrat James Blanchard won, with 53.2 percent of the vote. In Wayne County, the Democratic stronghold, the vote for Blanchard was 68.3 percent. But the outstate counties favored Headlee, giving him 51.3 percent of their vote.

Why is an understanding of the election so important to an analysis of the Michigan transition? The smoothness of a transition, we suggest, is dictated in large measure by the relationship of the outgoing incumbent and the incoming victor. Undoubtedly, there are exceptions, but when those who have been defeated must then assist those who have won, it seems unlikely that most losers will do much more than common courtesy requires. Some do considerably less.

But in this case, it was not Democrat Blanchard who brought an end to Republican Milliken's legacy. It was fellow Republican Richard Headlee who turned out "Millikenism" by defeating James Brickley and by campaigning against it in both the primary and general elections. And it was Blanchard who represented the continuation of "compassionate" government. We believe that these facts were fundamental to the quality and character of the transition period that followed.

The Months Between Election and Inauguration

Immediately after the election, as is customary, the governor-elect, with small briefing book in hand, went out of the state on vacation. He sent his lieutenant governor-elect, Martha Griffiths, to represent him at the new governors seminar sponsored by the National Governors' Association (NGA). Meanwhile, Blanchard's aides began thinking about managing the transition. Working with Blanchard's staff, a staff largely experienced in congressional rather than gubernatorial politics, was Jim Tait, a consultant for the NGA.

PREPARATIONS FOR TAKING OFFICE

Governor-elect Blanchard had spent the past eight years in Washington, D.C. When he visited Michigan, it was generally to spend time in his congressional district in Oakland County. Thus, despite the facts that he had been born and raised in Michigan, had graduated from Michigan State University, had worked in the election division of the secretary of state department, served as administrative assistant to the attorney general, had been legal advisor to the departments of Licensing and Regulation, Commerce and Agriculture, and had been active in Michigan

Democratic politics—he, at this point, was somewhat an outsider to the Lansing political scene.

The need for a Lansing political insider. Blanchard's most trusted aides, it soon became apparent, were from Oakland County, the booming suburban area north of Detroit. Beyond this was a smattering from Detroit and some from Washington. Consequently, what the governor-elect found was that neither he nor his aides knew much about the capital in 1983 or, indeed, about the government they were soon to dominate. This was later to show up in a few minor gaffes that gave the new administration a somewhat shaky beginning. What Blanchard sorely needed was a Lansing political insider, a person he had known for a long time, one whom he could trust and who could devote full time to Blanchard's interests.

Shortly after the primary victory, a Lansing lawyer, Lawrence D. Owen, associated with Miller, Canfield, Paddock, and Stone, perhaps the state's most prestigious law firm, offered to be that person for Blanchard. Owen, a former college classmate of Blanchard, was now mayor of suburban East Lansing. He had worked in state government and was an active Democrat. He was also a person of good political instincts.

Blanchard, though, seemed neither to accept nor reject Owen's offer. There were several reasons for his lack of action. The first was one that perhaps all primary victors face. Gearing up for a transition during a campaign may give the appearance of overconfidence—the impression that the victory is already in hand. And while an effective takeover of the executive suite was desirable, that goal was secondary. Winning the office was paramount at that point. A second reason, was that Owen did not meet two key conditions: he did not have the ability to make a long-term, full-time commitment to the governor, and he was not a person with whom Blanchard had had a long, close political association. A third difficulty was that the Democratic speaker of the house, Bobby D. Crim, had also offered to be "Blanchard's man in Lansing." Although Crim had already decided not to run for another term as state representative, accepting or rejecting Crim's offer presented its own set of difficulties in the middle of a campaign, especially because Blanchard was uncertain about all the implications of such an appointment. Hence, Blanchard delayed making a decision.

Meanwhile, Owen, along with George E. Ward, a Detroit associate from the Miller, Canfield firm, began informally to make some tentative preparations for the transition. After a month or so the two became a part of the circle of Blanchard's campaign advisors. Within that circle they began to make some suggestions about how the transition might be handled. Near the end of the campaign, when the outcome seemed clear, the law firm gave Owen leave to work for Blanchard as part of the transition team. Indeed, it was the two lawyers, together with several other persons close to Blanchard, who prepared the briefing book that the governor-elect took with him on his postelection vacation.

Transition documents. The twenty-five-page briefing book dealt with such items as how to fund the transition. Michigan had not had a genuine transition in twenty years. Most legislators were uncertain about the costs, although they appropriated $1 million. About $362,000 went for the Blanchard transition team and the inauguration ceremony. Adding to the uncertainty were unknown amounts—how much exiting officials would be entitled to for unused leave time, how much would be needed to pay accrued retirement benefits. Some $600,000 was allocated for these payments, and an additional $38,000 was allotted to pay Governor Milliken's expenses in leaving office. The governor-elect would have to pay for the inaugural celebration parties—significantly, parties were held both in Lansing and Detroit.

The briefing book identified office space, both in Detroit and Lansing, for the transition staff. It proposed a budget for the transition, outlined staff assignments, and recommended a compensation plan. Importantly, it also outlined detailed procedures for responding to the mail that was soon to deluge the transition offices. Other concerns addressed in the briefing book were the key appointments to be made early in the transition, the need for an early meeting of Governor Milliken and legislative leaders, a suggested plan for the new executive office, a list of essential first steps, and a program outline for the first 100 days.

The governor-elect, or his transition staff, did not follow the script in the briefing book in every detail. But the book proved a surprisingly accurate presager of the actions that would be taken during the period from November to the end of the first 100 days of the new administration. It was the unanticipated events that caused the ripples in what was otherwise a smooth transition.

The briefing book was supplemented by documents offering a wide variety of details about running the gubernatorial office. They were prepared under the direction of George Weeks, a principal aide to Governor Milliken. In addition, the Blanchard team received reports that the outgoing governor had requested from state agencies. Members of the Milliken and the Blanchard administrations characterized these departmental reports as being of uneven quality—some were very good and some not. (That, incidentally, should not be surprising. In these reports, administrators were asked to describe key department and program problems. Highly candid reports, for the most part, would have reflected negatively on department and program managers, some of whom were hoping to stay on.)

THE BLANCHARD VIEW OF THE TRANSITION

Governor-elect Blanchard seems to have been well aware that the months between election and inauguration should not be wasted. He seems to have planned his actions carefully for this period. Three kinds of activity were started.

Logistical concerns. First, the new administration had to prepare to handle the logistical problems of getting settled—assigning offices and getting phones installed and offices redecorated or rearranged. In addition, there were the arrangements for the inauguration and the balls that would follow, responses to the mail coming in—answering the thousands of letters from job-seekers and letters of endorsement, the letters of congratulation, and sending out the thank-you notes. Such planning could be left to trusted aides. It is doubtful that the transition staff was able to meet the goal in the briefing book of responding to most letters within twenty-four hours. But for the most part, the mail was answered, even if not always promptly.

Major appointments. A second level of transition concerned screening for major appointments. Part of this screening had already been done. In Michigan the party convention, following the nominee's suggestion, nominates the lieutenant governor. Blanchard chose a former member of Congress, Martha Griffiths—a personal friend from Detroit and, as it turned out, a valuable asset in a campaign in which feminism became a critical issue. Later, in governing, she would wield a heavy hand in keeping order in the senate.

But the pattern thus established had to be carried out in other appointments. The kinds of people the governor-elect wanted to recruit, as he began to make clear, were men and women who, like Griffiths, were Democrats, loyal to him, and competent but also as strongly committed to New Deal values as he himself was.

Short-term goals. The third level of transition is related to the second—

setting the immediate goals and style for the administration. He wanted first to show those who knew him only slightly that he could lead and govern. Second, he wanted to prepare Michigan for the kind of proposals he would sponsor. Blanchard had run on a "jobs, jobs, jobs" platform in a state with high unemployment, but the state also faced heavy budgetary and accrued deficits. He had to take decisive action in both areas.

Finally, he wanted to telegraph the methods he would follow and the interests that would benefit and those that might not. Blanchard believed in partisan politics rather than the consensus approach that had characterized the Milliken years. Blanchard respected competence. But above professional specialization, he placed commitment to welfare-state values, particularly those that benefited what some called the pretzel-and-beer Democrats and, less so, perhaps, those that appealed to the wine-and-cheese liberals in the party.

ACTIONS OF THE GOVERNOR-ELECT

In the following, we suggest what may at first sound like a slightly strained interpretation—that the governor-elect began modeling his actions on a hero of his youth, Franklin Delano Roosevelt. We suggest even that this may have been a conscious action. Whether the action was or was not conscious, the parallels stand out sharply.

No rush to Lansing. The governor-elect made an early decision to stay away from Lansing until he had the responsibility for governing. Roosevelt scholars will recall how FDR also refused to work with Herbert Hoover to attack the depression during the months between election and inauguration. FDR feared that the public might associate him with the failed policies of the outgoing administration. And so perhaps did Blanchard. At any rate Blanchard made his transition headquarters in Detroit, a location that meant a great deal of commuting for aides (about 170 miles per round trip). The commuting continued even through the first months of the administration; Lieutenant Governor Griffiths, for example, commuted by helicopter from her Armada Township farm in Macomb County.

What were the effects? It took longer for aides to be integrated into the Lansing scene. It added to their feelings of being overworked and overtired—inevitable during these hurried months. It also increased the uncertainty of the high-level civil servants who would not be exiting;

the distance kept them from getting to know their new superiors very well.

The distance from Lansing also resulted in some mistakes—mostly logistical. For example, a nonunion caterer was hired to prepare food for the inaugural ball in Lansing. The caterer, surprised at getting the contract, told reporters that he had kept preparations to a minimum because he had suspected a foul-up. Secretaries in Governor Milliken's office were not told that they would be transferred. When they reported to work at their regular stations on the first day of the new administration, the situation was awkward and slightly painful.

Milliken appointments. Being away from Lansing also contributed to a misunderstanding between the governor-elect and the Democratic senate. Governor Milliken asserted that his administration still had governing responsibilities and that he intended to exercise them as long as he held office. He proposed filling some seventy vacancies on boards and commissions.

Some of these appointments were to take care of loyal supporters. Others were appointments of specialists generally respected in their fields. Some were Democrats; one was the father of two Democratic members of the Michigan House of Representatives. Most of these appointments required senate confirmation. The senate Democratic leadership decided that it would be a good idea to reject all these appointments.

In a brief conversation with senate leaders, Blanchard agreed. Some observers were not sure that Blanchard had fully thought out the implications of his response to the senators. When the senate majority leader announced the strategy, some Democratic senators, including some of the ten who were then lame ducks themselves, indicated they would not go along on all the rejections—some appointees were friends and people from their districts. Thus the senate failed to reject some and rejected others in hit-or-miss fashion. Milliken then reappointed some twenty-three people to positions he judged critical. On the last possible day Governor Blanchard sent word that he wanted all these appointments killed. A senate committee did so.

This episode was perhaps a bit messier than it needed to be. Having the transition office in Detroit probably reduced communication between the incoming governor and the legislative leaders more than was desirable. The distance also may have made it more difficult for the two administrations to negotiate some of this dispute outside the public view.

Blanchard's appointment policies. A second major decision of this period was to delay making appointments until shortly before inauguration. The only exceptions were the major campaign aides who were shifted to Blanchard's personal staff. F. Thomas Lewand, a Detroit lawyer, former Oakland County commissioner, and Blanchard campaign manager, became chief of staff. Ronald Thayer, Blanchard's top aide in Congress and his campaign finance director, became executive secretary and patronage chief. Shelby Solomon, a congressional aide, was appointed policy coordinator. Blanchard appointed Conrad Mallet, Jr., a close associate of Detroit mayor Coleman Young, as legal aide. Blanchard also recruited trusted persons and campaign supporters to handle logistical details. These decisions added a sense of tension—a feeling that Blanchard was making a sharp break from the appointment practices of the previous administration.

Agency personnel, including those sympathetic to the governor-elect, complained openly that they were in limbo, not knowing whether political heads would be replaced and what agency priorities would be. They remembered that Blanchard, during the campaign, had promised that a rise in taxes would be a last resort. Some wondered what that campaign promise would mean for state services.

In late December, Blanchard appointed some of his first department heads. A pattern began to emerge that became even clearer after the January 1 inauguration. Blanchard was resolved to appoint persons whom he had known and worked with for some time. And he was willing to go out of the state to recruit others. What was the basic Blanchard standard? Blanchard was interested in partisan Democrats who were emotionally committed to a New Deal welfare-state kind of program. Unlike Milliken's criteria, Blanchard's first requirement, aside from loyalty, was not professional credentials. What he seemed to want most was emotional commitment combined with general competence.

His most controversial appointment—that of Sister Agnes Mary Monsour to head social welfare—illustrates this requirement. A public controversy ensued over her ability to supervise the program for abortions for welfare clients. Her archbishop finally ordered her to resign. (In May, under pressure from the Vatican, she ended her official affiliation with the Sisters of Mercy.) What the appointment illustrates so well is that the governor chose a person known to him from his home county, someone who had headed a college and who showed exceptional administrative ability, a close friend of Lieutenant Governor Griffiths, who had served on her college board, and someone deeply committed to serve to the less well-off in society. The fact that her professional degree was a Ph.D. in biochemistry was unimportant.

Other appointments also showed that the governor was intent on filling offices with Democrats who were loyal to him and committed to his kind of New Deal program. His efforts were more than just exercises in political patronage clout. He argued that if his administration was to be responsible for the policies of state government, he wanted his appointees to make the policy decisions. He suggested that directors of departments who were chosen by commissions should be appointed by the governor. The resignation of the head of the natural resources department, unpopular with enthusiasts of the outdoors, was followed by articles of foreboding in Detroit sports pages about how the governor would use partisan standards in getting a replacement. Later, the administration, picking up on FDR's court-packing strategy, suggested that the state Public Service Commission might be enlarged to enable Blanchard appointees to control utility rate setting. (That suggestion followed a Republican commissioner's refusal to resign.)

Blanchard also succeeded in easing out the professional who directed the state transportation department to make room for his own choice. Of the department heads who could be replaced, only two kept their positions. One, C. Patrick Babcock, director of the mental health department, had shown exceptional administrative competence as a troubleshooter heading several agencies—and was a Democrat. The other was Gerald Hough, director of the department of state police.

Financial crisis planning. A third obvious action that had to be taken was gathering information, particularly on the budget crisis. This now began in earnest. Milliken's director of the Department of Management and Budget (DMB), Gerald Miller, supplemented the report from agency heads with his own appraisal of the problems and key issues in these departments. Almost immediately, a longtime aide to Congressman Brodhead, Philip Jourdan, began round-the-clock meetings with Milliken's DMB director. Jourdan served on Blanchard's transition team as director of departmental liaison. The meetings between Jourdan and Miller were professional and cordial. Blanchard ultimately named Jourdan the new DMB director. The result was an effective transfer of responsibility in what is perhaps the single most important position in Michigan's administrative structure.

Blanchard concluded that the immediate issue facing the new administration was the bleak financial condition of the state government.

Miller, nearing the end of his job as DMB director, said with uncharacteristic candor that the state's economy was in a free fall. During the last weeks of the administration he estimated the budget deficit at $500 million.

Blanchard now used these transition months to orchestrate a campaign that would lead most citizens to conclude that a tax increase was inevitable. He appointed a distinguished advisory panel from labor and the business world. They reported to Blanchard just before the inauguration that the deficit was then about $750 million. A week or two into the new administration, the new governor, using information that his director of management and budget had collected, estimated the deficit at $900 million. Hence, by the time the administration reached office, Blanchard had expectations for action on the issue he considered paramount—the state had to get control of its financial condition. The jobs program, promised in the campaign, would have to wait.

The supreme court mess. The transition went relatively smoothly until the major transition crisis occurred. Again, a situation arose that touched on the outgoing governor's loyalty to his supporters. The situation began during the months before the inauguration but continued into the first few weeks of the governor's term.

Democratic justice Blair Moody, Jr., had been reelected to a new eight-year term. Only days later he had a fatal heart attack. The state constitution provides that the governor fill supreme court vacancies by appointment without senate confirmation. Normally, the appointee serves until the next election, then runs to fill out the rest of the term. The problem in this instance, however, was that the constitution was silent regarding the death of an incumbent during the transition period. Not unexpectedly, Republicans argued that this should be treated as a normal vacancy. Democrats said that the Milliken appointee should serve only the last weeks of the unexpired term. The new governor, they said, should appoint someone to serve the two years until the next election.

Governor Milliken appointed Dorothy Comstock-Riley, a state appeals court judge who had been the Republican runner-up in the November election. She had come in third, losing by 15,000 votes to a second Democratic nominee, Michael F. Cavanaugh. Milliken announced that she would serve until the next election. Governor-elect Blanchard urged the Democratic attorney general to challenge the Milliken appointment before the supreme court.

In January the supreme court announced its decision: three Democrats were opposed; two Republicans and an independent justice who had Democratic party ties supported seating justice Comstock-Riley. She, of course, abstained. The tie vote meant that she would remain on the court. Governor Blanchard announced that he would urge further legal action. During the weekend that followed, the independent justice had second thoughts. He shared them on Monday morning with chief justice and former Democratic governor G. Mennen Williams. After deliberations that afternoon, and without informing the Republican justices, the Democrats and the independent caucused in Williams's office. They then voted to remove justice Comstock-Riley from the court and sent a messenger to give her the news while she was at dinner.

A great deal of discussion followed in the newspapers. Former supreme court justices, both Republican and Democratic, criticized the court's action. Some pointedly argued that the state constitution explicitly forbids the supreme court's removing a judge. Governor Blanchard, after some delay, persuaded a federal judge to resign and take the appointment. The result was a supreme court composed of two Republicans, four Democrats, and an independent Democrat.

The composition was important because the court, six months or so before, had appointed a master to prepare a legislative apportionment. Democrats claimed that the redistricting favored Republicans. Moreover, it was an open secret that the new governor and the Democratic leadership were planning a new reapportionment for the 1984 and 1986 elections.

After the Inauguration

Only a few weeks into the new administration the new governor was ready for his first major policy decision: he announced that the personal income tax would have to be raised by 38 percent. He set the legislature's Easter recess in April as the deadline. In addition, budget cuts of some $225 million more would have to be made.

With sleeves rolled up, he dived in, calling local government association directors to tell them that their scheduled state-aid payments would be suspended indefinitely. Although these people did not like the message, they were impressed that the new governor called them directly. Blanchard went on the campaign trail anew, speaking in a number of the state's major cities. This time he urged support for his tax increase proposal. He sought and got the endorsement of Milliken and many other prominent persons throughout the state.

Then Blanchard approached the legislature. His commitment to a partisan style, as opposed to the Milliken style of consensus, compromise, and negotiation across party lines, became evident. Governor Blanchard's income tax proposal was unpalatable to many Democratic legislators. But part of the reason for the high level of partisan voting that followed was the word that a reapportionment bill was in the works and that the governor was monitoring the vote on the tax bill.

The tax increase was pushed through the house with no discussion. All but four Democrats favored it. No Republican voted for it—nor was asked to do so. In the senate, negotiations were necessary because one Democrat had announced opposition. Without that vote, Democrats could not pass the tax increase. The early briefing papers had suggested that one Republican in particular might be won over if attention were paid to his opinions (which had not been done for him under the Milliken administration). As governor-elect, Blanchard had invited this Republican senator to some briefings and was said to have paid attention to his suggestions. If true, the strategy paid off. Suddenly, during the bipartisan negotiations, the senator seized his moment and announced that for the good of the state he would vote for Blanchard's tax bill.

Immediately, the bill, containing only minor changes from the original version, went to a vote and passed. All other Republicans and Democrats voted along party lines. Miraculously, in a state not accustomed to prompt legislative action, the income tax became law. And the legislature had more than met the governor's Easter deadline.

In February the Democratic party held its regular winter convention. The main business of this meeting is usually the selection of the party chairman for a two-year term. Governor Blanchard recommended Rick Wiener of Detroit. He had been an aide to Congressman Brodhead and had directed U.S. Senator Carl Levin's Michigan staff. Wiener, of course, was elected.

The budget for the new fiscal year, usually delivered to the legislature in early February, had been put on the back burner. The legislature, at Milliken's urging, had obligingly passed a law deferring the deadline for the budget message until April. Governor Blanchard now introduced his first budget. He claimed that he was recommending increased appropriations for education and social welfare. Some Republican legislators noted that Blanchard's recommended increases, at least for education, were less than what Governor Milliken had recommended and less than the legislature had approved the previous year. (Because of budget cuts, education did not get the full appropriation, so Blanchard's recommendations were at least higher than what education actually received.) An economy measure (later abandoned) included the closing of eleven national guard armories—all in Republican districts.

In early May the governor announced his jobs program. It featured the creation of 80,000 public service jobs, including a summer youth corps of 25,000 modeled on the CCC of FDR days. Job corps workers would wear Blanchard buttons—green and white (Michigan State University colors)—as reminders, journalists said, of who had given them a summer job. The program included projects to resurface 414 miles of roads and bridges, weatherize 13,000 homes, and repair 230 miles of railroad track. Those who hired summer youth would get a state tax rebate, and small businesses would get new special tax breaks. As the governor buoyantly ticked off, in a televised address to a joint session of the legislature, item after item of his public works programs, one could almost hear the faint strains of "Happy Days Are Here Again" in the background.

Conservationists were critical when they found out that the governor proposed to finance part of the program by borrowing money from oil revenues dedicated to the state's land acquisition fund. Other, more conservative critics mounted a recall effort against the governor and selected Democratic legislators. At this point one could definitely say that the transition was over and the new governor had firmly set the pattern of his administration.

Both in style and content Governor Blanchard had put in place a program in the Franklin Roosevelt–New Deal mode. His only bobble during these first months was the mishandling of a chemical spill in the small community of Swartz Creek. The governor had announced that there would have to be a one-year delay in clean-up. A judge then ordered the state to clean up the dump site immediately.

We do not want to make too much of the incident. Yet it does suggest once more that Blanchard is a Democrat in an older mold, not one who gets emotional about the social issues of the 1960s and 1970s— nuclear power, environmental concerns, women's rights. It is not that he does not favor these issues. It is, rather, that they do not reach his consciousness in the way that the old New Deal battle cries of the 1930s do.

The Michigan Transition of 1983: An Evaluation

From outgoing Governor Milliken's vantage point, the transition out of office went reasonably well. Few blamed him for being loyal to those who had served him. Even Democrats did not blame him for appointing Comstock-Riley to the bench. He left office feeling that he had, to the end, given the state a professional and responsible administration.

From Blanchard's point of view, the transition was handled exceptionally well. The mistakes that were made tended to be in the less important area of logistics, and none did irreparable harm. The paperwork of information gathering for the new governor had a few gaps, but the governor-elect got the important political and financial information that he needed. That departmental reports could in some cases have been more thorough was, again, a matter of secondary importance.

The governor-elect did put his stamp on the new administration. He seems to have planned a clear break with his predecessor's style of governing. He laid the groundwork carefully and successfully for that break during the transition period. In office Blanchard made it clear very quickly that he would act—generally, with vigor and effectiveness. The sizable rise in income tax was accomplished with little haggling or delay. The handling of the court crisis case showed a governor who knew what he wanted and was willing to push for it. Legislators could hope that his actions on apportionment would be equally well planned and effective.

In terms of style the governor had demonstrated, at least to his own satisfaction, that party government was superior to the kind of compromising across party lines that had characterized Michigan governance for a generation. Even the controversy over Agnes Mary Monsour redounded to his benefit. Feminists could hardly fault him for his actions, even though, as we indicated, he probably chose Sister Monsour less because she was a woman than because she would make an effective administrator and was committed to the values that he held.

Governor Blanchard accomplished this change in less than six months. Whether the style of partisan governing he instituted can survive for his whole term, given the separation of powers system, remains to be seen. But what is not in dispute is that the transition initially accomplished, in general, the political results that the governor-elect had hoped for. And that is one standard by which we should judge transitions.

Epilogue: The Governorship Fifteen Months Later

If we judge the transition by its long-term effects, however, we may reach a different conclusion.

Michigan permits the recall of state officials for political cause, but none had ever faced such an election. Within three months after the tax increase, recallers launched a drive against Governor Blanchard but were unable to secure the 760,000 signatures needed within the ninety days allowed. Recalls were also attempted in more than twenty legislative districts. Two were successful; Democratic senators were replaced with Republicans, and control of the state senate changed from Democratic to Republican.

The governor's popularity within his own party and with the general public (as shown by the polls) slumped. Meanwhile the legislature was in a stalemate, unwilling to consider controversial legislation. Nevertheless, the governor continued to meet some of his goals—reinstituting his well-received summer job youth corps, having his veto sustained by one vote on a law forbidding state welfare abortions, and continuing to trim the state bureaucracy on schedule. But none of these victories required bipartisan negotiation. The youth corps was relatively noncontroversial, Governor Milliken's eleven vetoes on the abortion issue had left lines sharply drawn, and the reduction of the bureaucracy through attrition could be accomplished unilaterally.

As we suggested earlier, the American system of governing is difficult to adapt to party government.

The Gubernatorial Transition in Minnesota, 1982

VIRGINIA GRAY AND KAREN HULT

The transition from Republican Governor Albert H. (Al) Quie to Democrat Rudy Perpich was a smooth one, in part because Perpich was entering the governor's office for the second time. The shift from one incumbent to another was accomplished speedily, with a minimum of discord. Nevertheless, several criticisms can be made, including the questionable quality of some major appointments, delays in budget preparation, and the lack of a legislative program. In this chapter we examine the conditions leading to a smooth transition and the sources of problems, most notably the state's economy.

The Context

The transition took place during a period of budgetary crisis. After the election, lame-duck Quie called his seventh and last special legislative session to solve the state's latest financial woes. These prolonged budgetary difficulties were a consequence of several factors. One was the tax-reduction programs that Quie had initiated in 1978, particularly his tax indexation scheme. In practice, taxes were overindexed so that revenues fell further than predicted. Early in Quie's term the Democratic-Farmer-Labor (DFL) party contributed to the coming revenue shortfall by greatly enlarging the state's property tax relief program (the homestead credit). Another critical factor was the onset of a nationwide recession. Contrary to the conventional wisdom that Minnesota is relatively immune to economic downturns, this time Minnesota's economy performed worse than the nation's economy. Agriculture and mining were particularly hard hit. Quie's budgetary forecasts unfortunately were based on the assumptions of no recession and modest economic growth; thus, his revenue projections were way off base and far too optimistic. By August of 1980 the recession had reduced revenues to the point at which the first of several budgetary shortfalls occurred. The last factor in the budgetary equation was that mandated spending also exceeded budgetary assumptions.

Quie first dealt with these problems by unilaterally cutting expenditures. Burned by this experience, he joined with the legislature in 1981 to increase taxes and to shift some expenditures into the next biennium. By the end of that year he was no longer able to reach agreement with the legislature. Legislators solved the November 1981 shortfall by enacting, without Quie's signature, more shifts, more tax increases, and only a few cuts in spending.

It was the continuing specter of current and deferred budget deficits that led Quie to decide in March 1982 not to run for a second term. That decision was supported by most party leaders, who wanted to find a new candidate untainted by management problems. Still, the Independent-Republican (IR) party leadership did select Quie's lieutenant governor, Lou Wangberg, as their gubernatorial nominee. Wangberg was subsequently rejected in the IR primary in favor of millionaire businessman Wheelock Whitney. Whitney, in contrast to Wangberg and Quie, was moderate or even liberal on most social issues. But Whitney's most important qualification appeared to be his proven success as a businessman who had built a small stock brokerage firm into a regional leader. "A governor who can manage" was the refrain heard in his campaign ads.

The state's economic problems and its chronic inability to balance its budget similarly led the DFL to its final choice. Like the Republican party leadership, the DFL party convention chose a nominee who was subsequently rejected by his party's voters. He was Warren Spannaus, the attorney general. However, Spannaus lost at the polls to former Governor Rudy Perpich. Perpich had been elected lieutenant governor in 1974 and had succeeded Wendell Anderson into the governor's office. Anderson, in turn, had resigned the governorship after appointing himself U.S. Senator. Since being defeated by Quie in 1978, Perpich had been in Vienna, Austria, working as a trade representative for Control Data Corporation. He did not attempt to capture the convention endorsement but instead appeared in the summer of 1982 to wage a whirlwind primary campaign against Spannaus. In this battle Perpich was the more conservative candidate on social issues. He stressed his experience in both state government and private enterprise in contrast to Spannaus's exclusively governmental experience. Furthermore, Perpich represented the Iron Range, a northern Minnesota DFL stronghold long at odds with Twin Cities liberals. The DFL voters appeared to respond to the candidate with more business experience: Perpich won the primary.

Thus, economic issues were important in structuring the choices of both parties. Both parties chose candidates with business backgrounds, and both chose candidates with views on social issues that are atypical of the leadership and perhaps unrepresentative of the activists in each party. The election became a referendum on managing the state's economy rather than on the social issues that had so dominated Minnesota politics in recent years.

The Electoral Campaign and Transition Planning

The period covered by this study runs from the gubernatorial primary in mid-September 1982 through the delivery of and reaction to the governor's budget message in mid-February 1983. The sources include interviews with ten participants in the transition process, news accounts, and personal observation. The interviews were semistructured, with open-ended questions. Interviews were conducted with the head of Perpich's transition team, the staffers heading the transition effort for the state Department of Administration, and a member of the outgoing governor's staff both before and after the election, as well as with a member of Whitney's staff before the election. After the election, respondents included the new governor, the lieutenant governor, and key members of Perpich's transition (and later office) staff. Cooperation was excellent, especially considering the time constraints on those interviewed. All respondents except the governor and lieutenant governor were assured of the confidentiality of their remarks. In what follows, then, information is not attributed to particular individuals, though in some cases their positions are identified.

Transition planning evidently started first in the Perpich campaign. Several days before the primary election, a Perpich associate raised the issue with the candidate. Increasingly confident of Perpich's nomination and election, this individual stressed the importance of a confident, well-prepared beginning: "Quie never recovered from his shaky start. . . ." Immediately following his primary victory Perpich read and approved a transition plan that laid out strategies and timetables through inauguration day. By the end of September the initial transition team had been selected; all three of its members (Terry Montgomery, Tom Triplett, and Lynn Anderson) had held staff positions in the previous Perpich administration.

Activity in the Perpich organization triggered responses elsewhere. Republican candidate Wheelock Whitney appointed a transition manager, and Governor Quie directed his staff to cooperate with the candidates. Meanwhile, the state Department of Administration took on the responsibility of coordinating the transition, handling everything from equipping the temporary transition offices to serving as liaison between the candidates and the outgoing governor and his staff on matters such as budget procedures and revenue and expenditure projections. The two-member team from the Department of Administration worked with very little statutory direction and with what one of them termed a "ridiculously low" appropriation of $29,600 for transition activities. The use of the department as the primary information link and coordinating mechanism was novel, more a reflection of the current commissioner's desires than an institutionalized set of procedures.

Between the primary and the general election the attention paid to planning for the transition differed dramatically in the Whitney and the Perpich campaigns. The Whitney organization gave it little emphasis. A volunteer transition advisory committee, made up of ten people not involved in the campaign, met for the first time the Saturday before the general election. The sole paid staffer assigned to deal with transition planning—the campaign administrator—estimated that he spent less than 5 percent of his time on transition-related matters. And the Department of Administration staffers reported only minimal Whitney-initiated contacts. Nor did the candidate appear to be much involved in transition planning. Although he apparently set priorities for personnel selection and labeled the budget the primary focus of his transition activities, Whitney did not name a transition team, draw up lists of prospective appointees, or begin putting together a legislative package.

This general lack of emphasis probably reflects several factors. First, behind in the polls (by as much as 17 percent in early October),[1] Whitney directed his efforts toward almost desperate campaigning. The Whitney staff—brave optimism to the contrary—evidently did not expect to win the general election and thus did not devote resources to a "pointless" transition effort. Finally, Whitney staffers may have expected transition to be less of a problem for them than it would be for Perpich because they would be replacing a fellow Republican.

In sharp contrast was the attention paid to transition planning within the Perpich camp. As noted earlier, his transition team was functioning by mid-September. Its members met frequently and at least weekly with both Perpich and his running mate, Marlene Johnson. Department of Administration staffers reported significantly more contacts with the Perpich campaign; the transition team members spoke of interacting with state legislators, representatives of interest groups, and state agency personnel during the preelection period.

Candidate Perpich placed considerable distance between the transition team and the campaign staff. Although the two sometimes coordinated their efforts, those concentrating on the transition, with one exception, did not work on the campaign. Governor Perpich offered two justifications for this separation. The first underscored his concern with maintaining an active campaign despite his growing confidence of a victory: "I didn't want to let word out to the campaign staff that everything was in the bag. That doesn't send out good signals." However, the second reason reflected a longer-term focus. Perpich noted that he had asked "the people I wanted in my office not to be in the campaign. . . . Around here, they think you're a dummy . . . if you get involved in campaigns. . . . I resent it. I think people that help someone campaign . . . are doing a public service. But, if you put someone like that in a job, they call it 'political.' "[2]

The individuals that Perpich did ask to be on the transition team divided their responsibilities. Triplett handled policy issues and started assembling a policy staff for the governor's office; Montgomery concentrated on putting together lists of potential heads of state agencies; and campaign staffer Anderson dealt with more routine, administrative concerns (e.g., hiring temporary clerical and support personnel for the transition office). Triplett worked with a Policy Advisers' Group (a brain trust of prominent community leaders, businesspersons, and academics) in developing "concept papers," which were to serve as the basis of the new governor's legislative program. Although no counterbudget to the one being readied by the outgoing governor was prepared, the policy advisor, the candidate, and other staff members sketched budget "plans, guidelines, and standards . . . [to help] target spending and guide what we do with taxes." High priority was placed on developing a transition timetable that would permit key personnel decisions to be made and announced as soon as possible after the general election.

While this relatively detailed transition planning went on—mostly at the staff level—the Democratic candidates for governor and lieutenant governor seemed to be preparing for the transition in other ways. Through much of the fall Perpich campaigned as the "candidate with experience," appearing at times almost as the incumbent. As a headline in the Minneapolis paper pointed out, "Perpich's plans race past election day." For example, the candidate solicited suggestions for appointments, recruited prospective agency heads, and introduced plans for a postelection overseas trip to explore better marketing of state products.[3] Meanwhile, Perpich and Johnson spent their travel time on long campaign trips laying out the division of labor between the governor's and the lieutenant governor's offices.[4] Confident of the outcome of the general election, both candidates were able to begin their preparations for taking office early.

Overall, transition planning during the preelection period proceeded rather smoothly. Complaints about time pressures and lack of money were common, but all those interviewed remarked on the high degree of cooperation. The Department of Administration received outstanding marks for its service as messenger, linking the candidates and the outgoing governor, eliminating the awkwardness of direct interaction. Underscored, too, was the general spirit of helpfulness expressed by Governor Quie and his staff. The latter had had the opportunity to prepare for leaving office—to "grieve," as one respondent put it. Moreover, the 1978–79 transition had been so difficult that parties on all sides evidently resolved to "do better this time." Individuals spoke of having taken over offices after the 1978 election that had no furniture, stationery, or even staples, of spending weeks trying to reconstruct missing files. According to one observer, "when the new lieutenant governor moved into his office, the office had been stripped clean; there was nothing there except a rattrap with the sign 'the rats are here.' "

The Transition Period

But this time, in 1982, there were no reports of resistance or lack of cooperation during the period between the primary and the general election. And, at least in the short run, the planning in the Perpich camp paid off. Though the governor-elect was marooned in a snow storm in northern Minnesota the day after the election, his staff reported to work in the legislative hearing room already outfitted by the Department of Administration. Because of the planning of the department and the Perpich staff, no time was lost in organizing the transition staff. Rather, time could be devoted to the larger goal of organizing the new governor's administration.

By all accounts this was both the best-planned and best-executed transition that Minnesota has experienced. Those managing the shift from running to governing included the three previously mentioned Perpich staffers (Anderson, Montgomery, and Triplett) plus a fourth professional, Mike O'Donnell, on loan from Control Data Corporation. O'Donnell appears to have been a late but important addition; his name surfaced publicly only after the election. All four later joined the Perpich administration in significant capacities. During the transition, however, Montgomery served as head of the team, Triplett as the top policy advisor, Anderson as office manager, and O'Donnell as personnel manager. In practice, responsibilities were often shared. This sharing seemed to work for the people involved, though it sometimes mystified outsiders. These four people also managed the much larger group of people involved in diverse transition tasks, including the appointments of the heads of 33 agencies and, subsequently, their deputy or assistant commissioners (between 70 and 80 in number); the selection of the governor's personal staff, numbering about 30; the filling of approximately 400 positions on state boards and commissions; judicial appointments; and policy, legislation, and budgetary matters.

MAJOR APPOINTMENTS

Clearly, the most significant personnel task was the identification and selection of persons to head state agencies. The Perpich team set a goal of completing these thirty-three major appointments by December 15. One reason for the early deadline was the feeling that Quie's relatively slow start on appointments was a problem that he had not overcome. Others, too, urged speed; for example, the *Tribune* editorialized, "Perpich administration needs a fast start."[5]

The major positions had been ranked according to importance, with the most urgent ones being revenue, finance, welfare, transportation, natural resources, administration, economic security, and energy, planning, and development.[6] They were to be filled in ten days by Perpich's own search procedures. Advisory committees were established to conduct the searches for other positions, such as agriculture and veterans' affairs. Still other secondary positions were targeted to be filled in December. Moreover, before the election Perpich had decided which incumbents he would keep and which of his own commissioners he would bring back.

The postelection search procedure was quite formalized. O'Donnell processed approximately 2,000 solicited and unsolicited résumés. Every second day he furnished the governor and key staff with a list of candidates grouped by departments. Perpich, according to our sources, went through the list and indicated those worth pursuing. The transition team then contacted the individuals to determine interest and checked references. Following that investigation, senior staffers interviewed each candidate once or twice, sometimes joined by a confidant of the governor. Finally, the governor interviewed the finalist or finalists, allocating his time according to the importance of the position. Some he did not interview personally.

With the important exception of energy, planning, and development, Perpich and his staff met their mid-December goal. The order of making appointments appears to have been governed by the ease of selection rather than by the urgency principle. Among Perpich's first appointments were the current corrections commissioner and the incumbent military affairs director. Of the eight urgent posts, only three (revenue, administration, and economic security) were filled in November, and one of the appointees (head of economic security) accepted after the ten-day target. Welfare was one of the last posts filled because several people turned it down. The appointment of a commissioner of natural resources was delayed pending a grievance against the incumbent commissioner, who was finally reappointed. The relatively new combination of energy, planning, and development was targeted again for reorganization. Though offered to at least one candidate, the post had not been filled by January.

Appointments after the first ten days were more likely to have come about through the postelection search procedures. The appointment of the commissioner of finance, which came in early December, is illustrative: the man selected was recommended to Perpich by the Minnesota Business Partnership, which sponsored Perpich's trip to Boston in November.[7] The positions for which Perpich used formal screening procedures were also being filled well into December. For example, not until December 15 did Perpich announce his choice for commissioner of agriculture. Several people admitted to us that the screening commission was a bad idea that they would not repeat—it tied the governor's hands too much. Screening commissions had been contemplated for several other posts with important constituencies but had been rejected—fortunately so, most thought.

Throughout the transition Perpich continually mentioned the names of those under consideration, hinted at the identities of others, and announced offers well before they were accepted. For example, on Wednesday morning, the day after the election, he revealed his leanings on appointees for three positions; all were subsequently appointed. On Thursday it was reported that the present transportation commissioner would be replaced; in fact, the incumbent stayed on. On Friday, Perpich mentioned four additional leanings.[8] These open leaks appear to be one way by which Perpich ascertained the reactions of various constituency groups, though the method may have been embarrassing to those not appointed.

Overall, nearly one-third of the thirty-three positions were reappointments of Quie people, some of whom Quie had held over from the Perpich administration. Another third were people that Perpich had in mind when he was elected. The remaining third were people suggested by interest groups and individuals. In speed of selection and general quality, the outcome of the process clearly satisfied the Perpich team. The governor's sense of satisfaction appears to have come from his confidence in the judgments of his staff rather than the knowledge that he handpicked each commissioner. The governor said, "You put in people you would not put in if you were totally free to choose. There are lots of pressures. . . . Some groups think they own particular departments, and also you have to keep the legislators happy."[9]

The governor's direct involvement in appointments seemingly did not extend below the top level. The commissioners picked their own deputies and assistants, though some of the names may have been generated by O'Donnell's personnel system. Perpich claimed that he would not recognize five names on a list of deputy commissioners.[10] In fact, he admitted to a reporter who asked about certain controversial deputy selections, "as God is my witness, it's a big surprise."[11]

JUDICIAL APPOINTMENTS

Next in importance to the appointments of the agency heads were the judicial appointments. Perpich appointed an eleven-member screening commission, including one member from each judicial district plus a chairman. By appointing all the commission members Perpich departed from Quie's selection mechanism, in which the governor picked only half of the screening committee. Both the state bar association and the state's leading newspaper criticized the new process.[12] Undeterred, Perpich used the commission to suggest three to five names for each vacancy on municipal, county, and district courts as well as for the newly created intermediate appellate courts.

MINOR APPOINTMENTS

The third set of state appointments was the hundreds of positions on boards and commissions. By law, such openings were listed and advertised by the secretary of state's office. The selection came in sifting the thousands of names rather than in generating the names in the first place. As in his previous administration, Perpich appointed a screening commission that included one member from each congressional district. Chaired by the lieutenant governor, the commission recommended three to five people for each opening.

Though the lieutenant governor chaired the commission, it was clear that control was being exerted from the governor's office. O'Donnell was formally in charge of these appointments and assigned a staffer to keep track of the résumés, which were kept in the governor's transition office. The process was somewhat similar to that for the major appointments: boards were categorized according to whether they were policy making or purely advisory. The policy boards, of higher priority, were filled first; their candidates were interviewed personally by the commission. Advisory board openings were filled later; the selections were made from the résumés only, without interviews. Due to its lesser importance, this selection process did not get under way until after Perpich took office. A related factor in the slowness was the sheer volume of paper; 3,700 résumés for 439 jobs greeted Perpich when he came into office.

PERSONAL STAFF

The final group of appointees was the governor's personal staff. Though many were decided upon relatively early, their appointments were not announced until after the commission appointments were. For example, even the four top aides, the foursome who managed the transition, were not named formally until December 3. Montgomery returned to his old job as chief of staff; Anderson became deputy chief of staff for administration; Triplett was named deputy chief of staff for policy development; O'Donnell became special advisor to the governor and executive secretary to the cabinet. A little later the legislative liaison, Keith Ford, was announced.

Most of the staff decisions were also made early. One initial decision was that Perpich would hire only about thirty people, about half as many as had worked for the governor ten years before. This reduction was due to budgetary difficulties and to Perpich's desire to rely on department heads. The transition team prepared an organization chart and a list of names of possible candidates for the jobs. Included on the list were people from the last Perpich administration and from the current campaign, about half coming from each group.

POLICY PLANNING

Besides appointments, the major task of any transition group is planning for the policies that the new governor wants enacted: the translation of campaign issues into legislation, the search for other public problems and their possible solutions, and the design of a budget that will make these priorities possible or likely. Although there are fewer objective measures of whether the transition team achieved its policy goals, compared with its personnel goals, most observers agreed that the Perpich staff was less successful in achieving its policy goals. The primary reason for lethargy was the interruption caused by the special legislative session in December 1982 and the subsequent narrowing of budgetary options.

The Perpich team organized for policy planning through a series of commissions, one of which began work before the election. These groups focused on agri-processing, mineral development, international trade, tourism, investment and banking, and film and the video arts. Each task force was headed by a prominent citizen and was expected to produce a set of recommendations by February 15.

In addition to these sources of policy initiatives, Perpich's staff solicited ideas from each outgoing commissioner and from legislators. During the transition period his limited staff was involved primarily in gathering ideas and narrowing the options. The goal was to have only twelve to fifteen governor's bills for the legislative session. Thus, the transition period was a time for reducing the policy agenda rather than expanding it. Moreover, the absence of several policy advisors (only one person worked on policy) and the overwhelming attention paid to appointments (that one advisor spent less than half his time on policy) meant that there was little time to generate entirely new initiatives. Because of the press of time, the review of department bills (usually a technical review) was subcontracted to Quie's staff.

There was even less time to devote to the new budget. On Perpich's first day in his transition office, Governor Quie warned him of a possible revenue shortfall. By mid-November a new forecast predicted a deficit of $312 million in the current fiscal year ending in June 1983. For the next three weeks legislators were closeted with Governor Quie and his staff, trying to find a solution. Quie accepted responsibility for the state's financial woes and thus continued to act as chief negotiator with the legislature. Much to the dismay of his party's legislative leadership, the IR governor entered into yet another agreement with the DFL-controlled legislature to cover half the deficit through spending cuts and shifts and the rest through increased taxes. The bill passed without a vote to spare, and the governor signed it.

In his public role Perpich stood apart from the special session negotiations, taking the position that he did not want to interfere with the incumbent's prerogatives. Undoubtedly, Perpich saw little to be gained by public association with increased taxes and budget cuts. However, a Perpich representative, usually Triplett, attended all the legislative meetings, seeking to prevent expenditure shifts into the next fiscal year and to guard Perpich's campaign promises. At the same time DFL legislative leaders desired to solve fiscal problems then so that Perpich would have some leeway once he was in office. The net effect was that Perpich was not just a bystander to Quie's negotiations: "More people were running down to Perpich's office to see what to do than were going to Quie's."

Meanwhile, the three weeks devoted to the state's immediate budgetary problems necessarily curtailed Perpich's ability to scrutinize the biennial request already prepared by Quie. Perpich eventually had to postpone submission of the budget until late February because his staff simply did not have sufficient time to prepare an analysis of the ongoing budget.

Amid this intense pressure from the state's budgetary problems, the Perpich transition team by all accounts functioned very well in the two months available for the transition. Certainly, all the team members felt that the experience was a positive one and that the job was accomplished. Indeed, several said that this was the smoothest transition Minnesota had ever seen. Many outside the staff had positive evaluations but questioned the division of labor within the staff, specifically the combining of policy, legislation, and budget functions in one person. This weakness was exacerbated by the crunch brought on by the special session, but the weakness existed apart from that added burden.

Throughout the transition period the Perpich team had help from several sources. Without a doubt, the most significant source of help was the Department of Administration. Its work in planning the transition was considerable, but during the transition one staff member from the department spent about half his time on transition matters. Primarily, he helped with office management and administration: orienting new secretarial staff, acquainting people with state office procedure and procurement, and generally doing routine tasks that no one else had time to do.

Another source of expertise was the National Governors' Association (NGA). Perpich, his wife, and three staffers attended the new governors' seminar in Utah after the election. All pronounced it invaluable. For one thing, it offered an occasion for a staff retreat, an experience they repeated locally in late December. The published materials of the NGA were obviously familiar to the Perpich staff, yet their use was somewhat limited. Most people found the checklist of tasks useful, but their own planning usually went far beyond such a basic list. This limitation probably reflects the fact that the materials are intended for neophytes. Finally, the NGA assisted by sending a staff person to Minnesota for brief visits. Apparently, he designed some forms for them, helped to set up the lieutenant governor's office, and did other short-range jobs. The general impression was that his help, like any help, was appreciated but not crucial.

The Governor's Role

Thus far, we have described the major activities of any transition: filling positions and planning a legislative program. Most of these activities, however, took place without the new governor's personal attention because he spent most of his time traveling. During the campaign Perpich had often said, "I'll go anywhere I need to go, if it could help the state's economy."[13] In the first month after the election he certainly honored that pledge, visiting Boston, Japan, Ohio, Pennsylvania, New York, and Washington, D.C.

When he was in town Perpich worked out of the transition office, meeting with his staff, interviewing finalists for major positions, holding press conferences, and announcing policy initiatives. However, it was clear that he delegated much authority to his staff, preferring the ambassador role to the manager role. As the governor himself said, "They did most of the work. . . . I can trust them; they do a good job." In addition, Perpich probably took a less active role in the appointments process because this was his second time around. Moreover, Perpich is not a detail-oriented person as, for example, Jimmy Carter was. Rather he is a chairman-of-the-board type, who prefers not to be bothered by details. He asserted, "People are the most important thing. I have the best staff a governor could have. They're what makes things work. We just got back from spending five days away and everything was running smoothly. In fact, they may have been running better than when I'm here. I could go away for two months and things would still go on."[14] On this dimension Perpich's style resembles that of Ronald Reagan except that Perpich is a very active person who works long hours; one source mentioned eighteen to twenty hours a day seven days a week during the transition.

Another task for any governor during the transition phase is to determine the role that the lieutenant governor will play in his administration. As a former lieutenant governor, Perpich was especially sensitive to the role of his partner. Perpich had handpicked businesswoman and feminist Marlene Johnson as his running mate. They ran as a team—to a degree unusual even for Minnesota, where the two candidates are elected together. Perpich relied on Johnson to attract women, minorities, and liberals as well as to add business expertise to a DFL ticket. During the campaign they traveled and spoke together. He made it clear that Johnson would head the activities to increase tourism, one of his major priorities. However, as already noted, Johnson's role during the transition was much less visible and apparently less influential than during the campaign.

Overall, Perpich and his staff accomplished a great deal between November 3 and January 3. Planning before the election paid off: major appointments were made swiftly, and mechanisms for filling other positions were set up. Policy matters did not flow so easily, however; too many important and difficult decisions were left for the new administration. Although the staff gave careful attention to detail, the new governor was relatively detached from daily operations. The roles of both governor and staff presaged their roles in office.

Taking Office

Like most new governors, Rudy Perpich began his term amid an out-
pouring of congratulations and good wishes from all sides. The honeymoon period was brief, however, perhaps because Perpich, as an already
experienced governor, was allowed less leeway, perhaps due to the severe financial problems and difficult decisions confronting the state. By
mid-February, when the new governor presented his budget to the legislature, several areas of potential trouble for the administration could be
identified.

Even Perpich's inauguration raised some critical comment. The new
governor decided to take the oath of office in his hometown, Hibbing,
rather than in the state capital with the rest of the elected officeholders.
Still, the inaugural address, which underscored the governor's commitment to quality public education, was well received. Even Republican
legislators found themselves responding favorably to the state of the
state address, in which Perpich called for a partnership between business, labor, and government.[15]

THE BUDGET

After the ceremonies of the first week in office, attention returned once
again to the state fiscal crisis. Despite the emphasis evidently given the
budget during the transition, Perpich and his staff still found themselves behind in preparing a budget required by law to be submitted by
January 25. Almost immediately, therefore, the governor asked for and
received a three-week extension.

The struggle with the budget highlighted perhaps the major weakness in the Perpich transition. Certainly, the special session and the continually worsening revenue projections (including the announcement of
an $8.5-million shortage instead of the $32-million surplus expected after
the December changes)[16] would have posed considerable problems for
any incoming governor. Yet the lack of attention paid to the budget
during November and December, as well as the continuing overload on
top Perpich aides, further slowed budget making.

Press reports and interviews painted a picture of a governor actively
involved in assembling the budget. Upon taking office, the governor
hammered out the budget with a small group of advisors—his chief of
staff, policy advisor, legislative liaison, officials of the revenue and finance
departments, the state economist, and the chairman of the senate Tax

Committee. In a departure from the tradition of the previous Perpich administration, the commissioners of the various line agencies were not included in most of the deliberations. A good deal of the budget preparation took place in public, and various parts were announced before the deadline. Budget changes were also publicized. For example, the governor introduced, then abandoned, an extension of the sales tax to clothing. Unclear, however, was whether such instances were only so many trial balloons or whether, as the governor claimed, he merely "changed his mind."[17]

Governor Perpich defended his budget as a step toward achieving financial stability for the state and toward helping citizens in need. The $9.3 billion biennial budget—19 percent larger than that for the previous two years—contained a $250-million reserve fund to protect the state against faulty revenue projections. It also introduced the notion of "shared risk": school and local government aids would be cut by as much as 4 percent if state revenues dropped below budgeted amounts. On the revenue side it called for retaining a 10-percent income tax surcharge and a 6-percent sales tax, and proposed a 5-cent-per-gallon increase in the gasoline tax. In addition, the proposed budget made property tax circuit-breaker provisions (bringing state relief to property taxpayers) more sensitive to income level and the amount of tax paid. Proposed expenditures generally reflected Perpich's campaign priorities. A 16-percent increase was sought for the development of alternative energy resources and conservation programs. The governor also asked for a $75-million jobs program, under which the state would subsidize the costs of hiring new workers.[18]

Legislative reaction to the budget was predictable. Fellow Democrats expressed overall satisfaction. Republicans complained that spending levels were too high and that increased taxes would trigger further deterioration in the state's business climate. Interest group opposition to specific parts of the budget surfaced, too. We predict that, despite a convincing electoral victory and considerable thought and deliberation in putting together the budget, Governor Perpich will by no means have an easy time moving the budget through the legislature.

LEGISLATIVE PROPOSALS

Even more mixed have been the reactions to Perpich's policy proposals. Despite promises to narrow its legislative agenda, the administration began with a flurry of general ideas and priority areas, ranging from international marketing of the state and its products to developing indigenous energy sources and streamlining state government. Initially, the reaction to Perpich's recommendations was favorable. His promises to cut bureaucracy, decrease workers' compensation rates, and involve the state in creating jobs in the private sector drew support from Republicans; his evident concern with elementary and secondary education and the plight of the unemployed appealed to Democrats.

The new governor proved less successful, however, at translating these ideas into legislative proposals. By mid-March—halfway through the legislative session—Perpich had failed to introduce legislation on jobs, energy conservation and alternative fuels, and a variety of other top priorities. "Where's the Perpich whirlwind now?" wondered a *Tribune* editorialist.[19]

Several reasons for the gap between promise and performance can be identified. First, a good deal of staff time and energy was devoted to budget matters, leaving little opportunity to develop more substantive policy proposals. Second, some outside the governor's office argued that the policy staff was inadequate. Not only did the total size of the governor's staff shrink but policy might have been too much a one-man show, handled primarily by an overloaded staff assistant.[20]

Following through on particular ideas was even more difficult, given the governor's frequent shifts in interest and his readiness to change his mind on policy direction and substance. In addition, Governor Perpich at times became embroiled in controversies not directly related to his top priorities. For instance, much television time and newspaper ink was spent on the war of words between Perpich and South Dakota Governor William J. (Bill) Janklow on the relative merits of the two states. Finally, time and public attention were diverted from the governor's key initiatives by the sheer number of Perpich priorities; both the governor and his staff were subject to the criticism that they "spread themselves too thin."

However, after a shaky start, Perpich's public performance improved greatly. The DFL-controlled legislature gave him much of what he requested: fifty-five of sixty-three initiatives proposed, according to his aides' generous estimates.[21] The *Tribune*'s legislative scorecard, however, accorded Perpich only three clear victories on twenty major issues, though acknowledging his important role in negotiating settlements on total spending, taxes, and workers' compensation. In the eyes of most observers such successes overshadowed the setbacks during the transition.

Despite some significant successes, Perpich also faced problems in developing and maintaining links with various constituency groups. On the one hand he continued to hold and cultivate the support of fellow Iron Rangers. The new governor worked to keep plants open in the economically troubled area, proposed expanding research and technology activities at the University of Minnesota–Duluth campus, and appeared before northeast Minnesota audiences with Republican Senator Rudy Boschwitz to discuss jobs and the possible location of a federal enterprise zone in the region.[22] More striking were Perpich's efforts to woo business support. " 'Born again' in his attitude toward business," the governor approached economic recovery and development by relying heavily on private sector involvement, with the state as facilitator and investor.[23] Business seemed to respond favorably.

At the same time these strategies carried risks. Perpich's focus on the Iron Range led to complaints about a "regional governor." Moreover, the tilt toward business was unpalatable to many DFLers, traditionally hostile to government involvement in economic development on the grounds that it is a subsidy of the private sector. Disagreements between the governor and fellow Democrats arose in other areas as well. The Democratic state Central Committee publicly opposed Perpich on several issues. Less than a month into the new administration, the committee issued a " 'reminder' to the DFL governor that the party wants him to listen to them."[24] What remains to be seen, of course, is to what extent the governor will be able to balance and negotiate with some of these competing groups on specific pieces of legislation in the context of a tight budget.

In addition, some of Perpich's appointments to head state agencies led to conflict with constituency groups. Pro-choice advocates and the medical community objected to the naming of Sister Mary Madonna Ashton, an antiabortion activist and former hospital administrator, as commissioner of the Health Department, an agency traditionally headed by a physician. Cries of political patronage greeted the appointments of Len Levine, a St. Paul city council member, and Mike Hatch, state Democratic party chairman, as commissioners of the departments of Welfare and Commerce, respectively. Ashton and Levine generated further controversy when they removed career employees from top-level jobs. As mentioned earlier, the use of an advisory committee to suggest possible candidates to head the Agriculture Department caused problems, too. Complaints were also heard from minorities, who were dissatisfied with the number of positions they received in the new administration.

Yet Governor Perpich appeared to weather these storms relatively well. None of his nominations were rejected, and by mid-February legislators were commenting favorably on the performance and cooperativeness of the departments that were of particular concern.[25] More difficult to assess is whether any longer-term damage to constituency relationships (for example, with agricultural groups) has resulted from the appointments process and outcomes.

EXECUTIVE BRANCH RELATIONS

Also during this period, relationships within the executive branch began to sort themselves out. The image of a governor remote from the daily management and ongoing operation sharpened.

As noted, Perpich reduced the size of his personal staff. Programs attached to the governor's office were transferred to line agencies. Only three staffers were assigned to be the liaison with executive departments; no day-to-day links were maintained. Agencies were more autonomous than under previous administrations. Nor did the governor himself interact much with agency heads. Except for matters of particular concern (the budget, workers' compensation, high-technology industry), an advisor (O'Donnell), not the governor himself, meets with various subcabinets on particular issues; by March 3, however, only one such meeting had taken place.

Overall, Governor Perpich appeared to have little to do with affairs within the executive branch. Focusing his attention more on communicating ideas to the public and on cultivating constituency ties, the governor delegated management responsibilities to his staff. An open question was whether the new governor's goal of improving the performance of the state bureaucracy could be accomplished under such an arrangement.

Conclusions

The process of transition involves the shifting of activities and attention from running for office to governing. As the Minnesota transition illustrates, preparation and redirection continue well past inauguration day. Remaining to be considered are how successful the 1982–83 gubernatorial transition has been and why. To what extent has the transition period enhanced Rudy Perpich's ability to govern?

In a very real sense the Minnesota transition should be treated as a model for other states. The logistical aspects of the transition proceeded smoothly, marked by early, systematic planning and a high degree of cooperation. The winning candidate had a well-developed timetable and a set of transition strategies by the time of the general election. He made rapid decisions on appointments and assembled a team ready to "hit the ground running" on January 3.

These successes can be traced to a variety of factors. First, Perpich faced an easy general election battle, giving him time both to direct staff-level transition activities and to engage in more gubernatorial and less candidate-like activity. Second, his previous experience as governor had convinced him of the importance of moving rapidly after the election, particularly on appointments; it had also given him a head start in deciding matters such as his relationship with the lieutenant governor and the organization and activities of his personal staff. Perpich benefited also from having a pool of proven individuals from which to draw advisors and appointees. Third, unhappy memories of the previous transition and the fact that the incumbent was leaving office by choice fostered a general spirit of goodwill and cooperation among all transition participants.

Even with these advantages, however, problems in the Perpich transition can be identified. To some extent the transition was a triumph of form over substance. Despite the harmony, the speedy decisions on appointments, and the flurry of policy proposals, some critical tasks were not completed. Budget preparation moved slowly, if at all, between November and January, necessitating a request for an extension. After the inauguration, work on the budget intensified, but in comparison with previous years, corners continued to be cut. In addition, few concrete legislative proposals emerged from the governor's office in early months; among those that did, some were withdrawn (e.g., eliminating tuition reciprocity), and others were not clearly related to expressed priorities (e.g., reducing the size of the legislature). Too, there was at least the potential for constituency-based conflict because the new governor generally sought support from Republican sources but did not always keep his fences mended with Democratic legislators or traditionally DFL constituency groups.

Some of these problems might have been avoided. Observers attribute much of the difficulty with both the budget and the legislative package to the overloading of and the lack of detailed expertise among the governor's staff. Changes in staff organization, makeup, and size might have helped. In addition, a scaling down of the range of activities and interests, a more careful focusing of the governor's and staff's attention, might have produced quicker, more coherent decision making.

At the same time, the outcomes and accomplishment of the transition must be judged in the light of several other factors. For example, the budget crisis and general state economic troubles are critical constraints. The special session diverted time and energy from the preparation of the new budget. The persistent shortfalls in state revenues and the increasingly sharp conflict over imposing new taxes and targeting expenditure cuts complicated the already difficult tasks of assembling a budget and formulating feasible legislative proposals. Meanwhile, Perpich's views of the dynamics of the state's economic problems and the role of government in correcting them led him to cultivate certain sources of support at the risk of alienating others. In addition, the governor's personal style significantly shaped the character of the transition and the likely course of his administration. Perpich's desire to be an ambassador and communicator rather than a manager influenced not only his activities and priorities but also those of his staff. Further, his wide range of policy interests seemingly worked against the development and pursuit of a scaled-down list of key legislative proposals.

Overall, the 1982–83 Minnesota transition was a qualified success. Other states might well follow some of the strategies and procedures used in Minnesota. Arguably, changes in transition focus and activity might have improved the outcomes; perhaps not all of Rudy Perpich's approaches and decisions were appropriate. Ultimately, however, the new governor was left to face what no transition could ever fully prepare him for: governing in a setting marked by pressing demands, the shortage of resources, and considerable uncertainty about the best ways of addressing complex problems.

The Nebraska Transition

KEITH J. MUELLER AND MARGERY M. AMBROSIUS

In January 1983 Joseph Robert Kerrey became the thirty-fifth governor of Nebraska—thirty-nine years of age, the youngest governor elected since 1918 and, according to many observers, the most exciting new state politician in recent memory. Kerrey's rise to political importance constitutes a romantic story in American politics, a journey from political obscurity to prominent office in the span of nine months. It also indicates the problems such a victor—an "outsider"—can have during gubernatorial transition.

The campaign of candidate Robert Kerrey and the behavior of Governor Robert Kerrey show that the gubernatorial transition involves not only a change from one governor to another but also a personal transition from candidate to governor. Looking at the Nebraska transition in this way yields noteworthy information for two reasons that extend beyond the state's boundaries. First, Kerrey has been hailed by the national media as a rising star in the Democratic party; he is a handsome young politician who seems to fit the new Democratic model of fiscal conservatism blended with social liberalism. Second, as a new governor, he has confronted the budgetary problems all too common in state governments, particularly in the Midwest. Those problems, as Kerrey's experience reveals, make the care and feeding of past and potential campaign supporters more difficult at best and in some instances impossible.

The 1982 Nebraska Gubernatorial Campaign

After trailing incumbent Governor Charles Thone in opinion polls at the start of the campaign, Bob Kerrey finished with a narrow victory on

November 3, 1982. Given Kerrey's political inexperience, his defeat of an incumbent reflected a climate of disenchantment in Nebraska in 1982 like that in many regions of the country. Thone reaped the bitter harvest of the disappointment of Nebraska voters because he had not been able to protect the state from the consequences of the general economic downturn and because he appeared to many persons to be an inadequate and far too indecisive a leader.

A young and handsome man with a reputation for putting people at ease, Kerrey had the advantage during the election of looking the part of a leader. His background created a can-do image. As a young man Kerrey served in Vietnam, where he distinguished himself as a platoon officer by leading a Navy SEAL team in a raid, losing part of his right leg as a result. His having won the Congressional Medal of Honor for this heroic action gave him an image as a war hero among the voters. Kerrey also distinguished himself after returning from Vietnam. As a businessman he started and, in partnership, expanded a successful chain of local restaurants. He showed his personal determination to succeed by becoming an avid jogger and completing a local marathon despite his injury.

These personal characteristics enabled Bob Kerrey to offer an appealing alternative to Governor Thone, but it took hard work on the part of Kerrey's supporters to make him seem a viable governor rather than just an attractive candidate. An early poll in March of 1982 showed Kerrey trailing Thone 46 percent to 21 percent. By August that gap had closed to 42 percent favoring Thone, 38 percent favoring Kerrey, and 17 percent undecided. By October the tide had turned completely: Kerrey, 47 percent, Thone 37 percent, undecided, 15 percent.[1]

Several groups helped Kerrey turn the tide, but three assumed special importance. The Nebraska State Education Association (NSEA) supported Kerrey with both money and manpower, as did the state AFL-CIO and the Nebraska Association of Public Employees (NAPE), the state employees' organization. Their financial contributions appear in table 1, which shows all those contributing over $5,000 to the Kerrey campaign. Volunteers from these groups proved especially useful in helping Kerrey achieve a significant margin of victory in the two most populous counties of the state, Lancaster and Douglas, including, respectively, the cities of Lincoln and Omaha.

Other sources of support were also important to Kerrey, particularly the support he got from U.S. Senator and former Governor James Exon and his backers. Especially during the last push of the campaign, support

Table 1. Campaign Contributions to Bob Kerrey

Contributor	Amount
Nebraska Democratic Party	$ 5,000
NSEA-Commitment to Representative Government	7,500
Chapman, William	7,530
Democrats for the 80's	5,000
DNC Non-Federal Corporate Acct.	7,500
NE Democratic State Central Committee	26,191
Theisen, William	8,100
Transportation Political Education League	8,000

Note: Only those contributions of $5,000 or more are listed.

from this former governor gave Kerrey increased credibility among Democratic party loyalists. Kerrey also won the support of important local politicians in Lincoln and Omaha, particularly the mayors of those two cities. Other vital support came from the individuals who were his most important advisors during the campaign: Senator Exon; former U.S. representative John Cavanaugh; Lincoln state senator Steve Fowler; Lincoln attorney Bill Wright; Omaha businessman Bill Esping; former administrative aide to governors Exon and Morris, Norm Otto; former chair of the Lincoln-Lancaster County Committee on the Role and Status of Women, Donna Karnes; Omaha state senator Berniece Labedz; and state AFL-CIO president Gordon McDonald.[2]

Often, candidates win support from key groups and individuals by making promises. Yet the new governor evidently felt no obligation to produce specific changes early in his administration. When asked about obligations to NSEA, the largest financial contributor to his campaign, Kerrey responded, "I don't have any more obligation to them than I do to any other citizen."[3] Indeed, a careful reading of many of his campaign statements provides evidence of the lack of firm commitment on his part. In August of 1982, for example, he stated that he could not make a firm commitment to increase state general fund support for the university.[4] One person we interviewed recalled a meeting of NAPE in which Kerrey explicitly said that he could not promise a pay increase for state employees but he would at least promise to treat them better than the incumbent had. In light of the fact that Thone had said that employees who did not like the way he treated them could leave the state, Kerrey's must be regarded as a very minimal commitment. Although promising to work closely with municipalities on such matters as state mandates, he did not promise increased state aid to municipalities.[5] He did campaign on a platform to increase aid to education gradually in order to provide more property tax relief, but this goal took a lower priority than solving state fiscal problems.

The pressure of state budget woes made many of Kerrey's commitments to his supporters conditional. Nevertheless, the groups we identified did support him vigorously, a reflection of their deep dissatisfaction with the incumbent. Kerrey's image promised something better. His campaign stressed his ability to lead and his having the background to correct the budget problems of the state. Most of Kerrey's supporters, at least those whom we interviewed, expected him to make the budget his top priority. They hoped for favorable treatment, but they acknowledged the overriding constraint of fiscal concerns. Nevertheless, the promise of something better, raised implicitly when not explicitly by Kerrey, did lead to the expectation that the new governor would not behave in a manner similar to that of outgoing Governor Thone. This expectation later affected Kerrey's appointments and policy during the transition and his first few months in office.

The 1982 Nebraska gubernatorial election, following the national pattern, was more expensive than past elections. Thone and Kerrey spent a combined $1.9 million, more than double the $907,110 spent in the previous Nebraska gubernatorial election. Thone spent $1,028,532 of the total; Kerrey spent $868,833.[6] After these campaign expenditures and after all the months of hard work, Kerrey won by only 7,233 of the 559,422 votes cast. A high turnout brought 67 percent of registered voters to the polls.[7] Kerrey's electoral margin resulted from strong victories in the urban counties, including a 14,935-vote margin in Lancaster County and a 10,855-vote margin in Douglas County. Kerrey also did well in some outstate counties, particularly in those with greater populations, along the Platte River. He won in twenty-eight of ninety-three counties.

Election Aftermath

This gubernatorial transition shared with others the raised level of expectations on the part of citizens and supporters that is inherent in any change from old to new. In addition, this new governor, lacking political or governmental experience, came to office under conditions of state fiscal stress. Though a Democrat labeled a liberal by many supporters and critics, Robert Kerrey remained true to his conservative business background, a trait identified in a newspaper editorial. "Kerrey presented himself as a conservative businessman and there is no reason to believe that the voters expect anything other than a conservative governor."[8] Kerrey himself refused to accept any ideological labels, declaring, "I have friends who say I'm conservative. And I am in terms of not being wasteful. I am not that comfortable with accepting labels."[9]

Even if Kerrey could be called a liberal, even if he wanted to be a creative, innovative governor, and even if he possessed the political skill to make that possible, Nebraska politics militates against such gubernatorial behavior. A writer in the Lincoln Journal said that Kerrey would be in trouble politically if he tried to be more than a caretaker because that is all the state expects. "History has shown that a Nebraska governor who is creative and forceful in putting forth innovative ideas to meet the problems of his time has to struggle far more—with the Legislature and the citizenry—than a governor who isn't a boat-rocker, or whose judgments are expressed mainly through vetoes."[10] The last Nebraska governor widely recognized as being innovative (Norbert Tiemann, 1967–71) suffered defeat in his attempt to serve a second term.

The new governor would also have to work with a legislature that, although officially nonpartisan, included a majority of Republicans. Further complicating policy discussions, the legislature divided almost evenly between urban and rural senators. Nebraska's unicameral is composed of forty-nine senators: thirty are identified as Republicans, nineteen are identified as Democrats; nineteen are urban, thirty-one are rural (we count representatives from the Lincoln and Omaha areas as urban, others as rural). Working with these senators means compromise. Kerrey, however, needed to avoid too much negotiation and compromise; such action had been a political liability for Charles Thone. Thone's style had lacked the appearance of leadership.

The economic environment of the state was not encouraging to the governor-elect in November of 1982. The legislature convened in special session directly after the general election to balance that year's budget. Revenues were lower than forecast, so the budget had to be cut and/or new revenues raised. Governor Thone preferred the former option, calling a special session of the legislature to accomplish the necessary cuts. Even after the special session ended, the budget required an increase in Nebraska's income tax rate. The Board of Equalization did increase the income tax rate following the special session, but by only 1 percent, from 17 percent to 18 percent.[11] Because Nebraska states its rate as a percentage of federal income tax liability, the Reagan tax cuts meant that the increased tax rate did not represent an actual increase in taxes.

Governor-elect Kerrey highlighted his perception of the state's fiscal woes by calling these actions of the legislature and the Board of Equalization totally inadequate and by predicting a shortfall of as much as $142.6 million in the next budget year, beginning in July 1983. He anticipated budget reductions, saying, "I think we need to prepare people for additional cuts."[12] The incoming governor later added, "What we thought was a small crack is really a major flaw, not one we can quickly plaster over. . . . everyone who received state revenue or services needs to be on the alert as to how large a problem this is."[13] In sum, budget problems dominated the agenda during and immediately after the transition.

With the budget problems monopolizing legislative discussions, fiscal and economic issues usurped the policy agenda of the Kerrey administration in the early days. The new governor had to address the need to balance the budget and eliminate such previously unacceptable practices as interfund transfers and miscalculated estimates of both revenues and expenditures. The new governor's top economic priority had to be improving the economic stability of the state by shoring up the agricultural sector and by attracting other revenue producers to the state.

Thus, it did not surprise us that the Kerrey transition team members whom we interviewed identified budget considerations as the primary element in the state of the state during the election aftermath. The need to become familiar with the budget in as much detail as possible within a short time added to the burdens of a transition staff also responsible for administrative transition, personnel decisions, and other policy concerns.

The transition team and new administrators of the incoming administration were frustrated by the assumptions of outgoing administrators that were rooted in the inactivity of their administration. Officials in state government were not accustomed to the governor's staff members' following the budgetary process in detail. However, Kerrey's people immersed themselves in budgetary matters, searching for all possible means of righting the state's fiscal imbalance.

The other major characteristic of the state of the state after the election was the widespread expectation that Governor-elect Kerrey would appoint recognizably qualified Nebraskans to important state posts. During the campaign Kerrey made an issue of Governor Thone's use of cronies in important administrative positions, and he stressed the need to find highly qualified persons to head state agencies. In postelection interviews, including ones with the national media, Governor-elect Kerrey indicated that he would rely on talented Nebraskans to solve the major problems of the state. Not having predetermined solutions himself, Kerrey said he would bring together qualified persons from throughout the state and work with them to solve problems: "There are a lot of problems I don't have the answers to. But, with the tools they need, the people can find them. . . ." Recruiting would thus be crucial: "I am going to be very, very careful how I recruit. When I hire I will remember that I am using the people's money. And I will make certain that I hire the best I can find—even though I could hurt some feelings."[14]

As had been the case during the campaign, budget problems dominated the political and economic climate during the transition. Appointments had to be made with this problem in mind, with Kerrey seeking good managers, particularly for agencies that were expected to face budget reductions. Managerial skill would often be more important than substantive knowledge of a particular agency's activities. To keep his campaign promises, Kerrey needed to devote much attention to the appointment process.

Transition Activities

The task of changing leadership in state government during a two-month period between November 5 and January 10 can never be easy. Doing so in a year when budget problems dominated the political scene and when the legislature started work on the next budget as soon as the governor took office made the transition even more difficult. Kerrey's lack of governmental experience compounded these difficulties for him and his supporters, many of whom likewise did not have governmental experience. Their inexperience affected all dimensions of the transition, from the most mundane administrative details to the major budgeting and appointments decisions that had to be made.

ORGANIZING DAILY ACTIVITIES

According to one insider we interviewed, Kerrey supporters who stayed around after the election became the core transition team and staff.

Their first task was to organize the transition office and plan the activities. Some people involved in the transition at this time have told us they were comfortable with the way things were handled. One person called the activities "routine," since they merely involved setting up an office with some system of receiving and disseminating information.

Others took a less sanguine view of the transition. Even the person who labeled the organization of the transition office routine pointed out problems of confusion and indecision. Others identified similar problems, usually related to the inexperience of persons involved in the campaign who stayed on to help the governor-elect. No one adequately anticipated the demands that would be made on the transition workers and Kerrey himself. For example, the tasks of handling all the scheduling, responding to correspondence, logging all calls, and sitting in on all briefings originally were assigned to one person. That person soon put in long days doing scheduling alone. For another example, some assistants immediately committed the governor-elect to an extensive speaking schedule—before they realized that the budget briefings and appointments interviews, combined with meetings with state legislators, would consume all his time.

Governor-elect Kerrey did have problems during the transition because very few of those who helped had previous government experience, much less state government experience. Of the seven key people helping, only two had government experience, one in county government and one in state and national government. The person with state and national experience joined in after the transition started, admittedly too late to prevent the early problems. The other experienced member of the transition staff provided expertise for organizing the office. The campaign experience of the scheduler also brought an element of political responsiveness to that person's role in the transition; even when the governor-elect could not accept invitations or schedule appointments under the press of other concerns, backers might receive a personalized response because of the scheduler's knowledge of the campaign. However, the fact that the transition budget in Nebraska consisted of a mere $30,000 certainly restricted the staffing. During this transition at least one of the key persons drew salary from the campaign funds rather than from the transition budget.

Unlike previous governor's transition teams, which had been housed in a downtown office building, the Kerrey team opened its office in the state capitol. This location proved especially beneficial, as it provided the opportunity to use the computer system that would be used by the governor's office after the inauguration, saving later time and expense.

Participants in the transition formed two major efforts. One group of persons formed the transition "team," with responsibility for appointing personnel, reviewing the budget, and, as one person interviewed put it, "thinking the big thoughts." A transition "staff" carried responsibility for the more routine tasks of scheduling, handling correspondence, and developing the information system to run the office. Persons for both efforts were selected in part for their personal skills and talents and in part on the basis of their compatibility with the governor-elect and their agreement with his objectives. A local attorney with strong ties to the business community directed the transition as a member of the team. The team also included a strong campaign supporter with a background as an insurance firm attorney; the governor-elect's brother, who had a background in agriculture, economic development, and public budgeting; and the administrative assistant to U.S. Senator Exon, who had also been Exon's administrative assistant when Exon held the office of governor. Members of the staff included a former administrator in county government, a former schoolteacher who was important during the campaign and had gained the reputation of being a hard worker, as well as a legal secretary and a former insurance agent familiar with computerized information systems.

Given the inexperience of these people in running state government, we might have expected them to run frequently to outsiders for help. However, interviews with these staff and team members revealed that most had the impression that the job was not difficult to learn. According to respondents, completing transition activities may have been demanding and at times almost overwhelming because of the time required, but the tasks were not that difficult. Perhaps their attitude, which is retrospective, makes too little of how important the specific skills possessed by a few of the actors were to a successful transition.

Transition staff and team members made limited use of outside assistance. As is so often true, the precepts of effective administration proved to be less important than good judgment and common sense. Kerrey's transition team, in belittling the importance of outside assistance, implicitly admitted that they relied on their own good judgment. Our interviews showed them to be a proud group, yet willing to defer to knowledgeable members of the group for particular decisions. Several people read National Governors' Association (NGA) publications, but not everyone did. Our respondents, members of both the transition team and the staff, found the primary utility of these publications in the reinforcement they gave to existing knowledge or to good instincts. For example, the filing system used to organize the office appeared in one NGA publication but, perhaps more importantly, had been used successfully by the former county administrator when in office. Team members deemed an NGA transition team visit unnecessary, as they expected no insoluble problems to arise during the transition. In addition, one respondent expressed an unwillingness to spend time with an NGA team, indicating that time could be spent more productively by continuing to work on a successful, though hectic, transition.

BUDGETING

Learning how to shape the state budget into a balance between revenues and expenditures confronted the transition team as their major task. Governor-elect Kerrey's schedule allowed time for budget briefings every afternoon, but members of the transition team spent considerably more time than that on budget matters. Indeed, one team member stated to us that he devoted almost all his time to budgetary matters. Early in the transition, Kerrey and his team decided to keep the current budget director and his staff. They expected this decision to result in earlier, more knowledgeable attention to the details of the budget.

Governor-elect Kerrey surprised both administrators and state senators with his attention to the details of the budget during the transition. Normally, said one interviewee, they would expect an incoming governor only to "work at the margins" of the previous governor's budget. However, Kerrey chose to "go in and make major changes" in the budget. This strategy meant that Kerrey sacrificed other perhaps more pleasant tasks, such as making more public appearances.

By giving attention to the budget details, Kerrey displayed his background as a small businessman. He controlled personally much of the budget of his enterprise. Although one person cannot control most of state government, Kerrey seems to be trying to do so. One person interviewed commented that Kerrey has the style of a chief executive officer, even though that style, however, may lead to greater personal disenchantment among gubernatorial appointees who were attracted by the more informal style of the campaign. The same respondent said that much of what happens in state government remains beyond the control of the governor. Perhaps Bob Kerrey intends to put that assumption to the most severe test. Kerrey described himself as liking "to get in the midst of things." His style caused one important member of the previous administration to assert that Nebraska had gone from the "most laid-back governor to the most activist governor in the state's history."

Kerrey's approach to state budgeting became obvious very quickly. Expenditures needed to be reduced, and no agency was immune to the pressure. But the new governor did not favor the cutting-across-the-board approach of his predecessor. Under that approach, as one agency director pointed out, agencies with small budgets had borne disproportionately the burden of reducing expenditures. Again, Kerrey's managerial philosophy and background were evident, as he attempted to make reductions in the areas least likely to result in service reductions.

MAKING APPOINTMENTS

In making appointments the Kerrey team used a strategy consistent with the recommendations of the NGA. First, they decided to proceed deliberately, not rushing the process. Second, they chose to recruit as widely as possible, developing lists of the most qualified persons available for the important administrative posts. As undoubtedly always happens, Kerrey received many résumés and expressions of interest from persons who wished to be appointed to a position. In addition, task forces composed of leaders throughout the state acted in fourteen substantive areas to suggest names of persons highly qualified for particular positions. These persons were notified of the governor-elect's interest in them, and they were encouraged to apply. Kerrey and his transition coworkers thus availed themselves of a wide range of possible choices. Although one member of the team was given primary responsibility for developing the lists of candidates, all the "thinkers of big thoughts" participated in the screening of the top applicants.

The Kerrey transition team announced appointments in a purposeful order, according to one person intimately involved. In early December they made appointments to head the public safety agencies: Corrections, the fire marshal's office, state patrol, and National Guard. Kerrey reappointed the incumbents in all four agencies. The transition team believed these officials to be the least political of agency directors, as they had been chosen by previous governors of both parties because of their qualifications and not because of their politics. The security of the state merited a high priority; if any crisis arose, the Kerrey administration wanted someone with experience ready to handle the situation.

Because of the state's financial situation, several members of the team, including the governor-elect, pressed for appointment of core administrative departmental heads next. Accordingly, they proceeded to fill the positions of budget director, tax commissioner, personnel director, and head of the Department of Administrative Services. This timing enabled Kerrey and key advisors to familiarize themselves with the budget as quickly as possible, in order to prepare for the start of the legislative session. Next, the team decided to find agency heads for the three departments of greatest policy interest to Kerrey: Economic Development, Agriculture, and Public Welfare.

In the cases of two of these high-priority departments, specific persons were aggressively recruited by the Kerrey administration. One of those proved particularly difficult to attract to the state post, but after considerable recruiting effort, including up to thirty hours by the governor himself, Kerrey appointed the new head of the Department of Agriculture. The new director possessed the background desired by the administration, having worked with a university, having been a farmer, and having a reputation as a good public speaker.

The second appointment illustrates one problem encountered by Governor Kerrey in assembling the people he wanted. Officially, the governor appoints the head of the Department of Economic Development but must restrict the choice to one of the names submitted by the Economic Development Advisory Committee. When Kerrey made his appointments, this body was predominantly Republican. Kerrey's transition team had recruited a person with the background they wanted, which included business experience, an understanding of the state's economic problems, ability in public relations, and the image of a chief executive officer. The advisory committee needed to be convinced, at least in part, according to our informant, by the application of some hard-ball politicking, to submit the name Governor-elect Kerrey wanted for agency head. The resulting delay frustrated the transition team's efforts to address quickly the major issue of developing the state's economy, a policy over which they saw partisan control as being essential.

Some observers described the appointments process used by Kerrey's team as chaotic and, at best, uncertain. To some, it seemed as though the transition team did not know how to proceed, that it had no clear sense of direction. Although it is true that when they won the election they had no prepared list of who should direct state agencies, it goes too far to say that they lacked any sense of purpose or direction. Their procedure, they knew, fostered uncertainty, but they wished to find the best-qualified person for each job, someone who would be accepted by fellow workers. In this, as in other instances, the difference between observers with a great deal of political experience and the bulk of the transition team was obvious. Some decried the lack of political payoffs in the appointment process, but Kerrey and his team declared themselves free of obligation to groups or individuals, free to choose on the basis of merit as they saw it. In this, one member of the Thone administration noted, they succeeded.

Governor-elect Kerrey was intentionally vague about his requirements for agency directors, for he wanted good managers who understood his desire to retain absolute control over their activities. Compatibility with the governor was more important than substantive expertise. The new governor also wanted "tough" administrators, another vague concept that cannot be determined objectively. Finally, in some agencies the ability to sell the governor's programs would be important. Recruiting persons to meet these criteria proved difficult and frustrating, as so much depended on Kerrey's personal perceptions. Transition team insiders could have some notion of how recruits would do, for they themselves had good relations with Kerrey, but the final decisions still required a great deal of personal attention by Kerrey. The appointment process demonstrates the extent to which personalities, rather than administrative precepts, can influence the transition process.

The top people among the Kerrey supporters, particularly those on the transition team and staff, found places during the appointment process. As one respondent put it, the only transition movement that occurred before election day was the "jockeying for position" among these key individuals. Governor Kerrey's staff now includes his brother and also a former Exon administrative assistant. Other key campaign/transition people are the tax commissioner, the director of the energy office, and the staff of the Policy Research Office. Supporters at the lower levels could not hope for top positions, as the governor made only approximately twenty-five appointments. A shrinking state bureaucracy over the past five years has severely limited the governor's ability to reward campaign supporters.

In sum, the appointments process used by the Kerrey administration fulfilled their goals of deemphasizing political considerations and of restraining spending. They concentrated on finding qualified and acceptable persons, appointing their supporters only when they believed a particular position's requirements to be consistent with the qualifications and skills of a certain supporter. The director of the energy office, for example, has the reputation of being a good administrator and finds herself in an agency desperately in need of improved administration.

RELATIONS WITH THE OUTGOING ADMINISTRATION

Our respondents provided mixed reactions to a question about their relations during the transition with the previous administration. As one insider pointed out, after a close election and an increasingly bitter campaign, one should not expect a great deal of cooperation from the losers. Several of our interviews unearthed examples of some lack of cooperation; an unwillingness to share information was the most common complaint. And yet, more than one transition insider did compliment high-level officials in the Thone administration for their cooperation, though they suspected that in one or two instances others at lower levels deliberately withheld information. Although the outgoing administration did not provide a great deal of help to the new administration, the transition actors did not view this as a disadvantage. They recognized the difficulties inherent in a transfer across party lines, as well as from one governor to another whose personal styles differed considerably. Also, they did not view the tasks as sufficiently complicated to require a great deal of assistance. As one member of the transition team stated it, there was "not much in the way of a baton to pass."

Some persons who had been active in the administration of former Governor Exon, the last Democrat to occupy that position, provided assistance. The Democratic party also proved to be helpful. In addition, the experiences of other governors served as guides; the NGA assisted through its publications and the new governors' seminar. Finally, state government employees provided helpful briefings to the transition team.

Evaluating the Transition

Three problems characterized this transition: insufficient time, insufficient appropriations, and the inexperience of the key actors. Despite these problems, the transition from Thone to Kerrey and from candidate to governor was made successfully. Kerrey made the most important appointments, which were judged to be good appointments by close observers with whom we talked and by the media at the time. Kerrey and his staff examined the budget in a level of detail that surprised many observers.

The problems of time and money frequently plague transitions. As Governor Kerrey said at the outset, trying to replace the top management of any organization is difficult, and trying to do it in two and a half months during the holiday season is impossible. The limited time restricts what any transition team can do, which is unfortunate but not necessarily devastating. The time constraint does force the transition team to focus on top priorities first and to delay action on important matters. According to one transition team member, you cannot ignore problems; you have to deal with them by first taking a look and then postponing action if that is necessary and possible. As a top aide noted, the transition team members "have to have their ears open to hear all the things that are going on," or they risk having problems grow out of control before time is found to deal with them.

The small sum appropriated for transitions makes the time problem loom even larger because only a very small staff can be retained. Staff selection is critical, as staff members will be asked to work long hours at low pay. Fortunately, the most dedicated of the campaign supporters tend to be the ones who stay around after election night, and they are also the ones most likely to be willing to work long hours.

Inexperience did create special problems for this transition. As one observer said, Bob Kerrey needed to spend some time just "to find his way around." He had to work at establishing a network of connections in and out of government after coming into office; his background as a small businessman had not moved him into the circles of those who make the crucial decisions for the state. Consequently, his personal transition from candidate to governor proved more difficult than it might have been for an experienced politician. As one insider observed, the difficulty consisted of getting the candidate to start thinking like a governor. Kerrey overcame part of this problem by hiring within the first few weeks an administrative assistant who had previous experience in the state. But as one political powerhouse noted, the assistant's experience had been gained four years before, and in the interim the roles of "power actors" had in some cases shifted to new players.

The transition actors who tried to compensate for their inexperience by being quick studies were frustrated when they attempted to learn quickly about state administration in Nebraska. The management system in the state does not enable an outsider to learn readily what happens on the inside. Information remains decentralized and, in some instances, unrecorded. For example, to learn what particular agencies actually do with the budgeted dollars, a transition team or staff member had to invest a considerable amount of time.

Although inexperience creates problems for transition actors because they have such a short time in which to learn and to act to accomplish their objectives, little can be done about the problem of scarce time. In a close election, no one can afford the time to begin working toward transition; the time problem seems inevitable. Indeed, a top member of the transition staff expressed absolute unwillingness to work for a candidate who would dilute his concentration on the campaign by starting work on the transition prior to the election.

The problem of inexperience could be helped on one level if someone were able to provide clear, concise information about that particular state government's operations and politics. Whether the Kerrey administration's lack of what one powerful observer called a "hard, moxie politician" in the top echelons will prove troublesome remains to be seen. So far, Kerrey has been able to accomplish his most important objectives during the transition and to remain comfortable with the necessary delays in other actions.

Some of the expectations built by Bob Kerrey's aggressive can-do image were dashed during the transition. He did not come into office with a team of political tyros already assembled and ready to change dramatically the face of Nebraska government. His behavior was instead more consistent with the general expectation in Nebraska that all governors are caretakers. The interesting possibility is that Kerrey's inexperience in state government augurs something other than a caretaker administration as he gains experience in office.

After the Transition

At this writing Governor Kerrey has been in office five months, long enough to disappoint many who supported him in the days of campaign allegiances. The decisions made during the transition regarding the budget and appointments now affect Governor Kerrey's image in the state. Rectifying the state's financial problems constituted the obvious first priority of the Kerrey administration. One administrator we interviewed said that other policy initiatives, including some affecting that person's agency, had to be delayed while the transition team resolved budget matters. Nebraska's budget woes drew national attention in a *Wall Street Journal* article in March. As pointed out there, Kerrey's approach to the budget problem differed from his predecessor's. Consistent with his campaign statements, he decided to make financial cuts in selected programs in order to balance the budget. He also advocated delaying the proposed state takeover of Medicaid expenditures from county governments. The media characterized both of these approaches as politically courageous, as demonstrated by the national coverage already mentioned.[15]

The administrators we talked with found impressive the Kerrey approach to budget problems, particularly his understanding that agencies with very small operating budgets cannot make large cuts. Many observers have criticized Governor Kerrey's decision not to press for an early increase in the state tax rate, but one administrator admitted that had he done so, the pressure to pass a higher state budget would have been increased. The local press also reacted favorably to Kerrey's budget proposals.[16] Broadly speaking, in the area of the state budget he has done what he said he would do.

Much of Kerrey's success in resolving the budget problems resulted from his relationships with state legislators. Here, too, he has done more than other governors to keep matters as smooth as possible, earning in the process a description by a Thone administration insider as being "up to his ears in legislative advocacy." The *Wall Street Journal* story described some of his ingratiating habits: "The governor appears to be going out of his way to win favor with the lawmakers. He has dropped in on legislative committee sessions, has sought out senators in the Capitol hallways and has held luncheon meetings with many of them at the governor's mansion. In addition, he frequently stops by the Capitol's popular vending-machine room to get a diet drink and chat with legislators and staff members."[17]

The legislators we talked with, as well as ones quoted in the local press, appreciated the relations established between the new governor and the legislature. One legislative tyro said Kerrey was a "super, super quick study" and that what he accomplished in a short period vis à vis the legislature was "nothing short of miraculous." Another legislator we talked to appreciated Kerrey's openness and his ability to "say no nicely." He is seen as more aggressive than Thone but also more accessible. In contrast to Thone, he appeared more frank, direct, and accountable. "With Thone," reported one top legislator, "the word just came down that he didn't want a certain piece of legislation on his desk." Another important legislator, who labels himself the second most conservative senator in the legislature, found himself agreeing with Kerrey more often than not and had this to say: "People elected him on his promise to bring a business-like approach to state government and after a 90-day session I can say that he has carried out everything that he promised."[18]

Obviously then, some of Kerrey's success must be attributed to the fact that his fiscal conservatism appealed to many state legislators, among whom conservative Republicans predominate. Governor Kerrey accordingly attributed his harmony with the legislature to their common, serious problem, the state's economy: "It is very difficult to argue Republican and Democratic philosophies when you're talking about a state that is broke. The old conservative-liberal discussions tend to break down first of all when you face a common goal and secondly when you come up against mathematics, which is what happened this time."[19] These comments testify to the groundwork laid during the transition when Kerrey and his staff learned as much as quickly as possible about the budget. Further, Kerrey allocated time during the transition to meet individually with state senators as the first item of his day. Kerrey managed to convey directly to legislators his perception of the consonance of interests between the governor and state legislators.

Kerrey also acted quickly to improve the state's economic conditions. He made, and lobbied successfully for, policies to improve access to credit for major developments, housing, and agriculture. He also visited active or inactive states, most notably Massachusetts, to learn of other ideas that could help Nebraska. Most important, his public activity concentrated on his promotion of Nebraska's existing economic strengths, especially agriculture. His high visibility nationally as a young attractive Democrat from the Midwest has helped him promote Nebraska agriculture.

Governor Kerrey impressed the administrators we talked with by his efforts to establish new lines of communications. Governor Kerrey made an effort to visit all state offices, including some at a distance from the capital. Further, state agency directors find him to be accessible in his office. Governor Kerrey also surveyed state employees to determine their preferences in handling the upcoming increase in health insurance premiums, for which no state money was budgeted.

But Governor Kerrey did not find everything in the area of administrative relations to be a bed of roses, unless we bear in mind the accompanying thorns. In resolving the budget crisis, Governor Kerrey vetoed all pay raises for state employees. And though state employees appreciated receiving state funds to pay the increases in health insurance premiums, many state employees found Kerrey's lack of budgetary support for better wages disillusioning. Especially among higher level employees, who do not benefit as much in percentage terms from the health insurance coverage, this disillusionment seems severe.

Not all the people who supported Kerrey as candidate have reacted favorably to the actions of Kerrey as governor. We questioned actors on both sides, asking the members of Kerrey's transition how their supporters fared and asking some of the major support groups, through their spokespersons, how they thought the governor did. Staff members could point to a few groups of supporters who, in their view, obviously fared better under the new governor. Members of the agricultural community should be pleased with the new director of the state Department of Agriculture, a former farmer and leader among agricultural actors. Blacks, who registered 6,000 new voters in Omaha, should be pleased with the number of black appointees in the Kerrey administration, according to insiders interviewed.

Other groups, though, have not fared as well. State employees, a major support group in terms of manpower provided to the governor's campaign, suffered a disappointing lack of salary increase. However, a Kerrey administration spokesperson indicated that the major concern of the administration lay in improving professional growth in the personnel system by opening up more opportunities for training and promotion. Another disappointment came when Kerrey agreed with the state attorney general that state employees cannot bargain collectively with the legislature or with the governor, as they are not legal employers. This position, seen as legally questionable by some, came as a special blow to state employees after candidate Kerrey's clear statements that he would advocate state employee bargaining rights. On balance, we can say that state employees have mixed feelings about the new governor. Many of the higher ranking employees exhibit disillusionment, if not despair. They had read into Kerrey campaign statements an advocacy of state employee salary raises and more ample funding for state agency activities, results not seen in the first five months of the administration. One respondent predicted an "incredible exodus of competent people out of government" owing to the governor's "lack of political guts." Many state employees at lower pay scales, however, seem satisfied with the insurance benefits package and unsurprised by the lack of a salary increase.

The governor's quick agreement to cut the University of Nebraska's appropriation by $6 million, resulting in no salary increases, caused university staff members to be very disappointed. His actions magnified the feeling that the governor evidenced some hostility toward the university, an attitudinal problem that university people had hoped would change with the turnover in governors. His problems with the university have differed from his problems with state employees. The governor has sung the praises of state employees but has implicitly criticized the university.

Governor Kerrey has neither found nor created many opportunities to show his appreciation to some of those who supported him in the campaign. Kerrey, for example, did not seek to increase state aid to education, but that was not an issue in the legislative session just concluded. Mixed impressions predominate among supporters. Governor Kerrey had impressed campaign workers as industrious and as a good student of government. However, he appears at least to some supporters to be a poor practitioner of the art of politics. Some observers see a failure to attempt to compensate for his lack of hard-ball political experience in his reliance on other small business persons as advisors. He has accepted help, mostly in the form of money, from many business firms that supported Thone in the campaign. The mayors of Omaha and Lincoln, both strong Kerrey supporters, suffered direct disappointment from Kerrey's support of the repeal of the sales tax on food, costing the city of Lincoln over $1 million and the city of Omaha over $6 million in lost revenues, while raising questions among party insiders concerning the governor's political acumen.

In sum Kerrey's record presents a mitigated disaster or a mitigated success, depending on which supporter makes the assessment. The ambiguity results in part from his being in office for only five months, too little time to initiate great changes in policy. To a larger extent, though, it stems from the decision to focus nearly all the governor's attention on getting the Nebraska state budget balanced. Making this the top priority shaped specific decisions, especially the lack of pay increases for state and university employees, disappointing past and potential supporters and precluding his attending to other substantive issues.

Conclusion

The gubernatorial transition in Nebraska provides the opportunity to study the problems inherent in having an outsider assume the most important state elective office. Kerrey's actions have demonstrated both the advantages and disadvantages that result from inexperience. The disadvantages inhere in the process of making appointments without broad acquaintance and also in working with important political decision makers without being able to match their experience. The advantages result from the clean slate with which such a governor begins, especially in terms of the expectations of other political leaders. The newcomer can therefore develop a political role while in office, molding that role according to the actions and beliefs of those around the governor.

Governor Kerrey also had the advantage during the transition of taking his time making appointments. Most other actors knew he had no preselected slate of appointees ready to assume control, as he had not been in government. Although lack of previous government experience made it difficult to know initially whom to recruit, that problem was overcome by allowing more time for a deliberate process.

Kerrey's experience confirms once again the timeless political lesson that campaign images do not necessarily predict behavior in office. Because so many groups were so bitterly disappointed in Governor Thone, they invested a considerable amount of emotional energy in the Kerrey campaign. That emotional investment led them to believe in Kerrey as some sort of savior, which he never promised to be. Bob Kerrey has confounded armchair political analysts with his fiscal conservatism and apparent inattention to rewarding important constituents. Yet careful reading of his campaign statements reveals the underlying concern for solving the fiscal problems of the state, regardless of the costs to certain groups of people in the short run. Governor Kerrey would argue, and administrators we talked to agree, that the problems of state employee salaries and administrative budgets can be resolved only after the larger fiscal problems have been firmly and finally controlled. Thus, Bob Kerrey is one politician who asks for patience in reviewing his record, a request not always heeded in American politics.

The List-Bryan Transition
in Nevada, 1982–1983

DON W. DRIGGS

The Political and Economic Environment
in Nevada in 1982

After a long period of economic growth that began with the construction of several large hotel-casinos on the Las Vegas Strip in the 1950s, the recession that hit the state as well as the nation in 1982 provided a rude awakening for Nevada's political leaders. With its heavy reliance on revenues derived from tourism and gaming, state government had been able to avoid the fiscal problems that afflicted most other states in times of national recession. Indeed, during the 1973–74 economic downturn, Nevada's gaming revenues actually increased 20 percent, as casinos spent more money on advertising and free transportation to bring gamblers to the state. (The principal gaming taxes are levied on gross winnings, not net after expenses.) The economic recession of 1981–82 was harder on Californians than any of the other post–World War II downturns had been, and Nevada relies heavily on tourists from its large neighboring state to fuel its gambling industry. So instead of being recession-proof, as some observers had felt it was in 1974, Nevada's economy suffered along with most of the rest of the nation in the early 1980s.

The state fiscal outlook in 1978, as Mike O'Callaghan was completing his eighth and final year as governor had looked very rosy. The state's booming tourist economy had resulted in large surpluses in the state's general fund during those eight years, as the revenues consistently exceeded the predictions of the budget director. In the fall of 1978 legislative fiscal analysts were anticipating close to a $200-million surplus going into the 1979 legislative session. Then came the passage by the electorate in November 1978 of Question 6 (Nevada's twin of California's Proposition 13), which had been approved in the June primary. However, in Nevada a constitutional amendment that is proposed by initiative petition is not effective until it has been approved by the people in two consecutive general elections. So the Nevada Legislature and newly elected Governor Robert List had the opportunity to come up with a tax-reduction plan that would be viewed by the voters as superior to Question 6 and thus would lead the electorate to vote against the initiative proposal in 1980.

Governor List recommended and the 1979 legislature approved a tax plan that provided for sharp reductions in the property tax and placed on the ballot a proposal to take the sales tax off food. The latter measure was, not surprisingly, overwhelmingly approved by the people. Governor List and former Democratic governor Grant Sawyer then collaborated on a television campaign urging the people to vote "no" on Question 6 in the 1980 election. List went further and promised the people that he would recommend even more reductions in the property tax if they would defeat Question 6.

The electorate did vote down the initiative amendment in November 1980, so List proceeded to search for a new tax proposal for the 1981 legislative session. By January he had embraced a plan originally advocated by two Democratic assemblymen from northern Nevada for an increase in sales taxes that would make possible the further reduction in the property tax. In retrospect it seems that the so-called tax shift that was passed by the legislature might have worked out better if the budget office's predictions on sales tax increases had not been so optimistic. In other words the key people in the budget office and in the legislative money committees seemed to believe the rosy picture being painted by the Reagan administration, which said that supply-side economics would have an immediate favorable impact on the nation's economy.

As it turned out, by the fall of 1981 it was obvious that the sales tax revenues in Nevada were falling far short of the numbers that had been built into the 1981–83 biennial budget. Thus, the recession had a sharp impact on the sales tax so that there was not the expected compensation for the substantial property tax decreases. The shortfall in the sales tax revenues was to continue unabated for the next year and a half and was to be an important factor in the 1982 gubernatorial election.

The unpopularity of Robert List was another key variable in the election. He entered the governor's office under a cloud because of the disclosure a few days after the 1978 election that he had accepted complimentary rooms, food, and "other services" from a large Las Vegas hotel-casino that he was supposed to have been investigating for possible corruption in his former position as attorney general of the state. As governor, List was also accused by leaders of both parties of being inaccessible, especially when his policy was compared with the "open door" policy of his predecessor, popular Democrat Mike O'Callaghan. List's popularity seemed to hit an all-time low in the spring of 1982 when he injected himself into a school bond election in Clark County (Las Vegas); many community leaders believed that his public opposition was a factor in the defeat of the proposal.

List was also criticized almost from the start of his administration for choosing a personal staff that lacked political savoir faire and government experience and expertise. For example, in 1979 List appointed a junior high school art teacher as his planning assistant; then in 1980 he appointed a department store executive as his chief of staff. Thus, to add to his problems, political insiders who interacted with List's staff were negative about the administration.

The Gubernatorial Election Campaign of 1982

During the summer of 1981 Attorney General Richard Bryan informed many of his close friends throughout the state that he planned to run for governor in 1982. He realized at that time that his fate might well be determined by the success or failure of Reaganomics and its effect on Nevada's economy in 1982. Bryan's ambition for the governorship went back to his days at Las Vegas High School and was fueled by his service as student body president at the University of Nevada.[1] After serving as deputy district attorney and public defender in Clark County, Bryan had spent four years in the state assembly and six years in the state senate. In 1974, in the midst of his first term as state senator, he had run against Robert List, who was then seeking a second term as attorney general. Bryan came within 701 votes of defeating List at that time and gave some thought to running for governor in 1978 when Governor O'Callaghan announced his retirement. However, Bryan decided that the statewide exposure as attorney general would give him a better chance to be elected the state's chief executive. He had no serious opposition for attorney general in 1978 and decided to keep his options open on whether to go for the governorship in 1982 or 1986.

In deciding to challenge List in 1982, Bryan defied the odds, for of the ten previously elected governors who had run for a second term, seven had been successful, including all four since 1926. However, Bryan had a big advantage over List in having been a lifelong resident of Clark County (including Las Vegas), which now contains about 60 percent of the state's population. No native Las Vegan had ever been elected governor, and Bryan had always been a strong vote-getter in his home county, leading all candidates in the large multiseat state senate district in Las Vegas in 1972 and 1976. In 1974, when Bryan tried to deny List a second term as attorney general, the young Democrat had carried Clark County with 58.7 percent of the vote.

In addition to his big advantage in southern Nevada, Bryan also was encouraged as he started his campaign by reports that a substantial percentage of both Democrats and Republicans had given negative ratings to List's performance as governor.[2] Part of List's unpopularity was undoubtedly the consequence of economic conditions, but he was also viewed as "wishy-washy" on some of the main issues, including the proposed placement of the MX missile system in Nevada.[3]

Bryan had formed a campaign steering committee and was already heavily involved in fund raising by late summer 1981. There had never been any question that List would run for a second term, so the governor's fund raising had been under way for some time. State law at that time did not require the reporting of campaign contributions made prior to January 1 of the election year, and Bryan and List both declined to volunteer the amounts raised in 1981. Insiders estimated that Bryan raised about $200,000 and List about $300,000 before January 1, 1982.

Bryan formally announced his candidacy at news conferences in Reno and Las Vegas on February 2. The attorney general stated that Nevada could "no longer afford absentee administration, indecisiveness, or vacillation on major issues in the governor's office."[4] At the press conferences the forty-five-year-old Bryan promised to present later in the campaign a tax plan that would include a lowering of the sales tax that had been sharply increased in 1981. A short time later he admitted to campaign aides that it had been a mistake to promise a reduction in the sales tax in the face of evidence that a shortfall in state revenues was already occurring.

Over the course of the next few months Bryan distributed position papers and made campaign speeches on the following topics:

1. The need for a much greater effort on the part of state government to foster economic diversification and to promote tourism.[5]
2. The need to strengthen ethics-in-government legislation, including the requiring of fuller disclosure of campaign contributions and the assets of public officials and the prohibition of voting by public officials on "matters in which they have a direct personal financial interest."[6]
3. The need for tougher criminal laws, including a mandatory life term without possibility of parole for those convicted of a fourth felony and modification of the so-called exclusionary rule.[7]
4. The need to give a high priority to education, including higher education, so that the state could prepare its young people adequately for the future and attract new industry.

Bryan tried for as long as he could to fend off demands by List and reporters that he disclose his tax plan, for each monthly and quarterly report indicated that the state's economy was getting worse and that the revenue picture was even bleaker than he had anticipated at the start of the campaign. However, after a powerful member of his own party, senate majority leader James Gibson, blasted him publicly in early October for placing the blame on List for the state's fiscal crisis and for not coming up with an alternative plan, Bryan announced the tax proposal he would recommend if elected. The main provision of the plan was an increase in the property tax, accompanied by a proposed constitutional amendment to exempt from taxation altogether the first $20,000 or $30,000 of property owned. Under this Bryan proposal the large property holder would pay a proportionately higher percentage of the value than would a small homeowner.

In the meantime Governor List's problems increased as the economy continued to slide and the state's finances became precarious. As early as April, List ordered state agencies to establish contingency plans for cutting their budgets by 10 percent. By the fall the state's chief executive had cut over $19 million from state government, necessitating layoffs of state workers in addition to a continuation of the freeze on filling vacancies. The University of Nevada Board of Regents complied with an initial plea from List to cut 5 percent of its budget for the 1982–83 fiscal year but balked at List's request for a further cut because the state's school districts had refused to comply with the governor's first appeal.

In the face of the state's fiscal crisis, List refused to consider the plea from some educational groups that he call a special session of the legislature to deal with the money problems and the overly optimistic revenue projections that had been built into the 1982–83 budget. The governor and his advisors talked about going to court to force the school boards and the board of regents to comply with his cuts and hoped that his strong stand against tax increases and his large-scale cuts in public spending would appeal to the voters of the state. However, List's stands tended to solidify the support of state employees, schoolteachers, and university professors for his opponent. Bryan had already been endorsed by the State of Nevada Employees Association (SNEA) and the Nevada State Educational Association prior to the cuts; now, those public employees redoubled their efforts in behalf of electing the Democratic candidate. Bryan, in turn, spoke out against further cuts in the university's budget.

Analysis of the Outcome of the Election

Public opinion polls taken in the fall of 1981 showed that Governor List was in trouble and that Bryan had calculated correctly in believing that 1982 was a good year to run against the Republican incumbent. Even the strongest Bryan supporters found it hard to believe the results of a poll in May commissioned by Bob Cashell, a Democratic candidate for lieutenant governor; the attorney general was ahead of the incumbent governor by twenty-one percentage points. However, the incredulity of the Bryan people turned to euphoria a week before the primary in September when an independent poll commissioned by Nevada's leading newspapers showed Bryan ahead by twenty-two percentage points. Moreover, the latter poll showed that 50 percent of the potential voters polled had either a "somewhat unfavorable" or a "strongly unfavorable" opinion of List.

The reasons for Bryan's huge early lead were fairly obvious. In addition to the recession and accompanying unemployment in Nevada, which exceeded the national average, and an unusually negative attitude toward List by the public, there was the fact that Bryan had conducted a television and media blitz in June and early July to convince potential Democratic opponents not to file for the primary. As it turned out, the publication of private polls showing the governor as weak tended to encourage some of the Democratic leaders. Lieutenant Governor Myron Leavitt and state treasurer Stan Colton filed for governor, even though most political observers felt that they were much too late. Although he did not have strong primary opposition, Governor List did use some television and radio advertising just before the primary to try to head off too large a vote for the "none of these" category on the ballot.

The Bryan forces realized that the big lead would decline some when List went on the attack after the primary. The governor's media campaign concentrated on charges against Bryan in order to knock down the attorney general's popularity in the polls. (As one national campaign expert had stated, "positive is nicer, but negative is quicker.") List's attempt to paint Bryan as a liberal, emphasizing his earlier liberal voting record in the state assembly, had been foreseen by Bryan and his strategists. The early Bryan television ads had emphasized his "tough on crime" stance and were meant to blunt the effects of List's expected name-calling tactics.[8]

The independent newspaper poll that was taken two weeks before the general election showed that Bryan's lead had shrunk to nine percentage points and gave the incumbent hope to believe that he was back in the running. However, Bryan's ultimate twelve-point margin over List (in terms of the percentage of the two-party vote) showed the solidity of his support in his home county (63 percent of the two-party vote) and the big dent he had made in List's previously strong areas of Washoe County (Reno) and Carson City (50 percent of the two-party vote) since their 1974 statewide race for attorney general.

Bryan viewed his election as a mandate for strong leadership to deal with the state's economic crisis. He made it clear prior to his inauguration that his top priorities were education, economic diversification, and more state support for tourism. Governor List blamed his defeat on a number of factors, "including his tax package, his handling of the MX, the stagnant state economy, and superior Democratic voter registration figures."[9]

An examination of the campaign contributions to Bryan and List during the 1982 election shows that both depended heavily on the large hotel-casinos for funds. Because of the unreported sources before 1982, it is not possible to determine exactly the percentage of the total contributions that were made by gaming casinos and individuals connected with gambling; it appears to have been about 50 percent in each case. Overall, the gambling interests followed the traditional pattern of contributing to both major candidates, thus covering their bets no matter who won. As Bryan was the expected winner from early in the campaign, his contributions from gaming interests were probably larger than they otherwise would have been; List had promised the casino owners that he would not recommend any increases in taxes, despite the state's fiscal crisis. The substantial contributions to Bryan may have been a factor in the Democrat's decision not to recommend an increase in gaming taxes, although the more probable reason was the shaky financial condition of many of the casinos in the state.

Transition Procedures and Support in State Law

During the campaign Richard Bryan had indicated to some of his closest aides in the attorney general's office that he hoped to have them aboard his administration if he won the governorship, but he did not make any specific commitments before election day. Also, even though the polls showed him with safe leads throughout the campaign, he did not detach any personnel from his campaign to work on the possible transition.[10] On election day Bryan did go to the legislative building to ask William Bible, a fiscal analyst with the Legislative Counsel Bureau and former state deputy budget director, to be state budget director and head of the Department of Administration if the election turned out as expected. Bible is the son of former U.S. Senator Alan Bible and had been given high marks by legislators for the job he had done as fiscal advisor to the assembly Ways and Means Committee over the previous ten years.

The budget director's position had been a problem in previous gubernatorial transitions. A governor-elect has less than three months from election day to the date that he must present his biennial budget request to the legislature. It had been twenty-four years since the budget directorship had changed hands during the transition period. Faced with the short time, Governor-elect Grant Sawyer and his newly appointed budget aide were forced in 1958 to make an across-the-board percentage cut in almost all budgets in order to balance revenues and expenditures. Former governors Laxalt and O'Callaghan asked budget director Howard Barrett to stay on through the legislative session; when they found out that they worked well with Barrett, he was made a regular part of each administration. (On at least one occasion Barrett changed his party registration to match that of the new governor.) Governor List's relationships with Barrett had been excellent when the former was attorney general for eight years, so Barrett was asked once again to continue as budget director.

A coincidence of circumstances made it possible for Richard Bryan to change budget directors without significant disruption in the budget office. The first factor was that after twenty-one years as budget director, Howard Barrett resigned on August 1, 1982, and his deputy became acting director. Second, the Nevada Legislature had mandated some years before that the fiscal analysts who advised the two legislative appropriations committees would sit in on all budget hearings conducted by the budget director for departments, divisions, and other state agencies. Thus, Bill Bible had participated in the 1982 budget hearings and had done so for several previous biennial budgets. Having served as deputy budget director before he joined the Legislative Counsel Bureau, Bible understood the budget operation from both the executive and legislative perspectives. Furthermore, he immediately asked List's acting budget director to be his deputy, making the transition even smoother.

The third important circumstance was Bible's willingness to accept the position. His father had been a longtime friend of Bryan, and his brother Paul had been one of the governor-elect's closest advisors during the campaign. Bryan had also consulted Bill Bible on budget matters during the campaign, and some members of the Democratic candidate's campaign team expected Bible to be appointed. The public announcement was made at a press conference two days after the election, as Bryan and his family left for a short vacation in Hawaii.

At a breakfast meeting in Las Vegas the morning after the election, the governor-elect informed administrative assistant Marlene Lockard that she would be the transition coordinator and act as liaison with the outgoing List administration.[11] List, in turn, named one of his executive assistants, Noreen Barber, as his liaison with Bryan. Lockard and Barber worked very well together throughout the transition period.

During his four-day sojourn in the Islands, Bryan made numerous phone calls to Lockard to discuss possible appointments and transition procedures.[12] When the governor-elect returned, he immediately contacted Andy Grose, the head of the Research Division of the Legislative Counsel Bureau, to ask him to become his chief of staff. Grose readily agreed to accept the offer; the position was probably the only one that would have lured him away from his counsel bureau job.[13]

Governor-elect Bryan had thus in the first few days after the election lined up the three key people who would assist him during the transition period: transition coordinator Marlene Lockard, chief of staff Andy Grose, and budget director Bill Bible. In addition to following through on the necessary interactions with their counterparts in the List administration, the three would be important consultants to Bryan on appointments.

There are only two references to gubernatorial transition in Nevada law. In a section of the *Nevada Revised Statutes* that lists the powers and responsibilities of the state superintendent of building and grounds, there is the following provision: "The superintendent may provide, with the approval of the governor, suitable office space for the use of the governor-elect, and expend funds for incidental expenses connected therewith." The other mention of transition procedures is found in the following section listing the responsibilities of the governor:

The governor shall submit to his successor in office:
(a) A detailed record of all expenditures made in the preceding fiscal year by each of the departments of the state government supported by public funds.
(b) A record of fund balances, the income to each fund in the state treasury, and a record of the sources of income to each fund in the state treasury from or during the preceding fiscal year.
(c) A statement of the bonded debt and of the obligations and assets of the state as of the close of the preceding fiscal year.[14]

In the List-Bryan transition there was not a problem with office space, as was also the case in the O'Callaghan-List transition, because the attorney general's office was directly across the street from the capitol. With the cooperation of the Legislative Counsel Bureau, both Andy Grose and Bill Bible became involved full time in the transition shortly after the election. During most of November and December the two salaries were billed half to the Legislative Counsel Bureau and half to transition expenses.[15] As no money had been appropriated in the 1982–83 budget for a possible transition, a special request for $5,000 had to be submitted to the Interim Finance Committee (made up of members of the two appropriations committees for the 1981 legislative session) to cover the transition portion of the salaries. As Andy Grose later stated, an incumbent governor is not likely to include transition expenses in his or her budget request unless it is the last biennial budget of a second term.[16] The transition is likely to be more complicated when a person who is not a state official with an office in Carson City is elected governor.

The Guidelines Used for Transition Decisions

As soon as Richard Bryan had obtained Andy Grose's agreement to serve as chief of staff of the new administration, the governor-elect gave his new aide a copy of the National Governors' Association (NGA) booklet *Transition and the New Governor* and advised him to use it as a planning tool. Grose later stated that the booklet had indeed been of great assistance to him throughout the transition period.[17]

At the time that Bryan asked Lockard to be his transition coordinator, he also asked her to accompany him and his wife to the Seminar for New Governors that was held in Park City, Utah, a week and a half after the election. The three Nevadans found the training sessions to be a valuable introduction to the challenges and problems ahead. Lockard later commented that on many occasions during the transition and the early weeks of the new administration, Bryan would refer to statements or advice given at the seminar.[18]

The *Transition* booklet and other materials furnished by the NGA provided the main guidelines followed by Governor-elect Bryan and his transition team. The designated contact people in the outgoing List administration were helpful, but there were no written materials available that outlined previous transition procedures. The Bryan team had to proceed without an "institutional memory" of Nevada's earlier transitions.

Staffing Changes and Assignment of Staff Responsibilities

Many of the individuals who occupied the "unclassified" positions during the List administration were well known to the governor-elect, for Bryan had served for ten years in the legislature and four years as attorney general and had had frequent contact with certain department and agency heads. There were about eighty cabinet-level agency heads and deputies that could be changed.

As indicated earlier, the people Bryan relied upon most for advice in the appointment process were Bible, Grose, and Lockard. As legislative fiscal analyst for the assembly Ways and Means Committee for a period of years, Bill Bible had observed the agency heads present their budgets to the budget director and then to the legislature; consequently, his advice was especially valuable when the decisions about retaining existing agency directors were made. In addition to his three principal advisors, Bryan consulted three Reno attorneys—campaign manager Keith Lee, state senator Spike Wilson, and Paul Bible—and Las Vegas attorney and campaign finance director Frank Schreck about particular appointments.[19]

According to Lockard and Grose the most important criteria in the consideration of an individual for a particular position were qualifications and expertise. Only when the person was deemed qualified did the question of whether he or she had been a supporter of Bryan come into play.[20] However, the criteria used in deciding whether or not to retain an agency head or deputy included the amount of activity, if any, of the person in the List campaign. For example, the director of the Department of Human Resources was not considered for reappointment, as he had actively responded to some of Bryan's charges against List. Other List appointees had been closet supporters of Bryan; for example, the women who served as executive director of the Equal Rights Commission and as director of the Department of Community Services were retained. Many others had remained publicly neutral and, as it turned out, had better than an even chance of being retained. Roland Westergard, the director of the Department of Conservation and Natural Resources, had been removed from the Tahoe Regional Planning Agency by List, apparently because he was too pro-environmentalist. Bryan criticized List during the campaign for replacing Westergard with a developer and early in the transition period announced his decision to retain Westergard as a department head.

Bryan's appointments to the very sensitive positions on the Gaming Control Board and the Gaming Control Commission were influenced by an event that had taken place during the campaign. After Democratic senate majority leader James Gibson criticized Bryan's attacks on List's tax-shift plan, Gibson formed a committee to educate the people on the good points of the tax changes. In the course of raising funds for the committee, which was viewed by the media as a not-so-subtle front to assist List's reelection efforts, Gibson was notified by the owner of one of the large Las Vegas hotel-casinos on the Strip that he had a check for the committee. Gibson then phoned his good friend and fellow Mormon Richard Bunker, who just happened to be chairman of the Gaming Control Board, and asked if he would have his secretary pick up the check. Bunker complied with Gibson's request, and the disclosure in the media of this less-than-circumspect behavior on the part of the two leaders gave Bryan a chance to make political points and to call for the resignation of Bunker from the gaming board.[21] Bunker, though, made it clear during the campaign and again after Bryan's election that he intended to complete the final two years of his term. However, Bryan met with Bunker in December and by the end of the month the List appointee had submitted his resignation.

Following the revelation of Bunker's involvement with a casino in campaign fund raising, Carl Dodge, the chairman of the Gaming Control Commission to which the Gaming Control Board reports, announced that he would conduct an investigation into the extent of Bunker's involvement. After Dodge reported that there was no evidence that Bunker himself had been involved in securing the campaign donation from the hotel-casino, Attorney General Bryan wrote Dodge requesting the details of the investigation so that he (Bryan) might decide whether or not to launch his own investigation. Dodge and Bryan had served together in the state senate and had a high regard for each other, but the implicit contention by the attorney general that Dodge's investigation had been cursory and that the chairman of the Gaming Control Commission was being used by Governor List for political purposes caused Dodge to submit his resignation to Bryan shortly after the election. Bryan asked Dodge to serve out his term so that Paul Bible, who was named as his successor, could get his law practice in order before taking over on April 1.

All told, Bryan received over two thousand applications for the eighty political positions that he could have filled. As it turned out, forty-three appointees were named. Special attention was given to affirmative action in setting up the governor's personal staff; women were named to positions as the employment relations officer, the press secretary, and the appointments secretary, joining executive assistant Lockard. Bryan completed the appointment of executive assistants with the naming of Tim Hay, one of his top aides in the attorney general's office, as legal counsel. In filling other positions Bryan consulted widely with constituent groups and trusted political advisors. He contacted some individuals as a courtesy, knowing they would be pleased about being consulted and made part of the Bryan team.

In setting up his personal staff Bryan was handicapped by the fact that the 1981 Nevada Legislature had removed the position of assistant for planning from the budget for the governor's office. The governor-elect decided that Grose would have special responsibility for the area of economic development and tourism in addition to his general duties as chief of staff. Lockard was given the responsibility for liaison with the legislature, adding to her closing duties as transition coordinator. As legal counsel, Hay would examine all bills passed by the legislature and make recommendations to the governor about signing them. In addition, the various agencies were divided among the three executive assistants so that the bureaucratic contacts with the governor would be filtered through one of the aides.

Bryan's appointments were generally well received in the media. Government insiders were especially pleased with the appointments of Bill Bible as budget director, Grose as chief of staff, and Paul Bible as chairman of the Gaming Control Commission, as all were highly regarded.[22]

The Executive Budget
and Other Legislative Proposals

The most immediate policy problem confronting Governor-elect Bryan following his election was the question of how to get through the remainder of the 1982–83 fiscal year; the revenue shortfalls meant that the state might not be able to meet its payroll at the end of January. Governor List, as mentioned, had called upon the public school districts and the university system to make additional cuts, but they had waited to act until they knew the outcome of the election. Bryan had pledged to give top priority to education during the campaign, and the educational leaders clearly were hoping that his election would eliminate the need for cutbacks.

List had proposed that the legislature recall the $20-million loan that it had made to the Public Employees Retirement System in 1979. The interest from the investment of loan money had provided significant cost-of-living increases for retired state employees. Bryan concurred in the loan recall and so stated in his state of the state message to the legislature in January. The bill recalling the loan sailed through both houses as an emergency measure at the beginning of the session; thus, the state was able to meet the January payroll.

Additional legislative action was needed to ensure the state's solvency at the end of the 1983 fiscal year, so Bill Bible recommended that Bryan ask the legislature to recall the $7 million that it had transferred in 1981 from the state general fund to the state highway fund for the construction of highways. At the time of the appropriation transfer the state highway fund was in desperate shape because of the decline in tax revenues for motor vehicle fuel. However, the 1981 legislature had also increased those same taxes, and by 1983 the highway fund was in much better condition and the general fund was dry. Despite the opposition of the construction industry and other supporters of more highway construction, Bryan's recommendation for the transfer of the funds back to the general fund went through the legislature with little difficulty.

As part of the emergency fiscal proposal to the legislature, Bible also recommended to the new governor that permission be requested to collect the state tax on gambling revenues on a monthly rather than on a quarterly basis, so that the collections for April and May would be available to help the state get through the fiscal year. Once again the legislature went along with Bryan's recommendation, so that the speed-up in collections plus the recall of the aforementioned $27 million eliminated the need for further cuts in education and other essential services.

Once the legislative proposals to take care of the immediate fiscal problem had been agreed upon, Bryan and his advisors went to work putting together the legislative recommendations for the state of the state message and the 1983–85 budget. One of Bryan's campaign aides in Las Vegas had compiled a summary of all the campaign statements made by the Democratic candidate on the various issues, and this summary, along with the position papers that had been issued, was examined by the governor-elect and aides Bill Bible, Grose, and Lockard as they assembled the legislative proposals.[23]

One of the major problems confronting Bryan was the expected revenue shortfall of about $70 million a year for the 1983–85 biennium. He and his aides decided to recommend a 6 percent increase in public school funding and less than a 4 percent increase in university funding, with no cost-of-living increases for teachers or professors. (The schoolteachers would receive automatic step increases for satisfactory service, but the university faculty salary scale contained no such provision.) State employees were not given cost-of-living raises either, although most would be eligible to receive step increases within their grades. The state employees organization, SNEA, had endorsed Bryan's candidacy, and its executive director had struck a deal with the incoming governor by which SNEA would not push for a cost-of-living increase if the governor would support a legislative proposal that would provide for collective bargaining for state employees. (Local government employees and schoolteachers had been covered under a collective bargaining law since 1967.)

Bryan also decided to recommend an increase in the prison budget, for as a member of the Prison Board for four years he was well aware of the understaffing problems. He called, too, for more state involvement in economic development and the promotion of tourism. To pay for the increased expenditures for these activities, the new governor proposed a three-quarters of 1 percent state room tax on hotels and motels. To make up for the small increases in education funding, Bryan recommended the elimination of a number of top-level state administrative and supervisory positions over and above the cuts that Governor List had made in the summer and fall of 1982.[24] Bill Bible played the major role in putting together the budget figures once the governor-elect had decided the major issues. Taxes were then proposed to make up the expected $70-million difference between the expected revenues and the recommended expenditures for each year of the biennium. This amount was almost exactly the amount of shortfall that would have occurred for the 1982–83 fiscal year if there had not been the extraordinary mid-year cuts, the recall of funds, and the speed-up in collection of revenues mentioned above. As a consequence, the Bryan budget proposal was basically a "standstill" document when compared with the original 1982–83 budget passed by the 1981 legislature.

Bryan's main advisor on the taxation issue was Patrick Pine, the principal architect of the tax plan that was unveiled in the closing weeks of the campaign. In addition to Pine, who was named by the governor-elect to head the Department of Taxation, Bill Bible and Grose helped to put together the final tax package that was presented to the legislature in the state-of-the-state message. As Bryan had indicated in the later stages of the campaign, an important aspect of the proposal to increase the property tax was the recommendation of two constitutional amendments that would allow an across-the-board exemption (say, $20,000) and would provide for a separate tax plan for utilities, railroads, and airlines.[25] Because the proposed constitutional amendments could not be finally approved for over two years, Bryan came up with a stopgap rebate plan for the 1983–85 biennium. He recommended a property tax increase of 75 cents per $100 assessed valuation,[26] with all homeowners and renters receiving an $80 rebate. The rebate would erase the increase for very small property owners while providing only a small percentage decrease for large property owners. This property tax increase would be earmarked for the public schools.

In addition to these budget measures, Bryan in his state-of-the-state message called for the passage of a package of ethics-in-government bills, the establishment of an economic development commission to administer a department of tourism and economic development, the passage of an omnibus health care bill, a consumer protection bill to require better planning for the major utilities, a bill to increase the penalties for those convicted of crimes against the elderly, and a bill designating the birthday of Martin Luther King, Jr., a state holiday.[27]

Gubernatorial Relationships with the 1983 Legislature

Richard Bryan was the first Nevada governor with previous legislative experience since Charles Russell, who served from 1951 through 1958. As a Democrat he also had an advantage over List, who had served four years with both houses under control of the opposite party. However, the Democratic majority in the lower house had been reduced to a 23–19 edge in the 1982 election, and the Republicans were hoping to make some political points at the expense of the governor during the session in order to give them the campaign ammunition to gain control in 1984 for the first time since 1971 and only the third time since 1931. The 17–4 Democratic majority in the senate was deceptive, as many of the Democratic senators are conservative and there is traditionally little party-line voting in the upper house.

One of the main elements of Governor Bryan's legislative strategy was the establishment of a regular weekly luncheon meeting on Monday with the majority leadership in the two houses. One of the problems he faced in his relationship with the six leaders who were invited was that only two of them were strong supporters of his, and they were the two assistant majority leaders. These two tended to be considered more liberal than the average legislator and thus had some difficulties in trying to carry the ball for the governor's programs. Moreover, senate majority leader Jim Gibson had given support to List in the campaign and had blocked Bryan from gaining a seat on the powerful Finance Committee during the latter's service in the upper house.

In addition to the weekly luncheon meetings, which were very cordial affairs, Bryan usually invited one or two legislators to breakfast during the period that the legislature was in session. The governor also kept in close touch with the legislative proceedings through reports from his top aides at late afternoon meetings. In the latter half of the session, Bryan called on Keith Lee, his campaign manager, to use his considerable political skills as a part-time lobbyist for important bills.

The Bryan proposal for handling the immediate fiscal year budget crisis was approved by both houses of the legislature by large margins, but his most important defeat came on the taxation package he recommended for the 1983–85 biennium. The rebate proposal to give relief to small property owners and renters was rejected overwhelmingly in committee because of the large cost (over $1 million a year) of administering such a program. Without the rebate and with legislative approval of increases in minor taxes such as cigarettes and liquor, Bryan and his advisors believed a 35-cent increase in the property tax was needed to fund his budget proposals. However, the Republicans in the assembly decided early in the session to make the property tax their issue for the 1984 elections and so remained united in their opposition to the 35-cent increase. The Democrats had the votes to pass the increase in the assembly if they had been united, but two defections gave the Republicans their victory.

Even if the larger tax increase had passed the assembly, it is doubtful that the senate would have gone along, for majority leader Gibson claimed that the votes were not there for passage of more than a 30-cent increase. One of the reasons for the senate opposition, even though the Democrats had a 17–4 edge, was the strong lobbying effort by Lieutenant Governor Bob Cashell. A nominal Democrat, Cashell had heavily backed List in his successful election campaign of 1978 and had seriously considered running for governor in 1982. Because of problems with putting his gaming casinos into a blind trust in time for the election campaign, Cashell decided to run for lieutenant governor in 1982. However, his actions during the session seemed to indicate that he was looking toward a run for the top spot in 1986, even though he would have to challenge Bryan in a primary. At any rate, his opposition to the extra 5-cent increase in the property tax undercut the governor's attempt to gain more revenues for education. As it was, the legislature lopped off over $8 million from the public school budget after the failure of the 35-cent property tax proposal.

Only one part of Governor Bryan's ethics-in-government proposals made it through the legislature. Republican Senator Sue Wagner was actually the chief sponsor of the bill to require the reporting of all campaign contributions and the names of individual or corporate contributors who give over $500 during the entire period since the last election for the office. Bryan's chief legislative lobbyist Lockard worked very closely with Wagner and Speaker John Vergiels to gain passage. The other parts of the ethics package never emerged from the assembly Elections Committee, as the conservative legislators balked at more stringent disclosure and conflict-of-interest laws.

Bryan's proposal for a three-quarters of 1 percent room tax to support his economic development and tourism promotions ran into early opposition from the hotel and motel owners. However, the governor and Grose were able to work out a compromise by which the tax would be raised to 1 percent, with about half the amount to be returned to local convention authorities to be used at their discretion for promotional activities and "special events." The tax was then approved by large margins in the two houses. A compromise also resulted in the establishment of two different commissions: one for economic development and one for promoting tourism. When it came to the question of who should chair the two commissions, a tug-of-war developed between the governor and the lieutenant governor, the latter showing that he had considerable muscle with the legislators. Bryan's original bill provided that the chairman of each commission would be appointed by the governor. Cashell wanted the lieutenant governor designated as chairman of both committees. By using the argument that the lieutenant governor needed some important duties besides presiding over the state senate and the influence he had gained by contributing to the campaigns of most legislators, Cashell was able to get his amendment approved. Even with this minor setback, Bryan viewed the passage of his economic development package as one of his major victories of the legislative session.[28]

The 1983 legislature did enact most of the consumer, health care, and tougher criminal penalty legislation proposed by Governor Bryan. The proposal to declare the birthday of Martin Luther King, Jr., a state holiday was changed to a "day of remembrance" to be marked by special tributes in the public schools.

In summary Governor Bryan had mixed results in his first legislative session as the state's chief executive. He met with great success in his proposals to take care of the immediate fiscal emergency of the state, but he did not get the support for the type of revenue program he believed to be necessary. On other matters he fared well—as have most previous governors. Some observers believed that he did not exercise vigorous enough leadership early in the session, but his veto of two bills after the adjournment of the legislature will probably send a message to the 1985 session that he will not be a rubber stamp.

The Governor in His Bureaucratic,
Party, and National Roles

Bryan divided the state agencies among his three top executive assistants so that agency heads would normally communicate with him through the designated aide. There was some early grumbling on the part of a few bureaucrats about not having direct access to the governor. However, a two-day briefing program for policy executives held in early February appeared to improve communication between the governor's office and the agency heads and deputies.

The recommendation for the orientation program for top state executives came from James S. Roberts, professor of political science at the University of Nevada, Reno, and former state deputy budget director. Governor Bryan and chief of staff Grose embraced the idea enthusiastically and asked Roberts to proceed with his plans. Roberts patterned the orientation after the U.S. Civil Service Commission's briefing program in Washington for new policy executives on the federal level. About eighty agency heads and deputies were in attendance for all or part of the two-day program, at which they heard from the governor, other elected officials, legislative leaders, and several of the governor's aides, in addition to participating in panel discussions. One of the by-products of the meeting was the opportunity of many of the bureaucrats to interact with the other members of the new administration. The evaluation of the program by the participants was good, and Professor Roberts has been asked to put together follow-up programs for the same policy executives every six months.

Bryan showed very early that he planned to take a leadership role in state party affairs by hosting a meeting in January of the Democratic State Central Committee at the governor's mansion. He and former governor Grant Sawyer, who has been the Democratic national committeeman for fifteen years, also launched a fund-raising drive for a full-time state party director, each contributing a check for $5,000. Members of the committee afterward expressed the opinion that morale had never been higher and that the vigorous leadership displayed by Bryan at the meeting bodes well for the party's ability to organize the type of effort that will be needed to rebuff the Republican attempt to take control of the assembly in the 1984 election. (The Republicans have had a full-time paid executive director for several years.) Bryan has also attended many county Democratic party affairs since his election and seems to place more emphasis on party leadership than did Mike O'Callaghan, the last Democratic governor, who denounced parts of the Democratic platform when he first ran in 1970.

Bryan enjoyed very much the NGA Seminar for New Governors at Park City in November. However, he did not attend the 1983 annual meeting of the NGA in Washington because of the top priority he gave to remaining in the state throughout the legislative session. He had been critical of List's extended absences from the state and thus far has not given evidence of any intention of becoming greatly involved in national and regional gubernatorial affairs.

Overall Evaluation of the Transition

On the whole the List-Bryan transition went smoothly, especially considering the strained relations between the two during the long year and a half of the campaign. Most contacts between the outgoing and incoming administrations were at the staff levels. Noreen Barber from List's office and Bryan transition coordinator Marlene Lockard worked very well together, as did outgoing chief of staff Greg Lambert and Andy Grose. A crucial aspect of the smooth transition was the background and contacts that William Bible brought to the positions of budget director and director of the Department of Administration; his experience enabled him to assume the heavy responsibilities without any serious problems.

Most of the governor-elect's time between the election and the inauguration was taken up with appointing people to the key staff and agency head positions. Bryan did a commendable job in deciding which persons to retain and which ones to replace and with whom. The announcements following each of the decisions were also handled well; the press secretary staggered the releases in such a way that the public did not get the impression that the incoming governor was making wholesale changes for political reasons but that he was weighing each decision carefully.

The governor-elect did not have much time to devote to policy questions and legislative strategy before assuming the burdens of office. In retrospect it appears that Bryan should have consulted with more of the legislative heavyweights in the construction of his tax proposal during the campaign. Perhaps the fact that Democratic leaders Jim Gibson and Assemblyman Paul May had been heavily involved in the planning and enactment of the List tax shift in 1981 would have made such consultation awkward and difficult. Despite the fact that Gibson had not supported Bryan during the gubernatorial campaign, the legislature's most powerful individual did not prove to be a roadblock to Bryan's legislative program, with the exception of the taxation issue. The differences between Governor Bryan and Lieutenant Governor Cashell that surfaced in a few instances during the 1983 session are likely to be more in evidence in 1985, as skirmishing for the next gubernatorial election begins.

It appears obvious that future gubernatorial transitions in Nevada would be aided if written recommendations based on the 1982–83 experiences could be passed on to the next governor and staff. Guidelines similar to those published by the NGA, but with specific references to the Nevada scene, would be most helpful.

The New Hampshire Gubernatorial Election and Transition

RICHARD F. WINTERS

New Hampshire voters in 1982 must have had the sensation of being caught up in electoral and political theater. They might have expected colorful characters and engrossing drama, but they were hardly prepared for scenes that ranged from the ridiculous to the sublime, with episodes of the tragic and the unique.[1]

Eight candidates entered the Republican gubernatorial primary to qualify for the general election challenge to two-term incumbent Hugh Gallen, who ran unopposed in the Democratic primary. The Republican primary was hard fought on a wide range of ideological issues, with candidates spanning the ideological range of the party. The influence of the *Manchester Union Leader* figured importantly in the events and the outcome of the primary campaign.

Republican conservatives, ever fearful of a victory by a moderate or liberal in their party primary, posed a serious maverick challenge to the party by entering former Governor Meldrim Thomson in the general election as an independent candidate. To forestall pique challenges from sore losers, state law required such candidates to enter the race before the outcome of the primary was known. Thus, although Thomson's entry ensured that voters would have a right-wing choice in November, it also potentially posed a problem if an approved conservative won the Republican primary, thus pitting two conservatives against Gallen in the general election—hardly the intended result. However, conservative worries were unfounded, for conservative-to-moderate John Sununu won the primary.

Ideological conflict also appeared in the Democratic primary, where unopposed moderate-to-liberal Hugh Gallen captured fewer votes than more moderate—and also unopposed—Democratic candidates for other offices, most notably Congressman Norman D'Amours. Knowledgeable observers concluded that many conservative Democrats simply passed by Gallen's name, an indication of substantial disaffection among Democratic voters.

In the general election, normal Republican party and conservative issues and ideological forces reasserted themselves (after a four-year lapse), and Gallen lost to Sununu, the only incumbent Democrat to lose among the fourteen running nationally in 1982.

During a postelection vacation in the Caribbean, Gallen was taken ill and, after being flown to a hospital in Boston, he died on December 29, nine days before the end of his term. As there was no constitutional post of lieutenant governor, newly elected senate president Vesta Roy became interim governor. However, she refused to take the oath of office, thus putting into doubt whether New Hampshire had a governor from the time of Gallen's death until January 6, the date set by the constitution for the Sununu inauguration. In a peculiarly worded statement Roy declared the nine-day interim between Gallen's death and the inauguration a "temporary absence," thereby avoiding her own inauguration with its implied need to organize and select the leadership of the new state senate. In any case, between election day and the inauguration the state had five acting, or "real," governors: Gallen; senate president Robert Monier, as acting governor in Gallen's absence; Secretary of State William Gardner, during the thirteen hours between the expiration of Monier's term and Roy's swearing-in; and finally Sununu.

Crowding and Conflict in New Hampshire Elections

Eight Republican challengers sought the chance to face two-term incumbent Hugh Gallen. The number suggests that the candidates were confident that Gallen was vulnerable, a vulnerability due to short-term electoral forces as well as long-standing structural characteristics of the New Hampshire electoral system.

Although the state has slowly become more Democratic over the last several decades, the normal forces of party identification still favor Republican nominees. Typically, this would be heightened in an off-year election, with no presidential election to complicate the balance of political forces. Additionally, contextual factors important to understanding New Hampshire politics and elections favor the Republican nominee:

(1) the distribution of party support favors their nominees, (2) the ideological complexion of the voters is distinctly conservative, (3) the effects of critical issues in the state normally favor the Republican nominee, (4) the influence of business leaders in the state who gather around Republican primary candidates has surged; and finally, (5) the peculiar constitutional standing of the governor's office strengthens Republican and conservative nominees.

PARTY BALANCE

Since the Civil War, analysts have categorized New Hampshire as a strongly Republican state.[2] Using 1962–73 data, Ranney characterized it as a two-party state, but barely so, ranking eighth of the states in degree of "Republicanness" of its electoral contests.[3] However, the balance of party registration over the last twelve years has shifted. In 1968 the Republican party registered about 42 percent of the voters, whereas the Democrats accounted for about 26 percent. The remaining one-third of the voters declared themselves to be independents. Twelve years later, after experiencing a 38-percent increase in the number of registered voters, Republican registration dropped to 40 percent while Democratic registration increased to 32 percent and independents dropped to 27 percent. Thus, although the trend of new and changing party registration has slowly favored the Democrats, the balance of forces still clearly favors the Republican party and its candidates.[4] Though no survey figure has established what the normal gubernatorial vote might be in New Hampshire, the fragmentary data suggests that the Republican nominee is probably favored in the typical election by about 55 percent to 45 percent.

POLITICAL CONSERVATISM

A 1976 Cambridge Survey Research survey asked how the voters would ordinarily characterize their political philosophy. The survey established an important characteristic—the dominance of conservatism. Forty-six percent of the state's voters considered themselves conservatives, whereas only 20 percent labeled themselves liberals. Twenty-six percent claimed to be moderates. But for our purposes the most striking finding was that conservatives were just about equally spread between the two parties. Thirty-eight percent of all Democrats claimed to be conservative (29 percent were liberals) and 50 percent of all Republicans claimed to be conservatives (12 percent liberals). Self-designated conservatives numerically dominate both political parties, putting the parties' centers of gravity to the right, probably making New Hampshire's two-party system one of the most conservative among the northern states.

In addition to its normal Republicanness and conservatism, the state's electorate is also one of the nation's most active. Routinely, more voters are drawn to the state's gubernatorial elections than to presidential elections.[5] As Kim et al. discovered after controlling for the expected effects of registration laws and socioeconomic composition of its population, New Hampshire has one of the highest participation rates in elections among the fifty states.[6]

TAXES AND POLITICS

There is an important self-conscious aspect of electoral politics in New Hampshire—a conservatism that focuses on the issue of taxation in the state.[7] New Hampshire levies neither a broadly based retail sales tax nor a personal income tax on its citizenry. In New Hampshire taxation is the key issue. In many ways a person's position either favoring or not favoring a broadly based tax serves as a remarkably good proxy for his or her position on a wide number of other political issues.

This unusual level of conservatism has come about and been maintained in part by the presence of a unique factor in New Hampshire, the *Manchester Union Leader* newspaper, long owned and dominated by its late, very conservative publisher, William Loeb.[8] It is fair to say that the *Union Leader* is politically the most successful newspaper for its size in the country. The consensus among politicians is that it has profoundly shaped politics in the state for three decades, power that shows only a few signs of abating since Loeb's death in 1981.[9] The keys to its success are simple. First, it advocates a simple, practical, gritty conservatism of an uncomplicated politics. Opposition to new taxes, holding the line on increases in old taxes, opposition to growth in government, opposition to traditional liberal welfare and other redistributive programs, and favoritism to the business community have marked the *Leader's* positions.

The ideological cleavage over state taxes promoted by the *Leader* fits into a broader debate over expectations about the New Hampshire state government. One hears with surprising frequency such sentiments as "man's liberty is at stake whenever the legislature meets." Many citizens, leaders and followers alike, are deeply suspicious of the activities of government. When government acts, according to their logic, private freedoms shrink. They conceive of the relationship between public and private action as a sharp and negative trade-off. This is hardly an irrational or inexplicable view. Government does extract income from the private sector in order to fund its activities. But in New Hampshire the questioning of the worth of proposed government action is the general rule. And the presumption is that the value of the loss of private action foregone by new public taxation or regulation will be greater than the benefits that might flow from the new or expanded government program.

One obvious aspect of the *Leader*'s impact is the longevity of consistent philosophical control of the state's largest paper. Loeb assumed control in the late 1940s and kept up a steady, pervasive political presentation. Over time the paper's impact spread not only to the readership but also to the leadership of the state. The paper has been instrumental in drawing into politics many people, such as former Governor Meldrim Thomson and 1982 gubernatorial candidate Robert Monier, who, in my opinion, would not have been attracted into any other state's political arena. Another effective publicity and political device Loeb employed was to demand a pledge from the candidates in both parties that they would veto any broad-based (general sales or personal income) tax bill that would cross the governor's desk.

BUSINESS GROWTH

The tax debate also reflects the changing social and economic situation in the state. The rapid growth of New Hampshire over the last two decades was no accident. Businessmen moved in to take advantage of the low taxes, and workers followed to take the new jobs in the border towns or to commute to their old jobs in "Taxachusetts" from their tax havens in southern New Hampshire. The decision to move into the state was often straightforward and self-aggrandizing. And the prevailing public philosophy supports the private one of economic gain. The net effect over the last decade and a half has made New Hampshire the fastest-growing state east of the Mississippi, apart from Florida. Reaganomics is alive, well, and has been in control for many years in this state. Many people claim that New Hampshire itself is testimony to its success.[10]

Traditionally, the powerful interest groups in New Hampshire politics have been the commercial, industrial, and business groups. Historically, they have varied, from the railroads at the turn of the century, horse racing and gambling in the postwar era, to the modern economic mix that includes many recent arrivals such as Wheelabrator-Frye, Congoleum, AMCA International, Digital Equipment, and Anheuser-Busch, the first three having their international headquarters in the state.[11] The leaders of many of the old-line industrial firms as well as many of the newer ones have reinforced the moderate-to-conservative wing of the Republican party. The executives are often very active in political organizations for good government such as the Forum on New Hampshire's Future or volunteer their time to assist the state in achieving efficiencies and economy in operation. They participate, for example, in Gallen's volunteer Governor's Commission on Governmental Efficiency or fund academic studies that attempt to establish the validity of political viewpoints.[12] The business groups allied in the Business and Industry Association (and other traditional groups such as the chambers of commerce) are particularly concerned about the operation of the state revenue system.

Small businesses, especially small commercial interests, are important in the continuing tax battle. Their influence probably explains the difference between survey findings that the general public far prefers a sales tax to an income tax if new revenue is required, and my finding that a quite sizable majority of state legislators in 1975 favored an income tax—if forced to choose. The direct losers in the case of a new sales tax would be the small business interests. Other active business interests are those regulated by the state and towns. Good examples are trucking, land development, and insurance companies.

THE SINGULAR NATURE OF THE GOVERNOR'S OFFICE

A final factor that focuses Republican energies is the status of the office of the governor—it is the only statewide elective office in New Hampshire. There is no lieutenant governor, and the other statewide offices such as treasurer and secretary of state are either appointed by the governor (the former) or elected by the legislature (the latter).

An important by-product of this singular office is the high and sustained level of intraparty conflict over the party nomination to the post. The Republican gubernatorial party primaries with incumbents, for example, have been contested in each of the elections since 1970. During this period the Republicans held the governorship for four of the six biennia, and a serious challenge to the renomination of the incumbent was posed each time. In 1970 Republican Walter Peterson was challenged by Thomson. In the 1972 primary the Republican incumbent Peterson was challenged again in the party primary by Thomson, who won and went on to win the general election in a three-way race. In 1974 and 1976 Thomson, as the incumbent, faced a serious primary challenge from the moderate wing of the party. In 1978 he faced an even more conservative challenger in former Governor Wesley Powell. This unexpected independent candidacy from the right probably cost Thomson the election, as Democrat Hugh Gallen won the general election with slightly less than 50 percent of the vote.

Because of the unique electoral status of the governor's office, the *Union Leader* focuses its editorial and news column efforts—and usually in the Republican primaries—to enhance its influence. There is another, more subtle effect as well. Because politicians cannot establish their electoral and party credentials through races for intermediate offices, the state lacks natural electoral pathways to the governor's chair. Because politicians are unable to stake out widely agreed-upon claims to serious consideration for nominations based on past electoral support for lower offices, primary elections in the state often become (like 1982) free-for-alls to all comers.

The Primaries

By the summer of 1982 the Republican primary field had narrowed from eight to five reasonable candidates, by late summer only three candidates presented serious campaigns for the September primary: Robert Monier, John Sununu, and Louis d'Alessandro, respectively representing the conservative, moderate-to-conservative, and moderate wings of the party.

Monier was powerfully positioned for a successful run at the nomination. Endorsed by former Governor Thomson, he was also the president of the state senate, the second-ranking position in the state after the governor, where he had wielded power in a fashion to mobilize the powerful conservative wing of the party behind him. He was a direct, outspoken, and provocative spokesman for New Hampshire conservatives. He was also endorsed for the nomination by the *Union Leader*, which provided strength in the state's largest city. His constituency was in a small-town district in the northern half of the state, which gave him broad statewide support.

Monier was the early odds-on favorite in the primary campaign. His name recognition was high, and he had the backing of the *Union Leader* and the many activist conservative groups in the Republican party. He ran a campaign that resonated with what was conventionally thought to be the philosophy of the party faithful: opposition to the broad-based tax, hostility to government spending, and suspicion of government programs, agencies, and those who run them. But his campaign never accelerated. He steadily, almost diffidently, went through the motions. He brought to bear few resources either in advertising, direct mail, or television. He ran his own political shop with local, personally loyal advisors. Consequently, while the fortunes of other candidates bobbed up and down during the summer months, Monier's campaign tracked steadily, almost inexorably it seems in retrospect, to his second-place showing with 30 percent of the primary vote.

Louis d'Alessandro was a longtime favorite of the establishment moderates in the party. He was a veteran state officeholder, having served as a state representative and as one of five governor's councilors, a powerful quasi-legislative/quasi-executive council with large popular constituencies. He was, however, the bête noire of the *Manchester Union Leader* and its staff, who managed to keep alive the old antagonisms of its by now late editor, William Loeb.

D'Alessandro did have certain advantages. He was widely known as an educator and as a public servant, working all across the state in many public-spirited organizations. He had a wide network of colleagues and friends. He was assisted by the state's leading political consultant, Stewart Lamprey, in forcefully stating his own positions on the major issues in the state. Unlike Monier, most frequently described as abrasive, d'Alessandro was an attractive, photogenic, and appealing candidate. He was active from the start, building support in the traditionally liberal communities of Concord, Portsmouth, Hanover, Keene, and Lebanon. He was relying on these middle-sized communities for strong backing and for broad support among party moderates, independents, and a sizable reregistration of liberal Democrats disaffected with the moderate incumbent Gallen.

John Sununu was, in many ways, the mystery candidate in the race. He was a fairly recent (for New Hampshire) immigrant to the state, still working in Massachusetts. He was a college professor running in a state not known for its partiality to higher education.[13] And he was a nuclear engineer and a spokesman for the private nuclear power industry, running in a state where the Seabrook nuclear power plant was a

powerful and divisive issue. He had held only one elective position before the race, a two-year term as a state legislator. However, he was a
veteran campaigner, having lost in 1978 for the Executive Council and
in the 1980 Republican primary race for the U.S. Senate seat eventually
won by Warren Rudman. Each time he had bounced back with a more
successful and better-bankrolled campaign.

In this campaign he positioned himself squarely in the middle of the
political spectrum and created ties to all political camps. He was helped
in this by a sizable campaign budget, resources that few observers had
expected. Like the other two major candidates, he was an educator, and
it was clear that "he learns well." The secrets of his past campaigns
were brought to bear: big money (twice to three times the expenditures
of the other two), outside consultants and advice (Smith and Herroff
of Washington, D.C.), correct positioning on the issues (opposing the
broad-based tax pledge, yet less abrasively so than Monier), and the
devotion of many campaign hours to reach all corners of the state and
to make the pitch to all wings and factions of the party.

Sununu won with 32 percent of the vote, closely followed by Monier
with 30 percent and d'Alessandro with 29 percent. The other five candidates split the remaining votes. The evenness of the percentages is
again testimony to how fractured the party is in the state.

THE CONSERVATIVE CHALLENGE

Meldrim Thomson—a candidate in all eight gubernatorial primary and/or
general elections between 1968 and 1982, three-time governor of the
state (1973–79), defeated in 1978 by Democrat Hugh Gallen, and
widely recognized as the leading conservative in the state—filed as an
independent candidate for the gubernatorial general election the day
before the 1982 Republican primary (held on September 6). He wanted
to guard against the possibility of a contest in the general election between moderates of both parties (e.g., d'Alessandro versus Gallen).
Thomson publicly pondered this possibility early in the primary season,
thereby perversely damaging his own candidate, Monier. Thomson has
a sizable personal following in the state, and the prospect of a Thomson
candidacy might have been just enough to keep some of his supporters
at home on primary day.[14]

In an earlier article on political styles in New Hampshire, I used
Lloyd Etheredge's analysis of the "hard-ball political style" to examine

New Hampshire leadership style.[15] In my opinion Thomson's action was an excellent example of the characteristics of such style, in which "ends pursued politically seem to be largely self-centered, private and individual largely because of [the politician's] difficulty in forming '. . . strong bonds of mutual respect . . . with [other] autonomous individuals.' "[16]

Thus, the very possibility of a d'Alessandro victory in a Republican primary was so abhorrent that Thomson filed his candidacy without regard for the possible damage to fellow conservative Monier in the primary or to Monier and Sununu in the general election. As Etheredge would suggest, such "fundamental [intraparty] disagreement [with the moderate d'Alessandro] is perceived as disloyalty, and disloyalty will engender a powerful and emotional rejection" in the hard-ball political style.[17]

But more generally, his action was a blind stab on a darkened stage. He hoped that the light of election day would not reveal a wounded conservative such as Monier or Sununu. In fact, the wound inflicted was superficial. Thomson gained only about 4,000 votes in the Sununu-Gallen general election race, 1.5 percent of the total vote. He worked diligently on Sununu's behalf in a concerted conservative effort to defeat the incumbent. Thomson's foray into the general election field, risky as it was if a more acceptable candidate had won the primary, indicates the depth and intractable quality of the intraparty cleavages.

THE DEMOCRATIC PRIMARY

Gallen sought unopposed the nomination of his party for the governorship; despite the lack of opposition there were awkward signs of party disaffection. In the Second Congressional District unopposed Democratic Congressman d'Amours ran well ahead of Gallen, precisely in those areas where Gallen would have to hang on to protect his incumbency. The conventional wisdom of party politicians was that Gallen's problems centered on questions of political philosophy and the tax issue. Early on, Gallen had made it clear that he was rethinking the tax issue. He cautioned that he was unlikely to take the *Union Leader*–inspired pledge to veto any broad-based tax bill. Gallen intended to run on the platform of a close, hard look at the state's revenue system, with an eye on reform.

The Outcome of the General Election

Conservatives and Republicans nearly swept the election in New Hampshire. Gallen was the only Democrat (among fourteen incumbent Democratic governors) to lose reelection. Congressman Judd Gregg, a first-term conservative Republican, was easily reelected, while his more liberal Democratic colleague, Norman D'Amours, faced his most serious opposition in four terms in Congress, barely defeating Robert Smith, a candidate with little previous political experience but supported by the *Union Leader*. In Concord, Republicans retained control of both state legislative chambers.

Gallen's loss in the general election suggests that New Hampshire continues to build a record in gubernatorial elections that, I suspect, may be unparalleled in modern American state politics. Gallen is the third incumbent in a row and the fourth of five (since 1960) to be defeated in a bid for reelection either in the primary or the general election.

The tax issue in New Hampshire is the key, for it accounts, in my opinion, both for the critical margins of success of the victors and the incumbents' losses. That is to say, the effect of the tax issue is twofold in the state: it affects the winning of elections; whoever takes the pledge, or appears to be more faithful to an antitax stance, is benefited. The other side of the tax issue, its effect on incumbents' losing elections, will be spelled out shortly. In brief the tax issue is a powerful short-term force that both attracts and repels voters.

David Moore and Robert Craig, coauthors of the results of the University of New Hampshire poll, claim that the 1982 election was a "party" election.[18] It could be thought of as a statewide "reinstating" election in which the established forces of party and philosophy asserted themselves, and in this case a Republican and more conservative nominee won. The "normal electoral forces" of Republicanism and conservatism turned out the incumbent. Other factors reinforce this view of the 1982 election. John Sununu was in many ways the perfect Republican candidate. In addition to being right on the issues, he also presented them in a forceful yet nonthreatening way (unlike Monier). He was an articulate spokesman for the party and, as well, emphasized those valence issues, such as efficiency and more businesslike management, that appealed broadly to the electorate.

Sununu won the election, as Hugh Gallen put it, on the basis of "that stupid pledge." After the fact Gallen concluded that Sununu's simple pledge to veto any broad-based tax (personal income or general sales) presented a benign and, for the typical voter, a personally rewarding commitment that brought those faithful to the party, to the philosophy, and to the issue back into the Republican fold. Gallen's failure to take the pledge left him wide open to the double-barreled election attacks by Sununu, who claimed that both an income and a sales tax would be adopted if Gallen were reelected. Such a campaign charge is difficult to refute. Gallen could hardly counter with statements that he favored only one of the two broad-based taxes; he could only weakly counter that he simply refused to pledge a tax veto.

Such a characterization of the electoral outcome, however, begs the question somewhat, for Hugh Gallen was the only Democratic incumbent in the nation to lose reelection. Why did Gallen do so poorly, compared with other incumbents? I suggest that this election is not simply a Sununu victory, not just an expected reinstating election, but also an incumbent's loss, just as the last three of four incumbents, Wesley Powell (in 1962), Walter Peterson (in 1972), and Meldrim Thomson (in 1978), lost.

But I argue that the tax issue has a double-bind quality in New Hampshire politics. On the one hand the crucial winning margins of the past three governors in their initial victories have been based on their opposition to new taxes (a "quasi-tax" in the case of Gallen, who based his campaign on the promise to enact a ban on construction work in progress, or CWIP, charges by the Public Service Corporation of New Hampshire, the chief utility constructing the controversial Seabrook nuclear power plant).

Yet the very absence of a broadly based tax system precludes the incumbent governor from creating a long-lasting electoral coalition based on the mutual self-interest of voters and politicians. Without a broad-based tax in New Hampshire, the political resource base is insufficient to fuel programs to create successful gubernatorial reelectoral coalitions, term after term. That is to say, the New Hampshire governor is incapable of winning a succession of terms because he lacks the wherewithal to demonstrate to groups in the state that the government is actively involved in their political concerns. Over one or two terms, electoral coalitions slowly disintegrate as the incumbent is unable to reward followers with benefits. Democratic incumbents such as Gallen are probably more sensitive to this rate of erosion. Although this rate may vary across the incumbents of the two parties, the Republicans have the advantage of being able to call on other political forces to stave off defeat. But as the experiences of Peterson and Thomson indicate, Republican incumbents are also sensitive to tax-related electoral defeat because of the erosion of political support around them.

A further consequence of the tremendously deep cleavage generated by the tax issue in the state is that the incumbent will often be prone to challenge from the outside by a candidate (either in his or the other party) who can claim (legitimately so, in the Sununu-Gallen race) that the incumbent is soft on the tax issue.

The gubernatorial career of Governor Meldrim Thomson is the most ironic example of this in action. Thomson bested two-term moderate Republican Walter Peterson in a primary battle based largely on the tax issue. Over his successive three terms Thomson made a national name for himself and the state on the basis of the tax issue, praising the benefits that flowed to the state because it lacked taxes. "Axe the Tax" was his campaign slogan. Yet in 1978 Democrat Hugh Gallen, with little political experience, was able to fashion a successful coalition in the primary and in the general election to triumph over the antitax candidacy of Thomson by claiming that Thomson was soft on a utility tax, the CWIP charges to be levied as part of the consumers' utility bills.

The lesson here is that being against taxation is not a safe strategy for an incumbent governor. It may simply be impossible to base a credible reelection campaign on one's fidelity to an antitax posture. The very nature of modern American state politics, with its wide range and variety of taxes, large and small, with their natural growth and the many minor and major changes routinely made, and with numerous publicly established utility charges (such as CWIP) that can be made out to appear as if they are taxes, leaves an incumbent wide open to the charge of being soft on taxes.

Thus, Gallen, like many of his predecessors, acted out the inevitable scenario. His 1978 candidacy was created and made believable by a tax issue. During his first years in office, no politician was more adamantly or publicly opposed to new taxes. However, in 1982, as his coalition of support for reelection began to falter, he was caught in a dilemma. Reelection was contingent on producing proof positive of the worth of his candidacy. Worth of candidacy depended on an incumbency-generated flow of benefits to such key groups as educators, state employees, contractors, and others. But lacking a broadly based tax system, the governor had no way to make such commitments. Unquestionably, Gallen was supported by the traditional liberal and moderate constituencies, but their enthusiasm was not high, nor was that of self-aggrandizing groups such as state employees that did not have direct flows of benefits from a well-funded treasury.

The tax issue is a powerful political instrument in New Hampshire campaigns. Gallen and many of his predecessors used it to forge winning efforts. The final lesson of the Gallen governorship, and of those preceding his, is that although the tax issue often creates victory, it may also turn and destroy the victor.

Evaluating the Transition

Sununu turned out two-term incumbent Hugh Gallen decisively, with 53 percent of the two-party vote. The election left the party balance in New Hampshire unchanged, under Republican control and, as it turned out, decisively under the control of the moderate-to-conservative political forces sympathetic to the new governor.

Within a few weeks of the election Sununu signaled the start of an activist yet conservative regime, an administration that wished to push forward aggressively in fulfilling a short list of goals: balancing the budget with no new taxes, executive reorganization, and business development. His advisors were well aware of the importance of these transitional weeks in establishing momentum at the start. As one put it, "You can blow the first year of your term as governor in the first few weeks ahead of becoming governor, just by not doing those things or losing some early organizational contests."[19] Yet this same person, and many others, doubted that Sununu could succeed.

Their doubts were straightforward: Sununu had never held an executive office. His single term of elective office was one two-year term as a state representative—one that was, by all accounts, an unremarkable term of service. He was an academic with an oftentimes dogmatic lecturing style. His campaign was bankrolled, and his chief advisors were not from politics but from the business community, and they echoed Sununu's quite antipolitical themes of efficiency and frugality; his stance was antiwaste, antitaxation, and antigovernment. He was the new guy, successor to the late, defeated, though well-liked Governor Gallen, in a town full of politicians who had heard these same refrains from Gallen in 1978, Thomson in 1972, and others before them. And many of them were tired of hearing once again how the novice was going to balance the budget, save the tax system, and bring prosperity to New Hampshire. On inauguration day there was no clear sense that Sununu would succeed.

By the end of his first year it is clear from the accounts of many, Republican and Democrat, conservative and liberal, that Sununu had in fact succeeded, had performed more than creditably, and had in fact directed a smooth transition to a successful year. What were his successes, his few failures, and how can we account for the difference between modest expectations and high performance?

The not-yet-inaugurated governor discovered that his political activities began early and were focused upon battles for leadership in the senate, as control by Republican moderates was threatened. Sununu successfully intervened with Republican senators to deflect efforts to create a conservative bipartisan coalition around the candidacy of Democrat Norman Champagne. His energetic actions on behalf of moderate Republican Vesta Roy turned the election around for her. In many ways it was an extraordinary action by a newly elected governor. It set the tone for the administration early: Sununu was an activist; he clearly set out to impress upon the Concord establishment—elected and unelected—that he would energetically intervene wherever he thought his interests were threatened. It was a novel concept, distinct from the low-key Gallen style of cooperation and papered-over compromises and the earlier Thomson strategy of bulldogged confrontations. It also set the tone of his legislative strategy, which focused squarely on the importance of legislative leadership, that was now at least one-half directly obligated to him. However, he was less successful at ousting the nominally Democratic incumbent secretary of state and former state legislator William Gardner, who successfully won another term from his former legislative colleagues.

The governor also earned respect for his constant presence throughout the awkward transition during Gallen's illness and death. He was an intrusive, though respectful, presence at important Executive Council meetings and other gatherings. His requests were modest: Take no action; wait until after the inaugural and then let us gather and reconcile our differences.

Sununu came into office with a $30-million deficit looming in his first fiscal year in a total biennial budget of about $1.7 billion. Though not a large deficit by the standards of most states, this was serious stuff in New Hampshire, with its jerry-rigged system of taxation. Sununu and his part-time staff of imported aides and consultants from private industry presented a balanced budget that solved the deficit problem (at least for the time being) and, most importantly, with no new general and broad-based tax increases. It also contained some rather generous increases in the welfare programs and cuts well aimed at the University of New Hampshire, and was balanced by modest increases in liquor and other charges, taxes on business profits, and ultimately by a sophisticated and quite optimistic projection of revenue.

A by-product of these budgetary actions was the reinforcement of the highly visible image of the state's favorable business climate. A responsible Republican, sensitive to business interests in a state that remains the very embodiment of supply-side economics in action in a federal system, was safely ensconced in power.

Sununu also pushed through a ten-year reorganization plan that had as a by-product the stripping of all important functions from a key Gallen holdover appointee, comptroller Michael Cornelius. The plan reorganized and centralized the financial arms of the executive branch and will, over a ten-year period, bring state government close to a cabinet style of executive branch organization.

Freshman Governor Sununu was also highly visible outside the state, leading a key, though ultimately unsuccessful, effort in the National Governors' Association (NGA) to bring about a unified approach to the issue of acid rain.

Sununu had failures as well. Some of his budget-balancing strategies were turned back as being farfetched, even by New Hampshire standards (e.g., solving short-term tax anticipation and cash-flow problems by borrowing against the tangible inventory of the state liquor stores). And his efforts at bringing into the governor's office private business talent by asking their business corporations to pay the difference between their old (high) salary and their prospective (low) government salary—a peculiar admixture of private and public monies—was decisively rejected by the legislature.

The Sununu strategy for transition, in retrospect, was straightforward. He surrounded himself with highly placed and, one suspects, quite talented businessmen who advised him on budget numbers, revenue, and taxation. He also amassed a number of Republican party advisors, largely from the mainstream of the party. Third, he adopted an ambitious and energetic legislative style. However, the force that made this all stick together to create an effective and dominating first year was John Sununu's own drive and his abilities to persuade the legislature to focus its efforts on a limited number of items.

It was clear very early in the primary campaign that Sununu had friends in high and well-financed places. He had the largest and probably the best-organized media campaign in the Republican primary. That campaign carried through to the general election campaign as well. His first appointments were drawn from the ranks of traditional Republican administrators; several of them were in minor positions with the Thomson administration and others were from the big New Hampshire-based industries. The latter were in positions of importance, however. Donald McKittrick, former owner of American Metals, was appointed Sununu's chief of staff, and Terry Morton, a vice president of the Congoleum Corporation, was the governor's chief budget advisor. Other businessmen in the state were reputed to serve as informal advisors, most importantly, Signal Company executive Paul Montrone, land developer Samuel Tamposi, and others. The governor's business-oriented strategy was not without political cost, however. Morton, a part-time budget advisor, often arrived in Concord in a style somewhat irritating to the more traditional, earthbound local politicians (e.g. in his corporate helicopter from Congoleum). Such imagery simply cast the governer as the friend, if not the tool, of big business. On the other hand that image in the land of supply-side economics was not entirely negative. But what the business connection did endow the governor with was the imprimatur of expertise and the implicit promise of cooperation from the business establishment.

Sununu ably positioned himself in the middle of the Republican party. He drew on advisors and help from the wings of the party and made his office the centerpiece of Republican efforts in the state. This unifying strategy sharply contrasted with the efforts of other Republican governors and would-be governors, who chose to confront their party rivals (Meldrim Thomson and Robert Monier) or who were unable to position themselves or persuade others of their middle position (former Governor Walter Peterson).

Finally, Sununu's success in the end was a personal one. He put it all together as an energetic, inquisitive, hardworking, and persuasive individual. Whatever doubts the capital politicians had about his talents were quickly dispelled as Sununu rapidly became a well-regarded expert on budgetary and many other legislative matters. Rapid and quite favorable house and senate consideration of his original budget, his reorganization legislation, and other priority items resulted from his well-put-together and convincing presentations, and his energetic and convincing pursuit of legislative approval.

The 1982 Gubernatorial Transition in New Mexico: A Farewell to Patron Politics

JOSE Z. GARCIA

Background

THE ETHNIC AND DEMOGRAPHIC EQUATION

Recent ethnic, demographic, and economic changes in New Mexico are affecting the political system of the state—and influenced the 1982 elections—in various ways. Census data for 1980 record another decline in the proportion of Hispanic citizens, down from 40 percent of total population in 1970 to 36 percent,[1] caused by the significant in-migration, to urban centers, of relatively sophisticated non-Hispanics from all parts of the country but especially from the Southwest. All other southwestern states showed increases in the percentage of Hispanics.

Since the early 1940s New Mexico has been a one-party (Democratic) state, largely because about 90 percent of the state's voting Hispanics are registered in the Democratic party and because ethnic voting patterns are strong. In fact, Hispanic–non-Hispanic ethnicity measurements are better predictors of voting behavior than is party affiliation.[2] Ethnicity, for example, explains why a conservative Republican, Manuel Lujan, was able to capture and hold a U.S. congressional seat in a normally liberal Democratic district. A significant long-term decline in the proportion of Hispanics within the state, therefore, could be expected to cause major political changes. These began as early as the late 1960s.

The first of these changes was that Republican party candidates running for statewide offices became increasingly successful, in spite of a better than two-to-one registration advantage of Democrats over Republicans. Between 1966 and 1976 Republicans held the governorship for four years (1966–70) and captured both U.S. Senate seats (in 1972 and 1976) while retaining firm control over one of two congressional seats. Another important development has been that relatively liberal non-Hispanic and issue-oriented candidates in both parties have emerged as viable candidates statewide and in urban areas; these candidates appeal to a politically sensitive and increasingly significant sector of the population: urban and mostly non-Hispanic professionals. Finally, Democrats have had to search for new ways to get elected. Expanding the favorable base through voter registration and get-out-the-vote drives directed toward Hispanics—the most common tactic used in other Hispanic states—are less successful in New Mexico, where most eligible Hispanics are already registered and where voting rates of Hispanics are slightly higher than that of the overall population.[3] Other devices must be used.

But as Hispanic voting strength waned, a media assault on the traditional method of retaining Hispanic voting loyalty—the patronage system—intensified, especially in large urban areas such as Albuquerque, a city with one-third of the state's population. The media repeatedly deplored patronage systems, by implication tainting the Democratic party. The power of this assault was illustrated neatly by the case of Senator Joseph Montoya, who was depicted in the media as virtually the personification of the patronage system. He was defeated in 1976 by Republican astronaut Harrison Schmitt. Montoya received 25,000 more votes in 1976 than he had received in his successful reelection campaign in 1970 but still lost by a margin—58,000 votes—strikingly similar to the estimated number of out-of-state migrants who registered to vote in New Mexico from 1970–76—56,000. More than 90 percent of his losing margin was produced in the five largest urban concentrations of the state. By the early 1970s these factors had combined to produce a serious structural problem within the Democratic party.

In 1974 Jerry Apodaca, a Democrat who understood the implications of these changes, became the first Hispanic governor in half a century by combining traditional and modern techniques. He used an ideological and modern (nonpatronage) campaign style in the media and among Anglo populations, an approach that would appeal to urban liberals, but at the same time he used traditional patronage campaign techniques among Hispanics. In 1978 Democrat Bruce King became governor with a margin of less than 1 percent by reviving Hispanic and Anglo patronage systems on the one hand and appealing to rural non-

Hispanic concerns on the other. He nearly lost the election in large urban areas, though, where he was soundly defeated.

In 1982, after four years of further decline in the proportion of Hispanics, there was a decided movement in the Democratic party away from Hispanic patronage-style politics to a more modern issue-oriented campaign style to attract voters. The shift was combined with a renewal of the 1974 coalition of Hispanics and urban liberal Anglos within the Democratic party. Toney Anaya, a popular liberal Hispanic and former attorney general, forged this coalition in 1982 with the assistance of organized labor during the preprimary and primary campaigns to defeat a conservative Anglo Democrat. It landed him in the governor's office after a well-organized, modern, issue-oriented general election campaign. The political implications of these campaign trends upon the course of the transition and governing style of the new administration will be pointed out below.

THE STATE ECONOMY

State government income in New Mexico, like most western states rich during much of the 1970s in taxes on income from oil and natural gas and revenues from copper-, uranium-, and coal-mining severance taxes, suffered a significant decline when the national recession began during the preparations for the 1982 campaign. Because of technical difficulties encountered in accurately projecting revenues, however, a $137-million shortfall (9 percent of the entire state government budget) was not discovered until about two weeks after the election. Thus, prescriptions for alternative cutbacks did not emerge as issues during 1982. Candidates and public alike assumed that the recently normal severance-tax bonanza would permit both low taxes and a continually expanding range of government services.

Perhaps the most visible economic issue in the campaign was a scheme that both candidates toyed with: the state would invest money from a permanent severance-tax fund in low-interest-rate housing for middle-income families as a way of stimulating the economy and helping especially the ambitious and growing class of young professional and small business owners who have had difficulty buying housing at prevailing market interest rates. But if economic issues were not salient during the campaign, they were present in the governor's first legislative session and will likely be major issues for the next two or more sessions.

OTHER CAMPAIGN FACTORS

Outgoing Governor Bruce King, a Democrat and rancher elected with a margin in 1978 by oiling patronage machines and appealing to agricultural concerns, was constitutionally ineligible to run for another term. King's administration had been somewhat discredited in the press, which was disenchanted with his caretaker style. Rumors abounded that incompetence within the bureaucracy led to the most violent prison riot in U.S. history, the riot at the Santa Fe state prison in February 1981. Charges of nepotism and political favoritism in state government were frequent. King's administration had been fiscally blessed, however, with large revenue increases from severance taxes on the booming energy industry, which had permitted substantial tax cuts to all citizens and increases in state expenditures; these had reduced much of the public animosity that might otherwise have been expected. That fortuitous break, combined with Anaya's focus on serious issues in the campaign and the fact that a crew of articulate and attractive candidates were running for the lesser state offices, reduced the damage that the previous administration's perceived performance could inflict on the party's image. Republican candidate John Irick, a former state senator from Albuquerque, projected a caretaker demeanor from beginning to end, causing voters to associate him, rather than the Democratic candidate, with the previous administration.

All of this plus the normal off-year national trend away from the party in power produced a substantial and unanticipated margin (53 percent) for Toney Anaya. He won Albuquerque, with one-third of the state vote, an unusual outcome for a Democrat running for statewide office. It had been eighteen years since a Democratic gubernatorial candidate had won in Albuquerque. In assisting Anaya, the state Democratic party received significant technical and financial support from the Democratic National Committee, which chose New Mexico for a pilot program designed to maximize overall party strength through extensive polling and pinpoint targeting techniques for all statewide candidates.

Anaya himself should be credited with engineering some of these outcomes, since he was highly experienced in state races, having run successfully for attorney general in 1974 and unsuccessfully in a close race for U.S. Senate in 1978 against the most popular politician in the state, incumbent Senator Pete Domenici. In addition, he was able to attract talented young professionals, both Hispanic and Anglo, to help with his campaign. Finally, a strong tactical weapon he enjoyed was an almost uncanny ability to command and direct the attention of the press, a talent for which he had gained a well-deserved and long-standing reputation.

Transition Organization

Ahead in the polls from the beginning, Anaya anticipated victory and discussed transition plans at length during the campaign with two of his closest advisors, Shirley Scarafiotti and Harvey Fruman.[4] Anaya's preelection concept of the transition appears to have focused on two tasks: first, on filling high-level posts in state government only after superior applicants had been sought and professionally screened for evidence of high qualifications. He felt that his campaign strategy had freed him from the necessity of playing patronage politics. Second, Anaya was particularly interested in fulfilling many of his campaign promises during the first (sixty-day) legislative session. The second session, by constitutional mandate, lasts only thirty days and is devoted to financial affairs except for special gubernatorial requests for consideration. It was unlikely that a comprehensive package of legislation could be dealt with in so short a time. By the third session, again sixty days long, creeping lame-duckism would have set in and the legislature might not be so compliant.

Two days after the election Anaya held a meeting with roughly twenty campaign workers and supporters.[5] He outlined the goals of the transition. Shirley Scarafiotti and Steve Anaya, the governor-elect's twenty-six-year-old nephew, were placed in charge of the search for a highly qualified cabinet, and two days later Anaya, who wanted to spend most of his time on legislation and budgeting, engaged Harvey Fruman to help him with these matters during the transition. Within a few days Fruman, through the assistance of the National Governors' Association (NGA) representative, learned that a tight timetable must be followed by a governor in the process of presenting a budget to the legislature. By this time the staff had discovered that the statutes mention the gubernatorial transition only to the extent that $40,000 is appropriated for it. In addition, an office complex of three or four rooms was made available in the state capitol. This would mean cutting down expenses to a bare minimum and focusing on the highest priorities. To cut costs Anaya left open his campaign headquarters, donated by a supporter, rather than rent space.

New Mexico is a state with a long ballot, so the governor must share some responsibilities with other elected officials, including a lieutenant governor, attorney general, state auditor, land commissioner, secretary of state, three corporation commissioners, and a state treasurer. Normally, these are won by Democratic candidates, keeping partisan friction low, and 1982 was no exception. There are no provisions for a transition for any of these officials except the governor.

Transition Politics

A single overriding emotion colors the recollections of the transition by all the governor's people: anxiety over the lack of time. In two months a governor-elect must arrange his own office, make thorough revision of budget requests to the legislature, conceive and draft legislation for the session that begins the third week in January, recruit executives to fill cabinet posts, and fill approximately 300 bureaucratic positions exempted from civil service requirements of job continuity. There are flocks of job seekers, dozens of interest-group representatives and legislators anxious to meet the new governor, and an unrelenting herd of reporters begging for hard and soft news. There are cocktail parties to attend, new family relationships to sort out, and a final Christmas to go through as a private citizen. The campaign must be terminated, reports filed, and costs accounted for.

All of the major participants in the transition remember the transition period as being more hectic and harder to get through than the campaign or the legislative session that followed. The culture shock of the transition is like nothing that any of them had ever experienced. All other problems—substantive, personal, procedural—including the usual struggles for power during that period, are overwhelmed by the magnitude of tasks to be done and the short time available. The words *confusion, hectic, overwhelmed,* and *overtime* formed on the lips of insiders again and again as they recalled the period. Anaya, known to be extremely demanding as a boss, was demanding on himself, working long hours overtime to get things done. The relatively clear-cut priorities established by the governor-elect and the knowledge that the period would end soon were the only consoling features of the transition for the actors. Staffers wistfully deny having engaged in the usual carving out and defending of turf among themselves. The governor was to make all decisions, large and small, procedural and substantive. The staff's role was to find the information, articulate a set of alternatives, and carry out gubernatorial instructions.

It became obvious soon after the election that the sheer volume of work to be done would require unanticipated staffing arrangements during the transition. Anaya decided, however, that he could make do with a staff about one-third the size of his anticipated eventual needs and that his staff's functional responsibilities could evolve gradually as he was able to evaluate performances. But he did not assure members of his staff that a place would be made for them in the governor's office after the transition. This may have been to keep his own options open while evaluating staff members under noncampaign circumstances or simply to keep focused on higher priorities. In any event Anaya's use of a reduced staff that was working overtime and uncertain about personal futures was something he would later regret.[6] Staffing problems plagued at least the first six months of his administration.

As the transition moved into December a morale problem developed among some staffers who had not yet been assured of a job, some of whom had foregone adequate incomes for months during the campaign and some of whom had watched as more highly qualified "outsiders," who might not have participated in the campaign at all, received coveted appointments. Most staffers were screened for qualifications along with other applicants, several were selected for high positions, and eventually those whose ambitions outran their perceived qualifications were deftly removed by the governor to relatively minor positions within the bureaucracy.

The office in the capitol was used for the cabinet selection process; the headquarters was used by governor-elect Anaya, Scarafiotti, Fruman, and a few others recruited to work on budgetary and legislative matters. One's presence as a worker at the outer edges of these offices was either tolerated or not, according to the complex ethical codes that evolve among campaign survivors. It was clear there was little money to pay those who were physically present and willing to help, little time or money to recruit professional, noncampaign workers, and many, many things to be done.

Comings and Goings

Only a receptionist and a few lower-level office staffers from the previous administration were retained. But it was not until the fall of 1983 that the governor's official staff organization was complete. This delay had the effect of reducing to three or four the number of contact points available for direct input to the governor and of overloading these already busy persons with relatively unimportant decision-making tasks. More significantly, efficient and manageable divisions of labor did not evolve until a rather desperate staff reorganization the following summer, when six to ten staff positions for policy planning (a kind of in-house think-tank) were created to coordinate with scheduling, administrative, legislative, and other functions. How effective this will be in alleviating bottlenecks is still unknown.

Scarafiotti was placed in charge of talent search coordination and office administration, including gatekeeping to protect the governor's time. Fruman was given the responsibility of coordinating policy and the budget; he was also put in charge of internal staff control. Scarafiotti had been Anaya's secretarial and administrative assistant since before his election as attorney general. She had gained his confidence to the extent that she was allowed during the campaign to screen most requests for access to him. Fruman had worked in the attorney general's office before Anaya was elected in 1974 to that post and continued there two years after Anaya left in 1978, after which he joined Anaya in a law firm. Fruman handled a few campaign issues and helped with fund raising during the 1982 campaign.

The gatekeeper role during and after the transition was handled at several levels. For the mob of job seekers looking for regular civil service positions, the Anaya administration decided to retain the state personnel director, Leo Griego, a man closely associated with the outgoing King administration. Hundreds of job applicants were simply referred to his office, asked to fill out the regular civil service forms, and scheduled for qualifying examinations. Griego's continuation in the personnel office was significant for two reasons. First, in retaining a prominent member of the King administration in this sensitive position Anaya indicated that, although he felt he did not owe any patronage to patron leaders, he was not insensitive to the needs of Hispanic citizens, many of whom were accustomed to job hunting through personal contact. Griego knows people throughout the state. Hispanics, in fact, are overrepresented in state government employment but are concentrated at lower levels. Thus, a second reason for retaining Griego was that in him the governor could count on someone who was familiar with both the technical, bureaucratic side of affirmative-action hiring and the cultural needs of the Hispanic population. During the transition and first few months of the administration Anaya also hired men familiar with the black and Indian communities—part of his commitment to affirmative action.

Persons seeking gubernatorial appointments sent résumés to the talent search group. All nonstaffers wishing to see the governor were required to clear through Scarafiotti, except legislators; for them Anaya had, and still maintains, an open-door policy. Staffers wishing to see the governor were also required to go through Scarafiotti; exceptions were the press secretary, Fruman, and perhaps one or two others, including the governor's nephew, Steve Anaya, who was placed in charge of non-cabinet appointments. As a campaign coordinator Steve Anaya was in a position to know an applicant's campaign relationship to the governor-elect.

Coping with the Process

SETTING UP THE TRANSITION TEAM

Under the constant supervision of the governor-elect, Fruman and Scarafiotti set about organizing teams to handle the work load.[7] Bob McNeil, an unsuccessful primary candidate for lieutenant governor and an ideological friend and a former coworker with Anaya, joined Denise Fort and Paul Biderman in helping Fruman prepare legislative policy positions summarizing Anaya's campaign promises. Together, they checked each proposed item to see which promises could be accomplished by executive order and which might require legislation. McNeil was a major speech writer during the campaign, so this was, in effect, a continuation of his campaign job. During the transition these names were submitted to the talent search team. McNeil was chosen to be Secretary of Health and Environment, Biderman became Secretary of Energy, and Denise Fort became Secretary of the Department of Finance and Administration (DFA). Like Anaya, all were liberal lawyers.

Fort, Fruman, and Anaya also worked together on the budget. As there is very little time for a governor-elect to digest the details of a billion-dollar budget between election day and January, when the legislature must act on it, most new governors do little more than give a cursory glance at the previous administrations's projected budget. In 1982, however, the unexpected shortfall in revenues would make last-minute budget cuts necessary.

Characteristically, Anaya wanted to make sure he was the one to make these decisions and thus was willing to work overtime and to devote more time to the budget than perhaps any previous governor. DFA officials were asked to keep Anaya up-to-date on fiscal projections of revenues held in the four major state funds, and the previous administration's projected budget was inspected closely and modified substantially. Anaya himself spent countless hours poring over budget figures for each department, revising figures as he went along in response to revenue projections and his own priorities. Fruman estimates that Anaya spent two-thirds of his time overall with the legislative package and the budget, although he was forced to spend more time during the last few days interviewing cabinet aspirants. Fort, as head of DFA, is now the chief budget officer.

David Oakeley, campaign press secretary, continued in the same capacity during the transition and became the state press secretary on inaugural day. He did not, however, know of his appointment until December 31. Steve Cobble, a regional campaign staffer, stayed on to work on policy concerns. Dan Lopez, a top campaign staffer, became head of the Employment Security Department, and a few lesser job-seeking campaign workers stayed on in what amounted to courier roles.

The governor's wife, Elaine, headed up a large inaugural team composed of many persons, including several staffers, well-wishers, friends, and relatives. As in other areas, however, the governor was consulted on major decisions and was kept informed of all plans. The major costs of the inaugural were borne by those who paid $5 to attend the festivities. Another team was given the task of wrapping up the campaign. Pat Montoya, Orlando Romero, and Ron McDaniels headed this group; each had worked at the state campaign headquarters in Santa Fe during the election.

THE SEARCH FOR A CABINET

Anaya announced soon after the election that he would select his cabinet by December 1. This proved to be impossible for logistical reasons. A consulting firm was hired to assist in processing the host of applicants for top positions; nearly 300 persons applied for ten cabinet appointments. The governor-elect and Scarafiotti had envisioned computer matchings of the skills required for top jobs with the skills of applicants. In practice the system broke down, and much of the matching of applicants with jobs was done by hand in the state capitol office, where the talent search took place. It proved to be difficult to train volunteers to learn the word-processing programs well enough to input required data.

An interview team headed by a trusted volunteer was then set up for each of the ten cabinet posts. Most of these teams were composed of secondary campaign staffers, the leaders of whom, in most cases, ended up in secondary positions in the bureaucracy. Judy Basham managed the office, Steve Anaya screened applicants, and Willie Alire evaluated those who had survived the first screening. Governor-elect Anaya was finally given a list of three names for each cabinet post, data on each, and the schedule for interviews. Applicants whose credentials were not deemed good enough for cabinet-level positions were in many cases screened for secondary positions or for exempt positions in the bureaucracy.

The search for talent was active as well as passive. Interview teams for each cabinet position were asked to contact chambers of commerce, universities, interest group representatives, federal and state agencies, and other groups appropriate to the peculiar mission of each cabinet post to obtain the names of superior persons who might be available for consideration. Very quickly, word got out that an applicant with high professional credentials would be reviewed seriously, regardless of one's personal connection to Anaya or the campaign.

In the end, four of the ten cabinet posts were given to persons active in the Anaya campaign, and a fifth post went to a known supporter. Three had never met Anaya until the job interviews. What they all had in common were moderate-to-liberal ideologies, youth, and professional academic degrees. Several, like Anaya, were lawyers. Four were women, legacies of a campaign promise that ended up delaying the cabinet selection for several weeks while a reasonably successful effort was made to find qualified female applicants for executive positions. Four were Hispanics, one was a Republican, and one was an Indian.

Overall, the personnel chosen for these cabinet posts have won high ratings from experienced observers. A writer for the *Washington Post* wrote that Governor Anaya "has assembled what is perhaps the most liberal cabinet of any state in the country and has made government intervention, affirmative action, and high energy the watchwords of his young administration."[8]

The governor's nephew, Steve Anaya, was placed in charge of replacing board and commission members. Normally this is done haphazardly by contacting campaign and party workers for lists of names of people whose qualifications match roughly the legal and functional requirements. It is a tedious job that always results in a certain in-house backlash, as unsuccessful aspirants or those backing them register their disgruntlement with whoever will listen. Typically, campaign volunteers or contributors unrequited with some sort of status symbol from the governor are the first to express vocal opposition to a new administration. In Governor Anaya's case, opposition was stronger than usual.

There are some two thousand appointments to be made by a governor. Most of these are to boards and commissions that dispose of large volumes of official and semiofficial business for a governor—everything from a committee to regulate the hair-cutting industry to a commission making many day-to-day multimillion-dollar decisions about highway construction, location, and repair. Nearly 300 of these are for exempt positions in the state bureaucracy.[9]

For exempt jobs and boards and commissions, a tendency for the development of small fiefdoms has evolved, not unlike the case of J. Edgar Hoover and the FBI at the national level, when persons have occupied these positions and acquired expertise over the years. In many cases in New Mexico the occupants are prominent in Democratic party circles (Republicans have not controlled the governor's seat since 1970), contribute small sums of money to many campaigns, and have many friends with access to the governor. In fact, overlapping networks of such people have dominated much of the filling of party patronage positions in the past.

Until Governor Apodaca was able to consolidate many of these boards and commissions in 1976 into a cabinet system whereby each commission or board was required to report periodically to one of the cabinet secretaries, perhaps the most serious problem in state government was the logistical inability of a governor to control the direction of more than a handful of these nearly autonomous entities. The prob-

lem had been pointed out as early as 1952, and by 1976 the prolifera-
tion of state government services and their accompanying bureaucracies
had reached almost scandalous proportions.[10] Apodaca's most lasting
achievement as governor was his reorganization of state government to
place much of the bureaucracy under administrative supervision. Neither
he nor his successor, however, acted systematically to change the personnel in these agencies except when vacancies occurred. Anaya did.

During the 1982 campaign, as mentioned earlier, Anaya had chosen
to avoid patronage commitments. This freed Anaya, once he was elected,
perhaps more than any previous governor, to change the personnel holding the hundreds of salaried and nonsalaried state positions. During the
transition Anaya made clear that he expected to make many changes
where he could in exempt positions and in boards and commissions.
Most of the latter members were sent letters in December requesting
resignations. Because many of them belonged to the informal partisan
network discussed earlier, their indignation was predictable: they expected to be retained as usual and were chagrined to find that they had
sometimes (although not by any means always) been replaced by relative newcomers to politics. Exempt state employees, many of whom,
like board and commission members, were part of an informal partisan
network, were told they would be screened and evaluated; a handful of
employees Anaya fired on his first day in office. Many were eventually
replaced. For all of these reasons the reaction against Anaya was more
severe than is usual for a new governor.

Although these moves were unprecedented and unpopular, the governor was clearly acting within legal limits established many times over
by the state courts, which have maintained that exempt employees and
board appointees serve entirely at the pleasure of the governor.[11] Anaya
himself defends his wholesale changes in two ways: first, he argues, he
has eliminated patronage fiefdoms that have been closed to all but a
few insiders.[12] One might call this a reform move. Second—and this ap-
plies even where competent persons might have served in these positions—policy control is better served when all positions are filled by
persons loyal to the governor if not always of the same ideological commitments. This might be called a move to centralize more power in the
governor's office. Although higher priorities during the transition period
and first few months have delayed the recruitment of exempt and nonsalaried appointees, there seems little question that Anaya is gaining
control over many of the boards and commissions.

Thus far the news media have not connected these reform moves to the kind of campaign Anaya waged and the relative freedom he was granted thereby. Instead, they have often criticized Anaya for seeming to covet power over all decisions, no matter how insignificant.[13] Anaya has at times contributed to this view by making statements to the press on even insignificant issues. For example, he publicly entered an argument over a minor policy matter affecting the barber board and urged the board of regents of a major university to change the name of the student yearbook (it was called the *Swastica*, so named and symbolized since 1907, long before Hitler's use of the symbol).

One might disagree with some of Anaya's judgments, but, it is clear that he has broken precedent not so much in trying to control the selection of appointees as in conducting this process immediately and in public. Public response has been rather negative during the first few months of the administration, testifying indirectly not only to the weakness of the governor's office in New Mexico but also to the public's compliance with this weakness.[14]

Reaching Out from the Governor's Office

Having been elected with largely Hispanic and urban professional support, the Anaya administration was somewhat unconnected to the state's business and agricultural interests, which had been served well by the previous governor. Because the Secretary of Agriculture in New Mexico is named by the Board of Regents of New Mexico State University and not by the governor (the only cabinet position beyond the governor's control), Anaya was anxious to establish a rapport with agricultural interests. Though diminishing in overall importance, agriculture still accounts for 15 percent of employment and 20 percent of personal income in New Mexico. Few of his campaign workers had any knowledge of rural concerns. Anaya brought Bob Toberman, who had worked with the King and Apodaca administrations, to work with the transition specifically to establish contact with farmers and ranchers. Toberman was able to articulate their interests to the new governor and to maintain formal liaison between them and the governor.

The business community was sounded out through its ubiquitous lobby groups. Input was solicited, for example, from the Association of Commerce and Industry, the largest business lobby in the state. At the same time, however, tensions between the business community and the governor's office began to arise when Anaya appointed several active environmentalists to high positions in the administration. These tensions did not disappear during the first six months of the administration, although business leaders generally were not dissatisfied with Anaya's efforts to stimulate economic development.

The constituent relations of a governor have always been extremely important in New Mexico, where jobs with state and county governments are in many localities the only realistic alternative that many young persons have to moving away. In a state where the vagaries of patronage politics have determined one's relationship to the governor's office, people are extremely sensitive about a governor's efforts to tamper with the access that citizens have to state government agencies. In recent years several efforts have been made institutionally to ensure that citizens no longer must rely on inefficient local party chairpersons, friends of the governor, and personal contacts in their dealings with state government agencies.

In 1970 state statutes authorized the lieutenant governor to act as an ombudsman for state government. The lieutenant governor is authorized to "facilitate and promote the cooperation and understanding between the people of this state and the agencies of state government. . . ."[15] Since 1970 the job has been considered full time, and most knowledgeable persons agree that Roberto Mondragon, who occupied the position from 1970 to 1974 and from 1978 to 1982, did a superb job of establishing a systematic way of dealing with the public. Statutes passed in 1977 created Governor's Service Centers in several large cities, staffed by caseworkers selected by the governor; the centers provided essentially the same services as did the lieutenant governor. All but one of these were eliminated by the legislature in 1979, and two were restored by the legislature, with Anaya's backing, in 1983.

Anaya continued the recent tradition of concern with constituent relations by appointing his lieutenant governor, Mike Runnels, to an intergovernmental committee to maintain systematic liaison between the governor's office and other levels of government. This appears to be working well. Anaya also staffed the existing New Mexico Office in Washington, D.C., with experienced and energetic professionals who have had high-level political experience. The office has existed for several years and is instrumental in helping state agencies apply for grants from the federal government and generally keeps the governor's office abreast of relevant trends in Washington.

Aid and Assistance

Within days after the election the NGA had contacted Anaya and offered help. Anaya and Fruman attended the NGA's Seminar for New Governors in Utah. Fruman learned to his delight that the NGA had technical expertise that could be made available to him. An NGA staffer responsible for four states, including New Mexico, traveled several times to New Mexico to help organize the office staffing and to help Fruman on the policy and budget organization. He is also remembered fondly for helping to tighten up the schedule with his knowledge of the legislature's intricate calendar requirements for budget submissions. All in all, one has the impression that Anaya's staff found the NGA's expertise invaluable. Aside from the transition team's informal attempts to solicit input from interest groups and the assistance of a consulting firm to help with cabinet and subcabinet selections, Anaya's people appear to have relied on the NGA for technical assistance in setting up the administration.[16]

Party Politics and the New Administration

DEALING WITH THE COALITION AND THE INAUGURATION

The state house of representatives was dominated during the 1970s by an alliance of Hispanics from northern New Mexico and by urban liberals. Certain conservative Democrats from rural areas, especially the "Little Texas" ranching and oil sector of southeast New Mexico, were disssatisfied with the house leadership. In 1978 nine Democrats formed a coalition (referred to always, appropriately, as the Coalition) with the twenty-seven Republicans in the seventy-member house to defeat the incumbent speaker. Committee assignments reflected the relative party strengths of the Coalition. A more conservative cast was given to legislative output. When in power, Coalition leaders, like their predecessors, were vindictive toward the other side. Governor Bruce King, sensitive to rural needs, tried to work with the new leadership but found himself tugged and pulled by intense and often emotional pressures from both winners and losers. The controversies were recorded in detail in the news media. Some Democrats accused King of "working with Republicans." Coalition members accused non-Coalition Democrats of "playing party politics with state problems."[17]

The Coalition retained power in the house in 1980, giving its leadership control over reapportionment. The first house reapportionment, passed in early 1982, was quickly contested in the courts by aggrieved Democrat legislators and was declared unconstitutional. A special session in June 1982 reapportioned the state house and senate again, this time paying much stricter attention to maintaining constant population sizes and to preserving ethnic and partisan integrity.

Thus, as Anaya geared up his campaign during the primary and general election seasons, the issue of the control of the house was salient throughout the state, with legislators and interest groups polarized over it more than at any other time in the previous four years. Anaya, both a liberal and a Hispanic and searching for a winning coalition combining both groups, could not be expected to side with the Coalition. It was not, however, something that could be dealt with openly during the campaign by either Anaya or his opponent John Irick, lest they be charged with trying to interfere with the legislative branch of government. Also, of course, the winning candidate would have to work with the leadership of the house in any event, another factor calling for prudent campaigning. Both candidates stated their opposing preferences but urged voters to make the ultimate decision by voting for their legislative choices in each of the seventy house districts.

The campaign over, it appeared that the pro-Coalition forces might win the speaker's race by a vote or two, although there were several freshmen legislators whose preferences remained unknown. They and a few other relatively undecided house members became the objects of a concerted campaign by the incumbent speaker, Gene Samberson, and the anti-Coalition candidate, Ray Sanchez, who had been extremely powerful as a legislator during the pre-Coalition days of the 1970s. Both had been accused of vindictiveness, and both tried to repair injured feelings.

Anaya's options were limited. He could repeat King's strategy of staying neutral and working with the winners. King, however, had discovered that this merely made the winners unbeholden to the governor while the losers accused him of betrayal. His relations with the house were problematic throughout his term. Anaya, more liberal than King, might also face more ideological trouble with Coalition leadership. The governor-elect chose to offer his full support to the choice of the Democratic house caucus, which convened over Thanksgiving weekend. This move, in effect, constituted a stand against the Coalition, as only a small number of Democrats—between ten and twelve—favored the Coalition, and as Democrats outnumbered Republicans in the House forty-five to twenty-five. The caucus selected Sanchez by a vote of twenty-eight to seventeen. The caucus vote over, Sanchez, with the un-ambiguous support of the governor-elect, began to compete against Samberson for the thirty-six votes it would take to win the speakership.

For several weeks the tally among legislators was fluid, each side claiming to have thirty-five or thirty-six (out of seventy) "solid" votes. Rumors and anecdotes spread about the impact of logrolling agreements that may have been made during the previous reapportionment session and about the pressures both sides were exerting on individual members. In the end Samberson withdrew his candidacy on the first day of the session, Sanchez was elected speaker, and the Coalition was terminated.[18] Sanchez himself credits his election to the efforts of the governor, although of course many others assisted as well. Having been decisive in his support of Sanchez, the governor was in a relatively strong position to deal with the new leadership of the house. It is surely the single most important factor in explaining Anaya's success with the legislature during his first session.

The Anaya inaugural was the first in New Mexico history to extend beyond Santa Fe. Anaya felt strongly that the festivities should signal a sincere effort to reach out to all sectors of the state, geographic, ethnic, and partisan. For that reason he chose to hold events not only in Santa Fe but also in Albuquerque, where one-third of the state's population resides, and in Roswell, deep in the southern Little Texas area of the state, where Anaya had lost heavily in both the primary and general elections. A reception was given in Roswell, and balls were held in Santa Fe and Albuquerque. Tickets to the balls were held to $5 per person in an effort to make the event affordable to all, even though costs were somewhat higher. Everyone was invited and the event was viewed by Anaya as a governmental affair.

THE LEGISLATIVE SESSION

Having won the fight over house leadership, the administration found the legislative session to be almost anticlimactic.[19] The $137-million shortfall in state revenues was disposed of rather easily, although not without some give-and-take, especially with the senate. A 2 percent across-the-board cut in the budgets for all state agencies and schools was enacted. Teachers' salaries and most state employees' wages were frozen at least through the next school year. A $55-million bond swap was legislated to raise that amount of money in issuances of severance-tax bonds, and money was transferred from the operating reserve and other funds. These measures corrected the shortfall in revenues for expenses already incurred by the previous legislature. Revenue projections for the future were also low, requiring either more taxes or a cut in the budget. The tax issue was fraught with more controversy.

The governor, working closely with the house, asked for a raise in taxes of $140 to $195 million over a three-year period. Senate leaders balked at this, feeling that the governor could make do with an $80-million increase. Many house members, in fact, wanted to cut the budget, although in the end they compromised, increasing the budget by 1 percent, ($97.5 million) for a net loss after inflation of about 3–4 percent. Anaya was unwilling to compromise during most of the session, insisting not only on tax increases but also on budget increases. Senate leaders in the end forced him to accept either a reduced tax increase or, because of the lack of time, to call a special session to deal separately with the issue. When the governor realized he did not have the votes, he personally negotiated a compromise with the recalcitrant senators, got an agreement, and sold it to the house. Taxes were increased by $97.5 million, with a 32-percent increase in income taxes, a 20-percent emergency increase in oil and gas taxes, a 20-percent increase in corporate taxes, a .25-percent increase in gross receipts taxes, and a few other increases in minor taxes. The fiscal crisis, if it resulted in few winners, certainly had its share of losers: state employees and teachers in the public school system and universities. Neither of these groups is well organized in New Mexico.

In the end the governor got perhaps 90 percent of what he asked for from the legislature, a record that informed persons considered superb for a governor who began the session with a very shallow understanding of the legislative process, having never been a legislator himself or worked with the legislature. Nor did any member of his staff have solid experience with the legislature; the one exception was Fabian Chavez, a senior statesman in New Mexico politics who was hired as a liaison between the governor and the legislature. Without his help Anaya might well have had a stormy legislative session, but most legislators also favorably recall the governor's willingness to roll up his sleeves and work cordially with legislators to work our compromises. The fact that the fiscal situation of the state was unknown and hence not an issue during the cam-

paign may also have freed Anaya from having to fight during the session
to keep campaign commitments.

CREATING AN IMAGE

Anaya came to the governorship with a defined and favorable media
image. As attorney general he had maintained a high profile as a feisty
and fearless prosecutor. As a candidate for the U.S. Senate he had received more than his share of campaign news space by attacking his
opponent's record and defining issues sharply, and as a gubernatorial
candidate Anaya used his media experience brilliantly in both the primary and general elections. Thus, he did not have to create an image; it
was already there.

True, he had made some mistakes. During the campaign he announced
he would not permit a death sentence to be carried out during his tenure
in office, an admirably honest statement that also alienated those in
favor of the death sentence (a majority of the state) and inspired outright horror among the state's prison guards, still reeling from the most
violent prison riot in American history. This and other campaign gaffes
were relatively minor, considering his usual aggressive, hard-hitting style.

Once in office, however, Anaya has had unanticipated difficulty with
the media, even after an extremely successful legislative session. Attention has focused on his making out-of-state trips, most notably one to
Chicago to campaign for mayoral candidate Harold Washington. He
was also criticized heavily for chairing a conference in Santa Fe for out-
of-state Hispanic leaders to prepare a strategy for maximizing national
Hispanic political clout in the 1984 elections. Media commentary provoked by these episodes has suggested that the electorate chose him to
be governor of New Mexico only.

The intensity of this criticism, elicited by ethnically motivated behavior, is not easy to explain. Jerry Apodaca, the state's only other recent
Hispanic governor (1974–78), was never criticized for rather similar behavior. The difference seems to be that Apodaca never drew attention to
his ethnic background. Although he believed firmly in affirmative action
and practiced it, it was never an issue; in fact, ethnic concerns, though
real, were disguised. Anaya's openness about ethnicity seems to have
violated an unwritten code in a state where minority populations out-
number majority populations: it is permissible to feel strongly about,
and to act within limits on, ethnicity but not to discuss it. Subtle, com-

plex, and long-standing interethnic dynamics have caused this code to be rigorously enforced upon the state's major political personages.

Another problem that has surfaced is the perception that Anaya has a penchant for insisting on control over even minor decisions. As mentioned earlier, most exempt employees and commission appointees were replaced immediately following the inauguration. The governor has made no secret of his desire to have people in these positions who reflect his own views and who will be loyal to him. Occasionally the governor has even made clear to the press which course of action he expects a specific appointee to take. These traits have often been interpreted in the media as the pettiness of a man so consumed by ambition that he refuses to delegate decisions even on trivial matters.

The persistence of these criticisms have been made at the expense of a full evaluation by the media of the governor's undeniable accomplishments, especially during the first legislative session. They have added up to a growing image problem, something that must be quite new and unexpected for Anaya. After eight months in office Anaya's image problems had grown so large that it appeared they might well interfere with his effectiveness unless major steps were taken to reverse the trend. It would be a major irony indeed if Anaya, whose greatest asset during the campaign was his ability with the press, were to see his power significantly diminished by a negative image. Anaya's restless energy and strength of resolve, however, make such a scenario unlikely.

Evaluation of the Transition

The recent demographic and political changes in New Mexico dictated the campaign strategy that made Anaya's gubernatorial candidacy a success. In abandoning the traditional campaign promises of patronage, especially among Hispanics, Anaya's campaign acquired legitimacy in the mass media and, hence, in the all-important urban centers, where state campaigns are now won or lost. Moreover, his ethnic concerns and identity were sufficient to elicit strong support among the state's large nonurban Hispanic population. It is therefore not surprising that Anaya's postelection policies should reflect these considerations, especially as they affect the composition of appointees. Nor is it surprising that such an administration should be fraught with controversy. After all, Anaya is the first governor largely to abandon standard operating procedures and to embrace the politics of issues and ideologies rather than the politics of existing fiefdoms. His strategic forerunner, Jerry Apodaca, who

paved the way for an Anaya governorship in many ways, also faced organized resistance when he tried to centralize more power within the executive branch of government and when he ignored traditional patronage
expectations. What is perhaps most surprising is the relative ease with
which Anaya was able during the transition to lay the groundwork for
far-reaching changes.

On balance, the Anaya transition was quite smooth, especially when
one considers the conflict that could have arisen with state finances in
crisis. In spite of the fact that his staffing system was plagued with problems from the beginning and that he has received intense criticism in
the press, these problems apparently did not interfere with the governor's ability to accomplish his goals. Transition tasks (except for the
appointment of members to boards and commissions) were finished,
the legislative session was an undeniable success, and firmer control over
the bureaucracy was obtained. A conservative coalition failed to ma-
terialize in the legislature, and many of Anaya's campaign promises have
been implemented. Appointments to boards, commissions, and high-
level bureaucratic posts, though often painfully slow in coming and
sometimes rancorously received in the press, increasingly reflect the policy concerns and attitudes of the administration rather than the standard operating procedures of established fiefdoms, although not yet to
the extent anticipated by Anaya.

No single factor, of course, can account for these successes, and a final
evaluation even of the transition and first few months in office will not
be possible for several years. Several points, however, can be made. It
seems clear that the newly emerging political environment in New Mexico, caused by gradually shifting demographic patterns, favored not only
Anaya's candidacy but also his goals in office. As these are long-term
trends, they are likely to favor Anaya in the future.

The chaos, staff shortages, and lack of administrative support during
the transition appear to have been overcome by several factors. First,
Anaya had a clear plan for finding a cabinet and working on legislative
and budgetary programs. He had a defined set of priorities to which he
stuck tenaciously. Second, Anaya was willing to work long hours during
and after the transition to master the facts and details of legislation, the
budget, or applicants' qualifications. Rarely, if ever, was he caught unprepared. The NGA assistance was especially important to the staff, most
of whom were inexperienced in state government. The NGA was able to
provide perspective as well as guidance. Finally, Anaya was fortunate to
have a cooperative and responsive incumbent administration during the

transition. Facts, figures, histories, standard operating procedures—all kinds of information were willingly shared with the new administration.

Anaya's legislative successes can be attributed not only to his careful preparation during the transition but also to the defeat of the Coalition, a defeat he helped to engineer. It seems unlikely that the previous leadership in the house would have blended well with Anaya's style. In addition, when his back was against the wall, he was personally willing to enter the fray to compromise, negotiate, bargain, and eliminate bottlenecks in legislation, earning him the respect of most legislators.

Anaya's failures, thus far mainly in the area of style rather than substance, seem to lie, first, in the problematic staffing of his office, which has caused inefficiency and perhaps unequal access to the governor; second, in his seeming inability to delegate authority, which causes all kinds of minor decisions to be made in the governor's office; and, third, in his increasingly problematic relations with the press. The governor, who is known to be extremely demanding of himself and of his staff, has recently lost four of his top office staffers to other agencies, including Fruman, Oakeley, Steve Anaya, and Cobble. He seems to be quite aware of his staffing and stylistic problems. In the future, however, Anaya must convince the legislature and public that his first session was not a fluke, that he can correct at least some of the potential damage to his image caused by press criticism, and that only major decisions will require his direct attention most of the time.

Epilogue

Governor Anaya's popularity during the next two years declined precipitously. By early 1985 he was clearly the most unpopular governor in the state's history. All 112 legislative seats in both chambers were contested in 1984: Republican candidates almost universally tried to tag their opponents as being "pro-Anaya." In both the House and Senate leadership in 1985 fell to coalitions of anti-Anaya conservative legislators in both parties who went so far as to threaten impeachment in reprisal for gubernatorial item vetoes.

Staffing problems grew worse, alienating legislators and political elites. Anaya's appointments created enemies from the ranks of usual supporters. His personality became the focus of attention. In short, after the transition and first legislative session, things fell apart. Anaya himself became the lightning rod for complex social, economic, and ethnic forces at work in the state, and he was unable to lead or govern.

The Gubernatorial Transition
in New York

GERALD BENJAMIN

The candidate, backed by a coalition of great social and ethnic diversity, swept into the New York governorship on a flood tide of voters who turned out after a hard-fought campaign. The governor-elect had been considered a political long shot only months before his nomination. But by the time he took his oath on New Year's Eve, with his wife, five children, and a few close friends looking on, he had already impressed the state with his energy and the force of his personality. Still only fifty years old, the new governor, if successful in Albany, might look forward to national leadership in his party and even, perhaps, a presidential nomination.

Widely perceived as a liberal as the result of the press coverage of his campaign, the governor was in fact a pragmatist with little use for ideological labels or approaches. Indeed, he had made campaign commitments that, if examined for ideological consistency, would come up short. For example, he sought to enhance services to New Yorkers, especially those less fortunate citizens of the Empire State who were dependent upon government over the long term, but he also sought to stimulate the state's lagging economy and to achieve less costly government through tighter management, reorganization, and the elimination of wasteful programs.

His campaign and the words of his first public addresses notwithstanding, the new governor quickly came to realize that unless he found an early solution to the state government's financial problems, he could hope to accomplish little during his four-year term. With less than three months remaining in the current fiscal year, there was a substantial gap projected between revenues and expenditures. And for the coming fiscal year, the gap, widened by state legislative leaders' propensity to authorize increased spending in preparation for their reelection campaigns (they had met the previous spring), would be more than 10 percent of the state-funded budget if immediate action was not taken. Yet these leaders could not be openly criticized for their earlier decisions. Most had been returned to Albany. Their cooperation would be needed by the governor during the critical first few months ahead.

All the policy alternatives offered by close advisors to close the gap—program cuts, limiting growth of local assistance, tax increases—seemed equally unpalatable to the new governor; moreover, they contradicted campaign pledges repeated only weeks earlier. Furthermore, the budget process, initiated within a framework set up by his predecessor, was virtually completed by the time he took office. Thus, though he would be politically responsible for it, the governor could hope to have little more than an incremental impact upon the final budget document, and this despite the complete cooperation of the outgoing governor. How could he come out of this situation with his reputation for integrity intact, with his ability to govern over the rest of his term unimpaired?

Mario Cuomo in 1983? No . . . Nelson Rockefeller in 1959! But the uncommonly close parallels between these two transition years, separated by almost a quarter of a century, provide some important insights.

First, all transitions of executive power in New York state government face a number of similar problems and occur in similar contexts. Although just finished campaigning—a process that demands a sort of distributive position taking in order to build a large winning coalition in a very fluid and uncertain environment—the governor-elect in his or her moment of triumph must begin to govern—a very different process that, in a more structured and constrained environment, will often demand painful redistributive decision making. The essential problem for any new governor is to find the appropriate balance between continuity and change. Entering an ongoing process, the new governor must create a "discontinuity with the past; not a complete break," must seek "adaptive change within a stable system."[1] And, in a seeming paradox, it is precisely the demands of the continuities of government—the budget process, the annual state of the state address, the need to staff the new administration and establish its routines—and the real or perceived deadlines that are attendant on these that provide the opportunities for the discontinuities, for a new "definition of the situation."

A second common element for incoming New York governors is the context provided by the importance of the state and its chief executive in the national political system. With the exception of Malcolm Wilson, who served out the fourth term of Nelson Rockefeller and then failed of election in his own right, all recent New York governors have been considered more or less serious presidential contenders. The possibility of future high-level service in Washington surely assists the governor in some transition tasks (for example, the recruitment of a cabinet and staff) and affects in subtle ways early interactions with the legislature and the "permanent government" in Albany. And, because of both this possibility of a future presidential bid and New York City's prominence as a world media center, the early performance of a "fledgling" New York governor (as Mario Cuomo characterized himself during his first visit as a governor to Washington) is probably more closely watched, and by a broader audience, than in most other states.

Yet, however similar the circumstances and opportunities of transition are for all new governors, there are unique elements in each case. Unlike Averell Harriman in 1955, Nelson Rockefeller in 1959, or Hugh Carey in 1975, Mario Cuomo had substantial experience at the highest levels of state government before his election to the top job. Having served as lieutenant governor, the presiding officer of the state senate, Governor Cuomo knew the legislative leaders of the state well. From his earlier vantage, he could not help but observe and make judgments upon the effectiveness of Governor Hugh Carey's confrontational approach to legislative relationships. As lieutenant governor, Cuomo, though not in Carey's inner circle, was also well positioned to get to know key gubernatorial aides and the top managers of New York's sprawling bureaucracy and, not incidentally, to make private evaluations of their performance.

Other contrasts, too, are essential. In 1959, the start of the Rockefeller governorship, the United States was entering a period of economic expansion, and New York, still the biggest state in the union, seemed an unparalleled economic powerhouse.[2] Expectations of government, especially in New York state, were high, and resources were readily made available in support of the conviction that major social and economic problems were solvable through governmental action. By 1983, the start of the Cuomo governorship, government had come to be viewed as part of the problem rather than as part of the solution. A shrinking economic base made available fewer resources for state government and, after a frightening fiscal crisis in the mid-1970s, the consensus concern of New

York's political leaders had become the preservation and expansion of this base.

Then there is the political dimension. Mario Cuomo was the first governor of New York since World War II to assume the position by election following an incumbent of his own party. He was also the first in almost three decades to take over in a situation in which the incumbent was not seeking reelection. A governor who is running again has great incentives, both psychological and political, for ignoring the possibility that a transition might occur. And, however professional the approach of a defeated governor and his staff, the handling of a transition cannot help being affected by the differences that may have emerged in a hard-fought but losing primary or general election effort. In contrast, a governor (like Hugh Carey) who has chosen to leave office has the time to prepare for an orderly transfer of power, the command of staff not diverted to campaign tasks to use for this purpose, and—that not insignificant incentive—the desire to document a record so as to preserve an honored place in the history of the state.

By this reasoning it appears that the political conditions for a smooth transfer of power at the top in New York state were optimal in 1983. The transition was within the Democratic party, from a governor who had chosen to leave and had prepared to do so to a governor with long experience just beneath the top. But even in these optimal circumstances another unique element may complicate matters: the personalities of the men involved and the character of their relationship.

The Carey-Cuomo Relationship

"I got a genius nobody knows about. He's a law professor at St. Johns. Brilliant sonofabitch. Mario Cuomo. I begged him to run with me. Nobody knows him. The first time they ever hear of him, they'll be right there in his hands. But I just couldn't talk him into running."[3] As journalist Jimmy Breslin recalls it, the first time he heard Mario Cuomo's name was from Hugh Carey, during a losing campaign for city office in New York City in 1969. And so New York's outgoing governor in 1982 and its newly elected governor went back a long way together. Both graduates of St. Johns University Law School, one from Brooklyn and the other from Queens, they apparently encountered and impressed each other in the half-visible and byzantine world of New York City Democratic politics during the 1960s, while Carey was still an ambitious congressman and Cuomo had not yet gained his first visibility as a mediator of an explosive housing controversy in Forest Hills, Queens.

By 1974 Cuomo was trying very hard for a second slot, this time in a statewide campaign. Running for lieutenant governor on an informal ticket with Carey's primary opponent, Howard Samuels, Cuomo lost to Mary Anne Krupsak. Though the Samuels-Cuomo collaboration prompted Carey to ask, "What was the quid-pro-Cuomo for that?" for his efforts on behalf of the Democratic campaign after the primary, Cuomo was placed on the governor's transition team and later appointed secretary of state.[4] The position, Governor Carey insisted, was not for a "symbolic Italian-American chamberlain"; his appointee would be a "key figure in our efforts to make government sensitive to public needs." Later, in 1978, when he was challenged for renomination by Krupsak, Carey took Cuomo onto his ticket.

But the political relationship between the two men was not all positive. It is well known that Carey endorsed Ed Koch, mayor of New York City, rather than his own lieutenant governor shortly before the 1982 gubernatorial primary, leading Cuomo, who had once characterized his chief as a "brooding Celt," to remark, "Who knows why he does what he does?" What is less clearly remembered, however, is that the lieutenant governorship was a consolation prize for Mario Cuomo; what he really aspired to was the New York City mayoralty. An abortive race in 1973 (Cuomo was reportedly sandbagged by his county leader, Matthew Troy), was followed by a full-scale effort in 1977. At first Carey openly backed Cuomo. (As a result of having tried to work with Mayor Abe Beame during the city fiscal crisis, the governor desired his defeat.) After Ed Koch came in first by a narrow margin in a field of seven candidates and then went on to defeat Cuomo in a runoff primary, however, Governor Carey, despite his early pledge of backing all the way to November, sought to dissuade Cuomo from continuing the race on the Liberal party line and then switched to Koch. After this experience Cuomo is said to have commented about Carey to New York Daily News columnist Peter Hamill, "I like him but I don't really respect him."[5]

It is clear that Hugh Carey helped make Mario Cuomo. It is also clear that political self-interest at times caused each of these ambitious men to be less than fully supportive of the political career of the other. It was a complex and mixed relationship of two very different personalities. Carey is introspective, a man of enormous wit and intelligence, brilliant in crisis but uninterested in the everyday work of government. And Cuomo is an action intellectual, sharp and pragmatic, with a lawyer's penchant for detail and a negotiator's skill at compromise. By 1982 Cuomo still owed Carey, but not too much.

The Campaign

On the morning of his inauguration as New York's governor, Mario Cuomo called his victory "so implausible" as to be a "curiously beautiful thing."[6] Indeed, it was. As 1982 began, most political observers assumed that, despite discouraging polls, Hugh Carey would seek a third term. After Carey withdrew in mid-January, a large field of Democratic hopefuls began to jockey for position to seek the nomination. But when Mayor Ed Koch of New York City, encouraged by a *New York Post* write-in campaign orchestrated by publisher Rupert Murdoch, finally declared for governor in February, most others withdrew from the field. After all, hadn't Koch just won the mayoralty with 75 percent of the vote as the candidate of both the Republican and Democratic parties?

Thus, when Lieutenant Governor Mario Cuomo (who had been hinting interest in taking on Carey months before he withdrew) declared his candidacy on March 16, he was assured of a two-way contest within the party with Koch. At first, this hardly seemed an advantage. Koch appeared invincible. A national figure, he had been a winner for every office he had sought, commanded the preponderance of campaign funds and the services of media consultant David Garth, and was consequently able to quickly win endorsements from all the major New York City newspapers and an overwhelming majority of state Democratic leaders. Cuomo, in contrast, failed to play a central role in the Carey administration even after his election as lieutenant governor in 1978. Before his election as Hugh Carey's second, he had lost a bid for the same post in 1974 and had lost to Koch in the primary, the runoff, and the general election for mayor of New York City in 1977. A man with a lackluster reputation as a campaigner and a reputation for indecision, Cuomo was often portrayed as Hamlet in the musical comedy satires put on annually by New York political reporters.[7]

There are reasons, however, why no New York City mayor has gone on to higher office in the state in this century. Ed Koch, before his candidacy for governor, had characterized life in Albany as a "fate worse than death." This remark was typical of many (some quoted prominently in *Playboy* magazine just after his declaration for the governorship) that made Koch, in style and substance, a symbol of New York City to non–New Yorkers across the nation. In upstate New York, as in much of the United States, there is an ever-present, though sometimes latent, hostility to "the city." Koch's candidacy brought this to the surface.

As the mayor's sole primary election opponent, Mario Cuomo (though himself a New York City native) benefited from this "issue." Apparently, few upstaters recalled that he had refused to move to the capital from his home in Queens when appointed secretary of state by Carey eight years earlier. Cuomo also received the support of the mayor's major adversaries within the city, notably the minority groups and powerful municipal labor unions.

But Mario Cuomo did not win the primary simply because he was the single focal point within New York's Democratic party for anti-Koch sentiment. Both his stronger-than-expected showing at the state convention that designated Koch in June—Cuomo got 39 percent of the votes, with 25 percent needed to assure a place on the primary ballot—and his later successes in early debates against the mayor established him as a complex, thoughtful personality, knowledgeable and quick-witted, in short, a credible possible governor. Koch's strategy as a front-runner, to label Cuomo a liberal and to make the death penalty a core issue (he favored it while Cuomo, like Carey, opposed it), failed in the end to define the framework of the election. In contrast, Cuomo's final theme, that a victory for him would leave two good men in office—Koch as mayor and himself as governor—served to remind city Democrats of the mayor's often repeated pledge not to seek higher office, without opening the lieutenant governor to charges of "negativism."

In the end Koch's $3.5-million media campaign was overcome by a less expensive ($1.6 million) but massive grass-roots effort. Likely Cuomo voters, including 50,000 Italian-Americans, were identified by telephone and then turned out on primary day by 10,000 volunteers, most recruited from major labor unions. The field coordinator of this effort, Norman Adler, on leave from his regular position with the American Federation of State, County and Municipal Employees, commented on the contrasting approaches of the two campaigns: "Koch said you can win it on television. I said you win it in the streets."[8]

Cuomo and Koch ran even in New York City, and Koch's small margin in the city's suburbs was not enough to overcome losses by two- or three-to-one in upstate counties. Of 1,268,555 votes cast (the 38-percent turnout was much larger than usual), Cuomo prevailed by a margin of 73,053. His 670,804 was 52.9 percent of the total.

While Koch and Cuomo slugged it out, drugstore magnate Lew Lehrman coasted to an easy victory in the Republican primary over Paul Curran, a former state assemblyman and U.S. attorney. Yet in its early stages Lehrman's candidacy had looked as improbable as Mario Cuomo's. Immediately after his declaration for governor on January 11 (before Hugh Carey withdrew), Lehrman, a relative unknown who had never held public office, spent $2 million on a media campaign to familiarize New Yorkers with his name, face, fiscal conservatism, and law-and-order views. Lehrman's resources and organization overcame the effort by some county leaders to support a centrist Curran candidacy and thus block the capture of the nomination from outside the party organization. On the second day of the Republican convention in New York City, Lehrman reached an accommodation with Jim Emery, the assembly minority leader and an upstate gubernatorial hopeful. With Emery as his running mate for lieutenant governor, Lehrman went on to roll up 69 percent of the convention votes. Curran retained enough strength to win a place on the primary ballot but was abandoned by most of his early backers among the party leaders during the course of the summer and simply swamped on primary day. In getting 81 percent of the vote Lehrman spent $7 million, about twenty times Curran's total.

Lehrman thus won after having captured the designation of his party's convention, and Cuomo won despite his failure to get such a designation within his party. Ironically, Cuomo, the nondesignee, had long been active in his party and was more within its mainstream than Lehrman was in the mainstream of the state GOP. The designation, however, was not a great political resource; no nonincumbent who had captured it had gone on to the governorship since the preprimary convention system was established in 1968.

The massive Lehrman media campaign, targeted now on a known opponent, continued in the general election period. Principal themes included advocacy of the death penalty and massive tax reductions, including a 40-percent cut in the state individual income tax over eight years. Ignoring the incumbent administration's second-term record of tax cutting, Lehrman sought to identify Cuomo with the now unpopular Carey, and Carey with traditional New York liberalism. Commenting on this in the context of Mayor Koch's oft-repeated preprimary remark that he "had no record," Cuomo said, "It is amazing how quickly I have gotten a record."

Continuing to oppose the death penalty and massive tax cuts (though he did suggest a cap on state spending), Cuomo scored well against Lehrman, as he did against Koch, in televised debates. Again his campaign slogan was a masterful combination of positive and (understated) negative points, "Lieutenant Governor Cuomo for Governor: Experience Money Can't Buy."

Because of both men's advanced education and comfort with abstractions, the gubernatorial election came to be presented in the media as a clash of intellectuals and ideologies—Lehrman on the right, Cuomo on the left. The candidates helped foster these perceptions, with Cuomo calling Lehrman "a pristine radical arch-conservative Reaganomics believer" and Lehrman labeling Cuomo the man of "the most radical left wing elements of the Democratic party."[9] In fact, Cuomo in his positions was less an ideologue than a pragmatist. He appeared much less a true believer in a doctrine than Lehrman did over the course of the campaign, a factor that might have been reflected in his higher personal-approval ratings among voters in preelection polls.

Private polls released by Lehrman after the election showed him behind Cuomo for all of October, with the gap narrowest on the twenty-sixth of that month and again on election day. Lehrman, facing a Democratic and Liberal enrollment edge of over 900,000, spent a total of $13.5 million ($8 million of it his own). Cuomo spent $4.7 million.[10] All this effort—Lehrman's media and direct mail, Cuomo's marathon telephone organization—produced a turnout of more than 70 percent of those registered. Of the 5,124,745 votes cast, Mario Cuomo captured 51 percent. He was able, however, to carry only two counties outside New York City: Albany, the home of many state workers frightened by Lehrman's budget proposals and the feifdom of Mayor Erastus Corning III, a very early Cuomo backer; and Westchester, the base of Alfred Del-Bello, the Democratic candidate for lieutenant governor.

After delaying his concession because of the closeness of the contest, Lew Lehrman pledged to keep his staff together as a "loyal opposition" in preparation for another run at the governorship. "We shall be observing," he said. Mario Cuomo was ready. The day after his victory, asserting that he would form a government made up of an "army of brilliant young people," the governor-elect designated his son and campaign director, Andrew Cuomo, as executive director of his transition team.

Carey's Preparations

Having announced almost a year before the end of his second term that he would not seek reelection, Governor Hugh Carey had ample time to prepare for an orderly transition. The governor's conviction that such preparation was vital was based on his belief that the Rockefeller-Wilson administration had been "irresponsible" in failing to prepare adequately for his own assumption of the governorship.[11] As a "novice governor," Carey said, he had had little opportunity to "set priorities and get direction" before he got "involved in the catchup process of making . . . a transition budget."[12] As summarized by William Ellinghaus, president of AT&T and cochairman of Carey's transition group, the Council on State Priorities, "[The Governor] . . . said that when he entered office eight years ago, he was given inadequate information on the enormity of the fiscal crisis that the State and City of New York would face. He resolved that when he left office, he wanted his successor to have a full awareness of the most pressing problems facing the state, and, in dealing with those problems, to have the benefit of his administration's perspective and policies concerning those issues."[13]

Actually, the 1974–75 transition had been similar to others in New York up to that time. It entailed a change of partisan control of the executive branch and, as in 1958, the departure of a governor who had sought reelection. T. Norman Hurd, former state budget director and Malcolm Wilson's secretary, who had participated in both the transitions of 1954 and 1958, served as coordinator for the outgoing administration. He was in regular touch with Robert F. Wagner, Jr., former mayor of New York City and Governor-elect Carey's transition coordinator. As a result of the Hurd-Wagner meetings, Carey's task forces on various areas of state policy gained access to commissioners and their staffs for briefings. Though it was not required by law, as in some states, the incoming administration was provided office space and given a $100,000 budget for personnel and other expenses.[14]

In addition to these arrangements and at Governor Wilson's direction, Richard Dunham, the budget director, opened the state budget process to the incoming administration and agreed to make no major changes without the governor-elect's approval. "It's their budget," Dunham said.[15] The process was further facilitated when Howard Miller, Dunham's deputy, took charge of the transition budgeting team for Carey and then continued as the new governor's deputy budget director.

And the professional bureaucracy assumed a role as well when the education unit of the Budget Division prepared for the Carey transition team a briefing document that described the state budget process and the division's role in it.

Nevertheless, it would be too much to expect that Wilson, who had just weeks before been saying that to allow Hugh Carey to control the state budget would be "like putting Dracula in charge of a blood bank," would develop more than a correct relationship with his successor. Many sensitive political records regarding state appointments were shredded in Wilson's office, leaving the incoming Carey people with no central file of jobs exempt from civil service or of vacancies. Records kept by the counsel's office on legislation, the famous "Bill Jackets," were removed to a remote location in the State Education Building or remained in the hands of Wilson's counsel, Michael Whiteman.[16] When, in late November, the press learned of a letter from Carey asking Wilson for a hiring freeze and cutbacks in state agencies, Wilson responded that a freeze was unnecessary because the current year's budget was balanced, and that for 1975–76, "As you know, I have made it crystal clear that any and all decisions with respect to budget requests are to be made by you or your authorized representatives."[17]

In commenting that long-entrenched Republicans might find ways to give civil service protection to their jobs and "overload the circuitry with a layer of bureaucracy," Mary Anne Krupsak, the lieutenant governor-elect, was voicing another fear of top Democrats throughout New York in 1975, for they had been the "out party" for sixteen years.[18] In fact, Hurd, acting with Wagner's approval, advised top state officials at a cabinet meeting to file for retirement if they were eligible to do so, so as to be able to meet the thirty-day notice requirement of the state retirement system. This action, the exact opposite of what Krupsak feared, greatly upset Carey's secretary-designate, David Burke, who knew he could never staff all of these positions by January of 1975. Saying that Republicans might well be retained in some key jobs by the incoming administration, Burke urged "critical and important personnel" to continue "until further notice" and assured them of ample time to file for retirement if they did continue.[19]

These tensions aside, however, Malcolm Wilson had many incentives to cooperate with his successor. He desired an office and small staff for a few months after he left office in order to bring his state responsibilities to an orderly close and had loyal aides who needed only a short additional period in state service in order to have their retirement benefits vested, or to qualify for retirement. As for Carey, lacking a base of inside knowledge, he needed access, information, and cooperation in order to be able to hit the ground running after inauguration. There was, then, some mutuality of interest. The outgoing administration's admitted failure to take special steps to prepare the new governor for the fiscal crisis of 1975 was thus probably more the consequence of its members' not anticipating its severity than the result of partisanship or irresponsibility.

Nevertheless, Carey's recollection of the trauma of his first year gave him the incentive to prepare extensively for his own departure from office, and his early decision not to run for a third term provided the opportunity. His approach to the task of transition had two tracks, one for the "nuts and bolts" and the other for policy. In the area of policy, the governor sought a continuation of the coalition of labor, business and government that he had forged to deal with the fiscal crisis. In this incarnation, the coalition took the form of a Council on State Priorities, chaired by Carey and Ellinghaus and made up of an ethnically diverse group of twenty-one professional, business, labor, university, and religious leaders from across the state. A small professional staff of four, formed especially for the task and working within the executive chamber but apart from the ongoing daily process of governance, supported the council's work.

Established on June 1, 1982, within six months the council was to "prepare a series of reports on issues to be designated by the Governor, which reports shall include a concise analysis of present policy, identify the stress points of public administration, and suggest policy options to deal with those difficulties."[20] According to Orin McCluskey, its executive director, the governor, in selecting five policy areas for the council's consideration—public finance, housing, the care of dependent populations, economic growth and taxation, and education and human resource development—sought to cover matters that had not recently been studied, were within the purview of the executive department, and were interagency in nature. Interagency working groups chaired by a member of the governor's staff were formed within state government in these five areas. These facilitated the production of policy review papers by each of thirty-seven state agencies and formulated responses to data research requests to provide a current data base on state government operations. Then state agency heads met in September with panels of the council to "identify key stress points of public administration." Finally, the results of these meetings and prior research were used to produce an overall report to the governor.

Critical to the success of this effort was the detailed, continued, and enthusiastic involvement of Governor Carey in the meetings of the council, both in New York City and at a weekend retreat in the Adirondacks. This was particularly notable because of Carey's reputation in state government for being uninterested in engaging himself over time in the complexities of policy making.

Some analysts suggested that Governor Carey's unusual commitment of time and energy to the work of the Council on State Priorities was simply motivated by his desire to document his achievements in a legacy for New York. Carey denied this and also insisted that he had no interest in "precooking the next governor's agenda."[21] Certainly, however, the involvement on the council of major leaders from the private sector, who had ties to every serious candidate for governor, would serve to have the report treated "not as the plaintive cry of a lame duck" but as "the considered judgment of observers in the field, qualified people in business, labor, academics and management."[22] And, by convincing such luminaries as investment banker Felix Rohatyn and Ford Foundation president Franklin Thomas to act as advisors to the council, Carey took further steps to legitimize its work.

While the council's work on policy options went forward, the governor's acting secretary, Michael Finnerty, initiated the nuts-and-bolts track with the state agencies to "identify issues that must be addressed, decisions that must be made and actions that must be taken during the transition period and within the first six months of the new administration" so that "the new Governor may assume his responsibilities with minimal disruption."[23] Coordination was to be through personnel from the Management Systems Unit of the Division of the Budget on temporary assignment to the Governor's Office. Departments were asked to prepare two sets of documents: "Gubernatorial Decision Papers" and "Agency Action Reports." The first were to center on "issues with significant policy, program, budget and fiscal implications" that required attention in the governor's budget or legislative program. The second were matters that did not require top-level action but about which the governor needed to be informed because of their potential to generate public controversy or because they provided an opportunity for positive publicity.

In a separate but ultimately merged effort, the Division of the Budget prepared a comprehensive "Transition Documents" book for Governor Cuomo, which described the constitutional and legal base of the executive budget process, the budget cycle, and the organization and staffing of the division. This effort went considerably beyond that of 1974–75 in that it took up policy issues; it was a self-conscious effort to ensure that the new governor did not become captive of the viewpoints of a single agency on key matters early in his tenure.

As a result of these processes, the budget division was able to anticipate a number of the lesser problems of the transition, for example, the expiration of the lease on the governor's New York City office and the legality of the use of state aircraft by the governor-elect's staff. Two lists of deadlines of routine matters requiring gubernatorial action, one for the first ninety days and one for the first six months, were readied. In addition, a summary of the budget division's view of the fifty top issues facing the state in the coming year was prepared, with backup files, for the new governor's information and use. Throughout the election this preparatory process was informed by the public positions taken by the candidates, and research was augmented as necessary by white papers that addressed issues raised in the campaign.

After assuming office Governor Cuomo expressed appreciation to Michael Finnerty, now his budget director, for the preparatory work of the division. It did, in sum, seem to confirm the observation made by Ahlberg and Moynihan some two decades earlier that "the ease of transition in administration will be in inverse proportion to the professionalism of the bureaucracy."[24] The new governor also praised the work of the Council on State Priorities, telling his predecessor that it was "not good, but excellent." But would Mario Cuomo act upon what he had read?

Symbolism: Staffing and Management Style

The transition period offered the governor-elect many opportunities to send subtle, unifying messages to the people of New York. New Yorkers sympathized with his decision to retain the home in which he had raised his family, built by his father in Queens twenty-four years earlier. "We might need it in four years," Cuomo said.[25] They also took note of his desire to save money by moving the governor's office in New York City downtown and by having his campaign fund (there was a surplus!) share inaugural expenses with the state. And sports fans debated the former professional baseball player's view that NBA basketball would be made more exciting if each game were split in two, making it a double-header.

In an early postelection interview, Mario Cuomo revealed that he was quite conscious of these opportunities for symbolic leadership, for connecting himself with all the people of New York. "I want to convey a certain message," he said, "in everything I do."[26] This sensitivity about the subtleties of communication with the many publics that had him under scrutiny, so evident in small matters, was also evident in the governor-elect's handling of the more substantive aspects of the transition: the selection and announcement of aides and other appointees, the organization of his office, the content of the inaugural and state of the state addresses, and the early fullfilling of campaign pledges. Throughout the postelection period Cuomo sought to create an environment of accommodation and consensus in the state, one in vivid contrast to the conflict-ridden Carey years. To dramatize the difference, the governor-elect cited four lines from Edwin Markham's poem "Outwitted":

> He drew a circle that shut me out,
> Heretic, rebel, a thing to flout.
> But love and I had the wit to win;
> We drew a circle that took him in![27]

During the two months before Mario Cuomo took office the staffing and organization of his administration was the most watched aspect of the transition, and therefore the one that offered the greatest opportunities for the communication of its direction. A fifteen-person transition team (with some of the same membership as Carey's Council on State Priorities), chaired by former executive director of the Emergency Financial Control Board, Steve Berger, first met with Andrew Cuomo, the transition coordinator, on November 19. The principal task of this group—of evident racial, ethnic, and social diversity—was to "recommend the most talented and best available candidates nationwide" to fill some of the 2,400 jobs available to the new administration in Albany. Earlier, Andrew Cuomo had asserted that the "only standard [would be] merit and talent." But it clearly did not hurt to have helped and impressed his father, who explained, "A lot of names I stored in my mind."[28]

Governor-elect Cuomo's early personnel decisions took on a special importance because one criticism of him had been that as lieutenant governor he had not attracted good people to his staff. Bill Caban, his former chief of staff, was indicted in 1981 for putting fictitious people on the state payroll and pocketing the resultant salaries. He pleaded guilty and was sent to prison. Cuomo thus had to demonstrate the truth in the comment by Sandy Frucher, Carey's director of the state's Office of Employee Relations, that "the fact of the matter is that he hasn't had the jobs that attract strong people. Mario was standby equipment as Lieutenant Governor. That's not what Mario is. It's what the job was."[29]

By the time that the transition panel sent the governor-elect (characterized by Berger as "a lot new, some old, some borrowed") 410 names on December 21, Cuomo had already appointed his key executive chamber aides. Five weeks after election day the last of the "Big Five," Tim Russert, formerly of Senator Daniel P. Moynihan's staff in Washington, was named. The others were Michael J. Del Guidice, secretary to the governor; Michael Finnerty, budget director; Alice G. Daniel, counsel, and Fabian Palomino, special counsel. In these appointments, as in the transition advisory committee, there was balance. Russert and Finnerty were upstaters, Palomino an old friend experienced in state government, and Daniel the first woman ever to serve in her post. There was also continuity—Del Guidice and Finnerty had been top-level Carey aides—and change—the others had not, and Del Guidice was called back into state government after having gone to work, briefly, for Shearson–American Express. Interestingly, none had worked for Cuomo when he was lieutenant governor.

Actually, there were six people in the big five, for Andrew Cuomo was also to be in the governor's inner circle. The way in which "the son thing" (as Andrew Cuomo called it) was handled again demonstrated the governor's sensitivity to the symbolic content of the appointment process. Few were surprised when the transition team unanimously recommended Andrew Cuomo, the director of the governor's campaign and transition, for appointment to a top position because of the "superb job" he had done in these capacities. The governor, described as "reluctant" to bring his son into government, accepted the idea that he "deserved a chance to serve," as long as he "promised to take the bar exam."[30] Later, Andrew was appointed, at a salary of a dollar a year (he would save money by living with his father in the executive mansion), and became a central administration figure.

One question that arose early in the transition concerned whether Lieutenant Governor Alfred DelBello would be integral to Governor

Cuomo's team, as Malcolm Wilson had been in the Rockefeller administration, or more peripheral, as were Mary Anne Krupsak and Cuomo himself during the Carey years. Some thought that Cuomo, having been subordinated by Carey, might give DelBello a larger role. But the new lieutenant governor, not Cuomo's first choice as a running mate (as much because of his primary support of Ed Koch as because of traditional New York concerns about ethnic balance on the statewide ticket), soon found himself facing an integration of his office with that of the governor and a consequent budget reduction of 40 percent.[31] Though the separate status of DelBello's office was later restored by the Republican state senate over which he presided (majority leader Warren Anderson commented, tongue in cheek, "We take care of our own"), it did not appear that there would be much room for the lieutenant governor within the "circle of conciliation" into which his chief sought to invite other state leaders.

After the selection of key executive chamber staff, appointments to other posts in the Cuomo administration went more slowly. The governor-elect and his transition advisors had weighed the desirability of having all of the commissionerships filled by the time of the inauguration against the possible costs of major error and had decided to go slowly. Despite all the precautions that were taken, however, there were some self-inflicted wounds. The appointment of Martin Ives as state tax commissioner was publicly discussed by aides before being scotched by the governor. Another proposed appointment, of Lucille Falcone as counsel to the Urban Development Corporation, opened the new administration to the same charges of cronyism and extravagance in the payment of salaries that they had levied against Governor Carey.

Generally, early appointments of women and minority group members to cabinet-level jobs did signal Governor Cuomo's sensitivity to these portions of his constituency, and the designation of a special deputy for management and productivity indicated his continued interest in greater governmental efficiency. At the same time the reappointment of some Carey commissioners (Berger had said that they would "get a fair shake") added to the theme of continuity during the changeover at the top. By the end of his first hundred days in office Cuomo was still working to complete his management team in the state's departments and agencies, and some major jobs, such as in the Department of Mental Health, remained unfilled.

One other Cuomo appointment, though not to a post in his administration, was highly significant in the transition. This was the elevation of Judge Richard D. Simon, a Republican, to the state's highest court, the court of appeals. Governor Cuomo was unhappy with the judicial selection process that he had inherited, saying that it unduly hampered his choice of persons for the bench. (In this instance the Commission on Judicial Nomination offered him four white male sitting judges, and he had promised during his campaign to appoint a woman to the court.) Nevertheless, on his third day in office the new governor appointed Simon, who had been considered several times for the post over the previous ten years. Noting his own commitment to the court of appeals, which he had served as a clerk in the 1950s, Cuomo called Simon's party "not relevant" in his choice. The appointment, however, was seen throughout the state and especially in the Republican senate as concrete evidence that the governor was sincere about his desire to bring a new era of bipartisan cooperation to Albany.

During the last days of the campaign for governor, Lew Lehrman continually charged that the election of Lieutenant Governor Mario Cuomo would, in effect, produce four more years of the highly unpopular Carey administration. Consequently, in making his key staff appointment just after the end of the campaign Cuomo was quite sensitive about avoiding the appearance of too much "Carey over." But the principal contrast he sought to establish with his predecessor was not in whom he appointed to his staff but in how he intended to organize and managed it.

Though early in his first term Governor Carey was said to fear putting too much power in the hands of one aide, by his second he had come to rely on his secretary, Robert Morgado, as a "surrogate governor." Cuomo, in contrast, sought to take a more personal role in the direction of state affairs, dispersing power among five principal assistants, all of whom would have access to him. Interestingly, this management strategy did not require a reorganization of the governor's office; it was implemented simply by giving top-level access to the new occupants of staff positions that were already established.

In fact, by the end of his first two months in office, about twelve staff members were reporting directly to Governor Cuomo, and he was still insisting that "no bill will go up, no appointment will be made without crossing my desk." In addition, his personal calls to legislators, lobbyists, and other contacts developed over his years in state government guaranteed alternative sources of information and advice. "My style is to be eclectic," Cuomo said, "to use as much talent as I can. To use a team. That's much harder than using a single person."[32]

The effort to contrast this hands-on style with that of Carey was quite deliberate. Andrew Cuomo commented, "I think this Governor has a very different personal style than past administrations. . . . He does not delegate the decision making process itself as much as some past governors."[33] The danger, of course, was that Governor Cuomo, an ex-professor of legal writing who had once described himself as "a lawyer, a nit-picker, a footnote writer," might immerse himself in details to such an extent that he would lose policy control of the state government.[34]

Symbolism: Promises and Policy

Mario Cuomo's early policy-making actions, like his later behavior in budgeting, were designed to send a message of integrity, to signal to New Yorkers that they had elected a man who would keep his promises. The new governor expressed his intention to stop construction of the Arthur Kill power plant on Staten Island and to close a newly opened prison on the grounds of the Pilgrim Psychiatric Center in Brentwood, Long Island, as he had promised in his campaign. Both projects were strongly opposed by local community groups, though favored by others as being in the broader interests of the people of the state. In an editorial entitled "The Campaign for Governor Is Over" the New York Times scolded Cuomo for excessive rigidity about keeping his word regarding Arthur Kill: "It is a dubious virtue to keep campaign promises foolishly made. . . . With his new and wider perspective and authority, Mr. Cuomo might try to begin impressing the state by confessing his unworthy opportunism."[35]

But more important as policy vehicles for the governor than his campaign promises were two speeches that he gave within days of each other at the outset of his administration, his inaugural and state of the state addresses. Cuomo was reportedly attentive to every detail of the inaugural. His speech, delivered to an audience of 2,600 friends, supporters, and state leaders, was masterful. Quickly reviewing the themes of his campaign, the governor went on to assert his conviction that in New York, as elsewhere, government could be "a positive source for good." There was an obligation, Cuomo said, "to assist those who for whatever inscrutable reason have been left out by fate." "A society as blessed as ours should be able to find room at the table, shelter for the homeless, work for the idle, care for the elderly and infirm and hope for the destitute."[36]

Turning then to what was to become the unifying theme of his first months in office, Governor Cuomo offered the image of "the family of New York," "hard working and realistic." We must, he said, "feel one another's pain, share one another's blessings, equitably, honestly, fairly, without respect to geography or political affiliation. . . . No family that favored its strong children or that in the name of evenhandedness failed to help its vulnerable ones would be worthy of the name."

The acclaim for this speech was universal. Arthur Eve, a Democratic Buffalo assemblyman and one of the leading black politicians in the state, called it "the greatest . . . ever made by a governor." Perhaps surprisingly, this sentiment was echoed by Senate Republican leader Warren Anderson. It was "pretty near the top," he said.[37] And James Reston, in his nationally syndicated column, suggested that Cuomo's comments, "the best speech in recent months," might provide the new theme that the national Democratic party so clearly needed for its 1984 campaign.

Having explicated the soul of his administration in the inaugural, the governor, four days later, began to present its flesh and blood in his state of the state message. Much of it drew upon a major campaign theme, "Jobs and Justice," and reiterated positions taken in the fall. Reforming the state system of budgeting, borrowing, and planning was given prominence, as was a "partnership" (reminiscent of Carey's) of labor, government, and business to foster economic growth. Maintaining his opposition to the death penalty, Governor Cuomo offered instead a comprehensive plan for strengthening the criminal justice system that focused on the certainty of punishment for felony offenders, especially "career criminals." And in the wake of the passage of new taxes during a special legislative session in December to bolster the fiscal condition of the Metropolitan Transit Authority (MTA) in the New York City area, the new governor directed a review of the agency's structure, with the goal of putting it more directly under the control of the state's elected officials.[38]

To high-level state administrators, Governor Cuomo's first state of the state message was important as much for its silences as for what it said. As in previous years, state departments and agencies had submitted material for inclusion in the message, hoping to have their priorities become the governor's. By saying almost nothing about the programs of some of New York state's biggest departments—the state university and the Department of Mental Health, for example—Governor Cuomo was clearly signaling priorities. In these areas his interest was more in controlling costs and encouraging internal generation of resources than in program innovation.

Though of course important, the content of the state of the state message had less impact in New York than did its style and tone. Again the governor struck a note of conciliation and stressed the need for cooperative, bipartisan action by New York's political leaders. His speech to the legislature on January 5, for example, was the first in recent memory in which a governor had named legislative leaders and other state officials, acknowledging their past leadership and accomplishments. This symbolic demonstration of a willingness to share the credit for successes and initiatives, and Cuomo's earlier actions on the Simon appointment and other, less visible matters gave added strength to the growing perception that the governor really meant it when he said that he was willing to "believe, to work, to give . . . together." Warren Anderson, first elected to the senate in 1952, summed up the overall reaction in Albany when he commented, "I don't remember any governor reaching out this way before."[39]

Finally, like the inaugural, the state of the state address was nationally reported. It was thus an opportunity for Governor Cuomo to begin to assert on the national scene the leadership that is traditional for New York governors. Cuomo, who later offered to help the Democratic National Committee with fund raising and was soon being mentioned as New York's favorite son for president in 1984, did not shrink from this role. He used this speech not only to comment on federal programs that had direct impact upon state policy but also to decry President Ronald Reagan's proposed level of military spending and to endorse a mutual, verifiable nuclear freeze. In this approach, the governor's action presaged that taken by his colleagues collectively at the annual National Governors' Association (NGA) meeting in February.

A close reading of the inaugural and the state of the state addresses reveals much continuity in Governor Cuomo's early policy positions with those of his predecessor. Dramatic departures to keep particular campaign promises aside, it is clear that Cuomo accepted Carey's definition of the state's fiscal difficulties and the consequent need for austerity in government. In key areas of policy—budgeting reform and economic development, for example—Carey transition documents read as virtual catalogs of Cuomo proposals, though this may be as much because of Cuomo's experience and the continuation of top aides as because of the use of the documents themselves. (A former Carey aide, Henrik Dullea, was appointed director of state operations and coordinated the preparation of the state of the state message.)

Change came in the messages' implied messages. The governor would work hard, tell the truth, and keep his word. Arriving with a reputation as an effective negotiator, he would truly negotiate, taking suggestions, sharing credit—all, implicitly at least, in contrast to the puckish unpredictability and confrontational style of the previous governor. And in budgeting, New York would return to what one historian has called its tradition of positive liberalism, "balancing our books the way a family would—without abandoning our weak, without sacrificing the future of our young, without destroying the environment that supports us."[40]

Three Crises

A leading student of the presidency, Thomas E. Cronin, has pointed out the utility of crises for chief executives. "A president," Cronin said, "can appear more presidential if he can accentuate the nation's sense of being in a desperate predicament."[41] This observation holds true, as well, for governors. When seeming to have to work against close and externally imposed deadlines that, if passed, will result in unacceptable consequences, governors may be able to move others in the state's political system toward a resolution of conflicting views that might not otherwise be accomplished. Crises thus have utility for governors, and governors have a stake in enhancing the crisis-like aspects of the problems they face. "Because the important and critical problems are not necessarily those that people want to hear about, a self-enhancing technique is to place critical problems in an unreal light and pose illusory ones as if they were critical. . . ."[42] And the utility of the crisis atmosphere is never greater than during the transition, when it helps the outgoing governor augment his rapidly dwindling power and the incoming one demonstrate his capacity to do the job.

Having dealt with a very real and massive fiscal crisis during his first few months as governor, Hugh Carey came to understand intimately the utility of crises as action-forcing devices in state government. In fact, some in Albany observed that Carey, bored by the routines of government, could function at the peak of his considerable capacities only when dealing with a crisis, real or contrived. He appeared to be a man, Mario Cuomo said, "who enjoyed swimming along in the waves at the top of the turbulence his own actions had created."

Carey's crisis came in the form of a threat by Richard Ravitch, chairman of the New York City area MTA, to raise subway fares from 75¢ to $1 on December 20, 1982, unless the state acted to increase its subsidy to the authority by $225 million. Previous state action, taken in June 1981 and designed to maintain the fare at 75¢ for two years, was projected by the MTA to have fallen short by $300 million. When Ravitch suggested the necessity for a fare increase in June of 1982, state leaders prevailed upon him to wait until after the election and promised action then. He waited, and December arrived.

Governor Carey, now a lame duck, called the legislature into special session in early December in order to meet this commitment. He found, however, that he needed to include the governor-elect, his formerly neglected lieutenant governor, in the negotiations with the legislative leaders if they were to succeed. Majority leader Anderson of the Republican senate and speaker Stanley Fink of the Democratic assembly would make no commitments and deliver no majorities on matters that might have implications for the next fiscal year's budget unless the incoming governor was involved.

Both parties were committed to finding a solution to the MTA's fiscal problems, but each had a different answer. Democrats favored a payroll tax in the metropolitan region (it was business based), whereas Republicans offered a regional tax on sales. An attempt by Carey and Cuomo to use the special session to deal, in addition, with the massive current year budget deficit, over half a billion dollars, was scotched by Senator Anderson; the Republicans wanted this issue handled separately after Cuomo actually took office in January. Pursuing their preferences, the Democratic assembly passed a payroll tax, and the Republican senate passed one on sales.[43]

The wrangling proceeded for two weeks, with Ravitch holding firm to his deadline. As Carey, Cuomo, and the legislative leaders considered alternative tax proposals, Ravitch flew back and forth to Washington to seek clarification of the now murky picture on federal aid. Meetings of the MTA board and the Financial Control Board, which had to approve the fiscal plan for transit, were delayed. Making his contribution, Mario Cuomo, though not yet governor, offered to "take responsibility for the necessary taxes" if this would help to produce a solution.[44] Legislative leaders met with "the governors," the December 20 deadline came and went, the MTA board kept "vigil" and Christmas approached. "Will they postpone that too?" asked Robert Tierney, Mayor Koch's press secretary.[45] Finally, the crisis atmosphere produced action: a .25 percent increase in the sales tax in the twelve-county MTA region.

This solution was a victory for the Republican senate, as was the uncoupling of the MTA issue from the state budget deficit for the special session. But it allowed Carey to deliver on a commitment to Ravitch, and Cuomo to help resolve a nagging problem prior to his assumption of the governorship. A good illustration of how a governor-elect is empowered by election, not inauguration, the MTA crisis also demonstrates how an outgoing chief executive can retain a piece of the action. At the close of the MTA negotiations Governor Carey remarked, "If I had known this job was going to be so hard to get out of, I might not have tried so hard to get into it."[46] In fact, he later revealed that the MTA crisis was, in part, contrived. He bound himself to Ravitch's deadline because he chose to do so; as a lame-duck governor he needed the deadline to force action.

Two other crises presented themselves during the transition period. One, concerning the state budget, had long been publicized, and its parameters were well known. The other, a prison uprising at Ossining during which hostages were taken, occurred suddenly and threatened the viability of the Cuomo governorship just as it began.

On the evening of January 8, while Governor Cuomo dined with his wife and family at a restaurant in Manhattan, nineteen corrections officers were taken hostage at the Ossining Correctional Facility, formerly known as Sing Sing Prison. The precipitating incident was a dispute between some inmates in cell block B and a corrections sergeant over the enforcement of recreation rules. Within minutes of the event Governor Cuomo was located and informed. After consulting with aides he decided not to go to Ossining. Instead, the governor dispatched his corrections commissioner, Thomas A. Coughlin, to the scene. With Coughlin, who had previously served Governor Carey, went the department's crisis intervention team, and later, John Burke, head of the correction officers' union.

Cuomo, who announced that he would "devote my entire attention to this matter until it is resolved . . . ," set out two priorities in dealing with the crisis: first, "the lives of the corrections officers," and second, "the lives of potential hostages in prisons throughout New York [that might be] endangered by any agreement that would unduly erode respect for the state."[47] The governor remained in constant touch with his commissioner by telephone from a command post at the World Trade Center in New York City, speaking with him more than sixty times during the fifty-three hours of the incident. At times Coughlin was on the phone simultaneously with Cuomo and with his negotiating team in the prison.

The commissioner's strategy was to isolate cell block B from the rest of the prison, control media access, and enter into negotiations with the inmates. Cuomo directed, however, that no concrete concessions could be made while the hostages were still being held. Problems arose in identifying spokesmen who could effectively represent the views of the almost 500 prisoners involved. As some inmates left those in rebellion, however, and as two hostages were released—one in exchange for medicine and the other because of a need for medical attention—a clearer view of the situation within cell block B emerged. Reassured by the fact that no hostages had been harmed, the state's team continued to seek serious negotiations.

Despite a setback, when an announcement on television by Senator Ralph Marino that amnesty would not be offered to the angered inmates inside the prison, negotiations continued. Both sides proceeded with a clear recollection of the violent results of the uprising at Attica prison during the Rockefeller administration, over a decade earlier, and this helped sustain the ongoing process. Inmates hung out bedsheet banners declaring "we don't want another Attica," and the governor later commented, "you couldn't deal with this without thinking of Attica."[48]

Demands, later called "requests" by the governor, boiled down to ten. Most had to do with disparities in privileges between those inmates in transit through Ossining (in cell block B) and others being permanently held there. The stickiest problem, that of amnesty, was resolved by a promise of no "retaliation," a word later variously interpreted by inmates and the state. (Governor Cuomo insisted that it barred illegal acts but not prosecutions, if Westchester District Attorney Carl Vergari chose to undertake them.) The governor later pronounced these requests "not outlandish or unusual" and commissioner Coughlin commented, "I would have agreed to all those things from the beginning."[49]

The hostages were finally released on the evening of January 10 when inmate demands were broadcast on the eleven o'clock television news. Both the governor and the legislature undertook a general inquiry into conditions at Ossining and throughout the state prisons, and Coughlin sought to respond quickly to several of the grievances.

Cuomo later described these two and a half days as "the longest week of my life."[50] Certainly, this was not a crisis he would have chosen to face, nor did he manipulate it for political purposes. Nevertheless, a failure to deal with it effectively would have been very damaging to his governorship. Instead, the fact that he came through the Ossining uprising unscathed, in a state in which many of the top public officials shared a personal recollection of Attica, increased the governor's ability to lead in Albany during the early months of his first year.

In his mid-1982 report on the budget, Governor Carey, citing the impact of veto overrides in the spring and the legislature's continued refusal to enact a statutory cap on spending as the causes, announced a current-year deficit of $579 million. In addition, he said, there would be a shortfall for the coming fiscal year of $1.2 billion, bringing the total state deficit over eighteen months to $1.8 billion.[51] Because funds borrowed to fill the 1982–83 gap would have to be paid back in 1983–84, Mario Cuomo, in his first budget, had to find resources to cover the entire $1.8 billion.

Despite a recommendation to all new governors by the NGA, Cuomo declined to take a vacation after the election was decided in November, citing as his reason the need to "send a message" that he understood the gravity of the state's fiscal condition. Standard and Poor's, the bond rating agency, had lowered New York State's rating just eight days after Cuomo's victory. "Fiscal survival," the governor-elect said, "is the first order of business. Without it you can't do things for people in wheelchairs."[52]

Unlike governors-elect before him, Mario Cuomo did not send his representatives to Albany to monitor budget hearings and seize control of the budgetary process. His transition did not involve a change of party, and he had held high-level posts in the Carey government for eight years. In addition, two of those selected for his inner circle, Michael J. Del Guidice and Michael Finnerty, had been top aides to Carey, and Finnerty's career was rooted in budgeting. In short, an in-party transition and intimate familiarity with the budget from the inside seemed to obviate the need for any special effort at monitoring the process by the incoming administration.

During the last weeks of January the difficult fiscal choices that they faced were publicly discussed by the governor and his aides. Options being considered were carefully leaked to the press over the days before the actual delivery of the budget message. This was a long-established technique in New York, designed to get maximum coverage and create a receptive environment for gubernatorial proposals that might be overlooked if press coverage were limited to the day of the message alone.

Then, on February 1, Governor Cuomo offered a budget balanced by a $900 million tax increase and a reduction in state expenditures of the same amount. It was, Cuomo reiterated, an attempt to "balance our books as a family would, by sharing the burden." True to his campaign pledge, the new governor sought no raises in broad-based state taxes. And surprising to many because of the political support he had received from organized labor, budget cuts would be achieved, in part, through the speedy elimination of 14,000 state jobs, 8,400 of these by layoffs.[53]

The 50–50 division between new taxes and budget cuts in Governor Cuomo's budget plan was no accident. It symbolized his desire to spread the impact of austerity equally. The unions having been his strongest supporters, the governor thought it especially necessary that they visibly share the pain so that his commitment to equity for all New Yorkers, former supporters as well as opponents, be evident. In the symbolism of his budget submission and his determination to hold the line on broad-based taxes, Cuomo's credibility was again a principal concern. "Unless everybody understands that I am telling the truth when I say we are in deep, deep trouble," he insisted, "I won't be able to get the hard things done."[54]

In offering his budget the governor invited the legislature to "improve on it." Later, Cuomo extended this invitation to all who publicly questioned parts of the document. On two occasions when he was criticized in the letters column of the New York Times for cutting worthy programs, for example, the governor responded in kind, acknowledging the value of the programs but citing overriding fiscal considerations in a "season of hard choices." "Those who disagree," Cuomo wrote, "are free to suggest changes. But I hope that in making the suggestions the dissenters will tell us how to accommodate the changes. What other worthwhile programs would be cut instead? Or what taxes or fees should be raised to provide compensating revenue?"[55] By traveling through the state and speaking in defense of his budget despite widespread protests, and by responding at this level of detail in every forum in which criticism was offered, the governor successfully defended the integrity of his decision-making process and, in the end, the result of that process.

The 1983–84 state budget incorporated at the outset many legislative priorities that had traditionally been added later, after a period of hard bargaining. Thus, though the legislative leaders, after receiving the budget, remained interested in exploring alternatives on both the revenue and expenditure sides, they shared the feeling that unlike Carey, Cuomo had not "thrown the gauntlet down." The budget, speaker Fink said, "was honestly arrived at. I don't think anybody is trying to play any games. That is a welcome feeling."[56]

One consequence of Governor Cuomo's creation of an atmosphere of willingness to compromise was a reluctance by legislative leaders to challenge his revenue projections. The projections had been a major bone of contention between Governor Carey and the senate Republican majority in previous years. Though he had a study in hand showing that the governor was underestimating revenue by $200 million, senate majority leader Warren Anderson made little issue of it. Anderson, of course, was not influenced solely by the governor's accommodating posture. His majority liked Cuomo's conservative fiscal stance, and the revenue estimates he had acted upon in challenging Governor Carey in the previous session had been too high, contributing to some of the problems the state now faced. Finally, the governor got a major boost when, on March 11, 1983, New York's comptroller, Ned Regan, the only Republican official elected statewide, endorsed the tightness of Cuomo's budget and the soundness of his revenue estimates. (A few weeks earlier, R. Wayne Diesel, Regan's deputy, had been appointed first deputy director of the budget by budget director Finnerty, with the approval of Cuomo. Diesel, a Republican, had served on the staffs of Senator Anderson and governors Rockefeller and Wilson.)

In the end the legislature did not, as Hugh Carey had predicted, "dump a ton of mud on the Cuomo budget, and let him dig himself out."[57] Instead, the state produced its budget before the beginning of the fiscal year for the first time in four years. Tax increases totaled close to $1 billion. Programs added in the legislature amounted to $200 million, balanced by $140 million in cuts of the programs offered by Governor Cuomo. Education aid was increased substantially without reallocation from wealthy districts, a concession to the Republican senate, and layoffs were reduced to about 3,400 at the insistence of the Democratic assembly. Describing legislators and his staff as "near euphoria" over reaching agreement before the April 1 start of the fiscal year, the governor proclaimed himself "very grateful" to the legislature for producing "a better budget than the one I gave you. . . ."[58]

To the end Governor Cuomo insisted that his proposed layoffs were not "a strategy designed to create a certain kind of political environment."[59] But the fact remained that in every transition in New York since World War II the incoming governor had proclaimed a budget gap of at least 10 percent of expenditures over revenues and had sought to take extraordinary measures to deal with these crises. State fiscal crises are the norm, not the exception, during gubernatorial transition years. They are a cost of democracy, the result of the impact of the electoral cycle upon budgetary decision making in New York.

Incoming governors, like outgoing ones, have a stake in crisis. The atmosphere created by a crisis creates in the potential winners and losers the willingness to consider painful alternatives that they might otherwise not even permit to reach the table. And a crisis during his first legislative session is a unique opportunity for a governor, a time in which he can reveal fiscal problems and seek new resources or deep budget cuts without sharing the blame for them. The goodwill of the postelection honeymoon period had not yet dissipated. Those hopeful of preferment had not yet been disappointed and were thus muted in their criticism. And both the governor and the legislature would never, together, be more distant in time from the judgment of the electorate than during this period. There was ample time for those who would be hurt to forget.

A Governorship Well Begun

When, near the end of his third month in office, Mario Cuomo remarked, "I don't feel like governor," he was reflecting less a slowness in adjusting to his office than an emerging comfort in it.[60] In fact, Cuomo's management of the transition had been excellent. Always sensitive to the symbolic import of his speech and actions, the new governor was able to communicate a change in direction for state government while maintaining much-needed continuity in policy and operations. He weathered one unanticipated crisis in the prisons (good fortune as well as skill played a role here) and managed another in the budget, proving early that he could govern. Finally, he established himself as a force to be reckoned with in the national Democratic party.

These early successes were crucial, for they established the tone and competence of the Cuomo administration when some in the state were skeptical about the governor's toughness and decisiveness. As Richard Neustadt observed of the presidency over two decades ago, first successes create the context in which later successes can be achieved.[61]

In New York in 1982 the conditions for a smooth transition were optimal. The transfer of power took place within the Democratic party, from a governor who had not sought reelection and carefully prepared for the transfer, to a governor who had long experience in state government. In addition, governors Carey and Cuomo had a long-standing, though sometimes stormy, political and personal relationship.

The preparations of the Council on State Priorities and the state Budget Division contributed to the smoothness of the transition, despite the absence in New York of any law governing the process and providing resources for it. Bridges were built in part through the use of prestigious and well-connected notables in the private sector and in part by reliance on the professionalism of the state bureaucracy. But in order to make the process work, the governor-elect had to seize the opportunity. This he did, overcoming concerns about being coopted, reaching out in a spirit of cooperation to state leaders of both parties and using former Carey people in key roles in his new government. In doing this Governor Cuomo accepted the Carey commitment to austerity as a continuing theme of New York state government but sought again and again to emphasize compassion as a balancing element in his approach.

The success of the transition was, however, just a beginning. "Up to now we've been doing things the great 'they' told us we had to do," Cuomo said. "Now we can start doing the things we want to do. We've been liberated."[62]

But questions still remained. Could the governor sustain his hands-on approach to management of the state in the long term, or would his penchant for detail ultimately cause him difficulties? Would Mario Cuomo, like Hugh Carey before him, ultimately choose a chief of staff to ease some of the day-to-day burdens of his office? Could the morale problems among state workers caused by the trauma of rapid layoffs and the continual threat of further layoffs be overcome? Could the state really deliver "more for less" as thousands of experienced employees accepted early retirement incentives (put in place to avoid layoffs) and left their jobs simultaneously?

As early as April the revenue package so painstakingly put together in March began to unravel. There were victories—oil companies agreed to drop a lawsuit, pay some back taxes, and accept some new ones in exchange for modifications in the governor's proposals. And there was a major defeat—the federal government acted to delay withholding on interest and dividend income, thus scuttling similar piggybacked state provisions. As the transition ended the large question remained: Could its successes be sustained under the grind of everyday government? This was to be the test of the days and months ahead.

The 1982 Gubernatorial Transition in Texas:
Bolt Cutters, Late Trains, Lame Ducks, and Bullock's Bullets

CHARLES W. WIGGINS, KEITH E. HAMM,
AND HOWARD R. BALANOFF

In the early afternoon of cold and rainy January 18, 1983, shortly after officially being sworn in as the forty-first governor of Texas, Mark White stood with a group of celebrating supporters across from the capitol at the iron gate leading to the main entrance of the governor's mansion.[1] White and key representatives of his winning electoral coalition (three labor union officials, the Texas State Teachers Association president, a black state senator, and a Hispanic state senator) took turns applying a gold-colored bolt cutter to a chain that had been draped across the gate earlier in the day by campaign lieutenants. Upon successfully completing this symbolic exercise and with a charge to "come on in," White led a band of what was eventually estimated to be eight hundred supporters, media representatives, and well-wishers past a grazing donkey (provided by organized labor) on the mansion lawn, up the walk and steps, and into the antebellum structure. The former residents of the mansion, Bill and Rita Clements, who had raised $3 million in private contributions to redecorate and restore it, were not present to form a greeting party, having quietly slipped out of Austin late the afternoon before to return to their permanent abode in north Texas. Democracy had returned to the Lone Star State.

This event in many ways symbolizes the 1982 gubernatorial transition in Texas. Recently converted to a populist orientation, forty-two-year-old Democrat Mark White—Baylor law graduate, Houston attorney, protégé of moderate-to-conservative ex-Governor Dolph Briscoe, and former secretary of state and attorney general—had been successful in his bid to wrest control of the governor's office away from one-termer Bill Clements—sixty-five years old, crusty and outspoken, millionaire Dallas oil man, and the state's first Republican governor since Reconstruction. Virtually absolute control of state government was back in the hands of the dominant yet highly variegated Democratic party after the state's brief fling with Republicanism. To White, in particular, the governor's office was back in the hands of "the people," where it rightfully belonged.

We will examine several key dimensions of the 1982 gubernatorial transition in Texas: the major campaign and electoral developments that preceded the transition, and, the basic components of the transition following White's somewhat unexpected victory on election day, covering the period from the initial formation of his transition team up to the key activities associated with his inauguration and first six months in office. Two important aspects of the transition receive separate and special emphasis: (1) the controversy surrounding gubernatorial appointments to major positions in state agencies, boards, and commissions, and (2) the involvement of the new governor in the state budget process. Finally, we attempt to evaluate the transition process itself, at the same time making a suggestion or two about ways the transition process in Texas might be improved.

Campaign and Election

Unlike in 1978, Texas Democrats in 1982 were reasonably united as they headed into their fall general election campaign. The 1978 primary race had left the party bitterly divided between supporters of the incumbent governor, Dolph Briscoe, and his main challenger, attorney general John Hill, the latter having emerged as the nominee. Into the void created by the Democrat's disarray stepped political amateur Bill Clements, who conducted a very well-financed ($7.4 million, including $4.5 million of his own money) and aggressive campaign against his somewhat overconfident opponent, running on a platform that emphasized traditionally popular conservative themes—reducing taxes, crime, and the number of state employees, as well as opposing a personal or a corporate income tax and any changes in the state's right-to-work law.[2] Also capitalizing on the low popularity of the national Democratic administration in the state, Clements defeated Hill in what was regarded as one of the most stunning upsets in Texas political history and became the state's first Republican governor in over 100 years. Although victorious, Clements's margin was extremely narrow (four-tenths of 1 percent), and his vote total was over 350,000 less than his party's losing 1972 candidate had received, leading many analysts to attribute his unexpected victory at least partly to a general lack of interest in the election and a resulting low turnout of voters.

In seeking his party's renomination in 1982, Clements received only token opposition. On the other hand the Democratic primary began as a highly contested three-man race, pitting three of the party's highly visible and successful professional politicians against one another: attorney general Mark White, railroad commissioner Buddy Temple, and land commissioner Bob Armstrong. All three campaigned vigorously, with Temple and Armstrong appealing more to the liberal wing of the party and White to the conservative wing. The results of the May 1 primary showed White with a lead, but only by a plurality, over his two rivals, with Temple finishing in second place. Five days after the first primary Temple unexpectedly withdrew from the runoff contest against White, saying that such a race would not only be very costly but would also be too divisive to the Texas Democratic party. Temple's decision spared White the costs of further intraparty battle and allowed him to begin immediately his campaign against the incumbent Republican governor.

STYLE AND ISSUES

The campaign style adopted by both gubernatorial candidates was in many ways consistent with the rough-and-tumble of the traditional Texas political culture: hard hitting, expressive, and personal. At times the two candidates appeared more interested in exchanging barbs about each other's personal character than in discussing their disparate views on public policy questions. Although some observers attributed this focus on personality rather than issues to the fact that both candidates were political conservatives who basically agreed on the course of public policy much more than they disagreed, others argued that they genuinely did not like each other. Whatever the cause, the net result was a personality-oriented and highly charged style of campaign.

Throughout the campaign, for example, Clements frequently charged White with having been an "incompetent" (later mellowed to "mediocre" or "poor") attorney general, citing examples of occasions when the attorney general's office had either lost cases in federal courts on substantive grounds or had defaulted cases in state courts because of appearance and/or scheduling foul-ups. Furthermore, in mid-September, the Clements organization released a campaign tabloid (reportedly mailed to 1.2 million households) revealing that White had been arrested on a drunk-driving charge some nineteen years before while attending law school at Baylor University.[3] Acknowledging that such a wrongful act had occurred (with subsequent formal conviction on a reduced charge of public drunkenness), White countered that the exposé was "gutter stuff" being disseminated in a "scurrilous rag."

This episode even resulted a few days later in an intense shouting match between the two candidates after a regionally televised debate in Amarillo, with White charging Clements with degrading the governor's office by publishing such "garbage" and Clements countering that he considered such information important for the public, allowing them to "gauge the morality and integrity" of his opponent.[4] White regularly tried to portray his opponent as being abrasive, insensitive, and rather tactless. For example, during a statewide televised debate sponsored by the League of Women Voters in mid-October, White charged Clements with being "insensitive" to environmental matters during the time of the infamous oil spill in the Gulf of Mexico a few years before, an event at the time referred to by Clements as "much ado about nothing."[5] (The spill involved oil rigs on lease from Clements's own company to the Mexican public oil industry. As attorney general, White had sued Clements's company in 1979 for damages to the Texas coastline; the suit was resolved in an out-of-court settlement.) These are just a few examples of the highly volatile atmosphere that permeated the gubernatorial campaign debate in 1982.

Although oftentimes difficult to decipher because of the campaign rhetoric employed, the positions of the two candidates on some substantive public policy questions were communicated to the electorate. On general issues, both candidates agreed that the state's highways and roads needed to be improved, that the state's educational system needed more support, that the state's welfare programs should be streamlined, and that the state's criminal justice policies could be toughened, especially with regard to drug trafficking. Yet, throughout most of the campaign, Clements tended to assume the defensive posture of one compelled to justify or explain the record of his administration against the onslaught of an aggressive challenger. Having seized the initiative, White emphasized two key issues throughout the campaign: public utility regulation and public schoolteachers' salaries.

The issue of public utility regulation involved two dimensions. First, White charged that Texas utilities were reaping unreasonable benefits to the public's detriment by being permitted to impose an automatic fuel adjustment factor (FAF) on the monthly utility bills (reflecting recent increased costs in the purchase of basic fuels).[6] White thought that the Texas Public Utility Commission (PUC), the state regulatory agency in such matters, should ban the practice and require utilities to enter the competitive marketplace in their purchases of basic fuels. Such a practice, White reasoned, should reduce customers' utility bills. Clements countered that White was generating a "phony issue" and that consumers' utility bills would remain essentially the same even if the FAF portion of the bill was prohibited by the PUC. White also charged that Clements's use of his appointment powers had allowed the PUC to become a captive of the utility interests, which it was established to regulate, and that consumer representatives—his example was a housewife—should be appointed to the PUC at the earliest opportunity. In somewhat foot-in-mouth fashion, and drawing the ire of women's groups, Clements countered by arguing that he "didn't know of a housewife who was qualified to serve on the PUC," later qualified to mean that he was not aware of a housewife who had the technical expertise (i.e., the knowledge of accounting, procurement, and the legal aspects of utility operations) needed to serve as a commissioner.

The other key issue in the White campaign arsenal was the salaries of primary and secondary public schoolteachers. White thought that teachers' salaries in Texas were still too far below the national norm and that drastic action, such as a 24-percent increase, was needed to prevent good people from leaving the profession and to attract new ones. In numerous campaign appearances White was quick to point out that a guard at a Texas prison was paid more than a typical teacher and that improving the state's educational system via higher teacher salaries would most assuredly reduce the need for more prison guards. Although acknowledging that there was still room for improvement, Clements countered that teachers' salaries in Texas had improved during his administration, moving up from thirty-fourth to twenty-seventh in state ranking.

Although utility rates and teachers' salaries appeared to be White's main campaign themes, he increasingly stressed the state's worsening economic conditions as the campaign progressed, blaming both Clements and the national Republican administration for many of the state's ills. (Although polls showed that Reagan was continuing to enjoy relatively high personal popularity among Texans, they also revealed a growing disenchantment with his economic policies and programs.) By September the state's unemployment rate had reached an all-time high of 8.0 percent (compared with 10.1 percent nationally), and White charged Clements with not using either his good offices or influence with the national administration to alleviate the situation.

By emphasizing early in the campaign that the Texas economic situation was "recession-proof," Clements was actually encouraging unemployed residents from other states to migrate to the state at a time when an increasing number of current residents were being laid off or were unable to find jobs, or so White charged. Clements, on the other hand, argued that economic conditions in the state were still much better than in other states, that "recession-resistant" (as opposed to "recession-proof") might be a more appropriate term to employ in characterizing it, and ordered the Texas Employment Commission to send letters to its counterparts in other states indicating that job openings had dried up in the state. Although difficult to measure, the overall economic situation in the state—further influenced by devaluation of the Mexican peso, drought in west Texas, plus rain and hail damage and low cotton prices in the Panhandle—probably worked to the advantage of the challenger in his bid to unseat the incumbent governor.

ORGANIZATION, TACTICS, AND FINANCE

Any analysis of a political campaign should devote at least some consideration to its organization, tactics, and finances. In broad organizational terms, Texas statewide campaigns have traditionally been noted for their every-man-for-himself character. In addition to the governor's race, other major statewide races were conducted in 1982 for U.S. senator, lieutenant governor, attorney general, treasurer, agricultural commissioner, land commissioner, and comptroller. Although still running independent campaigns of their own in terms of staff organizations and financing, members of the Democratic ticket were more prone to engage in cooperative campaign ventures than were the Republicans. In many ways their perception of themselves as members of the "out party" in terms of the governorship led candidates, including of course White himself, to be more interested in joint campaign appearances and activities.

For the most part, incumbent Clements followed the traditional Texas model and ran a very independent campaign. The only exception to this pattern occurred shortly after the May primary when, in an effort to strengthen the state Republican ticket, he allegedly played a personal role in the sacking of the nominal Republican nominees for state treasurer and agricultural commissioner and in the recruitment of their replacements. However, indications were that he was never particularly enchanted with the visibility and campaign vigor of most of the other candidates on the state Republican ticket. Presumably, Clements's determination to go it alone became even stronger as the campaign progressed; he flatly turned down the suggestion by a close campaign consultant that he should provide financial and other assistance to ticket cohorts to enhance their public visibility.[7]

White, in contrast, viewed the state Democratic ticket as a major source of electoral strength, frequently tooting the party unity horn at rallies and press conferences around the state. In addition to himself, three other members of this ticket were highly visible and successful veterans of previous statewide campaigns: U.S. Senator Lloyd Bentsen, lieutenant governor Bill Hobby, and state comptroller Bob Bullock. Joining them on the ticket for the other offices were four individuals who had strong associations with the more liberal, or progressive, wing of the party: Jim Mattox (attorney general), Gary Mauro (land commissioner), Jim Hightower (agriculture commissioner), and Ann Richards (treasurer). To White and other Democratic supporters, the strength of the Democratic ticket could be found primarily in its political diversity—voters of any philosophical or ideological stripe could find someone to vote for on such a balanced ticket.

In narrower organizational terms, both Clements and White had candidate-centered campaign organizations that provided assistance in such areas as fund raising, scheduling, research, and volunteer coordination. If size is an indicator of organizational prowess, Clements's campaign appeared to have the advantage by a wide margin. From the spring until the general election, Clements's campaign organization reportedly had 119 individuals on its salary rolls, whereas White's paid staff at its peak was estimated to number only 30.[8]

Both candidates employed a wide variety of tactics in making their campaign appeals to the electorate and stimulating voter interest. Foremost among them was the use of television and, to a lesser extent, radio advertising. In a state as populous and large as Texas, and with the bulk of residents (over 80 percent) residing in well-scattered, highly urbanized areas, serious candidates for statewide office find it necessary to raise and spend large sums of money for advertising in the ten major media markets of the state. Approximately 50 percent to 60 percent of each candidate's total campaign expenditures went for this purpose in 1982. An aide to White reported late in the campaign that White was about even with Clements on prime-time television purchases but that Clements was spending significantly more during nonprime viewing periods. This same aide also noted that Clements was spending substantially more than White for direct mail, billboards, and newspaper advertisements.

In addition to advertisements, phone banks, polling, and endorsements were other especially significant techniques employed by both candidates. Phone banking reportedly had first been used extensively in a statewide campaign in Texas by Clements during his 1978 campaign, and several observers attributed much of his success to this particular technique.[9] Not to be outdone, Texas Democrats, under the organizational leadership of U.S. Senator Bentsen and Lieutenant Governor Hobby, lured a nationally recognized phone-bank specialist (Dan McClung) to Texas during the 1982 campaign and put him in charge of organizing a statewide bank.[10] As the campaign progressed, other Democratic candidates were plugged into this operation, which was designed to reach over 2 million voters, focus on the state's thirty-five largest cities, utilize at its peak some 600 workers, and deliver messages supportive of the Democratic ticket. In the end several of the major Democratic candidates shared the estimated $1-million cost of its operations, with the Bentsen, Hobby, and White campaign organizations paying the lion's share. (After the election the state Democratic party agreed to pick up slightly over $100,000 still owed by the White organization for its share of the bank's cost.) Clements's phone-bank operation, which also was estimated to cost in the neighborhood of $1 million, centered on fifty of the largest communities in the state and was strictly an independent enterprise, conveying only messages supportive of the incumbent governor.

Both candidates made extensive use of information from public opinion polls throughout the campaign, with Clements relying upon his

1978 pollster (Lance Tarrence and Associates of Houston) and White primarily upon Dressner, Morris, and Tortorella of New York City.[11] Throughout the campaign, although seldom releasing any specific polling results, Clements maintained that his polls and three others to which he had access indicated that he enjoyed a comfortable lead over White by anywhere from 5 to 16 percent. White, on the other hand, announced in June that a Dressner poll indicated that he had a four-point edge over Clements (48–44), with 8 percent undecided. Overall, uncertainties about turnout and how undecideds would actually vote (if they did) made predictions of the election outcome particularly difficult for pollsters in the 1982 gubernatorial race.

A major source of embarrassment to Clements was the release of the results of an August poll conducted by Arthur Finkelstein and Associates of New York City for the Republican U.S. Senate candidate, conservative congressman Jim Collins of Dallas, and paid for by the National Republican Senatorial Campaign Committee.[12] Collins, in releasing the results of the poll, indicated that it showed that he was not trailing Bentsen by as wide a margin as many speculated and that the poll also revealed that Clements was trailing White in the gubernatorial race. Collins's public disclosure of the latter fact irritated Clements, further cooling personal relations between the two candidates at the top of the state Republican ticket.

Clements and White also actively solicited or enjoyed the endorsement of leading politicians, interest group representatives, and newspaper editorialists. Republican Clements took great delight in announcing quite early in the general election campaign that he was being endorsed by three former Democratic governors (Shivers, Smith, and, of course, Connally); this was followed up in mid-August with endorsements from four former Democratic attorneys general (Carr, Wilson, Sheppard, and Mann).[13] None of the latter group, however, appeared to be particularly active or otherwise visible during his campaign. White, on the other hand, received the endorsement of ex-Governor Briscoe (his political mentor, who had appointed him secretary of state), John Hill (former attorney general, who had defeated Briscoe in the 1978 primary but lost to Clements in the general election), and his two opponents in the 1982 primary—Buddy Temple and Bob Armstrong.

Major interest groups or their leaders were also very visible during the campaign.[14] Two key teacher organizations—the Texas State Teachers Association (a 95,000-member National Education Association [NEA] affiliate) and the Texas Federation of Teachers (15,000-member AFL-CIO affiliate)—endorsed White, at the same time pledging much manpower and financial assistance to his campaign. Although neither group had supported his 1978 election bid, Clements's relations with teachers had deteriorated even further since the 1981 legislative session, when Clements had vetoed a bill mandating that all school districts provide their employees with health insurance programs. As was normal, the Texas Federation of Labor, AFL-CIO, also openly endorsed and supported White, but Hispanic leaders appeared to be divided on the question of which candidate to support. For example, the state leaders of five major Hispanic groups—the League of United Latin American Citizens (LULAC) and the American GI Forum—announced that they personally were supporting Clements, even though their organizations' policies prohibited official group endorsements.[15] Both cited previous actions by Clements that had been supportive of the Hispanic community, such as his 160 appointments of Hispanics to important state positions and his support for a documented workers program, and both indicated that they had reservations about some of White's activities while secretary of state and attorney general, such as his opposition to the extension of the federal Voting Rights Act in 1975. White countered with the endorsements of the national president and the general counsel of LULAC (both Corpus Christi residents) and a group called the Hispanic Mayors Advisory Committee, an ad hoc organization of some twenty Texas mayors of Mexican-American backgrounds.[16] Clements received the endorsements of the leaders of a major grass-roots group (MADD, or Mothers Against Drunk Driving) pushing for tougher drunk-driving and liquor-control laws, and White's lieutenants successfully discouraged a growing and politically sophisticated gay rights alliance based in Houston from publicly endorsing him. Black groups (the Progressive Action League in Houston, as well as several Baptist congregations in Houston and Dallas) sided with White.[17] Both candidates made appeals to a broad spectrum of business and professional interests, with Clements presumably receiving a disproportionate share of support from energy interests and White from the legal fraternity.

A strong advantage befell Clements in the form of newspaper editorial endorsements. Of twelve newspapers in the state for which information was readily available all endorsed Clements. However, they did at times acknowledge that he had certain weaknesses in record and leadership style.[18]

Both candidates conducted extensive and exhaustive campaigns throughout the state, using both personal appearances and the media. One apparent difference in geographical emphasis was that White personally campaigned more heavily in the more rural regions of east, central, and south Texas in an effort to attract traditional "Yellow Dog" Democrats (those Democrats whose partisan identifications can be traced to the Civil War period) to the fold. White tended to emphasize more his solicitation of support from blacks by making appearances among Baptist congregations in Houston and Dallas at their Sunday services.[19]

To pay for their numerous and expensive campaign activities, both candidates had to raise enormous sums of money.[20] Several facets of the financing of the 1982 gubernatorial campaign are worth noting. First, as might be expected, it was the most expensive gubernatorial campaign in Texas political history; the two candidates spent a total of $18.4 million. Second, Republican candidate Clements, as he had in 1978, substantially outspent his Democrat opponent, this time more than twice as much. Whereas Clements reported spending $13.3 million in his reelection bid, White reported spending "only" $5 million (excluding about $2.2 million spent for his primary race). In other words, the cost for each general election vote received by Clements and White was $9.07 and $2.94 respectively. Third, both candidates reported completing their campaigns with their treasuries substantially in debt. Clements's debts totaled $3 million, which he reportedly retired out of his personal assets, and White incurred a $2.4-million debt, an amount that he retired in a manner to be described in our analysis of the transition. Finally, Clements's fund-raising activities emphasized the big-banquet approach; $2.9 million was raised in a Dallas banquet in June 1981, and $3.5 million was garnered at a Houston banquet featuring President Reagan one year later. These two banquets alone netted over one-half of the funds raised by the Clements campaign, excluding his personal contribution.

ELECTION OUTCOME

On election day White scored what many media pundits considered an upset victory over the incumbent Clements; White received 53.2 percent of the vote, Clements 45.9, and the remaining 0.9 percent was divided between two minor party candidates. Foremost among the several factors deemed salient to White's victory was the tremendous voter turnout. In response to general economic conditions and a high-stimulus campaign, 3.2 million Texans exercised their right of franchise in 1982, compared with only 2.4 million in 1978. The number of votes Clements received in his reelection bid was actually higher than in 1978, but White's net gain (in comparison with 1978 Democratic candidate Hill) was 230,000 votes more than Clements's. Although the voting increase was spread quite evenly across the state among communities of all sizes, at least two analysts argue that higher selective turnout on the part of rural Democrats voting the straight ticket accounted for the largest share of White's net gain in votes over Clements.[21] Others attributed much import to the increased turnout of minorities and to the increments in White's share of their votes.[22]

Although the winner, White, in terms of proportion of the vote, still trailed other statewide candidates on the Democratic ticket by 4 percent to 10 percent.[23] For example, incumbent U.S. Senator Lloyd Bentsen, who headed the ticket and ran against a rather lackluster opponent (Congressman Jim Collins) whose campaign never really got off the ground, received 58.6 percent of the vote, or 5.4 percent more than White received.

The Transition

Overall, the Texas gubernatorial transition can best be described as a free-lance affair. No provisions have been incorporated into either the state's constitutional or statutory laws establishing duties and responsibilities for the orderly transfer of power from one administration to its successor. No public funds are appropriated to provide financial assistance to an incoming administration as it prepares to assume the reins of power. What happens during the transition period depends for the most part upon custom and the personal inclinations of the people involved. Thus, Texas transitions are not uniformly smooth. The Clements-White transition was no exception.

THE TEAM, COMMITTEES, AND ASSISTANCE

Shortly after his victory White appointed his principal assistant from the attorney general's office, John Fainter, to head his transition team, and Clements appointed a staff aide from his office, Hilary Doran, to coordinate the transition for his outgoing administration. For the most part these two individuals handled the transition on an informal ad hoc basis beginning about ten days after the election. No plan had been devised by the Clements administration before the election for orienting the new administration because it really had not anticipated defeat. On the other hand, the incoming administration did not expect or particularly want the Clements people to conduct an elaborate orientation program, one including well-prepared position papers and briefing sessions designed to bring them up to date on major state program developments. The White people preferred to go their own way.

It is also interesting to note that White and Clements never interacted during the transition period, apparently because of the personal animosity that had developed between them during their heated campaign. Instead, all interactions relating to the transition were conducted by staff aides. But both antagonists instructed their aides to act courteously and cooperatively, and, according to the media and other information sources, the atmosphere of the transition activity conducted by the two administrations was indeed cordial, though limited in scope.

No arrangements were made to provide the incoming administration with public office space in or near the capitol complex. Fainter, White's transition head, continued to operate out of the attorney general's office, and other aides operated out of campaign headquarters. White himself directed the transition from private office space in a commercial enterprise near the capitol that was provided by a longtime friend and supporter who was a prominent Austin businessman. Meetings were held at campaign headquarters and White's personal residence.

White's announcement immediately after the election of the appointment of Fainter as head of his transition team contained one ambiguity: no other members of this group were mentioned. Some argue that the ploy was intentional in that the governor-elect was very concerned about alienating some of his supporters by omitting them. Whether intentional or not, it had the net effect of allowing a wide array of campaign supporters and staff aides to feel that they were meaningfully involved in the transition.

White's somewhat loosely structured transition team can be broken down into three general groups. First, there were the members of White's formal campaign organization, with his campaign manager (Dwayne Holman) being the most visible from this group. The second group consisted of people who had served in major administrative posts under recent Democratic state administrations, particularly those of Preston Smith and Dolph Briscoe. Foremost among them were Ed Grisham, a San Antonio–based executive of an energy firm who had served as planning office director under Smith, and Dan Petty, a Dallas real estate executive and former Smith aide. (Grisham eventually assumed a major position within the White administration; Petty did not.) Members of this group reportedly had the largest impact on developments and activities associated with the White transition into office. The third group of team members consisted of personal friends and longtime supporters of White who had functioned as major fund raisers during his campaign. Foremost among the individuals belonging to this kitchen cabinet were Austin businessman Robert Baldwin (also owner of the private office space provided White during the transition), Dallas financier-investor Jess Hay, and Bryan savings and loan executive and former state Democratic party chairman (under Briscoe) Calvin Guest; Guest was the most actively involved.

The transition team was further expanded in mid-December when White announced that he was appointing a special 200-member transition committee to advise him on policy directions that his administration should take once it assumed office. Fainter was appointed to head the committee, which consisted of individuals from diverse social, occupational, and racial or ethnic backgrounds; the only common thread was that all had been White supporters during his bid for the governorship.

An analysis of the political connections of the transition committee members indicates that (1) 17 percent had been county chairpersons for White's election campaign, (2) 14 percent had received expenditures from White's campaign office, and (3) 4 percent had contributed at least $1,000 in a lump sum at some point during the campaign. Given the rough criteria for identifying political connections, it is reasonably safe to say that the transition committee was peopled by those who had actively supported White's election bid.

The committee was organized and operated primarily along subcommittee lines, with each of nine subcommittees devoting its attention to a state governmental public policy area, several of which had been emphasized during the gubernatorial campaign. It formally convened for two weekends of meetings consisting of presentations and deliberations at the University of Texas in Austin in early January and subsequently issued a 200-page report outlining its recommended goals and objectives for the new administration, plus specific strategies for achieving them.

Presumably a first for the state, this large and relatively broad-based citizens' committee provided advice to the incoming administration, but its overall impact upon later actions taken by the White administration is difficult to assess.

Transition assistance to the incoming administration was made available by several other individuals and groups. For example, the Austin office of Peat, Marwick, Mitchell, and Company, a private consulting firm, assisted with the development of a manual outlining the organizational structure for the governor-elect's top staff and specifying each staff member's duties and responsibilities. A few faculty members of the Lyndon Baines Johnson School of Public Affairs at the University of Texas—Austin, especially Terrell Blodget (professional public administrator and former city manager and Connally staff aide), also helped shape organization and staffing procedures. The services of the National Governors' Association (NGA) were also made available in two forms: a special seminar designed for new governors and the visit of a transition assistance team. The NGA new governor's seminar was held in mid-November in Utah, but White was unable to attend (because of a scheduled vacation), and Fainter was assigned responsibility for attending this meeting. In mid-December, an NGA transition assistance team, headed by Bert Wakeley of the NGA staff, visited Austin for several days to advise White's transition team. Although the Utah seminar was described by a staffer as very useful to White's transition planning and operations, some observers suggest that the impact of NGA's assistance team was limited, as locally based planning efforts were already in place before its arrival.

THE "LATE TRAIN"

The White campaign organization concluded its activities on election day with a debt totaling approximately $2.4 million. By December 11 it had successfully raised more than enough contributions to retire this debt. The way the White organization accomplished this constitutes one of the most interesting aspects of the transition.

For many years winning Texas politicians have capitalized on their electoral successes by holding fundraisers either to retire their campaign debts or to fortify special officeholder accounts authorized by state law. After the 1982 election newly elected state officials were confronted with a new constraint in the timing of fund-raising activities, in that the 1981 legislature passed a law banning such activities between December 11 (or thirty days prior to the convening of the 1983 legislative session) and the adjournment of the 1983 session in late May.[24] A political reform measure, the new law was designed to discourage charges made by news media and others over the years that conflicts of interest, if not downright political payoffs, had been occurring in conjunction with fundraisers conducted during legislative sessions. Because the new law applied to elected officials in both the legislative and the executive branch, Governor-elect White was confronted with the choice of either immediately raising funds for his debt-ridden campaign or waiting until mid-summer of the following year and having to deal with an even larger debt as the result of postelection transition expenses and the accrual of interest charges on his original campaign debt. He chose immediate action.

Between the election and December 11 the White organization raised slightly over $3 million in contributions.[25] The largest portion of these contributions was raised via five personal receptions held for the governor-elect in four cities (Austin, Dallas, Houston, and Midland). For example, individual tickets for the Midland reception, hosted by the local petroleum club, reportedly cost a minimum of $5,000. During this period of intensive fund-raising activity, White received contributions of $10,000 or more from each of at least ninety donors, including individuals and PACS.

Many of these postelection contributors had been supporters all along and were merely augmenting their previous contributions, but others had been major supporters of, and contributors to, the Clements campaign. In Texas political parlance, major contributors to the Clements campaign were now being afforded the opportunity to grab the "late train" and help the governor-elect retire his campaign debt, as well as meet his transition expenses.[26] For example, among previous donors to Clements's campaign, Dallas businessman W. O. Bankston reportedly contributed $19,500, Houston contractor George Brown $20,000, Houston developer and banker Walter Misher $15,000, and Dallas oil man Edwin Cox, Jr., $10,000 to the White organization following the election. On the PAC side of the ledger, previous Clements supporters who joined the late train by making contributions included the realtors ($25,000), physicians ($15,000), mobile home manufacturers ($15,000), bankers ($10,000), auto dealers ($10,000), dentists ($10,000), and insurance agents ($6,000).

POSTELECTION ISSUES: APPOINTMENTS AND SURPLUSES

Throughout the postelection period at weekly press conferences. White reiterated his campaign themes: increased teachers' salaries, more support for roads and highways, utility reform (the elimination of FAF and the appointment of consumer advocates to PUC), and prison reform and expansion. Two additional issues developed during this period, receiving increasing public comment and media attention: Governor Clements's lame-duck appointments to major state agencies, boards, and commissions, and a suddenly discovered budget crisis in the state. Although both issues receive more detailed discussion later, they require a brief discussion at this point.

Only a few weeks before the election, veteran Democratic state supreme court chief justice Joe Greenhill announced his immediate resignation in order to accept a position with an Austin law firm.[27] Greenhill's sudden departure came so late in the election calendar that the state Democratic central committee was not authorized by law to select a replacement for him on the general election ballot. Thus, the choice of his successor fell to the incumbent Republican governor, Clements. Shortly after the election and Clements's defeat, fifteen state Democratic senators (enough to block a senate confirmation) sent Clements a joint letter suggesting that the vacant supreme court position not be filled until after the inauguration of the governor-elect.[28] The governor refused their request, setting off the initial spark that eventually evolved into a major controversy over Clements's lame-duck appointment actions. Pending before the state senate during its 1983 session would be the confirmation of some 500 appointments made by Clements after the 1981 session. Furthermore, Clements could fill between 150 and 200 already vacant or soon-to-be-vacant positions before his term expired. The governor-elect publicly stated that he would have no problem with Clements's making the appointments as long as he was personally consulted about them and his advice heeded, an offer that Clements ignored. On November 24 Clements announced that he was appointing a scheduled-to-retire member of the court (Jack Pope) to serve as chief justice to complete Greenhill's term.[29] From this point on, the growing debate among Democrats, especially among senators and the governor-elect, was over whether or not to deny confirmation automatically to Clements's lame-duck appointments.

The second evolving issue dealt with the state's budgetary health.

Throughout the campaign both Clements and White had painted a rosy picture of the condition of the state treasury, in that Comptroller Bullock had projected at the end of July that an additional $5.1 billion in revenue ($1.3 billion remaining from 1982–83 and $3.8 billion in 1983–84 revenue growth) would be available to the 1983 legislature for current program expansions or new programs.[30] The comptroller's projections had provided the basis for the planks in the governor-elect's platform on increased teachers' salaries, welfare payments, highway funding, prison construction, and the like, all without a need for major tax increase. However, as the Texas economy gradually worsened after the election, the comptroller began to hint that his July estimate had been too optimistic and that he would more than likely have to revise his projection downward. By mid-December, Bullock was saying that his projected budget surplus was not materializing because of significant decreases in sales, as well as oil- and gas-production, taxes.[31] This sudden budgetary change placed a major constraint upon White's ability to follow through on his campaign program.

THE INAUGURATION

As one might expect, the inauguration of a governor is a major social and political event in Texas, especially to many residents of the Austin area. It usually involves many activities, much organizational planning, the expenditure of a tidy sum of money, and much media coverage and comment.

The main activities associated with the January 18, 1983, inauguration were as follows: 7:00 P.M. of evening before: victory dinner at $50 a plate sponsored by state Democratic central committee; 8:00 A.M.: governor's volunteer breakfast, by invitation only, hosted by White and Hobby to honor campaign workers—3,000 of those invited, or more than expected, showed up, and the breakfast was moved from a hotel ballroom to the city coliseum; 10:00 A.M.: nondenominational prayer service at a Baptist church, with early arrival suggested; high noon: the inaugural ceremony at south portico of the capitol—White was officially sworn in at 12:13 by Chief Justice Pope, taking the oath on the Sam Houston Bible; a nineteen-gun salute preceded White's delivery of a brief eight-point "foundations of greatness" address reportedly written by former LBJ speechwriter Robert Hardesty; 12:30 P.M.: inaugural luncheon at $6 each—people munched on fajitas and ice cream cones under two large and brightly striped tents erected on capitol grounds; 3:00 P.M.: inaugural parade along Congress Avenue, with university and high school marching bands, floats, precision military drill units, and fly-overs by various military aircraft; and evening: not just one but three inaugural balls, including an informal one at $15 per ticket and two separate black-tie affairs at $50 per head, one for north Texans and the other for south Texans—with White and his wife, Linda Gale, leading a grand march and dancing to "Waltz Across Texas" at each ball.[32]

Needless to say, such an array of activities required extensive organization. The group leading this effort was the Austin Inaugural Committee, its 130 members organized into twelve subcommittees. Appointment to this committee is customarily regarded as indicating one's closeness to the new fountainhead of power in state government. Members had been White supporters during the campaign. The lobbyist for the Texas Auto Dealers Association publicly lamented the fact that he could not chair the parade committee this time around because he had backed Clements during the campaign.[33] The Austin Inaugural Committee was chaired by two women, one the wife of the Austin businessman and White kitchen-cabinet member referred to earlier and the other the wife of the treasurer of White's campaign organization. The committee's operating budget reportedly totaled $500,000, with $300,000 derived from the sale of tickets to the inaugural activities and the remainder from private contributions. Again, it should be emphasized that no public funds were spent for this component of the gubernatorial transition.

ORGANIZING AND STAFFING THE GOVERNOR'S OFFICE

Before the inauguration transition team members directed much attention to the organizational format and staffing procedures to be employed by the incoming administration. Working closely with the Austin office of a national professional management consulting firm and others, White and his team eventually adopted an organizational structure arranged along pyramidal, hierarchal lines. (See figure 1.) Functionally, this new organization also reflected a synthesis of two focuses, one oriented toward clientele (press, legislature, selected publics) and one more oriented toward process and program (budget, planning).

Essentially, White's office was to have an executive assistant, or chief of staff, through which all staff communications to the chief executive

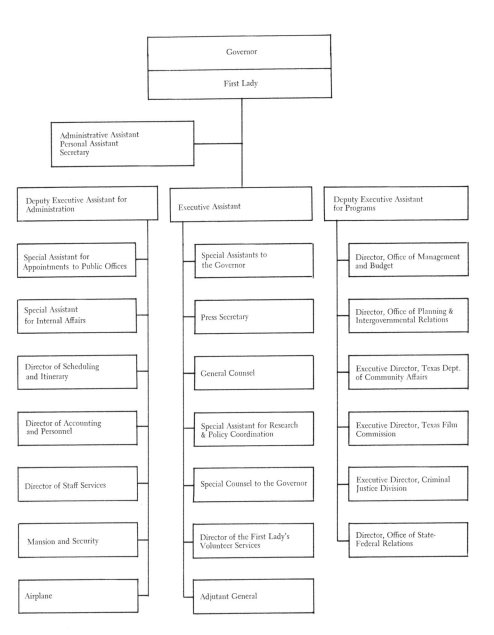

Figure I. Organization of the Governor's Office

would flow. Reporting to this executive assistant would be the two deputy executive assistants in charge of major divisions (administration and programs) and several key aides. The administration division, responsible for the internal administrative operations of the governor's office, contained seven sections, most of which were headed by a special assistant or director. The sections were appointments (coordinating gubernatorial appointments to state agencies, boards, commissions), internal affairs (a statutory office created in 1973 to deal with equal employment opportunity matters), scheduling (coordinating the governor's appointment/appearance schedule), accounting/personnel (purchasing, payroll, bookkeeping, clerical recruitment, personnel files), staff services (mail distribution, tracking correspondence, mailing list, word processing), mansion and security, and airplane. The program division consisted of six separate offices or agencies, each headed by a director or executive director and responsible for a designated program area. These offices were management and budget (budget preparation, veto messages, financial management), planning and intergovernmental relations (planning research, policy initiation, program review), department of community affairs (technical assistance to communities in the delivery of local services), criminal justice (promotion of crime prevention programs, criminal justice planning), film commission (promoter of the film industry's use of state), and federal-state relations (central office in Washington, D.C.). The organizational format provided that several key persons, in addition to the two division heads, should report directly to the chief of staff: press secretary, general counsel (bill review, pardon and parole review), research and policy coordinator (speech writing, position papers, issue research), special counsel (legislative liaison), first lady's volunteer services, adjutant general, and special assistants (ad hoc assignments tailored to the persons available or to specific problems, including staffing special task forces, assisting with legislative programs, or working as liaison with key constituent groups).

How did this organizational structure differ from that employed by White's predecessor? First, the Clements structure was more horizontal and diffuse; the directors of most program agencies or offices reported to him through his executive assistant. The rationale for the more centralized chain of command under the White scheme was to reduce significantly the increasing competition that had evolved among these agencies for the governor's personal attention during the preceding two administrations. A second main distinction between the White and

Clements formats was that the budget and planning functions were combined in one office under Clements, whereas each was assigned to a separate entity under White. White's people reasoned that the long-term state planning function of the governor's office should be substantially upgraded, or emphasized, during his administration and that this was less likely to occur if it continued to be closely associated with shorter-term budgetary considerations.

Most of those initially appointed to several of the key positions in the new governor's office were campaign operatives, supporters, or friends. For example, the chief of staff was Pike Powers, a personal friend and supporter who had most recently held a lobbying position in Austin for the prominent Houston-based law firm of Fulbright and Jaworski. Jim Nelson, a lawyer and former administrative aide in the attorney general's office, was appointed deputy assistant for administration, and Ed Grisham (a key member of the transition team) was selected to be deputy executive assistant for programs. Dwayne Holman, the governor's campaign manager, became the special assistant for appointments; Dennis Thomas, a former staff member of the previous two Democratic administrations, became the director of the office of management and budget. Women and minority supporters were duly recognized: Mary Hardesty (research and policy coordination special assistant), Sarah Weddington (state-federal relations director), Ralph Quintanilla (department of community affairs executive director), and Gilbert Pena (criminal justice executive director).

By mid-April the equivalent of 215 individuals were on the payroll of the governor's office full time. Some were permanent employees; others were temporary employees who had been hired for special tasks. (For example, Susan McBee, a former state representative from Del Rio, was a temporary special assistant on the staff whose work focused primarily upon legislative liaison activities.) Of these 215 people, 114 had been brought on board by the new administration, including at least 13 ex-staffers from White's attorney general's office. Of the people who had served in the previous administration, 79 (including 71 originally hired by Clements and 8 by Democrats Smith or Briscoe) had left the governor's office as the result of either resignation or involuntary termination. As has been the custom in Texas politics, the gubernatorial transition had resulted in a significant turnover in the staff of the governor's office.

What kind of people became members of the new governor's staff, and what was the general atmosphere in the governor's office after the

White staffers moved into the capitol on inauguration day? An observer points out some interesting qualities of this new environment, especially in comparison with the previous administration:

> Nowhere is the evidence of change more visible than in the capitol quarters of the governor and his staff; even a visitor who had spent the last six months in hibernation would know that power had changed hands. Under Bill Clements, the office had a corporate feel: women in tailored dresses, young men in three-piece suits and blow-dried hairstyles, clean air and clean ashtrays, and an aura of discipline and confidence. Under White, women wear skirts and blouses, many men are in short sleeves, and the atmosphere comes close to the chaos of a political boiler room.[34]

STATE OF THE STATE: A NEW ANGLE

On Thursday, January 27, White delivered a twenty-eight-minute state of the state message to the recently convened legislature.[35] In his message White recommended that the legislature take action on a number of the commitments that he had made during the campaign. Teachers' salaries should be increased by 24 percent, a measure so important that White placed an emergency tag on it so that the legislature could give it immediate consideration.[36] Other proposals included harsher penalties for DWI offenders, more narcotics enforcement officers, a new veterans' housing loan program, overhaul of the state's unemployment compensation program, and a new university building program.[37]

The issue that received the most attention, however, was utility regulation. White had concluded that the only way of making the PUC more responsive to consumer interests was by changing the method of selecting its members, from appointment by the governor to popular election.[38] White decribed the PUC as the "captive handmaiden of monopolistic utilities" and believed that the only way to make commissioners accountable to the public was to have them stand for election. White then announced the start of a nine-day media blitz in which he would attempt to persuade the public to support his position on the issue and contact their representatives and senators. The media campaign, consisting of thirty-second television and radio announcements, as well as newspaper ads, would cost approximately $180,000; this money would come out of his campaign treasury.[39]

Lawmakers' reactions to White's proposal were less than enthusiastic. Lieutenant Governor Hobby, normally a White supporter, argued that electing the commissioners would not make a great difference in utility rates and that the Texas ballot was already too long.[40] Consumer groups were split on the question; investor-owned utilities and cooperatives lined up against the proposal. Even after the extensive and expensive media campaign, few lawmakers who had been opposed changed their minds on the matter. On April 6, when voting on a sunset-generated measure to renew the life of the PUC, the senate turned down, 19 to 10, three amendments that would have made positions on the PUC elective. Subsequent efforts by White supporters in the house of representatives to resurrect this proposal on May 16 were tabled by substantial margins (105–39, 109–37, and 107–37). The legislature's action represented a key setback in White's efforts to implement his legislative program.

Appointments

One of the major political powers that the Texas governor traditionally wields is that of appointment. Most of the myriad departments and agencies that constitute the executive branch are governed by boards or commissions, service on many of which involves only part-time work. The common practice has been for the governor to appoint the members of these governing boards or commissions, the terms of members usually extending beyond the four-year term of the chief executive. Most governors have viewed their appointive powers as especially important in two regards. First, because the administrative heads of many departments and agencies are appointed by and responsible to their respective boards or commissions, a governor views the authority to appoint board or commission members as a means of playing a central role in overseeing the normal administrative operations and the decision making within such departments or agencies. Furthermore, Texas governors have traditionally regarded their appointment prerogatives as a means of rewarding their campaign workers and supporters.

Over the years, as the executive branch has expanded, the number of agency, board, and commission positions subject to gubernatorial appointment during a four-year period has grown to the point that today they number about 4,000, approximately 2,000 of them subject to a two-thirds confirmation vote by the senate. The expiration dates for members' terms are spread across the calendar year. No attention has been given to establishing one expiration date for all agencies and boards. Although there may be some advantage in having different dates—the governor's appointment work load is spread out over the year—such a system also has the potential for generating problems. Foremost among them is the ambiguity and possible controversy surrounding appointments that are made during gubernatorial transition periods—after a new governor has been elected but has not formally assumed office.

LAME-DUCK APPOINTMENTS

The 1982 transition was ripe for such a controversy. For the first time in over 100 years, the traditionally dominant party was reassuming power after a brief interruption. In addition, it was apparent that the personal bitterness between the two candidates generated during the long, exhausting campaign was lingering on. And although historical precedents in the area of interim appointments did exist, they were inconsistent and applied only to a few cases.

From election to inauguration day, White argued that unless he was closely consulted, Clements should dispense with making appointments to fill vacancies or regular terms on boards and commissions. After all, he had been elected by the people to be the state's chief executive for the next four years. Clements, on the other hand, argued that he was only following constitutional and statutory mandates by filling such positions and that departments and agencies would lack leadership and direction if vacancies were to go unfilled. Besides, Clements added, he had honored the midnight appointments of his predecessor after assuming office in 1979. As the number of Clements's appointments gradually increased during the transition period, White's criticisms also magnified. About one week before his inauguration White publicly charged Clements with trying to undermine his new administration and with being the only governor in the state's political history who was wishing his successor future ill fortunes.[41]

Although approximately 171 vacancies existed or occurred before Clements left office on January 18, he chose to fill 105 of them. A number of these appointments were to relatively prestigious positions. For example, Clements appointed ex-governor and Democrat-turned-Republican John Connally, along with two others, to the University of Texas regents, and long-term and retiring Democratic speaker of the state house of representatives Billy Clayton (who had tacitly supported him in the election), along with two others, to the Texas A&M regents. Clements also tried to reward some of his staff with these postelection appointments, including his executive assistant, special assistant for gubernatorial appointments, and director of the office of budget and planning. During this period he also filled major positions on the employment commission, the veterans' land board, the human resources board, the mental health and mental retardation board, various university boards, and others.

What was White's posture with regard to the senate confirmation of these 104 appointments, excluding the chief justice of the supreme court? Although not emphasized publicly because, as he noted on at least one occasion, some of these appointees were friends, indications are that White favored a blanket return of all 104 nominations to him by the senate once he was inaugurated.[42] Although White favored this blanket approach to resolving the controversy over lame-duck appointments, the senate votes needed to pass his proposed plan never materialized. At the most only twelve of the sixteen senators needed reportedly were willing to support him on the senate floor. Although having a 26-to-5 Democratic majority, a number of Democrats were not willing to back him because many had at least one of the 104 appointees as prominent constituents in their districts or regarded them as friends. Others argued that some of the appointments involved such minor positions that returning all of Clements's appointments was not warranted. Finally, all five Republicans in the chamber were disinclined to support a proposal that could be regarded as a slap in the face to their recently retired gubernatorial standard bearer.

The senate proceeded to vote on each of Clements's 104 appointments case by case. The chamber consented to return 59 of the appointments to White for his disposition. To what extent was the return of the appointments contested? Substantial disagreement existed over most appointments, except those on which senatorial courtesy was invoked. An analysis of the eighty-one contested roll calls (sometimes more than one appointment was voted on in a roll call) indicates that the moderate-liberal Democrats formed the base of White's support. Eight Democrats supported White 100 percent of the time, and another six Democrats voted against White on only one to five occasions. On the other hand, five Republicans and five conservative Democrats voted in all cases against White's requests, save one abstention on grounds of a personal relationship, and another three conservative Democrats gave only two, four, and ten supporting votes, respectively. The swing Democrats, who often provided the margin of victory, voted with the governor on thirteen to sixty-six of the eighty-one votes.

In general senators were more likely to return appointees to the major university boards of regents and to professional regulatory bodies. On the other hand White was less successful in persuading senators to return appointments to judicial offices, river authorities, soil conservation commissions, and such commissions as those dealing with history, the sesquicentennial, and the arts.

As for the appointments not returned to White, only two were subsequently rejected by the senate in the normal confirmation procedure. The governor, as of mid-May, had filled forty-five of the fifty-nine returned appointments. Somewhat surprisingly, given the amount of conflict surrounding these forty-five appointees, eleven were people who had initially been appointed by Clements and subsequently returned to White, including Clements's Harris County campaign manager.

One final question about appointments centers on the relationship between political support for the governor and subsequent appointment to a board or commission; that is, to what extent did the governor appoint individuals who (1) had made substantial contributions to his campaign, (2) had worked on his campaign, or (3) were part of the transition? To answer this question for the Texas governor during 1983, we operationalized the terms as follows. A significant contributor was designated as anyone who had provided a $1,000 contribution at any time during the campaign ($N = 631$). Working significantly in the campaign was more difficult to determine. We settled on two indicators: being a county coordinator ($N = 272$), or receiving campaign contributions from the campaign committee ($N = 320$). Working on the transition was operationalized as being a member of the 200-member transition committee.

Analysis of Governor White's first 128 appointments requiring senate confirmation indicates that 35 individuals, or 27 percent of appointees, were somehow tied to the campaign, with 17 contributors leading the way. Although these figures may not seem to provide overwhelming evidence of the linkage, they are moderately impressive for two reasons. First, included in the 128 are people who were returned to White by the senate and reappointed by him. Second, the operational indicators cannot capture all, or even most, of those who gave significant effort to the campaign.

The Budget

Several key factors are involved in the biennial budgetary decision-making process in Texas. Playing an especially critical role are the members who make up the Legislative Budget Board (LBB), which consists of the legislative leaders of both chambers and their designees. For several months before a new legislature convenes, the LBB, assisted by its professional staff, reviews the appropriations requests from the administrative departments and agencies and formulates an independent legislative budget proposal—one of a few in the United States—for submission to the next session. In addition, the governor puts together his own budget proposal and presents it to a joint session of the legislature. In point of fact, of course, two gubernatorial budget proposals are presented to the legislature when a transition occurs, the one proposed by the incoming administration usually receiving more serious consideration. After these proposals are made, the legislature, working through its appropriations committees, leaders, and others, must decide what programs to fund and at what levels. Even here, however, the Texas legislature does not have as much discretion as is the case in many states, for the state constitution mandates that it can appropriate (unless a four-fifths majority overrules) only a total sum that the state comptroller certifies will be available during the next biennium. Thus, the state's chief tax collector and accountant can impose a major constraint upon legislative budget decisions via revenue projections, or estimates.

Many of the programs advocated by Mark White during his successful 1982 campaign were based on the premise that ample resources would be available in the state treasury to fund them. Over the summer the state comptroller had estimated that $5.1 billion in additional revenues should be available for the 1984–85 biennium. Following the election, however, the outlook for the state's economy and revenue began to deteriorate to the point that, by mid-December, the comptroller generally acknowledged that his previously projected new revenues were drying up. About the same time White acknowledged at a press conference the strong possibility of a similar scenario and suggested that state taxes consequently might have to be raised (or modified in the case of the gasoline tax). As if he were still campaigning, he further speculated that a significant portion of the state's increasingly obvious financial problems could also be attributed to the blunders of the outgoing administration. A few weeks later, in releasing the LBB's $33.5-

billion proposed budget, Lieutenant Governor Hobby reiterated that the state's revenue outlook was no longer as promising as it had been and acknowledged that from $1.2 to $1.5 billion in new revenues would have to be raised to fund the board's biennial appropriations package, which included an 11-percent increase (exclusive of step increases) in teachers' salaries.[43] For the first time since 1971, Texas state government was on the verge of a financial crisis.

BULLOCK'S BULLETS

As the legislature convened in early January, Comptroller Bullock announced that he was reducing his previous revenue estimate by $1.5 billion, attributing the reduction to a major drop in collections of sales and severance taxes. Oddly enough, he also announced that he was becoming a candidate for the Democratic nomination for governor in 1986, thus putting himself in what appeared to be a nearly adversarial role with White. Some observers speculated that Bullock was not particularly fond of White, as the two had clashed on at least two occasions when White was serving as secretary of state and as attorney general. In addition, although generally regarded as a professionally competent administrator, Bullock had received much media attention over the years for his somewhat erratic personal behavior and his excesses (alcoholism, chain smoking, depression, and speeding).

Throughout the 1983 session Bullock announced further reductions in his revenue estimates. On March 8, for example, he announced a $861-million reduction in future additional revenues and followed this on April 8 with a further $1-billion reduction in conjunction with his final projecton. Projected new revenues had decreased by $3.4 billion over a three-month period.

THE GOVERNOR'S BUDGET

After some delay White delivered his budget message to the legislature in mid-March. The White budget provided for $32.9 billion in expenditures over the biennium, or $1.4 billion more than Bullock said would be available.[44] White based his recommendations on the budget originally proposed by the LBB; at this point the LBB's budget was $1.6 billion over the comptroller's estimates.

To what extent did Governor White deviate from either Governor

Clements's recommendations or those of the LBB? In answering this question, we combined budgetary figures for 1984 and 1985. Compared with Clements's budget, on slightly less than two-thirds of the budget items ($N = 213$), the White recommendation was within + or − 10 percent. In slightly over 22 percent of the budget items, the recommendation exceeded Clements's figures by at least 10 percent, thirty-two entries were more than 20 percent greater. Included among the major increases were those dealing with the various courts, as well as with some of the agencies that were tied to his campaign or constituencies, e.g., the Public Utilities Commission or the Industrial Accident Board. On the other hand, for eleven entries he slashed the budget by 10 percent to 20 percent, and in nineteen cases the cuts exceeded 20 percent. For example, White severely reduced Clements's requests for the Aircraft Pooling Board and the Texas National Guard Armory Board.

A comparison of White's budget figures with those of the LBB shows that more than 70 percent of the figures for the various agencies were within 10 percent of each other; 27 percent were in excess of the LBB proposal by 20 percent or more. White also made some severe cuts in comparison with the LBB recommendations, with eleven agencies receiving less than 80 percent of the LBB figure. In summary, White's figures did not completely diverge from the LBB or Clements's, but he did tend to establish different priorities.

White recommended increased funding for teachers' salaries (24 percent), AFDC recipients, narcotics enforcement, and highway programs but also advised some reduction in the LBB's recommendations for capital construction, corrections, and higher education. In addition, a major portion of his augmented highway construction program was to be funded through the sale of bonds, a measure immediately opposed by both the comptroller and the lieutenant governor. White also suggested that some additional revenues could be picked up by increasing automobile license fees and the "sin" taxes on alcohol, cigarettes, and amusement/video arcade machines.

Overall, legislative reaction to White's budgetary proposals was cool; the house was especially unresponsive. Although newly elected Democratic speaker Gib Lewis and others reportedly had initially flirted with the idea that some additional revenues could be raised by changing the automobile license fee formula from weight to value, they withheld their support for this proposal after criticism appeared in the media and a major lobbying effort by the auto dealers' group brought pressure to bear.[45] Although more prone than the house to sympathizing with White on his budget, the senate was prohibited by the state constitution from initiating a revenue bill designed to accomplish White's objectives. The result was a standoff between the governor and the legislature, with the legislature eventually deciding to pare back on LBB-recommended spending levels and not to increase taxes.

Feeling that a dramatic move was necessary if his legislative program was to prevail, White in mid-May proposed a $1.27-billion tax increase, which was to be derived primarily from increased levies on alcohol, cigarettes, and amusement games. Noting that these new revenues would be used primarily to finance a minimum 24-percent increase in teachers' salaries, White decided to reach out, or go public, again by launching a series of appearances and media events around the state, including visits to primary and secondary schools and even special luncheons with prominent bankers and investors. His efforts went for naught; the legislature successfully resisted his attempts to increase taxes to provide the funds for the programs that he had campaigned on so vigorously the previous year. In the end White's inability to generate a broad base of legislative support for his fiscal program, plus the ever-increasing constraints on the budget by the declining economy (as interpreted by recently announced gubernatorial candidate Bullock), sounded the death knell to his commitment to a minimum 24-percent increase for teachers' salaries.

The Transition: A Brief Postscript

Our sojourn through the 1982–83 Texas gubernatorial transition would be incomplete if we did not attempt to reflect at least briefly upon this process, pinpoint a few of its weaknesses, and suggest alternative courses of action. First, two important caveats are in order. Although the authors are supporters of a strong legislative branch of state government, many of our observations are based on the premise that a new state governor today should be provided with the mechanisms that permit him to be not only the chief administrator of the executive branch but also an effective initiator of public policies in his dealings with the legislative branch. Second, it should also be emphasized that the authors are cognizant of the fact that the dominant political culture of Texas is conservative, one so steeped in tradition and the status quo that any proposal for wholesale reform of the transition process would be unrealistic. Yet, because important changes are occurring in the state—increasing urbanization, industrialization, and two-party competition come immediately to mind—perhaps serious consideration should be given to a very select number of limited modifications in the transition process.

We have found that the gubernatorial transition can best be described as a free-lance affair, with most of its components at a given time stemming from a mixture of tradition and the personal predispositions of the key actors in it. Few, if any, expectations regarding the duties, obligations, and responsibilities of these actors have been formalized in constitutional or statutory law. Most support, financial and otherwise, for an incoming administration comes from the private sector. The newly inaugurated governor, as well as the upper chamber of the recently convened legislature, may be confronted with conflict and turmoil surrounding the disposition of important executive branch appointments made by the previous governor only a short time before he relinquishes office.

What alternative courses of action might streamline the transition process in Texas? First, some planning and implementation for the transition by the incumbent administration before the general election might be mandated by the legislature. For example, the administration could be required to prepare briefing books, or papers, providing updated basic information about major state governmental programs, the resources (including a space and equipment inventory) available to the governor's office, and alternative administrative formats for organizing the governor's office. Such information should be provided to a newly elected governor immediately following his election.

Second, the legislature should seriously consider providing some public funds to the governor-elect for several selected transition activities.[46] Foremost among the activities deserving such support would be those associated with the newly elected governor's efforts to organize and recruit staff, acquire temporary office space, equipment, and supplies, travel on necessary business, and research to prepare his policy recommendations to the legislature. A fixed amount should be available to a governor-elect the day following the general election, as has been the case for some time at the national level and, more recently, in an increasing number of states. Private financial support, on the other hand, can continue to be solicited for the more symbolic activities associated with the transfer of gubernatorial power, most of which occur on inauguration day.

Third, the appointments process could be streamlined to discourage the type of intense conflict that surrounded it during the 1982–83 transition. Although there is some advantage to spreading out the beginning dates for the new terms of board and commission members over a period of time, the problems that can occur when such dates fall during the November–January transition period were dramatically illustrated during the Clements-White transition; White had to devote much of his political energy and capital to the problem upon assuming office. In our opinion governors-elect should have the power to make such appointments, and although the 1982 legislature did undertake some changes to deal with the overall problem, further steps should be taken to streamline and rationalize the appointments process.

Fourth, and a somewhat related matter: perhaps the appointments process could be further streamlined if the senate relinquished its power to confirm appointments to key positions in the governor's office itself. For example, the head of the community affairs department must undergo senate scrutiny, a procedure that may extend several months into a new administration and limit the nominee's initial administrative effectiveness. If this agency performs salient staff functions for the governor, then we doubt the wisdom and need for the politically intrusive senatorial confirmation of its head. On the other hand, if the agency performs functions characteristic of a line department, it should probably be formally recognized as such and reorganized, taken out of the governor's office.

Fifth, and finally, if the Texas governor should play a more effective role in initiating and developing public policy, perhaps it would be appropriate to permit the new governor to assume office earlier than is now the case (approximately one week after the legislature formally convenes in mid-January of odd-numbered years). The new governor and staff would probably find such additional time beneficial for more adequately educating themselves on present state administrative programs and personnel as they prepare their recommendations—both substantive and budgetary—to the legislature. Or perhaps, especially since the present legislature only meets in regular session for 140 days during odd-numbered years, the newly inaugurated governor's policy role would be enhanced if the legislature were to convene at a later date, after the governor and his staff have had adequate opportunity to settle into their capitol offices.

Wisconsin's Gubernatorial Transition

WILLIAM T. GORMLEY, JR.

The Campaign

"THE VEST" RETIRES

On April 23, 1982, Republican Governor Lee Dreyfus and his wife, Joyce, grinned appreciatively as hundreds of admirers greeted their arrival at a noontime rally in Wisconsin's capitol rotunda with thunderous applause. Dreyfus, the fortieth governor of Wisconsin, was expected to seek reelection and was expected to win. Although Dreyfus was not invulnerable, he had returned a $1-million surplus to the taxpayers and had successfully promoted a variety of tax reforms, as promised four years earlier. He was photogenic in his bright red vest, a trademark over the years. Moreover, he was charismatic, persuasive, and charming. A former speech professor and university chancellor, Dreyfus had written his Ph.D. dissertation on the subject of mass propaganda. Even his detractors conceded that he was terrific on television and on the stump and that he would be tough to beat.

Thus, it came as a shock when Dreyfus announced that he would not seek reelection to a second term. Without elaborating, Dreyfus simply said that he and his wife had decided to return to private life. Some observers noted that growing budget deficits seemed to require tax increases and fierce political combat, neither of which appealed to Dreyfus. The thrill of being governor had long since faded. As for more personal considerations, Dreyfus and his wife seemed genuinely to enjoy each other's company, and as governor Dreyfus could spend little time with her. As a private citizen, he might recapture his lost leisure time.

If his decision was good for Dreyfus, it was disastrous for the Republican party. Republican politicians had assumed that Dreyfus would run again. His late withdrawal from the race left his party in the lurch. Republican representative John Albert vividly recalled his reaction to Dreyfus's announcement: "I felt like I had been kicked in the stomach." If Republicans were dismayed by his decision, Democrats were elated. Democrats Anthony Earl and James Wood, who had already announced for the governorship, recognized that the Democratic nomination had suddenly become a valuable prize. Former Governor Martin Schreiber, who was considering a race for the Democratic nomination, reached a similar conclusion and prepared to enter the race. Two Republicans, Terry Kohler and Lowell Jackson, also decided to run. The race for governor was on.

VISIBILITY AND IDEOLOGY

Although Schreiber waited until June to announce formally for the governorship, he was widely regarded as the Democratic front-runner. A former governor, Schreiber could argue that he had the best kind of experience a gubernatorial candidate could possibly have. The fact that Schreiber was popular in vote-rich Milwaukee and that he was certain to receive the strong endorsement of Milwaukee Mayor Henry Maier augured well for the Schreiber campaign. Schreiber was also expected to benefit from the popularity of his father, who had served as president of the Milwaukee Common Council. All in all, Schreiber's prospects seemed good.

Yet Earl was a formidable opponent. Intelligent, articulate, and personable, Earl was highly regarded by politicians of both parties. Indeed, Lee Dreyfus himself once referred to Earl as a "class act." Earl had considerable experience in government, as a legislator and as a bureaucrat. In 1969 he was elected to the state legislature from Wausau. Two years later he was chosen as house majority leader—a remarkable achievement for such a junior member. In 1975 Earl became secretary of administration under Governor Patrick Lucey. Later that year, he became secretary of the Department of Natural Resources, a post he held until 1980, when he resigned to practice law and lay the groundwork for the gubernatorial campaign.

Despite his experience in government, Earl lacked Schreiber's name recognition. In all probability Anthony Earl was less familiar to the Wisconsin electorate than Earl Anthony, the popular bowler. Yet Earl was building a strong, vital political organization. Long identified with the liberal wing of the Democratic party, Earl emphasized his support for such liberal causes as the women's movement, the environmental movement, and a nuclear-freeze referendum, which would be on the primary ballot. In doing so, he attracted an impressive corps of volunteers, whose enthusiasm for Earl was contagious. Earl's organization was exceptionally strong in Dane County and its largest city, Madison, long recognized as a liberal enclave.

Wood, a former Carroll College professor and head of the Wisconsin Center for Public Policy, was not considered a serious contender for the Democratic nomination. His only experience in government was as an aide to Earl, when Earl served as secretary of the Department of Administration. Moreover, Wood often seemed stilted, overly ambitious, and overly serious. But Wood could be a spoiler in the race. As a liberal from Madison, he was likely to siphon off votes from Earl.

If the Democratic primary looked interesting, the Republican primary promised to be a mismatch. As early as May, it appeared almost certain that Kohler would be the Republican nominee. Chairman of the board of the Vollrath Corporation, headquartered in Sheboygan, Kohler was a successful businessman at a time when Wisconsin needed to attract and retain business. Kohler also had name recognition in his favor because both his father and his grandfather had been governors of Wisconsin (and, less auspiciously, because the Kohler name appeared on plumbing fixtures across the state). In addition, Kohler had access to corporate money.

Jackson, a University of Wisconsin Extension professor until he joined the Dreyfus cabinet in 1979, suffered from a lack of visibility and a shortage of cash. Although Jackson received high marks for competence as secretary of transportation and, later, of industry, labor and human relations, he was not well known outside Madison. It would be extremely difficult for him to build an effective organization in time to win the Republican primary in September. Jackson's only hope was to lure Kohler into a series of damaging debates. In a battle of wits Jackson would come out on top.

In an effort to smoke Kohler out, Jackson challenged the front-runner to a debate at the Republican convention in Milwaukee, scheduled for June 4. When Kohler declined, as expected, Jackson asked Earl, who quickly agreed in an effort to remedy his own visibility problem. Both candidates scored a public relations triumph with that debate and impressed members of the press corps with their knowledge and intelligence. They also impressed each other, despite the fact that Jackson was as conservative as Earl was liberal. To their surprise, the candidates discovered that they agreed on a number of issues, such as the need for new highways.

Earl and Jackson debated a total of six times during the primary campaign. All five candidates also appeared together several times at candidate forums, two of which were televised statewide. In appearances with the other candidates Schreiber struck a moderate pose. On the need for taxes Schreiber equivocated, saying he would increase taxes only as a last resort. Earl, in contrast, openly predicted that a tax increase would be necessary and indicated a strong preference for an income tax surcharge as a progressive alternative to a sales tax increase (or higher property taxes). Earl's realism on the need for a tax increase further impressed members of the press corps, already smitten with Earl. As the primary election approached, Earl won endorsements from all but two of the twenty or more daily newspapers expressing a preference. Still, a private poll conducted by Schreiber three weeks before the primary election showed Schreiber leading Earl by a wide margin.

A DEFEAT FOR SCHLAFLY, FALWELL, AND WATT

September 14 was a gray, overcast, rainy day—the sort of day that discourages voter turnout. Yet voters turned out in record numbers, especially in liberal Dane County. As the returns rolled in, it became apparent that Kohler would win handsomely. Indeed, final returns showed Kohler trouncing Jackson 67 percent to 33 percent. In the Democratic primary, however, an upset was in the making. Early returns showed Earl doing surprisingly well in Schreiber's stronghold, Milwaukee County, and extremely well in Dane County. By midnight it was clear that Earl would be the winner.

Appearing at his campaign headquarters in Madison, Earl was jubilant. He noted with pleasure that voter approval of the nuclear freeze referendum coincided with his own electoral victory. As reported by Dan Allegretti in *The Capital Times* (September 15, 1982), he also happily reaffirmed his liberal faith: "Wisconsin in a very affirmative way said yes to the nuclear freeze. Wisconsin said yes to this state's progressive traditions. We said no to nuclear buildup. We said no to trickle down. We said no to Phyllis Schlafly (gleeful applause). We said no to James Watt and no to Jerry Falwell (wild applause)." Final returns gave Earl 46 percent, Schreiber 42 percent, and Wood 12 percent of the vote. Earl would be the Democratic nominee.

In trying to explain Earl's victory, many analysts have pointed to Earl's strong organization, described as the best in Wisconsin in thirty years. Certainly, the Earl organization was impressive. Volunteers telephoned and canvassed and licked envelopes until their tongues were dry. Fund-raising appeals were highly successful, and many people contributed small amounts of money to the Earl campaign. Thanks to these contributions, Earl was able to outspend Schreiber by about two to one.

Yet this begs the question of why so many people enthusiastically supported Earl to the point of campaigning for him or contributing money to his campaign. To understand that enthusiasm, it is necessary to recall the mood of November 1980. Wisconsin liberals, who had grown complacent, were jolted out of their lethargy by Reagan's victory (nationwide and in Wisconsin) and by the unexpected defeat of Senator Gaylord Nelson, principal spokesman for the Wisconsin left. Many liberals decided they could no longer remain on the sidelines. So they worked their tails off for Earl and for the nuclear freeze referendum.

This was especially apparent in Dane County, long a liberal bastion. Earl had a better telephone and canvassing operation in Dane County than anywhere else. He also received more contributions from Dane County than from Milwaukee County, despite the latter's greater size. In Dane County, as elsewhere, a broad cross section of citizens voted for Tony Earl. But the liberals got the Earl message across. Earl's margin of victory was provided by Dane County, which gave him a margin of 25,000 votes in an election decided by 14,000 votes. Without the strong support of Dane County liberals, Earl would have lost the primary election.

ISSUES AND IMAGES

Early in the campaign Terry Kohler identified the top three issues as he saw them: jobs, jobs, jobs. As chairman of the board of a $93-million-per-year firm, Kohler argued that he was well qualified to deal with the jobs issue: "I have met a payroll," he reminded audiences. "I have built a factory." Clearly, unemployment was a major issue. Throughout the campaign Wisconsin's unemployment rate exceeded the national average. In July the rate was 10 percent; in August the rate climbed to 10.7 percent; in September the rate reached 11.3 percent. In Beloit and Janesville, heavily dependent on the auto industry, the figures were even higher.

Yet the jobs issue backfired on Kohler. As the press reported, Kohler's company had created jobs, but most of them were in Tennessee and Alabama. The jobs Kohler seemed adept at creating were outside Wisconsin! Kohler even acknowledged that he was considering opening a new plant in Mexico. When Kohler sought to speak before the AFL-CIO in La Crosse, he was rebuffed. He showed up anyway and was unceremoniously escorted out of the hall. Earl, in contrast, was warmly received.

Throughout the campaign Kohler seemed to suffer from foot-in-mouth disease. A tax increase, he argued, would be unnecessary because projected budget deficits were too high. When the president of the Wisconsin Taxpayers Alliance, James Morgan, predicted a short-term deficit of $100 million, Kohler told a business group that Morgan was "flat wrong." Later, Kohler apologized to Morgan, noting that "too many numbers" left him confused. "I guess I can't handle them all," he conceded.

Not surprisingly, Earl capitalized on Kohler's apparent inability to cope with facts and figures. Earl's own mastery of details stood in sharp contrast. Earl's liberalism also stood in sharp contrast to Kohler's conservatism. Instead of tilting to the right in the general election campaign, Earl held steadfastly to liberal principles. He continued to stress the need for higher taxes. He continued to express a preference for progressive taxes. And he continued to articulate strong support for environmental protection, affirmative action, and freedom of choice for women. Philosophical differences between Earl and Kohler were crystal clear.

In other respects as well, it was a campaign of sharp contrasts. A burly man with broad shoulders and a thick neck, Kohler looked more like a noseguard than a statesman. A slow, unsteady speaker with a penchant for using his fingers as props, he often sounded like a high school debater who had been out partying the night before. Earl, in contrast, was lean and trim. Polished and articulate, he was a formidable debater, with a gift for clarifying and analyzing complex issues. Joint appearances by the candidates were almost always to Earl's advantage.

STICKS AND STONES

As the campaign wore on the two candidates grew weary and less polite. Increasingly, they took potshots at one another. Yet Earl managed somehow to seem both more gracious and more convincing. Ken Lamke of the *Milwaukee Sentinel* put it this way: "About the most frequently heard line in the campaign comes from Kohler: 'Tony, you just don't understand.' The second most frequently heard line may be Earl's: 'Terry, you're still confused.' The problem is that when Kohler says it, he looks and sounds like a playground bully. When Earl says it, he sounds like an altar boy offering to help the class dummy."

During the final days of the campaign Kohler staged a desperate media blitz, featuring some hard-hitting ads highly critical of Earl. One radio ad, aired in northern Wisconsin, charged that Earl "presided over the fight to take control of farmland away from farm families and give it to the bureaucrats in Madison." In a printed ad the Kohler camp charged that Earl had no jobs plan. In a televised debate with Kohler, Earl characterized both ads as "pure fiction" and demanded an apology. Although Kohler refused to back down, the ads appeared to do little damage.

Furthermore, Earl's campaign was gathering impressive momentum. Earl's intelligence, integrity, and consistency impressed the editorial boards of newspapers across the state. As election day approached, twenty-six of twenty-seven daily newspapers endorsed Earl. Earl's campaign organization, which had engineered his upset victory over Schreiber, mobilized canvassers and phone-bank operations. Earl also managed to raise nearly as much money as Kohler, so he was able to stage a media blitz of his own. Polls confirmed that Earl held a comfortable lead over Kohler.

THE LANDSLIDE

On November 2 Wisconsin voters chose Tony Earl to be their forty-first governor. By Wisconsin standards Earl's margin of victory was impressive. Earl defeated Kohler 57 percent to 43 percent—the largest margin of victory in a Wisconsin gubernatorial race in thirty years. Earl won by huge margins in Dane County (50,000 votes) and Milwaukee County (110,000 votes). He even carried Kohler's home county of Sheboygan.

Kohler was bitter, and he made no attempt to disguise his bitterness. In a speech to his supporters on election night Kohler borrowed a theme from Richard Nixon's 1962 concession speech. Noting that his father was a businessman "when that was not a bad word," Kohler blamed the mass media for his defeat. The media, he alleged, have made it impossible for a businessman to be elected governor: "The media now seem to feel that to be qualified for governor, it's necessary to be a bureaucrat." Kohler went on to predict that the tax increases Earl proposed would drive business out of Wisconsin.

Others disagreed with Kohler. "I don't think the fact that he was a businessman had anything to do with his loss whatsoever," Earl said the following day. Don Pfarrer of the *Milwaukee Journal* put it more bluntly: "The election returns seem to lead inevitably to the painful conclusion that it was Kohler himself whom the voters rejected." To many, it seemed that Kohler was not smart enough or experienced enough or articulate enough to be governor.

Yet it is doubtful that Earl could have been beaten by any Republican other than Lee Dreyfus. For if Kohler was an especially weak candidate, Earl was an especially strong one. A seasoned politician with considerable personal appeal, Earl was smooth but not slick, purposeful but not pigheaded. He was knowledgeable, capable, intelligent, consistent, and honest. He was a politician and a bureaucrat at a time when leadership and expertise were essential. He was too much for Terry Kohler.

Earl's ideology was far less important in the general election than in the primary election. Although his liberalism continued to motivate hard-core Earl supporters, the electorate as a whole was probably more impressed by his competence and intellectual integrity. Still, the election of a liberal Democratic governor in Wisconsin was an event of potential significance. In the wake of Reagan's breathtaking 1980 victory, the Democratic party was searching for a new identity. The behavior of liberal Democratic governors in economically troubled states such as Michigan, Ohio, and Wisconsin would provide insights into the viability of liberalism in a period of scarce resources and taxpayer rebellion. The Earl administration would be a crucible not just for Earl and Wisconsin but for the liberal wing of the Democratic party.

The Transition

THE PASSING OF THE BATON

In 1978 Lee Dreyfus became governor by ousting the incumbent, Martin Schreiber. The campaign left both camps tense and wary. Dreyfus, who had no real government experience, needed all the help he could get, yet he received very little. Perhaps he and his people did not ask the right questions. Perhaps the Schreiber people were hostile. Perhaps the Dreyfus people merely assumed the Schreiber people were hostile, with predictable results. In any case there was little communication between the offices of the governor and the governor-elect, exemplified by the fact that Schreiber and Dreyfus met only once during the transition period.

Schreiber, of course, had intended to win. As a result, there was no transition plan. Without a plan, arrangements were ad hoc, makeshift, and often unsatisfactory. For example, the governor-elect's transition office was squeezed into quarters so small that Dreyfus felt compelled to set up shop in a nearby hotel. The most annoying problems that arose concerned logistics—telephones, copying machines, the flow of mail, word-processing equipment. If armies cannot march without food, bureaucracies cannot operate without word processors. Yet the Dreyfus staff had to limp along without word processors for some time. More broadly, the transition from Schreiber to Dreyfus was marked by confusion, consternation, and chaos. As one Dreyfus cabinet member recalled, "In 1978 we were really bumbling around finding out where the faucets were for quite a while."

Well before the general election Dreyfus vowed that the 1982 transition would be smoother. In pursuit of that goal Dreyfus designated Lowell Jackson as his transition director. The appointment of such a prominent, capable individual signaled a commitment to be of service to the new governor, whoever he might be. There were other tangible indicators of this commitment. In mid-October, Department of Administration secretary Kenneth Lindner met separately with the two candidates and briefed them on the state's budgetary situation. At that time Lindner offered to appoint the winner's choice as budget director during the transition period. Later in October, Jackson consulted with the candidates on office space. As a result a suitable transition office for the governor-elect was available immediately after the general election. Coincidentally, the offices of the governor and governor-elect were side by side in a state office building while the governor's office in the state capitol was being renovated. This, as it turns out, facilitated communication between the outgoing and incoming staffs.

If Dreyfus was willing to help, Earl knew exactly what kind of help he needed. In a four-page memo to transition director Jackson the day after the election Earl outlined a series of specific requests for information and assistance. Earl also accepted the offer to install his own appointee as budget director. Jackson promptly set up several meetings requested by Earl. Jackson also instructed state agency heads to prepare detailed summaries of recent decisions and proposals under consideration. At Jackson's instructions, state employees prepared additional information on agency budget submissions, unclassified positions to be filled by the governor or his appointees, and other materials. In his communications Jackson stressed the need for speed and cooperation.

Although much of the information flow was handled by Jackson and by Earl's transition director, Dan Wisniewski, the governor and the governor-elect also played active roles. Earl conferred with Dreyfus the day after the election, and the two men met frequently throughout the transition process. The contrast with 1978 could not have been starker. Here was a retiring governor who was generously offering his assistance, an incoming governor who knew exactly what information he needed. The combination ensured that the transition from Dreyfus to Earl would be harmonious and efficient. Logistically and interpersonally, it is difficult to imagine a better transition.

Yet there is more to a transition than routing phone calls and mail to the right people. The challenges confronting Earl were enormous, and he knew it. In contrast to Dreyfus, who faced a huge budget surplus when he became governor, Earl faced a mammoth deficit that promised to grow even larger. House speaker Tom Loftus likened Dreyfus to the baseball pitcher who leaves the game with the bases loaded. Lowell Jackson, a more sympathetic observer, nevertheless conceded that the Earl administration faced a tougher crisis than the Dreyfus administration: "Our problem was how to get rid of $1 billion. Their problem is how to find $1 billion."

Clearly, the budget deficit would be the most immediate and the most difficult substantive problem the Earl administration would face. Appointments would also be critical, as hard times require a bureaucracy that can innovate without spending more money. Looking ahead, Earl acknowledged formidable problems, but he also expressed optimism: "There are only two things I know of that are unmanageable— New York City and the Chicago Cubs." In that spirit, Earl turned his attention to the challenges ahead.

THE DOMESTICATED CABINET

Wisconsin has long placed a premium on a strong civil service. This tradition has yielded rich rewards, in that Wisconsin's bureaucracy enjoys an excellent national reputation in a wide variety of fields. Yet

Wisconsin's emphasis on a strong civil service makes it extremely difficult for the governor to control the bureaucracy through the appointments process. Upon taking office, Earl was free to appoint a mere forty-nine full-time employees, only some of whom would have policy responsibilities. The forty-nine employees included thirty-three gubernatorial aides, six executive residence employees, seven cabinet secretaries, and three other people. Earl's appointees, in turn, would be free to appoint only sixty-three people—most of them deputies, executive assistants, and division administrators in cabinet departments. Other vacancies would occur—at the Public Service Commission, the Insurance Commission, the Banking Commission, and other agencies headed by term appointees. Indeed, some early vacancies were expected. Clearly, however, the governor's appointment powers were quite modest. Imagine the mayor of Chicago in such a setting! Well aware of these constraints, Earl resolved to play a very active role in the appointments process.

On November 1, one day before the general election, Earl huddled with several key staff members. If elected governor, Earl said, he hoped to appoint certain kinds of people to key state government jobs. Earl stated a strong preference for Wisconsin residents, on the grounds that an outsider would have difficulty adjusting to Wisconsin's unusual political culture. Earl also stressed the need to appoint people with program knowledge, system knowledge, and negotiating skills. In contrast to his Republican opponent, who viewed bureaucrats with unconcealed disdain, Earl felt that government experience in a job candidate was highly desirable. Earl also reaffirmed his campaign pledge to appoint women and minorities to key positions. More broadly, he emphasized the virtues of diversity in race, sex, age, and geography. Finally, he indicated that campaign experience was a plus and that loyal friends would not be forgotten.

Earl's cabinet appointments were largely consistent with these criteria. Of the seven appointees, two were women and one was black. Several had considerable experience in government (though not necessarily in the department they would head), and most had worked for Earl in the campaign. Only Lowell Jackson, whom Earl persuaded to head the Department of Transportation, was not a charter member of the Earl fan club. The remaining cabinet posts went to highly trusted Earl lieutenants. Michael Ley, who had worked for Earl at the Department of Natural Resources, would head the Department of Revenue. Linda Reivitz, an old friend with some experience in the health services area, would head the Department of Health and Social Services. Earl's running mate, Lieutenant Governor Jim Flynn, was tapped to run the Department of Development. Other cabinet appointees included Doris Hanson at the Department of Administration, Howard Fuller at the Department of Employment Relations, and Howard Bellman at the Department of Industry, Labor and Human Relations. All three had worked for Earl during the campaign.

Although Earl's cabinet appointees met Earl's criteria rather well, many supporters were disappointed and disillusioned, for Earl's criteria did not seem to include ideology or innovativeness. The appointment of Jackson to head the Department of Transportation struck many liberals as a betrayal of environmental principles with which Earl had been closely identified. Jackson was strongly committed to a variety of new highway projects opposed by environmentalists, whom Jackson publicly derided as "coercive utopians." The appointment of the state's most formidable conservative politician to a position of high responsibility left liberals chagrined. Liberals also expressed frustration over some of Earl's term appointments. The selection of Barbara Nichols, a former president of the American Nurses Association, to head the Department of Regulation and Licensing raised questions about the "revolving door" between regulated industries and regulatory agencies. The choice of Ness Flores, a judge with no expertise in the utilities area, to head the Public Service Commission (PSC) led consumer advocates to wonder whether consumers would have a strong, vigorous champion at the PSC. Both appointments enabled Earl to fulfill affirmative action promises. Still, liberals thought that Earl could have done better.

Admittedly, liberals are difficult to satisfy. Liberals favor affirmative action unless their preferred candidate is a white male. Liberals favor responsiveness until a taxpayer rebellion develops, at which point they retreat to a more elitist position. Liberalism costs money, and Wisconsin was in desperate financial straits. That Earl's appointees failed to satisfy liberals reflected as much on liberals as on Earl.

Yet, other qualities were also missing in Earl's appointees—outspokenness, creativity, innovativeness, a zest for reform. By and large, the Earl team consisted of people who would not menace the governor's program, people who would not challenge the governor's authority, people who would not steal the governor's limelight, people who would serve as friendly sounding boards and faithful implementors. Innovative thinkers and free spirits were conspicuous by their absence.

Of course, innovative thinkers are boat-rockers. But wasn't Earl a fellow boat-rocker? Apparently not. In his appointments Earl seemed more interested in loyalty than talent, more interested in consensus than reform, more interested in solving problems than in promoting new ideas. The progressive promised land, which seemed just over the horizon during the campaign, now seemed increasingly remote. By the time the dust had settled, the progressives were outside the executive branch. Inside the executive branch was a domesticated cabinet, a host of team players, and a governor whose liberal credentials were in doubt.

GUBERNATORIAL LEADERSHIP

If Earl's appointments raised questions about his political philosophy, they provided insight into his managerial philosophy. As Earl's values became blurred in the minds of his supporters, his style became clear. The weight of the evidence suggested that Earl would be energetic, strong, even stubborn. The governor would be in charge, and he would truly be the chief executive. The administration would speak with one voice, and that voice would be Earl's. Earl's brand of leadership would be decisive. In the final analysis, he would make all important decisions himself.

Throughout the transition period Earl's self-assurance was striking. In making cabinet appointments, for example, he demonstrated a willingness to override objections by prominent state legislators, important bureaucrats, and members of his own staff. Earl refused to reappoint Donald Percy, the highly respected secretary of the Department of Health and Social Services, despite strong support for Percy within the bureaucracy. Earl named Lieutenant Governor Flynn to head the Department of Development, despite staff objections that Flynn could promote economic development without wearing a second hat as a cabinet secretary. (With patronage so scarce, why dissipate it unnecessarily?) Earl appointed Michael Ley to head the Department of Revenue despite objections from Democratic legislators who preferred a bolder, more innovative choice. Democratic legislators also bitterly opposed the selection of Jackson, a probable Republican candidate for governor in 1986 and a man whose opinions on most issues gave Democrats high blood pressure. Earl was moved by none of these objections. Clearly, he would trust his own judgment in making appointments.

Furthermore, Earl's involvement in the appointments process extended well beyond the level of agency heads. From the outset Earl made it clear to his cabinet appointees that the selection of subcabinet officials would be a "consultative" process. Without being overbearing on this point, Earl nevertheless discussed potential assistants with each of his cabinet appointees. Earl's position was that a "short list" of qualified candidates prepared by his staff should be given very serious consideration. Moreover, Earl reserved the right to veto any appointments recommended by his cabinet secretaries (Jackson, the lone Republican in the cabinet, was given more leeway in his appointments than the other secretaries). Throughout the selection process Earl personally served as "the point person," offering suggestions to cabinet members and commenting on suggestions made by the cabinet members themselves. What developed, according to Earl's transition director, Dan Wisniewski, was "a mix of their choices and our suggestions." In this fashion Earl was able to partially overcome traditional limitations on the governor's appointment powers. As if they were loaves and fishes, he parlayed 49 appointments into 112 or more.

Once his appointments were made, Earl went a step further to solidify his control over the bureaucracy. In collaboration with his top assistants he assigned policy specialties to each of several gubernatorial aides. The purpose of this arrangement was to ensure that, on any given issue, Earl would receive advice not only from the agency head but also from a gubernatorial staff member with some expertise in that area. The governor fully expected that disagreements would arise on occasion. When they did, he would serve as arbitrator. Though time-consuming, this arrangement would ensure that the governor was in charge.

Earl also made it clear that he would leave his personal imprint on a wide variety of decisions. This was especially apparent in the budget-making process. During the two months between his election and his inauguration Earl devoted considerable attention to the budget. Although Earl left minor decisions in the hands of interim budget director John Torphy, he made major decisions himself and personally reviewed agency objections to decisions made by his budget staff. Once minor decisions were made, Earl made a point of attending every budget meeting himself. Certainly, his involvement in the process was more striking than that of his two most immediate predecessors—Dreyfus and Schreiber.

Overall, the picture that emerged was clear. The governor was an exceptionally energetic and determined individual who expected to make all important decisions himself. He would delegate authority only when absolutely necessary; furthermore, delegation would always be partial, tentative, and provisional, subject to revocation at any time. He would try to emulate the decision-making style of Franklin Roosevelt—getting advice from the bureaucracy and from his personal staff, in the hope of being sufficiently well-informed to function as chief executive. But he would also run the risk of succumbing to Jimmy Carter's decision-making style—that of the workaholic who tries to do too much.

Jimmy Carter, of course, also tried to get others to do too much. In his first year as president, he proposed so many new initiatives that Congress found it impossible to address them. Earl, a shrewder politician than Carter, would not make such a mistake. Also, he would try to persuade legislators not from a pulpit but from close range, eyeball to eyeball. In doing so, he would employ all of his considerable political and interpersonal skills.

Governance

STIFF MEDICINE

When Earl took office, Wisconsin faced two budget crises: a short-term crisis and a long-term crisis. In the short term Wisconsin faced a budget deficit eventually estimated at $330 million as of June 30, 1983. According to a report issued by the National Governors' Association (NGA) and the National Association of State Budget Officers, Wisconsin's immediate budget crisis was the second worst in the nation, just behind that of California. Wisconsin's long-term budget crisis was equally formidable. Although estimates varied, the Earl administration concluded in December that it would face a total budget deficit of nearly $2.5 billion by the middle of 1985.

From the start Earl defined the problem as primarily a revenue problem rather than an expenditure problem. Although he warned that some budget cuts would be necessary, he emphasized instead the need for tax increases, including permanent tax increases. With permanent expenditure commitments (or uncontrollables) increasing, he argued, the case for permanent revenue increases was compelling.

But which taxes would be increased? Throughout the campaign Earl expressed an aversion for the sales tax, a preference for the income tax. He pointed out that the sales tax is more regressive, the income tax more progressive. The case for a progressive tax increase seemed especially strong, given high unemployment rates and generally depressed economic conditions.

Yet the case was not crystal clear. For one thing the sales tax in Wisconsin, which does not apply to food, was less regressive than the sales tax in many other states. Moreover, Wisconsin's personal income tax, which ranged from 3.4 percent to 10 percent, was already high—the sixth-highest in the nation. An increase in that particular tax might well give Wisconsin the reputation of having an unfavorable tax climate. In a period of intense competition for jobs, such a reputation could be damaging. Furthermore, the state legislature seemed to regard an income tax increase, especially a permanent tax increase, with special fear and loathing.

In view of these economic and political realities Earl opted first for a pragmatic solution. On December 15 Earl announced that he would call a special legislative session on January 4, the day after his inauguration. He proposed an initial tax package that would eliminate $1.1 billion from the $2.5-billion deficit projected by the middle of 1985. The tax package included provisions that would (1) make permanent the 5-percent sales tax, scheduled to revert to 4 percent on June 30; (2) make permanent a 25-cent-per-pack cigarette tax, scheduled to revert to 20 cents on October 1; and (3) cancel a property-tax credit program approved but not funded by the state legislature the previous year.

Within two days after his inauguration Earl's first tax proposal was approved by the senate and house, both controlled by Democrats. The senate voted 17–13 in favor, strictly along party lines. In the house, six Democrats defected, but the house nevertheless approved the bill by a 52–45 vote. The sight of Democratic legislators voting en masse to support a regressive tax package was disconcerting to many liberals, but Democratic legislators, like Earl, viewed this as a necessary step if unacceptable spending cuts were to be avoided. Although no Republicans supported the bill, Earl refused to criticize the Republicans, noting that at least they were not obstructionistic. Nor did Earl criticize the Democratic defectors. Instead, he noted that he himself found the sales tax undesirable as a general rule.

A $1.1-billion tax increase within two days of the governor's inauguration was more than many taxpayers could swallow. One irate taxpayer sent Earl a trophy, featuring a horse's behind, to commemorate the occasion. Others sent critical letters to the editors of their local newspapers. Still, Earl seemed to sustain little political damage from this swift legislative victory, partly because he was merely continuing tax increases approved by his predecessor and partly because he was still basking in the glow of the honeymoon period. In the process he gave himself much more breathing room. With the projected deficit reduced by nearly a half, Earl was able to address a difficult but more manageable problem: how to come up with tax increases or spending cuts totaling $1.4 billion over the next biennium.

Having put pragmatism above principle in the special session, Earl put principle first in the regular session. In his budget message to the state legislature Earl proposed a tax package that included (1) a temporary surcharge in personal income taxes (10 percent the first year, 5 percent the second year); (2) a 5-percent permanent increase in personal income taxes; (3) a two-year freeze on the "indexing" of income-tax brackets; (4) a 10-percent permanent increase in corporate tax rates; and (5) an increase in the state gasoline tax, indexed to fuel consumption and highway maintenance costs. Earl also proposed more than $500 million in spending cuts—primarily reductions in agency spending requests but also some reductions in existing expenditure levels. If approved, these measures would result in a balanced budget, as required by law.

CUTTING WITH A LASER

Budget cutting is painful for any chief executive but especially so for a liberal. In the 1960s liberals held a naive faith that there were few problems that money could not solve. These hopes soured as program after program failed to meet its objectives. In the 1970s liberals decided that poor management and faulty implementation were responsible. With some fine-tuning, programs could be made to work. But taxpayers were unwilling to take such risks with their hard-earned money. Also, rising inflation threatened to reduce the real income of workers. In the wake of changing political and economic conditions, liberals adapted and a new form of liberalism began to emerge. The new liberalism was cost-conscious but humane, prudent but progressive. The new liberalism was preservationist, not expansionary. The aim was to preserve most social programs and to provide modest increases in those programs that could reasonably be related to economic development. Tony Earl, it seemed, was that kind of liberal.

Faced with the need to achieve substantial spending cuts, Earl took three steps. First, he ruled out the option of across-the-board spending cuts—the strategy favored by his predecessor, Lee Dreyfus. To Earl, this approach was an abdication of responsibility. If the budget was to be cut, distinctions would be made between essential and nonessential programs, between outstanding and good programs, between programs that aided economic recovery and ones that did not. In Earl's words, "I intend to amputate the least effective programs entirely, rather than inflict small and weakening wounds on all the vital organs of government." Second, Earl declined to specify a target figure for budget cuts. He told his staff and his cabinet secretaries to cut as much as they could, and he emphasized the importance of that effort. However, once such cuts were made, he would support tax increases to make up the difference. Finally, as noted earlier, Earl himself played the lead role in the budget-cutting process. As a result the budget reflected the governor's values and priorities to a substantial degree.

When Earl unveiled his budget proposal on February 8, he recommended spending cuts of approximately $500 million over the 1983–85 biennium. Earl proposed the elimination of an environmental agency (the Solid Waste Recycling Authority) and an environmental program (the DNR Inland Lakes Renewal Program). He also proposed cuts in environmental planning aids, mental health institutions, weatherization aids, Medicaid, the Council on Criminal Justice, municipal audit services, and various local aids programs. In addition, he proposed the elimination of 1,095 state jobs. The total number of state jobs at the end of the biennium would be 55,034—the same as in 1979.

In defending these cuts Earl admitted to a certain ambivalence. "Most of the programs being cut or eliminated are not wasteful or frivolous. We simply cannot afford them. We don't have the money." The new liberalism, it would seem, means always having to say you're sorry—apologies instead of dollars. Unfortunately, apologies seldom satisfy clientele groups, and many responded with consternation and indignation. A proposed cut in municipal fire aids triggered more than 2,000 angry letters. Nursing home operators warned that Medicaid cuts would force them to close some homes (or to cut services). The Wisconsin Difference Coalition, a human services group, objected to welfare spending that would not keep up with the rate of inflation. The proposed elimination of state subsidies for county fairs also caused much alarm. One could almost hear a chorus of cows mooing in protest across the state.

Although most state programs were held at or near existing levels, Earl selected education for "privileged status" in his budget. His budget for the public schools called for a real increase of 4.3 percent in the first year and 6.7 percent in the second, for a total of more than $120 million in new funds. In hard times, Earl argued, "our schools are a top priority. To talk about closing them or starving them is like talking about closing hospitals during an epidemic." Earl also asked the legislature to increase the University of Wisconsin's instructional budget by $8 million in state tax money over the biennium. Coupled with increased revenues from tuition and other fees, this would provide the university with an increase of 2 percent for the first year and 3 percent for the second, for a total of about $24 million in new dollars. Earl subsequently upset the university's applecart by recommending a faculty pay freeze during the first year of the biennium. Overall, though, the university had less to complain about than other state-funded institutions.

The Department of Transportation also fared well under Earl's budget. Modest cutbacks, such as a shift from two license plates per vehicle to one, concealed a dramatic increase in funds for new highway construction and a modest increase in money for road repair. These programs would be financed by issuing bonds and indexing the motor fuel tax. If approved, this would make possible fourteen new superhighways recommended by transportation secretary Jackson.

A LIMITED AGENDA

Well before inauguration day Earl announced that he would not introduce any major legislation unrelated to fiscal affairs. He also urged legislators not to "lard up the budget bill with policy." True to his word, Earl offered very few new programs in his budget bill. New initiatives might be possible in the future, but only after Wisconsin's fiscal crisis was solved. A limited agenda, Earl believed, would encourage legislators to concentrate on the budget bill. In keeping with this philosophy, Earl delivered no state of the state address to the state legislature. Instead, he simply appended a state of the state message to the budget bill. In an effort to sell his budget he visited newspaper editorial boards in Eau Claire, La Crosse, Milwaukee, Green Bay, Appleton, Sheboygan, Beloit, Janesville, and Waukesha.

Inevitably, minor crises distracted Earl from his central mission of securing a balanced budget. For example, Minnesota's governor Rudy

Perpich, facing serious fiscal problems of his own, threatened to terminate a tuition reciprocity agreement whereby Minnesota students paid Wisconsin resident tuition at Wisconsin campuses, with the state of Minnesota making up the difference between resident and nonresident tuition. Although Wisconsin students had the same opportunities in Minnesota, the state of Minnesota lost money every year because the gap between resident and nonresident tuition was higher in Wisconsin and because more Minnesota residents attended school in Wisconsin than vice versa. After conferring with Perpich, Earl worked out a compromise under which Minnesota students would pay Minnesota resident tuition to the state of Wisconsin. This arrangement, which enabled Minnesota to save $5.5 million over two years, mollified Perpich.

Earl also intervened to hasten a solution to Wisconsin's unemployment-compensation fund crisis. By March of 1983 Wisconsin, which had been borrowing from the federal government to pay unemployment benefits, was approximately $500 million in debt. The Unemployment Compensation Advisory Council, a ten-member body consisting of business and labor representatives, had been deadlocked for some time. Earl's first step was to set a firm deadline for a recommendation by the council to the state legislature. When the council failed to meet the deadline, Earl appointed a bipartisan legislative task force to forge a compromise solution. That group quickly agreed to a package of new employer taxes and unemployment benefit cuts that was less favorable to labor than a proposal previously rejected by labor representatives as unacceptable. Despite the bitter opposition of organized labor, Earl agreed to support the compromise.

Although Earl declined to play a strong leadership role on nonfiscal issues, he did express support for various initiatives recommended by others. On a proposal to raise the drinking age, Earl endorsed an increase from eighteen to nineteen but not higher. On a bill to extend a ban on phosphates in laundry detergents sold in Wisconsin, Earl reiterated his support for such a ban. For a proposal by his secretary of employment relations to reorganize the state's personnel structure, Earl expressed support. In general, though, Earl avoided policy controversies that might distract him from the state's fiscal problems or unnecessarily undermine his political support.

Earl also steadfastly refused to get involved in intramural disputes within the Democratic party. When the Democratic National Committee voted not to exempt Wisconsin from a party rule against open presidential primaries, Earl declined to press for changes in the open primary. Earl also distanced himself from the state Democratic party by setting up his own committee, Citizens for Wisconsin's Future, to pay for his political expenses as governor. "A lot of people who helped me are not Democrats and they are never going to become Democrats," Earl said. "I want to keep in touch with that broad coalition of people and this [the new fund] will enable me to do that."

Within Wisconsin, Earl was cautious, diplomatic, pragmatic. He avoided conflict when possible and encouraged his appointees to be team players. This strategy, it seemed, was most likely to facilitate passage of his budget bill. Outside Wisconsin, however, Earl presented a very different image. In occasional forays to Washington and in pronouncements on national issues, he was aggressive, outspoken, and stubborn. More than most governors, he made a strong effort to secure national publicity and attention.

Earl's "feistiness," as one newspaper put it, was most evident at the annual meeting of the National Governors' Association (NGA) in late February and early March. At that session Earl led a band of dissident Democratic governors who opposed an NGA deficit-cutting plan on the grounds that it did not emphasize strongly enough the need for more cuts in defense spending, fewer cuts in social service programs. Defying a tradition of public consensus, Earl objected to what he described as weak political tea. "You can be bipartisan without being bland," he asserted, as he led a group of Young Turks in dissent.

Earl also took on the Reagan administration in personal encounters with Treasury Secretary Donald Regan and the president himself. In a session with Regan, Earl complained about cuts in federal aid to the states. In a session at the White House, Earl told Reagan that his policies were "inherently unfair" to unemployed and low-income people. One can almost imagine the president muttering to himself, "Who is this upstart and what is he doing in my living room?" Although Earl's outbursts bothered the Reagan administration and some old hands at the NGA, they apparently impressed other midwestern governors. Before returning to Wisconsin, Earl was elected chairman of the Conference of Great Lakes Governors. Outside Wisconsin, Earl had established himself as a man of strong convictions and with the courage to express them.

Conclusions

We sometimes refer to the gubernatorial transition as a period or a process that begins on election day and ends on inauguration day. In fact, however, there are three transitions, not one: a logistical transition, an administrative transition, and a policy transition. The logistical transition refers to the establishment of a viable, functioning office for the governor-elect. It includes adequate space, reliable clerical help, the routing of phone calls and mail, knowledge about gubernatorial powers and pending decisions. The administrative transition refers to the selection of personnel and the institutionalization of decision-making patterns compatible with the new governor's personal style. It includes appointments to key positions, decision-making procedures, the flow of information and advice to and from the governor's office. Finally, the policy transition refers to the principles and programs with which the new governor is identified. It encompasses criteria for choice, issue priorities, and distinctions between firm principles and flexible positions. Each of these transitions may begin well before election day, and each may influence the other in important ways.

THE LOGISTICAL TRANSITION

The logistical transition from Lee Dreyfus to Tony Earl could not have been smoother. The outgoing administration was more than willing to help; the incoming administration knew exactly what kind of help it needed. Despite the fact that Dreyfus and Earl belonged to different parties, cooperation between the two men and their respective entourages was high. The two teams worked together harmoniously, expeditiously, effectively. It is difficult to imagine a better logistical transition.

Several factors contributed to the success of the logistical transition. First, the Dreyfus administration planned for the transition well before election day and included the two candidates—Kohler and Earl—in the planning process. As a result, office arrangements suitable to the governor-elect were already established by election day. Although the campaign is a hectic period, the week after election day is even more hectic for the victorious candidate. The time to settle logistics is before election day so that the governor-elect can quickly address more important matters.

Second, the Dreyfus administration appointed a prominent individual—Lowell Jackson—to direct the departing administration's transition effort. The outgoing administration transition director should be someone who knows state government and who has enough respect that his exhortations and remonstrations will be taken seriously by bureaucrats and departing gubernatorial aides. The appointment of such an individual sends a positive message to the incoming governor and to the "permanent" government: help is available and foot dragging will not be tolerated!

Third, the Dreyfus administration allowed the incoming governor to appoint his own person as budget director, effective immediately after the election. In most states the new governor must submit a new budget to the state legislature within one month after taking office or sooner. If the budget is to reflect the priorities of the new governor, rather than those of the old, the new governor needs a running head start. The opportunity to appoint a permanent budget director two months before inauguration day gives the new governor an early chance to send authoritative signals to the bureaucracy. The budget bill that results is more likely to reflect the new governor's values and secure his strong support.

Fourth, Tony Earl knew what questions to ask and where to turn for help. A veteran public servant with experience heading two state bureaucracies, Earl had a thorough knowledge of state government. A new governor who understands bureaucracies and budgets is better equipped to seize the reins of power. Goodwill on the part of the outgoing administration is not enough. The outgoing administration may stand ready to help, but it can only guess what information the new administration needs. A veteran bureaucrat or politician is better able to hit the ground running than is a neophyte.

Fifth, Earl and Dreyfus genuinely liked each other and communicated frequently with one another between election day and inauguration day. Both men were affable, good hearted, and good humored. A certain tension between outgoing and incoming governors is perhaps inevitable, but it need not preclude friendly cooperation. Cooperation between the principals, it should be added, is likely to have an impact on the respective staffs.

Finally, and perhaps most important, Dreyfus retired voluntarily. He was not ousted by Earl. This was undoubtedly a key factor in the smooth logistical transition. Few candidates for reelection doubt that they will win; fewer still admit it by arranging for a possible transition. If an incumbent is defeated, it takes a herculean effort for the vanquished and victorious organizations to work hand in hand for the betterment of the state. If an incumbent retires voluntarily, courtesy and cooperation are much more likely.

Thus, the Wisconsin experience suggests that friction between new and old governors is more likely when the new governor unseats the old than when the two are members of different political parties. The 1982 transition from a Republican to a Democrat was as smooth as the 1978 transition from a Democrat to a Republican was rocky. The key difference was voluntary displacement in 1982, involuntary displacement in 1978. The short-term tensions of a political campaign, it would seem, are greater than long-term tensions between the two political parties.

THE ADMINISTRATIVE TRANSITION

As the former head of two state agencies, Tony Earl knew more about the bureaucracy than most new governors. He also knew that a bureaucracy is more than standard operating procedures and routines, that individual bureaucrats matter, and that the bureaucracy can be shaped from above. Furthermore, he fervently believed that the bureaucracy should be controlled by the governor.

Earl had signaled as much during the gubernatorial campaign. When asked to comment on a proposal for the popular election of public utility commissioners, Earl not only opposed the idea (as most other candidates did) but went a significant step further. The governor, he argued, should be authorized to veto rate hikes approved by the PSC. Never mind the time and expertise required to evaluate a rate-hike request. Never mind the political flak the governor would take every time he "approved" a rate hike. A strong governor could find the time, acquire the expertise, and take the political heat.

In contrast to his predecessor, who delegated considerable authority to cabinet members, Earl would manage most agencies himself—by appointing people who would be highly responsive to the governor's policy directives and, if necessary, by getting involved in the details of the bureaucratic policy-making process. Ideally, the former would eliminate the need for the latter. With loyal people in place, Earl would not have to fret about unseemly credit claiming by cabinet officials, bureaucratic sabotage by subcabinet officials. His control over the bureaucracy would be complete but effortless.

Instead of appointing strong-willed, innovative individuals, Earl appointed safe, pliable individuals whose commitment to Tony Earl surpassed any commitment to an ideology or a set of ideas. There were exceptions to this general pattern. Lowell Jackson, the secretary of transportation, was an outspoken conservative with a strong commitment to new highway projects. Howard Fuller, the secretary of employment relations, was equally vocal as a spokesman for the black community. Yet Earl shared Jackson's enthusiasm for new highways, Fuller's enthusiasm for affirmative action. As a result, neither Jackson nor Fuller was likely to clash with the governor on public policy questions, at least not in the short run. Furthermore, no cabinet secretary could stray too far with Earl supporters underneath him.

In a state like Wisconsin, with a strong civil service, there is much to be said for intensive gubernatorial involvement in personnel selection and for occasional gubernatorial interventions in bureaucratic policy making. A hands-off approach to bureaucratic governance deprives a governor of valuable opportunities to shape public policy. The appointment of loyal people to key positions helps to reduce conflict within the executive branch. Gubernatorial vigilance and control help to promote consistency. Nevertheless, the chief executive role takes its toll, and the costs are considerable.

Managing the bureaucracy is time consuming, even when loyal subordinates are in place. A governor who is serious about directing major state agencies quickly discovers that it is impossible to devote enough time to this task. Tony Earl has incredible stamina and an amazing capacity for hard work. He reads memos extremely well, digests information rapidly, recalls details with enviable accuracy. He makes policy decisions easily. But no governor can do this for every agency. It drains him physically, emotionally, intellectually.

It also drains him politically. A governor who becomes identified with all major administration decisions runs the risk of losing vital political support. In the short run, critics are likely to give the governor the benefit of the doubt because of the traditional honeymoon period and because it is easy to blame the governor's appointees rather than the governor himself. Once it becomes clear that the governor makes the crucial decisions himself, however, he loses his protective shield. By minimizing internal dissent and consolidating power, a politician can outsmart himself.

A strong governor and a strong cabinet need not be mutually exclusive. Indeed, the two can be complementary. A cabinet secretary who is capable of taking the heat can deflect criticism from the chief executive. A governor who does not delegate authority gets a lot of credit but also a lot of blame. Unfortunately, the latter may be more enduring and more significant. People, it seems, remember injuries better than they remember favors. There is, in short, a need for flak catchers other than the governor himself.

There is also a vital need for creative tension within the executive branch. Without it, there is the danger that the chief executive will develop a bunker mentality—a we-they outlook when adversity presents itself, as it surely will. Under such circumstances the governor may lash out at outsiders—the legislature, the courts, other levels of government—when they threaten a program that his staff and cabinet assure him is right. He may forget his place in the constitutional scheme.

A related danger is that the governor will lose touch with his constituents. In one sense this has not happened to Tony Earl. Since his election Earl has been accessible to legislators, interest groups, members of the press. He has held frequent press conferences. He has crisscrossed the state and made numerous public appearances. Furthermore, his contacts with politicians, reporters, and ordinary people almost always do him some good. When visiting a farm, he remembers to ask to see the barn. There is no sign that Governor Earl has lost his touch with people.

Yet there is some evidence that he is losing the support of his liberal constituency. The head of the state AFL-CIO, John Schmitt, has publicly denounced the unemployment compensation plan supported by Earl as ridiculous and unconscionable. A liberal legislator, who was "all set to be a loyal slave," is miffed by Earl's support for new highway projects. Another liberal politician wonders about the depth of Earl's commitment to human services programs. The disenchantment of hard-core liberals need not be fatal if Earl finds support elsewhere. However, no politician can forsake his primary constituency without building another to take its place.

THE POLICY TRANSITION

Tony Earl, the darling of the liberal community during the gubernatorial campaign, proved a disappointment to many liberals during his first few months as governor. Did Earl deceive his liberal supporters? Did they deceive themselves? Is liberalism no longer fashionable? Is liberalism no longer practical? Does the governor lack deep-seated philosophical convictions? Or are his convictions at war with a desire to straighten out a terrible budget mess, a desire to build a better future for the state of Wisconsin, a desire to achieve political success?

Certainly, Tony Earl is a pragmatic politician. Schooled in the art of the possible, he is not a believer in lost causes. In his first few months as governor, he showed a willingness to be flexible in his dealings with the God-fearing, family-oriented citizens who truly believe in the American dream. In contrast to moderate Republicans, though, he sees public services, rather than tax relief, as the key to the government's pursuit of middle-class happiness. He sees government as a positive force, capable of improving the quality of life for average citizens, who want to send their children to good public schools during the week, take them to public parks on safe public roads over the weekend, and eventually send them to a fine public university. Tony Earl is neither a limousine liberal nor a ghetto liberal, but he is very much a middle-class liberal.

Earl's policy toward minorities helps to illustrate this facet of his thinking. There is no doubt that Earl believes that blacks, Chicanos, Indians, and women should share in the American dream. In keeping with that belief Earl and his appointees named thirty-seven women and twenty-five minorities to state positions, out of a total of 123 jobs. Earl believes in affirmative action and his appointments reflect that. Yet Earl has done more for minorities through the appointments process than through the appropriations process. This is not symbolic politics but middle-class politics. A good middle-class liberal promotes minority interests through appointments rather than through social reform.

In any event Earl is a problem-solver, not a reformer. His contribution to political discourse is a budget, not a vision. His fondest hope is to restore Wisconsin's fiscal solvency and end the trauma of annual budget crises. In his first six months as governor, Earl took significant steps toward reaching that goal. Although the state legislature rejected Earl's proposal for a permanent tax increase and insisted on additional spending cuts, legislators did agree to a variety of temporary tax increases, including a 10-percent surcharge on personal and corporate income taxes and a three-year freeze on income tax indexing. Earl's negotiating skills and his willingness to make key compromises enabled him to secure legislative support for a budget bill that substantially reflected his priorities. Moreover, the whole process was completed by July 1, for the first time in many years.

Nevertheless, it is unclear whether Earl's next three years as governor will be as successful as his first. Will he be able to shift gears from fiscal crisis management to policy innovation? Will he be able to promote new initiatives involving welfare reform and tax reform? Will he be able to provide long-range solutions to the dependence of Milwaukee, Racine, Kenosha, and other cities on declining industries for jobs? Will he be able to make state government more accountable to its citizens, not just to its leading politician?

Perhaps he will, but it will be difficult because certain patterns have already been set. The administrative transition is more than just a phase in the transfer of power. It sets parameters for the policy transition and determines the kinds of policies that can be pursued. It creates opportunities, but it also imposes constraints. The governor has appointed people who can be counted on to pursue his goals but who are unlikely to promote new initiatives themselves.

In the short run a strong governor may be one who runs a tight ship. In the long run, however, a strong governor is one who conserves his strength and husbands his political resources. With stronger agency heads Earl might pull back and delegate more authority to his subordinates. Under the circumstances, though, that is unlikely. The governor has, in a sense, painted himself into a corner.

Tony Earl is an extremely talented individual who needs less help than most politicians. This was evident during the campaign and the logistical transition, and it has been evident since. Yet even this gifted politician needs a considerable amount of help. The governor can generate only so many ideas. The governor can fight only so many brushfires. The governor can invest only so much intellectual and political energy in his job before both begin to dissipate. The governor must wear several hats but he cannot wear them simultaneously. If Earl's policy transition is to be as successful as his logistical transition, he needs the help that only creative, outspoken agency heads can provide.

What Guides Governors in Transition?
Some Conclusions Regarding
the National Governors' Association Guidelines

ROBERT P. HUEFNER AND MICHAEL L. NASH

What Guides Governors in Transition?

If the widely recognized limitations of the governorship are to be transformed into opportunities, what guidance can help governors-elect mold their visions into meaningful change? Can any general guidance be useful, given the constraints uniquely imposed by each state and by the problems and enthusiasms of the times?

This chapter looks at the 1982–83 gubernatorial transitions, comparing how new governors implement the National Governors' Association (NGA) guidelines with what these guidelines actually suggest. Our comparison draws upon the independent analyses of the 1982–83 gubernatorial transitions. In the state studies the selection of information and the lines of analysis reflect the analysts' own perceptions of what was most significant. As a result, our overview is not as quantitatively precise as a survey might be, but it is more sensitive to the difficulties and directions particular to each transition and is less likely to misunderstand them.

This comparison of practice and NGA guides aims at improving the guidance offered to new governors by identifying special circumstances that influence the nature and success of a transition and by providing a better understanding of how the governorship operates. Do governors lead as political brokers, as statesmen, as commanders, or as organizational managers? How do these approaches make a difference in the ways the governor shapes and uses the resources and processes of the office?

Our study suggests that the professionalism of state agencies, the backgrounds and relationships of the participants, the electoral mandates, and the current crises influence both the choice of guidelines to follow and the outcomes. In some transition activities there are few surprises and much consistency between guides and performance, most notably the high priority given to preparation of the new budget. In other activities there are striking differences, particularly in staffing the new administration, differences which suggest that the guidelines lean toward a view of the governor as commander whereas the governors themselves are more likely to lead through brokerage.

Advice versus Practice

The most recent and widely employed guides for new governors prepared by the NGA are *Governing the American States: A Handbook for New Governors* (1978) and *Transition and the New Governor: A Critical Overview* (1982).[1] Neither publication makes many absolute recommendations. Most suggestions are qualified, depending upon specific circumstances, and are presented with an analysis of choices, pro and con. However, from this advice general guidelines do emerge, offered with enough certainty to give direction to new governors and allowing comparison with what governors actually do.

Guidelines can be grouped into four issue areas. The first, personnel, contains the urgings that governors move quickly to make personnel appointments (particularly those for the key staff in the governor's office), seek persons of competence and personal loyalty, be cautious about carry-overs from prior administrations, and avoid using the same people in the campaign, the transition, and the state offices. The second issue area, administrative organization, includes suggestions about delegating transition functions, relating the governor's management framework to his or her personal style, and avoiding reorganization battles. In the third issue area, policy focus, the guidelines recommend that the new governor quickly select a limited policy agenda of high relevance to the state. In the final issue area, preparation of the new budget, the guides warn that revenue estimates deserve special attention and urge that the new budget be given a primary priority.

PERSONNEL ISSUES

What the guidelines say

Reconsider Retaining Incumbents. "Generally speaking, retaining an incumbent will give the Governor the least control over a department, and make it most difficult for him to shift general policy," though their useful experience should be considered, and exceptions made for transitions between governors of the same party and philosophy.[2]

Beware of Individuals with an Independent Base of Support. "Consider carefully the wisdom of appointing people with their own political or interest group constituencies. . . . An appointee with a significant and independent base of political power . . . will tend to resist the discipline of working through the new governor's staff."[3]

Be Cautious about Appointing Campaign Staff. "There is much utility in *not* assuming that your campaign staff will automatically make a good administrative staff. The new governor's role has just changed from candidate to chief executive; consequently, the personal team required . . . may also have to change." (An exception is made for the press secretary.) "An important guideline in recruiting staff is to broaden the Governor's political base by hiring individuals beyond those with personal or partisan commitments to the Governor." "Campaigns for office are oriented towards a specific individual and his immediate supporters . . . it is easily carried over as a philosophy into the immediate office of the Governor, where it is dangerous. . . . In a campaign it is essentially true that those 'who are not with us are against us.' This is not true in office."[4]

Separate the Campaign, Transition, and Administration Staffs. "The transition coordinator generally should not be the campaign chief . . . the activities of a transition are different from those of a campaign." "The Chief of Staff . . . should be selected very early in the transition and should *not* be assigned the transition coordinator role."[5]

Follow Hierarchical Lines in Personnel Selection. "Organizational doctrine in both public and private administration suggests that the scope of the chief executive officer in personnel selection and management should extend downward only one level . . . the presence of a subordinate in the top level of a department who owes his allegiance only to the Governor or his staff creates a difficult situation in the management of the agency."[6]

What the transition reports say. New governors in 1983 appeared to share the concern in the guides that appointees be personally loyal. They were most likely to carry over staffs from the previous administration when the transition was friendly and within the same party, as in Georgia, Iowa, and New York.[7] But the continuation of existing staff was not limited to these states. The other instances suggest that the loyalty sought was not a political or even permanent loyalty, but rather a professional integrity and commitment to the elected leadership, as appeared to be the case in Minnesota with its history of professionalism, as was stated by the analyst in the case of the budget office in Arkansas, and as was implied in the case of Nebraska by a decision to maintain the existing budget office staff.

Significant contrast between governors and guides emerge in the decisions about appointing campaign personnel to state government positions. The guideline is phrased as a suggestion rather than an absolute. Still, it is not so casual or qualified that it can be said to have been followed when most governors make significant, obvious, and immediate linkages between campaign and state staffs. Appointment guidelines were explicitly followed in Nevada, as well as in Minnesota (where the political culture itself presses for separation; as Governor Rudy Perpich put it, "around here they think you're a dummy . . . if you get involved in campaigns"). The guidelines were often followed in budget and finance appointments, influenced by a special concern for immediate technical competence (Arkansas, Georgia, Massachusetts, Nebraska, and Nevada). But a connection between campaign and appointments frequently emerges in cabinet positions, and it becomes the rule in the governors' personal staffs (Alabama, Alaska, Arkansas, California, Georgia, Iowa, Massachusetts, Michigan, Nebraska, New Mexico, Texas, and Wisconsin).

Perhaps the clearest difference between specific prescriptions and the governors' actions is the continuity from campaign to transition to gubernatorial staffs. Although the guidelines flatly advise against carrying over principal campaign staff as transition directors or making transition directors chief of the governor's staff, governors in Alabama,

California, Georgia, and Massachusetts carried the same persons through the top positions in all three stages, and, though organizational structures and titles differ, similar carry-over occurred in Arkansas, New Mexico, New York, and Texas.

The analyst for Massachusetts observed the context for this connection. Governor-elect Michael Dukakis's "policy agenda had been shaped . . . during the campaign." He drew his priorities from campaign pledges and pressures, and he built "support within the campaign organization" around these key issues. "Because there was so much overlap" in staffing the campaign, transition, and government, "the process for thinking about policy issues was already smooth and established early in the transition . . . dictated by the way it had been done in the campaign."

The guidelines are concerned with the different orientations, skills, and perhaps different loyalties appropriate for each role, and with overloading the same people with several functions. But many governors seemed more concerned with continuity and shared perspective, what the Massachusetts analyst described as the maintenance of "a team mentality." They do not just carry forward representative members of the campaign but make the core of the campaign staff the core of their state staff.

The extent to which the governors became involved in selecting staff below the first level sometimes strayed from the guideline because of circumstances, such as the independence of the bureaucracy in New Mexico and Wisconsin, and at other times because of the governor's style, as in Alaska and California. Such rationales notwithstanding, in each of these states the analysts noted that significant administrative problems were rooted in this practice, problems that added to the burden of the governor as well as to the cabinet officer whose authority is compromised.

ADMINISTRATIVE ORGANIZATION

What the guidelines say

Delegate Traditional Transition Functions. "Experienced governors stress that newly elected governors should delegate most responsibilities for the details of the traditional transition functions and concentrate on the longer-term issues of the style and substance of the new administration." "It is critical to an effective transition [that routine] functions be delegated as much as possible to junior staff members and volunteers, while the senior staff focuses immediately on key transition problems."[8]

Avoid Unnecessary Investments in Reorganization. "During the first six to nine months of his term, a governor generally should minimize 'down time' by not undertaking major reorganizations [or] large-scale personnel changes beyond normal top-level appointments . . . unless they are absolutely necessary." However "the sooner [reorganization] costs are incurred, the more likely they are to be forgotten by the next election . . . legislative bodies generally give governors more leeway in organizing their staff functions early in their term."[9]

Conform Office Organization to Personal Style. "Designing a management framework . . . is one of the most fundamental tasks to be accomplished during the transition period. . . . it is essential that the office structure be well thought out and that decisions on office organization be based on the preferences and management style of the governor-elect." Two "styles" are outlined: A "chief of staff" in which one person manages staff work and is the primary channel of access to the governor, and a "spokes of the wheel" with several persons having direct and independent access to the governor. "Each new governor will instinctively fall into a management style that suits him."[10]

What the transition reports say. Experience shows the necessity of delegating substantial responsibility during the transition. But to which key transition problems should the governor apply his personal time? Especially evident is the conflict between the time required for careful selection of important personnel and the time required for developing basic policy and the first budget. The experience reported for the 1982–83 transitions may say that the governor must balance attention between both or neither will be successful. This was clearly suggested in Nebraska, where the fiscal crisis prompted the new governor to quickly appoint "core administrative department heads" to facilitate budget preparation and to name "good managers" who could deal with budget reductions. This balance was carefully orchestrated in Massachusetts, where the budget preparation was delayed to provide a crucial "contract-setting mechanism" for the integration of the new appointees into the administration.

Some governors-elect (in Alabama, California, and Texas) used the period to set up task forces whose announced undertakings were key transition problems but whose actual functions were often more symbolic than substantive; only in Massachusetts did the task forces appear to be effectively employed. The 1982–83 experience urges caution in such assignments. In Alaska the use of "task forces for executive reorganization" produced unwanted influence, suggesting the "risks attendant to setting up essentially uncontrolled watchdogs."

There is uncertainty in the NGA's suggestions on the timing of reorganization and little clarification in the state reports. Although the most recent guide discourages first-year attempts at major reorganization, the 1978 guide encourages early efforts to take advantage of the honeymoon period. The state reports show that only two governors chose to make legislated reorganizations a significant issue during the 1982–83 transition: successfully in New Hampshire and unsuccessfully in Alaska. The different outcomes were dictated not by timing, but by the larger issues of policy focus and leadership approach.

What stands out in the reports is the substantial concern with shaping the staff and cabinet to fit the governor's personal style and perceived mandate, and to establish, or carry over from the campaign, an effective "team." Little staff reorganization occurred where new governors sought to continue the posture of the previous administration, as in Georgia and Iowa. Conversely, in Arkansas and Massachusetts, where new governors had learned hard lessons from election defeats after earlier incumbencies, the office was substantially reorganized in an attempt to strengthen political linkages. In the related case of Texas, where Democrats regained the statehouse after their first ouster in 100 years, there was a similar emphasis, with an atmosphere in the gubernatorial office that "comes close to the chaos of the political boiler room."

The 1982–83 experience does not completely support a conclusion that new governors will "instinctively" develop management frameworks appropriate to their personal approaches. A clash between structure and style emerged in Wisconsin. Governor Anthony Earl tried "to emulate the decision-making style of Franklin Roosevelt," using a competitive arrangement.[11] This approach provided independent and sometimes oppositional views from both agency heads and gubernatorial staff assigned to the same policy area, with Earl serving as "arbitrator" so that he would have sufficient information and access to personally control the bureaucracy. But he surrounded himself with a "domesticated cabinet," one lacking "innovative thinkers and free spirits," quelling confrontation so that "the administration would speak with one voice." Earl's structure promoted conflict while he demanded consensus. The analyst's principal criticism is that without "outspoken agency heads" Earl is politically liable for all decisions and is deprived of "vital creative tension" essential to policy development, losing the strengths of the competitive approach.

However, neither can it be assumed that consistency between style and organizational framework ensures good management. Governor Perpich's delegation of authority is consistent with his somewhat formal chairman-of-the-board style, but his approach has also decontrolled Minnesota's bureaucracy to the extent that the analysts question the governor's ability to lead. At the other extreme, in New Mexico, Governor Toney Anaya's unwillingness or inability to delegate authority is consistent with his style of making "all decisions large and small," but it has cost him in organizational support, staff morale, public image, and lost personnel.

POLICY FOCUS

What the guidelines say

Remain Neutral on National Issues. "It is important to remember that taking no position at all is an option, and frequently an attractive one. For a variety of reasons a Governor may have a position on major . . . national issues and may want to articulate that policy, but in many cases he is not obliged to do so."[12]

Limit the Agenda to Two or Three Issues. "Success in the governorship depends, first and foremost, on focus. Early in your term, pick a limited number of issues and concentrate on them throughout. . . . Initially, the new governor should select no more than three issues on which to concentrate." However, "a newly-elected governor should not pick a single issue on which to concentrate."[13]

What the transition reports say. Comparing the guidelines with recent transitions reveals rather high congruence on the topic of policy focus. The encouragement that new governors shy away from national issues was at least partially warranted by Governor Bill Clinton's experience in Arkansas, where his predilection for garnering "glowing recognition from the national press" created the impression that he was re-moved from the state's immediate concerns. This appearance of being "more eager for national acclaim than Arkansas acceptance" contrib-uted to his defeat in 1980 and then to a far more cautious approach in 1983. But some newly elected governors may have special reasons for ignoring this advice. Wisconsin's Governor Earl was elected in a politi-cal arena "crucial" to the viability of "the liberal wing of the Demo-cratic party." New York's Governor Mario Cuomo was elected to a post that is perennially of national importance, where the possibility of eventually serving in Washington provides leverage in recruiting cab-inet and staff. Still, it may be that unless a governor develops a strong base within the state or the state has special reasons for considering its governor a national leader, there are considerable risks in devoting substantial time to purely national issues. Perhaps the scope of a gov-ernor's agenda is best broadened after the first years of the term have been devoted to the state's immediate concerns. A recent effort to curb the federal deficit, for example, was spearheaded by a bipartisan group of four governors, all in at least a second term.[14]

The reports show that most governors did select only a few issues on which to concentrate, although several could not cut their lists to just three. The rationale was understood by Governor Dukakis, a seasoned veteran of legislative battles from his earlier term in Massachusetts, whose "focus was in keeping with [his] strongly held conviction that he could not come into office with a 'laundry list,' but instead needed to build support within the campaign organization and with external constituencies (particularly the legislature) around a limited number of issues." In general, the analysts credited those governors who focused on no more than four or five targets with effective strategy.

In Iowa, Governor Terry Branstad successfully pushed through a much longer agenda, probably aided by record popularity and the re-lated political momentum of an almost "transitionless transition." But analysts for four other states where the governor did not follow this advice (Alaska, Arkansas during Clinton's first administration, Min-nesota, and Texas) agree that the new governor encountered trouble when there was a lack of focus. In at least two of these states the lack of focus may have been a symptom of inexperience or problems in get-ting the new administration organized, rather than a primary cause of problems. Governors in Arkansas (in 1983), Nebraska, and Wisconsin technically violated the guideline by focusing exclusively on fiscal affairs, but this can be an umbrella issue offering substantial room for maneuver.

PREPARATION OF A NEW BUDGET

What the guidelines say

Obtain Good Revenue Estimates. "In recent years, there seems to have been no more politically perilous activity than revenue estimation. Little is more damaging than basing the budget on . . . bad revenue estimates." "If [the state's revenue estimates] are substantially off, a tremendous amount of political and operational damage will be inevitable."[15]

Give Top Priority to the Budget. "Priority attention to the first budget is one of the most important, if not *the* most important, activity that will occur during the transition period. . . . The memories of the press and public are extremely short. Problems inherent in the outgoing governor's budget become the new governor's problem when they crop up later in the year."[16]

What the transition reports say. The experiences of the 1982–83 transitions support the importance that the guidelines give the budget and revenue estimates during the transition period. The following observations are typical: "The [Alabama] state financial picture was the most important and probably the roughest aspect of the transition." "The [California] fiscal crisis and the budget battle dominated state politics for the first six months of the new administration." "The [Minnesota] struggle with the budget highlights perhaps the major weakness in the Perpich administration."

The question apparently is not whether to jump into the budget preparation but rather how and how soon. The especially severe financial problems for the states in 1982–83 present extreme conditions, which may offer special understanding. Governor Mark White's experience in Texas confirmed the critical nature of revenue projections: he was forced into a losing budget battle by dependence on the estimates of a political adversary. In both California and Minnesota, where fiscal problems necessitated special sessions after the election but before the inauguration, the governors-elect tried to remain apart from these sessions, then faced continuing fiscal problems and problems of leadership. Conversely, in Iowa, Michigan, and Wisconsin, where the new governors also faced severe fiscal problems but with no special sessions pressing preinauguration commitment, strong leadership in their first months brought emergency tax increases, breathing room, and early reputations for effectiveness. Governor Mario Cuomo's swift attention to a less demanding situation in New York led to the quickest budget resolution in four years. New Hampshire Governor John Sununu's careful attention to a small deficit avoided a broad-based tax increase. And in New Mexico, an NGA representative is given credit for "tightening up the schedule" for budget preparation, and the new governor overcame a 9 percent error in estimation to hammer out a favorable budget compromise.

The experiences in at least three states may warrant a new cautionary note. When preoccupation with the budget paints a governor into a corner, as apparently happened in California and Nebraska, other important aspects of a governor's agenda may be undermined through program cuts, depletion of political resources, or loss of ground that might be given in negotiations. The New Hampshire analyst argues that inflexible commitments to a no-tax-increase position perennially doom that state's incumbents to reelection defeat, partly because "the political resource base is insufficient to fuel programs to create successful gubernatorial reelectoral coalitions," partly because of the vulnerability inherent in this position. Though specific to the tax/budget issue, this argument adds credence to the guideline on policy focus urging the new governor not to concentrate on a single, narrow issue, even if it is the top priority.

However, governors in Arkansas (1983) and Wisconsin were more successful with an exclusive budget focus. The difference seems to be one of approach. In California and Nebraska the governors pushed specific proposals as nonnegotiable, whereas in Arkansas and Wisconsin the governors' focus communicated priority, allowing for negotiation. The real issue here may not be agenda size, but leadership style.

A Broader Look at the Comparisons

The individual state analyses used for this comparison of prescription and practice offer a rich context for the information provided, rather than a rigorous statistical base. Hence the value of the comparisons is in the broad insights they suggest rather than the specific hypotheses they document. These insights fall into several categories: First, in the questions raised by contrasts and in the agreement shown by congruence, the comparisons clarify what the guides and the new governors believe is effective. Second, in revealing uncertainties or vagueness in the guidelines, the comparisons spotlight aspects of the guides and of current understanding of the governor's office that deserve further attention. Finally, the contrasts illuminate alternative conceptions of the governor's office and the implications of these conceptions.

COMMANDER VERSUS BROKER

An especially intriguing difference between guidelines and practices is in personnel selection. The willingness of governors to link campaign, transition, and state staffs, at variance with the advice of the guides, suggests that many governors conceptualize their leadership more in terms of brokerage and less in terms of command than do the guides.

The guides question the suitability of campaign skills and perspectives for state administration. Campaign staffs garner support from interest groups and mobilize public opinion. But their success might later oblige them to favor those interests, and their reactions in tough policy decisions might be coopted by sensitivity to public opinion, at the expense of the state's ultimate interests. The guides raise concerns about existing agency heads' having established perspectives and commitments that could encumber the governor's own policy directions. Similarly, persons with separate political power bases may provide linkages, expertise, and perspective, but the guides are concerned that they may be too independent. The wording of the guides' indicates support for staff appointments that "broaden the Governor's political base" but imply that this is done by employing persons with broad perspectives even though they may lack the political connections of the campaign staff.

In summary, the governor is best served, the guides seem to suggest, by personal staff and major appointees who will form a governor's team, using intelligence, diligence, and cooperation to shape and implement a program furthering the interests of the state and the governor. Implicitly, the choice is for innate abilities and broad perspective over experience and connections.

The 1983 governors, on the other hand, showed a strong willingness to use the campaign and transition staffs, and perhaps persons from previous administrations or with outside ties and independent political bases. This could be interpreted as representing weak political position or timidity. It may be that these governors, as new governors or governors who have lost prior elections, are not yet exercising leadership like the strong, effective governors envisioned by the guides. Or these governors could be reacting intelligently to the circumstances of the governorship, particularly to the realization that their opportunities for leadership are not so much in formal powers[17] as in their abilities to lead a number of relatively independent power sources.[18] Rather than assuming a role of commander, they may see a necessity for acting as broker; they may be attempting to play that role as a means of building their own influence over public policy.

A brokerage approach reflects the broad dispersion of power in U.S. democracy.[19] It acknowledges, for example, what Norton Long found and what many newcomers forget, that the governor in dealing with the bureaucracy is "dealing with a system. This system, if it is to have any stability at all, must be highly resistant to change."[20] It recognizes that seldom can governors expect to outline state master plans in the privacy of their own administrative teams and expect to see them adopted.[21]

A fiat mentality appeared to underlie the approach taken in Alaska, where inexperience with political process resulted in several "political bungling[s]," leading the Alaska analyst to conclude that "cookbook recipes of the formal transition are far less important than political preparation by the governor and his staff. Indeed, the Alaska case suggests that a 'successful' formal transition might handicap a governor if not accompanied by effective political learning . . . because an easy transition may give . . . a false sense of control and security."

The commander and broker approaches were clearly contrasted in the first- and second-term strategies of the new governors who had previously won and lost the office: Clinton of Arkansas and Dukakis of Massachusetts. The earlier administrations of both were characterized by alienation from powerful political interests and an image of being "aloof," "arrogant," and "above politics." With the hindsight of defeat, both men structured and appointed their second staffs like campaign organizations, narrowed their agendas, and took calculated steps to fortify constituent relations. Governor Dukakis emphasized that he learned from his defeat "that being political . . . was an acceptable and perhaps even intelligent" approach. Governor Clinton described "the major difference in his two administrations as being that 'the populism of the heart now displays itself more in procedures,' that he had learned how to do things that were achievable . . . and, by all means, involve the people in them."

BROKERAGE: CONNECTIONS, COALITIONS, AND CONSTRAINTS

Does the governor's leadership potential come from being at the most central position for understanding and communicating with the state's widely distributed pockets of power? If so, the governor's unique and substantial opportunity is to use this communications focus to understand the state's needs, to spot the possibilities for trades that enhance the interests of the state, and then to fashion and implement effective agreements.[22]

Several of the analysts of the 1982–83 transitions support this perspective. The difficulties involved in establishing an effective communications network were cited as a major problem in the 1982 transition from candidate to governor for the then political neophyte Governor Robert Kerrey of Nebraska. Credit for a successful first year in New Hampshire was attributed to Governor Sununu's ability to personally shape a communications focus that integrated various corporate interests and legislative leadership. In New Mexico securing connections, particularly in the legislature and also among major business and agricultural interests, was "the single most important factor in explaining [Governor Anaya's] success with the legislature," from whom "the new governor got perhaps 90 percent of what he asked." Conversely, in Alabama, departing incumbent Governor Fob James's "distaste for the political process . . . meant that few of his reforms were actually institutionalized."

New governors may explain that carrying over their campaign and transition staffs amounts to their taking advantage of a team with proven effectiveness. The guides do not deny the "proven effectiveness" but suggest that the perspective needed for the administration is different from that of the campaign, where effectiveness means mobilizing the vote. However, if the proven effectiveness is in building, sustaining, and managing a focus of communication, and thus connecting the former candidate and now governor to interest groups throughout the state, the campaign staffs may have replaced the party as the most effective linkage to a range of political interests. Thad Beyle and Lynn Muchmore concluded in previous work: "the governorship seems to have developed in such a way that the party is no longer the most important instrument of political action. . . . When the emerging single-issue politics, the media, intergovernmental officials, and bureaucracies are factored into the equation, a sandlot analogy might be apropos:

The governor is an individual politician always having to create new and unstable alliances—a kind of sandlot politics, playing with and against pickup teams as they are created."[23] Campaign staffs may offer the primary tool for negotiating such transitory political alliances. An extreme example of "divided government"[24] in Alabama illustrates how the breakdown in party organization can affect staffing: a "one-party political environment has resulted in no-party politics . . . and almost necessitates a heavy overlap among key campaign, transition, and gubernatorial office appointees."

The governors could be quite aware of the risks and costs of staffing their administration with campaign workers and still find such staffing essential to their coalition-building strategy. The new administration must make such comparisons. Because the circumstances of each transition are unique, general conclusions about what these comparisons will show are not tenable. What continued analysis of actual transitions can do is investigate the presumed advantages and problems of primary transition decisions, such as those listed in table 1 and suggested by the pro-and-con analyses in the NGA guides. The analysis can help reveal the importance of each decision and how the decisions are affected by circumstances. This requires state evaluations covering more, or all, of the governors' terms.

If the governor's decisions reflect a correct assessment that leadership depends upon successful brokerage, it does not mean that there are only

Table 1. The Advantages and Disadvantages of Various Transition Personnel Decisions

Decision	Advantage	Disadvantage
Use campaign staff in state administration	Skilled brokerage team	Too narrow loyalty to partisans
Use transition staff in state administration	Continuity	Overload
Carry over agency heads	Administrative skill	Established perspective
Hire persons with independent power bases	Connections	Loyalty to interest groups
Involvement in second-level appointments	A check to help ensure loyalty	Administrative inefficiency
Take extra time on appointments	Better selection for long-term loyalty, skill, and connection	Early capability and record

minor problems with such an approach. The guides probably are correct in arguing that there is an important difference in the interests engaged by the campaign staff and those the governor must engage as the leader of state policy making and that the governor needs a broader range of communications and involvements to lead the state than are required to gain an electoral majority.[25] There must be risks in carrying over campaign staff who may not be able to reach out beyond the more friendly and ideologically limited support groups of the campaign to connect with the broader interests and activities of the state.

Another problem in relying on the campaign to produce state government staff is that the candidate may have a much more limited field of choice than does the governor-elect in selecting chief assistants. The uncertainties and the financial stress of the campaign can severely limit the rewards that a candidate can offer in order to attract competent personnel. This problem may be especially acute in smaller states.

There also are "groupthink" risks: "the tendency for cohesive groups to foster a shared illusion of invulnerability, which inclines them to minimize risks." The "more amiability and esprit de corps among the members of policy-making in-group, the greater is the danger that independent critical thinking will be replaced by groupthink, which is likely to result in irrational and dehumanizing actions directed against outgroups." The risks justify careful efforts to counteract groupthink tendencies, such as Janis's suggestions that the leader "might assign the role of critical evaluation to each member" and "when assigning a policy-planning mission . . . might adopt an impartial stance instead of stating preferences." Further, the leader can set up "several independent policy-planning and evaluation groups to work on the same policy question."[26] The states may be more subject to "groupthink" risks than is the federal government, because the press and Congress have more capacity to check executive abuses. This warrants special mechanisms to enhance access to information and feedback.[27]

Brokerage also can limit leadership if exercised in passive and reactive ways rather than as a tool to which the governor gives purpose. All these problems deserve attention and probably must be at least partly managed in a successful gubernatorial term.

CIRCUMSTANCES: CONDITIONS AND ENVIRONMENT

The guides do frequently consider special circumstances that may arise in a particular state or a particular transition. Virtually all the state reports note unique characteristics of the participants' political careers,[28] interpersonal relationships,[29] the states' political environments,[30] and the electoral mandate[31] that could constrain the applicability of maxims drawn from these transitions.[32] The analysis of the 1982–83 transitions is circumscribed by the fact that it includes only sixteen states, one point in time, and is dominated by one party (thirteen of the sixteen new governors were Democrats).[33] Still, it suggests some important contingencies to be considered in applying the guidelines and identifies several guidelines that deserve further study and clarification of the ways they relate to contingencies.

One area worth exploring is how political cultures affect the appropriateness of selecting campaign staff as the permanent staff members for the new gubernatorial term. A part of this question concerns the ways in which traditions within the state bureaucracy affect the loyalty that the new governor may presume he can claim from existing staffs. Loyalty may reflect a particular state political culture[34] such as that of Minnesota, or it may reflect the traditions of particular state agencies such as those of the Budget Office in Arkansas.

Another set of questions relates to the nature of the mandate the governor receives in the election. Does a narrow victory shift the priorities of the transition period? Does it change the appropriateness of undertaking various state or national roles? In Georgia and Iowa, where new governors were elected to succeed popular incumbents of the same party, the resulting "transitionless transitions" provided a "running start" for more ambitious agendas. Since the margins of victory were significantly different (26 percent in Georgia versus 6 percent in Iowa), a key ingredient would appear to be identification with a popular previous administration. In this circumstance governors may choose a more ambitious reorganization program or policy focus, perhaps even though the margin of victory is not large.

Contrast this situation with those in Alaska and California, where divisive elections empowered the political opposition, and confrontational stances with maverick or opponent-controlled legislatures deprived the new governor of a honeymoon period. The governors may or may not find the confrontations useful in gaining long-term electoral advantages,[35] but these confrontations certainly hampered short-term policy objectives. New governors facing such limitations should be especially cognizant of the cautions in the guides about too ambitious an agenda or reorganization and not underestimate obstacles, even if the mechanics of the transitions run smoothly.

CIRCUMSTANCES: THE GOVERNOR'S STYLE

The comparison of the guides and the reports raises questions about what *management style* means and what difference it makes. Both the guides and the reports are understandably vague. The most specific guidance provided is in *Transition and the New Governor*, where two basic options for organizing the governor's staff are outlined: one having a strong chief of staff and one having a number of persons reporting directly to the governor as "spokes of the wheel." The most common contrast in management style drawn by the reports is the extent to which the governor is involved in the details of the administration, with the polarities characterized as hands-on versus chairman-of-the-board approaches.

The available dimensions of executive style are far richer: Barber's two dimensions of active-passive and positive-negative, Johnson's continuum from formalistic through competitive to collegial, Koenig's five types of presidential-legislative relationships (fox versus lion, systematic versus buckshot, involved versus aloof, bipartisan versus partisan, independent), and Harrigan's four governors' styles (demagogue, program promoter, frustrated warrior, and caretaker) are among the most prominent.[36] The variation quickly becomes unmanageable in any single or comparative study. So there could be much value in articulating and applying a classification that reflects the richness of the situation, is simple enough for understanding, and is researchable (which Barber's classification, requiring sophisticated behavioral information, may not yet be at the gubernatorial level).

The classification could build upon the work done on the presidency, as well as that on the governors, recognizing such differences as the structural and political fragmentation of the states' executive branches, the governors' more limited formal powers, and the presidents' unique international and military roles.[37] (It also could add new depth to the presidential leadership literature because the governors offer a much larger population, allowing cross-sectional as well as longtitudinal comparisons.) If such a system of classification can be identified and then applied to future documentations of transitions, it would offer an additional and important opportunity for comparative analyses.

Such analysis would be especially useful if it showed how the governor's important transition decisions can reflect, support, or be confused by a particular style.[38] These decisions include the types of persons (campaign participants, holdovers) appointed to the governor's staff and state agencies; the mechanisms used in the talent search for appointees, including the charge given the searchers and the role of the governor; the extent to which the governor becomes involved in appointments at the subcabinet level; the timing of various appointments; the selection of policy priorities; and the decision about where to focus brokerage efforts—upon influentials, the legislature, or the general public.

These decisions become the governor's strategy. They depend upon the governor's purposes and upon an assessment of circumstances. They reflect a management style and might even adjust or change that style as the governor considers purposes and approaches. If future documentation of transitions can delineate management styles and the relationships of these styles to the primary decisions of the transition period, the choices could be more clearly articulated. For example, the choice between an aloof big-picture approach and an involved nit-picking approach to management could be analyzed, with emphasis upon how to reduce the problems of each approach, to better reveal to the new governors what their predilections imply. The comparison of a strong chief-of-staff and spokes-of-the-wheel organizations could be studied the same way. Thus, future studies could help adjust and elaborate an outline such as that presented in table 2.

THE PAYOFFS OF THE TRANSITION

As the Arkansas analyst noted, "the only good transition is an orderly transition," and that includes cordial and supportive relationships between the outgoing and the incoming governors and an effective organization by the incoming governor to manage budget preparation, personnel appointments, and inaugural and state of the state messages. An area of nearly universal agreement is that a good (orderly) transition is good politics. This is the consensus not only of the guides, the state reports, and the new governors but also of the outgoing governors (evidenced by the actions of governors Jay Hammond in Alaska, Frank White in Arkansas, Jerry Brown in California, William Milliken in Michigan, Albert Quie in Minnesota, and Lee Dreyfus in Wisconsin, all of whom provided substantial assistance to victors from the other party). The consensus presumes that a smooth transition will reflect well upon all the parties involved and thus be an important catalyst to the coming gubernatorial term as it was in Georgia, Iowa, and Michi-

Table 2. Examples of Style Tradeoffs and Adjustments

	Advantage	Disadvantage	Problem reduction
Reported Styles:			
Chairman of the Board	More chance for big picture	Loss of control	Strong management control system
Chief Administrator	Understanding and control of detail	Little time for molding broad strategy	Strong planning function in close personal contact with governor
Guide Styles:			
Chief of Staff	Completed staff work	Risk of being managed or limited by staff	Skill at questioning information and proposals, and good alternative sources of information and evaluation
Spokes of Wheel	More assurance of real options' surfacing	Administrative burden upon governor, and conflicting information and suggestions	Willingness to wait for issues to ripen and to then make definite choices

gan, and shape final judgments about the success of the concluding term. The consensus may reflect a present bias in the political culture toward cooperation rather than confrontation among public leaders. If so, it could be lost in future cultural changes. But at least for the moment it encourages apparently useful communications between the old and the new administrations to aid in achieving a smooth transition, even in situations, such as in California, where the relationships were otherwise much strained.

Reflecting this consensus, every governor made a nearly total personal commitment to the activities of this period, assigned substantial organizational and state resources to the effort, and usually made significant preparations even during the uncertainties and desperation of the final weeks of the campaign.

The implication of this consensus, beyond its threat to the governors' postelection vacations, is that separating the transition from either the campaign or the permanent staffing and operation of the governor's term becomes problematic. Any activity that deserves the candidate's personal time during the final months of the gubernatorial campaign can hardly be kept separate from the campaign itself and the campaign personalities. An effort that fundamentally shapes the policy agenda can hardly be turned off the day of the inauguration or the day of the state of the state message. Staff carry-over may not only be a key component of any brokerage strategy, it may be a practical necessity.[39]

None of this denies the substantial problems created by close linkages between campaign, transition, and state government, nor the limitations of brokerage without an effective sense of purpose and direction. But the contrast between guidelines and practice does suggest that these problems are not ended by urging away the linkages. Better to recognize the probability and even necessity of the linkages, to understand the problems they bring, and then seek adjustments and mechanisms to minimize the difficulties while building the capacity of the state staffs to broker effective gubernatorial leadership.

Appendix A
Outline for the State Analysts

1. *The milieu: The state's politics, government, and policies*
   At ease, crisis, tax problems, economy, social setting. The backdrop for the transition.
2. *Politics of the principals*
   Outgoing, incoming governors and their chief aides, supporters. The ambience of the situation. Was incumbency a critical variable, and how? Did the winner anticipate governing and detach personnel from the campaign to focus on transition? Was the state bureaucracy part of the campaign as participants or as an issue?
3. *The transition provisions, procedures, and support*
   Timing, state laws and provisions, budgetary considerations. How the state officially prepares for transition. How well do the principals and the staff work within the state's provisions?
4. *The politics of the transition*
   What really happens in the transition—outside the formal provisions and procedures? Where are the squeak points, the places where things work well? What interpersonal, intergroup, or intragroup problems are there?
5. *Comings and goings*
   Personnel turnover, appointments (what they are, who they are). The office staff, major departments, and so forth. How much holdover from previous administration? Shutting down the campaign and campaign organization. The inaugural, a political or governmental event? Who serves the gatekeeper role for the governor-elect, controlling the mob of job seekers?
6. *Coping with the processes*
   Getting an office working—the day-to-day mechanics. Becoming chief budget officer. Putting together the legislative program or package. Establishing a personnel screening process. Meshing the policy advisors and specialists with the more generalist process people. How is turf defined and territory staked out?
7. *Reaching out from the governor's office*
   Constituent relations and the ombudsman function—chaotic or organized? The

political party structures and the personnel. Staff's ability and understanding of the intergovernmental role in regard to:

—the local governments

—other states and regional entities

—the national level: Congress, the administration

—the decision whether to have a Washington representative and what that person(s) should do.

8. *Aid and assistance*

Where did governor and staff turn for help? Role and impact of the NGA Seminar for New Governors (November). Were the NGA written materials utilized, and did they have an impact? Role and impact of any NGA transition assistance teams. Others who impacted: the universities and their personnel, private industry, consultants, other state personnel. Who was impacted and how? What processes, if any, were impacted?

9. *The politics of the new administration*

Taking over and creating an image. The state of the state message—from campaign rhetoric to program and policy. The legislative program and its reception. The budget and the new administration's revisions. The team appointed to run state government. How the cabinet works and is perceived. The politics of reaching into the departments to seek loyalty (making the rounds, using the appointive cabinet heads, selecting the governors' person within an agency).

10. *Evaluation of the transition*

General findings and conclusions. Problems perceived and problems overcome, alleviated, ducked.

Appendix B   The Governors:
Provisions and Procedures for Transition

State or other jurisdiction	Legislation pertaining to gubernatorial transition	Appropriations available to gov.-elect	Gov.-elect participates in preparing state budget for coming fiscal year	Gov.-elect hires staff to assist during transition	State personnel made available to assist gov.-elect	Office space in buildings available to gov.-elect	Provisions for acquainting gov.-elect staff with office procedures and routine office functions	Provisions for transfer of information (records, files, etc.)
Alabama	...	...	...	...	...	...	...	...
Alaska	...	...	...	...	...	☆	...	☆
Arizona	...	...	☆	...	☆	☆	☆	☆
Arkansas	★	$ 60,000	★	★	...	☆	...	...
California	★	348,000	★	★	★	★	☆	☆
Colorado	★	10,000	★	★	...	★	★	★
Connecticut	★	10,000	☆	★	☆	★	...	★
Delaware	★	10,000(a)	...	...	☆	★	☆	☆
Florida	★	75,000	...	★	☆	★	☆	☆
Georgia	★	★	☆	☆	☆	☆	☆	☆
Hawaii	★	50,000	★	...	★	★	★	★
Idaho	★	15,000	★	★	★	★	...	...
Illinois	★	...	★	★(b)	★(c)	★	★	★
Indiana	★	40,000	★	★	★	★	★	★
Iowa	★(d)	10,000	★	★	☆(e)	...	★	★(f)
Kansas	★	100,000	★	★	★	★	★	★
Kentucky	★	Unspecified	★	★	★	★	★	★
Louisiana	...	10,000	★	★	...	★	☆	☆
Maine	★	5,000	★	★	★(g)	...	★	☆
Maryland	...	50,000	★	★	★	★	★	★
Massachusetts	...	★	☆	★	★	★	☆	☆
Michigan	...	...	...	...	...	...	☆	☆
Minnesota	★	29,600	★	★	★	★	☆	☆
Mississippi	★	25,000	★	★	★	★	★	★
Missouri	★	100,000	★	★	☆	★	...	...
Montana	★	30,000	★(h)	★	★	★	★	★
Nebraska	...	30,000(i)	☆	★	☆	☆	☆	☆
Nevada	...	...	★	...	☆	★	☆	☆
New Hampshire	★	5,000	★	★	★	★	★	...
New Jersey	★	150,000	★	★	★	★	☆	★

Appendix B (Continued)

State or other jurisdiction	Legislation pertaining to gubernatorial transition	Appropriations available to gov.-elect	Gov.-elect participates in preparing state budget for coming fiscal year	Gov.-elect hires staff to assist during transition	State personnel made available to assist gov.-elect	Office space in buildings available to gov.-elect	Provisions for acquainting gov.-elect staff with office procedures and routine office functions	Provisions for transfer of information (records, files, etc.)
New Mexico	★	25,000	★	★	☆	★	☆	☆
New York	...	...	☆	☆	☆	☆	☆	☆
North Carolina	★	3,500(j)	★	★	★	★	☆	☆
North Dakota	...	★	...	...	☆	...	☆	★
Ohio	★	30,000	...	★	★	★	...	☆
Oklahoma	★	10,000	★	★	...	☆	...	...
Oregon	★	20,000	★	★	★	★	★	★
Pennsylvania	★	100,000	...	★	☆	★	★	...
Rhode Island	...	...	★	...	...	★	...	...
South Carolina	★	50,000	★	★	...	★	...	☆
South Dakota	★	10,000	...	★	☆	★	☆	★
Tennessee	★	(k)	☆	★	★	★	☆	★
Texas	...	...	★(l)	★	☆	...	...	☆
Utah	...	5,000(m)	★	★	...	★	...	...
Vermont	...	18,000	★(n)	★	★	★	★	(o)
Virginia	...	40,000	...	★	★	★	★	★
Washington	★	80,000	☆	☆	☆	☆	☆	☆
West Virginia	...	...	...	...	...	☆	☆	...
Wisconsin	★	Unspecified	★	★	★	★	★	★
Wyoming	...	10,000(i)	★	★	...	...	...	...
American Samoa	...	Unspecified	★(p)	☆	☆	☆	☆	☆
Guam	...	...	...	...	...	...	...	...
No. Mariana Is.	...	...	...	...	...	...	...	...
Puerto Rico	...	56,000(a)	...	☆	☆	☆	☆	☆
Virgin Islands	...	...	...	...	...	...	...	...

SOURCE: *The Book of the States, 1982–83* (Lexington, Ky.: The Council of State Governments, 1982), 153.

... —No provisions or procedures.
★ —Formal provisions or procedures.
☆ —No formal provisions; occurs informally.
(a) Inaugural expenses are paid from this amount.
(b) On a contractual basis.
(c) Voluntary assistance.
(d) Pertains only to funds.
(e) Provided on irregular basis.
(f) Arrangement for transfer of criminal files.
(g) Budget personnel.
(h) Can submit supplemental budget.

(i) Made available in 1979.
(j) In addition, $1,500 is made available for the lieutenant governor-elect.
(k) Money made available from emergency and contingency funds.
(l) Outgoing governor and incoming governor present separate budgets to the legislature.
(m) Allocated from the governor's emergency fund.
(n) Responsible for the preparation of the budget; staff made available.
(o) Not transferred but use may be authorized.
(p) Can submit reprogramming or supplementa appropriation measures for current fiscal year.

Bibliography:
Gubernatorial Transition

Ahlberg, Clark D., and Moynihan, Daniel P. (1960). "Changing Governors—and Policies." *Public Administration Review* 20: 195–205. (New York).

Allen, David J. (1965). *New Governor in Indiana: The Challenge of Executive Power.* Bloomington: Indiana University, Institute of Public Administration.

Anonymous (1968). "Gubernatorial Transition in the States." *State Government Administration* 3: 18ff.

Arkansas Legislative Council (1971). *Pre-Inaugural Staff, Office and Other Allowances for Governors in Arkansas and Various States.* Little Rock: Arkansas Legislative Council.

Beyle, Thad L. (1984). "Gubernatorial Transitions: Lessons from the Past." *Publius* 14: 13–39.

——— (1984). "Transition Out of the Governor's Chair: The 1982 Experience." *State Government* 57: 79–84.

Beyle, Thad L., and Huefner, Robert (1983). "Quips and Quotes from Old Governors to New." *Public Administration Review* 43: 268–70.

Beyle, Thad L., and Wickman, John (1970). "Gubernatorial Transition in a One-Party Setting." *Public Administration Review* 30: 10–17. (Kansas and North Carolina).

Beyle, Thad L., and Williams, J. Oliver (1969). "New Governor in North Carolina: Politics and Administration of Transition." Unpublished report to the Governor's Office, Raleigh, N.C.

Blair, Diane, and Savage, Robert (1980). "The Rhetorical Challenge of a Gubernatorial Transition: Constructing the Image of Statecraft." Paper presented at the 1980 Conference of the International Communications Association, Acapulco, Mexico, May 1980 (Arkansas).

Bradley, Leonard K., Jr. (1973). "Gubernatorial Transition in Tennessee: The 1970–1971 Experience." Knoxville: Master's thesis, Department of Political Science, University of Tennessee.

Carter, Dale E. (1968). *When Governors Change: The Case of Mental Hygiene.* Institute of Governmental Affairs Research Report No. 2. University of California, Davis: (California).

———— (1968). *When Governors Change: Symbolic Output and Political Support.* Institute of Governmental Affairs Research Report No. 5. University of California, Davis: (California).

Caton, Bernard (1978). "Gubernatorial Transitions in Virginia." *Newsletter,* Institute of Government, University of Virginia 4: 9540–72.

Council of State Governments (1961). "Transition of Executive Administration from Governor to Governor-Elect." Memo prepared for the 53rd Annual Governors' Conference, Chicago.

———— (1968 and 1974). *Gubernatorial Transition in the States.* Lexington, Ky.: The Council.

———— (1970). "Bibliography: Seminar for New Governors-Elect." Lexington, Ky.: The Council, 5 pp.

———— (1972). *New Governors: Questions They Should Ask Immediately.* Lexington, Ky.: The Council.

———— (1984). "The Governors: Provisions and Procedures for Transition." *The Book of the States: 1984–85.* Lexington, Ky.: The Council. P. 54.

David, Paul T. (1961). *The Presidential Election and Transition 1960–1961.* Washington, D.C.: The Brookings Institution, 1961.

Gable, Richard W. (1983). *Changing Governors: The 1982–83 Transition in California.* Government Series II, No. 19. Davis, Calif.: Institute of Governmental Affairs.

Gibbons, Charles (1961). "Transition of Government in Massachusetts." *State Government* 34: 100–101.

Hopkins, Anne H. (1979). "Gubernatorial Transition in Tennessee." *Comparative State Politics Newsletter* 1:22.

Huefner, Robert P., and Nash, Michael L. (1984). "The Politics of Leadership: The 1982–83 Gubernatorial Transitions." *State Government* 57: 67–72.

Johnston, David A. (1963). "Problems in the Transition of Government." Columbus, Ohio: Legislative Service Commission Staff Research Report No. 57. (Ohio)

Kidman, Peter N. (1972). "Gubernatorial Transition in West Virginia." Ph.D. diss., Department of Political Science, University of West Virginia.

———— (1972). "Gubernatorial Transition in West Virginia." Paper delivered at the West Virginia Political Science Association Meeting, Morganton, October 1972.

Kress, Gunther (1968). *When Governors Change: The Case of the Controller's Office.* Institute of Government Affairs Report No. 4. University of California, Davis.

———— (1971). *When Governors Change: The Case of Medi-Cal.* Institute of Governmental Affairs Research Report No. 4. University of California, Davis. (California)

Long, Norton B. (1962). "After the Voting Is Over." *Midwest Journal of Political Science* 6: 183–200.

Mandeles, Mark (1977). "A Comparison of the 1966 and 1974 Gubernatorial Transitions." Master's thesis, Department of Political Science, University of California, Davis.

McGown, Wayne F. (1971). "Gubernatorial Transition in Wisconsin." *State Government* 44: 103–106.

National Governors' Association (1975). *The Critical Hundred Days: A Handbook for New Governors*. Washington, D.C.: The Association.

—— (1976). *The Governor's Office*. Washington, D.C.: The Association.

—— (1978). *Governing the American States: A Handbook for New Governors*. Washington, D.C.: The Association.

—— (1982). *Transition and the New Governor: A Critical Overview*. Washington, D.C.: The Association.

Ringham, Stuart R. (1972). "The Governor-elect to Governor: Transition in the American States." Ph.D. diss., Department of Political Science, University of Wisconsin.

Sabato, Larry (1983). *Goodbye to Good Time Charlie: The American Governorship Transformed*. Washington, D.C.: CQ Press.

Sanford, Terry (1967). *Storm Over the States*. New York: McGraw-Hill, 1967.

Schenker, Alan Evan (1969). *When Governors Change: The Case of the California Budget*. Institute of Governmental Affairs Research Report No. 8. University of California, Davis. (California).

—— (1972). "Comments." In Thad L. Beyle and J. Oliver Williams (eds.), *The American Governor in Behavioral Perspective*. New York: Harper and Row. Pp. 92–94.

Warner, Kenneth (1961). "Planning for Transition." *State Government* 34: 102–103.

Weeks, George (1984). "Gubernatorial Transition: Leaving There." *State Government* 57: 73–78.

Wisconsin (1970). *The Executive Office Transition*. Madison: Department of Administration. (Wisconsin)

Wyner, Alan J. (1970). "Staffing the Governor's Office." *Public Administration Review* 30: 17–24.

List of Contributors

Margery M. Ambrosius, Department of Political Science, University of Nebraska–Lincoln.

Howard R. Balanoff, Department of Political Science, Southwest Texas State University.

Gerald Benjamin, Department of Political Science, SUNY–New Paltz.

Thad L. Beyle, Department of Political Science, University of North Carolina, Chapel Hill.

Diane D. Blair, Department of Political Science, University of Arkansas, Fayetteville.

Don W. Driggs, Department of Political Science, University of Nevada, Reno.

Delmer D. Dunn, Department of Political Science, University of Georgia.

Richard W. Gable, Department of Political Science, University of California, Davis.

Jose Z. Garcia, Department of Political Science, New Mexico State University.

William T. Gormley, Jr., Department of Political Science, University of Wisconsin, Madison.

Virginia Gray, Department of Political Science, University of Minnesota.

Keith E. Hamm, Department of Political Science, Texas A&M University.

Robert P. Huefner, Center for Public Affairs and Administration, University of Utah.

Karen Hult, Department of Political Science, Pamona College.

Joel King, Institute of Governmental Affairs, University of California, Davis.

Gerald A. McBeath, Department of Political Science, University of Alaska, Fairbanks.

Keith J. Mueller, Department of Political Science, University of Nebraska–Lincoln.

Michael L. Nash, Political Science Department, University of Utah.

Laurence J. O'Toole, Jr., Department of Political Science, Auburn University.

Charles Press, Department of Political Science, Michigan State University.

Russell M. Ross, Department of Political Science, University of Iowa.

Terry Sanford, President, Duke University, and Governor of North Carolina, 1961–1965.

Mark Sektnan, Institute of Governmental Affairs, University of California, Davis.

Kenneth VerBurg, Department of Political Science, Michigan State University.
Martha Wagner Weinberg, Department of Political Science, Massachusetts Institute of Technology.
Charles W. Wiggins, Department of Political Science, Texas A&M University.
Richard F. Winters, Department of Government, Dartmouth College.

Notes

Introductory Chapter

Portions of this chapter appeared in *Publius* 14 (1984): 13–29.

1. For a sample of what these governors said, see Thad L. Beyle and Robert Huefner, "Quips and Quotes from Old Governors to New," *Public Administration Review* 43, no. 3 (1983): 268–70.
2. National Governors' Association (NGA), *The Critical Hundred Days: A Handbook for New Governors* (Washington, D. C.: NGA, 1975); *The Governor's Office* (Washington, D. C.: NGA, 1976); *Governing the American States: A Handbook for New Governors* (Washington, D. C.: NGA, 1978); *Transition and the New Governor: A Critical Overview* (Washington, D. C.: NGA, 1982).
3. NGA, *Transition and the New Governor*, v.
4. NGA, *Transition and the New Governor*, 6, 38, 54, 64, 78, 90, 100, and quotation on p. 5.
5. Clark D. Ahlberg and Daniel P. Moynihan, "Changing Governors—and Policies," *Public Administration Review* 20 (1960): 195–205 (New York); Norton B. Long, "After the Voting Is Over," *Midwest Journal of Political Science* 6 (1962): 183–200 (Illinois); David J. Allen, *New Governor in Indiana: The Challenge of Executive Power* (Bloomington: Institute of Public Administration, Indiana University, 1965); Dale E. Carter, *When Governors Change: Symbolic Output and Political Support*, Institute of Governmental Affairs Research Report No. 5 (Davis: University of California, Davis, 1968) (California); Thad L. Beyle and John Wickman, "Gubernatorial Transition in a One-Party Setting," *Public Administration Review* 30 (1970): 10–17 (Kansas and North Carolina); Peter N. Kidman, "Gubernatorial Transition in West Virginia" (Ph.D. diss., University of West Virginia, 1972); Leonard K. Bradley, Jr., "Gubernatorial Transition in Tennessee: The 1970–71 Experience" (M.A. thesis, University of Tennessee, Knoxville, 1973); Bernard Caton, "Gubernatorial Transitions in Virginia," *Newsletter*, Institute of Government, University of Virginia, 4 (1978): 9540–72; Diane Blair and Robert Savage, "The Rhetorical Challenge of a Gubernatorial Transition: Constructing the Image of Statecraft" (Paper delivered at the 1980

Conference of the International Communications Association, Acapulco, Mexico, May 1980) (Arkansas).

6. Stuart R. Ringham, "The Governor-Elect to Governor: Transition in the American States," (Ph.D. diss., University of Iowa, Iowa City, 1972).

7. Kenneth Warner, "Planning for Transition," *State Government* 34 (1961): 102–103.

8. Charles Gibbons, "Transitions of Government in Massachusetts," *State Government* 34 (1961): 100–101; Wayne F. McGown, "Gubernatorial Transition in Wisconsin," *State Government* 44 (1971): 103–6.

9. Ohio Legislative Service Commission (OLSC), *Problems in the Transition of Government*, Staff Research Report No. 57 (Columbus, Ohio: OLSC, 1963); Wisconsin, Department of Administration, *The Executive Office Transition* (Madison: Department of Administration, 1970); Arkansas Legislative Council, *Pre-Inaugural Staff, Office and Other Allowances for Governors in Arkansas and Various States* (Little Rock: The Council, 1971).

10. Gibbons, "Transition of Government in Massachusetts," 100; McGown, "Gubernatorial Transition in Wisconsin," 106; NGA, *Transition and the New Governor*, 1.

11. Ahlberg and Moynihan, "Changing Governors," 197; Beyle and Wickman, Gubernatorial Transition in a One-Party Setting," 15, 11.

12. Long, "After the Voting Is Over," 190; Beyle and Wickman, "Gubernatorial Transition in a One-Party Setting," 14–15; Blair and Savage, "The Rhetorical Challenge of A Gubernatorial Transition."

13. Ahlberg and Moynihan, "Changing Governors," 195; Long, "After the Voting Is Over," 196.

14. Beyle and Wickman, "Gubernatorial Transition in a One-Party Setting," 14; Long, "After the Voting Is Over," 188; quoted in Beyle and Huefner, "Quips and Quotes from Old Governors to New," 268.

15. ABC News, *The 1982 Vote: What Happened* (New York: ABC News, 1983), 177–79.

16. John F. Bibby, "State House Elections at Midterm," in Thomas E. Mann and Norman J. Ornstein, *The American Elections of 1982* (Washington, D.C.: American Enterprise Institute, 1983), 114–15.

17. Quoted in Beyle and Huefner, "Quips and Quotes from Old Governors to New," 268.

18. Long, "After the Voting Is Over," 192–94.

19. NGA, *Transition and the New Governor*, 76.

20. Quoted in Beyle and Huefner, "Quips and Quotes from Old Governors to New," 268.

21. NGA, *Transition and the New Governor*, 89.

22. Beyle and Huefner, "Quips and Quotes from Old Governors to New," 269.

23. Ibid.

24. Jack W. Germond and Jules Witcover, "Blanchard Faced the Music Early," *The Columbia Record* (S.C.), June 16, 1983.

25. Richard Neustadt, *Presidential Power* (New York: Wiley, 1960).

26. NGA, *Governing the American States*, 193.

27. NGA, *Transition and the New Governor*, 29–30.

Alabama

Among the research sources for this chapter were numerous interviews with political figures in Alabama, especially current and former members of the staffs of Governors Fob James and George Wallace. Unattributed quotations in the text are drawn from those interviews. Several members of both administrations were generous with their time, and some also provided me access to meetings, unpublished documents, and correspondence pertaining to the transition. Margaret Latimer offered the use of her comprehensive files of newspapers from the Alabama black community. The author thanks all these for their kind assistance and acknowledges with gratitude Gerald W. Johnson's many insights, research suggestions, and comments on an earlier draft.

1. V. O. Key, Jr., *Southern Politics* (New York: Knopf, 1949), 19.
2. For an analysis of political machines, political organizations reliant on material exchange for their continued sustenance, see Edward C. Banfield and James Q. Wilson, *City Politics* (New York: Vintage Books, 1963), 115–21.
3. Coleman B. Ransone, Jr., *Office of the Governor in the United States* (University: University of Alabama Press, 1956), 94; Larry Sabato, *Goodbye to Good-Time Charlie* (Lexington, Mass.: Lexington Books, 1978), 122.
4. Citizens' Conference on State Legislatures, *The Sometime Governments*, 2nd ed. (New York: Bantam Books, 1973), 49, 52–53.
5. Jon C. Ham, "Lobbyists and Legislators: Interaction in the Alabama Legislature" (M.A. thesis, Department of Political Science, Auburn University, 1981).
6. Council of Twenty-One, *Challenge—Obligation—Opportunity: The Imperative for Excellence in Higher Education* (Montgomery, Ala.: The Council, 1983), 4.
7. See, for instance, the results of the University of Alabama Capstone Poll data.
8. *New York Times*, June 14, 1983.
9. Clark D. Ahlberg and Daniel P. Moynihan, "Changing Governors—and Policies," *Public Administration Review* 20 (1960):195–205.
10. Keith J. Ward and Elton C. Smith, "Financing State Government," in *Alabama Issues 1982*, ed. Keith J. Ward (Auburn: Office of Public Service and Research, Auburn University, 1982), 21–34.
11. *Montgomery Advertiser*, Oct. 3, 1982.
12. University of Alabama Capstone Poll data.
13. Records at the Office of the Secretary of State, Montgomery.
14. *Montgomery Advertiser*, Nov. 1, 1982.
15. Ibid., Nov. 3, 1982.
16. Ibid., Jan. 16, 1983.
17. Ibid., Nov. 4, 1982.
18. Ibid., Nov. 7, 1982.
19. See the briefing by Faye S. Baggiano, commissioner of Pensions and Security, Office of the Governor, Montgomery, Nov. 19, 1982.
20. *Montgomery Advertiser*, Oct. 23, 1983.
21. Ibid., June 4, 1983 and Oct. 23, 1983.
22. Ibid., Jan. 16, 1983.
23. Ibid., June 13, 1983.
24. *Birmingham News*, May 8, 1983.

25. Harold W. Stanley, *Senate vs. Governor, Alabama 1971: Referents for Opposition in a One-Party Legislature* (University: University of Alabama Press, 1975), 23.

26. *Montgomery Advertiser*, Jan. 1, 1984.

27. Ibid., Apr. 8, 1984.

Alaska

My study of Alaska's executive transition began as part of the comparative study on gubernatorial transitions, described elsewhere in this volume. I thank Thad Beyle and Jim Tait for their advice, suggestions, and encouragement in this project.

The Alaska report is based on extensive review of the documents prepared for the Alaska gubernatorial transition by the Hammond and Sheffield administrations; interviews with the staff members of both administrations, with the Sheffield transition team and task forces, and with Alaska's governors; and review of Alaska's newspapers during and after the transition. Thanks are due the Sheffield administration, particularly Governor Sheffield, his special assistants and transition team members, and former Governor Hammond and his special assistants, for their support of my research.

I am particularly grateful to Barbara Sundberg, Sheri Layral, Linda Ilgenfritz, and Joe St. Sauver for their invaluable assistance in preparing the report. Colleagues and friends—Tom Morehouse, Vic Fischer, Carl Shepro, Brian Rogers, Pat O'Rourke, Andrea Helms, Claus Naske, and Scott Sterling—gave freely of their time in criticizing the draft.

Credit for this study belongs to many—informants who graciously gave of their time and colleagues who shared their expertise. I am solely responsible for errors and omissions.

1. The Alaska Constitution was drafted in 1955-56 to help gain statehood by proving to Congress and the nation that Alaska was a mature political entity. For information on the constitutional convention, see Victor Fischer, *Alaska's Constitutional Convention* (Fairbanks: University of Alaska Press, 1975), and Claus-M. Naske, *An Interpretative History of Alaska Statehood* (Anchorage: Alaska Northwest Publishing, 1973).

2. The five governors since statehood are: 1959-66, William A. Egan (D) (two terms); 1966-69, Walter J. Hickel (R); 1969-70, Keith Miller (R); 1970-74, William A. Egan (D); 1974-82, Jay S. Hammond (R) (two terms); 1982-86, Bill Sheffield (D). Biographical sketches of Alaska's governors are given in Evangeline Atwood and Robert DeArmond, *Who's Who in Alaska Politics* (Portland, Ore.: Binford & Mort, for the Alaska Historical Commission, 1977).

3. Political parties were strong in territorial days and into statehood. Use of the open primary system, among other factors, has greatly weakened their force in state politics and government.

4. In the statehood election of 1958 Alaskans voted Democrats into office—the governor, two U.S. senators and one representative, and fifty-two of sixty seats in the first state legislature. Since that time the Republican party has replaced the Democratic as the dominant organized political force. In 1984 the state has Republican U.S. senators and representatives. The last time Alaskans voted

Democratic in presidential elections was 1964. In state politics, as mentioned, party is a factor of declining importance, and coalitions organize the legislature. Yet thirty-two of the sixty seats in the 1983 legislature are held by Republicans. For an early survey of the Alaska electorate, see Thomas A. Morehouse and Gordon S. Harrison, *An Electoral Profile of Alaska* (Fairbanks: Institute of Social, Economic and Government Research, University of Alaska, 1973).

5. The other six propositions were a "Tundra rebellion" initiative, to assert state ownership over federal lands in the state; a proposition calling for a state constitutional convention; a measure to withdraw state funding for abortions; a proposed constitutional amendment to redesign the judicial qualifications commission; a proposed constitutional alteration in the veterans loan program; a proposed constitutional amendment to put a cap on state spending.

6. As aboriginal residents of Alaska, Natives are protected by federal law in their aboriginal occupancy and use of land. Native claims to land were resolved in the Alaska Native Claims Settlement Act of 1971 (ANCSA). Native rights to subsistence use were incorporated as a section of ANCSA and specifically provided for in the Alaska National Interest Conservation Act of 1980 (ANILCA). For interpretations of ANCSA, see Robert Arnold, *Alaska Native Land Claims* (Anchorage: Alaska Native Foundation, 1976), and Gerald A. McBeath and Thomas A. Morehouse, *The Dynamics of Alaska Native Self-Government* (Lanham, Md.: University Press of America, 1980). For information on Native sovereignty issues, see David S. Case, *The Special Relationship between Alaska Natives and the Federal Government* (Anchorage: Alaska Native Foundation, 1978).

7. The very expensive 1982 elections dried up funds for local races in many parts of the state. Legislative candidates were unable to raise as much money as usual for their campaigns because interest groups and individual contributions were directed to statewide races.

8. The transition team consisted of the following people:

Al Parrish—cochairman of campaign and transition team: president of Sheffield Hotels, Inc., and longtime business and personal associate of the new governor, CPA.

Norman Gorsuch—cochairman of campaign and transition team: attorney general in the Egan administration (1973–74) and partner of the Ely, Guess, and Rudd law firm (engaged in legislative lobbying, among other things) in Juneau.

Laurie Herman—campaign official and former employee of Sheffield Hotels, Inc.: Former executive director of the Alaska Republican party; longtime business and personal friend of the new governor.

Dave Walsh—campaign official and assemblyman: municipality of Anchorage; lawyer.

Lance Anderson—campaign finance official: executive vice president, Cook Inlet Region, Inc. (one of the largest Native corporations in the state); CPA.

Marlene Neve—member of statewide Democratic party organization: head of Fairbanks AFL-CIO COPE office; former council member, city of Seward, and former south-central election supervisor.

Emil Notti—member of statewide Democratic party organization: former president of both Doyon, Ltd., and the Alaska Federation of Natives; former deputy commissioner of the state Department of Health and Social Services under Governor Egan; former Democratic candidate for Congress (1973).

9. The transition team task forces reviewed the following departments:

Resources: Department of Fish and Game, Department of Natural Resources, Department of Environmental Conservation.

Human Services: Department of Health and Social Services, Department of Education, University of Alaska.

Public Protection and Labor: Department of Public Safety, Department of Labor, Deaprtment of Military Affairs.

Business Management: Department of Revenue, Department of Commerce and Economic Development.

Revenue Transfer: Department of Transportation and Public Facilities, Department of Community and Regional Affairs.

General Government: Office of the Governor, Office of the Lieutenant Governor, Department of Law, Department of Administration, boards and commissions.

10. In 1981 the state legislature enacted a plan to distribute permanent fund earnings to citizens according to the length of their residence in the state. The Zobels (two Anchorage attorneys) claimed that this plan violated the U.S. Constitution's equal protection guarantees and filed suit to halt the distribution scheme. The state supreme court supported the plan, but the U.S. Supreme Court did not, finding it in violation of the Fourteenth Amendment to the U.S. Constitution. The state legislature then decided to allocate dividends to residents equally, but the federal court action seemed to invalidate other programs based on residence—most of which have now been challenged in state court.

11. One Hammond administration official, John Katz (former commissioner of natural resources) was appointed to head the Alaska state office in Washington, D. C.

12. While the governor compiled a statewide list of capital projects, the legislature compiled local projects, particularly for rural, unorganized areas.

13. The 1982 legislative session authorized the allocation of more funds to the permanent fund than required by law (or available in the treasury), apparently binding future legislatures to make up the deficit. In 1983 legislators proposed to cancel this debt, but the bill did not pass.

14. The governor's executive order establishing the Office of Management and Budget was disapproved by legislators who objected to OMB's attempt to control the writing of fiscal notes (formerly done by agencies for committee chairmen). The executive order establishing a Department of Corrections was opposed because of failure to resolve the issue of juvenile corrections. Both were rejected so that the legislature could flex its muscles.

15. Departments of Transportation and Public Facilities, Community and Regional Affairs, Health and Social Services, and Environmental Conservation.

16. In his veto message for each of the bills the governor complained that the specialized-bill approach made it difficult for him to measure the overall impact of the spending proposals. He further objected to the high ratio of legislative add-

ons in the bills in comparison with agency requests and OMB-approved proposals.
17. I am indebted to Thomas A. Morehouse for this observation.

Arkansas

Much of the material in this chapter is based on personal interviews conducted between November 1982 and April 1983 with the following persons: Preston Bynum (1980 coordinator of Governor-elect Frank White's transition; 1981–82 Governor White's chief of staff); Rudy Moore (1978 Clinton campaign manager; coordinator of Governor-elect Clinton's 1978 transition; 1979–80 Governor Clinton's senior executive assistant); Joan Roberts (1978–80 IGR aide to Governor Clinton; 1982 Clinton campaign press secretary; 1983– Governor Clinton's press secretary); Steven Smith (1976–78 administrative assistant to Attorney General Bill Clinton; 1979–80 Governor Clinton's executive assistant for governmental agencies); Betsey Wright (1982 Clinton campaign director; member, Governor-elect Clinton's 1982 transition team; 1983– Governor Clinton's director of staff and management operations).

Information was also drawn from television broadcasts and from the following newspapers: *Arkansas Gazette, Arkansas Democrat, Northwest Arkansas Times, Springdale News.*

1. *The Governor's Press Relations* (Washington, D. C.: National Governors' Conference, 1976), 5.
2. Diane Kincaid Blair and Robert L. Savage, "The Rhetorical Challenge of a Gubernatorial Transition: Constructing the Image of Statecraft" (Paper presented to the Annual Conference of the International Communications Association, Acapulco, Mexico, May 20, 1980), 1.
3. *Springdale News,* Nov. 19, 1978; *Arkansas Gazette,* Jan. 9, 1979.
4. *Northwest Arkansas Times,* Dec. 12, 1982; *Arkansas Gazette,* Dec. 2, 1982; Nov. 4, 1982; Jan. 9, 1983.
5. Statement by Representative John Miller, quoted in *Arkansas Gazette,* Jan. 9, 1983.
6. The 1979 appointment was announced in tandem with two others, but Clinton made a point of stating that the black appointee, B. J. McCoy, had been his "first Cabinet choice." A previous minor cabinet appointment, of the state adjutant general, was made in December 1982, but Mahlon Martin's appointment was universally treated as Clinton's first major appointment of his new administration.
7. For discussion and examples, see Diane Kincaid Blair, "The Gubernatorial Appointment Power: Too Much of a Good thing?" *State Government* 55, no. 3 (1982): 88–92.
8. *Arkansas Gazette,* Jan. 9, 1983.

California

1. Norton Long, "After the Voting Is Over," *Midwest Journal of Political Science* 6 (May 1962): 200.
2. James R. Carroll, "Dull Tom and Cautious Duke," *California Journal* (July 1982): 229–31.

3. National Governors' Association, *Transition and the New Governor: A Critical Overview* (Washington, D.C.: NGA, 1982).
4. Ed Salzman, "Packing Deukmejian's Policies to Sell," *Sacramento Bee*, July 26, 1983.
5. Ibid.
6. Martin Smith, "The Reagans and the Mansion," ibid., Feb. 21, 1984.
7. Martin Smith, "Civility Loses Its Priority," ibid., July 26, 1983.
8. Martin Smith, "Willie Brown's Worst Experience," ibid., July 7, 1983.
9. Martin Smith, "Another Redistricting Battle," ibid., Nov. 22, 1983.
10. Claire Cooper, "Rocky Moments in Duke's 1st 6 Weeks," ibid., Feb. 24, 1983.
11. Ed Salzman, "Duke 'Unknown Man' Surveys Show," ibid., Oct. 30, 1983.
12. Ibid.

Georgia

Much of the information in this chapter came from interviews with the following: Governor Joe Frank Harris; former Governor George D. Busbee; Tom Perdue, executive secretary to Governor Busbee and chief administrative officer to Governor Harris; Tom Daniel, former administrative assistant to Governor Busbee and campaign coordinator for the Harris campaign staff; Griffith Doyle, administrative assistant to Governor Busbee; Gracie Phillips, executive assistant to Governor Harris; Mike deVetger, executive assistant to Governor Harris; Barbara Morgan, press secretary for Governor Harris; and Rusty Sewell, executive counsel for Governor Harris. All articles pertaining to the election and the transition that appeared in the *Atlanta Constitution* between election day and the inaugural were also used in preparing the chapter.

Iowa

1. National Governors' Association, *Transition and the New Governor: A Critical Overview* (Washington, D.C.: NGA, 1982).

Massachusetts

1. Interview with Michael Dukakis, Apr. 8, 1983.
2. Interview with Kristin Demong, treasurer of the Dukakis campaign, Jan. 27, 1983.
3. Interview with John Sasso, Mar. 3, 1983.
4. Interviews with Sasso, Mar. 3, 1983, and Charles Kireker, Feb. 9, 1983.
5. Interview with Dukakis, Apr. 8, 1983.
6. "Dukakis Begins Planning the Shape of Things to Come," *Boston Globe*, Nov. 4, 1982.
7. "Dukakis Names Teams for his Transition," *Boston Globe*, Nov. 11, 1982.
8. "Dukakis, Advisors Meet Again; Decision on Cabinet Is Near," *Boston Globe*, Dec. 1, 1982.
9. Interview with Dukakis, Apr. 8, 1983.

10. Interview with Demong, Jan. 27, 1983.
11. Interview with Kireker, Apr. 10, 1983.
12. Interview with Kireker, Feb. 9, 1983.
13. Interview with Barbara Salisbury, Feb. 24, 1983.
14. Interview with Dukakis, Apr. 8, 1983.
15. Interview with a member of the campaign staff who asked not to be named.
16. Ibid.
17. Interview with a member of the Human Services Task Force, Feb. 14, 1983.
18. Interview with Kireker, Feb. 9, 1983.
19. Interview with Sasso, Mar. 3, 1983.
20. Interview with Kireker, Feb. 9, 1983.
21. Interview with Sasso, Mar. 3, 1983.
22. Interview with an official from the Executive Office of Human Services, Feb. 23, 1983.
23. Interview with Salisbury, Feb. 24, 1983.
24. Interview with Dukakis, Apr. 8, 1983.
25. "Dukakis Budget Is $250 M. Short, Sen. Atkins Says," *Boston Globe*, Mar. 10, 1983.
26. Interview with Kireker, Feb. 2, 1983.
27. Interview with Tom Glynn, Jan. 19, 1983.
28. Interview with Sasso, Mar. 3, 1983.
29. Interview with deputy chief secretary Charles Baker, Apr. 11, 1983.

Minnesota

1. Minnesota Poll, *Minneapolis Tribune*, Oct. 3, 1982, pp. 1, 4A.
2. Interview with Gov. Perpich, Mar. 3, 1983.
3. *Minneapolis Tribune*, Oct. 25, 1982, pp. 1, GA.
4. Interview with Gov. Perpich, Mar. 3, 1983.
5. *Minneapolis Tribune*, Nov. 3, 1982, p. 14, A.
6. Ibid., Nov. 6, 1982, pp. 4, 5C.
7. Ibid., Dec. 2, 1982, pp. 3, 5B.
8. Ibid., Nov. 4, 1982, pp. 1, 4A; Nov. 6, 1982, pp. 4, 5C.
9. Interview with Gov. Perpich, Mar. 3, 1983.
10. Ibid.
11. Quoted in the *Minneapolis Tribune*, Jan. 26, 1983, p. 3B.
12. Ibid., Jan. 14, 1983, p. 14A.
13. Quoted in ibid., Dec. 3, 1982, p. 1A.
14. Interview with Gov. Perpich, Mar. 3, 1983.
15. *Minneapolis Tribune*, Jan. 5, 1983, pp. 1, 5A; Jan. 6, 1983, pp. 1, 6A.
16. Ibid., Jan. 19, 1983, p. 1A
17. Ibid., Feb. 14, 1983, pp. 1, 7A.
18. *St. Paul Dispatch*, Feb. 15, 1983, pp. 1, 4A.
19. *Minneapolis Tribune*, Mar. 13, 1983, p. 10A.
20. Ibid.
21. Ibid., May 29, 1983, pp. 1, 4A.

22. Ibid., Jan. 15, 1983, pp. 1, 6A.
23. Ibid., Jan. 31, 1983, pp. 1, 4A.
24. Ibid., Jan. 30, 1983, pp. 1, 8A.
25. Ibid., Feb. 20, 1983, pp. 1, 6B.

Nebraska

1. *Lincoln Journal*, Aug. 24, 1982, p. 17; Oct. 31, 1982, p. 6.
2. Ibid., Oct. 24, 1982, p. C1.
3. Ibid., Nov. 21, 1982, p. C1.
4. Ibid., Aug. 21, 1982, p. 6.
5. Ibid., Sept. 24, 1982, p. 13.
6. Ibid., Dec. 14, 1982, p. 6.
7. Ibid., Nov. 29, 1982, p. 18.
8. Ibid., Nov. 5, 1982, p. 39 (quoting an *Omaha World-Herald* editorial).
9. Ibid., Dec. 10, 1982, p. 1.
10. Ibid., Nov. 5, 1982, p. 39 (quoting an earlier *Lincoln Journal* editorial).
11. Nebraska's tax rate-setting board is composed of the governor, the tax commissioner, the secretary of state, the state treasurer, and the state auditor.
12. *Lincoln Star*, Nov. 18, 1982, p. 8, quoting Kerrey.
13. Ibid, Nov. 19, 1982, p. 8.
14. Ibid., Dec. 10, 1982, p. 1.
15. *Wall Street Journal*, Mar. 25, 1983, p. 1.
16. *Lincoln Journal*, Apr. 22, 1983, p. 6.
17. *Wall Street Journal*, Mar. 25, 1983, p. 21.
18. *Omaha World-Herald*, May 29, 1983, p. 8-B.
19. Ibid.

Nevada

1. *Reno Gazette-Journal*, Jan. 2, 1983, p. 1.
2. Press release of Market Systems Research, Inc., Reno, Dec. 10, 1981, and interview with Thomas Lorentzen, executive director of the Clark County Republican party, Feb. 6, 1982.
3. Martin Griffith, "Vegas Talk," *Nevada State Journal*, Nov. 29, 1981.
4. *Reno Gazette-Journal*, Feb. 3, 1982, p. 1.
5. Ibid., July 29, 1982.
6. Ibid., Oct. 10, 1982, p. 1C.
7. *Reno Evening Gazette*, Mar. 3, 1982, p. 4C.
8. In his successful 1978 campaign List had used the "liberal" tag to good advantage against Democratic candidate Bob Rose.
9. *Reno Gazette-Journal*, Nov. 3, 1982, p. 1A; Jan. 2, 1983, p. 17A; Dec. 18, 1982, p. 1A.
10. Interview with Marlene Lockard, Mar. 4, 1983.
11. Ibid.
12. Ibid.

13. Interview with Andrew P. Grose, Apr. 1, 1983.
14. *Nevada Revised Statutes,* 331.120 and 353.240.
15. Interview with Grose, Apr. 1, 1983.
16. Ibid.
17. Ibid.
18. Interview with Lockard, Mar. 4, 1983.
19. Interviews with Lockard and Grose.
20. Ibid.
21. *Reno Gazette-Journal,* Oct. 19, 1982, p. 1A.
22. Ibid., Jan. 2, 1983, p. 2F.
23. Interview with Lockard, Mar. 4, 1983.
24. *Reno Gazette-Journal,* Jan. 20, 1983, p. 1A.
25. Ibid., Oct. 13, 1982, p. 1A.
26. By law the assessed valuation is supposed to be 35% of market value.
27. *Reno Gazette-Journal,* Jan. 20, 1983, p. 1A.
28. Interview on radio station KUNR-FM, Reno, May 17, 1983.

New Hampshire

1. This chapter builds on and uses materials that have appeared in my earlier writings on New Hampshire politics: "Political Choice and Expenditure Change in New Hampshire and Vermont," POLITY (Summer 1980): 598–621; "Party Politics in New Hampshire" (with Robert Craig), in J. Milburn and W. Doyle, eds., *Party Politics in the New England States* (Boston: Schenkman, 1983); "Damn Yankees and Others: New Hampshire's Electorate and What It Represents," a paper presented before a N.H. Humanities Council Conference on New Hampshire (available from the author); and "The Political Culture of New Hampshire," in Alan Rosenthal and Maureen Moakley, eds., *Political Cultures of the American States* (New York: Praeger Press, 1984).

   The basic literature on New Hampshire politics includes my work in n. 1 and Duane Lockard, *New England State Politics* (Princeton: Princeton University Press, 1959); Eric Veblen, *The Manchester Union Leader in New Hampshire Politics* (Hanover, N.H.: University Press of New England, 1974); and Neal Peirce, *The New England States of America* (New York: W. W. Norton, 1976), 285–361. For an entertaining portrait of William Loeb, see Kevin Cash, *Who the Hell Is William Loeb?* (Manchester, N.H.: Amoskeag Press, 1975).

2. Sections of this part rely heavily on my more extended analysis in "Political Culture. . . ."

3. See the data in Austin Ranney, "Party Politics in the States," in H. Jacob and K. Vines, eds., *Politics in the American States* (Boston: Little, Brown, 1976), 51–92.

4. For a more extended analysis of political parties in New Hampshire, see Craig and Winters, "Party Politics. . . ."

5. For example, in 1976 the gubernatorial race between Harry Spanos and incumbent Meldrim Thomson drew 3,051 more votes than the presidential contest of

that year. Four years later the gubernatorial totals exceeded the presidential totals by 41 votes.

6. See the discussion in Jae On Kim et al., "Voting Turnout among the American States: Systemic and Individual Components," *American Political Science Review* (March 1975): 107–124.

7. The tax issue is discussed in detail in my "Political Choice and Expenditure Change. . . ."

8. Loeb is discussed at length in Peirce, *The New England States of America*; Veblen, *The Manchester Union Leader* . . . ; and Cash, *Who the Hell*. . . .

9. See the discussion about the future of the *Leader* and New Hampshire politics after Loeb's death in Charles Stein, "The Loeb Legacy," in the *Columbia Journalism Review*, Sept.–Oct. 1983, pp. 14–15.

10. See the discussion in a report of the Joint Economic Committee of the U.S. Congress, "State and Local Economic Development Strategy: A 'Supply Side' Perspective" (dated Oct. 26, 1981), a staff study of the Subcommittee on Monetary and Fiscal Policy.

11. For an excellent discussion of interest group forces in New Hampshire politics up to the 1950s, see Lockard, *New England State Politics*.

12. The best known and most controversial was Colin and Rosemary Campbell, "A Comparative Study of the Fiscal Systems of New Hampshire and Vermont: 1940–1974" (New Hampton, N.H.: Wheelabrator Foundation, 1976).

13. Peculiarly, all three Republican candidates were employed in higher education: Sununu as associate professor of engineering at Tufts University; Monier as professor of urban studies at St. Anselms College in Manchester, N.H.; and d'Alessandro as an administrator at Daniel Webster College.

14. This is another peculiarity of New Hampshire politics—very conservative state-wide politicians are able to mobilize sizable electoral followings. Both Thomson and former Governor Wesley Powell are reputed to have many thousands of votes at their disposal.

15. This discussion is elaborated in my "Political Culture . . ." article.

16. See Lloyd Etheredge, "Hardball Politics: A Model," *Political Psychology* (Spring 1979): 3.

17. Ibid., 6

18. As reported in David Moore, "The Margin of Vitriol" *New Hampshire Times*, Dec. 20, 1982, p. 26.

19. Former 1982 gubernatorial candidate, former state senator, former acting governor, and informal advisor to Sununu, Robert Monier, as quoted in the *New Hampshire Times*, Dec. 13, 1982, p. 5.

New Mexico

Many persons contributed to the author's understanding of the transition period. Formal interviews, varying in length from one to three hours, were held in Santa Fe with Shirley Scarafiotti, Harvey Fruman, Steve Cobble, David Oakeley, Steve Anaya, and Bob McNeil, all of whom were closely associated with the Anaya campaign, the transition, and the subsequent administration. Shorter discussions were also held with Rudy Valencia of the lieutenant governor's office; Mike Runnels, lieutenant governor; Hoyt Clifton, director of the state Bureau of Elections; Neal Gonzalez, executive director of the New Mexico AFL-CIO; Nick Franklin, chairman of the New Mexico Democratic party; Bob Toberman, of the Department of Agriculture; and Don Frederick, a reporter in the Santa Fe office of the *El Paso Times*. During the struggle over the leadership of the house and during the legislative session, discussions were held with Governor-elect Toney Anaya, Rep. Ray Sanchez, Rep. Mary Tucker (who also discussed with me several matters concerning the legislative session after its conclusion), Sen. Jimmy Rogers, Rep. Brent Westmoreland, Rep. Ralph Hartman, Rep. Ed Minzner, and several other legislators who were generous with their time. Many other informed observers, too numerous to name, also contributed useful insights. Factual and interpretive errors that may exist, of course, are the sole responsibility of the author.

My interpretation of demographic and ethnic influences on campaigns and on the transition and subsequent administration derives from two sources. First, it is based on several years of professional observation and writings on politics in New Mexico, in which I have been influenced greatly by four political scientists, F. Chris Garcia (no relation), Caleb and Janet Clark, and Paul Hain, cited in n. 2. And second, my understanding is rooted in several years of political activity as a campaign consultant and four years ending in April 1983 as chairman of the Dona Ana County Democratic party. Interested readers are urged to judge for themselves the degree to which these influences may have produced analytical, factual, or interpretive blind spots.

Notes

1. Summary Tape File 1A, table 7, U.S. Census Summary Tape File, Department of Commerce, Washington, D.C. Although it had been argued that the decline in the total proportion of Hispanics in New Mexico is due partly to statistical artifacts created by the use of different questionnaires in 1970 and 1980, countervailing trends in the age characteristics and registration propensities of the populations involved suggest that the proportion of registered Hispanic voters has declined from about 41 percent to about 36 percent.

2. Jose Z. Garcia and Paul Hain, "Voting, Elections, and Parties" (chap. 10), in F. Chris Garcia and Paul Hain, *Government in New Mexico* (Albuquerque: University of New Mexico Press, 1981), 218.

3. Derived from James D. Williams, testimony given before special three-judge panel, U.S. Circuit Court, Albuquerque, N.M., Apr. 1982. The trial concerned the 1982 reapportionment act passed by the legislature. Precise data on ethnic political behavior are difficult to obtain, and very little on the subject has been published.

4. Information for this paragraph was obtained through interviews with Shirley Scarafiotti, Harvey Fruman, and David Oakeley.

5. Information for this paragraph was obtained through interviews with Fruman.

6. Information for this and the following five paragraphs was obtained through interviews with Fruman, Scarafiotti, Cobble, McNeil, Steve Anaya, and Oakeley.

7. Information for this paragraph and the following eight was obtained from ibid.

8. *Albuquerque Journal*, Apr. 22, 1983, quoting Dan Balz, "Anaya Cabinet Most Liberal in Nation," *Washington Post*.
9. Interview with Steve Anaya.
10. Harold Rhodes, "The Cabinet and Other Appointive Agencies" (chap. 6), in *Government in New Mexico*.
11. Alan Reed, "The Plural Executive" (chap. 2), *Government in New Mexico*, 20.
12. Interview with Oakeley.
13. See, for example, "Anaya's Frenetic Pace even Impresses His Detractors," *Albuquerque Journal*, July 9, 1983, p. 2.
14. Political scientists have long felt the governor's powers in New Mexico are insufficient and should be enhanced. See, for example, Harold Rhodes, chap. 6, in Garcia and Hain, *Government in New Mexico*, and 1976 edition of same.
15. Reed, "The Plural Executive," 22–23.
16. Interview with Fruman.
17. For detailed information concerning the Coalition, see Cal and Janet Clark, "New Mexico: Moving in the Direction of a Republican Realignment," *Social Science Journal* V. 18: 3 (Oct. 1981) 75–85; and Cal Clark and Jose Z. Garcia, "Reapportionment in New Mexico: The Revolution that Wasn't" (Paper presented at the Annual Meeting of the Western Political Science Association, Seattle, March 1983).
18. The *Albuquerque Journal* published numerous articles on the Coalition struggle in Dec. 1982 and Jan. 1983.
19. Information for this section was obtained from interviews with Sen. Jimmy Rogers, R-Doña Ana County, who was instrumental in negotiating the agreements that led to the shortfall, budget, and tax-increase bills, and with H. (Doc) Weiler, executive director of the Association of Commerce and Industry.

New York

My thanks to T. Norman Hurd, Robert Kerker, Orin L. McCluskey, Harold Rubin, and Paul Veillette for their comments on an earlier draft of this chapter.

1. Norton Long, "After the Voting Is Over," *Midwest Journal of Political Science* 6 (1962): 183 and 187.
2. For an argument that New York State was already in a period of steep economic decline by this time, see Peter McClelland and Alan L. Magdovitz, *Crisis in the Making* (New York: Cambridge University Press, 1981).
3. Mario M. Cuomo, *Forest Hills Diary* (New York: Vintage, 1974), xii.
4. *New York Times* (hereinafter cited as NYT) Nov. 7, 1974, p. 34, and Dec. 28, 1974, p. 1.
5. Andy Logan, "Around City Hall," *New Yorker*, Nov. 21, 1977, p. 203. (This regularly appearing column will hereafter be cited as *New Yorker*.)
6. *New Yorker*, Feb. 7, 1983, p. 97.
7. Ibid., Nov. 22, 1982, p. 105.
8. NYT, Sept. 25, 1982, p. 31.
9. See, generally, *New Yorker*, Nov. 11, 1982; Maurice Carroll, "Lehrman: The New Right," and E. J. Dionne, "Cuomo: The Old Liberalism," *New York*

Times Magazine, Oct. 31, 1982, pp. 21 and 22; *Newsweek,* Oct. 25, 1982, p. 130; *Time,* Nov. 1, 1982, p. 21; and *National Review,* Oct. 15, 1982.

10. For polls see *NYT,* Nov. 7, 1982, p. 4E. For spending see Robert Marcus, "Campaign Spending: Is the Only Direction Up?" *Empire State Report,* Nov. 1982, pp. 20, 21, and 29.

11. *NYT,* Apr. 10, 1975, p. 28.

12. Office of the Governor, "News Conference of Governor Hugh L. Carey" (reproduced, Dec. 29, 1982), p. 5.

13. Council on State Priorities, *Report to the Governor* (Albany: The Council, 1982), 7.

14. Transition file of Dr. T. Norman Hurd (1974–75). This file, in the possession of Dr. Hurd, was lent to the author (hereafter cited as Transition File).

15. *NYT,* Nov. 7, 1974, p. 34.

16. Amy Plumer, "In Search of the Democratic Government," *Empire State Report,* July 1975, pp. 254–69.

17. "Dracula" quote is from *New Yorker,* Nov. 18, 1974, p. 203. Letter, Wilson to Carey, Nov. 26, 1974, from Transition File.

18. *NYT,* Nov. 7, 1974, p. 34.

19. Hurd Memo for the Record, Dec. 17, 1974, Transition File.

20. Executive Order No. 118 and Memorandum, Robert Morgado, Secretary to the Governor, to All Department and Agency Heads, both June 1, 1982. In author's files.

21. *NYT,* Aug. 25, 1982, p. B1.

22. Press conference transcript, p. 33.

23. Letter, Finnerty to Department and Agency Heads, Sept. 14, 1982, including "Instructions for Completion of Gubernatorial Decision Papers and Agency Action Reports." Author's files.

24. Clark D. Ahlberg and Daniel P. Moynihan, "Changing Governors—And Policies," *Public Administration Review* 20 (Autumn 1960): 205.

25. *NYT,* Dec. 30, 1982, p. 81, and Jan. 20, 1983.

26. Ibid., Nov. 22, 1982, p. B6.

27. Ibid., Nov. 7, 1982, p. E4.

28. Ibid., Nov. 7 and 22, 1982, and *Middletown Times Herald Record* (AP), Nov. 19, 1982.

29. *NYT,* Nov. 4, 1982, p. B8, and private interview.

30. *NYT,* Dec. 23, 1982, p. B2. Sources on the appointments process include: interview with Abe Levine, assistant to the governor; Pamela Tighe, "Send a Resume," *Empire State Reports,* Mar. 1983, pp. 32–33; and Mike Kramer, "Mario's Magicians," *New York Magazine,* Dec. 20, 1982.

31. *NYT,* Feb. 5, 1983, and Mar. 20, 1983, p. E8.

32. Ibid., Mar. 14, 1983, pp. B1 and B2.

33. Ibid.

34. Ibid., Nov. 27, 1982, p. B6.

35. Ibid., Dec. 17, 1982, p. 1, and Dec. 29, p. A18.

36. Text reprinted in ibid., Jan. 2, 1983, p. 22.

37. *New Yorker,* Feb. 7, 1983, pp. 88.

38. Gov. Mario Cuomo, "Message to the Legislature, January 5, 1983" (Albany: Office of the Governor, 1983). The effort to give the governor control of the MTA board failed in the legislature.

39. New Yorker, Feb. 7, 1983, p. 88.

40. "Message to the Legislature . . . ," p. 1. See Donald Roper, "The Governorship in History," in Robert Connery and Gerald Benjamin, eds., Governing New York: The Rockefeller Years (New York: Academy of Political Science, 1974), 16–30.

41. Cronin, The State of the Presidency, 2nd ed. (Boston: Little, Brown, 1980), 109.

42. Ibid.

43. NYT, Dec. 18, 1982, p. 1.

44. Ibid., Dec. 9, 1982, p. B4.

45. Ibid., Dec. 23, 1982, p. B2.

46. Ibid. The front-page headline of the New York Post for Dec. 30, 1982, was "Gov: I Faked Fare Crisis."

47. NYT, Jan. 11, 1983, p. B4.

48. Ibid., Jan. 12, 1983, p. B4, and New Yorker, Feb. 7, 1983, p. 92.

49. NYT, Jan. 12, 1983, p. B4.

50. New Yorker, Feb. 7, 1983, p. 92.

51. New York State Division of the Budget, Midyear Report, October, 1982 (Albany: New York State Division of the Budget, 1982), p. 5.

52. National Governors' Association, Office of State Services, Transition and the New Governor: A Critical Overview (Washington, D.C.: The Association, 1982), 18; NYT, Nov. 22, 1982, p. B6, and Mar. 28, 1983, p. B4.

53. See, generally, New York State Division of the Budget, Annual Budget Message, 1983–84 (Albany: The Division, 1983).

54. NYT, Jan. 21, 1983.

55. Ibid., Mar. 1, 1983, p. 22.

56. Ibid., Feb. 2, 1983, p. B1. For the comptroller's opinion see his press release entitled "Comptroller Regan's Review of the Governor's Budget," Mar. 11, 1983. Author's files.

57. NYT, Dec. 9, 1982, p. B4.

58. Ibid., Mar. 29, 1983, p. B4.

59. Ibid., Mar. 28, 1983, p. B4.

60. Ibid., Mar. 27, 1983, p. E6.

61. Richard Neustadt, Presidential Power (New York: Wiley, 1960).

62. NYT, Mar. 27, 1983, p. E6.

Texas

Research support for this project was provided in part by the Public Policy Resources Laboratory of Texas A&M University. The authors are grateful to the laboratory for its assistance. Special thanks are also extended to former Texas state representative Bill C. Presnal (D, Bryan), who commented on an earlier version of this manuscript. As usual, the authors assume full responsibility for the manuscript's final contents.

1. The description of the bolt-cutting event is taken from *Houston Chronicle*, Jan. 19, 1983; *Houston Post*, Jan. 19, 1983; and *Austin American-Statesman*, Jan. 19, 1983.

2. For an interesting portrait of Clements and his 1978 campaign activities see Stephen Harrigan, "The Governor's New Clothes," *Texas Monthly*, May 1981, beginning on 128.

3. *Houston Chronicle*, Sept. 23 and 24, 1982; *Bryan–College Station Eagle*, Sept. 24, 1982; *Dallas Morning News*, Sept. 22, 1982; and *Austin American-Statesman*, Sept. 22, 1982.

4. *Fort Worth Star-Telegram*, Sept. 25, 1982; *Austin American-Statesman*, Sept. 25, 1982; and *Bryan–College Station Eagle*, Sept. 25, 1982.

5. *Washington Post*, Oct. 13, 1982; *Austin American-Statesman*, Oct. 24, 1982.

6. *Houston Chronicle*, Oct. 12, 1982; *Houston Post*, Oct. 23, 1982.

7. *Fort Worth Star-Telegram*, Sept. 11, 1982.

8. Interesting descriptions of the White and Clements organizations are provided in the Aug. 1, 1982, issue of the *Houston Chronicle* by its veteran correspondent, Bo Byers. See also *Ft. Worth Star-Telegram*, Oct. 3, 1982, and Oct. 10, 1982; *Austin American-Statesman*, Oct. 28, 1982.

9. Clements's operation was masterminded by Nancy Brataas of Minnesota; see *San Antonio Express*, Aug. 8, 1982; *Bryan–College Station Eagle*, Sept. 27, 1982.

10. *Fort Worth Star-Telegram*, Oct. 10, 1982.

11. Ibid., Aug. 8, 1982.

12. *Dallas Times-Herald*, Aug. 13, 1982; *Houston Chronicle*, Aug. 13, 1982.

13. *Houston Chronicle*, Aug. 12, 1982; *Austin American-Statesman*, Aug. 12, 1982.

14. *Dallas Morning News*, Sept. 14, 1982.

15. *Dallas Times-Herald*, Sept. 14, 1982; *Houston Chronicle*, Sept. 14, 1982.

16. *Austin American-Statesman*, Oct. 2, 1983.

17. *Houston Chronicle*, Sept. 15, 1982.

18. For example, see endorsements in *El Paso Times*, Sept. 26, 1982, and *Dallas Times-Herald*, Oct. 10, 1982.

19. *Fort Worth Star-Telegram*, Oct. 17, 1982.

20. *Austin American-Statesman*, Dec. 3, 1982; *Dallas Times-Herald*, Dec. 3, 1982.

21. Gary Keith and Bruce W. Robeck, "Texas Democrats Find Victory in Unity," *Comparative State Politics Newsletter*, Dec. 1982, pp. 28–29.

22. *Houston Chronicle*, Dec. 26, 1982.

23. *Dallas Morning News*, Nov. 3, 1982.

24. *Houston Post*, Nov. 21, 1982.

25. *Austin American-Statesman*, Jan. 18, 1983.

26. Ibid.

27. *Austin American-Statesman*, Oct. 5, 1982.

28. *Dallas Morning News*, Nov. 13, 1982.

29. *San Antonio Light*, Nov. 24, 1982.

30. *Fort Worth Star-Telegram*, July 30, 1982.

31. *Austin American-Statesman*, Oct. 23, 1982; *Fort Worth Star-Telegram*, Dec. 24, 1982.

32. *San Antonio Express*, Jan. 20, 1983.

33. *Dallas Morning News*, Dec. 5, 1982; *Fort Worth Star-Telegram*, Jan. 19, 1983.
34. Paul Burka, "Mark White's Coming Out Party," *Texas Monthly*, May 1982, beginning on 138.
35. *Houston Post*, Jan. 28, 1983.
36. *Dallas Times-Herald*, Jan. 28, 1983; *San Antonio Express*, Jan. 28, 1983.
37. *Fort Worth Star-Telegram*, Jan. 28, 1983.
38. *Houston Chronicle*, Jan. 28, 1983.
39. *Dallas Times-Herald*, Jan. 28, 1983.
40. *Houston Chronicle*, Jan. 28, 1983.
41. Ibid., Jan. 12, 1983.
42. *Fort Worth Star-Telegram*, Jan. 20, 1983.
43. Ibid., Dec. 30, 1982.
44. *Houston Chronicle*, Mar. 10, 11, 12, and 13, 1983.
45. *Fort Worth Star-Telegram*, Jan. 26, 1983; *Dallas Times-Herald*, Jan. 28, 1983, and *Houston Post*, Feb. 2, 1983.
46. The only provision in Texas law dealing with state financial support for gubernatorial transition activities is a 1979 statute that authorizes the legislature to make appropriations to a special fund administered by the secretary of state's office for inaugural ceremonies and events (see *Vernon's Texas Annotated Civil Statutes*, Art. 6145–12, secs. 1–11). Although White's inaugural committee ran its operations through this fund, no public monies were appropriated to it. As indicated, White's less symbolic transition expenses were paid by his campaign fund.

Wisconsin

The author would like to thank Thad Beyle, Dennis Dresang, and James Gosling for helpful comments and suggestions. Only the author, however, is responsible for the opinions expressed in this report.

What Guides Governors in Transitions?

An earlier version of this chapter was prepared for delivery at the 1983 annual meeting of the American Political Science Association, The Palmer House, Chicago, Sept. 1–4, 1983, X.
1. According to the latest volume, its predecessor, *Governing the American States: A Handbook for New Governors* (Washington, D.C.: NGA, 1978), "continues to serve as the cornerstone for NGA's transition assistance . . . [providing] greater detail," whereas *Transition and the New Governor: A Critical Overview* (Washington, D.C.: NGA, 1982), "unlike earlier NGA publications, . . . is intended to be prescriptive in nature" (pp. ix–x, 3).
2. NGA, *Governing the American States*, 76, 64.
3. NGA, *Transition and the New Governor*, 57.
4. Ibid., 45; NGA, *Governing the American States*, 58, 39, 62.
5. NGA, *Transition and the New Governor*, 10, 45.
6. NGA, *Governing the American States*, 81.

7. Note, though, that the Arkansas report comparing Clinton's two transitions, one a friendly intraparty transition and one an interparty transition, points out that "in neither year were more than two of the previous governor's staff retained."

8. NGA, *Transition and the New Governor*, 9, see also 15; NGA, *Governing the American States*, 26.

9. NGA, *Transition and the New Governor*, 33; NGA, *Governing the American States*, 210.

10. NGA, *Transition and the New Governor*, 39, 41–44.

11. This evaluation uses Richard T. Johnson's typology of presidential styles: formalistic (Richard Nixon), competitive (Franklin Roosevelt), and collegial (John Kennedy). "Presidential Style," in *Perspectives on the Presidency*, ed. Aaron Wildavsky (Boston: Little, Brown, 1975), 262–300.

12. NGA, *Governing the American States*, 193.

13. NGA, *Transition and the New Governor*, 29–30.

14. Richard D. Lamm (D–Colo.), William J. Janklow (R–S.D.), Scott M. Matheson (D–Utah), and Richard A. Snelling (R–Vt.), "Hey Congress! Hey Reagan! We Are in Serious Trouble—A Cry from the Heartland: Deficits Will Impoverish Our Grandchildren," *Washington Post*, Jan. 22, 1984.

15. NGA, *Transition and the New Governor*, 84; NGA, *Governing the American States*, 154, see also 157.

16. NGA, *Transition and the New Governor*, 83.

17. See Ted F. Herbert, Jeffery Brudney and Deil S. Wright, "Gubernatorial Influence and State Bureaucracy," *American Politics Quarterly* 11 (Apr. 1983): 243–64; and H. Edward Flentje, "The Political Nature of the Governor as Manager," in *Being Governor: The View from the Office*, ed. Thad L. Beyle and Lynn R. Muchmore (Durham, N.C.: Duke University Press, 1983), 85–92.

18. See Joseph E. Kallenbach, *The American Chief Executive: The Presidency and the Governorship* (New York: Harper and Row, 1966), 253.

19. See Duane Lockard, *The New Jersey Governor: A Study in Political Power* (Princeton, N.J.: D. Van Nostrand, 1964), esp. chaps. 1, 6, 7.

20. Norton Long, "After the Voting Is Over," *Midwest Journal of Political Science* 6 (May 1962): 183–200.

21. See Thad L. Beyle, "The Governor as Chief Legislator," in *Being Governor: The View from the Office*, ed. Beyle and Muchmore, 143. See also the discussion of former Governor and President Carter's "command" in Nicholas Lemann's "Why Carter Fails: Taking the Politics Out of Government," in *Inside the System*, 4th ed., ed. Lemann and Charles Peters (New York: Holt, Rinehart and Winston, 1979), 83.

22. See the discussion of "six specific linkage and communication functions" in Eugene T. Kolb, *A Framework for Political Analysis* (Englewood Cliffs, N.J.: Prentice-Hall, 1978), 154–61.

23. Thad L. Beyle and Lynn R. Muchmore, "The Governor as Party Leader," in *Being Governor: The View from the Office*, ed. Beyle and Muchmore, 50–51.

24. "Divided government" refers to the widespread executive/legislative standoffs resulting from the governor's party's having such a large majority in the legislature that intraparty polarizations vitiate consensus. See Coleman B. Ransone,

Jr., *The American Governorship* (Westport, Conn.: Greenwood Press, 1982), 168–70.

25. See a brief outline of the different "exchanges" involved in presidential candidacy and governance in Robert J. Sickel's *Presidential Transactions* (Englewood Cliffs, N.J.: Prentice-Hall, 1974), 177–78.

26. Irving L. Janis, *Groupthink: Psychological Studies of Policy Decisions and Fiascoes*, 2nd ed. (Boston: Houghton Mifflin, 1983), 54, 13, and 172.

27. See Peter Tropp, "Governor's and Mayor's Offices: The Role of the Staff," *National Civic Review* 63 (May 1974): 243–49.

28. Alabama, Alaska, Massachusetts, Minnesota, New York, and Wisconsin.

29. California, Georgia, Iowa, Massachusetts, Michigan, New Mexico, New York, and Texas.

30. Alabama, Alaska, California, Nebraska, New Hampshire, and Texas.

31. Alaska, California, Minnesota, and New Mexico.

32. The "inherently individualistic" nature of transitions is the major conclusion of the Arkansas analyst.

33. Two of many potential differences between parties is that "Democratic governors tend to use smaller staffs" and "the conclusion is inescapable that Democratic governors tend to organize their staffs in a diffused, horizontal pattern and the Republican governors follow the classic pyramidal, hierarchically arranged model," according to Donald Sprengel, "Patterns of Organization in Gubernatorial Staffs," in *Comparative State Politics*, ed. Sprengel (Columbus: Charles Merrill, 1971), 315, 329. However, Sprengel's conclusion is challenged, at least in terms of organizational implications, by Charles H. Williams in "The 'Gatekeeper' Function on the Governor's Staff," *Western Political Quarterly* 33 (1980): 90–91.

34. See Daniel J. Elazar, *American Federalism: A View from the States*, 2nd ed. (New York: Thomas Y. Crowell, 1972), 84–126.

35. As noted in the Nebraska report, too much compromise with the legislature can damage reelection chances by creating the appearance of weak leadership.

36. James D. Barber, *The Presidential Character* (Englewood Cliffs, N.J.: Prentice-Hall, 1972). For an example of the application of Barber's typology to one governor, see Robert H. Connery and Gerald Benjamin, *Rockefeller of New York: Executive Power in the Statehouse* (Ithaca, N.Y.: Cornell University Press, 1979), 26–27. Johnson, "Presidential Style." Louis W. Koenig, *The Chief Executive*, 4th ed. (New York: Harcourt Brace Jovanovich, 1981), 173–79. John J. Harrigan, *Politics and Policy in States and Communities* (Boston: Little, Brown, 1980), 129–31.

37. For a discussion of the parallels between the presidency and governorship and the characteristics of state executive branches, see David R. Colburn and Richard K. Scher, *Florida's Gubernatorial Politics in the Twentieth Century* (Tallahassee: University Presses of Florida, 1980), 115–19. For other comparisons, see Eugene P. Dvorin and Arthur J. Misner, *Governments Within the States* (Reading, Mass.: Addison-Wesley, 1971), 49–54, and Sarah M. Morehouse, "The Governor as Political Leader," in *Politics in the American States*, 3rd ed., ed. Herbert Jacob and Kenneth N. Vines (Boston: Little, Brown, 1976), 277–79.

38. A useful "multiplicity of staff organizational characteristics" has been formulated by Sprengel, "Patterns of Organization in Gubernatorial Staffs," and Williams notes the possibility of using NGA survey information on governors' time allocation as an index of personal style in "The 'Gatekeeper' Function on the Governor's Staff," 91.

39. One recent study of gubernatorial transition concludes, "Rather than distinct elements, the campaign-transition-administrative tenure may be best viewed as an organic process, with each period growing from and building upon its predecessor." Eric B. Herzik and Mary L. Dobson, "Developing Executive Roles: Gubernatorial Concerns in the Transition Period" (Paper presented at the Annual Meeting of the Midwest Political Science Association, Apr. 12–14, 1984, Chicago), 7–8.

Index